REV. JEROME KNIES, O.S.A.
TOLENTINE CENTER
OLYMPIA FIELDS,
ILLINOIS 60461

About the Author

RICHARD WOODS is a Dominican priest with a doctorate in philosophy from Loyola University in Chicago, where he is currently Adjunct Professor in the area of spirituality at the Institute of Pastoral Studies. A frequent guest lecturer, he has also prepared several cassette tapes on a variety of religious subjects. In addition to books on the devil and the occult, Woods is the author of *Another Kind of Love* (available in Image Books in a revised edition) as well as *Mysterion/Mystical Spirituality as a Contemporary Lifestyle.*

UNDERSTANDING
MYSTICISM

Edited by Richard Woods, o.p.

IMAGE BOOKS

A Division of Doubleday & Company, Inc.
Garden City, New York
1980

Library of Congress Cataloging in Publication Data
Main entry under title:

Understanding mysticism.

   Bibliography
   Includes index.
   1. Mysticism—Comparative studies—Addresses,
essays, lectures.   2. Mysticism—Psychology—Addresses,
essays, lectures.   I. Woods, Richard.
BL625.U52   291.4'2

ISBN: 0-385-15117-9
Library of Congress Catalog Card Number: 78-22743
Copyright © 1980 by Richard Woods
All Rights Reserved
Printed in the United States of America
First Edition

Acknowledgments

The Nature and Meaning of Mysticism from AN INTRODUCTION TO MYSTICISM, by Margaret Smith, published by Sheldon Press, London. Copyright © 1977 Sheldon Press. Reprinted by permission of Oxford University Press, Inc.; *The Essentials of Mysticism* and *The Mystic as Creative Artist* from THE ESSENTIALS OF MYSTICISM AND OTHER ESSAYS, published by AMS Press, E. P. Dutton & Co., Inc., 1960; *Mysticism / An Essay on the History of the Word*, slightly abridged from MYSTERY AND MYSTICISM, London: Blackfriars Publications, 1956 (originally appeared under the title "Mysterium" in *La Vie Spirituelle*, 1952; *Mysticism Sacred and Profane* abridged from MYSTICISM SACRED AND PROFANE, by R. C. Zaehner, © Oxford University Press, 1961. Adapted by permission of Oxford University Press; *Interpretation and Mystical Experience*, reprinted from *Religious Studies*, Vol. 1, No. 1, October 1975 by permission of Cambridge University Press; *Superstructures* slightly abridged from EXPLORING MYSTICISM, Copyright © 1975 by The Regents of the University of California. Reprinted by permission of the University of California Press. *Sacrificial Mysticism* abridged from HINDU MYSTICISM, published by Frederick Ungar Publishing Co., 1927, 1959; *The Basis of Buddhist Philosophy* abridged from MYSTICISM: CHRISTIAN AND BUDDHIST, by Daisetz Teitaro Suzuki (Vol. 12 in the World Perspectives Series, planned and edited by Ruth Nanda Anshen). Copyright © 1957 by Daisetz Teitaro Suzuki. Used by permission of Harper & Row Publishers, Inc. and George Allen & Unwin Ltd.; *General Characteristics of Jewish Mysticism* abridged by permission of Schocken Books Inc. from MAJOR TRENDS IN JEWISH MYSTICISM, by Gershom G. Scholem. Copyright © 1946, 1954 by Schocken Books Inc. Copyright renewed © 1974 by Schocken Books Inc.; *Theology and Mysticism in the Tradition of the Eastern Church*, abridged from MYSTICAL THEOLOGY OF THE EASTERN CHURCH, 1957, reprinted by permission of James Clarke & Co. Ltd.; *The Mystics of Islam* from the Introduction to THE MYSTICS OF ISLAM, by Reynold A. Nicholson, published by Routledge & Kegan Paul Ltd., London and Boston, 1914, reissued 1963. Reprinted by permission of the publisher; *The Mystical Spirit and Protestantism* from PROTESTANTISM: INTERPRETATIONS, edited by William K. Anderson, published by Board of Education, United Methodist Church, Nashville, Tenn., 1944; *The Question of Mysticism within Native American Traditions, Mystical Experience as Cognition,* and *Unity and Diversity in the Interpretation of Mysticism* from MYSTICS AND SCHOLARS, edited by Harold Coward and Terence Penelhum, published by the Canadian Corporation for Studies in Religion, 1977. Reprinted by permission of the publisher; *A Suggestion about Mysticism* from COLLECTED ESSAYS AND REVIEWS, published in 1920 by Longmans Green; *The Meaning of Mysticism as Seen through Its Psychology* abridged from *Mind*, January 1912.

Reprinted by permission of Basil Blackwell Publisher Ltd.; *Deautomatization and the Mystic Experience* from *Psychiatry*, 1966, 29: 324–38. Copyright © 1966 by The William Alanson White Psychiatric Foundation, Inc. Reprinted by special permission of The William Alanson White Psychiatric Foundation, Inc.; *Bimodal Consciousness and the Mystic Experience* from SYMPOSIUM ON CONSCIOUSNESS, by Philip R. Lee, Robert E. Ornstein, Charles Tart, Arthur Deikman, and David Galin. Copyright © 1976 by Philip Lee, Robert E. Ornstein, Charles Tart, Arthur Deikman, and David Galin. All rights reserved. Reprinted by permission of Viking Penguin Inc.; *Two Sides of the Brain* slightly abridged from THE PSYCHOLOGY OF CONSCIOUSNESS, by Robert E. Ornstein. Copyright © 1972 by W. H. Freeman & Company. All rights reserved. Reprinted by permission of Viking Penguin Inc. and Jonathan Cape Ltd.; *A Cartography of the Ecstatic and Meditative States* slightly abridged from *Science*, Vol. 174, pp. 897–904, November 26, 1971. Copyright © 1971 by the American Association for the Advancement of Science. Reprinted by permission; *State-Bound Knowledge: I Can't Remember What I Said Last Night, but It Must Have Been Good* reprinted from *Psychology Today* magazine. Copyright © 1976 by Ziff-Davis Publishing Company. Used by permission; *The Creative Personality: Akin to Madness*, reprinted from *Psychology Today* (Vol. 6, No. 2). Copyright © 1972 by Seminar Press, Inc., New York and London; *Mysticism and Schizophrenia* from *The Journal of Transpersonal Psychology*, Vol. 1, No. 2 (Fall 1969), pp. 49–66. © Copyright Transpersonal Institute, 1969. Reprinted by permission of *The Journal of Transpersonal Psychology*, Box 4437, Stanford, Cal. 94305; *Cocoon Work: An Interpretation of the Concern of Contemporary Youth with the Mystical* from RELIGIOUS MOVEMENTS IN CONTEMPORARY AMERICA, edited by Irving I. Zaretsky and Mark P. Leone, pp. 255–71. Copyright © 1974 by Princeton University Press, reprinted by permission of Princeton University Press; *Mysticism, Action and Philosophy* abridged from "Dynamic Religion," Part III of THE TWO SOURCES OF MORALITY AND RELIGION, by Henri Bergson. Translated by R. Ashley Andra and Cloudesley Brereton with the assistance of W. Horsfall Carter. Copyright 1935, © 1963 by Holt, Rinehart and Winston. Reprinted by permission of Holt, Rinehart and Winston, Publishers; *Four Kinds of Mystical Experience*, abridged from the Introduction to THE PROTESTANT MYSTICS, edited by Anne Fremantle with an Introduction by W. H. Auden. Copyright © 1964 by Anne Fremantle and W. H. Auden. Reprinted by arrangement with the New American Library Inc., New York, N.Y.; *Mysticism and Rationalistic Metaphysics* reprinted from *The Monist*, Vol. 59, No. 4, 1976 with the permission of the author and the publisher; *The Mystical Experience of the Self and Its Philosophical Significance* from THOMAS AND BONAVENTURE, A Septicentenary Commemoration, Vol. XLVIII, Proceedings of the American Catholic Philosophical Association; *Ontology and Theology of Christian Mysticism* from STUDIES IN THE PSYCHOLOGY OF THE MYSTICS, translated by Algar Thorold, published by Benziger Brothers, 1927, reprinted by permission of the publisher; *The Natural Mystical Experience and the Void* slightly abridged from REDEEMING THE TIME, by Jacques Maritain, published by Geoffrey Bles Centenary Press, London, 1943, reprinted by permission; *Unitas Spiritus* abridged from THE MYSTICAL THEOLOGY OF ST. BERNARD, trans-

lated by A. H. C. Downes. Published by Sheed & Ward, 1940. Reprinted by
permission of Cecile J. Gilson; *What Is Mysticism?* from THE NATURE OF MYSTI-
CISM, reprinted by permission of Sheed & Ward Ltd.; *Liberation as an Encounter with Politics and Contemplation* from THE MYSTICAL AND POLITICAL
DIMENSION OF THE CHRISTIAN FAITH (Concilium, Vol. 96). Copyright © 1974
by Herder and Strichting Concilium. Used by permission of the Seabury Press;
Meister Eckhart and Karl Marx: The Mystic as Political Theologian slightly
revised from *Listening,* Vol. 13, No. 3 (Fall 1978). Reprinted by permission.

Contents

x   *Contents*

Introduction

Concurrent with the apocalyptic turbulence of the later sixties and early seventies, mysticism clearly became a significant factor in the lives of millions of people weary of war, racism, political corruption and religious institutionalism.[1] Not unrelated to the sudden mushrooming of interest in occultism, "neo-paganism," the pentecostal movement, the psychedelic revolution and "neo-orientalism"—the fascination with Eastern religions, a concern with the mystical dimensions of experience (or "neo-transcendentalism" in the phrase of Raymond Prince)—was particularly but not exclusively manifest among the young.[2] This upsurge of enthusiasm was, however, little more than a sudden wave visibly breaking on the shores of popular consciousness seventy years after the tide of interest in mysticism began rising steadily.

At present, the need for a comprehensive collection of critical studies of mysticism in both its past and contemporaneous manifestations is, I would think, self-evident. Several anthologies of mystical writings have appeared in recent years which included valuable and critical introductions, such as those of Happold, Stace, O'Brien, DeJaegher and Reinhold, and in particular the papers from the Calgary Conference on Mysticism, *Mystics and Scholars*, three of which are found in this collection. Other anthologies representing a broadly scientific or philosophical perspective have contributed to our understanding of mysticism, such as John White's *The Highest State of Consciousness* and Steven Katz's *Mysticism and Philosophical Analysis*. But to date there has been no attempt to provide a selection of critical studies, both "classical" and contemporary, particularly those written from a comparative viewpoint and exhibiting a wide range of inquiry.[3]

The studies in this volume represent at least the following disciplines: phenomenology, the history of religions, psychology, neuropsychology, sociology, literary criticism, philosophy and theology. But *Understanding Mysticism* is not intended to be exhaustive or even fully representative of the wide variety of approaches to and positions on mysticism current today or in the recent past. The essays were chosen primarily because of their original contribution toward understanding the phenomenon of mysticism. Accessibility was also a deciding factor. Many other articles, such as James's chapter on mysticism in *The Varieties of Religious Experience*, Bertrand Russell's unique essay "Mysticism and Logic" and Annemarie Schimmel's excellent introduction to *Mystical Dimensions of Islam* could well have found room, but are readily available in other works.

Most of the present essays appeared first in journals and in some cases are taken from works now out of print. Although all were composed in the present century, these articles reflect a chronological spread of over seventy-five years and are generally presented in that order. It is especially important in the study of mysticism to see our contemporary concern as continuous with an historically definite process beginning perhaps with Dean William Inge's *Christian Mysticism* in 1899. Today's commentators are the direct descendants of and greatly indebted to Inge, James, Evelyn Underhill, Margaret Smith and William Ernest Hocking, among others.

Furthermore, most of the essays were gathered as reference material for students in university courses on the psychology and theology of mysticism. Consequently, this collection bears at least a surface resemblance to a text book, and I hope it will find use as such. But it is much more and even much less. It is not, first, a balanced presentation of essays pro and con. All the authors share a common and positive, if critical, interest in the phenomenon and meaning of mysticism as an important factor in human experience and, as such, subject to rational investigation and analysis on many levels of inquiry. They do not presume that mysticism or mystical experience should or can be reduced to other, simpler elements of experience despite their psychological, physiological and sociological components. However, they neither evaluate mysticism in the same terms nor reach the same conclusions in all cases. On many points they are in strong disagreement, perhaps irreconcilably so. But, if I may say so, all regard mysticism *compassionately*. And all provide insight into and understanding of the phenomenon of mysticism.

Second, although the essays have been assembled into sections, this division is not rigorously systematic. In many articles, psychology, philosophy and theology mingle freely with literary analysis and the history of religions. The comparative study of mysticism has always been an interdisciplinary art. *Understanding Mysticism* is thus a collection of readings, a handbook of resources, an attempt to circumnavigate the mystical sphere, not to provide an atlas.

For a variety of reasons, the technical style of the original articles has been preserved in most instances. This has resulted in some variation in notation, particularly with regard to scientific articles in which bibliographical references are generally cited by author's name, the date of publication and frequently a page number within parentheses in the body of the text rather than as a footnote. Because of the abundance of references in scientific articles and the not insignificant fact that many of our authors cite the same authorities, a general bibliography has been appended to this volume which includes the scientific references as well as other important source material. Once again, however, this bibliography is not exhaustive; it is primarily a working tool for use with this volume.

Among the limitations of this collection, in addition to its somewhat partisan approach, is an overbalance of male writers in comparison to women. This should not be taken to signify a bias, much less that women have nothing to offer the comparative study of religion. A woman, Evelyn Underhill, can be credited with laying much of the groundwork for later studies. Further, most of the historical research as well as literary editing of medieval manuscripts in the early part of this century was conducted by outstanding women scholars whose work, I believe, has never been surpassed: Underhill, Margaret Smith, Grace Warrack, Geraldine Hodgson, Phyllis Hodgson, Hope Emily Allen and Hilda Graef, to name only a few. Nevertheless, whether by historical accident or a more regrettable problem of an imbalance of the sexes in the groves of academe, the great majority of psychological, philosophical and theological essays published in the recent past have been written by men.

Regrettably absent in these essays are critical studies of the scientific mysticism of Teilhard de Chardin, Carl Jung and Edith Stein. Similarly, space prohibits attention to such literary figures as Wordsworth, Tennyson, Dickinson and Flannery O'Connor, who certainly could be studied with great profit. Further, only passing concern is given to the great theological mystics, including St. John of the Cross, St. Bonaventure, St. Thomas Aquinas and St. Catherine of Siena. However, St. Teresa of Avila, the great favorite of most researchers, receives a good deal more attention.

Some Overarching Concerns

Despite the variety of topics and viewpoints, several common issues stand out when the essays are surveyed as a whole. An important and to some extent a perennial issue in comparative mysticism concerns the similarities and differences among mystical experiences and mystical doctrines. Is mystical experience in fact one and the same for all in its essential structure and function, or are there irreducibly plural forms of mystical experience? On one side of this issue stand Smart, Huxley, Fischer, Underhill, Hocking, Deikman and Wapnick. On the other side are found in no less uneasy alliance Zaehner, Maritain, Maréchal and Knowles.

The antagonists in this debate are generally the theologians, who opt for pluralism, as opposed to the philosophers and psychologists. The crucial argument for both sides concerns the role performed by interpretation in the drama of mystical and, indeed, all experience. If the differences manifest among reports of mystical experiences can be ascribed to interpretation alone, and can thus be reduced for the most part to extrinsic, cultural factors, then the uniformity of mystical experience and with it the relativity of doctrinal differences can be considered probable. However, if interpretation is itself an intrinsic part of experience, or if interpretation functions to a significant degree independently of cultural factors, then the differences among the mystics regarding experience may well be essential. If such be the case, it would be more appropriate to refer to mystical experiences and even "mysticisms" rather than treating them as if they were but variations of a common type.

Some light can be shed on this complex controversy by examining analogs of mystical experience, particularly episodes of schizophrenic behavior and creative states of consciousness in art and science (Fischer). But a solution will more likely depend upon a clarification of the structure of human experience itself. In this respect, the writings of Hocking are still remarkably instructive, particularly *The Meaning of God in Human Experience*.

More recently, the role of doctrinal structures (Deikman), mythologies (Fischer), credal ramifications (Smart), or superstructures (Staal) have been seen, I believe correctly, as component in mystical experiences as meaning-giving organizational patterns by which this immediate and ineffable awareness can be situated with respect to the whole system of ideas and values which provide the conceptual framework of the mystic's world view. As such an interpretative paradigm of reality, the system of beliefs (or *weltanschauung*), whether constructed by oneself in experiential interplay with the world, or having been accepted on the authority of others, or both, is part of experience because it is part of the *experiencer*. Thus, it is not *merely* a superstructure overlaying the "real" factors of experience (or *weltbild*) which can be freely disengaged without altering the intrinsic meaning of the experience itself. And thus interpretation would be built into experience. Moreover, there could be no experience which is meaningful without such interpretation.

This is not to deny, on the other hand, that interpretative schemes can be disengaged, to some extent at least, from the immediacy of an experience. This is especially true with regard to "second level" interpretations such as inferences, which are largely re-interpretations constructed on the basis of reflexively conscious and deliberate comparison with formal or informal belief systems. Such a process of disengagement can, in fact, bring us closer to an understanding of the pre-reflexive elements of original experience.

However, I also believe that the most recent commentators on the problem of mysticism and interpretation have not gone far enough in their evaluation of the part played by conceptual schemes in structuring mystical experience. For one thing, it seems evident that the doctrinal system partly inherited from the social matrix and partly an original construction, is relatively *open to reorganization.* Again, Hocking is instructive, being particularly attentive to the resulting *novelty* inherent in the mystics' experience, and to the profound force their experiences exerted toward recasting their whole system of beliefs. If anything, such a revaluation and reorganization of conceptual systems is *typical* of mystical experience. Such a possibly necessary reorganization of *weltanschauungen* can, of course, be a profoundly shaking psychological event. I am inclined to see in it the psychological correlate of the "dark night of the soul." Apart from a larger religious context (e.g. tradition) or its equivalent, within which this breakdown and restructuring can be managed safely, a schizophrenic episode is probably inevitable (see in this respect the essays by Wapnick, Fischer and Barron, as well as Mary Barnes' *Two Accounts of a Journey through Madness*).

It can be argued here that it is an important function of traditional mystical institutions to provide a "safe" mental and emotional environment for a process of disintegration and reintegration of idea and value systems on the part of their society's most sensitive and original members. The process of mystical development itself can be interpreted as just such a systematic recasting of the elements of experience.

There is another aspect of the conceptual and attitudinal reconstruction of experience frequently if not characteristically attendant upon mystical experience. That is the process by which *social* values, customs, beliefs and behaviors are altered by the mystics' particular self-transformation. Once again, Hocking was remarkably and almost solely attentive to this significant contribution of mysticism to society, although the role of social action was noted by Underhill, Bergson and among recent writers Kenneth Wapnick and William Johnston. In Hocking's view, the mystic is a social surrogate in whose apparently solitary adventure the most profound concepts and values of a culture are systematically isolated, evaluated and reconstituted in the social consciousness of an epoch, as in the instances provided by Eckhart, Joan of Arc and Gandhi.

The mystic's truly prophetic social function in this respect is not that of a rebel, but that of a reformer, an effort raising to *collective* consciousness the most important if often forgotten values and beliefs of a people. The mystic's torturous process of social and cognitive disengagement and re-engagement is, in effect, a psychic laboratory in which a society renews its spiritual vigor without itself being subject to the temporary immobilization necessary for the process.

Metaphorically speaking, the whole ship of state cannot go into drydock to have the encrusted habits or "automatisms" (Deikman) of gener-

ations scraped from its hull or to have its philosophical sails and rigging
repaired without disruption severe enough to endanger or even destroy
it. But individuals symbolically identified with the social body, whether
self-consciously or not, can in fact accomplish the process of renewal
vicariously and tentatively, depending upon, first, the effectiveness of
their identification with the essential values and beliefs of that society,
second, the thoroughness of the process of "deautomatization," and,
third, the success of their reentry into the social whole, especially their
ability to communicate and propagate what they have experienced. The
isolation and alienation of the mystics during their period of development is thus both provisional and contingent upon heightened social interaction later on, perhaps even long after their deaths, as in the case of
those whose message was heard only after that event or who continued
to affect generations of men and women into the indefinite future.

The greater mystics, then, are those whose identification with their
fellow human beings is more profoundly human, less specifically cultural,
and whose process of development is proportionately searching, their
subsequent activity more pervasive and penetrating. Such "scouts" or
"pioneers" of humanity (Underhill) are men and women of the future,
not of the past. They belong not to Germany, Spain or India, but to the
world.

An obvious and logical objection is that mysticism as I have been
describing it is a *religious* phenomenon. How then can it have a primarily social significance unless the society is similarly religious? Does the
mystic address only the religious issues of the society? Again, what of the
mystic (or the society) which is not explicitly religious, or even not at
all?

To begin with, however one feels about the separation of Church and
State, it can hardly be denied that the greatest mystics have been
religious figures, including those who have had the greatest political impact on their own cultures and others as well, e.g. Joan of Arc, Ignatius
of Loyola, and, of course, Gandhi again. Further, from the time of
Durkheim, it has been clear that the deepest values and beliefs of a culture are, in fact if not in name, religious. Or, to put it differently, from a
sociological viewpoint, religion consists of the deepest values and beliefs
of a culture. Whatever touches upon them will have the force of religious impact—even in officially atheistic societies. An explicit concept of
God is not necessary for the process to work. Moreover, if one accepts
the position that God can be active in the historical process outside the
sphere of manifest religion, i.e. the "Church," it may well follow that the
divine activity can be more effective in those societies in which an explicit God-concept is *not* in force. For the religious establishment seems
not only to have provided a large target for the mystics' prophetic

reform, but also to have opposed them even more strenuously than the State . . . in the name of "God."

As an established institution in society, religion seems to have functioned historically as a largely conservative force, whereas the mystical element in religion has been a reforming drive. Bergson's polarity of "static" and "dynamic" religion was not without an historical foundation. But as Hocking was able to show, as a religious phenomenon, the mystical dimension of experience is a function of the ability of religion itself to adapt to changing social and cultural situations. Mysticism, on this understanding, is not only society's way (nor its only one) of renewing itself, but also the Church's way of self-renewal. Resistance on the part of either the State or the Church may mean nothing more than that because of the dynamics of historical and social transactions, this process must be dialectical.

An interesting corollary in this regard concerns the mystics' notable antagonism toward *all* positive concepts of God. From the social-historical perspective, this opposition may simply reflect the inevitable tension between socially conditioned concepts of God which have a conservative force with regard to development, a case in point being that of the conflict between traditional and liberation theologies in Latin America. It is not by accident, then, that as Galilea indicates, the mystical dimension of religion in Latin America is more developed in liberation theology, which is obviously less reliant than classical theology on standard notions about God, utilizing instead Marxist and other nontraditional sources as well as the less "ramified" concepts of the Bible. Fox's analysis of Eckhart's political and religious opposition indicates that such conflicts probably follow a general pattern, rather than represent a special case.

It can hardly be denied that in the case of most, if not all, mystical movements, their founders were met by bitter hostility on the part of entrenched conservatives who saw them as dangerous, even heretical deviants from established traditions, to mention only the Buddha, Isaiah, Jesus, Sankara, Kabir, al-Ghazali, Eckhart, the Baal Shem Tov, Teresa of Avila, George Fox, Bernadette of Lourdes and the inevitable Gandhi. And yet in most cases, these mystics were in fact retrieving the most cherished and fundamental values and beliefs of their own traditions. The conflict, in this light, was actually between more pristine elements of religion as embodied in the mystics' reform movements and the more sophisticated versions elaborated by pedants for whom these ideas and values had little if any practical importance. The mystical element of religion can thus be seen as more rather than less tradition-conscious, but also as more flexible with regard to jettisoning attempts to define conceptually the more concrete, experiential elements of the original system. The mystic is both more and less conservative than his or her opponents. Mysticism, moreover, is revolutionary only in the sense that it insists upon a return to the fundamental elements of true religion.

The importance of the connection between mystical experience and social action is more widely recognized today than previously—an importance bearing on the political as well as the psychological sphere. But in the words of Hammarskjöld we hear a reflection of every mystic reformer:

> The 'mystical experience.' Always *here* and *now*—in that freedom which is one with distance, in that stillness which is born of silence. But—this is a freedom in the midst of action, a stillness in the midst of other human beings. In our era, the road to holiness necessarily passes through the world of action.[4]

Thomas Merton similarly insisted that "A theology of love cannot afford to be sentimental. . . . [It] must seek to deal realistically with the evil and injustice in the world—not merely to compromise with them."[5]

The liberation theology emanating from Latin America depends upon this connection for its spiritual continuity with the mystical tradition of Catholic Christianity. But many students of mysticism have been sensitive to this issue, as noted before, if their emphasis was overlooked by partisans of Ritschlean and Barthian viewpoints as well as that of the followers of Rauschenbusch, for whom mysticism represented the antithesis of social activism.

The necessary connection between action and the contemplative life, typically interpreted as a function of heightened compassion, individuation or even of an essential social process, has only recently begun to be examined critically. Not surprisingly, a social philosopher, Hocking, was the first clearly to articulate this connection from a comprehensive perspective, that is, as a psychological, social and specifically theological process by which both individual and social integration is accomplished.[6]

Sectional Concerns

The first section, "Description, Analysis and Methodological Concerns" introduces the topic of mysticism beginning with the now-classical viewpoint developed by Anglo-Catholic writers early in the present century, particularly by Evelyn Underhill and Margaret Smith. The seminal article by Louis Bouyer traces the evolution of the use and reference of the word "mystical" from its origins among the ancient Greeks through its transitional interpretation by Philo of Alexandria to its eventual reconception by the early Christian writers of that same city, where pagan, Jewish and Christian ideas and values clashed but also harmonized.

To Christian writers still laboring under the nineteenth-century assumption that *mystical,* both in usage and meaning, represents a particularly unhealthy intrusion of Neoplatonic thought into pristine Christian spirituality, Bouyer's article may prove to be disconcerting. But, in keeping with his conclusions, more recent scholarship is demonstrating that Christian mysticism is a more direct lineal descendant of first-century and earlier *Jewish* mysticism, with its admittedly *Middle*-Platonic Alexandrian veneer. Still, Christian mysticism is likewise a highly original phenomenon, springing from the spirituality of the Epistles and Gospels and post-Apostolic writings, quite distinct from any Hellenic influence.

I have included selections from R. C. Zaehner's *Mysticism Sacred and Profane* (1957) for several reasons. First, his debate with Aldous Huxley tilled the academic soil for an abundant crop of exchanges during the next twenty years and longer. The controversy figures prominently in the essays by Smart, Staal and Auden, for example. Secondly, Zaehner's discussion of mysticism is general and as a factor in world religions bears weightily on the following discussions. Then, too, Zaehner's treatment of Huxley's background and experiences with mescaline provide a rich if sometimes vulnerable specimen of the role inevitably played by interpretation in experience generally and mystical experience especially. Zaehner also introduces us to the controversy over the significance of drugs and mysticism, a subject which appears in the selections by James and Bergson and, more specifically, in those by Staal and Fischer.

The essays by Smart and Staal, and several references elsewhere, are also considerably concerned with the disagreement inaugurated by the Huxley-Zaehner dispute regarding the identity or difference among mystical experiences, whether "natural" or "artificial," i.e. drug-induced, etc. To comprehend the full significance of the controversy, one would need to read both *The Doors of Perception* and Zaehner's reply in their entirety. At stake is the fundamental tension in the comparative study of religion between universal and particular characteristics. Most contemporary commentators do not deny that "deep structures" exist among various, perhaps all, religions. Rather, the disagreement concerns apparently incompatible "superstructures" (Staal) or doctrinal "ramifications" (Smart), whether linguistic, credal or behavioral. Mystical experience and mysticism here provide a well-delineated area for investigation both as a common element in world religions and as the fullest development of consciously religious experience.

A more particularly defined example central to both recent as well as perennial controversies in comparative mysticism concerns the unitive phase of mystical experience. The terms of the debate are set out by Zaehner, Smart and Staal. Is the unity of mystical experience essentially the same everywhere and at all times? Or are there essential differences in the states described by Christian, Hindu, Buddhist and Sūfī mystics, among others? Is the "Self" absorbed by the "All," lost in a sea of some undifferentiated identity? Or is some form of perduring individual personality or subjectivity necessary for there to be an experience of mystical union at all? Is mystical union an "intentional" experience, always "of" another, or does it refer to the identity of pure self-consciousness? Further, can there be a "natural" mystical experience devoid of any consciousness of God's presence?

In the second section, we turn to the mysticism found concretely in world religions, which is uniform neither in depth nor in character. It is clearly more accurate in this regard to speak of mysticisms or of various manifestations of mysticism and mystical experience than of mysticism or mystical experience in the singular, abstract sense. But it is a debated point in many of the essays whether these types and variations can be reduced to a common pattern—one of the moot issues in comparative religion as a whole. For this reason, as well as for chronological completeness, I have begun this section with Dasgupta's essay on Hindu sacrificial mysticism. This, the earliest form of Indian mysticism and the first manifestation in recorded history, is also one of the most difficult to recognize in the welter of magic and ritualism of the ancient East. For, among other things, such primeval mysticism is devoid of particular theistic concerns of later, personalized religion. It thus sets the stage, as it were, for elaborating the Buddhist attitude toward the gods, as well as for the contemporary discussion of "atheistic" mysticism.

Selecting a single topic for analysis rather than a general trend, as in the case of Scholem and Lossky, has the advantage of exposing greater depth and detail, but at the loss of perspective proportionate to the restriction of the field of view. Thus, Suzuki's discussion of the doctrine of selflessness (*anatta*) in Buddhist experience and teaching may not have apparent relevance to the general issues regarding mysticism as treated elsewhere in this volume. However, the doctrine of *anatta* surely touches the central nerve of Buddhism, especially in comparison with Hinduism. And to grasp the full intent of Suzuki's analysis is to grasp in essence the genius of Buddhist mysticism, including some provocative resemblances to the teachings of Meister Eckhart and *The Cloud of Unknowing*.

Orthodox and Protestant Christian views are presented by Vladimir Lossky and William Ernest Hocking—neither of whom claims to speak with comprehensive authority, for various traditions exist within their respective branches of Christianity. Yet both are to a large degree representative and continue the main line of discussion regarding the *philosophia perennis*. A description of traditional Catholic mysticism, although the most common Western specimen, is not included in this section. But many of the later sections contain such descriptions, particularly in the articles by Joseph Maréchal, Jacques Maritain, Etienne Gilson and Dom David Knowles. In some respect, the theological essays in the concluding section of this book are *overly* Catholic, owing partly to the relative dearth of positive treatments of mysticism by Protestant theologians.

While dated in some respects, R. A. Nicholson's introduction to the mystics of Islam is still an outstanding example of critical scholarship, as noted most recently by Annemarie Schimmel in her authoritative work on this subject. Of particular interest is his attention to Hindu, Buddhist, Gnostic and Christian influences.

Finally, a tradition distinctly outside the *philosophia perennis* is eloquently described by Dr. Joseph Epes Brown in the context of that larger tradition, that is, North American "Indian" mysticism.

The scientific study of religion has developed more rapidly and constructively in the present century than any other branch of religious inquiry. The reciprocal effect on religions has been equally notable. The earlier hostility or condescension evident in the writings of T. H. Huxley, Spencer, Leuba, Durkheim and Freud, and embodied in the curricula of higher education as well as the agendas of learned bodies, has largely given way to a respectful rapport, even in the area of new religious movements, cults and sects. (The antagonism of religion toward science, symbolized by the infamous Scopes trial, has been less quickly reduced perhaps, but has diminished nevertheless.)

In the third section, James and Hocking have been selected to represent the changing scientific attitude in the early twentieth century. James's essay was written only months before his death, Hocking's two years later, just prior to the publication of his *magnum opus*, which was in good measure an extended philosophical commentary on his own essay.

A younger contemporary of Dewey, Hocking studied under James and Josiah Royce at Harvard, becoming one of America's foremost philosophers in the thirties and forties. Charles Hartshorne, the foremost contemporary process philosopher, was only one of Hocking's illustrious students at Harvard. Before his death in 1966 at the age of ninety-three, Hocking contributed more to the contemporary philosophical understanding of mysticism than perhaps any writer since Evelyn Underhill, having made it the focus not only of his 1912 masterpiece, *The Meaning of God in Human Experience,* but of many works throughout his prolific career. The selections in this volume include his first major statement about mysticism, and an important essay from his later period.[7]

Many of the scientific students of mysticism in the more recent past have concentrated especially on altered states of consciousness characteristic of mysticism. Four recent formulations have so greatly illuminated this largely undeveloped area that further psychological studies of mysticism will inevitably reflect their influence. The first concerns "deautomatization" or dishabituation, isolated and brilliantly analyzed by Dr. Arthur Deikman as the core process of mystical experience with regard both to perception and behavior. In second place, I locate the elaboration of the active and receptive modes of consciousness, possibly first articulated by French researchers at the end of the nineteenth century and later by Hocking, but here more succinctly presented by Dr. Deikman again. Third is the examination by Dr. Roland Fischer of the two directions of neurophysiological activity in the central nervous system which correspond to meditative as opposed to ecstatic mental states. Of particular interest is Fischer's discussion of the "rebound effect" by which ecstatic states pass instantaneously into the trance-like states of deep, unshakable peace or *samadhi*. Both his articles are instructive in this and other respects. The fourth item is the study of the "bicameral" nature of the human brain and its correlative conscious states, here discussed by Dr. Robert Ornstein. A promising field of inquiry in this regard concerns the possible "location" of the function of the ineffability of mystical experience in right-brain processes.

Our understanding of the psychological dynamics of mysticism from an interdisciplinary perspective has been greatly advanced by a comparison of related experiential situations, particularly those of artists, lovers and, perhaps not surprisingly, schizophrenic patients. Fischer's important *Science* article establishes significant connections concerning the activity of the central nervous system and correlative states of consciousness in terms of these situations. Likewise, Dr. Frank Barron explores similarities and differences between the behavioral states of artists and schizophrenics, whereas Dr. Kenneth Wapnick explores those of mystics and schizophrenics. Elsewhere, Bergson, Underhill and Maritain investigate the creative aspect of mysticism, thus establishing a kind of triangulation by which each situation illuminates aspects of the others. The article by Prince deals with the sociological parameters of mysticism, surveying North American religious history for origins as well as contemporary manifestations among youth groups.

The fourth section comprises both philosophical and aesthetic, mainly literary, analyses of mysticism. The selection from Bergson's last great work, *The Two Sources of Morality and Religion*, has been abridged from the whole of Part III of that work. Condensing the thought of an author of Bergson's literary genius as well as philosophical brilliance adumbrates argument as well as mars the beauty of presentation. The length of Bergson's treatment, which because of its historical importance and relative inaccessibility was particularly appropriate for this volume, in fact required rather extensive omissions. But the essential lines of his case are, I think, preserved, as well as his insights into the place of intoxicants, the value of action, his critiques of Greek and oriental mysticism, the question of morbidity and especially his application of mystical teachings to philosophical problems such as the existence and nature of God, and, finally, his soaring speculations on the ultimate significance of mysticism in the evolution of the cosmos.

Bergson, like many later students of mysticism, was not only interested in altered states of consciousness, but was alert to the important connections between artistic and mystical experience, a sensitivity shared in this case by Hocking, Maritain, Barron, Fischer and Underhill. Bergson's influence on Lossky is acknowledged, although the Russian author, like his American colleagues James and Hocking, emphasizes to a greater degree the *commonness* of mystical experience. Ranged with Bergson on this issue, however, stand the Catholic theologians Maréchal, the late Etienne Gilson, and "the peasant of the Garonne," Jacques Maritain.

The other articles in section four represent more recent views of outstanding contemporary thinkers. Those by Hick and Penelhum derive from the proceedings of the 1976 Calgary Conference on mysticism. Louis Dupré, T. L. Riggs Professor at Yale, takes up the question of the self as a metaphysical category, a much-debated item in the philosophical arena since the Buddha broke his silence half a millennium before Christ. His article should be read in close connection with those of Smart, Suzuki, Fischer and Maritain, for all of whom the "Self" versus the "I" is a major concern.

W. H. Auden's long introduction to *The Protestant Mystics* constitutes a brilliant and independently valuable piece of literary and philosophical analysis. Now out of print, both the introduction and the book, edited by Anne Fremantle, represent a unique contribution to Protestant theology. For reasons of spatial economy, Auden's introduction has been somewhat abridged for this volume.

The fifth and last section is composed of specifically theological appraisals of mysticism, from the dense speculations of Maréchal to the prophetic exhortations of Galilea and Fox, which have been described above in terms of liberation theology and dissent. To the contemporary reader, especially one versed in the psychological disciplines, Maréchal's style and content will seem even less familiar than those of James and Hocking. Although concerned primarily with philosophical or "rational" psychology, Maréchal was well acquainted with contemporary empirical science. His theological approach, while rooted in the Thomistic tradition, was nevertheless indebted to Kantian idealism as well as the authority of the mystics themselves.

Maritain and Gilson need little introduction to the professional theologian. Both distinguished themselves for a generation as the chief if somewhat differing lights of the neo-Thomist revival of the first half of the present century. Gilson's interests extended far beyond a single interpretative framework, however, as his exegesis of selected texts of St. Bernard's mystical theology manifests. While Maritain's article contributes valuably to an ecumenical theology of mysticism, Gilson's provides an example of painstaking, even meticulous historical and theological criticism.

The chapter from Maritain's *Redeeming the Time* was written when he was, perhaps, at the peak of his intellectual powers. It is even more significant insofar as in it he recasts portions of his major theological epistemology, *The Degrees of Knowledge,* precisely with respect to mystical experience. The later version is more balanced and respectful of non-Christian traditions, especially Buddhism. His article should be read in conjunction with those by Suzuki, Dupré, Bergson and Deikman.

Dom David Knowles' little essay represents an attempt to situate Catholic Christian mysticism within the historical context of the theological tradition and particularly with reference to the New Testament. A distinguished historian, Knowles is known chiefly for his studies of Western monasticism and his superb introduction to English mysticism, *The English Mystical Tradition.*

* * *

Preparing and presenting a large collection of critical essays on mysticism at least taught me that the process of selection is ultimately a reflection of one's own philosophical temperament. It is offered in hope that this "blue ribbon" panel of expert witnesses will contribute as much insight and enjoyment to others as it has to me and my students.

I wish to thank in particular those who stimulated my interest in this project and saw it through its various stages: Dr. Jack Miles and my support team at Doubleday, Patricia Kossmann and Debbie McCann. Gratitude is a faint term for the debt of thanks I owe my long-suffering friends and typists, Judy and Tim Rowan, Richard Hutt, Linda Condon and Patricia Kennedy. Many others have contributed to my education in this field and have supported my work, among them Rev. James Weisheipl, Dr. Francis Catania, Dr. Robert Barry, Rev. Robert Harvanek, Rev. Edward Maziarz, Rev. Kallistos Ware, Sir Alister Hardy, Mr. Edward Robinson, Rev. Antony Meredith, and my old friend, Todd Brennan. Possibly the greatest of my debts is to the man who started me off in the direction I have come in comparative mysticism, my "ghostly godfather," Dom Aelred Graham, to whom I respectfully dedicate this volume of studies.

Richard Woods, O.P., Ph.D.
Institute of Pastoral Studies
Loyola University of Chicago

NOTES

1. Cf. Adam Curle, *Mystics and Militants*. Unless otherwise noted, works referred to in the text will be found in the general bibliography at the end of this volume.

2. Cf. William Braden, *The Age of Aquarius;* Harvey Cox, *Turning East;* Martin Marty, "The Persistence of the Mystical"; R. E. L. Masters and Jean Houston, *The Varieties of Psychedelic Experience;* Jacob Needleman, *The New Religions;* Jacob Needleman, ed., *Religion for a New Generation;* and Richard Woods, *The Occult Revolution.*

3. Several important and critical studies of book length have appeared in the last two decades, however, including Hal Bridges' *American Mysticism from William James to Zen;* Margaret Lewis Furse's *Mysticism: Window on a World View;* Aelred Graham's *Zen Catholicism;* Georgia Harkness' *Mysticism: Its Meaning and Message;* William Johnston's *The Inner Eye of Love* and *Silent Music;* Ben-Ami Scharfstein's *Mystical Experience* and Illtyd Trethowan's *Mysticism and Theology.* In addition, several classic studies have been reissued, such as Ronald Knox's *Enthusiasm;* Rudolf Otto's *Mysticism East and West* and Evelyn Underhill's *Mysticism.*

4. Hammarskjöld, *Markings*, p. 122.

5. Thomas Merton, *Faith and Violence* (University of Notre Dame Press, 1968), p. 8. Cf. also his *Contemplation in a World of Action.*

6. For an analysis of Hocking's fundamental position, cf. Richard Woods, *The Social Dimension of Mysticism.*

7. For a further discussion of Hocking's contribution to the study of mysticism, see my article "Mysticism, Protestantism and Ecumenism: The Spiritual Theology of William Ernest Hocking," in *Western Spirituality, Historical Roots, Ecumenical Routes,* ed. Matthew Fox (Notre Dame: Fides Press, 1979).

PART I
Description, Analysis and Methodological Concerns

1

The Nature and Meaning of Mysticism

MARGARET SMITH

The word "Mysticism" itself comes down to us from the Greeks and is derived from a root meaning "to close." The mystic was one who had been initiated into the esoteric knowledge of Divine things, and upon whom was laid the necessity of keeping silence concerning his sacred knowledge. The term "mystical," then might be applied to any secret cult revealed only to the initiated. The philosophers took over the word from the priests and applied it to their own speculative doctrines and thence it passed over into the Christian Church, which held itself to be a body of initiates into a truth not possessed by mankind at large. The derivation of the word was later held to give it the meaning of closing the mind to the influence of all external things, so that it might be withdrawn into itself, and so be fitted to receive the Divine Illumination.

But the real meaning of the word, as we use it now, represents something much wider than its derivation. That for which it stands is a tendency not limited to the Greeks, either priests or philosophers, nor bounded by the far-reaching comprehensiveness of the Christian Church. It denotes something which is to be found, in a highly developed state, in the early religious doctrines of the East; in the Vedic literature; in Buddhism both in India and in China; in a form strangely attractive, considering the apparently barren soil in which this flower has bloomed, in Sūfism, the mysticism of Islam, which has spread itself and taken firm root in Persia, Turkey and India as well as in Arab lands; in Judaism, again an unpromising environment, to all appearances; and finally, as we have seen, in Greece and in the West.

It seems plain that a mystical doctrine found at an early period in the world's history, developing and persisting through the centuries, so that at one and the same time we find it, in an almost identical form, in the religions of the East, in the Western Christianity of Germany, France and Italy and in the Byzantine Church of Constantinople, represents a spiritual tendency which is universal, a tendency of the human soul which is eternal. As a great Oriental scholar[1] has put it:

There is hardly any soil, be it ever so barren, where Mysticism will not strike root; hardly any creed, however formal, round which it will not twine itself. It is, indeed, the eternal cry of the human soul for rest; the insatiable longing of a being wherein infinite ideals are fettered and cramped by a miserable actuality; and so long as man is less than an angel and more than a beast, this cry will not for a moment fail to make itself heard. Wonderfully uniform, too, whether it come from the Brahmin sage, the Persian poet, or the Christian quietist, it is in essence an enunciation more or less clear, more or less eloquent, of the aspiration of the soul to cease altogether from self and to be at one with God.

Mysticism, therefore, is not to be regarded as a religion in itself, but rather as the most vital element in all true religions, rising up in revolt against cold formality and religious torpor. Nor is it a philosophical system, though it has its own doctrine of the scheme of things. It is to be described rather as an attitude of mind; an innate tendency of the human soul, which seeks to transcend reason and to attain to a direct experience of God, and which believes that it is possible for the human soul to be united with Ultimate Reality, when "God ceases to be an object and becomes an experience." Mysticism has been defined as "the immediate feeling of the unity of self with God—it is the religious life at its very heart and center—it is the endeavor to fix the immediateness of the life in God as such—in this God-intoxication, in which the self and the world are alike forgotten, the subject knows himself to be in possession of the highest and fullest truth."[2]

The aim of the mystics, then, is to establish a conscious relation with the Absolute, in which they find the personal object of love. They desire to know, only that they may love, and their desire for union is founded neither on curiosity nor self-interest. That union which they seek is "the supernatural union of likeness, begotten of love, which is the union of the human will with the Divine. They seek to realize the unfelt natural presence of God in creation—by entering into a personal relationship with the concealed Presence which is the Source of being."[3] While religion in general separates the divine from the human, Mysticism, going beyond religion, aspires to intimate union with the Divine, to a penetration of the Divine within the soul and to a disappearance of the individuality, with all its modes of acting, thinking and feeling, in the Divine substance. The mystic seeks to pass out of all that is merely phenomenal, out of all lower forms of reality, to become Being itself.

On what do the mystics base their claim to be able to undertake this "tremendous journey towards the mysterious Isles of Fire, the Icelands of abstraction and of love"? Mysticism postulates certain articles of faith as the basis of its assumptions.

Firstly, it maintains that the soul can see and perceive, with that spiritual sense, of which St. Augustine speaks, which penetrates through the veils of matter and perceives the Light Unchangeable. This is that inner sense which is called intuition, by means of which man can receive direct revelation and knowledge of God, by which he perceives things hidden from reason, through which he is brought into a conscious fellowship and unity with God. "It is a spiritual sense opening inwardly, as the physical senses open outwardly, and because it has the capacity to perceive, grasp and know the truth at first hand, independent of all external sources of information, we call it intuition."[4] All possibility of spiritual revelation depends on such a spiritual faculty of the soul, capable of receiving it. Mysticism then denies that knowledge can be attained only by means of the senses, or the intellect, or the normal processes of consciousness, and claims that the highest knowledge can be attained, by this spiritual sense of intuition.

Secondly, Mysticism assumes that man must be a partaker of the Divine nature, if he is to know the Divine—only if the self is real can it hope to know Reality, and so it assumes that every creature is by nature akin to the Creator, there is within every living soul a divine spark, that which seeks re-union with the Eternal Flame. The mystics throughout the ages have contended that God Himself is "the ground of the soul" and that all men in the depths of their being have a share in one central, Divine, life. By the mystic, God is realized as the "foundation of the soul's being, and the soul's perception of its own essence is, in fact, the perception of its unity with the Divine nature."

In the third place, Mysticism assumes that none can attain to the knowledge of God except by purification from self. "Who shall ascend unto the hill of the Lord? or who shall stand in His holy place? Even he that hath clean hands and a pure heart," sang the Hebrew Psalmist, and the Greek philosopher Plotinus says also that as the eye could not behold the sun unless it were itself sunlike, so no more can the soul behold God unless it is Godlike. So the mystics both in East and West have maintained that the stripping from the soul of selfishness and sensuality is essential for the beholding of the Vision of God. Self-loss, withdrawal from self, self-annihilation, these are essential to those who would approach the Absolute. Only when all images of earth are hushed and the clamor of the senses is stilled and the soul has passed beyond thought of self can the Eternal Wisdom be revealed to the mystic who seeks that high communion with the Unseen.

Fourthly, the guide on the upward path of the mystic is, and must be,

Love. The Oriental mystic, seeking to overcome the element of Not-Being—all that is opposed to the one Reality, the Divine Being Itself—finds that self, the great hindrance, can be conquered only by Love. "By Love and Love alone can the dark shadow of Not-Being be done away: by Love and by Love alone can the soul of man win back to its Divine source and find its ultimate goal in reunion with the Truth."[5] To the mystic, wherever he is found, and to whatever type of religion he attaches himself, the Object of his search is conceived of as the Beloved, and the mystic regards himself as the lover, yearning for the consummation of his love in union with the One he loves. So the Flemish mystic Ruysbroeck writes: "When love has carried us above all things . . . we receive in peace the Incomprehensible Light"; and again: "The God-seeking man who has forsaken self and all things . . . can always enter into the inmost part of his spirit. There he feels himself to be an eternal life of love, which craves above all else to be one with God." And from this we see that the term Love as used by the mystics implies far more than a mere emotion: "it is to be understood in its deepest, fullest sense; as the ultimate expression of the self's most vital tendencies . . . the deep-seated desire and tendency of the soul towards its source. . . . Love, to the mystic, is the active expression of his will and desire for the Absolute and also his innate tendency to that Absolute."[6] Only Love can set the mystic free to pass from that which seems to that which is, to look upon the Light Unchangeable, to realize that he is one with that Transcendental Ideal, where is the Supremely Real.

While Mysticism has thus developed a speculative system which has for its chief theory the fundamental unity, and the religious necessity of the union, of the Divine spirit with the human, it is also practical, issuing in a life to be lived by a rule, the Mystic Way, which must be trodden by those who seek to enjoy the blessedness of actual communion with the Highest.

The stages of the Mystic Way vary somewhat in the different religions of East and West in which Mysticism has taken root, but the threefold division which has been accepted in the West will, to a large extent, cover the stages of that Way as set forth in the religious systems of the East. These three stages are those of the Purgative life, the Illuminative life and the Unitive life, and the old Sūfī teacher who said that Renunciation, which is the keynote of the Way, should be first of that which is unlawful, second of that which is lawful, and third of all save God Himself, was describing the three stages of the Mystic Way fairly accurately.

At the beginning of all must be the awakening or the conversion of the mystic, who becomes aware of what he seeks, and sets his face towards the Goal. But a long preparation is needed before he can expect to attain it, and the discipline of the Purgative life must first be endured.

By repentance, confession, amendment of life must the self be disciplined. To the Eastern mystics, and to many mystics of the West, a life of asceticism has seemed the only way by which the carnal soul could be purified from its sins, which have their root in the desires of self, sensuality and selfishness. For the mystic who lives in the world—and the best of the mystics have not withdrawn themselves from the business of life—this stage will mean the full development of the civic and social virtues and the discharge of all ordinary religious duties and the use of the ordinary means of grace. In this stage of the Way the soul seeks to be cleansed from the senses, to be stripped of all that is opposed to the Eternal Order and so to be fit to pass on to the second stage, that of Illuminative life.

The external life has been brought into accordance with the Good and now the struggle is transferred to the inner life. All the faculties, feeling, intellect and will must be cleansed and brought into harmony with the Eternal Will. This is the Sūfī doctrine of unification: an old Persian writer says that it means the cessation of human volition and affirmation of the Divine Will, so as to exclude all personal initiative. So also it is described by a modern writer as "the complete surrender of man's personal striving to the overruling Will of God and thus the linking up of all the successive acts of life with the Abiding."[7] Now is the soul walking in the light, looking upon a world illuminated by the effulgence of Unclouded Light, and the Presence of God is now an experienced reality, not simply a concept of the imagination.

The final stage of the Way is the Unitive life, in which the soul passes from Becoming to Being, man beholds God face to face, and is joined to Him in a progressive union, a union which is a fact of experience consciously realized. In terms of the most beautiful and glowing imagery have the mystics—who alone are qualified to speak, since they alone have seen and known that of which they speak—sought to describe the Beatific Vision and the Union to which it leads. Plotinus, who had seen and attained, speaks of it thus: "Beholding this Being—resting, rapt, in the vision and possession of so lofty a loveliness, growing to Its likeness—what beauty can the soul yet lack? For This, the Beauty supreme, the absolute and the primal, fashions Its lovers to Beauty and makes them also worthy of love."[8]

So also the Sūfī poet:

> With My Beloved I alone have been,
> When secrets tenderer than evening airs
> Passed and the Vision blest
> Was granted to my prayers,
> That crowned me, else obscure, with endless fame,
> The while amazed between

His Beauty and His Majesty
I stood in silent ecstasy
Revealing that which o'er my spirit went and came.
Lo, in His face commingled
Is every charm and grace;
The whole of Beauty singled
Into a perfect face
Beholding Him would cry,
"There is no God but He and He is the most High."[9]

We can set beside this the Franciscan concept of the Vision as "a rapture and uplifting of the mind intoxicated in the contemplation of the unspeakable savour of the Divine sweetness, and a happy, peaceful and sweet delight of the soul, that is rapt and uplifted in great marvel—and a burning sense within of that celestial glory unspeakable."[10] Suso, the German mystic of the fourteenth century, also seeks to give us a description of that which he finds words are too poor to depict: "This highest stage of union is an indescribable experience, in which all idea of images and forms and differences has vanished. All consciousness of self and of all things has gone and the soul is plunged into the abyss of the Godhead and the spirit has become one with God."

From the great Spanish mystic St. John of the Cross we have a similar testimony: "Thus the soul, when it shall have driven away from itself all that is contrary to the Divine Will, becomes transformed in God in love—the soul then becomes immediately enlightened by and transformed in God, because He communicates His own supernatural being in such a way that the soul seems to be God Himself and to possess the things of God—the soul seems to be God rather than itself and indeed is God by participation."

Mysticism, then, is spiritual and transcendent in its aims, but it holds that the Object of its quest, the World-Soul, the Absolute, the One Reality, is also the Beloved, and as lovers the mystics seek for union with the One. That union they believe can be attained only by passing through certain definite stages, which they call the treading of the Mystic Way, so that Mysticism is active and practical; it means discipline and a rule of life, and much upward striving before the mystic can hope to attain the heights. Mysticism, since it is permeated through and through by the power of Love, can never be self-seeking, for the end can only be attained by self-stripping; moreover, what is given in full measure to the mystic must be shared with others. That flooding of the mystic's soul with the Divine Life must mean a fuller, richer life lived in contact with other human lives. "The perfect life," said Plato, "would be a life of perfect communion with other souls, as well as with the Soul which animates the universe." This mystic consciousness of the Presence of God is not given simply to delight in as the most exquisite of pleasures, but is to inspire the mystic to a finer service of humanity; the purest Mysticism is found where the mystic "throws himself into action and life as though it were forever, and does it simply, without attempts to be isolated with the Absolute out of Time." So the active life of service in the world has been found necessary to the greatest of the mystics, who have felt themselves to be living in God, as in some measure deified in all their being and so in all their acts to be only instruments of God.

To sum up, then, in the words of a great modern teacher of Mysticism:

To be a mystic is simply to participate here and now in real and eternal life, in the fullest, deepest sense which is possible to man. It is to share as a free and conscious agent in the joyous travail of the universe, its mighty, onward sweep through pain and glory to its home in God. The ordered sequence of states, the organic development, whereby his consciousness is detached from illusion and rises to the mystic freedom which conditions, instead of being conditioned by, its normal world, is the way he must tread in order to attain. Only by this deliberate fostering of his deeper self, this transmutation of the elements of character, can he reach those levels of consciousness upon which he hears and responds to the measure "whereto the worlds keep time" on their great pilgrimage towards the Heart of God. The mystic act of union, that joyous loss of the transfigured self in God, which is the crown of man's conscious ascent towards the Absolute, is the contribution of the individual to this, the destiny of the Cosmos.[11]

NOTES

1. E. G. Browne in *A Year among the Persians*.
2. Pfleiderer.
3. A. B. Sharpe, *Mysticism: Its True Nature and Value*, p. 140.
4. R. W. Trine, *In Tune with the Infinite*, p. 40.
5. E. J. W. Gibb, *History of Ottoman Poetry*, i, p. 20.
6. E. Underhill, *Mysticism*, pp. 101ff.
7. E. Underhill, *Man and the Supernatural*, p. 246.
8. Plotinus, *Ennead* i. 7.
9. Ibn al-Farid, tr. R. A. Nicholson.
10. *Little Flowers of St. Francis*, tr. T. W. Arnold, pp. 290–91.
11. E. Underhill, *Mysticism*, p. 534.

2

The Essentials of Mysticism

EVELYN UNDERHILL

What are the true essentials of mysticism? When we have stripped off those features which some mystics accept and some reject—all that is merely due to tradition, temperament or unconscious allegorism—what do we find as the necessary and abiding character of all true mystical experience? This question is really worth asking. For some time much attention has been given to the historical side of mysticism, and some—much less—to its practice. But there has been no clear understanding of the difference between its substance and its accidents: between traditional forms and methods, and the eternal experience which they have mediated. In mystical literature words are frequently confused with things, and symbols with realities; so that much of this literature seems to the reader to refer to some self-consistent and exclusive dreamworld, and not to the achievement of universal truth. Thus the strong need for restatement which is being felt by institutional religion, the necessity of retranslating its truths into symbolism which modern men can understand and accept, applies with at least equal force to mysticism. It has become important to disentangle the facts from ancient formulæ used to express them. These formulæ have value, because they are genuine attempts to express truth; but they are not themselves that truth, and failure to recognize this distinction has caused a good deal of misunderstanding. Thus, on its philosophic and theological side, the mysticism of western Europe is tightly entwined with the patristic and mediæval presentation of Christianity; and this presentation, though full of noble poetry, is now difficult if not impossible to adjust to our conceptions of the Universe. Again, on its personal side mysticism is a department of psychology. Now psychology is changing under our eyes; already we see our mental life in a new perspective, tend to describe it under new forms. Our ways of describing and interpreting spiritual experience must change with the rest, if we are to keep in touch with reality; though the experience itself be unchanged.

So we are forced to ask ourselves, what is the essential element in spiritual experience? Which of the many states and revelations described by the mystics are integral parts of it; and what do these states and degrees come to, when we describe them in the current phraseology and strip off the monastic robes in which they are usually dressed? What elements are due to the suggestions of tradition, to conscious or unconscious symbolism, to the misinterpretation of emotion, to the invasion of cravings from the lower centers, or the disguised fulfillment of an unconscious wish? And when all these channels of illusion have been blocked, what is left? This will be a difficult and often a painful enquiry. But it is an enquiry which ought to be faced by all who believe in the validity of man's spiritual experience; in order that their faith may be established on a firm basis, and disentangled from those unreal and impermanent elements which are certainly destined to destruction, and with which it is at present too often confused. I am sure that at the present moment we serve best the highest interests of the soul by subjecting the whole mass of material which is called "mysticism" to an inexorable criticism. Only by inflicting the faithful wounds of a friend can we save the science of the inner life from mutilation at the hands of the psychologists.

We will begin, then, with the central fact of the mystic's experience. This central fact, it seems to me, is an overwhelming consciousness of God and of his own soul: a consciousness which absorbs or eclipses all other centers of interest. It is said that St. Francis of Assisi, praying in the house of Bernard of Quintavalle, was heard to say again and again: "My God! my God! what art Thou? and what am I?" Though the words come from St. Augustine, they well represent his mental attitude. This was the only question which he thought worth asking; and it is the question which every mystic asks at the beginning and sometimes answers at the end of his quest. Hence we must put first among our essentials the clear conviction of a living God as the primary interest of consciousness, and of a personal self capable of communion with Him. Having said this, however, we may allow that the widest latitude is possible in the mystic's conception of his Deity. At best this conception will be symbolic; his experience, if genuine, will far transcend the symbols he employs. "God," says the author of The Cloud of Unknowing, "may well be loved but not thought." Credal forms, therefore, can only be for the mystic a scaffold by which he ascends. We are even bound, I think, to confess that the overt recognition of that which orthodox Christians generally mean by a personal God is not essential. On the contrary, where it takes a crudely anthropomorphic form, the idea of personality may be a disadvantage; opening the way for the intrusion of disguised emotions and desires. In the highest experiences of the greatest mystics the personal category appears to be transcended. "The light in the soul which is increate," says Eckhart, "is not satisfied with the three Persons, insofar as each subsists in its difference . . . but it is determined to know whence this Being comes, to penetrate into the Simple Ground, into the Silent Desert within which never any difference has lain." The all-inclusive One is beyond all partial apprehensions, though the true values which those apprehensions represent are conserved in it. However pantheistic the mystic may be on the one hand, however absolutist on the other, his communion with God is always personal in this sense: that it is communion with a living Reality, an object of love, capable of response, which demands and receives from him a total self-donation. This sense of a double movement, a self-giving on the divine side answering to the self-giving on the human side, is found in all great mysticism. It has, of course, lent itself to emotional exaggeration, but in its pure form seems an integral part of man's apprehension of Reality. Even where it conflicts with the mystic's philosophy—as in Hinduism and Neoplatonism—it is still present. It is curious to note, for instance, how Plotinus, after safeguarding his Absolute One from every qualification, excluding it from all categories, defining it only by the icy method of negation, suddenly breaks away into the language of ardent feeling when he comes to describe that ecstasy in which he touched the truth. Then he speaks of "the veritable love, the sharp desire" which possessed him, appealing to the experience of those fellow mystics who have "caught fire, and found the splendour there." These, he says, have "felt burning within themselves the flame of love for what is there to know—the passion of the lover resting on the bosom of his love."

So we may say that the particular mental image which the mystic forms of his objective, the traditional theology he accepts, is not essential. Since it is never adequate, the degree of its inadequacy is of secondary importance. Though some creeds have proved more helpful to the mystic than others, he is found fully developed in every great religion. We cannot honestly say that there is any wide difference between the Brahman, Sūfī, or Christian mystic at their best. They are far more like each other than they are like the average believer in their several creeds. What is essential is the way the mystic feels about his Deity, and about his own relation with it; for this adoring and all-possessing consciousness of the rich and complete divine life over against the self's life, and of the possible achievement of a level of being, a sublimation of the self, wherein we are perfectly united with it, may fairly be written down as a necessary element of all mystical life. This is the common factor which unites those apparently incompatible views of the Universe which have been claimed at one time or another as mystical. Their mystical quality abides wholly in the temper of the self who adopts them. He may be a *transcendentalist:* but if so, it is because his intuition of the divine is so lofty that it cannot be expressed by means of any intellectual concept, and he is bound to say with Ruysbroeck, "He is neither This nor That."

He may be a *unanimist;* but if he is, it is because he finds in other men—more, in the whole web of life—that mysterious living essence which is a mode of God's existence, and which he loves, seeks and recognizes everywhere. "How shall I find words for the beauty of my Beloved? For He is merged in all beauty," says Kabir, "His colour is in all the pictures of the world, and it bewitches the body and the mind." He may be—often is—a *sacramentalist;* but if so, only because the symbol or the sacrament help him to touch God. So St. Thomas:

> Adoro te devote, latens Deitas,
> Quæ sub his figuris vere latitas.

The moment the mystic suspects that any of these things are obstacles instead of means, he rejects them, to the scandal of those who habitually confuse the image with the reality.

Thus we get the temperamental symbolist, quietist, nature-mystic, or transcendentalist. We get Plotinus rapt to the "bare pure One"; St. Augustine's impassioned communion with Perfect Beauty; Eckhart declaring his achievement of the "wilderness of God"; Jacopone da Todi prostrate in adoration before the "Love that gives all things form"; Ruysbroeck describing his achievement of "that wayless abyss of fathomless beatitude where the Trinity of divine persons possess their nature in the essential Unity"; Jacob Boehme gazing into the fire-world and there finding the living heart of the Universe; Kabir listening to the rhythmic music of Reality, and seeing the worlds told like beads within the Being of God. And at the opposite pole we find Mechthild of Magdeburg's amorous conversations with her "heavenly Bridegroom," the many mystical experiences connected with the Eucharist, the Sūfī's enraptured description of God as the "Matchless Chalice and the Sovereign Wine," the narrow intensity and emotional raptures of contemplatives of the type of Richard Rolle. We cannot refuse the title of mystic to any of these; because in every case their aim is union between God and the soul. This is the one essential of mysticism, and there are as many ways from one term to the other as there are variations in the spirit of man. But, on the other hand, when anybody speaking of mysticism proposes an object that is less than God—increase of knowledge, of health, of happiness, occultism, intercourse with spirits, supernormal experience in general—then we may begin to suspect that we are off the track.

Now we come to the next group of essentials: the necessary acts and dispositions of the mystic himself, the development which takes place in him—the psychological facts, that is to say, which are represented by the so-called "mystic way." The mystic way is best understood as a process of sublimation, which carries the correspondences of the self with the Universe up to higher levels than those on which our normal consciousness works. Just as the normal consciousness stands over against the unconscious, which, with its buried impulses and its primitive and infantile cravings, represents a cruder reaction of the organism to the external world; so does the developed mystical life stand over against normal consciousness, with its preoccupations and its web of illusions encouraging the animal will-to-dominate and animal will-to-live. Normal consciousness sorts out some elements from the mass of experiences beating at our doors and constructs from them a certain order; but this order lacks any deep meaning or true cohesion, because normal consciousness is incapable of apprehending the underlying reality from which these scattered experiences proceed. The claim of the mystical consciousness is to a closer reading of truth; to an apprehension of the divine unifying principle behind appearance. "The One," says Plotinus, "is present everywhere and absent only from those unable to perceive it"; and when we *do* perceive it we "have another life . . . attaining the aim of our existence, and our rest." To know this at firsthand—not to guess, believe or accept, but to be certain—is the highest achievement of human consciousness, and the ultimate object of mysticism. How is it done?

There are two ways of attacking this problem which may conceivably help us. The first consists in a comparison of the declarations of different mystics, and a sorting out of those elements which they have in common: a careful watch being kept, of course, for the results of conscious or unconscious imitation, of tradition and of theological preconceptions. In this way we get some firsthand evidence of factors which are at any rate usually present, and may possibly be essential. The second line of enquiry consists in a retranslation into psychological terms of these mystical declarations; when many will reveal the relation in which they stand to the psychic life of man.

Reviewing the firsthand declarations of the mystics, we inevitably notice one prominent feature: the frequency with which they break up their experience into three phases. Sometimes they regard these objectively, and speak of three worlds or three aspects of God of which they become successively aware. Sometimes they regard them subjectively, and speak of three stages of growth through which they pass, such as those of Beginner, Proficient and Perfect; or of phases of spiritual progress in which we first meditate upon reality, then contemplate reality, and at last are united with reality. But among the most widely separated mystics of the East and West this threefold experience can nearly always be traced. There are, of course, obvious dangers in attaching absolute value to number-schemes of this kind. Numbers have an uncanny power over the human mind; once let a symbolic character be attributed to them, and the temptation to make them fit the facts at all costs becomes overwhelming. We all know that the number "three" has a long religious history, and are therefore inclined to look with suspicion on its claim to interpret the mystic life. At the same time there are other significant numbers—such as "seven" and "ten"—which have never gained equal currency as the bases of mystical formulæ. We may agree that the mediæval mystics found the threefold division of spiritual experience in Neoplatonism; but we must also agree that a formula of this kind is not likely to survive for nearly two thousand years unless it agrees with the facts. Those who use it with the greatest conviction are not theorists. They are the practical mystics, who are intent on making maps of the regions into which they have penetrated.

Moreover, this is no mere question of handing on one single tradition. The mystics describe their movement from appearance to reality in many different ways, and use many incompatible religious symbols. The one constant factor is the discrimination of three phases of consciousness, no more, no less, in which we can recognize certain common characteristics. "There are," says Philo, "three kinds of life: life as it concerns God, life as it concerns the creature, and a third intermediate life, a mixture of the former two." Consistently with this, Plotinus speaks of three descending phases or principles of Divine Reality: the Godhead, or absolute and unconditioned One; its manifestation as *Nous*, the Divine Mind or Spirit which inspires the "intelligible" and eternal world; and *Psyche*, the Life or Soul of the physical Universe. Man, normally in correspondence with this physical world of succession and change, may by spiritual intuition achieve first consciousness of the eternal world of spiritual values, in which indeed the apex of his soul already dwells; and in brief moments of ecstatic vision may rise above this to communion with its source, the Absolute One. There you have the mystic's vision of the Universe, and the mystic's way of purification, enlightenment and ecstasy, bringing new and deeper knowledge of reality as the self's interest, urged by its loving desire of the Ultimate, is shifted from sense to soul, from soul to spirit. There is here no harsh dualism, no turning from a bad material world to a good spiritual world. We are invited to one gradual undivided process of sublimation, penetrating ever more deeply into the reality of the Universe, to find at last "that One who is present everywhere and absent only from those who do not perceive Him." What we behold, that we are: citizens, according to our own will and desire, of the surface world of the senses, the deeper world of life, or the ultimate world of spiritual reality.

An almost identical doctrine appears in the Upanishads. At the heart of reality is Brahma, "other than the known, and above the unknown." His manifestation is Ananda, that spiritual world which is the true object of æsthetic passion and religious contemplation. From it life and consciousness are born, in it they have their being, to it they must return.

Finally, there is the world-process as we know it, which represents Ananda taking form. So too the mystic Kabir, who represents an opposition to the Vedantic philosophy, says: "From beyond the Infinite the Infinite comes, and from the Infinite the finite extends." And again: "Some contemplate the formless and others meditate on form, but the wise man knows that Brahma is beyond both." Here we have the finite world of becoming, the infinite world of being, and Brahma, the Unconditioned Absolute, exceeding and including all. Yet, as Kabir distinctly declares again and again, there are no fences between these aspects of the Universe. When we come to the root of reality we find that "Conditioned and Unconditioned are but one word"; the difference is in our own degree of awareness.

Compare with this three of the great mediæval Catholic mystics: that acute psychologist Richard of St. Victor, the ardent poet and contemplative Jacopone da Todi, and the profound Ruysbroeck. Richard of St. Victor says that there are three phases in the contemplative consciousness. The first is called dilation of mind, enlarging and deepening our vision of the world. The next is elevation of mind, in which we behold the realities which are above ourselves. The third is ecstasy, in which the mind is carried up to contact with truth in its pure simplicity. This is really the universe of Plotinus translated into subjective terms. So, too, Jacopone da Todi says in the symbolism of his day that three heavens are open to man. He must climb from one to the other; it is hard work, but love and longing press him on. First, when the mind has achieved self-conquest, the "starry heaven" of multiplicity is revealed to it. Its darkness is lit by scattered lights; points of reality pierce the sky. Next, it achieves the "crystalline heaven" of lucid contemplation, where the soul is conformed to the rhythm of the divine life, and by its loving intuition apprehends God under veils. Lastly, in ecstasy it may be lifted to that ineffable state which he calls the "hidden heaven," where it enjoys a vision of imageless reality and "enters into possession of all that is God." Ruysbroeck says that he has experienced three orders of reality: the natural world, theater of our moral struggle; the essential world, where God and Eternity are indeed known, but by intermediaries; and the superessential world, where without intermediary, and beyond all separation, "above reason and without reason," the soul is united to "the glorious and absolute One."

Take, again, a totally different mystic, Jacob Boehme. He says that he saw in the Divine Essence three principles or aspects. The first he calls "the deepest Deity, without and beyond Nature," and the next its manifestation in the Eternal Light-world. The third is that outer world in which we dwell according to the body, which is a manifestation, image or similitude of the Eternal. "And we are thus," he says, "to understand reality as a threefold being, or three worlds *in one another.*" We observe again the absence of watertight compartments. The whole of reality is present in every part of it; and the power of correspondence with all these aspects of it is latent in man. "If one sees a right man," says Boehme again, "he may say, I see here three worlds standing."

We have now to distinguish the essential element in all this. How does it correspond with psychological facts? Some mystics, like Richard of St. Victor, have frankly exhibited its subjective side and so helped us to translate the statements of their fellows. Thus Dionysius the Areopagite says in a celebrated passage: "Threefold is the way to God. The first is the way of purification, in which the mind is inclined to learn true wisdom. The second is the way of illumination, in which the mind by contemplation is kindled to the burning of love. The third is the way of union, in which the mind by understanding, reason and spirit is led up by God alone." This formula restates the Plotinian law; for the "contemplation" of Dionysius is the "spiritual intuition" of Plotinus, which inducts man into the intelligible world; his "union" is the Plotinian ecstatic vision of the One. It profoundly impressed the later Christian mystics, and has long been accepted as the classic description of spiritual growth, because it has been found again and again to answer to experience. It is therefore worth our while to examine it with some care.

First we notice how gentle, gradual and natural is the process of sublimation that Dionysius demands of us. According to him, the mystic life is a life centered on reality: the life that first seeks reality without flinching, then loves and adores the reality perceived, and at last, wholly surrendered to it, is "led by God alone." First, the self is "inclined to learn *true* wisdom." It awakes to new needs, is cured of its belief in sham values, and distinguishes between real and unreal objects of desire. That craving for more life and more love which lies at the very heart of our selfhood, here slips from the charmed circle of the senses into a wider air. When this happens abruptly it is called "conversion"; and may then have the character of a psychic convulsion and be accompanied by various secondary psychological phenomena. But often it comes without observation. Here the essentials are a desire and a disillusionment sufficiently strong to overcome our natural sloth, our primitive horror of change. "The first beginning of all things is a craving," says Boehme; "we are creatures of will and desire." The divine discontent, the hunger for reality, the unwillingness to be satisfied with the purely animal or the purely social level of consciousness, is the first essential stage in the development of the mystical consciousness.

So the self is either suddenly or gradually inclined to "true wisdom"; and this change of angle affects the whole character, not only or indeed specially the intellectual outlook, but the ethical outlook too. This is the meaning of "purgation." False ways of feeling and thinking, established complexes which have acquired for us an almost sacred character, and governed though we knew it not all our reactions to life—these must be broken up. That mental and moral sloth which keeps us so comfortably wrapped in unrealities must go. This phase in the mystic's growth has been specially emphasized and worked out by the Christian mystics, who have made considerable additions to the philosophy and natural history of the soul. The Christian sense of sin and conception of charity, the Christian notion of humility as a finding of our true level, an exchanging of the unreal standards of egoism for the disconcerting realities of life seen from the angle of Eternity; the steadfast refusal to tolerate any claim to spirituality which is not solidly based on moral values, or which is divorced from the spirit of tenderness of love—all this has immensely enriched the mysticism of the West, and filled up some of the gaps left by Neoplatonism. It is characteristic of Christianity that, addressing itself to all men—not, as Neoplatonism tended to do, to the superior person— and offering to all men participation in Eternal Life, it takes human nature as it is; and works from the bottom up, instead of beginning at a level which only a few of the race attain. Christianity perceived how deeply normal men are enslaved by the unconscious; how great a moral struggle is needed for their emancipation. Hence it concentrated on the first stage of purgation, and gave it new meaning and depth. The monastic rule of poverty, chastity and obedience—and we must remember that the original aim of monasticism was to provide a setting in which the mystical life could be lived—aims at the removal of those self-centered desires and attachments which chain consciousness to a personal instead of a universal life. He who no longer craves for personal possessions, pleasures or powers is very near to perfect liberty. His attention is freed from its usual concentration on the self's immediate interests, and at once he sees the Universe in a new, more valid, because disinterested light.

> Povertate è nulla avere
> e nulla cosa poi volere
> ed omne cosa possedere
> en spirito de libertade.

Yet this positive moral purity which Christians declared necessary to the spiritual life was not centered on a lofty aloofness from human failings, but on a self-giving and disinterested love, the complete abolition of egoism. This alone, it declared, could get rid of that inward disharmony— one aspect of the universal conflict between the instinctive and the rational life—which Boehme called the "powerful contrarium" warring with the soul.

Now this "perfect charity in life surrendered," however attained, is an essential character of the true mystic; without it, contemplation is an impossibility or a sham. But when we come to the means by which it is to be attained, we reenter the region of controversy; for here we are at once confronted by the problem of asceticism, and its connection with mysticism—perhaps the largest and most difficult of the questions now facing those who are concerned with the restatement of the laws of the spiritual life. Originally regarded as a gymnastic of the soul, an education in those manly virtues of self-denial and endurance without which the spiritual life is merely an exquisite form of hedonism, asceticism was identified by Christian thought with the idea of mortification; the killing out of all those impulses which deflect the soul from the straight path to God. For the true mystic, it is never more than a means to an end; and is often thrown aside when that end is attained. Its necessity is therefore a purely practical question. Fasting and watching may help one to dominate unruly instincts, and so attain a sharper and purer concentration on God; but make another so hungry and sleepy that he can think of nothing else. Thus Jacopone da Todi said of his own early austerities that they resulted chiefly in indigestion, insomnia and colds in the head; whilst John Wesley found in fasting a positive spiritual good. Some ascetic practices again are almost certainly disguised indulgences of those very cravings which they are supposed to kill, but in fact merely repress. Others—such as hair shirts, chains, and so forth—depended for their meaning on a mediæval view of the body and of the virtues of physical pain which is practically extinct, and now seems to most of us utterly artificial. No one will deny that austerity is better than luxury for the spiritual life; but perfect detachment of the will and senses can be achieved without resort to merely physical expedients by those living normally in the world, and this is the essential thing.

The true asceticism is a gymnastic not of the body, but of the mind. It involved training in the art of recollection; the concentration of thought, will, and love upon the eternal realities which we commonly ignore. The embryo contemplative, if his spiritual vision is indeed to be enlarged, and his mind kindled, as Dionysius says, to "the burning of love," must acquire and keep a special state of inward poise, an attitude of attention, which is best described as "the state of prayer"; that same condition which George Fox called "keeping in the Universal Spirit." If we do not attend to reality, we are not likely to perceive it. The readjustments which shall make this attention natural and habitual are a phase in man's inward conflict for the redemption of consciousness from its lower and partial attachments. This conflict is no dream. It means hard work; mental and moral discipline of the sternest kind. The downward drag is incessant, and can be combated only by those who are clearly aware of it, and are willing to sacrifice lower interests and joys to the demands of the

spiritual life. In this sense mortification is an integral part of the "purgative way." Unless the self's "inclination to true wisdom" is strong enough
to inspire these costing and heroic efforts, its spiritual cravings do not deserve the name of mysticism.

These, then, seem essential factors in the readjustment which the mystics call purgation. We go on to their next stage, the so-called "way of illumination." Here, says Dionysius, the mind is kindled by contemplation
to the burning of love. There is a mental and an emotional enhancement,
whereby the self apprehends the reality it has sought; whether under the
veils of religion, philosophy or nature-mysticism. Many mystics have
made clear statements about this phase in human transcendence. Thus
the Upanishads invite us to "know everything in the Universe as enveloped in God." "When the purified seeker," says Plato, "comes to the
end, he will suddenly perceive a nature of wondrous beauty. . . .
Beauty absolute, separate, simple and everlasting." His follower Plotinus
says that by spiritual intuition man, "wrought into harmony with the
Supreme," enters into communion with *Nous,* the "intelligible world" of
eternal realities—that splendor yonder which is his home: and further
that this light, shining upon the soul, enlightens it, makes it a member of
the spiritual order, and so "transforms the furnace of this world into a
garden of flowers." Ruysbroeck declares that this eternal world "is not
God, but it is the light in which we see Him." Jacopone da Todi says
that the self, achieving the crystalline heaven, "feels itself to be a part of
all things," because it has annihilated its separate will and is conformed
to the movement of the Divine Life. Kabir says: "The middle region of
the sky, wherein the Spirit dwelleth, is radiant with the music of light."
Boehme calls it the "light-world proceeding from the fire-world"; and
says it is the origin of that outward world in which we dwell. "This
light," he says, "shines through and through all, but is only apprehended
by that which unites itself thereto." It seems to me fairly clear that these,
and many other descriptions I cannot now quote, refer to an identical
state of consciousness, which might be called an experience of Eternity,
but not of the Eternal One. I say "an experience," not merely a mental
perception. Contemplation, which is the traditional name for that concentrated attention in which this phase of reality is revealed, is an activity of all our powers: the heart, the will, the mind. Dionysius emphasizes
the ardent love which this revelation of reality calls forth, and which is
indeed a condition of our apprehension of it; for the cold gaze of the
metaphysician cannot attain it, unless he be a lover and a mystic too.
"By love He may be gotten and holden, by thought never," says the author of *The Cloud of Unknowing.* It is only through the mood of humble
and loving receptivity in which the artist perceives beauty, that the
human spirit can apprehend a reality which is greater than itself. The

many declarations about naughting, poverty and "holy nothingness" refer to this. The meek and poor of spirit really are the inheritors of Eternity.

So we may place the attitude of selfless adoration, the single-hearted passion of the soul, among the essentials of the mystic in the illuminated way. A very wide range of mystical experiences must be attributed to this second stage in man's spiritual growth. Some at least of its secrets are known to all who are capable of æsthetic passion; who, in the presence of beauty, know themselves to stand upon the fringe of another plane of being, where the elements of common life are given new color and value, and its apparent disharmonies are resolved. So, too, that deep sense of a divine companionship which many ardent souls achieve in prayer is a true if transitory experience of illumination. We shall probably be right in assuming that the enormous majority of mystics never get beyond this level of consciousness. Certainly a large number of religious writers on mysticism attribute to its higher and more personal manifestations the names of "divine union" and "unitive life"; thereby adding to the difficulty of classifying spiritual states, and showing themselves unaware of the great distinction which such full-grown mystics as Plotinus, Jacopone da Todi or Ruysbroeck describe as existing between this "middle heaven" and the ecstatic vision of the One which alone really satisfies their thirst for truth. Thus Jacopone at first uses the strongest unitive language to describe that rapturous and emotional intercourse with Divine Love which characterized his middle period; but when he at last achieves the vision of the Absolute, he confesses that he was in error in supposing that it was indeed the Truth Whom he thus saw and worshiped under veils.

> Or, parme, fo fallanza,
> non se' quel che credea,
> tenendo non avea
> vertá senza errore.

Thus Ruysbroeck attributes to the contemplative life, "the inward and upward-going ways by which one may pass into the Presence of God," but distinguishes these from that superessential life wherein "we are swallowed up, beyond reason and above reason, in the deep quiet of the Godhead which is never moved."

All the personal raptures of devotional mysticism, all the nature-mystic's joyous consciousness of God in creation, Blake's "world of imagination and vision," the "colored land" of Æ, the Sūfī's "tavern on the way," where he is refreshed by a draught of supersensual wine, belong to the way of illumination. For the Christian mystic the world into which it inducts him is, preeminently, the sphere of the divine Logos-Christ, fount of creation and source of all beauty; the hidden Steersman who guides and upholds the phenomenal world:

> Splendor che dona a tutto 'l mondo luce,
> amor, Iesú, de li angeli belleza,
> cielo e terra per te si conduce
> e splende in tutte cose tua fattezza.

Here the reality behind appearance is still mediated to the mystic under symbols and forms. The variation of these symbols is great; his adoring gaze now finds new life and significance in the appearances of nature, the creations of music and of art, the imagery of religion and philosophy, and reality speaks to him through his own credal conceptions. But absolute value cannot be attributed to any of these, even the most sacred: they change, yet the experience remains. Thus an identical consciousness of close communion with God is obtained by the non-sacramental Quaker in his silence and by the sacramental Catholic in the Eucharist. The Christian contemplative's sense of personal intercourse with the divine as manifest in the incarnate Christ is hard to distinguish from that of the Hindu Vaishnavite, when we have allowed for the different constituents of his apperceiving mass:

> Dark, dark the far Unknown and closed the way
> To thought and speech; silent the Scriptures; yea,
> No word the Vedas say.

> Not thus the Manifest. How fair! how near!
> Gone is our thirst if only He appear—
> He, to the heart so dear.

So, too, the Sūfī mystic who has learned to say: "I never saw anything without seeing God therein"; Kabir exclaiming: "I have stilled my restless mind, and my heart is radiant; for in Thatness I have seen beyond Thatness, in company I have seen the Comrade Himself"; the Neoplatonist rapt in contemplation of the intelligible world "yonder"; Brother Lawrence doing his cooking in the presence of God, reveal under analysis an identical type of consciousness. This consciousness is the essential; the symbols under which the self apprehends it are not.

Among these symbols we must reckon a large number of the secondary phenomena of mysticism: divine visions and voices, and other dramatizations of the self's apprehensions and desires. The best mystics have always recognized the doubtful nature of these so-called divine revelations and favors, and have tried again and again to set up tests for discerning those which really "come from God"—i.e. mediate a valid spiritual experience. Personally, I think very few of these phenomena are mystical in the true sense. Just as our normal consciousness is more or less at the mercy of invasions from the unconscious region, of impulses which we fail to trace to their true origin; so too the mystical consciousness is perpetually open to invasion from the lower centers. These invasions are not always understood by the mystic. Obvious examples are the erotic raptures of the Sūfī poets, and the emotional, even amorous relations in which many Christian ascetics believe themselves to stand to Christ or Our Lady. The Holy Ghost saying to Angela of Foligno, "I love you better than any other woman in the vale of Spoleto"; the human raptures of Mechthild of Magdeburg with her Bridegroom; St. Bernard's attitude to the Virgin; the passionate love songs of Jacopone da Todi; the mystical marriage of St. Catherine of Siena; St. Teresa's "wound of love"; these, and many similar episodes, demand no supernatural explanation, and add nothing to our knowledge of the work of the Spirit in man's soul. So, too, the infantile craving for a sheltering and protective love finds expression over and over again in mystical literature, and satisfaction in the states of consciousness which it has induced. The innate longing of the self for more life, more love, an ever greater and fuller experience, attains a complete realization in the lofty mystical state called union with God. But failing this full achievement, the self is capable of offering itself many disguised satisfactions; and among these disguised satisfactions we must reckon at least the majority of "divine favors" enjoyed by contemplatives of an emotional type. Whatever the essence of mysticism may turn out to be, it is well to recognize these lapses to lower levels as among the least fortunate of its accidents.

We come to the third stage, the true goal of mystic experience; the intuitive contact with that ultimate reality which theologians mean by the Godhead and philosophers by the Absolute, a contact in which, as Richard of St. Victor says, "the soul gazes upon Truth without any veils of creatures—not in a mirror darkly, but in its pure simplicity." The claim to this is the loftiest claim which can be made by human consciousness. There is little we can say of it, because there is little we know; save that the vision or experience is always the vision or experience of a Unity which reconciles all opposites, and fulfills all man's highest intuitions of reality. "Be lost altogether in Brahma like an arrow that has completely penetrated its target," say the Upanishads. This self-loss, says Dionysius the Areopagite, is the Divine Initiation: wherein we "pass beyond the topmost altitudes of the holy ascent, and leave behind all divine illumination and voices and heavenly utterances; and plunge into the darkness where truly dwells, as Scripture saith, that One Which is beyond all things." Some recent theologians have tried to separate the conceptions of God and of the Absolute: but mystics never do this, though some of the most clear-sighted, such as Meister Eckhart, have separated that unconditioned Godhead known in ecstasy from the personal God who is the object of devotional religion, and who represents a humanization of reality. When the great mystic achieves the "still, glorious, and absolute Oneness" which finally satisfies his thirst for truth—the "point where all lines meet and show their meaning"—he generally confesses how symbolic was the object of his earlier devotion, how partial his supposed communion with the Divine. Thus Jacopone da Todi—exact and orthodox Catholic though he was—when he reached "the hidden heaven," discovered and boldly declared the approximate character of all his previous conceptions of, and communion with God; the great extent to which subjective elements had entered into his experience. In the great ode which celebrates his ecstatic vision of Truth, when "ineffable love, imageless goodness, measureless light" at last shone in his heart, he says: "I thought I knew Thee, tasted Thee, saw Thee under image: believing I held Thee in Thy completeness I was filled with delight and unmeasured love. But *now* I see I was mistaken—Thou art not as I thought and firmly held." So Tauler says that compared with the warm color and multiplicity of devotional experience, the very Godhead is a "rich nought," a "bare pure ground"; and Ruysbroeck that it is "an unwalled world," "neither this nor that." "This fruition of God," he says again, "is a still and glorious and essential Oneness beyond the differentiation of the Persons, where there is neither an outpouring nor an indrawing of God, but the Persons are still and one in fruitful love, in calm and glorious unity. . . . There is God our fruition and His own, in an eternal and fathomless bliss."

"How, then, am I to love the Godhead?" says Eckhart. "Thou shalt love Him as He is: not as a God, not as a Spirit, not as a Person, not as an image, but as a sheer pure One. And in this One we are to sink from nothing to nothing, so help us God." "This consciousness of the One," says Plotinus, "comes not by knowledge but by an actual Presence superior to any knowing. To have it, the soul must rise above knowledge, above all its wandering from its unity." He goes on to explain that all partial objects of love and contemplation, even Beauty and Goodness themselves, are lower than this, springing from the One as light from the sun. To see the disc, we must put on smoked glasses, shut off the rays, and submit to the "radiant darkness" which enters so frequently into mystical descriptions of the Absolute.

It is an interesting question whether this consummation of the mystic way need involve that suppression of the surface-consciousness which is called ecstasy. The majority of mystics think that it must; and probably it is almost inevitable that so great a concentration and so lofty an intuition should for the time it lasts drive all other forms of awareness from the field. Even simple contemplation cannot be achieved without some deliberate stilling of the senses, a deliberate focusing of our vagrant attention, and abolishes self-consciousness while it lasts. This is the way that our mental machinery works; but this should not make us regard trance-states as any part of the essence of mysticism. The ecstatic condition is no guarantee of mystic vision. It is frequently pathological, and is often found along with other abnormal conditions in emotional visionaries whose revelations have no ultimate characteristics. It is, however, just as uncritical to assume that ecstasy is necessarily a pathological symptom, as it is to assume that it is necessarily a mystic state. We have a test which we can apply to the ecstatic; and which separates the results of nervous disorder from those of spiritual transcendence. "What fruit dost thou bring back from this thy vision?" is the final question which Jacopone da Todi addresses to the mystic's soul. And the answer is: "An ordered life in every state." The true mystic in his ecstasy has seen, however obscurely, the key of the Universe: "la forma universal di questo nodo." Hence he has a clue by which to live. Reality has become real to him; and there are no others of whom we can fully say that. So, ordered correspondence with each level of existence, physical and spiritual, successive and eternal—a practical realization of the proportions of life—is the guarantee of the genuine character of that sublimation of consciousness which is called the mystic way; and this distinguishes it from the fantasies of psychic illness or the disguised self-indulgences of the dreamworld. The real mystic is not a selfish visionary. He grows in vigor as he draws nearer and nearer the sources of true life, and his goal is only reached when he participates in the creative energies of the Divine Nature. The perfect man, says the Sūfī, must not only die into God in ecstasy (fana), but abide in and with Him (baqa), manifesting His truth in the world of time. He is called to a life more active, because more contemplative, than that of other men: to fulfill the monastic ideal of a balanced career of work and prayer. "Then only is our life a *whole*," says Ruysbroeck, "when contemplation and work dwell in us side by side, and we are perfectly in both of them at once."

Plotinus speaks in the same sense under another image in one of his most celebrated passages: "We always move round the One, but we do not always fix our gaze upon It. We are like a choir of singers standing round the conductor, who do not always sing in time, because their attention is diverted to some external object. When they look at the conductor, they sing well and are really with him. So we always move round the One. If we did not, we should dissolve and cease to exist. But we do not always look towards the One. When we do, we attain the end of our existence and our rest; and we no longer sing out of tune, but form in truth a divine choir about the One." In this conception of man's privilege and duty we have the indestructible essence of mysticism.

3

Mysticism / An Essay on the History of the Word

LOUIS BOUYER, *Cong. Orat.*

Very few subjects are as delicate and difficult to deal with as mysticism. When we consider all that has been said about it and the various judgments pronounced upon it, we see that there is no other subject in the whole vast field of religious studies which lends itself to such widely differing descriptions. In fact, this divergence of views is such that one is led to wonder whether all those who speak of mysticism can be speaking of the same thing. We must admit that, especially since the beginning of this century, the term has been so freely and diversely employed that it may well have become, for our contemporaries, almost completely equivocal. But we must look further back in history to find the roots of this misunderstanding.

Those who speak of mysticism do so with a certain number of prejudices which are as dangerously vague as they are generally implicit. The researches of nineteenth-century historians of Christianity have, in fact, led us to suppose that the word was connected with the Hellenistic invasion of Christianity, during the Patristic era. According to whether we admire Christian, or Christianized, Hellenism or, instead, distrust it, so must we regard mysticism, and particularly Christian mysticism, with favor or disfavor. Some see in it the very heart of religion, that aspect of Christianity in which the religious humanism common to all mankind can find the perfect fulfillment of its desires. Others, on the contrary, see it as a pagan leprosy which has gradually disfigured the countenance of the spiritual Christian, even to the point of finally obliterating therein the image of Christ. Most probably mysticism deserves neither this excess of honor nor that obloquy, which both derive from those false "clear ideas" by the light of which the nineteenth century examined so many problems, and which do not survive an examination of the facts. Much useless verbiage would have been avoided, in this field as in many others, if students had begun by examining the texts, all the texts, in which the word occurs in ancient times, and by seeking, according to the context and not in accordance with a priori theories, the meaning which it bears in these. Unfortunately, in spite of its positive claims, the nineteenth-century study of Christian doctrines was constantly being led astray by generic preconceptions, to the detriment of more humble, but more precise and certain, semantic research.

In the field of New Testament studies many so-called critical theories simply collapsed when in our own times there at last appeared a great number of genuinely critical studies, that is, studies which do not hasten to forge new theories before having grasped the facts themselves, in themselves, which in this case means grasping the words and their meaning. The *Theologisches Wörterbuch* compiled by G. Kittel has thus satisfied a need for clarification, in a highly significant and most satisfactory way. Unfortunately, as regards the Patristic era, studies of this kind are still too rare. . . .

* * *

The word μυστικός comes from the verb μύω, which means "to close," and more particularly, to close the eyes. The earliest use we find of it in pre-Christian times is in connection with the Mystery religions, that is, with those cults whose essential rites were kept hidden from all but the initiated. Thus, for Thucydides, τὰ μυστικά are the ceremonies of the Mysteries. Strabo calls the initiated themselves οἱ μυστικοί. But it is very important to bear in mind that in this first phase of the word's use the secret to which it refers is a purely ritual secret. What the initiated must forbear from revealing to their interrogators is not a doctrine, nor is it esoteric knowledge, but simply and solely the details of a ritual. This is proved by the fact that all the Greek philosophers, from Plato onwards, were forced to attempt, evidently at their own risk and peril and not at all according to any safe tradition, to find a meaning in the Mysteries without giving anyone cause to accuse them of having betrayed their secret. On the contrary, it is remarkable that no one has ever told us, for example, the nature of the essential ceremonies of the great Eleusynian Mysteries, although Alcibiades and his companions were accused of an inexpiable sacrilege in that they had, in a fit of drunkenness, mimed some part of them.

The comparison between these two series of facts may be considered as demonstrative proof. In Hellenistic religions the secret which is truly mystical is not the secret of any ineffable religious knowledge, but the secret of a rite in its purely material aspect. In fact, it becomes ever clearer that the Hellenistic Mysteries never authoritatively transmitted any aristocratic spiritual doctrine, in spite of the contrary suppositions of so many historians influenced by romanticism. All that was found in them, or rather all that was supposed to be found, was but the product of private speculations, which moreover never had anything mystical, that is secret, about them, for they were exposed to the light of day in the pages of Plato, Apuleius, and many other writers.

This preliminary conclusion is of the highest importance. A whole long line of historians of Christianity, from Harnack to Père Festugière, have considered mysticism, in the modern sense of the word, to mean an invasion of Christianity by Hellenistic religiosity. But the truth is that we do not find any trace of such a meaning having been given to the word in the pre-Christian era. This does not mean, of course, that the word "mystic," like all the rest of the liturgical vocabulary of the Mysteries, had not undergone some transposition before its acceptance by Christians. But this transposition, at that time, was merely of a literary character and never gave its name to any doctrine, still less to any particular religious experience. The secret ritual of the Mysteries furnished the lively imagination of the Greeks with a wealth of poetical symbols. Hence the tendency, at least from the time of Plato, and most noticeably among the Alexandrines, to evoke the ritual of the Mysteries and its relative terms when describing reflections and research concerning the enigma of the world: all metaphysical thought, whether religious or not, and, still more generally, all laborious discovery, whatever might be its object.

A very characteristic example of this use of a mystical term which shows how commonplace and insignificant it had become, is found in the words of St. Paul, in the New Testament. This text alone should have sufficed, long ago, to make the enthusiasts for comparisons more modest in their claims. St. Paul, whom they have often tried to explain by references to some doctrinal influence of the Mystery religions, borrows from these only their characteristic expressions. And for what purpose? "I am instructed (μεμύημαι)—both to be full and to be hungry."[1] One could wish for no clearer example to show how commonplace the transposed use of mystical expressions had become. Nothing can be deduced from this language to prove a religious influence!

However, to this negative text, the history of the word "mysticism" in Christian literature contributes a positive counterpart, which seems to us decisive. It not only does away with the theory of the dependence of Christianity upon Hellenism in this field, but it also shows this supposition to be both vain and untenable. It shows its vanity by explaining on quite different grounds the evolution of the word in the direction of the significance we attach to it today. It shows its untenability because, as soon as the word is seen to evolve in this way, it becomes part of a context in which Hellenism has nothing more to say. The Christian texts, in fact, in which the word μυστικὸς is acquiring the particular religious and doctrinal meaning which it has never had before may be classed, roughly speaking, in three great groups: biblical, liturgical and spiritual. The most ancient texts are found in the first category; those which have a liturgical character come later, and last of all appear those which belong most decidedly to the third group, that which interests us most directly. But—and this is most important—it is evident that nowhere can a clear boundary be drawn between these three different uses of the word. We pass from one to the other without any breach of continuity. An author who uses the word in one sense rather than in another always shows, by employing it adjacently in other senses, that he never loses sight of these also. In this way, to our mind, the real parentage of Christian mysticism is made evident: it stems from the Bible and from the liturgy, particularly from the eucharistic liturgy.

We shall try to put forward at least the main elements of this debate, leaving the reader to form his own conclusion.

I

It is very remarkable that at the moment when the language of Christians borrows the word "mystic" from the pagan tongue, it does not make use of it to describe either a ritual or a spiritual reality. In those two fields in which its use corresponds either to that which in fact the Hellenistic religion has known, or to Christian realities which are to be explained by references to pagan religious realities, it is not at first used, historically speaking, in connection with anything "Greek," but with earlier Christian significance. This usage applies it to the least Greek thing about Christianity: the Bible. It is quite true to say that the pre-Christian source of the word is always evident. But what is most evident is the very commonplace use to which it has been reduced, as we have already shown, a use which gives the Christians their chance to adopt it. An expression which has become of common use for their contemporaries is at their disposal to enable them to make known to others their own new and original teaching.

We have already said that it was in Alexandria that the most liberal philosophical use was made of the vocabulary of the Mysteries, understood in a purely metaphorical sense. The best example of this is in the writer Philo who, as Émile Bréhier has clearly shown, plunges into the most abstruse mystagogic declamations merely to introduce, in the majority of cases, the most arid (and the least mystical, in our sense of the word) scholarly distinctions in the realm of Stoical physics or psychology.

It is in Alexandria also that we find for the first time a current use of the word "mystical," already thus rendered commonplace, in Christian language. With Philo it was merely a way of poetizing about technical expositions of the most abstruse problems; with Clement and Origen it was generally employed for all that touched upon what was considered the most difficult theological problems presented by Christianity. We mean, of course, scriptural exegesis, as they understood it, that is, the discovery of the allegorical meaning of the Bible. We must, however, move warily in considering one of the thorniest of problems, and one which until recently, had been more confused than illuminated by modern research. We must not forget what has been clearly brought to light by von Balthasar's articles on Origen's *Mysterion* and by de Lubac's introductions to his *Homilies on Genesis and Exodus*. The essence of Origen's allegory is not the literary form itself, which may even repel modern minds; it is the notion, fundamentally evangelical and Pauline, that the whole Bible, and the whole history of God's people, find their final significance and, as it were, their key in Christ alone. The customary use of the word "mystical" by Alexandrian Christians derives precisely from this notion.

Clement already calls the allegorical interpretation of the Scriptures, understood as their explanation in a Christian sense, a "mystical interpretation."[2] Origen defines it more precisely as an "explanation of the mystical meaning (μυστικοῦ νοῦ) extracted from the treasury of the [divine] words."[3] It is interesting, moreover, to notice that the Pauline orientation, particularly in Origen but also in Clement before him, of this "mystical interpretation" (since it is always the μυστήριον in St. Paul's sense: the "Christ in us," "Jesus Christ and Jesus-Christ Crucified" which it seeks) endows the word "mystical" with truly supernatural splendor. Its use expresses the idea that in Christ alone that which is most profound in religion, the final designs of God and his very nature are communicated to us. This is clear in a fine text of Clement's: "The old law," he says, "like a pedagogue, ruled the people by fear and its word was but an angel. . . .[4] But for the new people Jesus himself is begotten as the mystical angel."[5]

The use of the word μυστικὸς to describe an interpretation directed towards Christ and his mystery was to continue. We find it again in Didymus, who speaks to us of the "mystical and spiritual understanding of the Scriptures,"[6] in the beautiful *Commentary on Isaiah* of Cyril of Alexandria,[7] in the *Chronicon Paschale* (found in Vol. XCII of Migne, col. 101 A), in the *Commentary on Isaiah* of Procopius of Gaza,[8] etc.

It is interesting to note that this use of the word is by no means confined to the Alexandrines and the authors under their influence. We find it used also even by those who showed most distrust of the exegetic methods in vogue in Alexandria. Theodoret, for example, called the Canticle of Canticles (evidently referring to Christ and his Church) the "mystical book of the Canticles."[9]

We find two other uses by the Fathers, with a meaning very much like the commonplace sense "mysterious," meaning "difficult of access," but nearly approaching the application of the word to Christian exegesis.

First of all they describe as mystical all doctrines which touch on the profoundest points of faith. Thus, Eusebius of Caesarea, in his *Evangelical Demonstration*, described as "more mystical" (μυστικωτέρα-θεολογία) the doctrine about the divinity of Christ, as contrasted with what we learn of his humanity.[10] Gregory of Antioch, in his *De Baptismo*[11] qualifies in the same way baptismal generation, as opposed to natural generation. In a *Fragment* of St. Cyril of Alexandria[12] we find the dogma of the Trinity described as "supremely ineffable and mystical," and Eusebius has already called the Trinity itself "the Mystical Triad."[13] In other texts, always concerned with the idea of scriptural revelation and its supernatural object, the word even comes to mean "sacred." Clement speaks of the name of Yahve as the "mystical tetragram,"[14] and even describes as mystical the explanation of the numbers seven and eight.[15] After these last texts we must place all those in which "mystical" becomes equivalent to "spiritual" (as opposed to "carnal" in the Pauline sense). Even if the reference here is not expressly to the Christ of revelation in contrast with the Old Testament, the thought is evidently always engaged with this contrast, clinging more to the truth itself, brought by Jesus, than to what is but an empty husk. In this sense Clement calls the teaching of Christ mystical and is followed in this by Eusebius, Procopius of Gaza and others.[16] He says also that the kiss of peace should always be mystical (that is, should contain the Christian reality which it implies).[17] Proclus of Constantinople formally contrasts mystical with carnal.[18] Maximus the Confessor follows the same trend when he speaks of "mystical circumcision."[19]

It seems to us that from this first collection of data a perfectly clear idea evolves. For the Greek Fathers the word "mystical" was used to describe first of all the divine reality which Christ brought to us, which the Gospel has revealed, and which gives its profound and definitive meaning to all the Scriptures. Moreover, mystical is applied to all knowledge of divine things to which we accede through Christ, and then by derivation, to those things themselves. Finally the word, evolving always in the same direction, comes to describe the spiritual reality of worship "in spirit and in truth," as opposed to the vanity of an exterior religion which has not been quickened to new life by the coming of the Savior. It is this fundamental agreement which must never be forgotten when we pass on to later meanings.

II

A text from St. Cyril, to which we have already referred, will show us the transition from the use of the word "mystical" in a biblical context to its use in a sacramental and, more particularly, a Eucharistic context. In his *Commentary on Isaiah* he writes: "We say that the Synogogue has been deprived of the support of bread and water. This saying is mystical. For it is we, who have been called to sanctification through faith, who possess the bread of Heaven, the Christ, to wit, his body."[20]

In fact, in a whole series of texts, we now find the word "mystical" used with reference to the Eucharist. This demonstrates in a striking manner the care taken to insist on its reality, which is Christ himself with all his inalienable attributes, and also on the fact that this reality is still in some way veiled. Just as there was something else to discern in the Old Testament, other than what the Alexandrines called "history," that is, the anecdote without lasting significance, so there is in the Christian sacraments something quite other than what sight reveals therein. And this other thing, here also, is Christ.

The Last Supper inspires a series of texts in which we see the sense pass from the idea of a fulfillment of the Scriptures to the idea of a sacramental reality. Thus in the *Chronicon Paschale,* already quoted,[21] as well as in the *Evangelical Questions* of Hesychius of Jerusalem,[22] the Supper is called a "mystical Pasch." Eutychius is more precise; in his Treatise on *The Pasch*[23] he says it is the "first fruits and mystical foretaste of the reality (τοῦ πραγματικοῦ) of the Cross."

On the other hand, by a transposition frequently found in cases of this kind, we find the *Apostolic Constitutions* (6.23.4.) calling the Eucharist itself "the mystical sacrifice of his body and blood," as opposed to the bloody sacrifices.

Considering at the same time both the reality of Christ present in the Eucharist, and the veiled form in which he hides himself, an Epistle of St. Nilus says that it must be approached "not as simple bread but as mystical bread."[24] St. Nilus also gives us one of the very rare examples of the expression "mystical body" in Patristic Greek: he says "we eat the mystical body and we drink the blood,"[25] with evident reference to the body of Christ in the Eucharist. In the same category must be classed and interpreted the frequent references to the mystical wine,[26] or mystical chalice.[27]

It is always with reference to the present but veiled reality of Christ that the communion itself is called "mystical" by Ammonius in his *Commentaries on St. John.*[28] St. John Chrysostom calls it "a mystical food" in his *Commentary on St. Matthew,*[29] and a "mystical banquet" in his *Commentary on the First Epistle to the Corinthians.*[30] A more detailed text of Cosmas Indicopleustes calls it "mystical food of the body and blood of Christ."[31] The altar itself is frequently called the "mystical table."[32] Theodoret apparently even calls the moment of communion "the mystical moment in which we receive the body of the Bridegroom."[33]

In texts in which this first reference to the supernatural reality of Christ seems still subjacent, but in which the first deliberate transference to the celebrations of the Christian mystery of terms of the pagan Mysteries it had supplanted cannot be excluded, the whole of the eucharistic liturgy is called a "mystical Cult,"[34] or a "mystical rite."[35] A striking feature of the liturgical terminology of the Fathers of the Constantine era is, in fact, the first application to Christian rites of expressions borrowed from pagan rituals.[36] But it is one of the general characteristics of this phenomenon that it superimposes the new allusions to the pagan mysteries on the traditional allusion to the Pauline mystery, without in the least suppressing or submerging this latter. Within this double context the word mystical becomes applicable to the general sum of Christian sacraments. St. Gregory of Nyssa[37] speaks of the "communion of customs and mystical symbols," and even[38] of the "mystical action" ($\pi\rho\alpha\xi\epsilon\omega\varsigma$).

In stricter parallelism with what we have said of the eucharistic rites or elements, we see Eusebius calling baptism "the mystical regeneration in the name of the Father, Son and Holy Ghost."[39] Similarly, Gregory of Nyssa described the baptized as "those who have been regenerated by this mystical process."[40] He also calls the water of baptism "mystical water."[41] Eusebius,[42] Epiphanius,[43] and Theodoret[44] all call chrism "mystical."

We must never lose sight of the general context of all these references. The quotations we have accumulated in this section and in the preceding one make it clear that the same authors, at a distance of some pages, or even of some lines, use the word "mystical" in what we have called its sacramental sense, while still continuing to use it in its biblical sense. It is therefore impossible for the fundamental sense, which is never lost sight of, not to give its strong color to the later sense. Thus we may say, on arriving at the end of this second section of our study, that the word evokes in the minds of the Fathers a complex of associations which are biblical and sacramental at the same time, and which it would certainly be erroneous to disassociate by limiting this use or that to a particular field.

We know moreover—this is perhaps the most solid and lasting contribution made by the researches at Maria Laach—to what extent the Patristic era was alive to the perpetual presence of the mystery of Christ, in the Pauline sense, in the Church, particularly in the Church's liturgical celebrations, and most of all in the eucharistic liturgy. This means that Patristic spirituality and theology are dominated by the idea of the permanent and active presence of the Head himself in the body, at one and the same time gathering its members into one, and giving them the power perpetually to reenact what had taken place in him once and for all: his glorifying Cross, his passing from the life of the old Adam to the life of the new Adam, his passing from this world to the world to come, from this world to the Father. . . . Therefore, through all the uses which we have so far seen, we may say that it is always this same reality, at the same time so various and yet profoundly *one*, which is expressed by the word "mystical." Whether this reality is described as the final revelation of God's plan, discernible through all the Scriptures, and elaborated throughout all human history, or whether it is represented under the guise of the sacramental symbol which itself contains the object of this revelation, and is the means of realizing it in us, it is always this central Christian truth which is described by the word "mystical."

This may be proved by references to other and later uses, such as, by derivation, its use in purely sacramental liturgy. The hymn of the cherubim, which accompanies the "great entrance" in the liturgies of the Byzantine group, preceding the central part of the eucharistic liturgy, is called the "mystical hymn" in the liturgy of St. Basil and St. John Chrysostom.[45] St. Gregory Nazianzus likewise calls the words pronounced by the faithful themselves, during the celebration, "mystical words."[46] This hymn and this response are evidently mystical because they accompany the supreme act of the ecclesiastical liturgy, that which perpetuates the sacred act of the Savior himself. It is by the same association that the *Our Father* is called the "mystical prayer."[47] But here, as can clearly be explained, the significance of special position in the liturgy is linked with the consideration of the supreme evangelical truth here revealed. We perceive in this the profound sense of unity, underlying the two aspects, which influences the primitive Christian use of the word "mystical."

III

The first uses of the word "mystical" applied to a certain way of knowing God, directly and as it were experimentally, are clearly to be found in Origen. It is very noteworthy that they are present in texts which are more or less directly concerned with the interpretation of Scripture. For him, indeed, this interpretation is not a merely scientific labor. No one may understand the Scriptures without a profound communion with the realities of which they speak. It follows that exegesis, without thereby ceasing to call upon all the resources of erudition and culture, must be a veritable religious experience. Conversely, one may say that all authentically Christian religious experience is, for Origen, linked with his meditation on the Scriptures.

It is precisely at this intersection of the two lines of thought that the word "mystical" is to be found, in the texts from Origen which we will now quote. He tells us that we have in Jesus Christ "the high priest of the order of Melchisedek, as our guide in mystical and ineffable contemplation."[48] The use which he habitually makes of the word θεωρία makes it clear that here he is speaking of profound understanding of the Scriptures. That this understanding is truly mystical, in a sense at least akin to that which the word has for us today, can be proved from another text in the same *Commentary*, evidently parallel with the preceding one. Here he tells us, in fact, that the "ineffable and mystical visions (θεωρήματα) give joy and impart enthusiasm."[49] We can now understand why Père Daniélou has hesitated over the interpretation to give to a text, strongly reminiscent of Origen, in which St. Gregory of Nyssa speaks of the "mystical contemplation of the Canticle of Canticles."[50] Is this a question of exegesis, or of mystical contemplation in our modern sense of the word? he asks.[51] Perhaps the wisest reply would be: here both are inseparably linked.

After these texts, which afford as it were the immediate prehistory of what we have called the third meaning of the word, we must now, of course, turn to the pseudo-Areopagite to find the earliest (and numerous) habitual uses of the word in this sense. It is to be noted that again they are to be found in connection with the problem of exegesis. The two texts in which Denis described to us the doctrine and the experience of Hierotheus, his supposed master, in which the word mystical is found in this sense, present, in fact, these very conditions.

The first passage, as sometimes translated,[52] might lead us to suppose an opposition between what Hierotheus learnt of God through the study of the Scriptures, and what he learnt of him through experience. But such a translation is distorted by our modern disjunctions. The only version which clings closely to the text must, on the contrary, present the opposition as being between a merely bookish understanding of the Scriptures and that understanding of them which they themselves inspire, which is not acquired by learning but by experience, or through a profound sympathy, which enables one to attain a "mystical union and faith which cannot themselves be taught."[53]

The truth of this interpretation is proved once more by a parallel instance in the same book, in connection with the same problem. Still speaking (in the *Treatise on Divine Names*)[54] of Hierotheus, and of his interpretation of the Scriptures, Denis declares to us that "quite rapt out of himself and into God he participated, interiorly and totally, in the very object of his celebrations." Then he passes on to another subject, referring to all he has just been saying, that is, about Hierotheus' exegesis and his spiritual experiences, as τὰ ἐκεὶ μυστικά.

In other uses which Denis makes of the word "mystical," in its application to an ineffable mode of experimental knowledge of divine things, it is generally in connection with the theme of the "cloud" that he introduces this word. But the position which Denis assigns to this theme in the general setting of his Christian views is most significant. A text of capital importance in his *Mystical Theology* reveals this to us. Note that it is based on an exegetical tradition concerning Moses to which Origen's *Homilies on the Exodus* and St. Gregory of Nyssa's *Life of Moses* are the principal witnesses. He tells us, substantially, that one enters "a truly mystical cloud of unknowing,"[55] when one attains to the sole Object of the Gospel, who is revealed to us through the multiplicity of its words, beyond all the details of liturgical consecrations and the particular illuminations of biblical revelation.[56] This sole Object of the Gospel, present but veiled, both in the Christian liturgy and beneath the letter of the Scriptures, is precisely what the Fathers, after St. Paul, call τὸ μυστήριον, that is, as Denis explains, still in the same context, "the God who dwells in an inaccessible light," and allows us to reach him mysteriously through Jesus Christ.

Here we must in fact insist on this second link in the Areopagitic mysticism, which is really the fundamental link in all Denis' thought: the Christian liturgy, and, still more precisely, the Byzantine liturgy of the Eucharist. In spite of his evident borrowings from the contemporary phraseology of Neoplatonism, we cannot forget that the framework in which Denis deliberately sets all his religious thought is that of the liturgical celebration. This mystical theology is but the hearth, which itself transcends all vision, around the glowing central flame which he discerns there, which may be likened to this ἕνωσις, this union with God, which merely transposes into the language of his own era the universal reconciliation and restoration in Christ which St. Paul had preached as "the mystery." The universe of the Areopagite is the universe of the eucharistic liturgy, extended and superimposed on the whole natural universe. There, in the heart of this liturgy, is inscribed for him the ineffable experience of union with God, to which he consecrates definitely the epithet "mystical." But now we see why, in doing this, he shows himself not as the heir of the Neoplatonists—whatever may be his debt to these—but instead as the heir to the whole Patristic tradition of the use of this word, with all the biblical and liturgical connotations which we have pointed out.

It may be said that the mystical life, or mystical experience as he understands it, is a life filled by the experience of the one sole reality of which all Scripture speaks, and which first inspired all Christian liturgy— an experience of union in the highest faith.[57]

If such is the case we finally understand why mysticism was never reduced by the Fathers to the level of a psychological experience, considered merely, or primarily, in its subjectivity. It is always the experience of an invisible objective world: the world whose coming the Scriptures reveal to us in Jesus Christ, the world into which we enter, ontologically, through the liturgy, through this same Jesus Christ ever present in the Church. For Denis, as for the Fathers who were contemporary with him, τα μυστικά, together with certain inseparable spiritual experiences, always represent the world to which they give access, this mystical world of which St. John Chrysostom speaks, where all the angels sing to God a mystical melody.[58] This world is revealed and given to us by what Denis calls also the "mystical reading of the sacred texts,"[59] a fundamental phrase which contains in itself all the three meanings of mystical: biblical, liturgical and spiritual. This world, "the world to come," is that of which the great commentator of Denis, St. Maximus the Confessor, speaks when he says we shall in the end find the "mystical fulfillment of him who is the natural object of our desire: God."[60]

Finally, as we see in a magnificent text of Theodoret, paradoxically similar to Origen, for whom the Christ is the αὐτοβασιλεία, the Kingdom in his own person, this world is the mystical body of Christ, which in this instance undoubtedly refers neither to the Church nor to the eucharistic bread, but to Christ risen and ascended into heaven where he becomes, as it were, the center of gravity toward which must soar all the impulses of faith: "In the holy Gospels, in fact, he calls those eagles who have stripped themselves of all earthly things and who strain upwards toward his mystical body. For, speaking of the saints who were rapt to the heavens at the time of his resurrection he says 'there where the body is shall the eagles be assembled together.' "[61]

* * *

It seems to us that after the reading of all these texts it has become impossible to present Christian mysticism as an element imported from Neoplatonism into Christianity. The links of Denis, the first and most influential of the great mystical theologians (in our sense of the word "mystical") with Neoplatonism are undeniable. But precisely that which, *for Denis himself*, constitutes mysticism, is not what these experiences which he describes may have in common with, for example, those of Plotinus. It is, on the contrary, their position at the intersection of a whole specifically Christian spiritual tradition of scriptural interpretation and the ecclesiastical experience of the liturgy, the eucharistic liturgy. His mystical theology, as he understands it himself, is his manner of recognizing the Christ, at the breaking of bread, in all the Scriptures.

The counterproof of all this is easy to find. If anyone cares to search the *Enneads* from beginning to end, he will never find a single example of the use of the word μυστικός. Only the adverb μυστικῶς is to be found, once—to indicate the significance of the rôle attributed to Hermes as the agent of creation, that is, in a context which has no connection whatever with anything spiritual.[62] This must surely decide the question once and for all.

NOTES

1. Phil. 4, 12.
2. Τὴν μυστικὴν ἑρμηνείαν: *Strom.* 5.6; P.G., ed. Migne, Vol. IX, col. 64 A.
3. *In Joan.* 1, 15; P.G., Vol. XIV, col. 49 B. cf. ibid. 13, 40; P.G., Vol. XIV, col. 469 C; also *De Princip.* 4, 2, 9; P.G., Vol. XI, 376 A, etc.
4. Allusion to Acts 7, 53, Gal. 3, 19, and Heb. 2, 2.
5. *Paedag.* 1, 7; P.G., Vol. VIII, col. 321 A; cf. *Protrept.* 1; P.G., Vol. VIII, col. 65 C.
6. Psalm 1, 3; P.G., Vol. XXXIX, col. 1160 A.
7. 1.2; P.G., Vol. LXX, col. 96 C.
8. 7, 10–17; P.G., Vol. LXXXVII, col. 1960 D.
9. *De provid.*, 5; ed. Schultze, Vol. IV, p. 550.
10. 3.7; P.G., Vol. XXII, col. 248 B.
11. 2.2; P.G., Vol. LXXXVIII, col. 1873 A.
12. *Fragm.* 1; P.G., Vol. LXXVI, col. 1424 A.
13. *Contra Marcellum*, 1.1; P.G., Vol. XXIV, col. 716 C: *De Laudibus Constantini*, 6; P.G., Vol. XX, col. 1348 B.
14. *Stromates*, 5.6; P.G., Vol. IX, col. 60 A.
15. Ibid., 6.16; col. 376 B.
16. *Stromates*, 6.15; P.G., Vol. IX, col. 352 A: *Quis Dives Salvetur*, Ibid., col. 609 C; etc.
17. *Paedag.* 3.11; P.G., Vol. VIII, col. 660 B.
18. *Orat.* 6.14; P.G., Vol. LXV, col. 748 D.
19. *Capit.* 5.41; P.G., Vol. X, col. 1365 A.
20. Loc. cit.; P.G., Vol. LXX, col. 96 C.
21. P.G., Vol. XCII, col. 548 C.
22. 34; P.G., Vol. XCIII, col. 1421 D.
23. 4; P.G., Vol. LXXXVI, col. 2397 A.
24. 3.39; P.G., Vol. LXXIX, col. 405 B.
25. Epist. 2.33; P.G., Vol. LXXIX, col. 320 C.
26. Eusebius: *Evangelical Demonstration*, 8.1; P.G., Vol. XXII, col. 596 A.
27. St. Athanasius: *Second Apology*, 8; P.G., Vol. XXV, col. 264 A; Philostorge: *Ecclesiastical History*, 2.11; P.G., Vol. LXV, col. 476 B; St. John Chrysostom: *Commentary on the Ephesians*, Bened. ed., Vol. XI, col. 6 D; Theodoret: *Questions on Genesis*, 110; ed. Schultze, Vol. I, p. 115; Procopius of Gaza: *Commentary on Isaiah*, 65, 13–25; P.G., Vol. LXXXVII, col. 2689 B.
28. 6.57; P.G., Vol. LXXXV, col. 1440 B.
29. Bened. ed., Vol. VII, col. 551 B.
30. Vol. X, col. 218 D.
31. In his *Topographia Christiana*, P.G., Vol. LXXXVIII, col. 308 B.
32. St. Gregory of Nazianzus: *Orat.* 40, 30; P.G., Vol. XXXVI, col. 404 A; Gregory of Antioch: *De Baptismo*, 2.10; P.G., Vol. LXXXVIII, col. 1881 D; etc.
33. *Commentary on the Canticle of Canticles*, 1.1; ed. Schultze, Vol. II, p. 25.

34. Μυστική λατρεία: *Apostolic Constitutions*, 8.5.11.

35. Μ, λειτουγία, Eusebius: *Vita Constantini*, 4.71; P.G., Vol. XX, col. 1225 C; Theodoret: *Epist*. 146; ed. Schultze, Vol. IV, p. 1260.

36. Eusebius: Ibid.; 4.45; col. 1196 B; Theodoret: *Religious History*, 13; ed. Schultze, Vol. III, p. 1208; Eutychius: *Treatise on the Pasch*, 3; P.G., Vol. LXXXVI, col. 2393 D.

37. *Contra Eunomium*, 11; P.G., Vol. XLV, col. 880 B.

38. *On the Baptism of Christ*, P.G., Vol. XLVI, col. 581 A.

39. *Contra Marcellum*, 1.1; P.G., Vol. XXIV, col. 728 C.

40. *Catechetic Discourse*, 34; P.G., Vol. XLV, col. 85 C.

41. Ibid., 35; col. 92 C.

42. *Evangelical Demonstration*, 1, 10; P.G., Vol. XXII, col. 89 D.

43. *Contr. haer*. 30.6; P.G., Vol. XLI, col. 413 D.

44. *Commentary on Isaiah*, 61.2; ed. Schultze, Vol. II, p. 383.

45. Cf. Brightman, p. 319.

46. *Orat*. 18.9; P.G., Vol. XXXV, col. 996 B.

47. St. John Chrysostom: *Commentary on the Romans*, Bened. ed., Vol. VII, col. 578 E; Theodoret: *Commentary on the Romans*, 8.15; ed. Schultze, Vol. III, p. 86.

48. *Commentary on St. John*, 13, 24; P.G., Vol. XIV, col. 440 C.

49. Ενθουσιᾶν ποιοῦντα, the force of "enthusiasm" in ancient religious literature is well known: Ibid., 1, 33; col. 80 B.

50. *Commentary on the Canticle*, P.G., Vol. XLIV, col. 765 A.

51. *Platonisme et théologie mystique*, p. 192.

52. For example Maurice de Gandillac: *Oeuvres complètes de Denys*, Paris, 1943, p. 86.

53. *Treatise on Divine Names*, 2.9; P.G., Vol. III, col. 648 B.

54. 3.2.3; Ibid., col. 681 D to 684 A.

55. 1.3; P.G., Vol. III, col. 1001 A.

56. Cf. the whole context, from 1000 B.

57. Cf. text above quoted.

58. *Commentary on St. Matthew*, Bened. ed., Vol. VII, col. 248 C.

59. *Ecclesiastical Hierarchy*, 3.2; P.G., Vol. III, col. 425 C.

60. *Opusculi*, P.G., Vol. XCI, col. 24 C.

61. *De Providentia*, 5; ed. Schultze, Vol. IV, p. 550.

62. III, 6, para. 19, line 26.

4

Mysticism Sacred and Profane

R. C. ZAEHNER

From the Introduction

In *The Doors of Perception* Mr. Huxley seemed to assume that preter-natural experiences, conveniently described by the all-embracing term "mysticism," must all be the same in essence, no matter whether they be the result of intensive ascetic training, of a prolonged course of Yoga techniques, or simply of the taking of drugs. In making these assumptions, of course, Mr. Huxley was doing nothing new. We have been told *ad nauseam* that mysticism is the highest expression of religion and that it appears in all ages and in all places in a more or less identical form, often in a religious milieu that would seem to be the reverse of propitious. This view has recently been reaffirmed by Professor A. J. Arberry who writes: "It has become a platitude to observe that mysticism is essentially one and the same, whatever may be the religion professed by the individual mystic: a constant and unvarying phenomenon of the universal yearning of the human spirit for personal communion with God."[1] Similarly Dr. Enid Starkie, in discussing Rimbaud's ecstasies, writes: "In his experience of God Rimbaud reached, without orthodox beliefs, the stage which mystics seek to attain, where there is no longer possibility for belief or disbelief, for doubt or for reflection, but only pure sensation, ecstasy and union with the Almighty."[2] And again we are told: "In *Les Illuminations* is found expressed, as nowhere else—except perhaps in the poems of Saint John of the Cross—man's eternal longing for spiritual satisfaction and beauty."[3] In actual fact there would appear to be nothing in Rimbaud to show that the poet ever considered that he had attained to union with God or that his ecstasies had any direct connection with Him: nor does Dr. Starkie see fit to develop the interesting comparison with St. John of the Cross, nor is any attempt made to establish its validity. This is only too typical of the great majority of writers on mysticism. It will suffice to quote only one more example, for, as Professor Arberry has rightly remarked, "it has become a platitude."

The platitude was earlier enunciated by Professor Arberry's eminent predecessor in the Chair of Arabic at the University of Cambridge, E. G.

Browne, the great Orientalist who did so much to familiarize the English-speaking world with Persian civilization. On the subject of mysticism he wrote:

> There is hardly any soil, be it ever so barren, where it (mysticism) will not strike root; hardly any creed, however stern, however formal, round which it will not twine itself. It is, indeed, the eternal cry of the human soul for rest; the insatiable longing of a being wherein infinite ideals are fettered and cramped by a miserable actuality; and so long as man is less than an angel and more than a beast, this cry will not for a moment fail to make itself heard. Wonderfully uniform, too, is its tenor: in all ages, in all countries, in all creeds, whether it come from the Brahmin sage, the Greek philosopher, the Persian poet, or the Christian quietist, it is in essence an enunciation more or less clear, more or less eloquent, of the aspiration of the soul to cease altogether from self, and to be at one with God.[4]

Always it is *assumed* that mysticism is "essentially one and the same": rarely is any attempt made to substantiate the assumption, and rarely are the equally significant differences analyzed. We are greatly indebted to Mr. Huxley in that, in *The Doors of Perception*, he has carried the popular view to its logical conclusion: for since he has proved that preternatural experience of the most vivid kind can be acquired by the taking of drugs and since the state of the drug-taker's consciousness bears at least a superficial resemblance to that of the religious mystic in that time and space appear to be transcended, must it not follow that this experience is "one and the same" as that of the generally accredited mystics?

Huxley could, and should, have gone further. Mescaline is clinically used to produce artificially a state akin to schizophrenia, more specifically the manic phase of the manic-depressive psychosis. It must therefore follow, if we accept the fatal "platitude," that not only can "mystical" experience be obtained artificially by the taking of drugs, it is also naturally present in the manic. It must then follow that the vision of God of the mystical saint is "one and the same" as the hallucination of the lunatic. There would appear to be no way out, unless the original "platitudinous" premise is unsound. . . .

In the analysis we have attempted of the various types of mysticism we have necessarily had to draw on Indian religion, and particularly on the Vedānta, as well as on the Christian and Muslim mystics. Here again we have been forced to the conclusion that the extreme non-dualist Vedānta of Śankara and his followers represents something different from the main stream of Christian mysticism as well as from the "orthodox" Muslim mysticism as formulated by Abū'l-Qāsim al-Junayd and

Ghazālī. The realization of this difference (if difference it be) is, from the academic point of view, of considerable interest; for until we are tolerably clear in our own minds what the varieties of mystical experience actually are, it would be futile to attempt to sift out the various strands which meet in Sūfism and which make it so puzzling a phenomenon. . . . I at least have become convinced that purely monistic ideas in Sūfism can be traced back to Abū Yazīd of Bisṭām who appears to have been directly influenced by the Vedānta.[5] From this it follows that purely monistic ideas in Abū Yazīd or in his successors cannot be treated as independent evidence for the ubiquity of the monist philosophy which is sometimes held to underlie all the manifestations of mysticism.

. . . In seeking to draw what seems to me to be a valid as well as an obvious distinction between monism on the one hand and theistic mysticism on the other, it should not be thought that I am in any way seeking to belittle the enormous Indian contribution to religious thought. It is true that absolute monism is characteristic of much in Indian thought though it is by no means peculiar to it. It is, however, only one of many streams that go to make up the complex mosaic that is Hinduism. It is moreover a doctrine that has been vigorously disputed in India itself from the time of Rāmānuja onwards; and though it may, with plausibility, claim to represent the authentic teaching of the Upaniṣads, it is plainly at variance with the main teachings of the Bhagavad-Gītā; for both monism and monotheism are strongly represented in Indian religion. Thus when I argue that the monist completely misunderstands the position of the theistic mystic rather than vice versa, so far from arguing against Hinduism as such, I am arguing against a trend in *all* religions which is in most cases an aberration from the doctrine generally held by the main body of mystical thought within a given religious tradition. That it is actually impossible to hold monistic and theistic opinions as both being *absolutely* true at one and the same time, seems obvious.

From Chapter I: Mescaline

. . . It is, of course, a well-known fact that certain drugs—and among them one may include alcohol—modify the normal human consciousness and produce what can literally be called ec-static states—states in which the human ego has the impression that it escapes from itself and "stands outside" itself. Indian hemp and hashish have long been used in the East to produce precisely such a result. In the West, however, it has never been taken for granted that such states are necessarily associated with religion, while in the East there have always been sober spirits who regarded such "religion surrogates" with the gravest suspicion. Mr. Huxley appears to have no such scruples, for he implies unmistakably that what he experienced after taking mescaline was explicable in terms of "contemplation at its height."[6] Herein lies the importance of Mr. Huxley's thesis; preternatural experience, whether produced by drugs or not, is equated with specifically religious experience.

It is essential that we should pause for a moment here in order to consider what Mr. Huxley and his friends understand by religion since, obviously, it is not what Protestant Christians normally understand by the word. Since the Reformation we have drifted more and more into a position of identifying religion with an ethical code; and despite the regrettable fact that the vast majority of those who call themselves Christians make no noticeable effort to follow the more difficult and paradoxical commandments of Our Lord, we like to think that the Christian ethic is the most perfect that has ever been propounded and that therefore Christianity is the best and for that reason the true religion. On turning to the Oriental religions, however, we will see that in India and in those parts of Asia which have come under Indian influence, such views are far from finding universal acceptance. Religion for the Hindu or Buddhist, we are repeatedly told by the modern advocates of those two religions, is primarily a matter of experience: it is not so much something to be believed as something to be lived. By belief or faith, too, they do not understand a series of propositions to which assent is given, they mean not only faith in, but contact with, a suprasensory world. Religion, for them, is not so much something to be professed as something to be experienced; and such experience, in its higher forms, is usually called mystical experience. In the West the reverse is true: we have lost contact with the suprasensory world to such an extent that many of us have come to deny it altogether. This is no place to discuss the effects of such an attitude on society at large; here we must be content to note that it leaves many people profoundly dissatisfied, and of these Mr. Huxley would seem to be a notable example.

Huxley's life would appear to have been one consistent revolt against the values of the nineteenth century, purely material values to which an air of respectability was lent by a decadent Christianity. Later in life he came into contact with the religious classics of the East which obviously attracted him strongly. Moreover, the fact that the Eastern religions had a far cleaner record than Christianity in the matter of persecution, was one more point in their favor; and in the life of reflection, concentration, and contemplation which they stressed far more exclusively than did the Christian Church, Huxley thought that at last he had found a sure anchor and lasting resting-place. Struck by the similarity of thought and expression he found in all the mystics, whether Hindu, Buddhist, Taoist, Muslim, or Christian, he reached the comforting conclusion that behind the great religions of the world there could be discerned a *philosophia perennis*, an ultimate truth of which all religions were only partial expressions. It was, however, the great religious systems of India which principally attracted him, particularly the Vedānta and those forms of Buddhism which are most akin to it. Just why this should have been it is difficult to say. Prima facie one might have supposed that his attraction was based on some profound religious experience and that this experience was felt to be in accordance with what the Vedānta taught rather than with what the Christian mystics described. Huxley himself, however, gives the lie to this in *The Doors of Perception*, for he there admits that until, thanks to mescaline, he came to know "contemplation at its height," he had not in fact had any experience to which the word "mystical" could possibly be applied. We can only conclude that Huxley's "conversion" to a Vedāntin way of life was due to little more than a total rejection of everything that modern civilization stands for and to a deepseated aversion to historical Christianity which, though it may not have directly given birth to the modern world, at least condoned it when it was born.

So it was that when Huxley came to take mescaline, his mind was permeated through and through with Vedāntin and Mahāyāna Buddhist ideas, and these ideas seem actually to have affected his vision; for as Baudelaire has rightly observed, drugs can add nothing new to a man, but can only raise to a higher power what is already within him.[7]

Despite its diminutive compass *The Doors of Perception* is an important book, for it presents a challenge to all who are interested in religious experience; and the mere fact that mescaline does not always produce such satisfactory results does not invalidate the argument that even if there is only a 5 per cent chance of beholding something that seems to approach the Beatific Vision, surely such a chance is worth taking. Further, Huxley's experiences under the influence of mescaline as recorded by himself are interesting from the point of view of what we may call "clinical" religion. They provide a case-history parallel to those collected by William James in his *Varieties of Religious Experience*, and as such they are of value. Secondly the book is important in that Huxley draws definite conclusions from his experience. Coming from so eminent an author these conclusions cannot decently be simply brushed aside.

From Chapter II: Mescaline Interpreted

. . . Before proceeding to the discussion of Huxley's experiences after taking mescaline and before seeking to explain it by similar experiences which others have had, and before we attempt to fit it into a general pattern, it would be as well to summarize the conclusions that Huxley has himself drawn from his excursion into the extratemporal world and to study his recommendations for the greater use of drugs in the furtherance of the happiness of the human race. These recommendations and conclusions will be found in the epilogue to *The Doors of Perception.* They are remarkable. But nowhere does Huxley seem to face up to the main problem: what is the relationship between the ecstasies of persons of heroic sanctity and those of the mescaline-taker?

In the concluding section of his book Huxley implies that the taking of drugs is, or should be, part and parcel of all religion; and on this basis he criticizes Christianity for not "baptizing" mescaline or similar drugs and incorporating them into Christian worship. This sounds outrageous: but it is not really so if we continue to bear in mind his major premise that "the urge to escape from selfhood and the environment is in almost everyone almost all the time."[8] The premise seems false, for it does not correspond to observed fact; and it would be only sidestepping the issue to say that this "urge" is more often than not unconscious, since until the urge has been brought up into consciousness, it cannot be stated that it is there at all. The premise should be emended to some such formula as this: "the urge to escape selfhood and the environment (which are two very different things) is in almost every introspective introvert who is naturally retiring, overcerebral, and oversensitive, and who has been brought up in a materialist and industrialized environment, almost all the time." If we are prepared to "emend" the premise in this way, Huxley's panacea for society becomes intelligible—except, of course, that we can no longer speak of society as such, but only of a limited number of hypercivilized persons in search of their soul. In lumping together "the urge to escape from selfhood" and "the urge to escape from the environment" Huxley is confusing two quite separate things. It is what William James calls the "sick soul" which longs to escape from itself, and it is what Coomaraswamy calls the "spiritual proletariat" that aspires to escape from its environment. This "proletariat" now forms a large part of any industrial society. Its members are occupied in doing intrinsically boring jobs, and if they seek relief in the cinema, television, and the "comics," they do so not in order to escape from themselves, but in order to project themselves into what seems to them a more meaningful existence. Their plight is the exact opposite of that of the neurotic intellectual; for the latter lives by and on introspection and is bound, sooner or later, to long to escape from a subject that has become a monomania, whereas the former has not yet got as far as finding a "self" from which he could wish to escape. He feels no urge to escape from himself, only an urge to escape from the dullness of everyday life in which no "self" of any sort has any chance to develop.

On the subject of how mescaline could be utilized for the good of humanity, Huxley's ideas appear to be extraordinarily confused. He oscillates in the most alarming manner between identifying the mescaline experience with the Beatific Vision on the one hand and regarding it as a safe substitute for alcohol on the other. The baffled reader finds himself wondering whether he regards the highest states of the mystics as being not only comparable to, but identical with, the effects of alcohol and drugs, or not. "The Beatific Vision, *Sat Chit Ananda,* Being-Awareness-Bliss—for the first time I understood, not on the verbal level, not by inchoate hints or at a distance, but precisely and completely what those prodigious syllables referred to." This is what he says on pages 12–13. If this means anything, then surely it must mean that what he was experiencing at the time was a near approximation to what Christians call the Beatific Vision and what the Hindus mean by *Sat Chit Ananda.* Yet when he comes to describe his own experience in detail, he describes it as follows:

> I continued to look at the flowers, and in their living light I seemed to detect the qualitative equivalent of breathing—but of a breathing without returns to a starting point, with no recurrent ebbs but only a repeated flow from beauty to heightened beauty, from deeper to ever deeper meaning. Words like Grace and Transfiguration came to my mind, and this of course was what, among other things, they stood for. My eyes travelled from the rose to the carnation, and from that feathery incandescence to the smooth scrolls of sentient amethyst which were the iris.

Possibly I am wrong, but I had always understood that the Beatific Vision means a direct appreciation of God, not through a glass, darkly, but face to face, with all the veils of sense stripped aside, as the Muslim mystics would say. Unless Huxley's descriptive powers have failed him altogether, I am afraid that I cannot discern any likeness between what he experienced and what is generally understood by the Beatific Vision. Why should we be asked to believe that a vision of nature transfigured in any way corresponds to the vision of God Himself? Though Zen Buddhists may speak of the Dharma-Body of the Buddha *being* the hedge at the bottom of the garden, Christian mystics use no such terminology to describe the unitive state. The only way to emphasize how great the difference is between Huxley's mescaline-induced visions and the experiences of Christian mystics is to quote the texts side by side. Let us then turn to Blessed Henry Suso who, as being a pupil of Meister Eckhart, a near-monist, on the one hand, and a *beatus* of the Catholic Church on the other, should meet the requirements of most religious tastes. The quotation is from *The Little Book of Truth,* and can be regarded as being fairly typical of Christian mysticism. We shall have occasion to quote further passages from theistic mystics, both Christian and Muslim, in our later chapters. This is what Suso says:

It happens, no doubt, that, when the good and faithful servant enters into the joy of his Lord, he become intoxicated with the immeasurable abundance of the Divine house. For in an ineffable manner, it happens to him as to a drunk man, who forgets himself, is no longer himself. He is quite dead to himself, and is entirely lost in God, has passed into Him, and has become one spirit with Him in all respects, just as a little drop of water that is poured into a large quantity of wine. For, as this is lost to itself, and draws to itself and into itself the taste and color of wine, similarly it happens to those who are in the full possession of blessedness. In an inexpressible manner all human desires fall away from them, they melt away into themselves, and sink away completely into the will of God. If anything remained in man, and was not entirely poured out of him, then the Scripture could not be true that says: God is to become all things to all things. Nevertheless, his being remains, though in a different form, in a different glory, and in a different power. And all this comes to a man through his utter abandonment of self.[9]

Literally hundreds of passages from Christian and Muslim mystics could be quoted which depict the union of the soul with God and which are closely parallel to the passage we have just quoted from Suso. But where is the likeness to Huxley's experience under the influence of mescaline? True, Suso spoke of "utter abandonment of self," and Huxley describes himself as a "Not-self, simultaneously perceiving and being the Not-self of the things around me."[10] Even allowing for the Buddhist convention of using the word "Not-self" to mean something other than the ego which has direct experience of both the subjective self and of objective phenomena, there still seems to be no parallel, unless one accept the proposition that God, as understood by Suso, means the same as the Dharma-Body of the Buddha which in turn is the hedge at the bottom of the garden. Yet even if we make this enormous concession, there is still no real parallel. In the case of Huxley, as in that of the manic, the personality seems to be dissipated into the objective world, while in the case of Suso, as of other theistic mystics, the human personality is wholly absorbed into the Deity Who is felt and experienced as being something totally distinct and other than the objective world. Suso is describing a state in which both the subject, "I," and the object, "the world," are momentarily excluded from consciousness, and in which the soul is literally "filled" through and through "with the Holy Ghost": in such a state, however we choose to interpret the "Dharma-Body of the Buddha," one thing at least is certain, and that is that "the hedge at the bottom of the garden" and, with it, all hedges and all gardens have ceased to exist for the soul rapt in God. How is it possible for a sane man seriously to maintain that such an experience which excludes all sensation of the objective world is the same as "not merely gazing at those bamboo legs, but actually *being* them—or rather being myself in them; or, to be still more accurate . . . being my Not-self in the Not-self which was the chair"?[11] In the first case we have the "deification" of a human soul in God, the loss of consciousness of all things except God; in the second we have the identification of the self *via* the "Not-self" . . . with the external world to the exclusion, it would appear, of God; for, significantly enough, even Huxley under the influence of mescaline fails to identify his Not-self with God, though he does not feel this to be incongruous in the case of the "Dharma-Body of the Buddha." The sensation that the individual human being and his external surroundings are not really distinct is not so uncommon as is normally supposed. . . . It is, however, unusual to find a serious author identifying this experience, sometimes called the "natural" mystical experience, with the Beatific Vision.

The confusion of thought that mescaline seems to have induced in Mr. Huxley is best illustrated in the epilogue. For here he says: "I am not so foolish as to equate what happens under the influence of mescaline or of any other drug, prepared or in the future preparable, with the realization of the end and ultimate purpose of human life: Enlightenment, the Beatific Vision."[12] It should merely be regarded, he says, as "what Catholic theologians call 'a gratuitous grace,' not necessary to salvation but potentially helpful and to be accepted thankfully, if made available." This is indeed a serious modification of his former position; and it is a modification by which he seems to stand. Yet from this it follows that intoxication of any sort must also be a "gratuitous grace," and in so far as the Church teaches that the fruit of the vine and the beverages that derive from it are a gift of God and to be enjoyed in moderation, this view does not seem to be objectionable. His position, however, becomes much more shaky when he assails the Church for not enlivening her ceremonies with a little sacramental mescaline as the "Native American Church" apparently does.

. . . Huxley is admittedly both incoherent and self-contradictory. Nevertheless, if I understand him correctly, what he seems to be arguing is this: Religion means principally escape from the ego. What have all the great mystics of all time done? They have shaken off their egos, they have become gods, Not-selfs, or what you will. What do alcohol and mescaline do for you? They do precisely this: they enable you to shake off the ego and give you a glorious feeling of release. Therefore they must be of the same nature as religion: therefore they are good.

. . . It would . . . be a grave mistake to underrate the challenge thrown down by Mr. Huxley and by many who think like him. What, then, is this challenge? It is this: that religion is a matter of experience, almost of sensation; that religious experience means "mystical" experience; and that mystical experiences are everywhere and always the same. Acting on this assumption, Huxley first became interested in the Vedānta philosophy of the Hindus since only in that philosophy is preternatural experience, deduced from the contents of the Upaniṣads, made the basis of all speculation. This teaching, in its extreme form, is the philosophy, not so much of the oneness of all things, but of the actual identity of the individual soul with the Brahman which can best be translated as "the Absolute." All mystical experience, according to this school of thought, ultimately leads to this identity—a conclusion that Westerners may find surprising. By a mystical experience Huxley seems to understand not only the experiences of all the recognized mystics, but experiences such as his own under the influence of mescaline; and, since he is honest, he would be forced to add, the experiences of madness. . . .

It is not easy to see what Huxley's intention was when he wrote *The Doors of Perception:* for hitherto he had been one of the most stubborn defenders of what he calls the *philosophia perennis,* that philosophy which maintains that the ultimate truths about God and the universe cannot be directly expressed in words, that these truths are necessarily everywhere and always the same, and that, therefore, the revealed religions which so obviously differ on so many major points from one another, can only be relatively true, each revelation being accommodated to the needs of the time and the place in which it was made and adapted to the degree of spiritual enlightenment of its recipients. Thus, as Coomaraswamy, another exponent of the *philosophia perennis,* has said,[13] the only real heresy is to maintain that one religion only is in exclusive possession of the truth. All are rather facets of the same truth, this truth being presented in a different manner at different times in accordance with the spiritual development of the society to which it is directed. The truth itself is that experienced by the mystics whose unity of thought and language is said to speak for itself.

There seem to be two very strong objections to such a theory. The first is that few of these authors can or will define what precisely constitutes a mystical experience, and that until that is done, we do not really know what we are talking about. The second is that to assert that all mystics speak the same language and convey the same message does not seem to be true even within one particular religious tradition. For our present purposes we may as well follow Mr. Huxley in including his own experiences under the influence of mescaline in the category of "mysticism." If we do this, however, we must also include the experiences of manic-depressives since mescaline is clinically used to reproduce artificially the state of mind typical of that distressing psychosis, and because, in fact, the experiences of manic-depressives show a marked resemblance not only to Huxley's experience, but also to that of some more conventional mystics. We will, then, first be dealing with those experiences which are usually termed pantheistic, the experience which tells you that you are all and that all is you, "when I am inseparably this and that and this and that are I; when I experience the other person as myself and the other, as myself, experiences me."[14] This experience is described clearly and with admirable concision in the Kauṣītakī Upaniṣad[15] in the memorable formula, "Thou art this all." This is the experience of the "nature mystic": it is the experience of all as one and one as all. It is common in the later Ṣūfī writers and can also be found in the works of modern authors who are not otherwise known as mystics. To call it "pantheistic" is wrong, for in the proposition "Thou art this all," neither term represents or can be construed as "God," and "pantheism," when translated into English, of course, means "all-God-ism." It would be far more accurate to describe this experience as "pan-en-hen-ism," "all-in-one-ism," for that is what in fact the experience tells us. It is, of course, the experience of Huxley not only perceiving his chair legs transformed, but actually being them, "being his Not-self in their Not-self," as he accurately puts it.

Is this experience the same as that described by the so-called mahāvākyāni or "great sayings" which are the key texts of the Vedānta? These are four in number, and together they may be said to sum up the whole of Vedāntin monism. They read as follows: (1) "Thou art that";[16] (2) "This ātman is *Brahman*," "This individual soul is the Absolute";[17] (3) "I am *Brahman*";[18] and (4) "Consciousness is Brahman."[19] What is meant by this? *Brahman* is the word used to represent the Absolute: it is the sole truly existing and eternal reality, beyond time and space and causation and utterly unaffected by these which, from its own standpoint, have no existence whatever. *Ātman* means "self," the individual soul. The proposition, then, that "*Ātman* is *Brahman*" means that the individual soul is substantially and essentially identical with the unqualifiable Absolute. From this it follows that the phenomenal world has no true existence in itself: from the point of view of the Absolute it is absolutely non-existent. Therefore, the soul which realizes itself as the Absolute, must also realize the phenomenal world as non-existent. This, then, is to experience one's own soul as being the Absolute, and not to experience the phenomenal world at all. To say that this is identical with the pan-en-henic experience, is to say something that is patently and blatantly untrue. For what sort of sense does it make to say that to experience oneself as actually being three chair legs which represent a minute proportion of the phenomenal world, is the same as to experience oneself

as the Absolute for which the phenomenal world is simply not-being?
Here, then, we already have two wholly distinct forms of "mystical experience."

Thirdly, there is the normal type of Christian mystical experience in
which the soul feels itself to be united with God by love. The theological
premise from which this experience starts is that the individual soul is
created by God in his own image and likeness from nothing and that it
has the capacity of being united to God, of being "oned" to Him as the
mediaeval English mystics put it. Here again we have a third type, distinct, it would appear, from the other two. For whereas both the Christian and the Vedāntin experiences are wholly different from the pan-en-
henic, so do they differ from each other. No orthodox Christian mystic,
unless he is speaking figuratively or in poetry as Angelus Silesius does,
can well go further than to say that his individual ego is melted away in
God by love: something of the soul must clearly remain if only to experience the mystical experience. The individual is not annihilated, though
transformed and "deified" as St. John of the Cross says: it remains a distinct entity though permeated through and through with the divine substance. For the non-dualist Vedāntin this is not so: the human soul IS
God; there is no duality anywhere. Superficially, at least, there is an
enormous difference between the two.

From Chapter III: Some Nature Mystics

. . . Any enquiry which aims at an unbiased approach to the phenomenology of mysticism is liable to be met with opposition not so much from
the orthodox of the various creeds as from the advocates of a *philosophia
perennis* which would set itself above creed and which therefore interprets all creeds from its own a priori notions. This tendency has been associated with the names of the late Ananda Coomaraswamy and René
Guénon, the first an unusually well-equipped Oriental scholar, the second a self-appointed interpreter of the Vedānta with a pronounced
animus against Orientalists. Their mantle now seems to have fallen on
M. Frithjof Schuon who has developed this "metaphysic" at some length
in his *Transcendent Unity of Religions*.[20]

. . . Fortunately, we are not concerned with comparative theology;
we are concerned only with the comparative study of mysticism and of
mystical experience, and whether all such experiences are reducible to
one pattern. Before proceeding to discuss this theme in detail, however,
it would be just as well to have a fairly clear idea of what we mean by
mysticism. In Christianity the word is usually held to mean a direct apprehension of the Deity. Sanctifying grace, according to orthodox doctrine, does in fact establish a relationship between the soul and God:

God is said actually to dwell in the soul that is in a state of grace. It is, however, obvious that the average soul in this state has no sensible experience of the presence of God. Persons technically in a state of grace do not look different or behave in a noticeably different manner from their fellows who may be in a state of mortal sin. Again orthodox doctrine holds that on receiving Holy Communion the soul is united to God. The recipient is only very rarely indeed actually aware of this ineffable union, whereas the onlooker may be permitted to doubt it. In a mystical experience, on the other hand, there is a direct apperception of the Deity; the mystic *knows* that God is in him and with him; his body has literally become a "temple of the Holy Ghost." This is no longer a dogma accepted on faith, but, the mystic would allege, an experienced fact. The experience has nothing to do with visions, auditions, locutions, telepathy, telekinesis, or any other preternatural phenomenon which may be experienced by saint and sinner alike and which are usually connected with an hysterical temperament.[21] It is true that some advanced (and canonized) mystics have been subject to these disturbances, but they have no essential connection with the mystical experience itself, the essence and keynote of which is union. Preternatural phenomena that may or may not accompany it are subsidiary, accidental, parasitic.

In Christian terminology mysticism means union with God: in nontheistical contexts it also means union with some principle or other. It is, then, a unitive experience with someone or something other than oneself. In Huxley's case it was union with and direct experience of three chair legs, grey flannel trousers, and, by extension, with all natural objects within his vision. If, then, we define a mystical experience as a sense of union or even identity with something other than oneself, Huxley can claim to have had a mystical experience, and this experience can be, and was, induced by mescaline. According to this definition are we entitled to class the experience of the *advaita*, that is, the strictly non-dualist, Vedāntins as mystical? The difficulty is that in this case it is not strictly proper to speak of union at all; for according to the proposition "I am Brahman," which means that I am the sole unqualifiable Absolute, One without a second, I cannot logically speak of being united to Brahman, since I am already He (or It). Just as, according to Christian doctrine, the Christian in a state of grace is a temple of the Holy Ghost, so, according to Vedāntin doctrine, is man, whether in a state of grace or not, identical with the Absolute. In both cases, in the ordinary course of events, they are unaware of it; and in both cases mystical experience brings to light an already existing state of affairs. There is, of course, a difference between the two. The Christian mystic, if he is orthodox, will not go so far as to say that he actually *is* God in any absolute and unqualified sense. It is possible that Suso did actually feel in ecstasy that this would have been a true description of what he felt, but that he was prevented from saying so because this happened to have been one of the propositions of his master, Eckhart, which had been condemned by the Pope. However that may be, this is a manner of expressing the ineffable experience which Christians normally avoid. Sticking strictly to the letter, then, for the moment, a distinction must be drawn between the Christian experience in which the individual soul is united or "oned" with God, to use the expression of the *Cloud of Unknowing*, and the Vedāntin experience which is one of absolute identity with Brahman—"I am Brahman" and "What thou art, that am I."[22] In any case, for the purposes of this work we propose to extend the meaning of "union" to include actual "unity," for no treatment of mysticism that claims to be serious can afford to ignore the all-important Indian contribution.

Though there is a difference, and a real difference, between the Vedāntin and Christian ways of defining the unitive experience, the difference may well be only one of terminology. There is, however, a radical difference between both of them and Huxley's experience under the influence of mescaline. For in strictly religious mysticism, whether it be Hindu, Christian, or Muslim, the whole purpose of the exercise is to concentrate on an ultimate reality to the complete exclusion of all else; and by "all else" is meant the phenomenal world or, as the theists put it, all that is not God. This means a total and absolute detachment from Nature, an isolation of the soul within itself either to realize itself as "God," or to enter into communion with God. The exclusion of all that we normally call Nature is the sine qua non of this type of mystical experience: it is the necessary prelude to the further experience of union with God in the Christian and Muslim sense, or the realization of oneself as Brahman in the Vedāntin sense. To state, then, or to imply, as Huxley does, that his own experience is either identical with, or comparable to, either the Christian Beatific Vision or to what the Hindus call *Sac-cid-ānanda* (*Sat Chit Ananda*), "Being-Awareness-Bliss," is to state or to imply an obvious untruth. If we take the extreme Vedāntin position that the individual soul *is* Brahman, and that the realization of oneself as Brahman means the destruction of what the Vedāntins call *upādhis* or "illusory adjuncts," then there can be no participation in the illusory or transient life of those adjuncts; there is only the realization of oneself as the only true One without a second. This is the exact opposite of being a "Not-self in the Not-self of three chair legs." The experiences are not comparable and need to be explained in different ways. . . .

From the Conclusion

. . . Our investigations have led to the tentative conclusion that what goes by the name of mysticism, so far from being an identical expression of the selfsame Universal Spirit, falls into three distinct categories. Under the general heading of mysticism we have . . . confined ourselves to preternatural experiences in which sense perception and discursive thought are transcended in an immediate apperception of a unity or union which is apprehended as lying beyond and transcending the multiplicity of the world as we know it. Because these experiences are recorded at all times and from all parts of the world, it is fatally easy to assume that because they are, one and all, preternatural, that is, not explicable in the present state of our knowledge, and because the keynote of all of them is "union," they must necessarily be the same. It is not realized often enough that once these experiences are assumed to be identical and of identical provenance, the conclusion that the transports of the saint and the ecstasies of the manic are identical cannot be escaped. If this were really so, and if these preternatural experiences were what religion is principally concerned with, then the only sensible course to adopt would be that which Rimbaud followed: we should all attempt to induce in ourselves an attack of acute mania; and this is in fact the solution that Mr. Huxley seems to propound in *The Doors of Perception.*

That "nature mysticism" exists and is widely attested is not open to serious doubt. How the experience is to be explained is quite another matter. To identify it with the experience of Christian or Muslim saints, however, is hardly admissible, as I hope to have shown, however inadequately. . . .

Though it is easy enough to dismiss the experiences of the nature mystic as mere hallucination, this is really begging the question; for, in all cases of this experience, the impression of *reality* they leave behind is quite overwhelming. In every case—whether the experience comes unheralded or whether it is produced by drugs or Yoga techniques—the result is the same; the person who has had the experience feels that he has gone through something of tremendous significance beside which the ordinary world of sense perception and discursive thought is almost the shadow of a shade. Huxley expresses this with the German word *Istigkeit,* and he has thereby fully caught the mood. The experience seems overpoweringly *real;* its authority obtrudes itself and will not be denied. It is this quality in it, I believe, which makes those who have been the subject of such a visitation assume that this must be identical with what the mystical saints have experienced. The Ṣūfīs reply to their critics by saying that their criticism is about as valid as that of a teetotaler who vainly tries to understand the pleasures of drunkenness without ever having tasted wine. It will not help him to know that wine is the fermented juice of the grape or what its chemical constituents are: until he has actually drunk deeply, he will never understand the exhilaration of the drinker. Similarly no child who has not reached the age of adolescence can understand what pleasure there can possibly be in the sexual act which seems to him revolting. So with the nature mystics—it is extremely difficult for the purely rational man to understand in what the excitement and the joy consist, or why it should be that the sensation of losing one's individuality should be so intensely prized. No comparison is adequate: the nearest, perhaps, as Huxley saw, is an intense absorption in music or painting, or in dancing, for all these can be used as aids to produce such a condition, and the Ṣūfīs introduced song and dance, and the contemplation of beautiful boys, very early as aids to the attainment of preternatural states. Yet even so, they can serve only as the faintest adumbrations, they can scarcely claim even to approximate to the real thing.

Ṣūfism is, in this respect, perhaps more instructive than either Christian or Indian mysticism. The distinction that Qushayrī drew between *basṭ*, or the sense of one's personality expanding indefinitely, and actual communion with God, is rarely met with again, and the opposition of the conservatives to the use of song and dance as stimulants broke down all too soon, because, as Ṣūfism degenerated, the achievement of ecstasy as such became the Ṣūfī's goal regardless of whether such ecstasies proceeded from the hand of God or not. The later Ṣūfīs came to assume that all ecstasy was divine, and thereby put a ready weapon into the hands of the orthodox, for whereas sanctity is its own argument, mania is not, and no genuinely religious person is likely to be impressed by one who claims either to be in direct communion with God or actually to be identical with Him, if his conduct is, in fact, subhuman. Thus the confusion that is popularly made between nature mysticism and the mysticism of the Christian saints can only discredit the latter. By making the confusion one is forced into the position that God is simply another term for Nature; and it is an observable fact that in Nature there is neither morality nor charity nor even common decency. God, then, is reduced to the sum total of natural impulses in which the terms "good" and "evil" have no meaning. Such a god is subhuman, a god fit for animals, not for rational creatures; and to experience such a god has rightly been termed "downward transcendence" by Mr. Huxley.

. . . I am painfully aware that all the explanations I have offered for the natural mystical experience have been inadequate: we are always reduced to similes, and can only hope that the similes throw some light on the nature of the problem. But the problem is there and must be faced:

and it is the problem of preternatural experiences which take account of neither good nor evil. If my halting explanations seem childish, then I can only hope that qualified theologians will produce something more convincing. The problem, however, seemed worth stating.

Secondly, a word must be said in conclusion about the validity of Jung's researches and the effect they are likely to have on religion. It will not, I hope, be unfair to say that Jung does not know himself where he stands theologically since he is not concerned with the God of any theology but with the God-archetype as he finds it in his patients; and this archetype appears in protean and ambivalent forms. I have pointed out in another chapter that Jung's attitude toward evil seems to be fundamentally Manichaean. The "dark, feminine," instinctive side of human nature is what we have inherited from the animals; it is neither good nor evil, but has, as Jung has demonstrated, great potentialities for both. That it must be integrated into the total psyche, few will deny; but to equate it with moral evil or with the Devil, and then to assert that evil as such has to be integrated into the whole psyche, shows a certain confusion of thought. Because the Manichees did precisely this, because they identified matter with concupiscence[23] and asserted that this, rather than pride, was the root of all evil, they were condemned by the Church as the *pessima haeresium*. What Jung appears to mean is that the material, instinctive, and non-rational side of our nature must be given its proper place in the integrated psyche. Ghazālī somewhere likens the relationship between the rational soul and the twin faculties of lust and anger to a man, his pack animal, and his dog, the proper place of the two latter being that of an obedient servant. So too the Hindus speak of "taming" the passions (*dam-, dānta*). This relationship which, in Islam, goes back to Plato's *Republic* seems as good a way of describing the integrated personality as any. Beyond integration, however, there is again separation, the separation of the immortal soul from all its mortal trappings, of *yang* from *yin*, of *puruṣa* from *prakṛti*. This would normally take place in the second half of life when the instincts lose much of their force and the isolation of the spirit seems less "unnatural." This is what is prescribed by the Sāṁkhya-Yoga: it is the natural preparation of the soul for life after death. Given the immortality of the soul, it is little more than a reasonable precaution, for it can be readily believed that a discarnate existence for which one is unprepared can be as profoundly disquieting as that described by Mr. Huxley in *Time Must Have a Stop*.

However, if there is a God, and if it is true that our relations with Him will be very much more intimate after death, then "it is not enough to know only that He exists, but one must know His nature and His will."[24] This is even more important for the mystic than it is for the ordinary man, for the mystic is in fact the man who has a foretaste in this life of life after death; and just as the experiences of those who have taken mescaline have, to a certain extent, varied according to their beliefs, so will the experiences of persons who tame their senses and discipline their minds with a view to reaching a higher reality.

Indian religion is right in describing the object of religious disciplines as being *mokṣa* or liberation. By this they mean liberation from what St. Paul calls "the flesh," that is, the life of blind instinct, the animal in man. Beyond this they also seek liberation from the third of Avicenna's three components of the lower soul, "imagination" or distracting thought. As their final goal the Sāṁkhya-Yogins seek their own immortal soul in its nakedness and isolation. Having no clear idea of God, they cannot seek union with Him, nor do they claim to.

The Vedāntins are in a different case. The Upaniṣads teach that Brahman is both the source of all things and that He includes all things. Greater than all the universe, he is yet the fine point without magnitude which is the deep center of the human heart. Insofar as they teach this, they are fully at one with the mystical teaching of the Catholic Church. However, they also teach that Brahman *is* the universe and that he *is* the human soul. Rāmānuja and his followers interpret this as being a metaphor and as meaning that the universe and human souls are what he calls the "body" of God whereas God or Brahman remains distinct from them though they are wholly dependent on Him. Here again there is full agreement between Rāmānuja and Catholic mystical tradition. Whether Rāmānuja or Śankara more accurately represents the general trend of Upaniṣadic teaching must be left to the Hindus to decide. It is, however, fair to point out that the concept of *māyā*, the cosmic illusion, is only adumbrated and never formulated in the classical Upaniṣads themselves. Śankara and his followers, by establishing complete identity between the human soul and the Absolute, do in fact accept the Sāṁkhya-Yoga view *in practice*, for self-realization means for them, no less than for the Sāṁkhya-Yogin, the isolation of the immortal soul from all that is not itself. As we have tried to point out in another chapter there is much in the Vedānta philosophy which fits in with what Mr. Custance says when in a manic state, particularly the claim that the "released" individual must make to be identical with the creator (of an imaginary universe). Precisely these views were attacked by Ruysbroeck who rightly saw that all people who firmly held them, must think that they had reached the highest possible mystical state, what the Hindus call the *paramā gatiḥ*, whereas they had only reached the stage of self-isolation, of rest and "emptiness" within themselves. Believing this to be union with God, they were prevented from taking any further step because they believed there was no further step to take. This, for Ruysbroeck, as for any Christian, was manifestly absurd, for how, as Abū Yazīd once said, could one ever come to the end of the Godhead?

Here, then, are two distinct and mutually opposed types of mysticism —the monist and the theistic. This is not a question of Christianity and Islam *versus* Hinduism and Buddhism: it is an unbridgeable gulf between all those who see God as incomparably greater than oneself, though He is, at the same time, the root and ground of one's being, and those who maintain that soul and God are one and the same and that all else is pure illusion. For them Christian mysticism is simply *bhakti* or devotion to a personal god carried to ludicrous extremes, whereas for the theist the monist's idea of "liberation" is simply the realization of his immortal soul in separation from God, and is only, as Junayd pointed out, a stage in the path of the beginner. He is still in the bondage of original sin.

Hinduism has its theists as well as its monists; and the Bhagavad-Gītā as well as Rāmānuja stand nearer to St. John of the Cross than they do to Śankara. This is a quarrel that cuts clean across the conventional distinctions of creeds. In each of the great religions there have been upholders of both doctrines. Even Christianity has not completely avoided the monistic extreme even though it makes nonsense of its basic doctrine that God is Love. Meister Eckhart, for instance, at times adopted a fully monistic position, and Angelus Silesius could well be interpreted monistically though a literal interpretation of the *Cherubinischer Wandersmann*, taken out of the context of his other work, is scarcely permissible since mystics, when writing in verse, allow themselves, like all poets, the boldest figures of speech.

Nevertheless, the Christian mystical tradition is, on the whole, strongly opposed to monism for the reasons already stated. The same is true of Indian theists; and the fact that the two traditions have existed in India side by side seems to be sufficient refutation of the theory, which is a half-truth only, that sectarian dogma necessarily modifies the actual nature of the mystic's experience. Rāmānuja's quarrel with Śankara is as fundamental as Ruysbroeck's with the Beghards. For neither was this a question of different paths leading to one goal; it was the goal itself that was in question. The fact that there has never been an official orthodoxy in India makes the struggle there the more interesting, for the mystical current could not thus be diverted, if diversion it is, into any one theological channel. The mystic was (and is) free to follow the most rigid monism or some type of theism. Hence the interest of Rāmakrishna who, though a professed non-dualist Vedāntin, nevertheless is at his best and most convincing when he worships God as the "Mother" as Julian of Norwich had done in Europe in very different circumstances. Rāmakrishna succeeded in breaking through the monistic shell because his nature was naturally expansive and his whole attitude to life was one of love. His case shows that the grace of God is withheld from no one, whatever his inherited theology, provided he is animated by charity. This could not be, if what Christians affirm is not true, namely, that God is Love.

Similarly, although the strictly orthodox among the Muslims maintained that it is not legitimate to speak of the love of God because love implies kinship and God is unlike His creation in every respect, the Ṣūfīs nevertheless made love the foundation of their relationship with God and finished up (in Junayd and Ghazālī) by reaching a position that approaches very closely to that of St. John of the Cross. All this goes to show that where there is genuine love, there will God be: and not only will He be there, He will make His presence deeply felt. Christian mysticism and Muslim mysticism at its best are not, whatever they may be, the mere upsurge of the God-archetype from the unconscious. They are what they claim to be, an intimate communion of the human soul with its Maker; and since God is holy and absolute goodness, the mystic, so far as he is united with God, will be absolutely free from sin. He will not be either above or beyond good and evil, but evil will not be able to touch him, since in God who is perfect there is no possibility of evil, the essence of imperfection.

In the words of Suso, "In so far as man remains in himself, he can fall into sin, as Saint John says: 'If we say that we have no sin, we deceive ourselves, and the truth is not in us.' But in so far as he does not remain in himself, he does not commit sin, as Saint John says in his *Epistle*, that the man who is born of God does not sin, nor err, for the Divine seed remains in him."[25] This doctrine must be true for any soul that is actually "deified" in God, as St. John of the Cross would say. No living man, however, can presume that the union he enjoys with God can be so perfect that a lapse is no longer possible. This is precisely what Ruysbroeck accused the Beghards of doing. By mistaking a monistic "possession of their own souls" for identification with the Deity, they considered that whatever they did or did not do must be perfect because divine. This Junayd called *isqāṭ al-a' māl*, "the falling away of works," and condemned it in the strongest possible terms. Ghazālī went further still and, being an orthodox Muslim at least insofar as conforming to the religious law was concerned, he considered the slaughter of such heretics to be a pious work. Such passions are not raised in humane men except when they see a gross perversion of what they hold to be the truth. Thus it seems that theists and monists cannot ever agree; for the former see in the latter's final state only the isolation of the soul in "natural rest," while the latter regard the transports of the former as an early stage on the way to isolation, the stage of *bhakti* which, for the monist, means paying homage to a deity which one has oneself imagined. This is, perhaps, because in India the available deities as represented in legend could not satisfy the religious mind as being undistorted images of the one true God.

Ruysbroeck attacked the monists of his time on the grounds that the mysticism they practiced was devoid of love: hence they could not possibly get beyond their "self" in the Jungian sense, their *ātman*. Because they were able to find within themselves "sufficient rest," they thought they had reached the highest bliss attainable by man. In actual fact, Ruysbroeck maintained, they were shutting themselves off from God; and this is bound to happen to the mystic whose religion only offers him an inadequate image of God.

NOTES

1. A. J. Arberry, *Sūfism, An Account of the Mystics of Islam,* London: George Allen and Unwin, 1950, p. 11.
2. Enid Starkie, *Arthur Rimbaud,* revised ed., London: Hamish Hamilton, 1947, p. 422.
3. Ibid., p. 423.
4. E. G. Browne, *A Year amongst the Persians,* London: Adam and Charles Black, 3d ed., 1950, p. 136. Quoted by Margaret Smith, *An Introduction to the History of Mysticism,* London: Macmillan, 1930, p. 2.
5. See *Mysticism Sacred and Profane,* pp. 161*ff.*
6. Cf. *The Doors of Perception,* London: Chatto and Windus, 1954, p. 31.
7. *Le Poème du Haschisch,* iii, in *Œuvres,* Bibliothèque de la Pléiade, Paris: Gallimard, 1954, p. 445.
8. *The Doors of Perception,* p. 50.
9. Henry Suso, *Little Book of Eternal Wisdom* and *Little Book of Truth,* tr. J. M. Clark, London: Faber and Faber, 1953, p. 185.
10. *The Doors of Perception,* p. 27.
11. Ibid., pp. 15–16.
12. Ibid., p. 58.
13. A. K. Coomaraswamy, *The Bugbear of Literacy,* London: Dobson, 1949, p. 49.
14. John Custance, *Adventure into the Unconscious,* London: Christopher Johnson, 1954, p. 4 (quoting Jung).
15. *Kauṣ. Up.* 1.6 (*idaṁ sarvam asi*).
16. *Chāndogya Upaniṣad* 6.9*ff* (*tat tvam asi*).
17. *Māṇḍūkya Up.* 2 (*ayam ātmā brahma*).
18. *Bṛadāraṇyaka Up.* 1.4.10 (*ahaṁ brahmāsmi*).
19. *Aitareya Up.* 5.3 (*prajñānaṁ brahma*).
20. English translation by Peter Townsend, London: Faber and Faber, 1953.
21. On this subject the reader may consult Herbert Thurston, S.J., *The Physical Phenomena of Mysticism,* London: Burns, Oates, 1955.
22. *Kauṣītakī Upaniṣad,* 1.6 (*yas tvam asi so 'ham asmi*).

23. The Greek ὕλη appears in the Middle Persian Manichaean texts as āз, "concupiscence."

24. *Škand-Gumānīk Vičār*, ed. Menasce, Fribourg, 1945, p. 117 (ch. 10, no. 37).

25. *The Little Book of Truth*, p. 196.

5

Interpretation and Mystical Experience

NINIAN SMART

I. THE MEANING OF 'MYSTICISM'

Unfortunately the term "mysticism" and its relations ("mystical," etc.) are used by different people in different senses. For the purposes of this article I shall treat mysticism as primarily consisting in an interior or introvertive quest, culminating in certain interior experiences which are not described in terms of sense-experience or of mental images, etc. But such an account needs supplementation in two directions: first, examples of people who typify the mystical life should be given, and second, mysticism should be distinguished from that which is *not* (on this usage) mysticism.

First, then, I would propose that the following folk typify the mystical life: St. John of the Cross, Tauler, Eckhart, al-Hallāj, Shankara, the Buddha, Lao-Tze (if he existed), and many Yogis.

Secondly, mysticism is *not* prophetism, and can be distinguished from devotionalism or *bhakti* religion (though mysticism often intermingles with these forms of religious life and experience). I would propose that the following are *not* mystics in the relevant sense in which the Buddha and the others *are* mystics: Isaiah, Jeremiah, Muhammad, Rāmānuja, Nichiren and Calvin.

Needless, perhaps, to say, such expressions as the "mystical body of Christ" have no necessary connection with mysticism in the proposed sense. It is unfortunate that a word which etymologically means sacramentalism has come to be used in a different sense. Since, however, "mysticism" now is most often used to refer to the mode of life and experience typified by men like St. John of the Cross and Shankara, I shall use the term, though "contemplation" and "contemplative" can be less misleading.

Thus "mysticism" will here be used to refer to the contemplative life and experience, as distinguished from prophetism, devotionalism and sacramentalism (though we must keep in mind the fact mentioned above

—that prophetic and sacramental religion are often interwoven with that of mysticism).

II. PROFESSOR ZAEHNER'S ANALYSIS AND THEORY

In a number of works, Professor Zaehner has distinguished between three categories of mystical experience:

(1) Panenhenic or nature mysticism (as exemplified by Rimbaud, Jeffries and others).

(2) Monistic mysticism (as found in Advaita, Sāinkhya-Yoga, etc.).

(3) Theistic mysticism (as in the Christian tradition, the Gītā, etc.).

His distinction between (1) and the other two is correct and valuable. The sense of rapport with nature often comes to people in a striking and intimate way; but it is to be contrasted with the interior experience in which, as it were, a man plumbs the depths of his own soul. It is probable that Zen *satori* is to be equated with panenhenic experience, though Zen also makes use of the general pattern of Buddhist Yoga which elsewhere culminates in an interior rather than a panenhenic type of experience.

But is Zaehner's distinction between (2) and (3) a valid one? He criticizes those who believe that mysticism is everywhere the same—a belief sometimes held in conjunction with the neo-Vedāntin thesis that behind the various forms of religion there is a higher truth realizable in contemplative experience and best expressed through the doctrine of a universal Self (or Ātman). On Zaehner's view, monistic mysticism is "realizing the eternal oneness of one's own soul" as contrasted with the "mysticism of the love of God."[1] The latter attainment is typical of Christian, Muslim and other theistic contemplation.

Zaehner believes in an eternal soul, as well as in God, and is thus able to claim that there is a real entity which the monistic mystic experiences, even if it is not the highest entity (which is God). In addition, he holds, or has held, that monistic mysticism can be explained through the doctrine of the Fall. Thus he is not merely concerned to analyze mysticism, but also to explain it through a (theological) theory. He writes as follows:

Assuming, as we are still encouraged to do, that man developed physically from the higher apes, we must interpret the creation of Adam as an original infusion of the divine essence into what had previously been an anthropoid ape. Adam, then, would represent the union of the orders of nature and grace, the order of coming to be and passing away which is created from nothing by God, and the infused spirit of

God. Adam, after he sinned, brought bodily death into the world, but did not and could not destroy his soul, because the soul was infused into him from God and therefore was itself divine. Though Adam may have repented, he was no longer able to take the supreme step of offering himself back completely and entirely to God, because he had lost contact with his source and could no longer find it again. Thus, tradition has it, at death his soul departed to Limbo, where, like all disinterested Yogins who have sought to separate their immortal souls from all that is transient and ungodlike, yet who cannot acknowledge God, it enjoyed the highest natural bliss, the soul's contemplation of itself as it issued from the hand of God and of all created things as they are in the sight of God. . . . The proof, it seems to me, that I am not talking pure nonsense is in the complete difference of approach which separates the theistic from the monistic mystic. The latter achieves liberation entirely by his own efforts since there is no God apart from himself to help him or with whom he can be united. In the case of the theistic mystic, on the other hand, it is always God who takes the first step, and it is God who works in the soul and makes it fit for union.[2]

Thus Zaehner not only distinguishes types of mysticism: he links his distinction to a theology of the Fall. Though it is not the main concern of this article to consider this theological theory, it may be useful to go into certain criticisms which can be leveled at it, since some of them are relevant to Zaehner's doctrine of types of mysticism.

III. THE THEORY EXAMINED

In linking his analysis of mysticism to a theory about the special creation of Adam and his Fall, Zaehner weakens his position, since his interpretation of the Adam story may be radically questioned. The doubts and objections which arise are, briefly, as follows:

(a) The biblical narrative, which is the principal basis for people's belief in the existence of Adam, says nothing about anthropoid apes and nothing about an eternal soul as such. Still less does it make Adam out to be like a Yogin.

(b) Adam cannot have brought bodily death into the world, since the apes were not immortal. But let us assume that Adam was different, and was initially immortal, because of the divine essence infused into him. How does this imply that there was no bodily death for him? Does it mean that God did something to the bodily side of Adam, making the flesh and bones which Adam inherited from the apes into something mysteriously imperishable? It is not a likely story.

(c) Not all Christians would accept the theory of a substantial eternal soul. But in any case, it does not follow that this is what the monistic mystic realizes in his inner contemplative experience. The Advaitin would believe that he has realized the oneness of the Ātman with the divine being; while the adherent of Yoga would not. This is a big difference of interpretation, and if we were to take it at its face value we might be inclined to say that the Advaitin and the Yogin have attained different states. But do we have to take their claims at face value? This raises important methodological issues.

Does the Advaitin make his claim simply on the basis of an inner contemplative experience? It is not so. The concept of Brahman as a divine Reality ultimately derives from an extension of the idea of the sacred Power implicit in pre-Upanishadic sacrificial ritual. The famous identification of Ātman with Brahman involves bringing together different strands of religious thought and life. It is not something yielded by contemplative experience alone, even though the latter is highly relevant to it.

Likewise, the theistic mystic, in thinking that he has attained a kind of union with God must already have the concept of God—as a personal Being, creator of the world, author of revelation, etc. His description of his experience, where this includes mention of God, is thus not derived *simply* from the nature of that experience. The mystic does not know that God is creator from a mere inspection of an interior state; rather he relates that inner state to beliefs which he already has.

Zaehner's theory, too, obviously includes data derived from sources other than those contained in mystical literature. In interpreting what happens to the Yogin, he draws on certain elements in the Christian tradition. It therefore seems that the truth of his theory depends partly on the truth of Christianity (at least negatively: if Christianity were false, Zaehner's theory would be false, though the falsity of his theory is compatible with the truth of Christianity, since the latter is not necessarily committed to beliefs about anthropoid apes and the like).

These points indicate that we must examine in more detail the methodology of the evaluations and interpretation of mystical experience.

IV. EXPERIENCE AND INTERPRETATION (AUTO- AND HETERO-)

That some distinction must be made between experience and interpretation is clear. For it is generally recognized, and certainly by Zaehner, that there are types of mystical experience cutting across different religions and theologies. That is to say, it is recognized that a mystic of one religion and some mystic of another faith can have what is substantially a similar experience. Thus as we have noted, both Christian and Muslim mystics come under Zaehner's category of theistic mysticism; while, for him, Advaitin and Yogin mysticism belong to the monistic category. But the interpretations within a type differ. We have seen a large doctrinal distinction between Advaita and Yoga. The latter believes in a plurality of eternal *purushas,* not in a single Ātman. Consequently its account of liberation, and therefore of contemplative experience, differs from that of Advaita. Thus on Zaehner's own thesis it becomes very necessary to distinguish between experience and interpretation, when two experiences belong to the same class but have rather different modes of interpretation.

Nevertheless, the distinction between experience and interpretation is not clear-cut. The reason for this is that the concepts used in describing and explaining an experience vary in their degree of ramification. That is to say, where a concept occurs as part of a doctrinal scheme it gains its meaning in part from a range of doctrinal statements taken to be true. For example, the term "God" in the Christian context gains part at least of its characteristic meaning from such doctrinal statements as: "God created the universe," "Jesus Christ is God," "God has acted in history," etc.

Thus when Suso writes "In this merging of itself in God the spirit passes away," he is describing a contemplative experience by means of the highly ramified concept *God,* the less ramified concept *spirit* and the still less ramified concept *pass away.* In order to understand the statement it is necessary to bear in mind the doctrinal ramifications contained in it. Thus it follows, for Suso as a Christian, that in this merging of itself in the Creator of the universe, the spirit passes away; and so on.

By contrast, some descriptions of mystical experience do not involve such wide ramifications. For instance "When the spirit by the loss of its self-consciousness has in very truth established its abode in this glorious and dazzling obscurity"—here something of the nature of the experience is conveyed without any doctrine's being presupposed as true (except insofar as the concept *spirit* may involve some belief in an eternal element within man). This, then, is a relatively unramified description. Thus descriptions of mystical experience range from the highly ramified to those which have a very low degree of ramification.[3]

It is to be noted that ramifications may enter into the descriptions either because of the intentional nature of the experience or through reflection upon it. Thus a person brought up in a Christian environment and strenuously practicing the Christian life may have a contemplative experience which he sees *as* a union with God. The whole spirit of his interior quest will affect the way he sees his experience; or, to put it another way, the whole spirit of his quest will enter into the experience. On the other hand, a person might only come to see the experience in this way after the event, as it were: upon reflection he interprets his experience in theological categories.

In all descriptions of mystical experience, then, we ought to be on the lookout for ramifications. Their degree can be crudely estimated by asking: How many propositions are presupposed as true by the description in question?

It would also seem to follow, if we bear in mind the notion of degrees of ramification, that the higher the degree of ramification, the less is the description guaranteed by the experience itself. For where there is a high degree of ramification, some statements will be presupposed which have to be verified in other ways than by immediate mystical experience. Thus a mystic who claims to become united with Christ presupposes that the historical Jesus is the Christ; and the historicity of Jesus is guaranteed by the written records, not by an interior experience. Again, where contemplation is regarded as a means of liberation from rebirth, the description of the mystical experience may involve reference to this doctrine (thus the concept *nirvana* presupposes the truth of the rebirth doctrine). To say that someone has in this life attained the peace and insight of nirvana is also to claim that he will not be reborn. But the truth of rebirth is not discovered through mystical experience as such. It is true that the Buddhist Yogin may claim supernormal knowledge of previous lives: but this is in the nature of memory, if anything, and is to be distinguished from the formless, imageless inner experience which accrues upon the practice of *jhāna*. Also, Buddhists appeal to other empirical and philosophical evidence in support of the claim that the rebirth doctrine is true.[4]

The idea of degrees of ramification may help to clarify the distinction between experience and interpretation. But a further methodological point is also important. Descriptions, etc., of religious experience may be made from various points of view. There is the description given by the man himself, in terms of his own tradition. There is the description which others of his own tradition may give. Also, men of another tradition may describe his experience in terms of *their* tradition or standpoint. Thus if a Christian says that the Buddha's Enlightenment-experience involved some kind of interior vision of God, he is describing the experience from his own point of view and not from that of the Buddha. We crucially, then, should distinguish between a mystic's interpretation of his own experience and the interpretation which may be placed upon it from a different point of view. In other words, we must distinguish between what may be called *auto*-interpretation and *hetero*-interpretation.[5]

The difference between the auto-interpretation of an experience and the hetero-interpretation of it will depend on, first, the degree of ramification involved and, secondly, the difference between the presupposed truths incorporated in the ramification. For example, the Christian evaluation of the Buddha's Enlightenment-experience posited above uses the concept *God* in the Christian sense. The Buddhist description on the other hand does not. Thus, the Christian hetero-interpretation presupposes such propositions as that God created the world, God was in Christ, etc., and these propositions are not accepted in the Buddhist auto-interpretation. By contrast the Jewish and Christian interpretations of Isaiah's experience in the Temple overlap in great measure. This is because the beliefs presupposed coincide over a reasonably wide range.

These methodological observations, though rather obvious, need stating because they are too commonly neglected.

We may conclude so far, then, that a description of a mystical experience can fall under one of the following heads:

(a) Auto-interpretation with a low degree of ramification
(b) Hetero-interpretation with a low degree of ramification
(c) Auto-interpretation with a high degree of ramification
(d) Hetero-interpretation with a high degree of ramification

These can conveniently be called for short:

(a) Low auto-interpretation
(b) Low hetero-interpretation
(c) High auto-interpretation
(d) High hetero-interpretation

We may note that a high hetero-interpretation of experience will usually imply the falsity or inadequacy of a high auto-interpretation of experience, and conversely. It would therefore seem to be a sound principle to try to seek a low hetero-interpretation coinciding well with a low auto-interpretation. In this way an agreed phenomenological account of experience will be arrived at, and this will facilitate the attempt to distinguish experience from interpretation. But since experience will often be affected by its high auto-interpretation, it is also important to understand this high auto-interpretation, without obscuring it by means of a high hetero-interpretation.

I shall argue that Zaehner's distinction between monistic and theistic mysticism partly depends on his own high hetero-interpretation, and partly on his not distinguishing between high and low auto-interpretation.

V. ZAEHNER'S DISTINCTION BETWEEN MONISTIC AND THEISTIC MYSTICISM CRITICIZED

A difficulty about Zaehner's classification arises once we examine Buddhism. It is undoubtedly the case that Buddhism—and very clearly in

Theravāda Buddhism—centers on mystical experience. The Eightfold Path incorporates and culminates in a form of Yoga which may bring the peace and insight of nirvana to the saint. Crucial in this Yoga is the practice of the *jhānas* or stages of meditation. It is thus necessary for any account of mysticism to take Buddhist experience and tradition seriously. But regrettably (from Zaehner's point of view) Buddhism denies the soul or eternal self. Zaehner, in order to fit Buddhism into the monistic pigeonhole, denies this denial, and ascribes an *ātman* doctrine to the Buddha.

This will not do, for a number of reasons.[6]

First, even if (incredibly) the Buddha did teach an *ātman* doctrine, we still have to reckon with the Buddhists. The phenomenon of Buddhist mysticism, not involving an *ātman*-type auto-interpretation, remains; and it is both widespread and important in the fabric of man's religious experience.

Secondly, it is asking too much to make us believe that a doctrine which has been eschewed by nearly all Buddhists (with the possible exception of the *pudgalavādins,* who significantly did not dare to use the term *ātman,* even though their Buddhist opponents castigated them for wanting to introduce the idea) was explicitly taught by the Buddha. The *anattā* teaching is about the strongest bit of the earliest tradition which we possess.

Thirdly, it is easy enough to play around with the texts by translating *attā* with a capital, as "Self." Thus Zaehner translates *attagarahī*[7] as "that the Self would blame," and so on. He refers us to *Dhammapada* 165 to show that evil is done by the empirical ego; so that in vs. 157, when we are enjoined to treat the self as dear, it must be the eternal Self which is being referred to. But consider the former passage. It reads: "By oneself is evil done; one is defiled by oneself . . . by oneself one is made pure; the pure and the impure stand and fall by themselves; no one can purify another." Does one really want to translate: "By oneself is evil done; . . . by one's Self is one made pure"? The point could have been expressed more clearly if the author had wanted to say *this.* The whole purport of such passages is that one should be self-reliant and responsible (and I do not mean Self-reliant!). The fact is that the word *attā* is very common, and has an ordinary usage. It is a gross strain on the texts to read into them the meaning ascribed to them by Zaehner.

Fourth, Zaehner thinks his case is confirmed by the passages "illustrating what the Self is not"[8]—it is not the body, feelings, dispositions, etc. But these passages in no way help Zaehner. Their import is clearly explained in the famous passage of the *Milindapañha* (40–45), where a Humean analysis of the individual is given. The Buddha himself, furthermore, is reported as having asserted that though it is wrong to identify the self with the body, it is better for the uninstructed man to make this mistake than to commit the opposite error of believing in an eternal soul.[9]

For these and other reasons, Zaehner's interpretation cannot seriously be defended. But embarrassing consequences flow from this conclusion. It means that a main form of mysticism does not involve a monistic auto-interpretation.

Nevertheless, Zaehner could still argue as follows. Admittedly a monistic auto-interpretation is not present among Buddhist contemplatives: but it is still reasonable to hetero-interpret their attainment in a monistic fashion. We can still say (can we not?) that what the Buddhist *really* achieves in and through contemplation is the isolation of his eternal soul.

Such a defense, however, implies that there can be a misunderstanding on the part of a mystic as to what it is he is attaining. It implies that auto-interpretations can be widely mistaken, insofar as they are ramified.

Likewise, since Zaehner classifies both Yoga and Advaita together as monistic, and since their doctrinal auto-interpretations differ very widely, within the Hindu context it has to be admitted that wrong auto-interpretation can occur.

Let us bring this out more explicitly. According to Zaehner, Buddhist, Yoga and Advaitin mystics belong together, and fit in the same monistic category, and yet the following three doctrines of liberation are propounded by them:

(1) That there are no eternal selves, but only impermanent individuals who are, however, capable of liberation, through attaining nirvana in this life, in which case they will no more be reborn.

(2) That there is an infinite number of eternal selves, who through Yoga can attain isolation or liberation, a state in which the soul exists by itself, no longer implicated in nature and in the round of rebirth.

(3) That there is but one Self, which individuals can realize, and which is identical with Brahman as the ground of being (which at a lower level of truth manifests itself as a personal Lord and Creator)— such a realization bringing about a cessation of the otherwise continuously reborn individual.

Now these are obviously very different doctrines. Why should the crucial difference lie between them and theism? Is not the difference between (2) and (3) equally striking? If the monistic category includes heterogeneous high auto-interpretations, there is no guarantee that we should not place *all* mystics, including theists, in the same category; and explain their differences not in terms of radically different experiences, but in terms of varied auto-interpretation. The gaps within the monistic category are big enough for it not to seem implausible to count the gap between monism and theism as no wider.

Admit that high auto-interpretation can be mistaken, and there is no great reason to isolate theistic mysticism as belonging to a separate category.

If I am right in proposing this on methodological grounds, we can go on to explain the difference between Yoga (say) and theism by reference to what goes on outside the context of the mystical life. The devotional and prophetic experiences of a personal God—prophetism and *bhakti* religion—these help to explain why the theist sees his contemplative experience in a special way. He already considers that there is evidence of a personal Lord and Creator: in the silent brightness of inner contemplative ecstasy it is natural (or supernatural) to identify what is found within with the Lord who is worshiped without.[10] A priori, then, there is no special call to assign theistic mysticism to a special pigeonhole. Of course, there are theological motives for trying to do this. It avoids some ticklish questions, and it suggests that there is something very special about theistic mysticism. It is a covert means of preaching theism. Now doubtless theism should be preached; but *fairly*. Methodologically, the assignment of theism to a special pigeonhole is suspect. The arguments are more complex and difficult than we think.

But it may be replied to all this that the discussion has been largely a priori. Do we not have to look at the actual words of theistic mystics? Of course. I shall, however, content myself with examining some passages which Zaehner quotes in favor of his own position.

VI. SOME PASSAGES FROM THEISTIC MYSTICS EXAMINED

An important part of Zaehner's argument rests on a couple of passages from Ruysbroeck. I quote from these.

> Now observe that whenever man is empty and undistracted in his senses by images, and free and unoccupied in his highest powers, he attains rest by purely natural means. And all men can find and possess this rest in themselves by their mere nature, without the grace of God, if they are able to empty themselves of sensual images and of all action.[11]

Zaehner comments that Ruysbroeck here has in effect described (Advaita) Vedāntin mysticism. Talking of men who have attained this "natural rest," Ruysbroeck goes on:

> Through the natural rest, which they feel and have in themselves in emptiness, they maintain that they are free, and united with God

without mean, and that they are advanced beyond all the exercises of the Holy Church, and beyond the commandments of God, and beyond the law, and beyond all the virtuous works which one can in any way practise.[12]

Now it will be noted that Ruysbroeck's criticism chiefly rests on moral grounds. He condemns quietists for arrogance, complacency and ethical sterility. They do not properly connect their inner experience with the God taught by the Church, who makes demands upon men, and who wishes that they may love him. But the ordinances and teachings of the Church do not spring from mystical experience: they have other sources. And moral insights are not simply derived from contemplation. In other words, the criteria for judging mystical experience are partly exterior to the contemplative life. Thus, even given that Ruysbroeck is a good guide in these matters (and this need not be so), we might still say: the trouble with "monistic" quietists is a failure in their auto-interpretation of their experience. They do not really see the God of the Bible and of the Church there. But this does not at all entail that, given a low interpretation (i.e. a relatively unramified account) of their experiences, these experiences differ radically in character from those of theistic mystics. In short, these Ruysbroeck passages are quite compatible with my thesis, and thus do not strongly support the Zaehner analysis.

Quietists, for Ruysbroeck, are not sufficiently aware of the working of God's grace. But the doctrine of grace (and by contrast, nature) is a theological account of God's activity. A person could have a genuine mystical experience, but be wrong in not ascribing it to God's grace. Ruysbroeck's high hetero-interpretation of monistic quietism conflicts with the latter's high auto-interpretation. But the experiences for all that could belong to the same type.

Zaehner also makes use of a very interesting passage from al-Ghazālī, part of which reads as follows:

> The mystics, after their ascent to the heavens of Reality, agree that they saw nothing in existence except God the One. Some of them attained this state through discursive reasoning, others reached it by savoring and experiencing it. From these all plurality entirely fell away. They were drowned in pure solitude: their reason was lost in it, and they became as if dazed in it. They no longer had the capacity to recollect aught but God, nor could they in any wise remember themselves. Nothing was left to them but God. They became drunk with a drunkenness in which their reason collapsed. One of them said, "I am God (the Truth)." Another said, "Glory be to me. How great is my glory," while another said, "Within my robe is naught but God." But the words of lovers when in a state of drunkenness must be hidden

away and not broadcast. However, when their drunkenness abates and the sovereignty of their reason is restored—and reason is God's scale upon earth—they know that this was not actual identity. . . . For it is not impossible that a man should be confronted by a mirror and should look into it, and not see the mirror at all, and that he should think that the form he saw in the mirror was the form of the mirror itself and identical with it. . . .[13]

What Ghazālī is saying here—to translate into my own jargon—is that the mystic's auto-interpretation of his experience as involving actual identity with God is mistaken, and that the correct interpretation must say that there is some distinction between the soul and God. In the passage quoted he goes on to explain how the mystic, in his self-naughting, is not conscious of himself (or even of his own unconsciousness of himself), and this is a main reason for the language of identity.

This seems to me a clear indication that the monistic and theistic experiences are essentially similar; and that it is the correct *interpretation* of them which is at issue. The theist must maintain, in order to make sense of worship and devotion, that there is a distinction between the human individual and God. The non-theist, not being so much concerned with devotion (though he may allow a place for it at the popular level), can more happily speak of identity with ultimate Reality, or can even dispense (as in Yoga and Theravada Buddhism) with such a concept of the Absolute. Thus the question of what is the best hetero- and auto-interpretation of mystical experience turns on whether devotion and worship are important. Or more generally: the question of interpretation is the same as the question of God. One cannot answer this by reference to auto-interpretation of mystical experience alone; for these auto-interpretations conflict, and they have ramifications extending far beyond the sphere of such experience itself.

This is why my thesis, that maybe there is no essential distinction between what Zaehner has called monistic and theistic mysticism, does not at all entail that proponents of neo-Vedāntin views of a "personal philosophy," involving a doctrine of the Absolute Self,[14] are right. The thesis "All introvertive mysticism is, as experience, essentially the same" does not entail any doctrine. Truth of doctrine depends on evidence other than mysticism, and this is true even of the doctrine of the Absolute Self.

I have tried to argue that the interpretation of mystical experience depends at least in part on evidence, etc., not given in the experience itself; and that therefore there is always a question about the degree to which nonexperimental data are incorporated into ramified descriptions of mystical experience. I can best illustrate this, finally, with a passage written by Zaehner himself.

We have already said that when the mystic claims attributes that are necessarily divine and demonstrably not human—such as omnipotence and omniscience—it is fairly clear that he is not enjoying union with God, but rather some sort of natural mystical experience. Apart from this important consideration it would seem that the mystic who is genuinely inspired by the divine love, will show this to the world by the holiness of his life and by an abiding humility in face of the immense favors bestowed which he always will see to be God's doing, not his own. Only such criteria can enable us to distinguish between the genuine state of union with God and the "natural" or rather "preternatural" phenomena we have been discussing.[15]

The two criteria here mentioned can be called respectively the theological and the moral. The theological criterion shows, or is claimed to show, that the mystic cannot have enjoyed real union with God because he makes false theological claims (omniscience, etc.) on his own behalf. The moral criterion can show that a mystic has not enjoyed real union with God because his life is not holy, or not humble. Some comments are in order.

First, *both criteria are indirect.* If they are, as Zaehner here says, the *only* criteria that distinguish genuine union with God from something else, then *one cannot establish this latter discrimination on the basis of a phenomenological account of the experience itself,* but rather on the basis of the verbal and other behavior of the contemplative. This supports my thesis that phenomenologically there is no need to distinguish between monistic and theistic mystical experience (auto-interpretations apart).

Secondly, the first criterion depends on the truth of theism. This is why the interpretation and evaluation of mystical experience from a doctrinal point of view cannot be separated from the general question of the truth of theism. The theological criterion could not work for a Vedāntin.

Thirdly, to some extent the same is true of the moral criterion. For humility is a virtue for the theist, who sees the wonder and holiness of the divine Being but need not be a virtue for the non-theist. Insofar as moral ideas depend on theology (and they do in part), one cannot really separate the moral from the theological criterion.

VII. CONCLUSION

The above arguments by themselves do not establish the truth of my thesis that monistic and theistic contemplative experiences are (except insofar as they are affected by auto-interpretations) essentially the same: but I hope that they are sufficient to cast doubt on the Zaehner analysis.

Mysticism is not the same as prophetism and *bhakti* religion; but it may gain its auto-interpretations from these latter types of religion. But there is no need to take all interpretations as phenomenological descriptions; and this is the main point of this paper. To put the possibility which I am canvassing in a simple form, it can be reduced to the following theses.

(1) Phenomenologically, mysticism is everywhere the same.

(2) Different flavors, however, accrue to the experiences of mystics because of their ways of life and modes of auto-interpretation.

(3) The truth of interpretation depends in large measure on factors extrinsic to the mystical experience itself. Thus, the question of whether mysticism is a valid means of knowledge concerning the Transcendent is only part of a much wider set of theological questions.

Finally, let me express my debt to Zaehner's learning and fertility of ideas. If I have criticized a main thesis of his, it is because it is itself an important contribution to the discussion of mysticism. In my view, his analysis is wrong; but interestingly false propositions are worth far more than a whole lot of boringly true ones.

NOTES

1. *At Sundry Times*, p. 132.
2. *Mysticism Sacred and Profane*, pp. 191–92.
3. See my "Mystical Experience," in *Sophia*, Vol. I, no. 1 (April 1962), pp. 19ff., discussing the distinction between experience and interpretation as propounded by W. T. Stace in *Mysticism and Philosophy*, p. 37.
4. See my *Doctrine and Argument in Indian Philosophy*, ch. xii.
5. *Op. cit.*, p. 37.
6. A fuller criticism is to be found in my *Doctrine and Argument in Indian Philosophy*, pp. 211ff. Zaehner's account of Buddhism is discoverable in his *At Sundry Times* (see, for example, his argument on p. 98).
7. *Sutta-nipata* 788: see *At Sundry Times*, pp. 98–101.
8. *At Sundry Times*, p. 101.
9. *Saṁyutta-nikāya* ii, 95.
10. See *Doctrine and Argument in Indian Philosophy*, ch. x, where an analysis along these lines is worked out in some detail.
11. *Mysticism Sacred and Profane*, p. 170.
12. Ibid., p. 171.
13. *Mysticism Sacred and Profane*, pp. 157–58.
14. See, for example, W. T. Stace, *Mysticism and Philosophy*, who comes to this conclusion.
15. Ibid., p. 193.

6

Superstructures

FRITS STAAL

Earlier[1] we have made two distinctions. On the one hand, the distinction between the difficult ways of contemplation and the easy way of drugs. On the other hand, the distinction between the types of mysticism that can be induced by human effort and may therefore be difficult, and those that cannot be so induced and are therefore not in a position to be difficult. The difference between the latter type and the drug-induced experiences is that what does not depend on human effort can be said to be easy, provided only it occurs; while the other kind is generally easy because it is brought about by the mere act of ingestion. The effect of a drug still depends on the cultural background, on general psychological factors and on the individual's receptivity and mental attitude. Some people are unaffected at least by the milder drugs and others get high when they merely come close. In fact, there is much more significant variety (see e.g. Claridge 1972, chs. 2 and 6). The same kind of variety surrounds other mental experiences.

The attainment of an experience is furthermore easy for a natural mystic, i.e. a person who is capable of attaining mystical states because he is born that way. This is what was indicated by the word *janma*, "birth," in the *Yogasūtra* and in the *Abhidharmakośa*. The nineteenth-century Indian saint Rāmakṛṣṇa Paramahaṃsa and the twentieth-century sage Rāmaṇa Maharṣi were such mystics, and went into trances frequently. But the aim of such complicated processes of training as we meet with in the Yoga are the same: they produce a *yogin* who can enter a state of *samādhi* easily and at will.

What is suggested by the parallel between these distinctions of easy and difficult ways? Since a mystical experience is like entering a mental state or like gaining access to a domain of the brain, there are different methods which can bring this about, just as a house can be entered by various means: by climbing through a window, by breaking a wall, by digging a tunnel to reach the cellar, or by opening the front door with a key. Some methods are easier than others, which may be reflected in different evaluations, competing with each other. Someone who has just broken the wall of his home is irritated when he afterwards finds in his pocket a key that fits. Moreover the house he has entered is no longer the same; it is now quite drafty and difficult to heat. Of course, entering a house with the help of a key, and obtaining the right key may be as difficult as digging a tunnel.

This analogy is only valid in some respects. For in the realm of mysticism, we do not know whether it is the same state which is reached in different ways. Also, a mystical experience is to a larger extent a mental event than entering a home. But even if it were possible to reach the same state by different methods, e.g. after expending great effort or effortlessly, the resulting effect would not be experienced in the same way. The different methods and techniques of mysticism therefore have a much more dissimilar impact on the total personality than the attainment of an allegedly identical physical or brain state might seem to suggest. Hence the tendency to claim that different mystical methods do lead in different directions. But these differences may in fact result from different religious or moral evaluations and may have little to do with the mystical states themselves. It is therefore important to distinguish between mystical experiences and superstructures.

I have paid some attention to the distinction between easy and difficult methods in mysticism because it is apparent, in this case, that the distinction is largely a moral one, so that the resulting mystical and corresponding brain states need not be different. Let me try to be more precise. Let us assume that there are two methods, α and β, one easy and one difficult, which induce, among other things, an identical state of the brain C, which corresponds in turn to a certain mystical experience. In such a case, the subjective experience will not only be of C, but will also reflect the preceding methods α and β. The different results of α and β will also be located in the brain, say through different brain conditions A and B, respectively. Now the resulting experience will in the one case correspond to a condition of the brain which incorporates A and C, and in the other case, B and C. Though the resulting state which incorporates A and C (or respectively, B and C) may present itself as a unified experience, one should distinguish between on the one hand A, which reflects past experience, expectation, degree of satisfaction, confirmation of existing beliefs, etc., and on the other hand C, which reflects the mystical state itself.

In this construction, which is of course simplified, artificial and schematic, the distinction between "easy" and "difficult" does not play an essential part. The same reasoning would apply to any two different methods α and β. And so we can conclude that different methods may well result in different experiences, and yet incorporate an identical mystical experience.

The same reasoning might apply to the distinction between mystical states that can be induced by conscious effort and mystical states that cannot be so induced. In the Western monotheistic view, and in several medieval Hindu sects, the latter states are attributed to the workings of grace. But in Advaita the concept of grace receives a special interpretation. The grace of the semipersonal divinity *īśvara*, who is nothing but a reflection on a lower level of *brahman*, is interpreted as his mere permission that the effects of *karman* be wiped out and the chain of transmigration be interrupted (see Staal 1961b, p. 146). In general, grace is postulated whenever no other source is known or acknowledged. The difference between mystical states that can be induced, and those that cannot, might therefore be only in degree of awareness. However, we may have to reckon with an unconditioned state that would seem to account for some specific properties of the mind, to which I shall return. Whatever the correct interpretation will turn out to be, the subjective experience in both cases may be expected to be quite different, which does not by itself establish that we are dealing with states that are necessarily different from each other.

Before turning to specifics, let me summarize the significance of these observations. I am not claiming here that many different states *must* lead to the same mystical state. They *may* lead to different states. I am only claiming that multiplicity of states is not inconsistent with an alternative possibility, and that the resulting states *may* be identical, or at any rate more closely related than the different approaches suggest.

Differences between easy and difficult and between based upon effort and not so based, are partly related to the level of mystical techniques and methods, but partly they reflect what I have called superstructure.[2] In the case of easy and difficult, this is fairly straightforward: we assign, on moral grounds, greater merit to the performance of a difficult task than to that of an easy one. In Christianity, for example, the Protestant doctrines that salvation can be reached by faith alone (*sola fide*) or by grace alone (*gratia sola*) strike believers in the effectiveness of good works as irresponsible because they seem too easy. It seems a kind but unfair thought that a sinner should be saved without any great effort on his part. The Greek philosopher Diogenes, when told about the Mysteries of Eleusis, said: "What do you mean? Is Pataikion the thief going to have a better lot after death than Epaminondas, just because he was initiated?" (Cornford 1923, p. 51.)

In Hinduism, the medieval *bhakti* cults advocate personal and emotional expressions of affection which offer a simple and popular alternative to ritual or asceticism. A feature of some of these cults is the chanting of a divine name (e.g. Hare Kṛṣṇa). In Rāmānuja's *Viśiṣṭādvaita*, *karman*, "(ritual) activity," and *jñāna*, "knowledge, insight," are subordinate to *bhakti*, "loving devotion," and the grace of God, which will bring about salvation (studied in Otto 1930 as *Indiens Gnadenreligion:* "India's religion of grace"). But since Rāmānuja was after all a theologian and moralist, his *bhakti* is not simple or easy. In fact, it is confined to the twice-born castes (which in South India, means: the Brahmans) and one of its prerequisites is that the person who wishes to engage in *bhakti* must first be *jñānaniṣṭha*, "firmly established in knowledge" (Muneo Tokunaga, personal communication). But acts also are important when one engages in *bhakti* (Buitenen 1968, p. 23). Rāmānuja regards *prapatti*, "surrender," (to Viṣṇu) as the first step in *bhakti*. This notion is developed in one school of the later *Viśiṣṭādvaita*, where it finally becomes an easy path which is open to all.

In Japan, in the Jōdo or Amida (Amitābha) Buddhism of Hōnen and his pupil Shinran we have another similar, easy and popular method. Here, as in some forms of Protestantism in Christianity, the sufficiency of mere faith is stressed. But now the moralistic superstructure is inverted, and these new doctrines are advocated with slogans intended to shock the piously toiling practitioners of virtue. A saying of Hōnen runs: "Even a bad man will be received in Buddha's land, how much more a good man." Shinran turned this into "Even a good man will be received in Buddha's land, how much more a bad man" (Anesaki 1963, pp. 182–83).

To interpret such passages correctly it should be borne in mind that the Pure Land Buddhism of Shinran was obsessed by a morbid sense of sin, to which only Manicheism and Christianity offer parallels. Nakamura, after quoting statements by Shinran like "There is no end of evil nature, man's mind is as abominable as a viper," characterizes this doctrine as follows: "Man is by nature evil, and because he is evil . . . he is entitled to be saved by the great benevolence of Amitābha" (Nakamura 1964, p. 515; for literary illustrations see Niwa 1966). When Jōdo Buddhism and Christianity came into direct contact, these similarities were not discussed. This may be so because, as Nakamura has shown, the encounter of the two was primarily a confrontation between political powers, not a confrontation between different ways of thinking (Nakamura 1967, I, 111–49).

In all these cases we may be concerned with mystical experiences which have nothing to do with the superstructural distinction between easy and difficult. I shall now survey some other superstructures which may also have to be evaluated in a similar manner. Such surveys constitute a necessary part of the study of mysticism, because superstructures generally express mystical doctrines and offer interpretations of mystical experience. Since they always involve religious or philosophical considerations, differences between them need not reflect differences in mystical experience. If we wish to isolate mystical experiences, we must disentangle them from such superstructures. Moreover we ourselves approach mystical experiences, like any other kind of experiences, always within existing perspectives and superstructures. We should be aware of these before we can remove them. Lastly, the theory of mystical experience which the student of mysticism must evolve, is itself such a superstructure. In fact, it might turn out to be related to one of the existing superstructures. After all, many philosophers, especially in the Orient, have constructed superstructures in order to make sense of mystical experience.

In Hinduism, the "easy" way of *bhakti* has to be understood within a wide perspective. In Indian religion, *bhakti* appears relatively late (in the *Śvetāśvataropaniṣad* and in the epic). But the controversy on the value and efficacy of *karman* and *jñāna* runs through the centuries. In Vedic ritualism as described in the later Vedic texts, codified in the ritual Sutras and systematized in the orthoprax[3] philosophy of the (Karma-) Mīmāṃsā, it is claimed that only the correct performance of *karman,* "(ritual) activity," will lead to the desired result (e.g. wealth, offspring, heaven, immortality). Subsequently the notion of *karman* is developed into a doctrine of retribution, the strict law of cause and effect is extended to all human activity, aims and ends, in this life and beyond, and the belief in transmigration appears. This generalization does not lead to fatalism, as is sometimes said, or at any rate not to any greater extent than any other religious notion does (fatalism seems to occur all over the world, especially among the poor and uneducated). On the contrary, human freedom presupposes the law of *karman.* Past activity may lead to a certain birth which restricts possibilities in a certain way; but within these restrictions, man is free to do his *karman* as he sees fit. One can influence the forces of *karman,* for example, by performing the austerities of *tapas.* . . .

In the Upaniṣads, the doctrine and the efficacy of *karman* are challenged and often rejected, and the notion of *jñāna,* "insight, knowledge," takes their place. The older notion of *svarga,* "heaven," which is reminiscent of "paradise" in Western monotheism, is replaced by *mokṣa,* "liberation." The *Muṇḍakipaniṣad* (1.2.7–10), for example, states that fools think that they will attain the highest good by performing sacrifices. But in fact, after a suitable period in heaven, they are reborn in this world or in a lower one (cf. Staal 1961, p. 76). This criticism, too, is generalized. Later it is denied that any activity whatsoever can contribute to the emergence of *jñāna.*

The notion of *jñāna* developed in a great many ways especially in the Vedānta, which also uses the term *vidyā,* and in Buddhism, where the corresponding term is *prajñā,* generally translated as "wisdom." In comparison with *karman*, which refers to physical activity, *jñāna* is a purely mental notion. In some of the systems of Indian philosophy, *jñāna* is regarded as a *vṛtti*, "fluctuation," of the mind. As such it would be one of the fluctuations of the mind which according to the Yoga have to be brought to a standstill. But in most Buddhist and Vedāntic thought, the concept of *jñāna* is divested of all traces of activity, mental as well as physical. It develops into what may be called a mystical concept. In order to understand this I shall trace a few steps in the development of this concept, which illustrate a development from ritualism to mysticism.

The Upaniṣadic reaction against ritualism took many different forms. Sometimes the ritual was interpreted symbolically, sometimes the ritual activity itself was "interiorized." It was also related to the ancient speculations on *prāṇa*, "breath." As distinct from *agnihotra*, a purely ritualistic sacrifice to the Vedic god Agni, mention is made of a more spiritual variant, the *agnihotra* of breath (*prāṇāgnihotra*). Then there developed the idea that it is not necessary to perform the ritual acts physically, but that it is sufficient to concentrate mentally on their sequence (this is called *upāsanā*, "contemplation," or *vidya*, "knowledge"). We come across references to "mental cups" along with the physical cups from which the Soma is drunk. In these practices we witness a transition from the Vedic ritual to the practice of meditation. In the final stages, the ritual is rejected outright (as in the above passage from the *Muṇḍakapaniṣad*) and the notion of *jñāna* takes its place.

In contemporary circles, where religion and irrationalism are regarded as inseparable, it is often emphasized that this *jñāna*, like the γνῶσις of the Gnostics and mystical knowledge in general, is altogether different from so called "intellectual" knowledge. Such semantic demarcation may well be justified, but it is not very informative, and is mostly advocated only negatively as an expression of anti-intellectual provincialism. So let us look more closely. The concept of *jñāna* may certainly be regarded as a "mystical" notion if only by definition or in the sense that such usage would in turn help to determine the meaning of the term "mystical" itself. At any rate, whether we deal with the Vedāntic *brahmajñāna*, "knowledge of brahman," or with the Buddhist *prajñā*, "wisdom," it is clear that the object of such knowledge is different from more mundane objects. Moreover, the object may coincide with the subject itself, as in the ordinary notion of "self-knowledge," or vanish altogether, as in *śūnyatā*. But we know already that all knowledge is not "intellectual" or taught in universities. There are many different kinds of knowledge, differing not only with regard to their object, but also with regard to the kind of object to which they are related, and with regard to the kind of relation to such an object. Since Ryle (1949, ch. 2), many philosophers, now supported by linguists, distinguish between "knowing that" and "knowing how." Knowing how to swim is different from knowing when to stop, knowing that the earth is round, knowing Mr. Nixon or knowing mathematics (the Dutch mathematician G. Mannoury held that knowing mathematics is not a knowing that, but a knowing how). No wonder, then that knowing *brahman* might again be different.

It is very important to bear in mind that the Indian notion of *jñāna*, whether it is called mystical, intellectual or anti-intellectual, is regarded as objective and true. Śaṅkara is very explicit on this point. He distinguishes between subjective: *puruṣabuddhyapekṣa*, "depending on man's notions," or *purrṣatantra*, "depending on man," and objective: *vastutantra*, "depending on things." That *jñāna* is objective is explained in the following passage, where it is contrasted with "option" (*vikalpa*): "There is no option as to whether a thing is thus or thus, is or is not. Option depends on human notions. Knowledge of the nature of a thing does not depend on human notions. It depends only on the thing itself. To say with regard to a pillar 'it is a pillar, or it is a man, or it is something else' does not result from correct knowledge. To say that it is a man or something else does result from false knowledge. To say that it is a pillar results from correct knowledge, because it depends on the thing itself. Therefore the means of knowing objects, that are existent things, depend on the things themselves" (*Brahmasūtrabhāṣya* I.1.3, quoted in Staal 1962a, p. 62).

In Advaita Vedānta, *jñāna* is regarded as objective and often as descriptive, and it is conceived of as having for its object something that is *siddha*, "established." This term is contrasted with the term *sādhya*, which denotes something that is "to be established." "To be established" are the objects not only of *vikalpa*, "option," but also of *dharma*, "duty," *karman* "activity" and *dhyāna* "meditation." Concepts like the latter four refer to entities which are related to what is subjective and which are often prescriptive. In elaborating on this contrast between *siddha* and *sādhya*, the Advaitins were undoubtedly thinking of their adversaries, the philosophers of the Mīmāṃsā. For in the Mīmāṃsā, which is a kind of hermeneutic of the Veda, each Vedic expression is interpreted as, or related to, a *vidhi*, "injunction," which prompts to, or enjoins, *karman*, "activity." Therefore the Mīmāṃsā is concerned with what is *sādhya*, not *siddha*.

Śaṅkara regards *dhyāna*, "meditation," also as an activity, which is therefore dependent on man, subjective, and relates to what is *sādhya*. Meditation, unlike knowledge, therefore has "effects," which are generally referred to by the term *siddhi*, another derivative of the same root. (This term acquired later, . . . the more specific meaning "supernatural power.") In thus subordinating *dhyāna*, Śaṅkara probably had the Yoga in mind. It is known that he was familiar with the *Yogasūtra*, and according to Hacker [1968], he was an adherent of the Yoga system before he converted to Advaita. Whatever his career may have been, Śaṅkara regarded meditation, even though it is assigned a definite place in the training of the mystic, as subjective and not concerned with objective truth.

In Sanskrit there is another term derived from the same root as *siddha, siddhi* and *sādhya:* namely, *sadhana,* literally "means of establishing," viz. "religious practice." In advocating knowledge which is confined to what is *siddha,* and in rejecting or subordinating all these other notions which pertain to what is *sādhya,* the Advaitins undermined in fact the foundations of religious practice. But unlike the Buddhists, they adhered to the Vedic tradition, and adopted in practice a kind of compromise. They could do this because they accepted the distinction of two levels, which originated with Nāgārjuna. . . . This distinction enabled Buddhists as well as Advaitins to justify in theory whatever practice they chose to adhere to.

Śaṅkara's pupil Suresvara (second half of the eighth century), who according to the Indian tradition was first a proponent of the Mīmāṃsā, and was then converted to Advaita by Śaṅkara, refers to these notions, which he directly attaches to the Upaniṣadic tradition of reaction against the ritual. He says for example in the *Sambandhavārtika,* the introduction to his subcommentary on Śaṅkara's commentary on the *Bṛhadāraṇyaka Upaniṣad* (Mahadevan 1958, pp. 49–50; cf. Hacker 1950, pp. 1993–95 and Van Boetzelaer 1971, pp. 10–16):

> Therefore, he who knows the truth of the Veda will realize the futility of rites, and seek the knowledge of the one self, purifying himself through austerity.

> Free from all desires on account of practice in a previous birth, he is eligible even in his first stage of life.[4] He does not need any more action.

> He who is detached and desires knowledge does not require anything other than knowledge. For action is required in respect of what is to be established (*sādhya*). In respect of the established (*siddha*) it is of no use.

In the earlier speculations on *karman* and in the extension of the notion of universal causality also to the domain of the mind, we witness a concept of man which may be characterized as mechanistic. The term *sādhya* expresses man's urge to establish things in accordance with the causal mechanisms of *karman,* leading to merit and demerit. There is here a kind of principle of conservation: nothing gets lost and nothing is added. Hara (1968–69 and 1970) has compared these exchanges and transactions to the transfer of property or money. Though no scientific theories were developed which describe and explain the laws underlying these mechanisms, we read again and again that every activity leads to a result and that the sum total of these results, at the moment of death determines a new birth. Mechanistic world views in the West developed quite differently. They were worked out in detail, subjected to experimentation and theory formation, but they largely remained confined to the physical world. Only during the last few centuries have there been attempts to deal with the science of man along mechanistic lines; attempts which on the whole have remained unsuccessful. It is tempting to conclude from ancient Indian and recent Western experience that man cannot be explained along these lines.

In India the experience of the mystic suggested something altogether different. Here seemed to be a state which is unconditioned and unrelated to previous activity. It is experienced as *siddha*, not as *sādhya*. It is conceived of as *mokṣa*, "liberation" and as *nirvāṇa*, "extinction." It is *jñāna*, "knowledge," because it does not through activity establish an object, but appears to reflect a situation which was already there and a condition already attained.

While the Yoga is concerned with the methods which lead to *samādhi*, the Upaniṣads begin to develop a notion of *mokṣa* which is beyond all methods. In the development of the Advaita Vedānta this is expressed in terms of the contrast between *siddha* and *sādhya*. These terms reflect of course interpretations, and belong to the superstructure. In Buddhism, the unconditionality of *nirvāṇa* is present in the superstructure almost from the beginning; but it was especially expounded by Nāgārjuna. In his philosophy, *nirvāṇa* is never attained because it is already there, and so there is no seeker of *nirvāṇa* and no process of liberation.

Gauḍapāda described these notions in lines which use almost identical expressions (*Māṇḍūkyakārikā* 2.32):

> There is none in bondage, none aspiring for wisdom,
> No seeker of liberation and none liberated.

Because of such similarities, several scholars have claimed that Gauḍapāda was not merely familiar with Nāgārjuna, but was himself a Buddhist. But Mahadevan (1960) maintains that he was an early Advaitin.

To the followers of a religion, doctrines like these are very hard to swallow. Philosophers can take them, since they don't commit anybody to anything and philosophers are anyway not interested in *sādhanā* or religious practice. But most people turn to religion for guidance and comfort, and expect to be told what they should do or avoid. Here they are told that there is no path, and in the final resort they are not told anything at all. Such pristine ideas are therefore always mixed with others and tend to develop into new cults and disciplines. This happened in India and, since Buddhism disappeared from Indian soil, in Buddhist civilizations elsewhere in Asia. I shall give only one example, but it is striking. Although *Ch'an* in China and *Zen* in Japan grew out of these Indian doctrines of "no effort," these Far Eastern traditions gave rise to schools which again preached that the seeker after enlightenment must undergo arduous training and be subjected to numerous tests. *Zen* is therefore noted for the stress on spontaneity which is present in its theory and expressed in its art, and for painful and military discipline which characterizes its practice. The two tendencies survive in somewhat modified form in the contemporary conflict between what Watts has called "Straight Zen" and "Beat Zen" (Watts 1967, pp. 77–110).

If we wish to eliminate superstructure as much as possible, what are we finally to make of these doctrines of "no effort"? Possibly we should reckon with a property of the mind, which is manifest in a mystical state or in mystical states, and which is independent of previous conditioning of any kind. This would be consistent with the fact that elsewhere in the superstructures of mystical religions and philosophies, we find many competing paths and methods advocated as leading to mystical states of mind. Such methods may be aids which in unexplained ways help to reach a point which is quite independent of each of them. Each of these methods is therefore dispensable. But just as certain mystical states can perhaps not be reached by any particular method to the exclusion of all others, they cannot perhaps be explored by any particular method to the exclusion of all others. For methods of mystic training, or methods of exploration, attach to themselves specific activities, observables, prescripts and disciplines. The student of mysticism needs such support, and in my discussion of methods I need methods to discuss. Therefore the Yoga, with its amplification of methods and poverty of superstructure, provides excellent laboratories and testing grounds. But as a special challenge to the student of mysticism, it remains to be explored whether there are states of mind which are beyond all methods. Such states would by definition be beyond methodical exploration, so the student of mysticism could only be successful if at some point he happened to turn into a mystic. The available evidence suggests that he could still return, and be therefore in a position to evolve his theory.

So far I have described and discussed superstructures which are related to *bhakti* and to *jñāna*. Though *bhakti* appears late in the chronological development, it serves as a useful introduction to Indian forms of mysticism, especially for those who are raised in a Western monotheistic environment. The concept of *jñāna* introduces a notion which appears to be more basic to mysticism in general, and which may help us to understand some fundamental features of certain kinds of mystical experience.

But *jñāna* itself appeared in a *milieu* of *karman,* and though I have often referred to this background, it has remained unexplained. Why should people advocate ritualism as the highest aim of life? In order to explore this, I shall move further back into Indian history. To pave the way, I shall first consider some efforts at synthesis.

In Indian philosophy there have been many attempts at a synthesis between this extreme view of "no-liberation," found in the Upaniṣads, in Buddhism and in the Advaita Vedānta, and the tradition of ritual *karman* of the late Vedic period which culminated in the Mīmāṃsā. In the philosophical works, a particular combination was called *jñānakarmasamuccaya* "the combination of works and insight." This view was defended in some form or other by early philosophers of the Vedānta like Brahmadatta and Bhartṛprapanca, by the Advaitin Maṇḍanamiśra and by the Mīmāṃsā philosopher Kumārila Bhaṭṭa (Hiriyanna 1925, pp. xxii–xxix; Kuppuswami Sastri 1937, pp. xlvi–xlix; Dasgupta 1932, pp. 44, 100).

The popularity of the *Bhagavad Gītā* is partly due to the fact that it advocates another such synthesis. Combining Hindu conservatism with the revolutionary ideas of mystics, the *Gītā* insists that actions should be performed in accordance with one's prescribed duty, but it teaches that this should be done without any attachment to the fruits of action (*karmaphalatyāga*). By adding this restriction it introduces renunciation and prevents activities from being regarded as methods or ways. The *Gītā* teaches many different things, but it is this doctrine which it propounds as its basic teaching:

> But these actions,
> Abandoning attachment and fruits,
> Must be performed, O Pārtha.
> This is my definite and highest doctrine
> (*Bhagavad Gītā,* 18.6).

In the domain we are concerned with, there are other efforts at synthesis. We have seen that the effectiveness of drugs varies not only with the circumstances and with one's frame of mind, but also with the manner and extent to which one has prepared oneself. It is an illusion to imagine that drugs take effect with the inevitability of an avalanche. The effects are linked not only with the preceding state of the body, but also with that of the mind. Conscious volition may pave the way, and may also continue after the drug has taken effect. And so it is not surprising to find that drugs are also often combined with works.

An interesting illustration of what might be called *oṣadhikarmasamuccaya,* or the combination of *karman* and drugs, was communicated by Slotkin (the investigator of the Peyote cult who joined the Native American Church) to Fischer, who describes and interprets it in the following terms:

> The greater the distance from the source of Peyote—the Rio Grande Valley—the scarcer is the supply; this appears to account for the fact that Indian tribes of the Northern Plains incorporate less Peyote during the ceremony than do Southern tribes. It is noteworthy, therefore, that it is in the Northern Plains that ceremonial cleansing precedes the rite; this takes the form of purges, sweatbaths and fasting [Slotkin, 1957]. One is tempted to speculate about this trend. Do the Northern Plains tribes supplement the smaller quantities of Peyote available to them with stressful stimulation and thus produce an experience of similar intensity to that evoked solely by larger doses of Peyote? (Fischer 1958, p. 401)

We have already seen that the ceremony, with which a drug is dispensed, contributes to its effect. Ritualistic circumstances must also account for the mild "contact high" observed by contemporary users of drugs: in a small group, more people get high than have actually taken a drug. There are ancient precursors. The *Rgveda* contains the solemn verse: "Soma unpressed has never intoxicated Indra, nor the pressed juices unaccompanied by sacred hymns" (*Rgveda* 7.26.1, quoted in Brough 1971, pp. 338–39). The term "intoxicated" is actually misleading, since the reference is not to alcohol: Soma was in all likelihood a hallucinogenic, as we shall see. But the development of the Soma cult was unexpected. It offers a large scale parallel in India to the Peyote phenomena observed by Slotkin. When the tribes of Indo-European speech who composed the Vedas, having entered the subcontinent from the Northwest, moved deeper into India in eastern and southern directions, when the Soma cult moved farther away from the mountains where the original Soma grew, when the plant became increasingly rare and substitutes were beginning to be used, there developed the Vedic ritual, in all likelihood the most elaborate ritual mankind has devised.

To call the Soma ritual "stressful stimulation" would merely be casting a behaviorist spell. But it would be correct to say that such ritual was in part a means to attain a certain state of mind, especially on the part of the main sacrificer (the *yajamāna*) who had undergone the consecration ceremonies (*dikṣā*), but quite possibly also on the part of the priests, sixteen in number in the classical prototype, who drank small quantities of the Soma liquid.

That originally the real Soma produced an extraordinary high seems to be indicated in the *Rgveda* by descriptions of Indra and Rudra after they drank it. Later the quantities became symbolical (like wine in Christian churches or saké in Shinto shrines); moreover, substitutes were introduced. The *karman* of ritual, which yielded the sacred *brahman* power, made up for these physical deficits. Finally, the ritual may have deteriorated into mere ceremonialism, and we come extremely close to the "distilled water, dispensed with appropriate ceremony," mentioned by Claridge. This entire development, which was spread out over many centuries, explains at least in part the extraordinary emphasis on the Soma ritual, and on ritual in general, which characterizes early Indian civilization. It is the replacement of a hallucinogenic by ritualism. But when ritualism lost, or was believed to have lost, its efficacy, it was replaced by more purely mental concepts. This was in some ways a return to the Vedic experience, at least in that it produced direct access to a mental state. Hence the importance of these discussions on *karman* and *jñāna*, to some features of which I have drawn attention. With these discussions we enter the domain of Indian philosophy proper.

The possibility of attaining certain mental states by means of hallucinogens, rituals, or combinations of both appears to be a basic feature of the mind that has to be taken into account in the study of mysticism. The option between these alternatives suggests, for instance, that one could train oneself to obtain the same experience repeatedly, but by gradually decreasing the doses of a drug, just like people who jump down from great heights using smaller and smaller parachutes. Whether or not the final result is the same, such training would in effect be an exercise in a certain kind of meditation or jumping. In fact, what Castaneda learned with the help of drugs was to achieve certain results also without the aid of drugs. In both cases it is attempted to bring forces that first eluded us under control. Conversely, people who are so inclined meditate easily under the influence of a drug.

Having surveyed some of the Indian superstructures, I shall now briefly discuss a few modern ones. The double fallacy, that drugs affect our body (*casu quo,* our brain) without having anything to do with our state of mind, and that their effects are completely determined and beyond our control, is committed by Zaehner. That his own single experiment with mescaline was "utterly trivial" throws light on the drug, but also on Zaehner, obviously (see also Smith 1964, pp. 523–24). Moreover, Zaehner's statement: "when Huxley came to take mescaline, his mind was permeated through and through with Vedāntin and Mahāyāna Buddhist ideas" (Zaehner 1961, pp. 2–3) may be a true statement (though Huxley 1946, contained a lot from Eckhart, St. John of the Cross, William Law, Santa Teresa, Philo, Rūmī, Kabīr, Ruysbroeck, etc.), but it is not a valid argument against Huxley. On the other hand, that Zaehner's own mind "was permeated through and through with Christian and ancient Iranian ideas" (as he does not say) goes a long way to explain the triviality of his own experience. For if Huxley is right, he says, "the conclusions . . . are alarming" (Zaehner 1961, p. 12); but they would be much less alarming within the perspective of less uptight religious traditions. Zaehner is moreover inconsistent, for he admits, at least half-seriously: "The fact that I am an assiduous reader of *Alice through the Looking-Glass* is probably not irrelevant to the nature of my experience" (Zaehner 1961, p. 226). Must we conclude that Zaehner was not prepared to take his mescaline experiment seriously, or that Alice's adventures made a deeper impression on him than the wide range of religious and mystical literature with which he is so familiar?

All of this shows that mysticism and drugs can certainly not be effectively studied or compared if the subjective aspects of experience are left out of consideration. It also indicates that different causes, physical as well as mental, and also combinations of these, may bring about particular states of the mind. That, of course, should not surprise anyone who has ever given the mind a thought. The specific character of the cases I have referred to reflects the specificity of these particular states of the mind. It would therefore not be surprising either if it were found that these states constitute a separate domain of the mind, and that this domain is linked with a separate area of the brain. To Castaneda the separateness of this area of experience was sufficiently striking to adopt *A Separate Reality* as the title for his second book.

Such a view also seems to be implicit in the words of Smythies (the same scholar who administered the drug to Zaehner) to the effect that the drug experiences are "the work of a highly differentiated mental compartment, without any apparent connection, emotional or volitional, with the aims, interests, or feelings of the person concerned" (quoted in Huxley 1963, p. 97). Though the first clause of this statement is probably correct, and the drift of the rest is not entirely unclear, the severance of connections which Smythies postulates is certainly presented in excessive terms. A person's will or feelings may well be affected under the influence of a drug, but they are by no means abolished and do not even seem restricted. They are surely different and differently oriented, and this may have something to do with the claim of many mystics that the ego can be and should be abolished: for the identity of the ego is largely felt to be determined by its own characteristic feelings and emotions.

* * *

Though I find Huxley's speculations very often reasonable and certainly suggestive, and wish the experts had taken them more seriously (as Zaehner did), I am not convinced of the correctness of the Bergsonian theory he received via Broad and developed into the view that drugs give access to the "Mind at Large," viz. the total awareness of all that has happened and is happening to the individual, and from which everything that is not useful is under normal circumstances eliminated by the brain and the nervous system. Instead of the hypothesis that drugs widen the mind, one could adopt the hypothesis that they narrow the mind—a theory which has actually been defended, through rather unconvincing criticisms of Huxley, by Cazeneuve (1959). Both theories are bold but exceedingly premature. Some information is now beginning to become available about the filtering or screening of stimuli by brain mechanisms under the influence of certain drugs (Claridge 1972, ch. 8). Deikman's work, which partly points in an opposite direction, is also a step forward. But one needs to know a great deal more about the world and about ourselves before one could come up with even a semblance of an argument in support of such grand theories as the "Mind at Large" or its opposite which might be called the "Mind Reduced." It is not improbable that the truth lies somewhere in between, and that drugs in some respects widen, and in others narrow the mind.

*   *   *

The moral and religious criticisms of the thesis that drugs and mysticism are related, and of the exploration of drugs and their effects on the mind in general, are not only similar to the age-old moral criticisms of religious movements that stress easy methods such as faith, but they are also simple reflections of the characteristic conservatism of institutionalized religion. Watts is certainly justified in comparing the use of a drug to explore the mind to the use of a microscope or telescope to explore the universe (Watts 1962, p. 20: "mystical insight is no more in the chemical itself than biological knowledge is in the microscope"). He might have added in support of this analogy that Galileo was in fact criticized by Aristotelians among the clergy for inspecting God's work with the help of such a diabolic device as a telescope. The analogy goes still further. The excessive use of drugs might adversely affect the mind, just as the excessive looking through microscopes might adversely affect the eyes. But such risks are not generally censured. The evaluation of dangers and risks by society, or worse, by a government acting as a moral guardian, clearly reflects prejudices that happen to be prevalent in a certain area and during a certain period. It may be recalled that Muslim orthodoxy censured hashish, opium, contemplation of boys, and coffee. Nowadays we are warned by columnists, priests and government agents that a person who uses drugs risks his mind or even his soul; and it is useful to bear in mind that this might very well be true. But the same agencies induce us to admire people who explore new continents, climb Mount Everest, go to the moon, experiment with radiation, germs, new medicaments, and devices designed for destruction, or risk their lives in many other ways. In fact, the greatest adventures of science are considered great partly because of the risks they involve. The scientific exploration of drugs should be evaluated in the same spirit. It should moreover be obvious, apart from the public search for truth, that no government should have the right to forbid adult citizens the freedom to explore their inner consciousness in private.

This last phrase takes me to the Harvard experiments of Alpert and Leary (compare the evaluation of this alleged "academic débâcle" in LaBarre 1970, 230–37). What Leary and Alpert might be criticized for is not that they experimented with drugs, but that they did not provide or continue to provide critical evaluation of their discoveries. They seemed to have lost their rational mind, and founded instead a religious sect. Alpert, in fact, has since turned to some kind of Yoga (Alpert 1971). This by itself is valuable in that it constitutes the latest evidence to date for the thesis that drug experience, when combined with the expectation of some sort of salvation, leads to religion. So does the persecution (in the guise of American justice) of Leary as if he were a heretic, instead of the much more relevant rational evaluation of his claims. Unfortunately, the publicity surrounding these events has caused many sensible people to believe that the use of drugs permanently affects, or causes a person to lose his mind. But this is clearly not always, and not even generally the case. Moreover, such a loss of mind may be apparent and similar to the state which Lao Tzu referred to when he wrote:

> Mine is indeed the mind of a very idiot,
> So dull am I.

Christian critics may recall I Corinthians 1:19: "For it is written, I will destroy the wisdom of the wise, and will bring to nothing the understanding of the prudent."

We have surveyed some of the many religious and philosophical evaluations and interpretations of mystical experiences, and some of the discussions on methods which may lead to the attainment of these experiences. This immense variety is consistent with an equally immense variety of experiences, but it is also consistent with a very small number of basic experiences, or even with one kind of basic experience. We cannot determine this at present. But since we have seen that such variety is often due to psychological and cultural circumstances, it would be safe to assume that the experiences themselves are to some extent independent of their interpretations and evaluations. This suggests even more strongly than my earlier demonstrations that we can only make progress in the study of mysticism if we direct our attention to the experiences themselves.

NOTES

1. Cf. *Exploring Mysticism*, ch. 11, pp. 167*ff.*, pp. 100–1. (Ed. note.)
2. Cf. *Exploring Mysticism*, pp. 56*f.* (Ed. note.)
3. Orthopraxy, "adherence to right activity," is different from orthodoxy, "adherence to right opinion." It is the former that characterizes the traditional advocates of *karman* and good works (cf. Staal 1959).
4. This refers to the four stages of life (*āśrama*) advocated in Hinduism: the first is that of the student (*brahmacārin*), the second that of the householder (*gṛhastha*), the third that of the hermit (*vanaprastha*), and the fourth that of the wandering ascetic (*saṃnyāsin*).

PART II
The Field of Inquiry:
Mysticism in World Religions

7

Sacrificial Mysticism

S. N. DASGUPTA

The Hindus possess a body of sacred compositions called the Vedas. Of these there are four collections. Two of them comprise original hymns. The contents of the others consist largely of poems derived from the former two. The collections of original hymns, known as the Rig Veda and the Atharva Veda, include, respectively, 1,028 original hymns of about 10,600 stanzas and 731 hymns of about 6,000 stanzas. All of these were kept in memory and transmitted by recitation and close memorizing on the part of teachers and pupils in an unbroken chain of early traditions from a time when writing was probably not known. The opinions of scholars vary greatly regarding the antiquity of this literature; some think that the hymns were composed about 6000 B.C. or at a still earlier date, while others think that they were composed about 1200 or 1000 B.C. The Vedic hymns are probably the earliest important religious documents of the human race.

The hymns of the Atharva Veda contain among other things descriptions of charms for curing diseases, prayers for long life and health, imprecations against demons, sorcerers and enemies, charms pertaining to women—to secure their love or arouse jealousy, and the like—charms for securing harmony and influence in an assembly, charms for securing the prosperity of household, fields, cattle, business, gambling, etc., charms in expiation of sins and defilement. The hymns of the Rig Veda, on the other hand, are often praises of various deities, who are frequently mere personifications of the different powers of nature, such as the rain-god, the wind-god, the fire-god, and the like. The prayers in these hymns are praises of the greatness and power, the mysterious nature, and the exploits of these deities, as well as prayers for various favors. Often the favors sought are of the nature of material blessings, such as long life, vigorous offspring, cattle and horses, gold, etc. Prayers for the advancement of the inner spiritual achievements of man, for righteousness or moral greatness, prayers expressing a passionate longing for the divine or a humble submission of the mind to the divine will are not so frequent. Most of these prayers were recited in the performance of certain prescribed rituals. Though from the praises of the gods one might infer that it was the gods who were supposed to bestow the benefits, it was in fact the complete set of ritualistic performances that was considered to be the cause of the showering of the benefits. It was supposed that these ritualistic performances when carried out in all their details, precisely and accurately, could by their joint and mysterious effect produce a mysterious something whereby the prayers were fulfilled.

I shall omit from my discussion the hymns of the Atharva Veda which deal only with spells, witchcraft and incantations. But while I take for examination those hymns of the Rig Veda which express beautiful ideas about the nature-deities and which voice personal requests for material comforts or for advantages, it should be understood that they also were chanted in connection with the performance of rituals and sacrifices. It is difficult to determine whether in the earliest period definite theories had been formulated regarding the intimate and indispensable connection between the chanting of these hymns of personal appeal and the performance of the rituals. But if we judge by the Vedic literature of the Brahmanas (probably composed shortly after the hymns, and later appended to them) which indicate authoritatively the place of these hymns in the ritualistic observances and specify what hymns were to be uttered under what ritualistic conditions and in what order or manner, it seems almost certain that the prevailing form of what is commonly called the Vedic religion may in strictness not be considered as a religion in the ordinarily accepted meaning of this term. Many of the ritualistic observances, or *yajna*, required the help of a large number of priests, and large quantities of butter, rice, milk, animals, etc. They had to be performed with the most elaborate details from day to day, for months together and sometimes even ten or twelve years; and it was enjoined that all the observances should be performed in exact accordance with the prescriptions laid down in the Brahmana literature. Even the slightest inaccuracy or the most trifling inexactness would be sufficient to spoil the entire effect of the sacrifice. But if the sacrifices were performed with the strictest accuracy, then the material advantages for which they were performed were bound to come regardless of the good will or the ill will of the gods to whom the prayers were offered. Tvashtar had performed a sacrifice for the birth of a son who might kill Indra, but owing to a slight error in pronunciation the meaning of the prayer was changed and the sacrifice produced a son who was not a killer of Indra but of whom Indra was the killer.

This idea of sacrifice is entirely different from anything found in other races. For with the Vedic people, the sacrifices were more powerful than the gods. The gods could be pleased or displeased; if the sacrifices were duly performed the prayers were bound to be fulfilled. The utterance or chanting of the stanzas of the Vedic hymns with specially prescribed accents and modulations, the pouring of the melted butter in the prescribed manner into the sacrificial fire, the husking of rice in a particular way, the making and exact placing of cakes, all the thousand details of rituals—often performed continuously for days, months and years with rigorous exactness—was called a *yajna* (frequently translated into English, "sacrifice"). All the good things that the people wanted, be it the birth of a son, a shower of rain, or a place of enjoyment in heaven, were believed to be secured through the performance of these sacrifices. It is possible that when these hymns were originally composed, they were but simple prayers to the deified powers of nature, or that they were only associated with some simple rituals. But the evidence that is presented to us in the later Vedic and non-Vedic records containing descriptions of these sacrifices and discussions respecting their value, convinces us beyond doubt that it was the performance of these sacrifices, perfect in every detail in accordance with the dictates of the sacrificial manuals, the Brahmanas, that was believed to be capable of producing everything that a man could desire. A direct consequence of this apparently unmeaning necessity of strictest accuracy of ritualistic performances is a theory that came to be formulated and accepted in later periods, namely, that the sacrificial rites revealed such supernatural wisdom that they could not have been made by any one but were self-existent. It came to be held that the hymns of the Vedas, as well as the sacrificial manuals, were without authorship; that they existed eternally, prescribing certain courses of ritualistic procedure for the attainment of particular advantages and prohibiting certain undesirable courses of action. Consistently with the sacrificial theory it was also believed that the meanings of the hymns, so far as they described events or facts of nature or the exploits and the conduct of the gods, were of a legendary character, that their true value consisted in the enjoining of particular courses of action or of dissuading people from other courses of action.

Religion in its ordinarily accepted sense means a personal relationship with some divine or transcendent person to whom we submit and to whom we pray for material advantages or for spiritual or moral enlightenment. But here was a belief in the divinity or the uncreatedness of a literature—the Vedas—which was believed to contain within itself the secret laws of the universe. Here there was a conception of commands, categorical in nature and external in character, without the least suggestion of any commander. Though these commands were supposed not to have emanated from any person, they may nevertheless in some sense be described as transcendent, for they were regarded as far above human wisdom. No reason could be given why a particular sacrificial perform-

ance should produce any particular kind of material advantage. There
stand the commands—commands which had revealed themselves to the
minds of the various sages, which had no beginning in time, which do
not imply any commander, and which are absolutely faultless and unerr-
ing in their directions.

The sacrifices, thus, were supposed to possess a mysterious power capable of regulating and modifying the workings of the universe for the
advantage of individuals; and the Vedic commands were thought to em-
body omniscience respecting the ways of the world. Though the repository of omniscience, the Vedas were not conceived as divulging to us
their secrets but merely as providing a body of directions which, if followed, would give whatever advantages one craved in this life or the
next. The sacrifices (*yajna*) or their mysterious powers are called
dharma, a term which in Indian vernaculars is often used wrongly to
translate the English word "religion." The Vedic hymns, the priests, and
the sacrifices are also called "the great" by the application of the term
brahman, which in later Indian philosophy and religion had such a momentous history.

What we have described is no ordinary magic of spells and incantations, but a repository of the cosmic secrets and cosmic forces. These impersonal commands unite in them the concepts of an unalterable law and
perfect omniscience; they imply therefore the possibility of reaping all
the comforts of this life and of the afterlife by submission to them and
compliance with them. But they involve no lawgiver, no divine person,
no author of the universe or of the destinies of human beings who must
be pacified, obeyed or loved, and by whose grace we receive the blessings of life. We can control our own destinies, and have whatever we
may want, if we only follow the commands. There is no other mystery of
life save this great mystery of the Vedic commands, and these are absolutely inscrutable. These commands do not teach ordinary laws of social
life or of behavior toward our fellow beings, or anything that we could
discover by our own intelligence and wisdom. Neither do they teach us
anything that we could learn by experience or reason. They give direction for the attainment of the good things of this life or of the afterlife
only insofar as the means thereto are absolutely undiscoverable by us.
They are not a body of facts, but a body of commands and prohibitions.
Yet they do not represent commands of the inner conscience or of the
spirit within us; they do not give us any food for the spirit. They represent an objective and unalterable law realistically conceived, and they
relate to desires for material comforts in this life or the life in heaven.
This concept gives us all the principal elements of religion except that of
a divine person. The acceptance of the blessings of this life as gifts from
God, and a sense of our duty to please Him by submission and prayer

are, therefore, not implied in this system of Vedic sacrifices. What is implied is some great impersonal force which harmonizes ourselves and our destinies with the happenings and events of the world of nature. Instead of God we find here a body of commands which demand our obedience and reverence; but the source of their power and the secret of their omniscient character and uncreatedness cannot be determined by us through reason or experience. But this ritualistic mysticism—if we may be permitted thus to call it—must be distinguished from the simple feelings and ideas that are found in the hymns themselves. In all probability the latter did not originally imply the complicated ritualistic hypotheses of the later period.

The forces of nature with their wonderful manifestations of inexplicable marvels appeared to the early sages like great beings endowed with life and personality. They were treated at times as friendly, but again as hostile. Sometimes the mystery of the natural phenomena seemed stupefying in its psychological effect. The laws of nature were at that time unknown, and there was no obstacle to the free flight of the imagination. When the Vedic sage saw the sun proceeding in his upward and downward course through the sky he cried out in wonder:

> Undropped beneath, not fastened firm, how comes it
> That downward turned he falls not downward?
> The guide of his ascending path—who saw it?[1]

The sage is full of wonder that "the sparkling waters of all rivers flow into one ocean without ever filling it." He perceives the unalterable course of the sun from day to day, and the succession of day and night, and he exclaims with delight: "Every day, in unceasing interchange with night and her dark wonders, comes the dawn with her beautiful ones to reanimate the worlds, never failing in her place, never in her time." Again, he is puzzled when thinking whither the shining ones of the sky disappear, and he cries forth in amazement:

> Who is it knows, and who can tell us surely
> Where lies the path that leads to the Eternals?
> Their deepest dwellings only we discover,
> And hidden these in distant secret regions.

In how many hymns does the singer express his wonder that the rough red cow gives soft white milk. To the god Indra he cries:

> Grant me, O God, the highest, best of treasures,
> A judging mind, prosperity abiding,
> Riches abundant, lasting health of body,
> The grace of eloquence, and days propitious.

To the God of the destroying storm he prays:

> Let me through thy best medicines, O Rudra,
> My life on earth prolong a hundred winters.
> From us dispel all hatred and oppression,
> On every side calamity drive from us.
>
> Where then, O Rudra, is thy hand of mercy,
> The hand that healing brings and softens sorrow,
> That takes away the ills which the gods send?
> Let me, O mighty one, feel thy forgiveness.
>
> The hero gladdened me amid tumult
> With greater might when I his aid entreated;
> Like some cool shade from the Sun's heat protected
> May I attain to Rudra's grace and refuge.

Again when he is penitent he would ask forgiveness of the god Varuna, the personification of the all-embracing heaven, and say:

> If we to any dear and loved companion
> Have evil done, to brother or to neighbor,
> To our own countryman or to a stranger,
> That sin do thou O Varuna forgive us.

＊　　　＊　　　＊

But besides these prayers, we sometimes find poems composed by the Vedic people, descriptive of their varied experiences of ordinary life. Thus a gambler gives his experience as follows:

＊　　　＊　　　＊

> The gambler hurries to the gaming table,
> "Today I'll win," he thinks in his excitement.
> The dice enflame his greed, his hopes mount higher;
> He leaves his winnings all with his opponent.

When we read these hymns we see in them the simple prayers of a simple primitive people impressed with the inexplicable and varied phenomena of a tropical climate. They turn to the forces behind the latter as personified deities, describing the phenomena and offering their simple prayers. We find in these prayers experiences of simple wonder, of sufferings and of simple enjoyments. But when we come to the sacrificial stage of development we find a religious outlook in which the independent simple meanings of the hymns possess importance only for their sacrificial utterance in particular contexts. During the particular ritual observances, the different verses were often torn out of their contexts and were combined with others which apparently had little or no relation with them and no conceivable bearing on the performances during which they were chanted or uttered. They were simply the means for the performance of the sacrifices. Their simple meanings as descriptions of things or events of phenomena or ideas were dropped from consideration. The value attached to them centered about their being uttered or chanted in particular Vedic sacrifices in accordance with certain sacrificial canons of interpretation. The entire significance of these hymns consisted either in their use as directions for the performance of certain sacrificial duties or in their utterance in these sacrifices under prescribed conditions as found in the sacrificial manuals, the Brahmanas, which were considered as part of the Vedas. Thought and feeling were driven from their places of importance in human nature, and the whole emphasis was laid on the interpretation of the Vedic literature as a system of duties involving commands and prohibitions, and nothing else. Some of these duties were compulsory, while others were voluntary in the sense that they had to be performed only when one wanted to secure some desired end unattainable by any means discoverable by his reason or experience.

The authority which this system of Vedic injunctions and prohibitions was supposed to possess was so high as to demand the entire submission of one's will and thought. Their claims did not stand in need of any justification by reason or logic, for they were supposed to be guides in a sphere where reason and experience were utterly helpless. The only fruitful way in which reason could be employed with regard to these Vedic commands was by accepting their authority and then trying to explain them in such a way that their mysterious nature might be reconciled to us. These Vedic commands cannot be described as "revelations" in the ordinary Christian sense of the term; for the latter presupposes the existence of a living God able and willing to bestow the body of truths that man requires, whereas the Vedic commands are devoid of any notion of a lawgiver. This sacrificial mysticism, if it may be so called, does not recognize any God or supreme being from whom these commands emanate or who reveals them to man. The commands are taken as eternal truths, beginningless and immortal, revealing themselves to man and demanding man's submission to them. Nevertheless they are not spiritual or inner truths revealed from within man himself; they are external and impersonal commands which contain within themselves the inscrutable secrets of nature and of the happiness of man.

The fact that the Vedas were regarded as revelations of eternal truths, truths which no human reason could ever challenge, naturally divested reason of confidence in its ability to unravel the mysteries of man and of the world. Even in the somewhat later days of the evolution of Vedic culture, when there grew up a school of thinkers who disbelieved the claim that the whole of the Vedas were nothing but a body of commands and prohibitions and who held that there were at least some particular portions of the Vedas which dealt with the eternal truths of spiritual facts and experiences of reality, the belief remained unshaken that what the Vedas gave one as truths were unshakable and unchallengeable by reason or by experience. This means a definite lowering or degradation of reason in its capacity as truth-finder. Reason calls for counterreason and leads through an endless regressus without ever being able to lead to truth. The Vedas, then, are the only repository of the highest truths, and the function of reason is only to attempt to reconcile these truths with our experience and sense-observation.

❖ ❖ ❖

The word "mysticism" is a European word with a definite history. Most European writers have used it to denote an intuitive or ecstatic union with the deity, through contemplation, communion, or other mental experiences, or to denote the relationship and potential union of the human soul with ultimate reality. But I should for my present purposes like to give it a wider meaning which would include this and the other different types of mysticism that I may be discussing in the course of this series of lectures. I should like to define mysticism as a theory, doctrine, or view that considers reason to be incapable of discovering or of realizing the nature of ultimate truth, whatever be the nature of this ultimate truth, but at the same time believes in the certitude of some other means of arriving at it. If this definition be accepted, then this ritualistic philosophy of the Vedas is the earliest form of mysticism that is known to India or to the world. This Vedic mysticism prepared the way for the rise of the other forms of mysticism that sprang up in India.

❖ ❖ ❖

The main elements of the sacrificial mysticism of the Vedas may be summarized as follows. First, a belief that the sacrifices when performed with perfect accuracy, possess a secret, mysterious power to bring about or produce as their effect whatever we may desire either in this life or in the hereafter. Second, the conception of an unalterable law—involved in such invariable and unfailing occurrences of effects consequent upon the performance of these sacrifices. Third, an acceptance of the impersonal nature of the Vedic literature, as having existed by itself from beginningless time and as not created or composed by any person, human or divine. Fourth, the view that the Vedic literature embodies nothing but a system of duties involving commands and prohibitions. Fifth, a recognition of the supreme authority of the Vedas as the only source of the knowledge of ultimate truths which are far beyond the powers of human reason. Sixth, the view that truth or reality, whether it be of the nature of commands or of facts (as was maintained by the later Vedic schools of thought, the Upanishads), could be found once for all in the words of the Vedas. Seventh, the belief that the Vedic system of duties demands unfailing obedience and submission. Two definite characteristics emerge from these: first, the transcendent, mysterious, and secret power of the sacrifices, replacing the natural forces personified as gods; second, the ultimate superiority of the Vedas as the source of all truths, and as the unchallengeable dictators of our duties, leading to our material well-being and happiness. The assumption of the mysterious omnipotence of sacrifices, performed by following the authoritative injunctions of the Vedas independently of reason or logical and discursive thought, forms the chief trait of the mysticism of the Vedic type. There is nothing here of feeling or even of intellect, but a blind submission, not to a person but to an impersonal authority which holds within it an unalterable and inscrutable law, the secret of all powers which we may want to wield in our favor.

The next step in the development of this type of mysticism consists in the growth of a school of thought which sought to intellectualize the material sacrifices. It encouraged the belief that it was quite unnecessary actually to perform the sacrifices requiring the expenditure of enormous sums of money for the collection of materials and for labor. The same results might be as well obtained through certain kinds of meditation or reflection. Thus, instead of the actual performance of a horse sacrifice, in which the immolation of a horse is accompanied by other rituals engaging the services of large numbers of men and the expenditure of funds such as kings alone could provide, one might as well think of the dawn as the head of a horse, the sun as its eye, the wind as its life, the heaven as its back, the intervening space as its belly, the sky as its flesh and the stars as its bones. Such a meditation, or rather concentrated imagining of the universe as a cosmic horse, would, it was maintained, produce all the beneficial results that could be expected from the performance of an actual horse sacrifice. Thus, these attempts to intellectualize sacrifices took the form of replacing by meditation the actual sacrifices, and this substitution was believed to produce results which were equally beneficial. This meditation by substitution gradually took various forms: certain letters of the alphabet had, for example, to be thought of, or meditated upon, as Brahman or some other deity, or as vital functions of the body, or as some personified nature deity. This meditation was supposed to produce beneficial results. It should not be supposed that the sacrificial forms were entirely supplanted by these new forms of substitution-meditations. Rather did they spring up side by side with them. These forms of meditation did not mean prolonged contemplation, or any logical process of thinking, but merely the simple practice of continually thinking of one entity, process, or letter as another entity or process.

Even in modern India there are still many men who believe that the repetition of mystical formulas (apparently meaningless combinations of letters, or the names of some deities) is capable of producing beneficial results. Even the worship of a round or an oval stone as the god Vishnu or Siva, or again the worship of a water jug or an image as a particular god or goddess, is nothing but a modified form of substitution-meditation, one thing being considered and meditated upon as another. These practices are to be distinguished from the ordinary spells and incantations commonly believed in by uneducated people. These substitution-meditations are often believed to be productive of virtue. They form the normal modes of worship of the ordinary Hindu and have now taken the place of the old sacrifices. Nevertheless the old Vedic sacrifices are also to a certain extent performed on occasions of marriages and other domestic ceremonies, as an indispensable part of those ceremonies which still claim to belong entirely to the Vedic order.

But, refraining from further references to modern India, let us pick up our thread of discussion and note the next stage in the development of the substitution-meditations. Although the latter were in their conception doubtless as mystical and magical as the old sacrifices, they represent an advance. For in them the mystical powers are supposed to reside not in external performances, but in specific forms of meditation or thinking. This represents an approach toward a consciousness of self and toward a recognition of the mystical powers of thought and meditation of a peculiar type. But it was only after an almost endless and fruitless search that the highest idea of self and the highest idea of world mystery and its solution dawned in the minds of the Vedic thinkers. What we find at this stage is merely that the Vedic thinkers had become conscious of the activity of thought and of imagination, and had begun to realize that the activity involved in thinking ought to be considered to be as potent a power as the activity involved in the actual performances of material sacrifices. Man's inner thought and his performance of sacrificial duties in the world outside are both regarded as capable of producing mysterious changes and transformations in nature which would benefit man. Passages are to be found in the literature where the vital and other inner processes of the self are compared with a sacrifice. The three periods of human life are considered as being the same as the three bruisings of the sacrificial plant soma; and the functions of hungering, eating and begetting are considered to be the same as the different ceremonies of the soma sacrifice.

✥   ✥   ✥

By a similar loose process of generalization the word "Brahman" came to denote the Vedic verses, truth, sacrifices, and knowledge. Etymologically the word means "The Great." Probably it signified vaguely and obscurely the mysterious power underlying these sacrifices and the substitution-meditations. Both the ideas involved in the conception of Brahman as the highest power and the highest knowledge were derived from the notion of the sacrifices. Thus we read in the celebrated man-hymn of the Rig Veda that the gods offered the supreme man as a sacrifice and that from this great oblation all living creatures, as well as the atmosphere, sky, earth and the four quarters, came into being. Three parts of this supreme man transcend the world while one part of him is the whole world about us; and yet, he is himself both the sacrifice and the object of the sacrifice.

But while I have just emphasized the importance of the mysticism of sacrifice in the development of the mystical conception of Brahman as the supreme being, it would be wrong to hold that the mysticism of the sacrifices is alone responsible for the evolution of the great concept of Brahman. Side by side with the concept found in the Rig Veda of the many gods as personifications of the forces of nature, there was also growing a tendency toward the conception of one supreme being, and this tendency gradually gained in force. Thus, in Rig Veda X. 114.5 we find a verse in which it is said that the deity is one, though he is called by various names. One of the hymns (R.V.X. 129), again, runs as follows:

Then there was neither Aught nor Naught, no air nor sky beyond.
What covered all? Where rested all? In watery gulf profound?
Nor death was then, nor deathlessness, nor change of night and day.
That one breathed calmly, self-sustained; naught else beyond it lay.
Gloom hid in gloom existed first—one sea eluding view.
The one a void in chaos wrapt, by inward fervor grew.
Within it first arose desire, the primal germ of mind,
Which nothing with existence links, as ages searching find.
The kindling ray that shot across the dark and drear abyss—
Was it beneath or high aloft? What bard can answer this?
There fecundating powers were found and mighty forces strove—
A self-supporting mass beneath, and energy above.
Who knows and who ever told, from whence this vast creation rose?
No gods had then been born. Who then can e'er the truth disclose
Whence sprang this world, whether framed by hand divine or no—
Its lord in heaven alone can tell, if he can show.[2]

Again, in the Atharva Veda (X. 7) we find a hymn dedicated to Skambha where the different parts of this deity are identified not only with the different parts of the material world but also with a number of moral qualities such as faith, austere fervor, truthfulness, etc. All the thirty-three gods of the Vedas are contained within him and bow down to him. He is also called Brahman, "The Great." In the next hymn of the Atharva Veda (X. 8) Brahman is adored and spoken of as presiding over the past and the future, and he is said to be residing within our hearts and to be the self which never decays but is self-existent and self-satisfied. This appears to be very much like the idea of the Upanishads. . . . In the Shatapatha Brahmana, also, we hear of Brahman as having created the gods; and in the Taittiriya Brahmana, Brahman is said to have created the gods and the entire world.

Thus we find that the conception of one great being who created the world and the gods, and who is also the power presiding over our lives and spirits, was gradually dawning in the minds of a few people. And though the sacrificial theory tended to lead away from the ordinary meanings of these Vedic hymns, the development of the sacrificial theory itself also made for the conception of some mysterious force which reconciled the destinies of the world and nature with those of men and their desires. This mysterious power, it was held, is resident not only in things external but also in activities of the inner life; it manifests itself in the power of thought, as is exemplified by the mysterious efficacy of the substitution-meditations. What was the nature of this mysterious power? It is difficult to answer this question. We have seen that its conception varied in significance according to the mode of its development and the sources from which it evolved. But when once the conception was formed, all these constituent notions were mixed together. People regarded Brahman as the highest, but they did not know how Brahman was to be known. Those who started with the sacrificial bias thought substitution-meditations to be the way to a knowledge of Brahman. And so we find various instructions regarding meditation upon objects, such as the wind, life, fire, etc.—even upon unmeaning letters.

But parallel with this tendency went another, viz. an intellectual search after Brahman, the highest, which displayed a contempt for sacrifices. We find Brahmins going out of their own sphere to warrior castes and kings for secret instruction about the nature of Brahman. There are narratives in which we find that kings belonging to the warrior caste fill proud Brahmins with a sense of discomfiture by exposing the ignorance of the latter concerning the secret nature of Brahman. Thus Balaki Gargya approached King Ajatashatru with the request to be allowed to explain to him the nature of Brahman. He then tried twelve times in succession to define Brahman as the presiding person in the sun, moon, lightning, ether, wind, fire, water, etc.; and in each case King Ajatashatru refuted him by showing the lower position that such presiding persons occupy in the whole of the universe, whereas Brahman should be that which is the highest. Again, we find another narrative in which five Brahmins meet and discuss the question, "What is our Atman and what is Brahman?" They proceed to Uddalaka Aruni with the question. When Uddalaka mistrusts his ability to answer the question, all six go to King Ashvapati Kaikeya for instruction. King Ashvapati first asks them what it is that they worship as Atman or Brahman, anticipating their error that they still regard Atman or Brahman as a new kind of external divinity. The six Brahmins explain Atman in succession as the heaven, the sun, the wind, space, water, and the earth, and in so doing assume it to be an objective and an external deity more or less like the old Vedic deities. This shows us a stage of thought in which people somehow understood Brahman to be the highest principle, but yet found it difficult to shake off their old conceptions of external deities or personifications of nature. Again we find Sanatkumara instructing Narada regarding the nature of Brahman. In so doing Sanatkumara starts from "Name," by which he probably understands all conceptual knowledge. With his peculiar logic, which is difficult for us to follow, he observes that speech is greater than name, that mind is greater than speech, that imagination is greater than mind, and so on. Passing in succession through a number of such concepts, from lower to higher, he ultimately stops at that which is absolutely great, the unlimited, beyond which there is nothing and within which is comprehended all that is to be found in the outer and the inner world.

The most important point to be noted in the development of this stage of thought is that worship or prayer is possible only as directed toward a deity conceived with limited powers and as occupying a subordinate position in the universe. But with reference to that which is conceived as the highest truth and the highest power, there is no longer the possibility of external forms of worship. We shall find . . . not only that it is not possible to worship Brahman but that it is not possible to reach Brahman by logical thought or any kind of conceptual apprehension. Thus in a Upanishadic story, referred to by Shankara, we are told of a person who approached a sage Bahva and sought from him instructions regarding the nature of Brahman. Bahva did not speak. He was asked a second time; still he did not speak. Yet again he was asked, but still he did not speak. When the inquirer became annoyed by this, Bahva told him that he was, from the first, by his silence telling him how Brahman was to be described: Brahman is silence and so cannot be represented in speech. There are, however, unmistakable indications that there were still some who believed that even the highest could be worshiped and adored and that men could still submit themselves to Him as to the highest personal God who comprehends us all and controls us all. But the idea that was gradually gaining ground with some of the most important sages, and which will be expounded in the next lecture, was that Brahman, as the highest, is no ordinary personal God who can be induced by worship to favor us or who can be approached by the pure intellect or even by feeling. Brahman still retains its mysterious character as the highest power, truth, being and bliss which can neither be worshiped nor known by ordinary means of knowledge. But its nature can be realized, and realized so perfectly that the realization will be like the bursting of a shell of light, a revelation which will submerge the whole of one's life together with all that it contains. . . . This type of mysticism of the Upanishads . . . represents one of the highest and best, and undoubtedly one of the most distinctive, types of mysticism that India has produced.

The Upanishads form the concluding portions of the Vedic literature, both chronologically from the point of view of the development of ideas. They were composed later than the priestly manuals, the Brahmanas, and the manuals of substitution-meditations in the Aranyaka literature, and they form the most authoritative background of all later Hindu philosophical thought. They possess the high authority of the Vedas and are the source of the highest wisdom and truth. The word "Upanishad" has been interpreted etymologically by Shankara to mean "that which destroys all ignorance and leads us to Brahman." It has also been interpreted to mean a secret or mystical doctrine, or a secret instruction, or a secret and confidential sitting. . . . Being the concluding portions of the Vedas, they are called the Vedanta. Their interpretations by different later writers gave rise to different systems of Vedanta philosophy. . . . The Upanishads themselves, however, do not seem to have been written in a systematic, well-connected and logical form. They are mystical experiences of the soul gushing forth from within us; they sparkle with the beams of a new light; they quench our thirst, born at their very sight. It was one of these that the German philosopher Schopenhauer said: "How does every line display its firm and definite and throughout harmonious meaning. From every sentence deep, original, and sublime thoughts arise and the whole is pervaded by a high and holy and earnest spirit. . . . In the whole world there is no study, except that of the originals, so beneficial and so elevating as that of the Upanishads. It has been the solace of my life, it will be the solace of my death." Cases are known in which even Christian missionaries, sent out to India to teach church doctrines to clergymen or to preach Christianity among the Indians, became so fascinated by the high and lofty teachings of the Upanishads that they introduced the teaching of the Upanishads in the Church and as a consequence were compelled to resign their posts. To Hindus of all denominations there is nothing higher and holier than the inspired sayings of the Upanishads.

NOTES

1. This translation is from Kaegi-Arrowsmith, *The Rig Veda*, p. 35. The immediately following translations are taken from the same work.
2. The translation is taken from Muir's *Original Sanskrit Texts*, Vol. V.

8

The Basis of Buddhist Philosophy

D. T. SUZUKI

Buddhist philosophy is based on the experience Buddha had about twenty-five centuries ago. To understand, therefore, what Buddhist philosophy is, it is necessary to know what that experience was which Buddha had after six years' hard thinking and ascetic austerities and exercises in meditation.

We generally think that philosophy is a matter of pure intellect, and, therefore, that the best philosophy comes out of a mind most richly endowed with intellectual acumen and dialectical subtleties. But this is not the case. It is true that those who are poorly equipped with intellectual powers cannot be good philosophers. Intellect, however, is not the whole thing. There must be a deep power of imagination, there must be a strong, inflexible willpower, there must be a keen insight into the nature of man, and finally there must be an actual seeing of the truth as synthesized in the whole being of the man himself.

I wish to emphasize this idea of "seeing." It is not enough to "know" as the term is ordinarily understood. Knowledge unless it is accompanied by a personal experience is superficial and no kind of philosophy can be built upon such a shaky foundation. There are, however, I suppose many systems of thought not backed by real experiences, but such are never inspiring. They may be fine to look at but their power to move the readers is nil. Whatever knowledge the philosopher may have, it must come out of his experience, and this experience is seeing. Buddha has always emphasized this. He couples knowing (*ñāṇa, jñāna*) with seeing (*passa, paśya*), for without seeing, knowing has no depths, cannot understand the realities of life. Therefore, the first item of the Eightfold Noble Path is *sammādassana*, right seeing, and *sammāsankappa*, right knowing, comes next. Seeing is experiencing, seeing things in their state of suchness (*tathatā*) or is-ness. Buddha's whole philosophy comes from this "seeing," this experiencing.

The experience which forms the basis of Buddhist philosophy is called "enlightenment-experience," for it is this experience of enlightenment which Buddha had after six years of hard thinking and profound reflection, and everything he taught afterward is the unfolding of this inner perception he then had.

What then was this enlightenment-experience?

2

Roughly speaking, we can say that there are two ways of approaching this question: What is the enlightenment-experience Buddha had? One is objective and the other subjective. The objective approach is to find out the first rationalized statements ascribed to Buddha after the experience and understood as forming the basis of his teaching. That is, what did he first teach? What was the main thesis he continued to preach throughout his life? This will be to discover what characteristically constitutes the Buddhist teaching as distinguished from that of the rest of the Indian thinkers. The second approach, called subjective, is to examine Buddha's utterances reflecting his immediate feelings after the experience of enlightenment. The first approach is metaphysical whereas the second is psychological or existential. Let us start with the first.

What is universally recognized as Buddhist thought regardless of its varieties of interpretation is the doctrine of anattā or anātman, that is, the doctrine of non-ego. Its argument begins with the idea: (1) that all things are transient as they are composites (skandha or khandha) and go on disintegrating all the time, that there is nothing permanent; and (2) that there is therefore nothing worth clinging to in this world where every one of us is made to undergo all kinds of sorrow and suffering. How do we escape from them? Or, how do we conquer them? For we cannot go on like this. We must somehow find the way out of this torture. It was this feeling of fear and insecurity individually and collectively that made Buddha leave his home and wander about for six long years seeking for a way out not only for himself but for the whole world. He finally discovered it by hitting upon the idea of non-ego (anattā). The formula runs thus:[1]

> All composite things (sankhāra) are impermanent. When a man by wisdom (paññā) realized [this], he heeds not [this world of] sorrow; this is the path of purity.
>
> All composite things are sorrowful. When a man by wisdon realizes [this], he heeds not [this world of] sorrow; this is the path to purity.
>
> All things (dhammā) are egoless. When a man by wisdom realizes [this], he heeds not [this world of] sorrow; this is the path to purity.

The one thing I wish to call to the readers' attention is the term "wisdom," paññā, or prajñā in Sanskrit. This is a very important term throughout Buddhist philosophy. There is no English equivalent for it.

"Transcendental wisdom" is too heavy, besides it does not exactly hit the mark. But temporarily let "wisdom" do. We know that seeing is very much emphasized in Buddhism, but we must not fail also to notice that seeing is not just an ordinary seeing by means of relative knowledge; it is the seeing by means of a *prajñā*-eye which is a special kind of intuition enabling us to penetrate right into the bedrock of Reality itself. I have elsewhere[2] given a somewhat detailed account of *prajñā* and its role in Buddhist teachings, especially in Zen Buddhism.

The doctrine of non-ego not only repudiates the idea of an ego-substance but points out the illusiveness of the ego-idea itself. As long as we are in this world of particular existences we cannot avoid cherishing the idea of an individual ego. But this by no means warrants the substantiality of the ego. Modern psychology has in fact done away with an ego-entity. It is simply a workable hypothesis by which we carry on our practical business. The problem of the ego must be carried on to the field of metaphysics. To really understand what Buddha meant by saying that there is no *ātman,* we must leave psychology behind. Because it is not enough just to state that there is no *ātman* if we wish really to reach the end of sorrow and to be thus at peace with ourselves and with the world at large. We must have something positive in order to see ourselves safely in the harbor and securely anchored. Mere psychology cannot give us this. We must go out to a broader field of Reality where *prajñā*-intuition comes into play.

As long as we wander in the domain of the senses and intellect, the idea of an individual ego besets us, and makes us eternally pursue the shadow of the ego. But the ego is something always eluding our grasp; when we think we have caught it, it is found to be no more than a slough left by the snake while the real ego is something else. The human ego-snake is covered with an infinity of sloughs, the catcher will before long find himself all exhausted. The ego must be caught not from outside but from within. This is the work of *prajñā*. The wonder *prajñā* performs is to catch the actor in the midst of his action, he is not made to stop acting in order to be seen as actor. The actor is the acting, and the acting is the actor, and out of this unification or identification *prajñā* is awakened. The ego does not go out of himself in order to see himself. He stays within himself and sees himself as reflected in himself. But as soon as a split takes place between the ego as actor and the ego as seer or spectator, *prajñā* is dichotomized, and all is lost.

Eckhart expresses the same experience in terms of Christian theology. He talks about Father, Son, Holy Ghost, and love. They sound unfamiliar to Buddhist ears but when they are read with a certain insight we will find that "the love with which he [God] loves himself" is the same as the *prajñā*-intuition that sees into the ego itself. Eckhart tells us: "In giving us his love God has given us his Holy Ghost so that we can love him with the love wherewith he loves himself. We love God with his own love; awareness of it deifies us."[3] The Father loving the Son and the Son loving the Father—this mutual love, that is, love loving itself is, in Zen terminology, one mirror reflecting another with no shadow between them. Eckhart calls this "the play going on in the Father-nature. Play and audience are the same." He continues:

> This play was played eternally before all natures. As it is written in the Book of Wisdom, "Prior to creatures, in the eternal now, I have played before the Father in an eternal stillness." The Son has eternally been playing before the Father as the Father has before his Son. The playing of the twain is the Holy Ghost in whom they both disport themselves and he disports himself in both. Sport and players are the same. Their nature proceeding in itself. "God is a fountain flowing into itself," as St. Dionysius says.

Prajñā-intuition comes out of itself and returns to itself. The self or ego that has been constantly eluding our rationalized scrutiny is at last caught when it comes under *prajñā*-intuition which is no other than the self.

Buddhists generally talk about the egolessness (*anattā* or *anātman*) of all things, but they forget that the egolessness of things cannot really be understood until they are seen with the eye of *prajñā*-intuition. The psychological annihilation of an ego-substance is not enough, for this still leaves the light of *prajñā*-eye under a coverage. Eckhart says, "God is a light shining itself in silent stillness" (Evans, p. 146). As long as our intellectually analytic eye is hotly pursuing the shadow of Reality by dichotomizing it, there will be no silent stillness of absolute identity where *prajñā* sees itself reflected in itself. Eckhart is in accord with the Buddhist experience when he proceeds: "The Word of the Father is none other than his understanding of himself. The understanding of the Father understands that he understands, and that his understanding understands is the same as that he is who is understanding. That is, the light from the light" (*ibid.*, p. 146).

The psychological analysis that cannot go further or deeper than the egolessness of the psychological ego fails to see into the egolessness of all things (*dharma*), which appears to the eye of *prajñā*-intuition not as something sheerly of privative value but as something filled with infinite possibilities. It is only when the *prajñā*-eye surveys the nature of all things (*sarvadharma* or *sabbe dhamma*), that their egolessness displays positive constructive energies by first dispelling the clouds of Māyā, by demolishing every structure of illusion, and thus finally by creating a world of altogether new values based on *prajñā* (wisdom) and *karuṇā* (love). The enlightenment-experience therefore means going beyond the world of psychology, the opening of the *prajñā*-eye, and seeing into the realm of Ultimate Reality, and landing on the other shore of the stream of *samsāra*, where all things are viewed in their state of suchness, in the way of purity. This is when a man finds his mind freed from everything (*sabbattha vimuttamānasa*),[4] not confounded by the notions of birth-and-death, of constant change, of before, behind, and middle. He is the "conqueror" to whom *The Dhammapada* (179) gives this qualification:

> He whose conquest nobody can conquer again,
> Into whose conquest nobody in this world can enter—
> By what track can you trace him,
> The awakened, of infinite range, the trackless?

Such an awakened one is an absolute conqueror and nobody can follow his tracks as he leaves none. If he leaves some, this will be turned into the means whereby he can be defeated. The realm where he lives has no limiting boundaries, it is like a circle whose circumference is infinite, therefore with no center to which a path can lead. This is the one Zen describes as a man of *anābhogacaryā* ("an effortless, purposeless, useless man").[5] This corresponds to Eckhart's man of freedom who is defined as "one who clings to nothing and to whom nothing clings" (Evans, p. 146). While these statements are apt to suggest the doctrine of doing-nothing-ness we must remember that Buddhists are great adherents of what is known as the teaching of *karuṇā* and *praṇidhāna*, to which the reader is referred below.

3

When "the egolessness of all things seen with *prajñā*,"[6] which makes us transcend sorrows and sufferings and leads to "the path of purity," is understood in the sense herein elucidated, we find the way to the understanding of the lines known as "hymn of victory."

The hymn is traditionally ascribed to Buddha who uttered it at the time of his enlightenment. It expresses more of the subjective aspect of his experience which facilitates our examination of the content of the enlightenment. While the egolessness of things is Buddha's metaphysical interpretation of the experience as he reflected upon it, the hymn of victory echoes his immediate reaction, and we are able to have a glimpse into the inner aspect of Buddha's mind more directly than through the conceptualization which came later. We can now proceed to what I have called the second approach. The hymn runs as follows:

Looking for the maker of this tabernacle
I ran to no avail
Through a round of many births;
And wearisome is birth again and again.
But now, maker of the tabernacle, thou hast been seen;
Thou shalt not rear this tabernacle again.
All thy rafters are broken,
Thy ridge-pole is shattered;
The mind approaching the Eternal,
Has attained to the extinction of all desires.[7]

*   *   *

The most essential thing here is the experience that Buddha had of
being released from the bondage in which he had been kept so long. The
utmost consciousness that filled his mind at the time of enlightenment
was that he was no longer the slave to what he calls "the maker of the
tabernacle," or "the builder of this house," that is, *gahakāraka*. He now
feels himself to be a free agent, master of himself, not subject to anything external; he no longer submits himself to dictation from whatever
source it may come. The *gahakāraka* is discovered, the one who was
thought to be behind all his mental and physical activities, and who, as
long as he, that is, Buddha, was ignorant, made him a slave to this au-
tocrat, and employed Buddha—in fact anybody who is ignorant of the
gahakāraka—to achieve the latter's egocentric impulses, desires, cravings.
Buddha was an abject creature utterly under the control of this tyrant,
and it was this sense of absolute helplessness that made Buddha most
miserable, unhappy, and given over to all kinds of fears, dejection, and
moroseness. But Buddha now discovers who this *gahakāraka* is; not only
does he know him, but he has actually seen him face to face, taken hold
of him at work. The monster, the house-builder, the constructor of the
prison-house, being known, being seen, being caught, ceases at last to
weave his entrapping network around Buddha. This means what the
phrase "*visankhāragatam cittam*" means, the mind freed from the bondage of its conditioning aggregates (*sankhāra*).

We must however remember that the *gahakāraka* is not dead, he is
still alive, for he will be living as long as this physical existence continues. Only he has ceased to be my master; on the contrary, I am his
master, I can use him as I wish, he is ready now to obey my command.
"Being free from the tyranny of its binding conditions" does not mean
that the conditions no longer exist. As long as we are relative existences,
we are to that extent conditioned, but the knowledge that we are so conditioned transcends the conditions and thus we are above them. The
sense of freedom arises from this, and freedom never means lawlessness,

wantonness, or libertinism. Those who understand freedom in this latter sense and act accordingly are making themselves slaves to their egotistic passions. They are no longer masters of themselves but most despicable slaves of the *gahakāraka.*

The seeing of the *gahakāraka* therefore does not mean the "seeing of the last of all desire," nor is it "the extinction of all desires." It only means that all the desires and passions we are in possession of, as human beings, are now under the control of one who has caught the *gahakāraka* working out his own limited understanding of freedom. The enlightenment-experience does not annihilate anything; it sees into the working of the *gahakāraka* from a higher point of understanding, which is to say, by means of *prajñā*, and arranges it where it properly belongs. By enlightenment Buddha sees all things in their proper order, as they should be, which means that Buddha's insight has reached the deepest depths of Reality.

As I have said before, the seeing plays the most important role in Buddhist epistemology, for seeing is at the basis of knowing. Knowing is impossible without seeing; all knowledge has its origin in seeing. Knowing and seeing are thus found generally united in Buddha's teaching. Buddhist philosophy therefore ultimately points to seeing reality as it is. Seeing is experienced enlightenment. The *Dharma*[8] is predicated as *ehipassika*, the *Dharma* is something "you come and see." It is for this reason that *sammādassana* (*sammādiṭṭhi* in Sanskrit) is placed at the beginning of the Eightfold Noble Path.

What is the *gahakāraka?*

The *gahakāraka* detected is our relative, empirical ego, and the mind freed from its binding conditions (*sankhāra*) is the absolute ego, *Atman*, as it is elucidated in the *Nirvāna Sūtra.* The denial of *Atman* as maintained by earlier Buddhists refers to *Atman* as the relative ego and not to the absolute ego, the ego after enlightenment-experience.

Enlightenment consists in seeing into the meaning of life as the relative ego and not as the absolute ego, the ego after enlightenment-experience.

Enlightenment consists in seeing into the meaning of life as the interplay of the relative ego with the absolute ego. In other words, enlightenment is seeing the absolute ego as reflected in the relative ego and acting through it.

Or we may express the idea in this way: the absolute ego creates the relative ego in order to see itself reflected in it, that is, in the relative ego. The absolute ego, as long as it remains absolute, has no means whereby to assert itself, to manifest itself, to work out all its possibilities. It requires a *gahakāraka* to execute its biddings. While the *gahakāraka* is not to build his tabernacle according to his own design, he is an efficient agent to actualize whatever lies quiescently in the *Atman* in the sense of the *Nirvāna Sūtra*.

<h2 style="text-align:center">4</h2>

The question now is: Why does the absolute *Atman* want to see itself reflected in the empirical *Atman?* Why does it want to work out its infinite possibilities through the empirical *Atman?* Why does it not remain content with itself instead of going out to a world of multitudes, thereby risking itself to come under the domination of *sankhara?* This is making itself, as it were, a willing slave of the *gahakāraka*.

This is a great mystery which cannot be solved on the plane of intellection. The intellect raises the question, but fails to give it a satisfactory solution. This is in the nature of the intellect. The function of the intellect consists in leading the mind to a higher field of consciousness by proposing all sorts of questions which are beyond itself. The mystery is solved by living it, by seeing into its working, by actually experiencing the significance of life, or by tasting the value of living.[9]

Tasting, seeing, experiencing, living—all these demonstrate that there is something common to enlightenment-experience and our sense-experience; the one takes place in our innermost being, the other on the periphery of our consciousness. Personal experience is thus seen to be the foundation of Buddhist philosophy. In this sense Buddhism is radical empiricism or experientialism, whatever dialectic later developed to probe the meaning of enlightenment-experience.

Buddhist philosophy has long been wrongly regarded as nihilistic and not offering anything constructive. But those who really try to understand it and are not superficially led to misconstrue such terms as demolition, annihilation, extinction, breaking up, cessation, or quiescence, or without thirst, cutting off lust and hatred, will readily see that Buddha never taught a religion of "eternal death."

"Eternal death," which is sometimes regarded as the outcome of the Buddhist idea of egolessness, is a strange notion making no sense whatever. "Death" can mean something only when it is contrasted to birth, for it is a relative term. Eternal death is squaring a circle. Death never takes place unless there is a birth. Where there is birth there is death; where there is death there is birth; birth and death go together. We can never have just one of them, leaving out the other. Where there is eternal death there must be continuous birth. Where eternal death is maintained there must be a never-ceasing birth. Those who talk about total annihilation or extinction as if such things were possible are those who have never faced facts of experience.

Life is a never-ending concatenation of births and deaths. What Buddhist philosophy teaches is to see into the meaning of life as it flows on. When Buddhists declare that all things are impermanent, subject to conditions, and that there is nothing in this world of *samsāra* (birth-and-death) which can give us the hope for absolute security, they mean that as long as we take this world of transiency as something worth clinging to we are sure to lead a life of frustration. To transcend this negativistic attitude toward life we must make use of *prajñā* which is the way of purity. We must see things with the eye of *prajñā*, not to deny them as rubbish but to understand them from an aspect closed to ordinary observers. The latter see nothing but the impermanence or transiency or change-ability of things and are unable to see eternity itself that goes along with time-serialism which can never be demolished. The demolition is on our side and not on the side of time. Buddha's enlightenment-experience clearly points to this. The ridgepole smashed and the rafters torn down all belong to time-serialism and not to eternity which suffers no kind of demolition. To imagine that when serialism is transcended eternity goes out of sight as if it were something relatively coexistent with time is altogether an erroneous way to interpret Buddha's utterance. It really requires the *prajñā*-eye to see into the "*sankhāra*-freed mind," which is in fact no other than Eckhart's eye: "The eye wherein I see God is the same eye wherein God sees me: my eye and God's eye are one eye, one vision, one knowing, one love." Time is eternity and eternity is time. In other words, zero is infinity and infinity is zero. The way of purity opens when the eye sees inwardly as well as outwardly—and this simultaneously. The *prajñā* seeing is one act, one glimpse, one *cittakṣāna*. Unless this truth is seen with *prajñā*-intuition, the "hymn of victory" will never yield its full meaning. Those who read it otherwise cannot go beyond negativism or nihilism.

The following from Eckhart will shed much light:

> Renewal befalls all creatures under God; but for God there is no renewal, only all eternity. What is eternity?—It is characteristic of eternity that in it youth and being are the same, for eternity would not be eternal could it newly become and were not always.[10]

"Renewal" means "becoming" which is "transiency." What is eternal never knows "renewal," never grows old, remains forever "youthful," and transcends "demolition" or "annihilation" of all kinds. Enlightenment is to know what this "eternity" is, and this knowing consists in "knowing eternity-wise his [God's] is-ness free from becoming, and his nameless nothingness."[11] Eckhart is quite definite in giving us what kind of God he has in mind in this matter of knowing and not knowing:

Know'st thou of him anything? He is no such thing, and in that thou dost know of him anything at all thou are in ignorance, and ignorance leads to the condition of the brute; for in creatures what is ignorant is brutish. If thou wouldst not be brutish then, know nothing of the unuttered God.—"What then shall I do?"—Thou shalt lose thy thyness and dissolve in his his-ness; thy thine shall be his mine, so utterly one mine that thou in him shalt know eternalwise his is-ness, free from becoming: his nameless nothingness.[12]

Eckhart's God of nameless nothingness is in Buddhist terms no other than the egolessness of all things, the *sankhāra*-free mind, and the cessation of all cravings.

5

In this connection I think it is opportune to say a few words about the negative statements liberally used in Buddhist and other texts dealing with problems of ultimate reality. I may also touch a little on the frequency of paradoxical propositions used to express a certain experience popularly known as mystic.

Considering all in all, there are two sources of knowledge, or two kinds of experience, or "two births of man" as Eckhart has it, or two forms of truth (*satya*) according to the upholders of the "Emptiness" doctrine (*śūnyavāda*). Unless this is recognized we can never solve the problem of logical contradiction which when expressed in words characterizes all religious experiences. The contradiction so puzzling to the ordinary way of thinking comes from the fact that we have to use language to communicate our inner experience which in its very nature transcends linguistics. But as we have so far no means of communication except the one resorted to by followers of Zen Buddhism, the conflicts go on between rationalists and so-called mystics. Language developed first for the use of the first kind of knowledge which was highly utilitarian, and for this reason it came to assert itself over all human affairs and experiences. Its overwhelming authority is such that we have almost come to accept anything language commands. Our thoughts have now to be molded according to its dictates, our acts are to be regulated by the rules it came to formulate for its own effective operation. This is not all. What is worse is that language has now come even to suppress the truth of new experiences, and that when they actually take place, it will condemn them as "illogical" or "unthinkable" and therefore as false, and finally that as such it will try to put aside anything new as of no human value.

The Sūnyatā school distinguishes two forms of truth (*satyā*): (1) *samvṛitti* of the relative world and (2) *paramārtha* of the transcendental realm of *prajñā*-intuition. When Buddha speaks of his enlightenment in the *Saddharmapuṇḍarīka Sūtra* ("Lotus Gospel"), he describes his experience as something which cannot be comprehended by any of his followers because their understanding can never rise up to the level of Buddha's. It is another Buddha who understands a Buddha, Buddhas have their own world into which no beings of ordinary caliber of mentality can have a glimpse. Language belongs to this world of relativity, and when Buddha tries to express himself by this means his hearers are naturally barred from entering his inner life. . . . Evidently Buddhas can understand one another by whatever means they may employ in conveying their inner acts, because they all know what they are through their experience. But where there are no such corresponding experiences, no amount of technique one may resort to will be possible to awaken them in others.

In Aśvaghoṣa's *Awakening of Faith* reference is made to two aspects of *Tathatā* ("Suchness") one of which is altogether beyond speaking or writing, because it does not fall into the categories of communicability. Language here has no use whatever. But Aśvaghoṣa continues: if we did not appeal to language there is no way to make others acquainted with the absolute; therefore language is resorted to in order to serve as a wedge in getting out the one already in use; it is like a poisonous medicine to counteract another. It is a most dangerous weapon and its user has to be cautioned in every way not to hurt himself. The *Lankāvatara* is decisive in this respect:

> . . . word-discrimination cannot express the highest reality, for external objects with their multitudinous individual marks are non-existent, and only appear before us as something revealed out of Mind itself. Therefore, Mahāmati, you must try to keep yourself away from the various forms of word-discrimination.[13]

Word-discrimination belongs to the *samvṛitti*, to things of the relative world, and is not meant for communicating anything that goes beyond this world of numbers and multiplicities. For here language ceases to be supreme and must realize that it has its limitations. Two of the three kinds of knowledge distinguished by Eckhart are of *Samvṛtti*, whereas the third corresponds to the *paramārtha*. To quote Eckhart:

> These three things stand for three kinds of knowledge. The first is sensible. The eye sees from afar what is outside it. The second is rational and is a great deal higher. The third corresponds to an exalted power of the soul, a power so high and noble it is able to see God face to face in his own self. This power has naught in common with naught, it knows no yesterday or day before, no morrow or day after

(for in eternity there is no yesterday or morrow): therein it is the present now; the happenings of the thousand years ago, a thousand years to come, are there in the present and the antipodes the same as here.[14]

The first two kinds apply to the world of senses and the intellect where language has its utmost usefulness. But when we try to use it in the realm where "the exalted power of the soul" has its sway it miserably fails to convey the activities going on there to those whose "power" has never been "heightened" or enhanced to the level indicated by Eckhart. But as we are forced to make use of language inasmuch as we are creatures of the sense-intellect, we contradict ourselves, as we see in Eckhart's statements just quoted. In this respect Eckhart and all other thinkers of Eckhart's pattern go on disregarding rules of logic or linguistics. The point is that linguistics or logicians are to abandon their limited way of studying facts of experience so that they can analyze the facts themselves and make language amenable to what they discover there. As long as they take up language first and try to adjust all human experiences to the requirements of language instead of the opposite, they will have their problems unsolved.

❖   ❖   ❖

Our language is the product of a world of numbers and individuals of yesterdays and todays and tomorrows, and is most usefully applicable to this world (*loka*). But our experiences have it that our world extends beyond that (*loka*), that there is another called by Buddhists a "transcendental world" (*lokauttara*) and that when language is forced to be used for things of this world, *lokottara*, it becomes warped and assumes all kinds of crookedness: oxymora, paradoxes, contradictions, contortions, absurdities, oddities, ambiguities and irrationalities. Language itself is not to be blamed for it. It is we ourselves who, ignorant of its proper functions, try to apply it to that for which it was never intended. More than this, we make fools of ourselves by denying the reality of a transcendental world (*lokottara*).

Let us see how impossible it is to bring a transcendental world or an "inner power" onto the level of linguistic manageability.

There is something, transcending the soul's created nature, not accessible to creatures, non-existent; no angel has gotten it for his is a clear[15] nature, and clear and overt things have no concern with this. It is akin to Deity, intrinsically one, having naught in common with naught. Many a priest finds it a baffling thing. It is one; rather unnamed than named, rather unknown than known. If thou couldst naught thyself an instant, less than an instant, I should say, all that this is in itself would belong to thee. But while thou dost mind thyself

at all thou knowest no more of God than my mouth does of color or
my eye of taste: so little thou knowest, thou discernest, what God
is.[16]

What "a baffling thing" this "something" or "somewhat" is! But it is no
doubt a light and if you can get a glimpse into it even "less than an instant" you will be master of yourself. Plato describes the light in the following words: It is "a light which is not in this world; not in the world
and not out of the world; not in time nor in eternity; it has neither in
nor out."[17] Linguistically considered, how could a thing be said to be
"neither in the world nor in out-of-the-world"? Nothing can be more absurd than this. But, as Eckhart says (Evans, p. 227), when we transcend
time (*zit*), body (*liplicheit*), and multiplicity (*manicvaltikeit*),[18] we
reach God, and these three things are the very principle of linguistics.
No wonder that when things of the *lokottara* try to find their expression
through language, the latter shows every trace of its shortcomings. This
is the reason why Zen Buddhism strives to avoid the use of language
and quite frequently denounces our shortsightedness in this respect. Zen
does not object to language just for the sake of opposition; it simply realizes that there is a field in which our words fail to communicate events
taking place there. One of the statements Zen is always ready to make is:
"No depending on words." Yengo, commentator of the *Hekigan-shu*
("Blue Rock Collection"), a work of the Sung dynasty, thus remarks:

> Bodhidharma observing that the Chinese minds are matured enough
> to accept teachings of Mahāyāna Buddhism came over here [China]
> via the southern route and started to prepare the people for "the
> transmission of mind-seal." He said, "I am not going to build up a
> system of thought which depends on letters or words. I want
> straightforwardly to direct you to the Mind itself and thereby to see
> into the Buddha-nature and attain Buddhahood. When Zen is under-
> stood in this way, we shall be able to attain freedom. Let us not there-
> fore follow the way of letters of any kind, let us take hold of Reality in
> its nakedness. To the question of Wu the Emperor of the Liang,
> Bodhidharma simply answered, "I do not know, your Majesty!" When
> Eka, who became the second patriarch of Zen in China, confessed that
> he could not locate the Mind, Bodhidharma exclaimed, "There, I have
> your mind pacified!" In all these situations which confronted him,
> Bodhidharma just faced them without hesitation, with no prepared an-
> swers concocted beforehand, he had nothing premeditated or deliber-
> ately schematized in his concept-filled mind. With one swing of the
> sword he cut asunder every obstacle that lay in our way, thereby
> releasing us from the fetters of linguistic discrimination. We are now
> no more to be troubled with right and wrong, gain and loss.[19]

The following *mondo*[20] will demonstrate how free Zen is in dealing, for instance, with the ultimate problem of being:

A monk asked Daizui Hoshin of the T'ang dynasty: "I am told that at the end of the universe a great fire takes place and everything is destroyed. May I ask you whether or not, 'this' also shares the fate?"

Daizui replied, "Yes, it does."

The monk went on, "If this is the case, it must be said that 'this' follows others."

Daizui: "Yes, it does."

The same question was later asked of another master whose name was Shū. Shū the master answered, "No, it does not." When he was asked "Why not?" the master replied, "Because it identifies itself with the whole universe."

From the logical linguistic point of view the two Zen masters defy each other and there is no way to effect a reconciliation. One says "yes" while the other says "no." As long as the "no" means an unqualified negation and the "yes" an unqualified affirmation, there is no bridge between the two. And if this is the case, as apparently it is, how can Zen permit the contradiction and continue the claim for its consistent teaching, one may ask. But Zen would serenely go its own way without at all heeding such a criticism. Because Zen's first concern is about its experience and not its modes of expression. The latter allow a great deal of variation, including paradoxes, contradictions, and ambiguities. According to Zen, the question of "is-ness" (*isticheit*) is settled only by innerly experiencing it and not by mere arguing about it or by linguistically appealing to dialectical subtleties. Those who have a genuine Zen experience will all at once recognize in spite of superficial discrepancies what is true and what is not.

*   *   *

7

It is now time, after these lengthy excursions, to come back to the original topic and see if we cannot get once more into the subjective approach to Buddha's experience of enlightenment. The experience cannot merely be designated as a kind of feeling and thus done away with as if this designation exhausted all the contents of enlightenment. For, as I understand it, the enlightenment cannot be said to be devoid of any noetic elements which yield to a certain extent to a linguistic and intellectual treatment. The feeling of enlightenment has something profoundly fundamental and gives one a sense of absolute certainty and finality which is lacking in the ordinary kind of feeling we generally have. A feeling may occasionally give one the sense of exaltation and self-assurance, but this will after a while pass away and may leave no permanent effect on the being of one who has the experience. The enlightenment feeling on the other hand affects the whole personality, influencing his attitude toward life and the world not only morally and spiritually but in his metaphysical interpretation of existence as a whole. Buddha's experience was not just a matter of feeling which moves on the periphery of consciousness, but something awakened in the deepest recesses of a human being. In this sense only is his utterance recorded in *The Vinaya* and *The Majjhima Nikāya* and elsewhere to be understood. In the *gāthā* already quoted above from *The Dhammapada* (vv. 153, 154), something similar to the one below is noticeable, but the positive and dynamic aspect comes forward more strongly and conspicuously in the following:[21]

> I have conquered and I know all,
> I am enlightened quite by myself and have
>   none as teacher.
> There is no one that is the same as I in the whole
>   world where there are many deities.
> I am the one who is really worth,
> I am the most supreme teacher.
> I am the only one who is fully enlightened.
> I am tranquilized.
> I am now in Nirvana.

This victory song is expressive of the supreme moment of the enlightenment-experience which Buddha had. In the first verse depicting the discovery of the *gahakāraka* (house-builder) and demolition of his handiwork, we see the negative aspect of Buddha's experience, while in the second one dealing with the exalted feeling of victory, the realization of the highest knowledge (*prajñā*) and the consciousness of one's own value as he is, we see its positive aspect coming out in full view.

The consciousness of conquest such as was awakened in the mind of Buddha at the time of enlightenment cannot be regarded as the product of a self-conceit which is often cherished by minds tarnished with schizophrenia and the wielders of political or military powers. With him however whose ego-centered desires have been shattered to pieces the consciousness of victory rises from the deepest sources of being. So the feeling of conquest is not the outcome of a struggle of powers belonging to the low level of existence. The enlightenment-experience is the manifestation of a higher power, a higher insight, a higher unification. It is beyond the sphere of relative consciousness which is the battleground for forces belonging to the same order. One force may temporarily proclaim its victory over another, but this kind of victory is sure before long to be superseded by another. This is in the nature of our relative consciousness. Enlightenment is the experience a man can have only when a higher realm of unification is revealed, that is, when the most fundamental basis of identification is reached.

The enlightenment-experience, therefore, is the one which we can have only when we have climbed up to the highest peak from which we can survey the whole field of Reality. Or we can say that it is the experience which is attained only when we have touched the very bedrock which sustains the entire system of multiple worlds. Here is the consciousness of intensive quantity to which nothing more could be added. All is fulfilled, satisfied; everything here appears to it such as it is; in short, it is a state of absolute Suchness, of absolute Emptiness which is absolute fullness.

Buddhist philosophy, therefore, is the philosophy of Suchness, or philosophy of Emptiness, or philosophy of Self-identity. It starts from the absolute present which is pure experience, an experience in which there is yet no differentiation of subject and object, and yet which is not a state of sheer nothingness. The experience is variously designated: in Japanese it is *sono-mama;* in Chinese it is *chih mo,* sometimes *tzu-jan fa-erh* (Japanese: *jinen hōni*); there are many technical names for it, each denoting its specific features or characters as it is viewed in various relationships.

In fact, this Suchness, or "is-ness" (*isticheit*) in Eckhart's terminology, defies all characterization or denotation. No words can express what it is, but as words are the only instrument given us human beings to communicate our thought, we have to use words, with this caution: Nothing is available for our purpose; to say "not available" (*anupalabda* in Sanskrit and *pu k'o tê* in Chinese) is not to the point either. Nothing is acceptable. To say it is, is already negating itself. Suchness transcends everything, it has no moorings. No concepts can reach it, no understanding can grasp it. Therefore, it is called pure experience.

In pure experience there is no division between "ought" and "is," between form and matter or content, and therefore there is no judgment in it yet. There is the Christ who says "I am before Abraham was," or God who has not yet uttered his fiat. This is Buddha who, according to *The Dhammapada* (179), is the *anantagocara* ("one whose limits are infinite"), the *apada* ("the pathless"), whose conquest can never be conquered again and into whose conquest nobody in this world can enter, and who is where there is no track leading to it. If it were a Zen master, he would demand that you show your face, however ugly it might be, which you have even before your birth into this world of multiplication.

The Buddhist philosophy of Suchness thus starts with what is most primarily given to our consciousness—which I have called pure experience. But, in point of fact, to say "pure experience" is to commit oneself to something already posited somewhere, and thus it ceases to be pure. *The Dhammapada* reflects this thought when it designates the starting point of Buddhist philosophy as trackless (*apada*), unboundable (*anantagocara*), abodeless (*aniketa*), empty (*śuñña*), formless (*animitta*), delivered (*vimokkha*). In psychological terms, it is described thus: sorrowless (*vippamutta*), released on all sides (*sabbaganthappahīna*), fearless (*asantāsin*), without craving (*vītataṇha*). These psychological terms are apt to be very much misunderstood because they point to negativism when superficially and linguistically interpreted. But I will not dwell upon this here.

One thing that must be noted in this connection is that pure experience is not pure passivity. In fact there is nothing we can call pure passivity. This does not make sense and does not lead us anywhere. As long as passivity is also an experience, there must be one who experiences passivity. This one, this experiencer, is an actor. Not only is he an actor, but he is a knower, for he is conscious of experiencing. Pure experience is not an abstraction or a state of passivity. It is very much active, and creative. Eckhart voices this idea when he states: "In this sense thy unknowing is not a defect but thy chief perfection, and suffering thy highest activity. Kill thy activities and still thy faculties if thou wouldst realize this birth in thee."[22]

Another thing I should like to emphasize in this *gatha* of conquest is that Buddha calls himself "all-conqueror" and also "all-knower," showing that his victory is absolute and that his knowledge is not at all fragmentary. He is omniscient as well as omnipotent. His experience has something noetic and at the same time something conative or affective, reflecting the nature of Reality itself which consists in *prajñā* and *karuṇā*. As regards *prajñā*, which is sometimes translated as "transcendental wisdom," I have written about it elsewhere. Therefore I shall speak here about *karuṇā*. *Karuṇā* corresponds to love. It is like the sands on the Ganges: they are trampled by all kinds of beings: by elephants, by lions, by asses, by human beings, but they do not make any complaints. They are again soiled by all kinds of filth scattered by all kinds of animals, but they just suffer them all and never utter a word of ill-will. Eckhart would declare the sands on the Ganges to be "just" (*gerecht*), because "the just have no will at all: whatever God wishes it is all one to them, however great the discomfort may be."[23]

The just are so firmly devoted to justice and so wholly selfless that whatever they do, they regard neither the pains of hell nor the joys of heaven. . . . To the just person, nothing is so hard to bear or so painful as anything opposed to justice, that is to say, as not feeling impartially the same about everything that happens.[24]

"Justice" savors a great deal of legalism contrary to the idea of love. But when, as Eckhart interprets it, justice is considered from the affective point of view as meaning "impartiality," "sameness," "universality," or "all-embracing," it begins to approach the Buddhist idea of *karuṇā*. I may add that Mahāyāna Buddhism further developed the idea of *karuṇā* into that of *praṇidhāna* or *pūrvapraṇidhāna* and made each one of the Bodhisattvas an incarnation of a certain number of *praṇidhāna;* for example, Amitābha has forty-eight *praṇidhāna,* Samantanhadra has ten, and Kṣitigarbha also has ten. *Praṇidhāna* is generally translated as "vow" or "fervent wish" or "prayer," or simply "the will," but these English terms do not convey the full meaning of the Sanskrit as it is used in the Mahāyāna. Roughly speaking, we may interpret *praṇidhāna* as love specified or itemized or particularized and made applicable to each practical situation in which we may find ourselves in the course of an individual life. Amitābha has his Pure Land where he wants us to be born; Mañjuśtri is the Bodhisattva of *prajñā* and whoever comes to him will be rewarded with an amount of transcendental wisdom.

This being the case, we will see that "the destruction of desires or cravings (*taṇhānam khayam*)" so much emphasized in the teaching of earlier Buddhism is not to be understood negativistically. The Buddhist training consists in transforming *tṛiṣṇā* (*taṇhā*) into *karuṇā,* ego-centered love into something universal, eros into agape.

When Jōshu (778–897) was asked, "Could Buddha cherish any desires (*kleśa*)?" he answered, "Yes, he decidedly has." The questioner demanded, "How could that be?" The master replied, "His desire is to save the whole universe."

One day Jōshu had another visitor who asked, "I hear so much of the stone bridge reputed to be on one of the sites in your monastery grounds. But as I see it, it is no more than an old log. How is that?"

The master said, "You see the log and don't see the stone bridge."

"What is the stone bridge, then?" the visitor demanded.

The master's answer was, "It permits horses to pass and also asses to pass."

Someone's *praṇidhāna* is too rickety for safe crossing whereas the other's is strong and broad, allowing anything to pass over it safely. Let *taṇhā* be destroyed but we must not forget that it has another root which reaches the very ground of being. The enlightenment-experience must realize that, though ordinarily Buddhists are more or less neglectful in bringing out the *karuṇā* aspect of the experience. This is due to their being too anxious and therefore too much in a hurry to destroy all the obstacles lying on the way to enlightenment, for they know that when this is accomplished what is to come therefrom is left to itself as it knows full well how to take care of it. When the devastating fire is extinguished the forest will not wait for any external help but will resume its biological functions by itself. When a man is shot by a poisonous arrow the first thing to do is to remove it before it is embedded too deeply into the flesh. When this is done the body will heal the wound by its own power of vitality. So with human passions, the first work is to destroy their root of ignorance and egoism. When this is thoroughly accomplished, the Buddha-nature which consists in *prajñā* and *karuṇā* will start its native operation. The principle of Suchness is not static, it is full of dynamic forces.

NOTES

1. *The Dhammapada,* tr. S. Radhakrishnan (Oxford University Press, 1951) verses 277–79, pp. 146–47. I do not however, always follow him in my quotations. . . .

2. *Studies in Zen* (London: Rider and Company, 1955), 85–128.

3. Evans, pp. 147*ff.* There are two English translations of Eckhart, one British and the other American. The British, in two volumes, is by C. de B. Evans, published by John M. Watkins, London, 1924. The American translation is by Raymond B. Blakney, published by Harper & Brothers, New York, 1941. Neither of them is a complete translation of all of Eckhart's known works in German. Franz Pfeiffer published in 1857 a collection of Eckhart's works, chiefly in the High German dialect of Strassburg of the fourteenth century. This edition was reprinted in 1914. Blakney's and Evans' translations are mainly based on the Pfeiffer edition. In the present article, "Blakney" refers to the Blakney translation and "Evans" to the Evans, Vol. I, while "Pfeiffer" means his German edition of 1914.

4. *The Dhammapada,* verse 348, p. 167.

5. *Studies in the Lankāvatāra Sūtra,* pp. 223*ff.*

6. "*Sabbe dhamma anattā' ti yadā paññāya passati.*"

7. *The Dhammapada,* pp. 153–54. (Published by Oxford University Press, 1936.)

8. *Dhamma* in Pali. It has a multiple meaning and is difficult to render it uniformly. Here it stands for Truth, Reality, Norm.

9. "O taste and see that the Lord is good; blessed is the man that trusteth in him." (Psalm 34:8.)

10. Evans, p. 246.

11. Pfeiffer, p. 319. "*Du mit ime verstandest ewichliche sine ungewordene istikeit under sine ungenanten nihtheit.*"

12. Evans, p. 246.

13. *Lankāvatāra Sūtra,* tr. D. T. Suzuki (London: George Routledge and Sons, Ltd., 1932), p. 77.

14. Evans, p. 228.

15. *"Ein luter wesen"* in German. *Luter* means "intellectually or analytically clear and distinct," opposed to what may be called "metaphysically indefinite."

16. Evans, pp. 204–5.

17. Quoted by Eckhart, Evans, p. 205.

18. Pfeiffer, p. 296.

19. A more or less modernized interpretation given to Yengo's terse and loosely knit Chinese.

20. Literally, "question and answer."

21. *The Vinaya,* I, 8. *The Majjhima Nikāya* (translated by Lord Chalmers, published by Oxford University Press), 26, p. 12.

22. Evans, p. 14. "This birth" in this sermon means "the newborn Being" or "the child of man turned into the child of God." It also means "hearing of the Word" which is revealed to "one who knows aright in unknowing."

23. Blakney, p. 179.

24. Ibid.

General Characteristics of Jewish Mysticism

GERSHOM G. SCHOLEM

2

Since Jewish mysticism is to be the subject of these lectures, the first question bound to come up is this: what is Jewish mysticism? What precisely is meant by this term? Is there such a thing, and if so, what distinguishes it from other kinds of mystical experience? In order to be able to give an answer to this question, if only an incomplete one, it will be necessary to recall what we know about mysticism in general.

* * *

A good starting point for our investigation can be obtained by scrutinizing a few of these definitions which have won a certain authority. Dr. Rufus Jones, in his excellent "Studies in Mystical Religion" defines his subject as follows: "I shall use the word to express the type of religion which puts the emphasis on immediate awareness of relation with God, on direct and intimate consciousness of the Divine Presence. It is religion in its most acute, intense and living stage."[1] Thomas Aquinas briefly defines mysticism as *cognitio deo experimentalis*,[2] as the knowledge of God through experience. In using this term he leans heavily, like many mystics before and after him, on the words of the Psalmist (Psalm xxxiv 9): "Oh taste and see that the Lord is good." It is this tasting and seeing, however spiritualized it may become, that the genuine mystic desires. His attitude is determined by the fundamental experience of the inner self which enters into immediate contact with God or the metaphysical Reality. What forms the essence of this experience, and how it is to be adequately described—that is the great riddle which the mystics themselves, no less than the historians, have tried to solve.

For it must be said that this act of personal experience, the systematic investigation and interpretation of which forms the task of all mystical speculation, is of a highly contradictory and even paradoxical nature. Certainly this is true of all attempts to describe it in words and perhaps, where there are no longer words, of the act itself. What kind of direct relation can there be between the Creator and His creature, between the finite and the infinite; and how can words express an experience for which there is no adequate simile in this finite world of man? Yet it would be wrong and superficial to conclude that the contradiction implied by the nature of mystical experience betokens an inherent absurdity. It will be wiser to assume, . . . that the religious world of the mystic can be expressed in terms applicable to rational knowledge only with the help of paradox. . . . It is well known that the descriptions given by the mystics of their peculiar experiences and of the God whose presence they experience are full of paradoxes of every kind. It is not the least baffling of these paradoxes—to take an instance which is common to Jewish and Christian mystics—that God is frequently described as the mystical Nothing. I shall not try now to give an interpretation of this term, to which we shall have to return; I only want to stress the fact that the particular reality which the mystic sees or tastes is of a very unusual kind.

To the general history of religion this fundamental experience is known under the name of *unio mystica,* or mystical union with God. The term, however, has no particular significance. Numerous mystics, Jews as well as non-Jews, have by no means represented the essence of their ecstatic experience, the tremendous uprush and soaring of the soul to its highest plane, as a union with God. To take an instance, the earliest Jewish mystics who formed an organized fraternity in Talmudic times and later, describe their experience in terms derived from the diction characteristic of their age. They speak of the ascent of the soul to the Celestial Throne where it obtains an ecstatic view of the majesty of God and the secrets of His Realm. A great distance separates these old Jewish Gnostics from the Hasidic mystics one of whom said: "There are those who serve God with their human intellect, and others whose gaze is fixed on Nothing. . . . He who is granted this supreme experience loses the reality of his intellect, he finds it full of divine and inflowing splendor."[3] And yet it is the same experience which both are trying to express in different ways.

This leads us to a further consideration: it would be a mistake to assume that the whole of what we call mysticism is identical with that personal experience which is realized in the state of ecstasy or ecstatic meditation. Mysticism, as an historical phenomenon, comprises much more than this experience, which lies at its root. There is a danger in relying too much on purely speculative definitions of the term. The point I should like to make is this—that there is no such thing as mysticism in the abstract, that is to say, a phenomenon or experience which has no particular relation to other religious phenomena. There is no mysticism as such, there is only the mysticism of a particular religious system, Christian, Islamic, Jewish mysticism and so on. That there remains a common characteristic it would be absurd to deny, and it is this element which is brought out in the comparative analysis of particular mystical experiences. But only in our days has the belief gained ground that there is such a thing as an abstract mystical religion. . . . As it is our intention to treat of a certain definite kind of mysticism, namely Jewish, we should not dwell too much upon such abstractions. Moreover, as Evelyn Underhill has rightly pointed out, the prevailing conception of the mystic as a religious anarchist who owes no allegiance to his religion finds little support in fact. History rather shows that the great mystics were faithful adherents of the great religions.

*   *   *

Jewish mysticism in its various forms represents an attempt to interpret the religious values of Judaism in terms of mystical values. It concentrates upon the idea of the living God who manifests himself in the acts of Creation, Revelation and Redemption. Pushed to its extreme, the mystical meditation on this idea gives birth to the conception of a sphere, a whole realm of divinity, which underlies the world of our sense-data and which is present and active in all that exists. This is the meaning of what the Kabbalists call the *world of the "Sefiroth."* I should like to explain this a little more fully.

The attributes of the living God are conceived differently and undergo a peculiar transformation when compared with the meaning given to them by the philosophers of Judaism. Among the latter, Maimonides, in his "Guide of the Perplexed," felt bound to ask: How is it possible to say of God that He is living? Does that not imply a limitation of the infinite Being? The words "God is living," he argues, can only mean that he is not dead, that is to say, that he is the opposite of all that is negative. He is the negation of negation. A quite different reply is given by the Kabbalist, for whom the distinction, nay the conflict, between the known and the unknown God has a significance denied to it by the philosophers of Judaism.

No creature can take aim at the unknown, the hidden God. In the last resort, every cognition of God is based on a form of relation between Him and His creature, i.e. on a manifestation of God in something else, and not on a relation between Him and Himself. It has been argued that the difference between the *deus absconditus*, God in Himself, and God in His appearance, is unknown to Kabbalism.[4] This seems to me a wrong interpretation of the facts. On the contrary, the dualism embedded in these two aspects of the one God, both of which are, theologically speaking, possible ways of aiming at the divinity, has deeply preoccupied the Jewish mystics. It has occasionally led them to use formulas whose implied challenge to the religious consciousness of monotheism was fully revealed only in the subsequent development of Kabbalism. As a rule, the Kabbalists were concerned to find a formula which should give as little offense as possible to the philosophers.

* * *

The mystic strives to assure himself of the living presence of God, the God of the Bible, the God who is good, wise, just and merciful and the embodiment of all other positive attributes. But at the same time he is unwilling to renounce the idea of the hidden God who remains eternally unknowable in the depths of His own Self, or, to use the bold expression of the Kabbalists "in the depths of His nothingness."[5] This hidden God may be without special attributes—the living God of whom the Revelation speaks, with whom all religion is concerned, must have attributes, which on another plane represent also the mystic's own scale of moral values: God is good, God is severe, God is merciful and just, etc. As we shall have occasion to see, the mystic does not even recoil before the inference that in a higher sense there is a root of evil even in God. The benevolence of God is to the mystic not simply the negation of evil, but a whole sphere of divine light, in which God manifests Himself under this particular aspect of benevolence to the contemplation of the Kabbalist.

These spheres, which are often described with the aid of mythical metaphors and provide the key for a kind of mystical topography of the Divine realm, are themselves nothing but stages in the revelation of God's creative power. Every attribute represents a given stage, including the attribute of severity and stern judgment, which mystical speculation has connected with the source of evil in God. The mystic who sets out to grasp the meaning of God's absolute unity is thus faced at the outset with an infinite complexity of heavenly spheres and stages which are described in the Kabbalistic texts. From the contemplation of these "Sefiroth" he proceeds to the conception of God as the union and the root of all these contradictions. Generally speaking, the mystics do not seem to conceive of God as the absolute Being or absolute Becoming but as the union of both; much as the hidden God of whom nothing is known to us, and the living God of religious experience and revelation, are one and the same. Kabbalism in other words is not dualistic, although historically there exists a close connection between its way of thinking and that of the Gnostics, to whom the hidden God and the Creator are opposing principles. On the contrary, all the energy of "orthodox" Kabbalistic speculation is bent to the task of escaping from dualistic consequences; otherwise they would not have been able to maintain themselves within the Jewish community.

I think it is possible to say that the mystical interpretation of the attributes and the unity of God, in the so-called doctrine of the "Sefiroth," constituted a problem common to all Kabbalists, while the solutions given to it by and in the various schools often differ from one another. In the same way, all Jewish mystics, from the Therapeutae, whose doctrine was described by Philo of Alexandria,[6] to the latest Hasid, are at one in giving a mystical interpretation to the Torah; the Torah is to them a living organism animated by a secret life which streams and pulsates below the crust of its literal meaning; every one of the innumerable strata of this hidden region corresponds to a new and profound meaning of the Torah. The Torah, in other words, does not consist merely of chapters, phrases and words; rather is it to be regarded as the living incarnation of the divine wisdom which eternally sends out new rays of light. It is not merely the historical law of the Chosen People, although it is that too; it is rather the cosmic law of the Universe, as God's wisdom conceived it. Each configuration of letters in it, whether it makes sense in human speech or not, symbolizes some aspect of God's creative power which is active in the universe. And just as the thoughts of God, in contrast to those of man, are of infinite profundity, so also no single interpretation of the Torah in human language is capable of taking in the whole of its meaning. It cannot be denied that this method of interpretation has proved almost barren for a plain understanding of the Holy Writ, but it is equally undeniable that viewed in this new light, the Sacred Books made a powerful appeal to the individual who discovered in their written words the secret of his life and of his God. . . .

5

Like all their spiritual kin among Christians or Moslems, the Jewish mystics cannot, of course, escape from the fact that the relation between mystical contemplation and the basic facts of human life and thought is highly paradoxical. But in the Kabbalah these paradoxes of the mystical mind frequently assume a peculiar form. Let us take as an instance their relation to the phenomenon of speech, one of the fundamental problems of mystical thought throughout the ages. How is it possible to give lingual expression to mystical knowledge, which by its very nature is related to a sphere where speech and expression are excluded? How is it possible to paraphrase adequately in mere words the most intimate act of all, the contact of the individual with the Divine? And yet the urge of the mystics for self-expression is well known.

They continuously and bitterly complain of the utter inadequacy of words to express their true feelings, but, for all that, they glory in them; they indulge in rhetoric and never weary of trying to express the inexpressible in words. All writers on mysticism have laid stress on this point.[7] Jewish mysticism is no exception, yet it is distinguished by two unusual characteristics which may in some way be interrelated. What I have in mind is, first of all, the striking restraint observed by the

Kabbalists in referring to the supreme experience; and secondly, their metaphysically positive attitude toward language as God's own instrument.

If you compare the writings of Jewish mystics with the mystical literature of other religions you will notice a considerable difference, a difference which has, to some extent, made difficult and even prevented the understanding of the deeper meaning of Kabbalism. Nothing could be further from the truth than the assumption that the religious experience of the Kabbalists is barren of that which, as we have seen, forms the essence of mystical experience, everywhere and at all times. The ecstatic experience, the encounter with the absolute Being in the depths of one's own soul, or whatever description one may prefer to give to the goal of the mystical nostalgia, has been shared by the heirs of rabbinical Judaism. How could it be otherwise with one of the original and fundamental impulses of man? At the same time, such differences as there are, are explained by the existence of an overwhelmingly strong disinclination to treat in express terms of these strictly mystical experiences. Not only is the form different in which these experiences are expressed, but the *will* to express them and to impart the knowledge of them is lacking, or is counteracted by other considerations.

It is well known that the autobiographies of great mystics, who have tried to give an account of their inner experiences in a direct and personal manner, are the glory of mystical literature. These mystical confessions, for all their abounding contradictions, not only provide some of the most important material for the understanding of mysticism, but many of them are also veritable pearls of literature. The Kabbalists, however, are no friends of mystical autobiography. They aim at describing the realm of Divinity and the other objects of the contemplation in an impersonal way, by burning, as it were, their ships behind them. They glory in objective description and are deeply averse to letting their own personalities intrude into the picture. The wealth of expression at their disposal is not inferior to that of their autobiographical confreres. It is as though they were hampered by a sense of shame. Documents of an intimate and personal nature are not entirely lacking, but it is characteristic that they are to be found almost wholly in manuscripts which the Kabbalists themselves would hardly have allowed to be printed. There has even been a kind of voluntary censorship which the Kabbalists themselves exercised by deleting certain passages of a too intimate nature from the manuscripts, or at least by seeing to it that they were not printed. . . . On the whole, I am inclined to believe that this dislike of a too personal indulgence in self-expression may have been caused by the fact among others that the Jews retained a particularly vivid sense of the incongruity between mystical experience and the idea of God which stresses the aspects of Creator, King and Lawgiver. It is obvious that the absence of the autobiographical element is a serious obstacle to any psychological understanding of Jewish mysticism as the psychology of mysticism has to rely primarily on the study of such autobiographical material.

* * *

My second point is that Kabbalism is distinguished by an attitude toward language which is quite unusually positive. Kabbalists who differ in almost everything else are at one regarding language as something more precious than an inadequate instrument for contact between human beings. To them Hebrew, the holy tongue, is not simply a means of expressing certain thoughts, born out of a certain convention and having a purely conventional character, in accordance with the theory of language dominant in the Middle Ages. Language in its purest form, that is, Hebrew, according to the Kabbalists, reflects the fundamental spiritual nature of the world; in other words, it has a mystical value. Speech reaches God because it comes from God. Man's common language, whose prima facie function, indeed, is only of an intellectual nature, reflects the creative language of God. All creation—and this is an important principle of most Kabbalists—is, from the point of view of God, nothing but an expression of His hidden self that begins and ends by giving itself a name, the holy name of God, the perpetual act of creation. All that lives is an expression of God's language—and what is it that Revelation can reveal in the last resort if not the name of God?

* * *

6

. . . What is to be regarded as the general characteristic of mysticism within the framework of Jewish tradition? Kabbalah, it must be remembered, is not the name of a certain dogma or system, but rather the general term applied to a whole religious movement. This movement, with some of whose stages and tendencies we shall have to acquaint ourselves, has been going on from Talmudic times to the present day; its development has been uninterrupted, though by no means uniform, and often dramatic. It leads from Rabbi Akiba, of whom the Talmud says that he left the "Paradise" of mystical speculation safe and sane as he had entered it—something which cannot, indeed, be said of every Kabbalist—to the late Rabbi Abraham Isaac Kook, the religious leader of the Jewish community in Palestine and a splendid type of Jewish mystic.[8] I should like to mention here that we are in possession of a vast printed literature of mystical texts which I am inclined to estimate at three thousand.[9] In addition, there exists an even greater array of manuscripts not yet published.

Within this movement there exists a considerable variety of religious experience, to use William James' expression. There have been many different currents of thought, and various systems and forms of speculation. There is little resemblance between the earliest mystical texts in our possession, dating from Talmudic and post-Talmudic days, the writings of the ancient Spanish Kabbalists, those of the school which later flourished in Safed, the holy city of Kabbalism in the sixteenth century, and finally the Hasidic literature of the modern age. Yet the question must be asked whether there is not something more than a purely historical connection uniting these *disjecta membra,* something which also provides us with a hint as to what renders this mystical movement in Judaism different from non-Jewish mysticism. Such a common denominator can, perhaps, be discovered in certain unchanging fundamental ideas concerning God, creation and the part played by man in the universe. Two such ideas I have mentioned above, namely the attributes of God and the symbolic meaning of the Torah. But may it not also be that such a denominator is to be found in the attitude of the Jewish mystic toward those dominant spiritual forces which have conditioned and shaped the intellectual life of Jewry during the past two thousand years: the Halakhah, the Aggadah, the prayers and the philosophy of Judaism, to name the most important? It is this question which I shall now try to answer, though without going into detail.

As I have said before, the relation of mysticism to the world of history can serve as a useful starting point for our investigation. It is generally believed that the attitude of mysticism toward history is one of aloofness, or even of contempt. The historical aspects of religion have a meaning for the mystic chiefly as symbols of acts which he conceives as being divorced from time, or constantly repeated in the soul of every man. Thus the exodus from Egypt, the fundamental event of our history, cannot, according to the mystic, have come to pass once only and in one place; it must correspond to an event which takes place in ourselves, an exodus from an inner Egypt in which we all are slaves. Only thus conceived does the Exodus cease to be an object of learning and acquire the dignity of immediate religious experience. In the same way, it will be remembered, the doctrine of "Christ in us" acquired so great an importance for the mystics of Christianity that the historical Jesus of Nazareth was quite often relegated to the background. If, however, the Absolute which the mystic seeks is not to be found in the varying occurrences of history, the conclusion suggests itself that it must either precede the course of mundane history or reveal itself at the end of time. In other words, knowledge both of the primary facts of creation and of its end, of eschatological salvation and bliss, can acquire a mystical significance.

"The Mystic," says Charles Bennett in a penetrating essay,[10] "as it were forestalls the processes of history by anticipating in his own life the enjoyment of the last age." This eschatological nature of mystical knowledge becomes of paramount importance in the writings of many Jewish mystics, from the anonymous authors of the early *Hekhaloth* tracts to Rabbi Nahman of Brazlav. And the importance of cosmogony for mystical speculation is equally exemplified by the case of Jewish mysticism. The consensus of Kabbalistic opinion regards the mystical way to God as a reversal of the procession by which we have emanated from God. To know the stages of the creative process is also to know the stages of one's own return to the root of all existence. In this sense, the interpretation of *Maaseh Bereshith*, the esoteric doctrine of creation, has always formed one of the main preoccupations of Kabbalism. It is here that Kabbalism comes nearest to Neoplatonic thought, of which it has been said with truth that "procession and reversion together constitute a single movement, the diastole-systole, which is the life of the universe."[11] Precisely this is also the belief of the Kabbalist.

But the cosmogonic and the eschatological trend of Kabbalistic speculation which we have tried to define, are in the last resort ways of escaping from history rather than instruments of historical understanding; that is to say, they do not help us to gauge the intrinsic meaning of history.

There is, however, a more striking instance of the link between the conceptions of Jewish mysticism and those of the historical world. It is a remarkable fact that the very term *Kabbalah* under which it has become best known, is derived from an historical concept. Kabbalah means literally "tradition," in itself an excellent example of the paradoxical nature of mysticism to which I have referred before. The very doctrine which centers about the immediate personal contact with the Divine, that is to say, a highly personal and intimate form of knowledge, is conceived as traditional wisdom. The fact is, however, that the idea of Jewish mysticism from the start combined the conception of a knowledge which by its very nature is difficult to impart and therefore secret, with that of a knowledge which is the secret tradition of chosen spirits or adepts. Jewish mysticism, therefore, is a secret doctrine in a double sense, a characteristic which cannot be said to apply to all forms of mysticism. It is a secret doctrine because it treats of the most deeply hidden and fundamental matters of human life; but it is secret also because it is confined to a small elite of the chosen who impart the knowledge to their disciples. It is true that this picture never wholly corresponded to life. Against the doctrine of the chosen few who alone may participate in the mystery must be set the fact that, at least during certain periods of history, the Kabbalists themselves have tried to bring under their influence much wider circles, and even the whole nation. There is a certain analogy between this development and that of the mystery religions of the Hellenic period of antiquity, when secret doctrines of an essentially mystical nature were diffused among an ever-growing number of people.

It must be kept in mind that in the sense in which it is understood by the Kabbalist himself, mystical knowledge is not his private affair which has been revealed to him, and to him only, in his personal experience. On the contrary, the purer and more nearly perfect it is, the nearer it is to the original stock of knowledge common to mankind. To use the expression of the Kabbalist, the knowledge of things human and divine that Adam, the father of mankind, possessed is therefore also the property of the mystic. For this reason, the Kabbalah advanced what was at once a claim and an hypothesis, namely, that its function was to hand down to its own disciples the secret of God's revelation to Adam.[12] Little though this claim is grounded in fact—and I am even inclined to believe that many Kabbalists did not regard it seriously—the fact that such a claim was made appears to me highly characteristic of Jewish mysticism. Reverence for the traditional has always been deeply rooted in Judaism, and even the mystics, who in fact broke away from tradition, retained a reverent attitude toward it; it led them directly to their conception of the coincidence of true intuition and true tradition. This theory has made possible such a paradox as the Kabbalah of Isaac Luria, the most influential system of later Kabbalism, though the most difficult. Nearly all the important points and major theses in Luria's system are novel, one might even say excitingly novel—and yet they were accepted throughout as true Kabbalah, i.e. traditional wisdom. There was nobody to see a contradiction in this.

7

. . . The peculiar affinity of Kabbalist thought to the world of myth cannot well be doubted, and should certainly not be obscured or lightly passed over by those of us to whom the notion of a mythical domain within Judaism seems strange and paradoxical and who are accustomed to think of Jewish Monotheism as the classical example of a religion which has severed all links with the mythical. It is, indeed, surprising that in the very heart of Judaism ideas and notions sprang up which purported to interpret its meaning better than any others, and which yet represent a relapse into, or if you like a revival of, the mythical consciousness. This is particularly true of the Zohar and the Lurianic Kabbalah, that is to say, of those forms of Jewish mysticism which have exerted by far the greatest influence in Jewish history and which for centuries stood out in the popular mind as bearers of the final and deepest truth in Jewish thought.

* * *

The secret of the success of the Kabbalah lies in the nature of its relation to the spiritual heritage of rabbinical Judaism; both have lost the simple relation to Judaism, that naïveté which speaks to us from the classical documents of Rabbinical literature. Classical Judaism expressed itself: it did not reflect upon itself. By contrast, to the mystics and the philosophers of a later stage of religious development Judaism itself has become problematical. Instead of simply speaking their minds, they tend to produce an ideology of Judaism, an ideology moreover which comes to the rescue of tradition by giving it a new interpretation. It is not as though the rise of Jewish philosophy and of Jewish mysticism took place in widely separated ages, or as though the Kabbalah, as Graetz saw it, was a reaction against a wave of rationalism. Rather the two movements are interrelated and interdependent. Neither were they from the start manifestly opposed to each other, a fact which is often overlooked. On the contrary, the rationalism of some of the philosophical *enlighteners* frequently betrays a mystical tendency; and conversely, the mystic who has not yet learned to speak in his own language often uses and misuses the vocabulary of philosophy. Only very gradually did the Kabbalists, rather than the philosophers, begin to perceive the implications of their own ideas, the conflict between a purely philosophical interpretation of the world, and an attitude which progresses from rational thought to irrational meditation, and from there to the mystical interpretation of the universe.

What many mystics felt toward philosophy was succinctly expressed by Rabbi Moses of Burgos (end of the thirteenth century). When he heard the philosophers praised, he used to say angrily: "You ought to know that these philosophers whose wisdom you are praising, end where we begin."[13] Actually this means two things: on the one hand, it means that the Kabbalists are largely concerned with the investigation of a sphere of religious reality which lies quite outside the orbit of mediaeval Jewish philosophy; their purpose is to discover a new stratum of the religious consciousness. On the other hand, though R. Moses may not have intended to say this, they stand on the shoulders of the philosophers and it is easier for them to see a little further than their rivals.

* * *

Let us take, as an example of what I have said, the idea of "creation out of nothing." In the dogmatic disputations of Jewish philosophy, the question whether Judaism implies belief in this concept, and if so, in what precise sense, has played an important part. . . . Viewed in its simplest sense, it affirms the creation of the world by God out of something which is neither God Himself nor any kind of existence, but simply the non-existent. The mystics, too, speak of creation out of nothing; in fact, it is one of their favorite formulae. But in their case the orthodoxy of the term conceals a meaning which differs considerably from the original one. This *Nothing* from which everything has sprung is by no means a mere negation; only to us does it present no attributes because it is beyond the reach of intellectual knowledge. In truth, however, this Nothing—to quote one of the Kabbalists—is infinitely more real than all other reality.[14] Only when the soul has stripped itself of all limitation and, in mystical language, has descended into the depths of Nothing does it encounter the Divine. For this *Nothing* comprises a wealth of mystical reality although it cannot be defined. "Un Dieu défini serait un Dieu fini." In a word, it signifies the Divine itself, in its most impenetrable guise. And, in fact, *creation out of nothing* means to many mystics just *creation out of God*. Creation out of nothing thus becomes the symbol of emanation, that is to say, of an idea which, in the history of philosophy and theology, stands furthest removed from it.

8

Let us return to our original problem. As we have seen, the renaissance of Judaism on a new plane is the common concern of both the mystics and the philosophers. For all that, there remains a very considerable difference, a good example of which is afforded by the conception of *Sithre Torah*, or "Secrets of the Law." The philosophers no less than the mystics talk of discovering these secrets, using this esoteric phraseology with a profusion hardly distinguishable from the style of the real esoterics and Kabbalists. But what are these secrets according to the philosopher? They are the truths of philosophy, the truths of the metaphysics or ethics of Aristotle, or Alfarabi or Avicenna; truths, in other words, which were capable of being discovered outside the sphere of religion and which were projected into the old books by way of allegorical or typological interpretation. The documents of religion are therefore not conceived as expressing a separate and distinct world of religious truth and reality, but rather as giving a simplified description of the relations which exist between the ideas of philosophy. The story of Abraham and Sarah, of Lot and his wife, of the Twelve Tribes, etc., are simply descriptions of the relation between matter and form, spirit and matter, or the faculties of the mind. Even where allegorization was not pushed to such absurd extremes, the tendency was to regard the Torah as a mere vehicle of philosophic truth, though indeed one particularly exalted and perfect.

In other words, the philosopher can only proceed with his proper task after having successfully converted the concrete realities of Judaism into a bundle of abstractions. The individual phenomenon is to him no object of his philosophical speculation. By contrast, the mystic refrains from destroying the living texture of religious narrative by allegorizing it, although allegory plays an important part in the writings of a great many Kabbalists. His essential mode of thinking is what I should like to call symbolical in the strictest sense.

This point requires a little further explanation. Allegory consists of an infinite network of meanings and correlations in which everything can become a representation of everything else, but all within the limits of language and expression. To that extent it is possible to speak of allegorical immanence. That which is expressed by and in the allegorical sign is in the first instance something which has its own meaningful context, but by becoming allegorical this something loses its own meaning and becomes the vehicle of something else. Indeed the allegory arises, as it were, from the gap which at this point opens between the form and its meaning. The two are no longer indissolubly welded together; the meaning is no longer restricted to that particular form, nor the form any longer to that particular meaningful content. What appears in the allegory, in short, is the infinity of meaning which attaches to every representation. The "Mysteries of the Torah" which I just mentioned were for the philosophers the natural subject of an allegorical interpretation which gave expression to a new form of the mediaeval mind as much as it implied a veiled criticism of the old.

Allegorization was also, as I have said, a constant preoccupation of the Kabbalists, and it was not on this ground that they differed from the philosophers; nor was it the main constituent of their faith and their method. We must look for this in the attention they gave to the symbol—a form of expression which radically transcends the sphere of allegory. In the mystical symbol a reality which in itself has, for us, no form or shape becomes transparent and, as it were, visible, through the medium of another reality which clothes its content with visible and expressible meaning, as for example the cross for the Christian. The thing which becomes a symbol retains its original form and its original content. It does not become, so to speak, an empty shell into which another content is poured; in itself, through its own existence, it makes another reality transparent which cannot appear in any other form. If allegory can be defined as the representation of an expressible something by another expressible something, the mystical symbol is an expressible representation of something which lies beyond the sphere of expression and communication, something which comes from a sphere whose face is, as it were, turned inward and away from us. A hidden and inexpressible reality finds its expression in the symbol. If the symbol is thus also a sign or representation it is nevertheless more than that.

For the Kabbalist, too, every existing thing is endlessly correlated with the whole of creation; for him, too, everything mirrors everything else. But beyond that he discovers something else which is not covered by the allegorical network: a reflection of the true transcendence. The symbol "signifies" nothing and communicates nothing, but makes something transparent which is beyond all expression. Where deeper insight into the structure of the allegory uncovers fresh layers of meaning, the symbol is intuitively understood all at once—or not at all. The symbol in which the life of the Creator and that of creation become one, is—to use Creuzer's words[15]—"a beam of light which, from the dark and abysmal depths of existence and cognition, falls into our eye and penetrates our whole being." It is a "momentary totality" which is perceived intuitively in a mystical *now*—the dimension of time proper to the symbol.

Of such symbols the world of Kabbalism is full, nay the whole world is to the Kabbalist such a *corpus symbolicum*. Out of the reality of creation, without the latter's existence being denied or annihilated, the inexpressible mystery of the Godhead becomes visible. In particular the religious acts commanded by the Torah, the *mitswoth*, are to the Kabbalist symbols in which a deeper and hidden sphere of reality becomes transparent. The infinite shines through the finite and makes it more and not less real. This brief summary gives us some idea of the profound difference between the philosophers' allegorical interpretation of religion and its symbolical understanding by the mystics. . . .

9

The difference becomes clear if we consider the attitude of philosophy and Kabbalah respectively to the two outstanding creative manifestations of Rabbinical Jewry: Halakhah and Aggadah, Law and Legend. It is a remarkable fact that the philosophers failed to establish a satisfactory and intimate relation to either. They showed themselves unable to make the spirit of Halakhah and Aggadah, both elements which expressed a fundamental urge of the Jewish soul, productive by transforming them into something new.

Let us begin with the Halakhah, the world of sacred law and, therefore, the most important factor in the actual life of ancient Jewry. Alexander Altmann, in raising the question: What is Jewish Theology? is quite justified in regarding as one of the decisive weaknesses of classical Jewish philosophy the fact that it ignored the problem presented by the Halakhah.[16] The whole world of religious law remained outside the orbit of philosophical inquiry, which means of course, too, that it was not subjected to philosophical criticism. It is not as if the philosopher denied or defied this world. He, too, lived in it and bowed to it, but it never became part and parcel of his work as a philosopher. It furnished no material for his thoughts. This fact, which is indeed undeniable, is particularly glaring in the case of thinkers like Maimonides and Saadia, in whom the converging streams meet. They fail to establish a true synthesis of the two elements, Halakhah and philosophy, a fact which has already been pointed out by Samuel David Luzzatto. Maimonides, for instance, begins the *Mishneh Torah*, his great codification of the Halakhah, with a philosophical chapter which has no relation whatever to the Halakhah itself. The synthesis of the spheres remains sterile, and the genius of the man whose spirit molded them into a semblance of union cannot obscure their intrinsic disparity.

*   *   *

Entirely different was the attitude of the Kabbalists. For them the Halakhah never became a province of thought in which they felt themselves strangers. Right from the beginning and with growing determination, they sought to master the world of the Halakhah as a whole and in every detail. From the outset, an ideology of the Halakhah is one of their aims. But in their interpretation of the religious commandments these are not represented as allegories of more or less profound ideas, or as pedagogical measures, but rather as the performance of a secret rite (or *mystery* in the sense in which the term was used by the Ancients).[17]

Whether one is appalled or not by this transformation of the Halakhah into a sacrament, a mystery rite, by this revival of myth in the very heart of Judaism, the fact remains that it was this transformation which raised the Halakhah to a position of incomparable importance for the mystic, and strengthened its hold over the people. Every *mitswah* became an event of cosmic importance, an act which had a bearing upon the dynamics of the universe. The religious Jew became a protagonist in the drama of the world; he manipulated the strings behind the scene. Or, to use a less extravagant simile, if the whole universe is an enormous complicated machine, then man is the machinist who keeps the wheels going by applying a few drops of oil here and there, and at the right time. The moral substance of man's action supplies this "oil," and his existence therefore becomes of extreme significance, since it unfolds on a background of cosmic infinitude.

The danger of theosophical schematism or, as S. R. Hirsch put it,[18] of "magical mechanism" is, of course, inherent in such an interpretation of the Torah, and it has more than once raised its head in the development of Kabbalism. There is a danger of imagining a magical mechanism to be operative in every sacramental action, and this imagination is attended by a decline in the essential spontaneity of religious action. But then this conflict is inseparable from any and every fulfillment of a religious command, since every prescribed duty is also conceived as assumed willingly and spontaneously. The antinomy is, in fact, inescapable, and can only be overcome by religious feeling, as it is strong and unbroken. When it begins to flag, the contradiction between command and freewill increases in proportion and eventually gathers sufficient force to become destructive.

By interpreting every religious act as a mystery where its meaning was clear for all to see or was expressly mentioned in the written or oral Law, a strong link was forged between Kabbalah and Halakhah, which appears to me to have been, in large part, responsible for the influence of Kabbalistic thought over the minds and hearts of successive generations.

A good deal of similarity to what I have said about the Halakhah is apparent in the attitude of the philosophers and mystics, respectively, to the Aggadah. Here, too, their ways part from the beginning. The Aggadah is a wonderful mirror of spontaneous religious life and feeling during the rabbinical period of Judaism. In particular, it represents a method of giving original and concrete expression to the deepest motive-powers of the religious Jew, a quality which helps to make it an excellent and genuine approach to the essential of our religion. However, it was just this quality which never ceased to baffle the philosophers of Judaism. Their treatment of the Aggadah, except where it pointed an ethical moral, is embarrassed and fumbling. They almost certainly regarded it as a stumbling block rather than as a precious heritage, let alone a key to a mystery. And thus it is not surprising that their allegorical interpretation of its meaning reflects an attitude which is not that of the Aggadah. Only too frequently their allegorizations are simply, as I have said, veiled criticism.

Here again the Kabbalists conceive their task differently, although it also involves a transformation of the subject's meaning. It would be too much to say that they leave the meaning of the Aggadah intact. What makes them differ from the philosophers is the fact that for them the Aggadah is not just a dead letter. They live in a world historically continuous with it, and they are able, therefore, to enhance it, though in the spirit of mysticism. Aggadic productivity has been a constant element of Kabbalistic literature, and only when the former disappears will the latter, too, be doomed to extinction. The whole of Aggadah can in a way be regarded as a popular mythology of the Jewish universe. Now, this mythical element, which is deeply rooted in the creative forms of Aggadic production, operates on different planes in the old Aggadah and in Kabbalism. The difference between the Aggadic production of the Kabbalah and that of the early Midrash can be easily gauged: in the Aggadah of the Kabbalists the events take place on a considerably wider stage, a stage with a cosmic horizon. Earth and heaven meet already in the ancient Aggadah, but now an even greater stress is laid on the heavenly element which comes more and more to the fore. All events assume gigantic dimensions and a wider significance; the steps of the heroes of the Kabbalistic Aggadah are directed by hidden forces from mysterious regions, while their doings react, at the same time, upon the upper world.

*   *   *

10

What has been said of the Halakhah and the Aggadah is also true of the liturgy, the world of prayer; the last of the three domains in which the religious spirit of post-biblical Judaism has found its classical expression. Here too the conclusion is inescapable that the philosophers had little of value to contribute. Of entire prayers written by philosophers only a few have been preserved, and these are often somewhat anaemic and half-hearted in their approach, especially where the authors were not, like Solomon ibn Gabirol and Jehudah Halevi, motivated in the last resort by mystical leanings. There is in many of them a curious lack of true religious feeling. The case is entirely different when we return to the Kabbalistic attitude toward prayer; there is perhaps no clearer sign that Kabbalism is essentially a religious and not a speculative phenomenon. The novelty of its attitude to prayer can be viewed under two aspects: the vast number of prayers whose authors were mystics themselves, and the mystical interpretation of the old traditional community prayers—the backbone of Jewish liturgy.

To begin with the former, it is hardly surprising that the new religious revelation, peculiar to the visionaries of the Kabbalah, for which there existed no liturgical equivalent in the older prayers, strove after some form of expression and had already inspired the earliest mystics to write their own prayers. The first prayers of a mystical character, which can be traced back to the Kabbalists of Provence and Catalonia,[19] are carried forward by a long and varied tradition to the prayers in which, about 1820, Nathan of Nemirov, the disciple of Rabbi Nahman of Brazlav, gave valid expression to the world of Hasidic Zaddikism.[20] This mystical prayer, which bears little outward resemblance to the older liturgy, and in particular of course to the classical form of communal prayer, flows from the new religious experience to which the Kabbalists were entitled to lay claim. Often these prayers bear the mark of directness and simplicity, and give plain expression to the common concern of every form of mysticism. But not infrequently their language is that of the symbol and their style reveals the secret pathos of magical conjuration. This has found a profound expression in the mystical interpretation of the phrase of Psalm cxxx 1 "Out of the depths I have called unto Thee"; which according to the Zohar, means not "I have called unto Thee from the depths [where I am]" but "from the depths [in which Thou art] I call Thee up."[21]

But side by side with these original productions of the Kabbalistic spirit we find from the earliest beginnings down to our time another tendency, that of mystical reinterpretation of the traditional community liturgy which transforms it into a symbol of the mystical way and the way of the world itself. This transformation, which has meant a great deal for the true life of the Kabbalist, has become crystallized in the conception of *Kawwanah*, i.e. mystical intention or concentration, which is its instrument.[22] In the words of the liturgy as in the old Aggadahs, the Kabbalists found a way to hidden worlds and the first causes of all existence. They developed a technique of meditation which enabled them to extract, as it were, the mystical prayer from the esoteric prayer of the community the text of which followed a fixed pattern. The fact that this form of prayer was conceived not as a free effusion of the soul but as a mystical act in the strict sense of the term, as an act, that is to say, which is directly linked with the inner cosmic process, invests this conception of *Kawwanah* with a solemnity which not only approaches but also passes the border of the magical. It is significant that of all the various forms of Kabbalistic thought and practice this meditative mysticism of prayer has alone survived and has taken the place of all the others. At the end of a long process of development in which Kabbalism, paradoxical though it may sound, has influenced the course of Jewish history, it has become again what it was in the beginning: the esoteric wisdom of small groups of men out of touch with life and without any influence on it.

11

As I have already said, mysticism represents, to a certain extent, a revival of mythical lore. This brings us to another and very serious point which I should like at least to mention. The Jewish mystic lives and acts in perpetual rebellion against a world with which he strives with all his zeal to be at peace. Conversely, this fact is responsible for the profound ambiguity of his outlook, and it also explains the apparent self-contradiction inherent in a great many Kabbalist symbols and images. The great symbols of the Kabbalah certainly spring from the depths of a creative and genuinely Jewish religious feeling, but at the same time they are invariably tinged by the world of mythology. . . . Failing this mythical element, the ancient Jewish mystics would have been unable to compress into language the substance of their inner experience. It was Gnosticism, one of the last great manifestations of mythology in religious thought, and definitely conceived in the struggle against Judaism as the conqueror of mythology, which lent figures of speech to the Jewish mystic.

The importance of this paradox can hardly be exaggerated; it must be kept in mind that the whole meaning and purpose of those ancient myths and metaphors whose remainders the editors of the book *Bahir*, and therefore the whole Kabbalah, inherited from the Gnostics,[23] was simply the subversion of a law which had, at one time, disturbed and broken the order of the mythical world. Thus through wide and scattered provinces of Kabbalism, the revenge of myth upon its conqueror is clear for all to see, and together with it we find an abundant display of contradictory symbols. It is characteristic of Kabbalistic theology in its systematical forms that it attempts to construct and to describe a world in which something of the mythical has again come to life, in terms of thought which exclude the mythical element. However, it is this contradiction which more than anything else explains the extraordinary success of Kabbalism in Jewish history.

Mystics and philosophers are, as it were, both aristocrats of thought; yet Kabbalism succeeded in establishing a connection between its own world and certain elemental impulses operative in every human mind. It did not turn its back upon the primitive side of life, that all important region where mortals are afraid of life and in fear of death, and derive scant wisdom from rational philosophy. Philosophy ignored these fears, out of whose substance man wove myths, and in turning its back upon the primitive side of man's existence, it paid a high price in losing touch with him altogether. For it is cold comfort to know that their troubles are but the workings of their own imagination.

The fact of the existence of evil in the world is the main touchstone of this difference between the philosophic and the Kabbalistic outlook. On the whole, the philosophers of Judaism treat the existence of evil as something meaningless in itself. Some of them have shown themselves only too proud of this negation of evil as one of the fundamentals of what they call rational Judaism. . . . To most Kabbalists, as true seal-bearers of the world of myth, the existence of evil is, at any rate, one of the most pressing problems, and one which keeps them continuously occupied with attempts to solve it. They have a strong sense of the reality of evil and the darker horror that is about everything living. They do not, like the philosophers, seek to evade its existence with the aid of a convenient formula; rather do they try to penetrate into its depth. And by doing so, they unwittingly establish a connection between their own strivings and the vital interests of popular belief—you may call it superstition—and all of those concrete manifestations of Jewish life in which these fears found their expression. It is a paradoxical fact that none other than the Kabbalists, through their interpretation of various religious acts and customs, have made it clear what they signified to the average believer, if not what they really meant from the beginning. Jewish folklore stands as a living proof of this contention, as has been shown by modern research in respect of some particularly well-known examples.[24]

It would be idle to deny that Kabbalistic thought lost much of its magnificence where it was forced to descend from the pinnacles of theoretical speculation to the plane of ordinary thinking and acting. The dangers which myth and magic present to the religious consciousness, including that of the mystic, are clearly shown in the development of Kabbalism. If one turns to the writings of great Kabbalists one seldom fails to be torn between alternate admiration and disgust. There is need for being quite clear about this in a time like ours, when the fashion of uncritical and superficial condemnation of even the most valuable elements of mysticism threatens to be replaced by an equally uncritical and obscurantist glorification of the Kabbalah. I have said before that Jewish philosophy had to pay a high price for its escape from the pressing questions of real life. But Kabbalism, too, has had to pay for its success. Philosophy came dangerously near to losing the living God; Kabbalism, which set out to preserve Him, to blaze a new and glorious trail to Him, encountered mythology on its way and was tempted to lose itself in its labyrinth.

12

One final observation should be made on the general character of Kabbalism as distinct from other, non-Jewish, forms of mysticism. Both historically and metaphysically it is a masculine doctrine, made for men and by men. The long history of Jewish mysticism shows no trace of feminine influence. There have been no women Kabbalists; Rabia of early Islamic mysticism, Mechthild of Magdeburg, Juliana of Norwich, Theresa de Jesus, and the many other feminine representatives of Christian mysticism have no counterparts in the history of Kabbalism.[25] The latter, therefore, lacks the element of feminine emotion which has played so large a part in the development of non-Jewish mysticism, but it also remained comparatively free from the dangers entailed by the tendency toward hysterical extravagance which followed in the wake of this influence.

This exclusively masculine character of Kabbalism was by no means the result of the social position of Jewish women or their exclusion from Talmudic learning. Scholasticism was as much exclusively a domain of men as Talmudism, and yet the social position of women in Islam and in Mediaeval Christianity did not prevent their playing a highly important part among the representatives—though not the theoreticians—of Islamic and Christian mysticism. It is hardly possible to conceive Catholic mysticism without them. This exclusive masculinity for which Kabbalism has paid a high price, appears rather to be connected with an inherent tendency to lay stress on the demonic nature of woman and the feminine element of the cosmos.

It is of the essence of Kabbalistic symbolism that woman represents not, as one might be tempted to expect, the quality of tenderness but that of stern judgment. This symbolism was unknown to the old mystics of the Merkabah period, and even to the Hasidim in Germany, but it dominates Kabbalistic literature from the very beginning and undoubtedly represents a constituent element of Kabbalistic theology. The demonic, according to the Kabbalists, is an offspring of the feminine sphere. This view does not entail a negation or repudiation of womanhood—after all the Kabbalistic conception of the Shekhinah has room for the, to orthodox Jewish thought, highly paradoxical idea of feminine element in God Himself—but does constitute a problem for the psychologist and the historian of religion alike. Mention has already been made of the dislike shown by the Kabbalists for any form of literary publicity in connection with mystical experience, and of their tendency toward objectivization of mystical vision. These traits, too, would appear to be connected with the masculine character of the movement, for the history of mystical literature shows that women were among the outstanding representatives of the tendency toward mystical autobiography and subjectivism in expressing religious experience.

If, finally, you were to ask me what kind of value I attach to Jewish mysticism, I would say this: Authoritative Jewish theology, both mediaeval and modern, in representatives like Saadia, Maimonides and Hermann Cohen, has taken upon itself the task of formulating an antithesis to pantheism and mystical theology, i.e. to prove them wrong. In this endeavor it has shown itself tireless. What is really required, however, is an understanding of these phenomena which yet do not lead away from monotheism; and once their significance is grasped, that elusive something in them which may be of value must be clearly defined. To have posed this problem is the historic achievement of Kabbalism. The varying answers it supplied to the question may be as inadequate as you like; I shall certainly be the last to deny that its representatives often lost their way and went over the edge of the precipice. But the fact remains that they faced a problem which others were more concerned to ignore and which is of the greatest importance for Jewish theology.

The particular forms of symbolic thought in which the fundamental attitude of the Kabbalah found its expression, may mean little or nothing to us (though even today we cannot escape, at times, from their powerful appeal). But the attempt to discover the hidden life beneath the external shapes of reality and to make visible that abyss in which the symbolic nature of all that exists reveals itself: this attempt is as important for us today as it was for those ancient mystics. For as long as nature and man are conceived as His creations, and that is the indispensable condition of highly developed religious life, the quest for the hidden life of the transcendent element in such creation will always form one of the most important preoccupations of the human mind.

NOTES*

1. Rufus Jones, *Studies in Mystical Religion* (1909), p. xv of the Introduction.
2. I owe this quotation from Aquinas' *Summa Theologiae* to Englebert Kreb's little book *Grundfragen der kirchlichen Mystik* (1921), p. 37.
3. Levi Isaac, the "Rabbi" of Berditchev, in his work *Quiddushat Levi: The Sanctification of Levi* at the end of section *Piqqudé: Duties*.
4. Molitor, *Philosophie der Geschichte*, Vol. II (1834), p. 56.
5. This term *'Omegē ha-eyn*: in the depths of (his) nothingness is a favorite metaphor of the thirteenth-century Kabbalists, cf. my remark in the Gaster Anniversary Volume (1936), p. 505.
6. Cf. Philo's *De Vita Contemplativa*, ed. Conybeare, p. 119.
7. Cf. Martin Buber's eloquent dissertation on this point in the introduction to his anthology, *Ekstatische Konfessionen* (1909).
8. Rabbi Kook's great work entitled *Oroth ha-Qodesh: Lights of Holiness*, the first two volumes of which were published in Jerusalem in 1938 from papers left by the author, is a veritable *theologia mystica* of Judaism equally distinguished by its originality and the richness of its author's mind. It is the last example of productive Kabbalistic thought of which I know.
9. A bibliography of Jewish mystical literature is still *a pium desiderium* of Kabbalistic research. My "Bibliographia Kabbalistica" (1927) lists only the scholarly literature on the subject of Jewish mysticism, not the texts themselves.
10. Charles Bennett, *A Philosophical Study of Mysticism* (1931), p. 31.
11. E. R. Dodds, in his commentary on Proclus' *Elements of Theology* (1933), p. 210.
12. This thesis is elaborated particularly by Meir ibn Gabbai in *Abodath ha-Qodesh: Service of Holiness*, Part III (written in 1531). The idea that the Kabbalah represented the lost tradition of the earliest state of mankind was familiar also to the "Christian Kabbalists" of the late fifteenth and sixteenth centuries, such as Pico della Mirandola and Johannes Reuchlin.
13. Quoted by Isaac of Acre, cf. *Tarbiz* 5 (1934) 318.
14. David ben Abrahan Ha-Laban, *Massorat ha-Berith: Traditions of the Covenant* (written about 1300), published in *Qobetz*, n.s. I (1936) 31. Exactly

---

* Scholem's Hebrew titles and phrases have been transliterated and translated for this edition by Dr. Benedict Viviano, O.P., of the Aquinas Institute of Theology, Dubuque, Iowa.

the same imagery is used by Dionysius the Pseudo-Areopagite (quoted by Inge, *The Philosophy of Plotinus*, Vol. II, p. 112)˙ and by John the Scot, called Erigena, in *De Devisione Naturae*, liber III, 19–23.

15. Friedrich Creuzer, *Symbolik und Mythologie der alten Voelker*, Second Edition, First Part (1816), p. 70.

16. Alexander Altmann, *Was ist juedische Theologie?* (Frankfurt-on-Main, 1933), p. 15.

17. Since the days of the Kabbalistic school of Gerona (about 1230), Kabbalistic writings are full of such mystical interpretations of *taame' ha-mitzwoth:* reasons for the commandments. Specifically Ezra ben Solomon and Jacob ben Sheshet (the true author of the *Sepher ha-emunah ve-ha-bittaḥon: The Book of Faith and Trust,* which has been ascribed to Nahmanides) were the first to treat at considerable length on such questions.

18. Samson Raphael Hirsch, *Neunzehn Breife ueber Judentum,* fourth edition (1911), p. 101.

19. To this category belong the prayers grouped under the title *Tephillat hayihud: Prayer of Union (with God)*, which are ascribed to Rabbi Nehuniah ben Hakanah and Rabban Gamaliel but the style of which is the enthusiastic one of the Kabbalistic Neoplatonists. Cf. also the great prayer of Jacob Hacohen of Segovia (Castile, about 1256), published by me in *Madui' ha-Yehadut,* Vol. II (1927), pp. 220–26.

20. *Liquthē tephilot le-nora tehiloth: Defects of Prayers before the Awesome One of Praises* printed first at Brazlav, 1822.

21. Zohar II, 63b and III, 69b; cf. also Joseph Gikatila, *Shaave-Oraḥ: Gates of the Path* (Offenbach, 1715), f. 40bff.

22. Cf. H. G. Enelow, "Kawwana, the Struggle for Inwardness in Judaism," in *Studies in Jewish Literature issued in honor of Professor K. Kohler* (1913), pp. 82–107, and my exposition "Der Begriff der Kawwana in der alten Kabbala," in *Monatsschrift für Geschichte und Wissenschaft des Judentums* 78 (1934) 492–518.

23. See my article "Buch Bahir" in *Encyclopedia Judaica,* Vol. III, cols. 969–79.

24. Cf. Jacob Lauterbach's studies: "The Ritual for the Kapparot-Ceremony," in *Jewish Studies in Memory of George A. Kohut* (1935), pp. 413–22; "Tashlik, A Study in Jewish Ceremonies," in *Hebrew Union College Annual* 11 (1936) 207–340.

25. The single case of a woman, Hannah Rachel, "the Maid of Ludomir," who became the spiritual leader, or Zaddik, of a Hasidic community (in the middle of the nineteenth century), constitutes no convincing evidence of the contrary. Cf. about her, S. A. Horodezky, *Leaders of Hasidism* (1928), pp. 113ff.

Theology and Mysticism in the Tradition of the Eastern Church

VLADIMIR LOSSKY

It is our intention, in the following essay, to study certain aspects of Eastern spirituality in relation to the fundamental themes of the Orthodox dogmatic tradition. In the present work, therefore, the term "mystical theology" denotes no more than a spirituality which expresses a doctrinal attitude.

In a certain sense all theology is mystical, inasmuch as it shows forth the divine mystery: the data of revelation. On the other hand, mysticism is frequently opposed to theology as a realm inaccessible to understanding, as an unutterable mystery, a hidden depth, to be lived rather than known; yielding itself to a specific experience which surpasses our faculties of understanding rather than to any perception of sense or of intelligence. If we adopted this latter conception unreservedly, resolutely opposing mysticism to theology, we should be led in the last resort to the thesis of Bergson who distinguishes, in his *Deux Sources*, the "static religion" of the Churches from the "dynamic religion" of the mystics; the former social and conservative in character, the latter personal and creative.

To what extent was Bergson justified in stating this opposition? This is a difficult question, all the more so since the two terms which Bergson opposes on the religious plane are rooted in the two poles of his philosophical vision of the universe—nature and the *élan vital*. Quite apart from this attitude of Bergson, however, one frequently hears expressed the view which would see in mysticism a realm reserved for the few, an exception to the common rule, a privilege vouchsafed to a few souls who enjoy direct experience of the truth, others, meanwhile, having to rest content with a more or less blind submission to dogmas imposed from without, as to a coercive authority. This opposition is sometimes carried to great lengths, especially if the historical reality be forced into a preconceived pattern. Thus the mystics are set up against the theologians, the contemplatives against the prelates, the saints against the

Church. It will suffice to recall many a passage of Harnack, Paul Sabatier's *Life of St. Francis,* and other works, most frequently by Protestant historians.

The Eastern tradition has never made a sharp distinction between mysticism and theology; between personal experience of the divine mysteries and the dogma affirmed by the Church. The following words spoken a century ago by a great Orthodox theologian, the Metropolitan Philaret of Moscow, expresses this attitude perfectly: "none of the mysteries of the most secret wisdom of God ought to appear alien or altogether transcendent to us, but in all humility we must apply our spirit to the contemplation of divine things."[1] To put it in another way, we must live the dogma expressing a revealed truth, which appears to us as an unfathomable mystery, in such a fashion that instead of assimilating the mystery to our mode of understanding, we should, on the contrary, look for a profound change, an inner transformation of spirit, enabling us to experience it mystically. Far from being mutually opposed, theology and mysticism support and complete each other. One is impossible without the other. If the mystical experience is a personal working out of the content of the common faith, theology is an expression for the profit of all of that which can be experienced by everyone. Outside the truth kept by the whole Church personal experience would be deprived of all certainty, of all objectivity. It would be a mingling of truth and of falsehood, of reality and illusion: "mysticism" in the bad sense of the word. On the other hand, the teaching of the Church would have no hold on souls if it did not in some degree express an inner experience of truth, granted in different measure to each one of the faithful. There is, therefore, no Christian mysticism without theology; but, above all, there is no theology without mysticism. It is not by chance that the tradition of the Eastern Church has reserved the name of "theologian" peculiarly for three sacred writers of whom the first is St. John, most "mystical" of the four Evangelists; the second St. Gregory Nazianzen, writer of contemplative poetry; and the third St. Symeon, called "the New Theologian," singer of union with God. Mysticism is accordingly treated in the present work as the perfecting and crown of all theology: as theology par excellence.

Unlike gnosticism,[2] in which knowledge for its own sake constitutes the aim of the gnostic, Christian theology is always in the last resort a means: a unity of knowledge subserving an end which transcends all knowledge. This ultimate end is union with God or deification, the θέωσις of the Greek Fathers. Thus, we are finally led to a conclusion which may seem paradoxical enough: that Christian theory should have an eminently practical significance; and that the more mystical it is, the more directly it aspires to the supreme end of union with God. All the

development of the dogmatic battles which the Church has waged down
the centuries appears to us, if we regard it from the purely spiritual
standpoint, as dominated by the constant preoccupation which the
Church has had to safeguard, at each moment of her history, for all
Christians, the possibility of attaining to the fullness of the mystical
union. So the Church struggled against the gnostics in defense of this
same idea of deification as the universal end: "God became man that
men might become gods." She affirmed, against the Arians, the dogma of
the consubstantial Trinity; for it is the Word, the Logos, who opens to us
the way to union with the Godhead; and if the incarnate Word has not
the same substance with the Father, if he be not truly God, our deification is impossible. The Church condemned the Nestorians that she might
overthrow the middle wall of partition, whereby, in the person of the
Christ himself, they would have separated God from man. She rose up
against the Apollinarians and Monophysites to show that, since the
fullness of true human nature has been assumed by the Word, it is our
whole humanity that must enter into union with God. She warred with
the Monothelites because, apart from the union of the two wills, divine
and human, there could be no attaining to deification—"God created
man by his will alone, but He cannot save him without the cooperation
of the human will." The Church emerged triumphant from the icono-
clastic controversy, affirming the possibility of the expression through a
material medium of the divine realities—symbol and pledge of our
sanctification. The main preoccupation, the issue at stake, in the questions which successively arise respecting the Holy Spirit, grace and the
Church herself—this last the dogmatic question of our own time—is always the possibility, the manner, or the means of our union with God.
All the history of Christian dogma unfolds itself about this mystical center, guarded by different weapons against its many and diverse assailants
in the course of successive ages.

The theological doctrines which have been elaborated in the course of
these struggles can be treated in the most direct relation to the vital end
—that of union with God—to the attainment of which they are subser-
vient. Thus they appear as the foundations of Christian spirituality. It is
this that we shall understand in speaking of "mystical theology"; not
mysticism properly so-called, the personal experiences of different
masters of the spiritual life. Such experiences, for that matter, more often
than not remain inaccessible to us: even though they may find verbal expression. What, in reality, can one say of the mystical experience of St.
Paul: "I knew a man in Christ above fourteen years ago (whether in the
body, I cannot tell; or whether out of the body, I cannot tell: God knoweth); such an one caught up to the third heaven. And I knew such a
man (whether in the body, or out of the body, I cannot tell: God know-

eth); how that he was caught up into paradise, and heard unspeakable words, which it is not lawful for man to utter."[3] To venture to pass any judgment upon the nature of this experience it would be necessary to understand it more fully than did St. Paul, who avows his ignorance: "I cannot tell: God knoweth." We deliberately leave on one side all question of mystical psychology. Nor is it theological doctrines as such that we propose to set forth in the present work, but only such elements of theology as are indispensable for the understanding of spirituality: the dogmas which constitute the foundation of mysticism. Here, then, is the first definition and limitation of our subject, which is the mystical theology of the Eastern Church.

The second limitation circumscribes our subject, so to say, in space. It is the Christian East, or, more precisely the Eastern Orthodox Church, which will form the field of our studies in mystical theology. We must recognize that this limitation is somewhat artificial. In reality, since the cleavage between East and West only dates from the middle of the eleventh century, all that is prior to this date constitutes a common and indivisible treasure for both parts of a divided Christendom. The Orthodox Church would not be what it is if it had not had St. Cyprian, St. Augustine and St. Gregory the Great. No more could the Roman Catholic Church do without St. Athanasius, St. Basil or St. Cyril of Alexandria. Thus, when one would speak of the mystical theology of the East or of the West, one takes one's stand within one of the two traditions which remained, down to a certain moment, two local traditions within the one Church, witnessing to a single Christian truth; but which subsequently part, the one from the other, and give rise to two different dogmatic attitudes, irreconcilable on several points. Can we judge the two traditions by taking our stand on neutral ground equally foreign to the one as to the other? That would be to judge Christianity from a non-Christian standpoint: in other words, to refuse in advance to understand anything whatever about the object of study. For objectivity in no wise consists in taking one's stand outside an object but, on the contrary, in considering one's object in itself and by itself. There are fields in which what is commonly styled "objectivity" is only indifference, and where indifference means incomprehension. In the present state of dogmatic difference between East and West it is essential, if one wishes to study the mystical theology of the Eastern Church, to choose between two possible standpoints. Either, to place oneself on western dogmatic ground and to examine the eastern tradition across that of the West—that is, by way of criticism—or else to present that tradition in the light of the dogmatic attitude of the Eastern Church. This latter course is for us the only possible one.

*   *   *

If we are often led to minimize the importance of the dogmatic question which determined all the subsequent development of the two traditions, this is by reason of a certain insensitivity toward dogma—which is considered as something external and abstract. It is said that it is spirituality which matters. The dogmatic difference is of no consequence. Yet spirituality and dogma, mysticism and theology, are inseparably linked in the life of the Church. As regards the Eastern Church, we have already remarked that she makes no sharp distinction between theology and mysticism, between the realm of the common faith and that of personal experience. Thus, if we would speak of mystical theology in the eastern tradition we cannot than consider it within the dogmatic setting of the Orthodox Church.

Before coming to grips with our subject it is necessary to say a few words about the Orthodox Church, little known down to the present day in the West. Father Congar's book *Divided Christendom,* though very remarkable in many respects, remains, despite all his striving after objectivity, subject, in those pages which he devotes to the Orthodox Church, to certain preconceived notions. "Where the West," he says, "on the basis at once developed and narrow of Augustinian ideology, claimed for the Church independence in life and organization, and thus laid down the lines of a very definite ecclesiology, the East settled down in practice, and to some extent in theory, to a principle of unity which was political, non-religious, and not truly universal."[4] To Father Congar, as to the majority of Catholic and Protestant writers who have expressed themselves on this subject, Orthodoxy presents itself under the form of a federation of national churches, having as its basis a political principle—the state-church. One can venture upon such generalizations as these only by ignoring both the canonical groundwork and the history of the Eastern Church. The view which would base the unity of a local church on a political, racial or cultural principle is considered by the Orthodox Church as a heresy, specially known by the name of *philetism.*[5] It is the ecclesiastical territory, the area sanctified by more or less ancient Christian tradition which forms the basis of a metropolitan province, administered by an archbishop or metropolitan, with the bishops from every diocese coming together from time to time in synod. If metropolitan provinces are grouped together to form local churches under the jurisdiction of a bishop who often bears the title of patriarch, it is still the community of local tradition and of historical destiny (as well as convenience in calling together a council from many provinces), which determines the formation of these large circles of jurisdiction, the territories of which do not necessarily correspond to the political boundaries of a state.[6] The Patriarch of Constantinople enjoys a certain primacy of honor, arbitrating from time to time in disputes, but without exercising a jurisdiction over the whole body of the oecumenical Church. The local churches of the East had more or less the same attitude toward the apostolic patriarchate of Rome—the first see of the Church before the separation, and symbol of her unity. Orthodoxy recognizes no visible head of the Church. The unity of the Church expresses itself through the communion of the heads of local churches among themselves, by the agreement of all the churches in regard to a local council—which thus acquires a universal import; finally, in exceptional cases, it may manifest itself through a general council.[7] The catholicity of the Church, far from being the privilege of any one see or specific center, is realized rather in the richness and multiplicity of the local traditions which bear witness unanimously to a single Truth: to that which is preserved always, everywhere and by all. Since the Church is catholic in all her parts, each one of her members—not only the clergy but also each layman—is called to confess and to defend the truth of tradition; opposing even the bishops should they fall into heresy. A Christian who has received the gift of the Holy Spirit in the sacrament of the Holy Chrism must have a full awareness of his faith: he is always responsible for the Church. Hence the restless and sometimes agitated character of the ecclesiastical life of Byzantium, of Russia and of other countries in the Orthodox world. This, however, is the price paid for a religious vitality, an intensity of spiritual life which penetrates the whole mass of believers, united in the awareness that they form a single body with the hierarchy of the Church. From this, too, comes the unconquerable energy which enables Orthodoxy to go through all trials, all cataclysms and upheavals, adapting itself continually to the new historical reality and showing itself stronger than outward circumstances. The persecutions of the faithful in Russia, the systematic fury of which has not been able to destroy the Church, are the best witness to a power which is not of this world.

The Orthodox Church, though commonly referred to as *Eastern*, considers herself nonetheless the universal Church; and this is true in the sense that she is not limited by any particular type of culture, by the legacy of any one civilization (Hellenistic or otherwise), or by strictly Eastern cultural forms. Moreover, *eastern* can mean so many things: from the cultural point of view the East is less homogeneous than the West. What have Hellenism and Russian culture in common, notwithstanding the Byzantine origins of Christianity in Russia? Orthodoxy has been the leaven in too many different cultures to be itself considered a cultural form of Eastern Christianity. The forms are different; the faith is one. The Orthodox. It is for this reason that her missionary work has been able to expand so prodigiously: witness the conversion of Russia to

Christianity during the tenth and eleventh centuries, and, at a later date, the preaching of the Gospel across the whole of Asia. Toward the end of the eighteenth century Orthodox missions reached the Aleutian Islands and Alaska, passed thence to North America, creating new dioceses of the Russian Church beyond the confines of Russia, spreading to China and Japan.[8] The anthropological and cultural variations which one encounters from Greece to the remotest parts of Asia, and from Egypt to the Arctic, do not destroy the homogeneous character of this kinship of spirituality, very different from that of the Christian West.

There is a great richness of forms of the spiritual life to be found within the bounds of Orthodoxy, but monasticism remains the most classical of all. Unlike Western monasticism, however, that of the East does not include a multiplicity of different orders. This fact is explained by the conception of the monastic life, the aim of which can only be union with God in a complete renunciation of the life of this present world. If the secular clergy (married priests and deacons) or confraternities of laymen may occupy themselves with social work, or devote themselves to other outward activities, it is otherwise with the monks. The latter take the habit above all in order to apply themselves to prayer, to the interior life, in cloister or hermitage. Between a monastery of the common life and the solitude of an anchorite who carries on the traditions of the Desert Fathers there are many intermediate types of monastic institution. One could say broadly that Eastern monasticism was exclusively contemplative, if the distinction between the two ways, active and contemplative, had in the East the same meaning as in the West. In fact, for an Eastern monk the two ways are inseparable. The one cannot be exercised without the other, for the ascetic rule and the school of interior prayer receive the name of spiritual *activity*. If the monks occupy themselves from time to time with physical labors, it is above all with an ascetic end in view: the sooner to overcome their rebel nature, as well as to avoid idleness, enemy of the spiritual life. To attain to union with God, in the measure in which it is realizable here on earth, requires continual effort, or, more precisely, an unceasing vigil that the integrity of the inward man, "the union of heart and spirit" (to use an expression of Orthodox asceticism), withstand all the assaults of the enemy: every irrational movement of our fallen nature. Human nature must undergo a change; it must be more and more transfigured by grace in the way of sanctification, which has a range which is not only spiritual but also bodily—and hence cosmic. The spiritual work of a monk living in community or a hermit withdrawn from the world retains all its worth for the entire universe even though it remain hidden from the sight of all. This is why monastic institutions have always enjoyed great veneration in every country of the Orthodox world.

The part played by the great centers of spirituality was very considerable not only in ecclesiastical life but also in the realm of culture and politics. The monasteries of Mount Sinai and of Studion, near Constantinople, the monastic republic of Mount Athos, bringing together religious of all nations (there were Latin monks there prior to the schism), other great centers beyond the bounds of the Empire such as the monastery of Tirnovo, in Bulgaria, and the great *lavras* of Russia—Petcheri at Kiev and the Holy Trinity near Moscow—have all been strongholds of Orthodoxy, schools of the spiritual life, whose religious and moral influence was of the first importance in the molding of peoples newly converted to Christianity.[9] But if the monastic ideal had so great an influence upon souls, it was, nevertheless, not the only type of the spiritual life which the Church offered to the faithful. The way of union with God may be pursued outside the cloister, amid all the circumstances of human life. The outward forms may change, the monasteries may disappear, as in our own day they disappeared for a time in Russia, but the spiritual life goes on with the same intensity, finding new modes of expression.

Eastern hagiography, which is extremely rich, shows beside the holy monks many examples of spiritual perfection acquired by simple laymen and married people living in the world. It knows also strange and unwonted paths to sanctification: that, for instance, of the "fools in Christ," committing extravagant acts that their spiritual gifts might remain hidden from the eyes of those about them under the hideous aspect of madness; or, rather, that they might be freed from the ties of this world in their most intimate and most spiritually troublesome expression, that of our social "ego."[10] Union with God sometimes manifests itself through charismatic gifts as, for example, in that of spiritual direction exercised by the *starets* or elder. These latter are most frequently monks who, having passed many years of their life in prayer and secluded from all contact with the world, toward the end of their life throw open to all comers the door of their cell. They possess the gift of being able to penetrate to the unfathomable depths of the human conscience, of revealing sins and inner difficulties which normally remain unknown to us, of raising up overburdened souls, and of directing men not only in their spiritual course but also in all the vicissitudes of their life in the world.[11]

The individual experiences of the greatest mystics of the Orthodox Church more often than not remain unknown to us. Apart from a few rare exceptions the spiritual literature of the Christian East possesses scarcely any autobiographical account dealing with the interior life, such as those of Angela of Foligno and Henry Suso, or the *Histoire d'une âme* of St. Thérèse of Lisieux. The way of mystical union is nearly always a secret between God and the soul concerned, which is never confided to others unless, it may be, to a confessor or to a few disciples. What is published abroad is the fruit of this union: wisdom, understanding of the divine mysteries, expressing itself in theological or moral teaching or in advice for the edification of one's brethren. As to the inward and personal aspect of the mystical experience, it remains hidden from the eyes of all. It must be recognized that it was only at a comparatively late period, toward the thirteenth century in fact, that mystical individualism made its appearance in Western literature. St. Bernard speaks directly of his personal experience only very seldom—on but a single occasion in the *Sermons on the Song of Songs*—and then with a sort of reluctance, after the example of St. Paul. It was necessary that a certain cleavage should occur between personal experience and the common faith, between the life of the individual and the life of the Church, that spirituality and dogma, mysticism and theology, could become two distinct spheres; and that souls unable to find adequate nourishment in the theological *summae* should turn to search greedily in the accounts of individual mystical experience in order to reinvigorate themselves in an atmosphere of spirituality. Mystical individualism has remained alien to the spirituality of the Eastern Church.

Father Congar is right when he says: "We have become *different men*. We have the same God but before him we are different men, unable to agree as to the nature of our relationship with him."[12] But in order to estimate accurately this spiritual divergency it would be necessary to examine it in its most perfect manifestations: in the different types of sanctity in East and West since the schism. We should then be able to give an account of the close link which always exists between the dogma which the Church confesses and the spiritual fruit which it bears. For the inner experience of the Christian develops within the circle delineated by the teaching of the Church: within the dogmatic framework which molds his person. If even now a political doctrine professed by the members of a party can so fashion their mentality as to produce a type of man distinguishable from other men by certain moral or psychical marks, a fortiori religious dogma succeeds in transforming the very souls of those who confess it. They are men different from other men, from those who have been formed by another dogmatic conception. It is never possible to understand a spirituality if one does not take into account the dogma in which it is rooted. We must accept facts as they are, and not seek to explain the difference between Eastern and Western spirituality on racial or cultural grounds when a greater issue, a dogmatic issue, is at stake. Neither may we say that the questions of the procession of the Holy Spirit or of the nature of grace have no great importance in the scheme of Christian doctrine, which remains more or less identical among Roman Catholics and among Orthodox. In dogmas so fundamental as these it is this "more or less" which is important, for it imparts a different emphasis to all doctrine, presents it in another light; in other words, gives place to another spirituality.

NOTES

1. *Sermons and Addresses of the Metropolitan Philaret,* Moscow, 1844, Part II, p. 87 (in Russian).
2. See the article by M.H.-Ch. Puech: "Où en est le problème du gnosticisme?," *Revue de l'Université de Bruxelles,* 1934, Nos. 2 and 3.
3. II Cor. 12, 2–4.
4. M. J. Congar, O.P., *Chrétiens désunis. Principes d'un "oecuménisme" catholique,* Paris, 1937, p. 15. English translation by M. A. Bousfield, *Divided Christendom,* London, 1939, p. 13.
5. Synod of Constantinople, 1872, v. Mansi, *Collectio Concilliorum,* Vol. 45, 417–546. See also the article by M. Zyzykine: 'L'Eglise orthodoxe et la nation,' *Irénikon,* 1936, pp. 265–77.
6. Thus the Patriarchate of Moscow includes the dioceses of North America and that of Tokyo beyond the frontiers of Russia. By contrast, the Catholicate of Georgia, though within the bounds of the U.S.S.R., does not form part of the Russian Church. The territories of the Patriarchates of Constantinople, Alexandria, Antioch and Jerusalem are politically dependent on many different powers.
7. The name *Oecumenical Council* given in the East to the first seven general synods corresponds to a reality of a purely historical character. These are the councils of the "oecumenical" territories, that is to say of the Byzantine Empire which extended (theoretically, at least) throughout the Christian world. In later epochs the Orthodox Church has known general councils which, without bearing the title of "oecumenical" were neither smaller nor less important.
8. See S. Bolshakoff, *The Foreign Missions of the Russian Orthodox Church,* London, 1943.
9. There is some useful information about Eastern monasticism in the little book by Fr. N. F. Robinson, S.S.J.E., entitled *Monasticism in the Orthodox Churches* (London, 1916). For Mount Athos, see Hasluck: *Athos and Its Monasteries* (London, 1924) and F. Spunda, *Der heilige Berg Athos* (Leipzig, 1928). For the monastic life in Russia, see the following studies of Igor Smolitsch, "Studien zum Klosterwesen Russlands," in *Kyrios,* No. 2 (1937) 95–112, and No. 1 (1939) 29–38, and above all, the same author's "Das altrussische Mönchtum" (XI–XVI Jhr.), Würzburg, 1940, in *Das östliche Christentum,* XI, and *Russischer Mönchtum,* Würzburg, 1953.
10. See on this subject E. Benz, "Heilige Narrheit," in *Kyrios* Nos. 1 and 2 (1938) 1–55; Mme. Behr-Sigel, "Les Fous pour le Christ et la sainteté laïque dans l'ancienne Russie," in *Irénikon* 15 (1939) 554–65; Gamayoun, "Etudes sur la spiritualité populaire russe: les fous pour le Christ," in *Russie et Chrétienté,* 1938–39, I, 57–77.
11. Smolitsch, *Leben und Lehre der Starzen,* Vienna, 1936.
12. Congar, n. 4, p. 47.

Sūfīs:
The Mystics of Islam

REYNOLD A. NICHOLSON

The title of this book (*The Mystics of Islam*) sufficiently explains why it is included in a Series "exemplifying the adventures and labors of individual seekers or groups of seekers in quest of reality." Sūfism, the religious philosophy of Islam, is described in the oldest extant definition as "the apprehension of divine realities," and Mohammedan mystics are fond of calling themselves *Ahl al-Haqq*, "the followers of the real."[1] In attempting to set forth their central doctrines from this point of view, I shall draw to some extent on materials which I have collected during the last twenty years for a general history of Islamic mysticism—a subject so vast and many-sided that several large volumes would be required to do it anything like justice. Here I can only sketch in broad outline certain principles, methods, and characteristic features of the inner life as it has been lived by Moslems of every class and condition from the eighth century of our era to the present day. Difficult are the paths which they threaded, dark and bewildering the pathless heights beyond; but even if we may not hope to accompany the travelers to their journey's end, any information that we have gathered concerning their religious environment and spiritual history will help us to understand the strange experiences of which they write.

In the first place, therefore, I propose to offer a few remarks on the origin and historical development of Sūfism, its relation to Islam, and its general character. Not only are these matters interesting to the student of comparative religion; some knowledge of them is indispensable to any serious student of Sūfism itself. It may be said, truly enough, that all mystical experiences ultimately meet in a single point; but that point assumes widely different aspects according to the mystic's religion, race, and temperament, while the converging lines of approach admit of almost infinite variety. Though all the great types of mysticism have something in common, each is marked by peculiar characteristics resulting from the circumstances in which it arose and flourished. Just as the Christian type cannot be understood without reference to Christianity, so the Mohammedan type must be viewed in connection with the outward and inward development of Islam.

The word "mystic," which has passed from Greek religion into European literature, is represented in Arabic, Persian, and Turkish, the three chief languages of Islam, by "Sūfī." The terms, however, are not precisely synonymous, for "Sūfī" has a specific religious connotation, and is restricted by usage to those mystics who profess Mohammedan faith. And the Arabic word, although in course of time it appropriated the high significance of the Greek—lips sealed by holy mysteries, eyes closed in visionary rapture—bore a humbler meaning when it first gained currency (about A.D. 800). Until recently its derivation was in dispute. Most Sūfīs, flying in the face of etymology, have derived it from the Arabic root which conveys the notion of "purity"; this would make "Sūfī" mean "one who is pure in heart" or "one of the elect." Some European scholars identified it with σοφός in the sense of "theophist." But Nöldeke, in an article written twenty years ago, showed conclusively that the name was derived from *sūf* (wool), and was originally applied to those Moslem ascetics who, in imitation of Christian hermits, clad themselves in coarse woolen garb as a sign of penitence and renunciation of worldly vanities.

The earliest Sūfīs were, in fact, ascetics and quietists rather than mystics. An overwhelming consciousness of sin, combined with a dread—which is hard for us to realize—of Judgment Day and the torments of Hell-fire, so vividly painted in the Koran, drove them to seek salvation in flight from the world. On the other hand, the Koran warned them that salvation depended entirely on the inscrutable will of Allah, who guides aright the good and leads astray the wicked. Their fate was inscribed on the eternal tables of His providence; nothing could alter it. Only this was sure, that if they were destined to be saved by fasting and praying and pious works—then they would be saved. Such a belief ends naturally in quietism, complete and unquestioning submission to the divine will, an attitude characteristic of Sūfism in its oldest form. The mainspring of Moslem religious life during the eighth century was fear—fear of God, fear of Hell, fear of death, fear of sin—but the opposite motive had already begun to make its influence felt, and produced in the saintly woman Rābiʻa at least one conspicuous example of truly mystical self-abandonment.

So far, there was no great difference between Sūfī and the orthodox Mohammedan zealot, except that the Sūfīs attached extraordinary importance to certain Koranic doctrines, and developed them at the expense of others which many Moslems might consider equally essential. It must also be allowed that the ascetic movement was inspired by Christian ideal, and contrasted sharply with the active and pleasure-seeking spirit of Islam. In a famous sentence the Prophet denounced monkish austerities and bade his people devote themselves to the holy war against unbelievers; and he gave, as is well known, the most convincing testimony in favor of marriage. Although his condemnation of celibacy did not remain without effect, the conquest of Persia, Syria, and Egypt by his successor brought the Moslems into contact with ideas which profoundly modified their outlook on life and religion. European readers of the Koran cannot fail to be struck by its author's vacillation and inconsistency in dealing with the greatest problems. He himself was not aware of these contradictions, nor were they a stumbling block to his devout followers, whose simple faith accepted the Koran as the Word of God. But the rift was there, and soon produced far-reaching results.

Hence arose the Murjite, who set faith above works and emphasized the divine love and goodness; the Qadarites who affirmed, and the Jabarites who denied, that men are responsible for their actions; the Mu'tazilites, who built a theology on the basis of reason, rejecting the qualities of Allah as incompatible with His unity, and predestinarianism as contrary to His justice; and finally the Ash'arites, the scholastic theologians of Islam, who formulated the rigid metaphysical and doctrinal system that underlies the creed of orthodox Mohammedans at the present time. All these speculations, influenced as they were by Greek theology and philosophy, reacted powerfully upon Sūfism. Early in the third century of the Hegira—the ninth after Christ—we find manifest signs of new leaven stirring within it. Not that the Sūfīs ceased to mortify the flesh and take their pride in their poverty, but they now began to regard asceticism as only the first stage of a long journey, the preliminary training for a larger spiritual life than the mere ascetic is able to conceive. The nature of the change may be illustrated by quoting a few sentences which have come down to us from the mystics of this period.

Love is not to be learned from men: it is one of God's gifts and comes of his grace.

None refrains from the lusts of this world save him in whose heart there is a light that keeps him always busied with the next world.

When the gnostic's spiritual eye is opened, his bodily eye is shut: he sees nothing but God.

If gnosis were to take visible shape all who looked thereon would die at the sight of its beauty and loveliness and goodness and grace, and every brightness would become dark beside the splendor thereof.[2]

Gnosis is nearer to silence than speech.

When the heart weeps it is because it has lost, the spirit laughs because it has found.

Nothing sees God and dies, even as nothing sees God and lives, because His life is everlasting: whoever sees it is thereby made everlasting.

O God, I never listen to the cry of animals or to the quivering of trees or the murmuring of water or the warbling of birds or the rustling wind or to the crashing thunder without feeling them to be evidence of Thy unity and a proof that there is nothing like unto Thee.

O my God, I invoke Thee in public as lords are invoked, but in private as loved ones are invoked. Publicly I say, "O my God!" but privately I say, "O my Beloved!"

These ideas—Light, Knowledge, and Love—form, as it were, the keynotes of the new Sūfism . . . Ultimately they rest upon a pantheistic faith which deposed the One transcendent God of Islam and worshiped in His stead One Real Being who dwells and works everywhere, and whose throne is not less, but more, in the human heart than in the heaven of heavens. Before going further, it will be convenient to answer a question which the reader may have asked himself—Whence did the Moslems of the ninth century derive this doctrine?

Modern research has proved that the origin of Sūfism cannot be traced back to a single definite cause, and has thereby discredited the sweeping generalizations which represented it, for instance as a reaction of the Aryan mind against a conquering Semitic religion, and as the product, essentially, of Indian or Persian thought. Statements of this kind, even when they are partially true, ignore the principle that in order to establish an historical connection between A and B, it is not enough to bring forward evidence of their likeness to one another, without showing at the same time (1) that the actual relation of B to A was such as to render the assumed filiation possible, and (2) that the possible hypothesis fits in with all the ascertained and relevant facts. Now, the theories which I have mentioned do not satisfy these conditions. If Sūfism was nothing but a revolt of the Aryan spirit, how are we to explain the undoubted fact that some of the leading pioneers of Mohammedan mysticism were natives of Syria and Egypt, and Arabs by race? Similarly, the advocates of a Buddhistic or Vedāntic origin forget that the main current of Indian influence upon Islamic civilization belongs to a later epoch, whereas Moslem theology, philosophy and science put forth their first luxuriant shoots on a soil that was saturated with Hellenistic culture. The truth is that Sūfism is a complex thing, and therefore no simple answer can be given to the question of how it originated. We shall have gone far, however, toward answering that quesion when we have distinguished the various movements and forces which molded Sūfism, and determined what direction it should take in the early stages of its growth.

Let us first consider the most important external, i.e. non-Islamic, influences.

I. CHRISTIANITY

It is obvious that the ascetic and quietistic tendencies to which I have referred were in harmony with Christian theory and drew nourishment therefrom. Many Gospel texts and apocryphal sayings of Jesus are cited in the oldest Sūfī biographies, and the Christian anchorite (*rāhib*) often appears in the rôle of a teacher giving instruction and advice to wandering Moslem ascetics. We have seen that the woolen dress, from which the name "Sūfī" is derived, is of Christian origin: vows of silence, litanies (*dhikr*), and other ascetic practices may be traced to the same source. As regards the doctrine of divine love, the following extracts speak for themselves:

Jesus passed by three men. Their bodies were lean and their faces pale. He asked them, saying, "What hath brought you to this plight?" They answered, "Fear of the Fire." Jesus said, "Ye fear a thing created, and it behoves God that He should save those who fear." Then he left them and passed by three others, whose face were paler and their bodies leaner, and asked them, saying, "What hath brought you to this plight?" They answered, "Longing for Paradise." He said, "Ye desire a thing created, and it behoves God that He should give you that which ye hope for." Then he went on and passed by three others of exceeding paleness and leanness, so that their faces were as mirrors of light, and he said, "What hath brought you to this?" They answered, "Our love of God." Jesus said, "Ye are the nearest to Him, ye are the nearest to Him."

The Syrian mystic, Aḥmad al-Hawārī, once asked a Christian hermit:

"What is the strongest command that ye find in your Scriptures?" The hermit replied: "We find none stronger than this: 'Love thy Creator with all thy power and might.'"

Another hermit was asked by some Moslem ascetics:

"When is a man most persevering in devotion?" "When love takes possession of his heart," was the reply; "for then he hath no joy or pleasure but in continual devotion."

The influence of Christianity through its hermits, monks, and heretical sects (e.g. the Messalians or Euchitae) was twofold: ascetic and mystical. Oriental Christian mysticism, however, contained a pagan element: it had long ago absorbed the ideas and adopted the language of Plotinus and the Neoplatonic school.

II. NEOPLATONISM

Aristotle, not Plato, is the dominant figure in Moslem philosophy, and few Mohammedans are familiar with the name of Plotinus, who was more commonly called "The Greek Master" (*al-Sheykh al-Yaunānī*). But since the Arabs gained their first knowledge of Aristotle from his Neoplatonist commentators, the system with which they became imbued was that of Porphyry and Prolus. Thus the so-called *Theology of Aristotle*, of which an Arabic version appeared in the ninth century, is actually a manual of Neoplatonism.

Another work of this school deserves particular notice: I mean the writings falsely attributed to Dionysius the Areopagite, the convert of St. Paul. The Pseudo-Dionysius—he may have been a Syrian monk—names as his teacher a certain Hierotheus, whom Frothingham has identified with Stephen Bar Sudaili, a prominent Syrian gnostic and a contemporary of Jacob of Sarūj (A.D. 451–521). Dionysius quotes some fragments of erotic hymns by this Stephen, and a complete work, the *Book of Hierotheus on the Hidden Mysteries of the Divinity*, has come down to us in a unique manuscript which is now in the British Museum. The Dionysian writings, turned into Latin by John Scotus Erigena, founded medieval Christian mysticism in western Europe. Their influence in the East was hardly less vital. They were translated from Greek into Syriac almost immediately on their appearance, and their doctrine was vigorously propagated by commentaries in the same tongue. "About A.D. 850 Dionysius was known from the Tigris to the Atlantic."

Besides literary tradition, there were other channels by which the doctrines of emanation, illumination, gnosis, and ecstasy were transmitted, but enough has been said to convince the reader that the Greek mystical ideas were in the air and easily accessible to the Moslem inhabitants of western Asia and Egypt, where Sūfī theosophy first took shape. One of those who bore the chief part in its development, Dhu 'l-Nūn the Egyptian, is described as a philosopher and alchemist—in other words, a student of Hellenistic science. When it is added that much of his speculation agrees with what we find, for example, in the writings of Dionysius, we are drawn to the conclusion (which, as I have pointed out, is highly probable on general grounds) that Neoplatonism poured into Islam a large tincture of the same mystical element in which Christianity was already steeped.

III. GNOSTICISM[3]

Though little direct evidence is available, the conspicuous place occupied by the theory of gnosis in early Sūfī speculation suggests contact with Christian Gnosticism, and it is worth noting that the parents of Ma'rūf al-Karkhī, whose definition of Sūfism as "the apprehension of divine realities" was quoted on the first page of this Introduction, are said to have been Sābians i.e. Mandaeans, dwelling in the Babylonian fenland between Basra and Wāsit. Other Moslem saints had learned "the mystery of the Great Name." It was communicated to Ibrāhīm Adham by a man whom he met while traveling in the desert, and as soon as he pronounced it he saw the prophet Khadir (Elias). The ancient Sūfīs borrowed from the Manicheans the term *siddīq*, which they apply to their own spiritual adepts, and a later school, returning to the dualism of Mānī, held the view that the diversity of phenomena arises from the admixture of light and darkness.

The ideal of human action is freedom from taint of darkness; and the freedom of light from darkness means the self-conscious of light as light.[4]

The following version of the doctrine of the seventy thousand veils as explained by a modern Rifā'ī dervish shows clear traces of Gnosticism and is so interesting that I cannot refrain from quoting it here:

Seventy Thousand Veils separate Allah, the One Reality, from the world of matter and sense. And every soul passes through these seventy thousand. The inner half of these veils are light: the outer half, veils of darkness. For every one of the veils of light passed through, in this journey toward birth, the soul puts *off* a divine quality: and for every one of the dark veils, it puts *on* an earthly quality. Thus the child is born *weeping*, for the soul knows its separation from Allah, the One Reality. And when the child cries in its sleep, it is because the soul remembers something of what it has lost. Otherwise, the passage through the veils has brought with it forgetfulness (*nisyān*): and for this reason man is called *insān*. He is now, as it were, in prison in his body, separated by these thick curtains from Allah.

But the whole purpose of Sūfism, the Way of the dervish, is to give him an escape from this prison, an apocalypse of the Seventy Thousand Veils, a recovery of the original unity with The One, *while still in this body*. The body is not to be put off; it is to be refined and made spiritual—a help and not a hindrance to the spirit. It is like a metal that has to be refined by fire and transmuted. And the sheikh tells the aspirant that he has the secret of this transmutation. "We shall throw you into the fire of Spiritual Passion," he says, "and you will emerge refined."[5]

IV. BUDDHISM

Before the Mohammedan conquest of India in the eleventh century, the teaching of Buddha exerted considerable influence in eastern Persia and Transoxania. We hear of flourishing Buddhist monasteries in Balkh, the metropolis of ancient Bactria, a city famous for the number of Sūfīs who reside in it. Professor Goldziher has called attention to the significant circumstance that the Sūfī ascetic, Ibrāhīm ibn Adham, appears in Moslem legend as a prince of Balkh who abandoned his throne and became a wandering dervish—the story of a Buddha over again. The Sūfīs learned the use of rosaries from Buddhist monks, and, without entering into details, it may be safely asserted that the method of Sūfism, so far as it is one of ethical self-culture, ascetic meditation, and intellectual abstraction, owes a good deal to Buddhism. But the features which the two systems have in common only accentuate the fundamental difference between them. In spirit they are poles apart. The Buddhist moralizes himself, the Sūfī becomes moral only through knowing and loving God.

The Sūfī conception of the passing-away (*fanā*) of individual self in Universal Being is certainly, I think, of Indian origin. Its first great exponent was the Persian mystic, Bāyazīd of Bistam, who may have received it from his teacher, Abū 'Alī of Sinde (Scinde). Here are some of his sayings:

> Creatures are subject to changing "states," but the Gnostic has no "state," because his vestiges are effaced and his essence annihilated by the essence of another, and his traces are lost in another's traces.

> Thirty years the high God was my mirror, now I am my own mirror, i.e. according to the explanation given by his biographer, "that which I was I am no more, for 'I' and 'God' is a denial of the unity of God. Since I am no more, the high God is His own mirror."

> I went from God to God, until they cried from me in me, "O Thou I!"

This, it will be observed, is not Buddhism, but the pantheism of the Vedānta. We cannot identify *fanā* with Nirvāna unconditionally. Both terms imply the passing away of individuality, but while the Nirvāna is purely negative, *fanā* is accompanied by *baqā*, everlasting life in God. The rapture of the Sūfī who has lost himself in ecstatic contemplation of the divine beauty is entirely opposed to the passionless intellectual serenity of the Arahat. I emphasize this contrast because, in my opinion, the influence of Buddhism on Mohammedan thought has been exaggerated. Much is attributed to Buddhism that is Indian rather than specifically Buddhistic: the *fanā* theory of the Sūfīs is a case in point. Ordinary Moslems held the followers of Buddha in abhorrence, regarding them as idolaters, and were not likely to seek personal intercourse with them. On the other hand, for nearly a thousand years before the Mohammedan conquest, Buddhism had been powerful in Bactria and eastern Persia generally; it must, therefore, have affected the development of Sūfīsm in these regions.

While *fanā* in its pantheistic form is radically different from Nirvāna, the terms coincide so closely in other ways that we cannot regard them as being altogether unconnected. *Fanā* has an ethical aspect: it involves the extinction of all passions and desires. The passing-away of evil qualities and of the evil actions which they produce is said to be brought about by the continuance of the corresponding good qualities and actions. Compare this with the definition of Nirvāna given by Professor Rhys Davids:

> The extinction of that sinful, grasping condition of mind and heart, which would otherwise, according to the great mystery of Karma, be the cause of renewed individual existence. That extinction is to be brought about by, and runs parallel with, the growth of the opposite condition of mind and heart; and it is complete when that opposite condition is reached.

Apart from the doctrine of Karma, which is alien to Sūfīsm, these definitions of *fanā* (viewed as a moral state) and Nirvāna agree almost word for word. It would be out of place to pursue the comparison further, but I think we may conclude that the Sūfī theory of *fanā* was influenced to some extent by Buddhism as well as by Perso-Indian pantheism.

The receptivity of Islam to foreign ideas has been recognized by every unbiased inquirer, and the history of Sūfīsm is only a single instance of the general rule. But this fact should not lead us to seek in such ideas an explanation of the whole question which I am now discussing, or to identify Sūfīsm itself with the extraneous ingredients which it absorbed and assimilated in the course of its development. Even if Islam had been miraculously shut off from contact with foreign religions and philosophies, some form of mysticism would have arisen within it, for the seeds were already there. Of course, we cannot isolate the internal forces working in this direction, since they were subject to the law of spiritual gravitation. The powerful currents of thought discharged through the Mohammedan world by the great non-Islamic systems above mentioned gave a stimulus to various tendencies within Islam which affected Sūfism either positively or negatively. As we have seen, its oldest type is an ascetic revolt against luxury and worldliness; later on, the prevailing rationalism and skepticism provoked countermovements toward intuitive knowledge and emotional faith, and also an orthodox reaction which in its turn drove many earnest Moslems into the ranks of mystics.

How, it may be asked, could a religion founded on the simple and austere monotheism of Mohammed tolerate these new doctrines, much less make terms with them? It would seem impossible to reconcile the transcendent personality of Allah with an immanent Reality which is the very life and soul of the universe. Yet Islam has accepted Sūfism. The Sūfis, instead of being excommunicated, are securely established in the Mohammedan church, and the *Legend of the Moslem Saints* records the wildest excesses of Oriental pantheism.

Let us return for a moment to the Koran, the infallible touchstone by which every Mohammedan theory and practice must be proved. Are any germs of mysticism to be found there? The Koran, as I have said, starts with the notion of Allah, the One, Eternal, and Almighty God, far above human feelings and aspirations—the Lord of His slaves, not the Father of His children; a judge meting out stern justice to sinners, and extending His mercy only to those who avert His wrath by repentance, humility, and unceasing works of devotion; a God of fear rather than of love. This is one side, and certainly the most prominent side, of Mohammed's teaching; but while he set an impassable gulf between the world and Allah, his deeper instinct craved a direct revelation from God to the soul. There are no contradictions in the logic of feeling. Mohammed, who had in him something of the mystic, felt God both as far and near, both as transcendent and immanent. In the latter respect, Allah is the light of the heavens and the earth, a Being who works in the world and in the soul of man.

"If My servant ask thee about Me, lo, I am near" (Koran 2.182); "We (God) are nearer to him than his own neck-vein" (50.15); "And in the earth are signs to those of real faith, and in yourselves. What! do ye not see?" (51.20–21).

It was a long time ere they saw. The Moslem consciousness, haunted by terrible visions of the wrath to come, slowly and painfully awoke to the significance of those liberating ideas.

The verses which I have quoted do not stand alone, and however unfavorable to mysticism the Koran as a whole may be, I cannot assent to the view that it supplies no basis for a mystical interpretation of Islam. This was worked out in detail by the Sūfis, who dealt with the Koran in very much the same way as Philo treated the Pentateuch. But they would not have succeeded so thoroughly in bringing over the mass of religious Moslems to their side, unless the champions of orthodoxy had set about constructing a system of scholastic philosophy that reduced the divine nature to a purely formal, changeless, and absolute unity, a bare will devoid of all affections and emotions, a tremendous and incalculable power with which no human creature could have any communion or personal intercourse whatsoever. That is the God of Mohammedan theology. That was the alternative to Sūfism. Therefore, "all thinking, religious Moslems are mystics," as Professor D. B. Macdonald, one of our best authorities on the subject, has remarked. And he adds: "All, too, are pantheists, but some do not know it."

The relation of individual Sūfīs to Islam varies from more or less entire conformity to a merely nominal profession of belief in Allah and His Prophet. While the Koran and the Traditions are generally acknowledged to be the unalterable standard of religious truth, this acknowledgment does not include the recognition of any external authority which shall decide what is orthodox and what is heretical. Creeds and catechisms count for nothing in the Sūfī's estimation. Why should he concern himself with these when he possesses a doctrine derived immediately from God? As he reads the Koran with studious meditation and rapt attention, lo, the hidden meanings—infinite, inexhaustible—of the Holy Word flash upon his inward eye. This is what the Sūfīs call *istinbāt*, a sort of intuitive deduction; the mysterious inflow of divinely revealed knowledge into hearts made pure by repentance and filled with the thought of God, and the outflow of that knowledge upon the interpreting tongue. Naturally, the doctrines elicited by means of *istinbāt* do not agree very well either with Mohammedan theology or with each other, but this discord is easily explained. Theologians, who interpret the letter, cannot be expected to reach the same conclusions as mystics, who interpret the spirit; and if both classes differ amongst themselves, that is a merciful dispensation of divine wisdom, since theological controversy serves to extinguish religious error, while the variety of mystical truth correspond to the manifold degrees and modes of mystical experience.

. . . It is only a rough-and-ready account of the attitude of the Sūfīs toward positive religion to say that many of them have been good Moslems, many scarcely Moslems at all, and a third party, perhaps the largest, Moslems after a fashion. During the early Middle Ages Islam was a growing organism, and gradually became transformed under the influence of diverse movements, of which Sūfism itself was one. Mohammedan orthodoxy in its present shape owes much to Ghazāli, and Ghazāli was a Sūfī. Through his work and example the Sūfistic interpretation of Islam has in no small measure been harmonized with the rival claims of reason and tradition, but just because of this he is less valuable than mystics of a purer type to the student who wishes to know what Sūfism essentially is.

Although numerous definitions of Sūfism which occur in Arabic and Persian books on the subject are historically interesting, their chief importance lies in showing that Sūfism is undefinable. Jalāluddīn Rūmī in his *Masnavī* tells a story about an elephant which some Hindus were exhibiting in a dark room. Many people gathered to see it, but, as the place was too dark to permit them to see the elephant, they all felt it with their hand, to gain an idea of what it was like. One felt its trunk, and said that the animal resembled a water pipe; another felt its ear, and said it must be a large fan; another its leg, and thought it must be a pillar; another felt its back, and declared that the beast must be like an immense throne. So it is with those who define Sūfism: they can only attempt to express what they themselves have felt, and there is no conceivable formula that will comprise every shade of personal and intimate religious feeling. Since, however, these definitions illustrate with convenient brevity certain aspects and characteristics of Sūfism, a few specimens may be given.

Sūfism is this: that actions should be passing over the Sūfī (i.e. being done upon him) which are known to God only, and that he should always be with God in a way that is known to God only.

Sūfism is wholly self-discipline.

Sūfism is, to possess nothing and to be possessed by nothing.

Sūfism is not a system composed of rules or sciences but a moral disposition; i.e. if it were a rule, it could be made one's own by strenuous exertion, and if it were a science, it could be acquired by instruction; but on the contrary it is a disposition, according to the saying, "Form yourselves on the moral nature of God"; and the moral nature of God cannot be attained either by means of rules or by means of sciences.

Sūfism is freedom and generosity and absence of self-constraint.

It is this: that God should make thee die to thyself and should make thee live in Him.

To behold the imperfection of the phenomenal world, nay, to close the eye to everything imperfect in contemplation of Him who is remote from all imperfection—that is Sūfism.

Sūfism is control of the faculties and observance of the breaths.

It is Sūfism to put away what thou hast in thy head, to give what thou hast in thy hand, and not to recoil from whatsoever befalls thee.

The reader will perceive that Sūfism is a word uniting many divergent meanings, and that in sketching its main features one is obliged to make a sort of composite portrait, which does not represent any particular type exclusively. The Sūfis are not a sect, they have no dogmatic system, the *tarīqas* or paths by which they seek God "are in number as the souls of men" and vary infinitely, though a family likeness may be traced in them all. Descriptions of such a Protean phenomenon must differ widely from one another, and the impression produced in each case will depend on the choice of materials and the prominence given to this or that aspect of the many-sided whole. Now, the essence of Sūfism is best displayed in its extreme type, which is pantheistic and speculative rather than ascetic or devotional. This type, therefore, I have purposely placed in the foreground. The advantage of limiting the field is obvious enough, but entails some loss of proportion. In order to form a fair judgment of Mohammedan mysticism, the following chapters [of this book, i.e. *The Mystics of Islam*] should be supplemented by a companion picture drawn especially from those moderate types which, for want of space, I have unduly neglected.

NOTES

1. *Al-Haqq* is the term generally used by the Sūfis when they refer to God.
2. Compare Plato, *Phaedrus* (Jowett's translation): "For sight is the keenest of our bodily senses; though not by that is wisdom seen; her loveliness would have been transporting if there had been a visible image of her."
3. Cf. Goldhizer, "Neuplatonische und gnostische Elemente im Hadīt," in *Zeitschrift für Assyriologie* 22, 317ff.
4. Shaikh Muhhamad Iqbal, *The Development of Metaphysics in Persia* (1908), p. 150.
5. *"The Way"* of a Mohammedan Mystic, by W. H. T. Gairdner (Leipzig, 1912), pp. 9f.

12

The Mystical Spirit and Protestantism

WILLIAM ERNEST HOCKING

There was a time when it took courage to be a Protestant. And courage is poor business unless there is a groundwork of conviction to start from. The moral core of Protestantism is not any love of dissent for its own sake but a regretful sense of necessity because of what one surely sees to be true. We cannot understand the beginnings of Protestantism nor, indeed, the major part of its history unless we can discern the sources of the assurance that undergirded its tragic choice: "Here I stand. I can do no other; God help me!"

Now, assurance of a sort was abundant in the European world at the birth of the modern era. What *is* this modern era except a glorious burst of self-confidence, in which man notifies the powers above that he now proposes to take charge of his own destiny by the aid of science and has very little need for their further attention? This feeling has lasted well over three centuries and, after falling into shallows, is now going out in a pall of tragedy.

But the confidence of humanism and of the scientific spirit is not the confidence on which Protestantism has based its position.

And, indeed, so far as knowledge is concerned, self-confidence and self-management are only half the story of the modern spirit. It is astonishing how soon that rational self-assurance which worked out the principles of scientific method and summoned all theology to justify itself before a man-built theory of the cosmos began to share the field with symptoms of self-doubt. The modern era might as fairly be called an era of *distrust of reason*. For it created a new science—the science of knowledge, in which reason is occupied with pointing out the limits of reason. And it bred at least two new brands of skepticism—that of Hume, based on this theory of knowledge; and that of scientific relativity, based on psychology. John Locke, the ancestor of both of them, stands well toward the beginning of this great era.

And what is still more striking is the fact that the great critics of reason—Locke and Kant—as well as the great skeptics, spring rather from the Protestant than from the Catholic vein of modernity. How can it be that Protestantism, which could neither begin nor continue to exist without certitude, could even indirectly yield such fruits as these?

Protestantism's Certitude is Moral and Mystical

The answer to this riddle has to be found in the fact that the certitude on which Protestantism builds is *not primarily rational but moral and mystical* and, at bottom, more mystical than moral. Let me briefly illustrate this point.

During the last century Protestantism, making valiant efforts to build for itself a positive theological foundation, has made much use of the distinction between affirmations of thought on one side and affirmations of our moral nature on the other. Religious faith was considered to be not an intellectual hypothesis but a decision, a launch of the will, an act of loyalty. Older writers had made much use of the Catholic Pascal's remark that "the heart has its reasons which the mind will never know." But the nineteenth century found greater help in Kant's famous distinction between theoretical and practical reason. It was said of him that he had "robbed reason to pay back to faith"—a statement that is roughly true if you are not very particular what you say. Kant, whose whole range of thought was deeply influenced by the Protestant Pietism in which his father's family was steeped, held that speculative reason could accomplish nothing in getting at the ultimate realities of the world—a fact that is perhaps fortunate if "dealing with reality instead of appearance" is something in which every man has a vital concern. There would be something wrong with a world in which finding God, if there is a God, would be reserved for men of high speculative talent. Our direct access to reality, Kant taught, is by way of our sense of duty, which is present in everyone. The most important truth is accessible on the most completely democratic terms. But in what sense does duty show us reality?

Schopenhauer had a simple answer to the effect that the will is the realest thing about us, as about all other living things, the intellect being but a servant of the will. When we "think," we are occupied with surfaces and symbols; when we act, we heave against the world, and we have to be as real as the world is. The will is therefore the place "where appearance and reality coincide"—a phrase of masterly penetration.

But Kant would not have endorsed without caveat this view of his ardent disciple. I think he would have foreseen the dangers both to theology in making thought a mere servant of a will power that must then be literally irrational, to religion in making faith purely a pragmatic choice or wager, and to civilization itself in making "I will" the ultimate ruler of the world. What Kant taught was that we are real, not because and when we "will" (that is, resolve, decide, act), but only because and when we will *according to duty.*

For when conscience speaks, and we acknowledge its authority, we are getting outside the will of our "natural man," which it is our business to master. The self of psychology, the stream of consciousness, is no more real than the stream of sensations that make up the apparent world of physical things. Both one and other are "phenomena" and nothing more. But the whole issue of life is to keep these appearances in their place. Conscience is the awareness of our calling, or vocation, to master "nature" in ourselves; and to do this we must step over the boundary line from appearance to reality. It is only the man aware of duty who knows the direction in which reality lies. And, since duty is the place where the veil of appearance breaks, whatever is implied in duty must itself be real, including the being of God.

This searching and cautious analysis comes very close to the central vein of Protestant religious experience. Protestantism has not alone insisted that the fruits of religion are visible in the moral aspects of living and that the soundness of religion is to be tested that way, but also that there are conditions for perceiving religious truth which are primarily moral: "If any man willeth . . . he shall know." It is not surprising that a line of distinguished thinkers have seen first the philosophy of religion and then Protestant theology through this insight: Lotze, Ritschl, William James, and, to some extent, Josiah Royce. But I doubt whether this is the deepest source of Protestant certitude, nor do I think we shall find it until we realize how nearly Kant was a mystic; yet how clearly he misses what the mystic has given to Protestant certitude!

The term "mysticism" has come to mean two distinct things in the Occident—a theory of reality and a doctrine regarding the way in which the human individual may gain union with reality. In the first sense mysticism is the theory that there is one all-inclusive real being, but that this being can have no further description. It is "ineffable" in the sense that all descriptives falsify its nature, even those which we take to be laudatory—such as "good," "holy," "omniscient," "Spirit," "Creator," "loving," "personal," "impersonal," "finite," "Infinite." This falsification involved in these epithets arises from what they deny, since every descriptive asserted carries with it the denial of its opposite. Thus, that which is "good," as we conceive goodness, cannot be not-good in the same sense; whereas the One cannot be assigned a quality, distinct from its being, to which our human distinction of good and not-good applies.

If the theoretical mystic were simply one who makes a thoroughgoing principle of being wary of the traps set by our "concepts," he would have a great deal of company in modern times. Bergson would join him on that ground, assigning all conceptual knowledge to the intellect, which has to be content with aspects of things, while the full-rounded truth, at least regarding everything that has life and "inwardness," can be had only through intuition, which can "coincide" with that inwardness. He would be joined also by a great group of thinkers and non-thinkers who, on various grounds, simply doubt that our minds were given us to know metaphysical reality at all. Dewey and James would unite here with Kant and Spencer and many of the "average man," for whom thought is a kind of adjustment, and truth a matter of getting a working hypothesis regarding the environment with which we actually deal—ergo, essentially "relative." These would agree with "logical positivism," and all with the mystic, that the question whether reality is "mental" or "non-mental" is "nonsense," because there is no way to decide between them. The real eludes our judgments about its nature; but this is another way of saying that it makes no difference to us what it is (since all significant differences can be embodied in concepts), and that we may as well ignore it entirely.

But the mystic is a better logician than all these. He has, in fact, made a fundamental logical discovery—that there is an important middle course between yes and no. If you ask the mystic whether there is a God, yes or no, he ought not to answer without knowing what you mean by "God"; at which point he should say, "No, not that God." He is not a theist. On the other hand, he is not an atheist; for he believes "that God is." He stoutly affirms "that" God exists while denying that he knows "what" God is. He throws himself open to the rebuke that if you have no idea *what* God is, your affirmation *that* he is becomes wholly meaningless; or, in other words, if you mean anything at all when you say, "God is," you must have some notion of God. The mystic replies that his affirmation is of the utmost significance for (1) it saves him from despair regarding the reality of the world and therefore the seriousness of life; and (2) it keeps him in active search for that grasp of God's nature which no concept can contain. There must be, he maintains, some other way of apprehending God than by concepts.

The mystic has the better of the argument, and his final answer reminds us strongly of Kant's proposal that reason in metaphysics should be used to "regulate," not to "construct." It directs our thinking processes without offering us solutions. It commands activity without promising any goal. But it is at this point that *the theoretical mystic ought to turn into the practical mystic*, who has a way of gaining union with God other than by concepts. Indeed, it is only in the Occident that these two sides of mysticism fall apart. In the Orient, speculative mysticism as we find it in the Vedanta, Taoism, and Mahayana Buddhism of the Nagarjuni school, is a way of salvation. The theory is a mere auxiliary, explaining why the devotee carries on his peculiar way of finding God.

Now, practical mysticism continues to exist only because men in considerable numbers have come to believe that there is a mode of experience which can properly be called "an experience of God" or "an experience of union with God," and that this mode of experience is (1) of the utmost practical importance and (2) attainable by following the right discipline. Heroic leaders have found "the Way." Their instructions may guide their followers to a similar success. Here the mystic falls into war with the entire recent trend of modernity, since the trend of our time, looking at the mystic's person and his accomplishments (with special emphasis upon the oddity of the specimens chosen as typical), is to judge (1) that, far from being important, the mystic's achievement only makes him queer, subjective, and out of gear, and (2) that he has no way of distinguishing his "experiences" from various types of autosuggestive exhilaration.

It is not my purpose to enter into this debate. The debate itself is a chapter little creditable to modern scholarship, whether in philosophy, theology, or science. For if there is any spectacle less edifying than that of the blind leading the blind, it is that of the blind fighting the blind. Those who disparage the mystic are in the position of denying something solely on the ground that they do not see it; which is not evidence in any court, whether of law or of science. The denial proves nothing but their own incapacity to see; which point might be conceded without any contest. The mystics, on the other hand, often treat their opponents with a certain arrogance as if to say that their mere assertion is itself a proof, whereas it can be nothing more than an invitation to test the matter by following the same path. Historically speaking, the mystics have not been free from the vanity of separatism. They have been inclined to turn the assertion "I have found a way" into the assertion "I alone have found a way, and it is the only way," and have called for exclusive following on the ground of this enlightenment or discovery or revelation. The position of mankind toward the whole wonderful history of mysticism would be vastly improved if attention were given to the extent to which the reports of the great mystics corroborate one another and indicate a common nature in the paths proposed; and if it were further shown how deeply the more extraordinary varieties of mystical experience are akin to very normal and, indeed, inescapable experiences of men everywhere.

In my judgment, mysticism is strongest where it is most universal, and I believe that it is precisely here that it has had its great contribution to make to Protestantism.

The characteristic assertion of mysticism in all its forms is that there is a vitally important and non-conceptual experience of God available to men who meet its conditions. The simplest and most usual expression of this thesis is that all men at all times are directly dealing with God, whether they know it or not. They must breathe air whether or not they know it to be air; they must eat food whether or not they know that it feeds them; if they move, they must thrust against something that resists; if they have weight, they must be in a gravitational field; if they achieve effects, they must enter the network of causes. And if any of these appearances is a mere sign of some deeper reality (as, doubtless, they all are), then through those signs we are in actual traffic with that more real, just as through language we move the mind of our neighbor; and whatever is more real is embedded in what is Most Real so that the whole basis and response of their living is the Real. The mystic simply denies that this battle is with appearances—an absurdity equivalent to saying that because one's adversary is clothed, one fights *the clothes* of his adversary. The principle of the mystical consciousness in the *transparency of intermediaries*. Vital awareness deals with what intermediaries *represent*. And if the Real is God, it is with God that we have to do from moment to moment of daily living. For each action the world concentrates itself into a point of resistance and support; and that point is a Thou, not an It.

Kant missed this, because for him the intermediaries were not transparent. There they stood—the "phenomena"—and the mind of man could not peer behind them. Hence, for Kant, the best that man can do is to have an *immediate awareness of duty*, from which he may infer the existence of God. The mystic reverses the order. Man has (or can have) an *immediate awareness of God*, from which fact he perceives that he is under obligation and must live his life in careful listening to the voice of duty.

In my own view it is the mystic who is right, not Kant; and it is the mystic who speaks for the position of Protestantism and who represents the permanent inner strength of that movement. Let me develop this point in several special aspects of Protestant experience:

On Mysticism and Authority

The following statements are incompatible with one another, and all of them have been made by mystics of different types:

Man is always aware of God.

Man must struggle to become aware of God.

Man is neither aware of God by nature, nor can he win this awareness by his own efforts; but God must, by his own act, make himself known to man—the essential act of grace.

The tradition of mysticism, however, has shown itself capable of uniting these three positions which have done so much to rend Christian bodies asunder. For (to speak of the second and third) the mystic has not infrequently asserted, on the basis of his own experience, that there comes a stage of effort in which effort must be set aside in favor of a purely receptive attitude. His effort has been chiefly (as the "negative path" suggests) to put aside the obstacles in his own nature to receiving that vision. He recognizes the danger that his "trying" may be trying toward some preconceived goal and therefore impede his perception of the true goal, whose character is such that it cannot have been preconceived. He must render himself passive and wait in hope that God will vouchsafe to reveal himself.

It is the first assertion that appears to set itself most squarely against the other two. For if God is always present, it becomes foolish to make a problem of finding him. But this very sensible proposal forgets two things: first, that it is remarkably easy to overlook what is always present, just because it is an invariable element of experience; there is no absurdity—on the contrary, it is one of the commonest events—that we discover what it is that we have been presupposing or unconsciously relying on; secondly, that if the God found were different from the power that always surrounds and sustains our being (and in this sense is always "there") it would not be God that was found. In this respect there is an important truth in that somewhat misleading paradox of Pascal's: "Thou couldst not seek me, hadst thou not already found me." It is a question often put to the mystic by his psychological critics: "How do you know that it is God whom you experience?"; to which the apposite answer is simply that the object now so impressively discerned is *the same object* as that which he has always known in a far less adequate manner.

Thus a fully understood mysticism may hold together what the accidents of Church history in the fifteenth and sixteenth centuries put asunder. The historic Church took the view that the life of God must be brought to individual men through the channels of revelation and the spiritual body of the Church. The Protestant view was that the life of God is already in the souls of men, and that this must be their guide in recognizing any outer authority.

It is sometimes held that mysticism is hostile to any authority whatever, but this is clearly not the case. As we have already seen, those mystics who announce their discoveries of "the Way" become authoritative to their followers. But, apart from this, the mystic, in claiming his own personal and original God-awareness, knows that this is only the beginning of his religious life. As his private religion it is a solitary religion. It has its own need of steadying, corroboration, interpretation, development. This he must find in the equally original experiences of other minds and in whatever has become for them the guide of the community. It is the Protestant position, certainly, not that authority is unnecessary, but that every man, since he has, by faith, his own access to the Highest, knows how to distinguish true authority from falsely claimed authority and knows how to use the authority he recognizes as valid. He has, for example, that in himself by which the Bible can be recognized as God's word and can be so read that God speaks personally to him through its language. In this sense it may be argued that the Protestant has *more use* for authority than anyone else.

But there is another sense in which the mystic is likely to be a thorn in the side of all existing authorities and so to be a person under suspicion.

The mystic experience of God's presence is either important to the mystic or it is fraudulent. It cannot be regarded by him as a commonplace. In principle it is *his* revelation and has the character of all revelation—that it authorizes him to speak, and with assurance. Perhaps, through him, God is attempting to open a new chapter of religious insight, as many in our time have thought—Mrs. Eddy, Joseph Smith, the prophets of Bahaism, the founders of new sects of Shinto, enthusiastic groups of all sorts from the peasants with whom Luther dealt so severely to Jehovah's Witnesses in our own day. The founder of Islam was himself a mystic of this type, wholly reverent toward earlier authorities except at the point where they declared the Book of Revelation closed. Bidden by the angel, he added to that book, revised its earlier statements, and then, not learning from his own experience the danger of premature closure, sealed the amended book, not with seven seals, but with seventy; in spite of which brave souls, equally respectful of their predecessors, continue to reopen and revise.

From the standpoint of the custodians of a finished revelation, therefore, the mystic is never a safe companion until he is dead. Not only may he add to the received truth, but he is bound to test the particular doctrines of earlier authority by his own vision of truth. This is that rill of "private judgment" which brings him into most frequent clash with the constituted religious channels and leads to division after division within Protestantism itself.

Originality and Private Judgment

I shall not resolve the dilemma created by these corollaries of the mystic's certitude by trying to suppress any one of the three values involved —the actuality of certitude, the possibility of new religious insight, the importance of a stable corpus of faith.

As to certitude, it stands at the opposite pole from that footless relativity—the moral disease of contemporary intellectual self-criticism, which neither has for itself nor allows others to have a point of solid ground on which to set their feet. The mystic is not in error in being certain; he may easily be in error in being certain of too much. When he is, the cure would lie in a firmer application of the mystic principle itself —the element of finality in all insight lies in the "that" rather than in the "what." It will lie, further, in a recognition by the mystic that his insight, while not achievable by pure reason, is not immune from criticism by the canons of reason. The convictions of its mystics are too precious for the race to lose even by the rational insistence that true insights must agree. But it belongs to the Protestant principle itself that the access to God's truth is democratic so that the long, slow suffrages of the race are pertinent to the ultimate judgment as to what is and what is not a truly interpreted word of God.

As to novelty in revelation, this possibility is contained in the very center of Christian tradition. Jesus expressly taught that his teaching was necessarily unfinished, and that the process of leading his followers "into all truth" was a further work of God, which the Church, in view of the uniqueness of that teaching among organized religions, quite justly expressed in a symbol of the highest emphasis: they ascribed it to a third "person" of the Trinity. It is thus a fundamental disloyalty to the Christian tradition to regard that tradition as closed against growth.

We should not be too much disturbed if the implied "liberty of prophesying" does, in the course of history, lead to an amount of aberrant religious experimentation. We have every reason, however, to cooperate with the application of such criteria for distinguishing the true prophet, as the civil order and the common sense of mankind by degrees develop. There is no way to avoid the clash of mystic with mystic; neither, on the other hand, is there any way in which the bearer of a genuinely new insight can avoid the fate of the prophets even in a world where "freedom of speech" is promoted by the heirs of a Protestant disposition to give every new speaker the benefit of the doubt. Truth getting and truth spreading remain an adventure whose risks and prizes and penalties can never be reduced to the tame measure of "received standards."

But we have much to gain by distinguishing *originality* in religion from *deviation*. Christianity may be defined as the religion that insists upon the originality of the religious experience of each believer. Jesus was original in the sense that he took tradition for what it meant to him. He did not reject it; he relived it. He wanted no followers who were imitators. Whatever truth he had to give them had to be born in them anew. To be a follower of an original soul is to be original. This does not necessarily imply deviation; it implies verification from one's own center of life. Originality implies the *risk* of deviation in order that corroboration, when it comes, shall be the endorsement of an independent spirit. The Protestant, as mystic, stands for this originality, which is the charter of all true liberty; he has no stake in deviation per se.

When this is understood, Protestantism will be ready not alone to admit but also to assert our third value—the importance of a stable corpus of faith. Growth cannot be stopped until there are no more "accents of the Holy Ghost" for a heedless world to treasure; but growth can be *within* a body of truth as well as by addition or correction. Science may glory in the rapidity with which it discards old conceptions and frames new ones. Its "Principia" lose their pertinence and require to be rewritten. But religion's whole meaning to mankind depends on a contrast with this sort of supersession: Unless there is a truth that is changeless, religion becomes a branch of anthropology, chiefly of historical interest. So, too, the whole point of mysticism is that the individual mind, wherever it is in space or time, may have its own tryst with the eternal. While the vanity of man takes a pride in novelty and invention, the good faith of the mystic—and his true anchor—lies in his testimony to the underlying unanimity of the mystics. Through their freedom they can best confirm the stability of a central corpus of religious truth.

Organization and Personal Religion

Where there is a consensus of faith in a body of believers who are also mystics—in the sense that their whole religious experience is contained within the frame of their own direct awareness of God as a constant presence—there can be a corporate mysticism as well as a private mystical experience. There are a few experiences in life in which a new perception is not "mine" alone but "ours," in which personal separateness is not destroyed but somehow outpassed. Augustine's memorable account, in his *Confessions*, of one such experience comes to mind. This is the purpose of *ritual*, which aims to conserve moments of common feeling and elevation within an existing community of many members and to reinstate them.

But the very ambition of ritual (usually set in opposition to the mystical element of religion) is so great and so difficult of realization that one may fairly say that it requires for its success a parallel development of private mysticism. It is for this reason that highly organized and highly ritualistic churches give rise from time to time, as if by reaction, to movements emphasizing "personal religion." It is for this reason, too, that the non-conformist branches of Protestantism, especially in England, including Independents, Puritans, and Quakers, have been most pronouncedly mystical in their beliefs and practices. The older Oxford Movement and the recent Group Movement have at least one thing in common besides the name—an attempt to reanimate the fundamental springs of religion in personal relationship to God.

If I were asked what qualities these mystical movements have lent to Protestantism as a whole, I should answer: seriousness, sincerity, dignity. The corporate life of the Church, not intentionally but by its very majesty, lifts something away from the individual feeling of responsibility. The mystic recalls himself to the thought:

> A charge to keep I have,
> A God to glorify,
> A never-dying soul to save
> And fit it for the sky.

There is a recovery of *seriousness*—that is, of the aloneness of destiny and of the mystery of individual calling, which made so much of the "character" of our American ancestry. Then, there is *sincerity*, which is closely allied: sincerity in the sense of an unwillingness to use general terms and ideals without a close inquiry to what extent I am carrying these out in my personal conduct. It is the disposition to bring my ethical code into direct relation with my religious experience. And there is *dignity*, which results from resuming, by the individual, the role which ritual allows to become specialized—that of the priesthood. In Christianity the goal is that every man shall be the minister to all, and every man the potential priest to all. But man attains his dignity only as he actually fulfills the function of priesthood, first in his own family and then for groups in which he may speak the reuniting word. This function has become difficult for the modern man and, I regret to say, for the modern Protestant as well as for others. But here Protestantism is false to its own deepest inheritance. It is its special mission to restore to our shallow lives the great qualities of seriousness, sincerity, dignity. And to do this it must renew its hold upon its birthright in the mystical spirit of the individual.

13

The Question of "Mysticism" within Native American Traditions

JOSEPH EPES BROWN

Contemporary uses of the term "mysticism" and its cognates have come to apply to a wide variety of often disparate phenomena, frequently far removed from the early Christian or original Greek sense of the terms. It may indeed be said that the term has become so often abused, and levels of reality so confused, that in certain contemporary contexts "mysticism" may actually express the inverse of, or the grossest parody on, those great mysteries and mystics of the legitimate and orthodox great religious traditions of the world.

Examples of abuse and misuse could be cited from a plethora of modern cults, "the new religions," popular parodies on legitimate spiritual or mystical ways, not to mention experimentations with instant "mystical experiences" afforded through the agencies of various drugs. . . . To underline . . . at least certain dimensions of such problems one may recall the statement of Aldous Huxley in *The Doors of Perception*, written in 1954:

> It has always seemed to me possible that, through hypnosis, for example, or auto-hypnosis, by means of systematic meditation, or else by taking the appropriate drug, I might so change my ordinary mode of consciousness as to be able to know, from the inside, what the visionary, the medium, even the mystic were talking about.[1]

That contemporary confusions concerning the prerequisite conditions for true spiritual realization abound in the world today is eminently comprehensible and evident to many. Under the forces of a pervasive materialistic outlook, spreading essentially from the Western world, and causally related to the erosion of the great spiritual legacies of this world, man has become increasingly a prisoner of the limits of his vision and the manner in which he experiences his world. In seeking release from this constricting experience of a continually changing physical multiplicity, and motivated by a nostalgia for a lost, more real world of true freedom, many have turned in every possible direction for alternate answers. Due, however, to the erosion and spiritual impoverishment of one's own proper tradition, or rather, due to man's inability in these times to understand the true nature of these traditions, there is left no real criteria for discrimination, evaluation, and eventual choice rooted in true knowledge. In addition, there is the problem that motivation in the quest, often undertaken with the greatest sincerity, may actually be, through the self-will of the ego, sentimentality, or the desire, self-defeating in itself, for some otherworldly, liberating mystical experience which nevertheless still appears within the realm of limiting phenomena. Under such conditions there is no guarantee that what is found will not lead to further frustrations, and often, as is the case with altered states of consciousness through the use of drugs, to a sinking within the lower chaotic depth of one's being, and thus to a deepening intensification of the original problem.

One response to this dilemma, which has already been implied above, may perhaps best be phrased through the following question: Is it still possible, given the force of contemporary circumstances, for man to reestablish his broken links with one of the great world religious traditions, that is, with one of those particular and providential expressions of what has been called the *philosophia perennis,* that perennial and timeless wisdom valid nowever and forever? That such may be the only way has been affirmed by an increasing number of scholars of the sacred such as Ananda Coomaraswamy, René Guenon, Seyyed Hossein Nasr, or the great contemporary European theologian and metaphysician, Frithjof Schuon, who has unequivocally stated that:

> . . . there is no possible spiritual way outside of the great orthodox traditional ways. A meditation or concentration practiced at random and outside of tradition will be inoperative, and even dangerous in more than one respect; the illusion of progress in the absence of real criteria is certainly not the least of these dangers.[2]

It is suggested that these general introductory considerations are particularly relevant to the discussion to follow on Native American religions, and specifically on the nature of "mysticism" as expressed and experienced within the context of these spiritual traditions.

It has, first of all, long been necessary to situate correctly the so-called "primitive religions" within the context of the world's historical religions, and in so doing to recognize, or at least that is the hope, that in spite of many elements unfamiliar to the outsider, these Native traditions, at least where there has not been excessive compromise to the modern world, are in no sense inferior, but indeed are legitimate expressions of that same universal *philosophia perennis*. The injustices suffered by these world views, ritual practices, and lifeways, through ignorance and ill-will, through deeply rooted prejudices and willful falsifications, all commencing with the first European contacts with the "new world," now demand that a reevaluation take place and that proper recognition and respect be given. There are indeed signs today that such positive reassessment is taking place, and what is especially encouraging is the extending realization on the part of many Native Americans themselves, who had lost or neglected their proper religious traditions, that such traditions and related lifeways do constitute within the world of today not only a viable reality in themselves, but also a valid and powerful response, in terms of fundamental values, to many of the problems faced by the contemporary world. That there is a progressive strengthening of this realization is nothing short of miraculous when one considers those pressures for abandoning these traditions, in the name of "progress" and "civilization," which have been exercised against the people over the past centuries.

One explanation for the current new willingness to understand Native Americans and their lifeways is the fact that, being rooted in this American land for thousands of years, the Indians' otherwise very diverse cultures have all come to express rich spiritual relationships with this American land; indeed the forms and symbols bearing these values are all drawn from the details of each people's particular geographic environment. Native Americans lived, and many still do live, what one might call a metaphysic of nature, spelled out by each group in great detail, and defining responsibilities and the true nature of that vast web of man's cyclical interrelationships with the elements, the earth, and all that lives upon this land. They are the echoes of such a message that above all have caught the attention of at least a few within a society that finally has been forced by hard circumstances to recognize the gravity of our ecological crisis, and thus to seek answers that speak to root causes rather than continually treating the ever recurring symptoms of the problem.

Many of the younger generations especially, who formerly had turned to distant lands and seemingly exotic traditions for answers to the problems of our world, have now come to see in expressions of Native American wisdom a more meaningful message, because these sacred traditions, as has been expressed above, are rooted in, and take their expressions from, elements of this very land with which many today, in their sense of alienation, seek meaningful relationships. Further, many individuals discern a deep mystical element in these sacred traditions of the Indian, and it is within something of this vision that they themselves would participate.

The problems, however, for the outsider who would personally relate to the sacred vision and practices of the American Indian are just as critical as, or even more problematic than, the attempt to relate to any of the orthodox traditions of East or West. The problem essentially lies in the tendency for the individual not rooted in any tradition to use an alien and thus often exotic religious tradition as a screen upon which to project all that one seeks yet finds lacking in one's own world. Rarely is the prerequisite effort made to understand the alien tradition on its own terms, through the categories of its proper language, and thus for what it really is in all its profundity and complexity, and with its impelling sacrificial demands. One is too easily satisfied merely to "touch the earth," to nourish one's own personal sentiment and nostalgia, and to hope thereby that somehow some mystic vision of ultimate meaning will automatically and easily come through.

Against the background of the above considerations, it is now possible to speak more directly to the theme of this conference, and to ask the following question: If "mysticism," in its original and thus deepest sense, is an experiential reality within Native American spiritual traditions, what are the conditions under which such experience becomes operative, and what are some of the contours of its manifestations? To answer this difficult question with any degree of justice, and within the necessarily brief space allowed, it is suggested that certain illustrative examples be drawn from the peoples and traditions of the Plains and Prairies because the place of this Conference is within this vast geographic and native culture area, and also because the major living and academic experiences of this present author have been with the peoples and religious traditions of the Plains, specifically with the Lakotas, the Assinoboine, the Crow, and the Blackfeet. It should initially be stressed that obviously there are rich differences across the cultures of the diverse Plains peoples, and yet at the same time, and particularly at the level which especially concerns us here, there is also a homogeneity of means and spiritual experience which allows generalizations within certain limits.

The essential thesis which it is intended to develop in that which follows is that "mysticism," insofar as it is a reality within these native traditions, is not, as the outsider has tended to view it, a vague quality of some supernatural experience which spontaneously comes to individuals whom providence has allowed to live close to nature. Rather, attempt will be made to demonstrate that such "mystical" experiences are first of all prepared for, and conditioned by, lifelong participation in a particular spoken language which bears sacred power through its vocabulary, structure, and categories of thought, and which serves as a vehicle for a large body of orally transmitted traditions, all the themes of which also express elements of the sacred. Secondly, such "mystic" experiences become more available to those persons who have participated with intensity and sincerity in a large number of exacting rites and ceremonies which have been revealed through time, and which derive ultimately from a transcendent source. There are also, through the nature of the peoples' lifeways rooted in hunting activities, interrelationships, informed by the rich oral traditions, with all the animal beings and the forms and forces of the natural environment. Further, there comes into plan the supporting exposure to a rich heritage of art forms, both visual and audible, many of which are representations of a supernatural experience received by the executor of the form. One may also mention the support offered by the dynamic rhythm of continually living out the myriad details of an everyday life, all the forms and acts of which are enriched by the inherent dimensions of the sacred. All these elements, and more, provide a specific, all-encompassing, supporting frame within which each individual lives out his or her life. It is essentially through the conditioning support and force of such spiritual forms and orientations that the individual becomes open to the possibility of receiving through dream or true vision glimpses of sacred realities borne perhaps by the forms of the Natural world, yet more real and permanent than the fleeting relative reality of this immediate world. The force of such traditions is so pervasive that it is understandable why it was expected that every man and woman should in solitude and with suffering participate in the so-called vision quest, or should seek a "guardian spirit," not only at the time of puberty, but indeed continuing regularly throughout their lives. A vision or guardian spirit helper may not always come to every seeker, but there is much evidence that such experiences did come to many of the people with great frequency. The fact, incidentally, that among many of the groups outside of the Plains the vision quest tended to be the exclusive province of the shaman, has led Robert Lowie and others to refer to the Plains experience by the intelligible, yet somewhat unhappy term—"democratized shamanism."

It is necessary to the clarification of our thesis to define in greater detail not the specific and often ritual requirements of the formalized vision quest, which time will not allow, but rather to speak of what one might call the spiritual contours and implications of the quest. In such necessarily condensed treatment one is impressed by the remarkable parallels to be found with expressions of the historical religions, and which have been so beautifully expressed by the statements of our colleagues in this conference. Not that such parallels suggest borrowings, but rather one may say that where the hearts and souls of men are exposed to the powers inherent to legitimate sacred traditions, there appears a common quality of spiritual realization which transcends cultural differentiations.

In Plains cultures no person should seek the vision experience without the help of a wise spiritual guide, an older person who has experienced visions and who has received special powers through guardian spirit helpers. Only such a person is aware of the dangers facing the seeker, and only he will be able to interpret for the novice that which might come to him or her in either an intense dream or a vision. Interpretation is important, for it is believed that the nature of the experience received indicates the directions and qualities a person's life should take. In the case of an especially strong experience the recipient will be instructed to secure some particular form or being from the natural world, and this will become part of a "medicine bundle," which will continue to actualize the particular power or quality received. Many of the sacred symbolic and often abstract paintings, such as those found on shields, represent such concrete representations of the supernatural experience, and these thus ensure continuity of the power inherent to the experience throughout the person's life.

The vision quest must always be preceded by rites of purification through the use of the sweat lodge. Here the novice is helped to enter into the necessary state of humility, to undergo, as it were, a spiritual rebirth. The person also, through rites and prayers, and through the form and materials of the lodge itself, is aided in establishing relationships with the primary elements, earth, air, fire, and water, and with all the beings of the earth, the animals, the winged creatures, and all that grows from the earth. Such relationships are additionally strengthened in these rites of purification through the use of a sacred pipe, the communal and sacramental smoking of which establishes a ritual relationship with all of creation and with the very source of life.

The quest itself must be undertaken in solitude and in silence upon a mountain, or some isolated place well away from the camp. The seeker's state of concentration is aided through the delineation of a protecting sacred area within which the person must remain and move about only in accord with a prescribed ritual pattern, usually defined by the four directions of space in their relation to an established center. One must always be attentive and listen, for it is believed that the sacred powers may manifest themselves through any form or being of the natural world, which may appear visually, or which may wish to communicate through some audible message. The presence and word of the Great Mystery is within every being, every thing, every event. Even the smallest being, a little ant for example, may appear, and communicate something of the power of the Great Mystery that is behind all forms of creation. The powers and beings of the world wish to communicate with man; they wish to establish a relationship, but may only do so where the recipient is in a state of humility, and is attentive with all his being. Since such humility is fostered through sacrifice, the seeker must neither eat nor drink for the duration of his quest, often three or four days. Being there alone and almost naked, he will realize the force of the elements through exposure and suffering. It has been said by many that the greatest support in the quest, and in the course of life itself, is silence, for ultimately silence is the very voice of the Great Mystery. The man or woman, however, is also enjoined to pray, indeed to pray continually, either silently, in an audible voice, or through song. The old Lakota sage, Black Elk, once told the writer of a prayer he often repeated continually during his quests. It was simply: "Grandfather, Great Spirit, have pity on me." In prayer, he also said, one should express thankfulness, gratitude, for all those gifts which are upon and above this earth.

Throughout that sacred lore given in sincerity and generosity to the outside world by many Plains peoples, there is ample evidence that through their sacred traditions and ritual practices, true mystical experiences in intense dream or vision did come to many seekers, and indeed they became such an accepted reality within these cultures that it was believed that no man or woman could ever be anybody, or could ever be successful in any undertaking important to the people's lives, unless one had received the spiritual power of the mystical vision experience. It is also true, as must always be the case, that some did not receive. Such persons, nevertheless, could participate in something of the power of the experience of others, even though less directly, due to the frequent obligation on those who received to express their experiences, as has been mentioned earlier, in concrete manner through paintings, song, or sacred forms of dance.

It should be added that mystical experiences did not come to the people exclusively through the actual vision quest, for often such experiences came through participation in other rites and ceremonies such as those of purification, through participation in the great annual sacrificial Sun Dance, or due simply to the general conditioning powers and sacred content of the totality of their traditions, men occasionally did receive such experiences at any time in their daily lives. Good evidence of this is found, for example, in the life of an exceptional man such as the Lakota, Black Elk. It may also be said of such a man that his frequent experiences, and the weight of their message and requirements, placed an enormous burden upon him, causing intense suffering throughout his entire life.

It may also be added at this point that mystical experiences such as the vision, which after all does appear in some phenomenal form, need not be a necessary criterion for, or a proof of, a true and integrated spiritual realization. The experience may simply provide probable evidence that the recipient has achieved at least a certain state of realization. Many traditions, it should be recalled, view visions, and mystical experiences generally, with suspicion, and suggest that such could provide dangerous distractions to a true spiritual way.

If at this point the question be raised as to what criteria can be used to affirm the spiritual authenticity of religious traditions such as those of the Native Americans, and the reality of mystical experiences to which such traditions give rise, at least one response, of one who may be so bold as to walk such dangerous ground, might be as follows:

The tradition in question must have its origins in a sacred source which is transcendent to the limits of the phenomenal world. All the expressions and extensions of this tradition will then bear the imprint of the sacred, manifested in terms appropriate to the time, place, and condition of man. In relation to man's active participation, the tradition will provide the means, essentially through sacred rites, for contact with, and ultimately a return to, the transcendent Principle, Origin, or by whatever name or term this be called. True and integrated progress on such an inner journey demands the means for accomplishing the progressive yet accumulative integration of the following elements or spiritual dimensions: (1) *Purification,* understood in a total sense, that is, of all that man is, of body, soul and spirit; (2) *Spiritual Expansion,* by which man realizes his totality, his relationship to all that is, and thus his integration with, and realization of, the realm of the virtues; (3) *Identity,* or final realization of unity, a state of oneness with the ultimate Principle of all that is. Spiritual expansion is impossible without the prerequisite purification, and ultimate identity is impossible outside of the realm of virtue, wholeness, or spiritual expansion.

These themes of purification, expansion, and identity, however they may be termed, are inherent, it is suggested, to all the true spiritual ways of the orthodox and thus legitimate traditions of the world. In regard to the situation of the Native American Traditions, it is hoped that sufficient evidence has been provided to demonstrate that these traditions, where they are still relatively intact, do not lie outside of such criteria, but rather, in accord with their primordial origins, they represent legitimate spiritual dialects of that *philosophia perennis* already referred to.

The dominant question raised in this presentation concerned those individuals who seek for a way which will provide answers to the multiple problems posed by the crises and spiritual poverty of the contemporary world. In terms of answers being found within Native American spiritual traditions, it was suggested that in spite of the initial attractiveness of these traditions, because they are rooted in this land, and because of their seeming "mystical" qualities, such traditions are nevertheless generally inaccessible to the non-Native American for reasons which one trusts have been made clear through the discussions in this paper. What is a possibility, however, is that by taking the pains to learn what one can from Native traditions, one who as yet is affiliated with no true tradition will be aided in knowing what *a* tradition is in all its complexity, depth, and richness of cultural expressions. This being understood, it is then possible to undertake the work of rediscovering the roots of what normally, or historically, should be one's own spiritual heritage, and now seeing and committing oneself to that heritage with the new vision that distance and perspective often allows. This is a way which demands sacrifice, as all spiritual ways do in any case, but it is now a way that is not an escape, but has that integrity and rigor which must always provide hope.

NOTES

1. Aldous Huxley, *The Doors of Perception* (London: Chatto & Windus, 1954).

2. Frithjof Schuon, "Des stations de la Sagesse," *Franc-Asie* (Saigon, 1953), No. 85–86, pp. 507–13.

PART III
Scientific Investigations

14

A Suggestion about Mysticism

WILLIAM JAMES

Much interest in the subject of religious mysticism has been shown in philosophic circles of late years. Most of the writings I have seen have treated the subject from the outside, for I know of no one who has spoken as having the direct authority of experience in favor of his views. I also am an outsider, and very likely what I say will prove the fact loudly enough to readers who possibly may stand within the pale. Nevertheless, since between outsiders one is as good as another, I will not leave my suggestion unexpressed.

The suggestion, stated very briefly, is that states of mystical intuition may be only very sudden and great extensions of the ordinary "field of consciousness." Concerning the causes of such extensions I have no suggestion to make; but the extension itself would, if my view be correct, consist in an immense spreading of the margin of the field, so that knowledge ordinarily transmarginal would become included, and the ordinary margin would grow more central. Fechner's "wave scheme" will diagramatize the alteration, as I conceive it, if we suppose that the wave of present awareness, steep above the horizontal line that represents the plane of the usual "threshold," slopes away below it very gradually in all directions. A fall of the threshold, however caused, would, under these circumstances, produce the state of things which we see on an unusually flat shore at the ebb of a spring-tide. Vast tracts usually covered are then revealed to view, but nothing rises more than a few inches above the water's bed, and great parts of the scene are submerged again, whenever a wave washes over them.

Some persons have naturally a very wide, others a very narrow, field of consciousness. The narrow field may be represented by an unusually steep form of the wave. When by any accident the threshold lowers, in persons of this type—I speak here from direct personal experience—so that the field widens and the relations of its centre to matters usually subliminal come into view, the larger panorama perceived fills the mind with exhilaration and sense of mental power. It is a refreshing experience; and—such is now my hypothesis—we only have to suppose it to occur in an exceptionally extensive form, to give us a mystical paroxysm, if such a term be allowed.

A few remarks about the field of consciousness may be needed to give more definiteness to my hypothesis. The field is composed at all times of a mass of present sensation, in a cloud of memories, emotions, concepts, etc. Yet these ingredients, which have to be named separately, are not separate, as the conscious field contains them. Its form is that of a much-at-once, in the unity of which the sensations, memories, concepts, impulses, etc., coalesce and are dissolved. The present field as a whole came continuously out of its predecessor and will melt into its successor as continuously again, one sensation-mass passing into another sensation-mass and giving the character of a gradually changing *present* to the experience, while the memories and concepts carry time-coefficients which place whatever is present in a temporal perspective more or less vast.

When, now, the threshold falls, what comes into view is not the next mass of *sensation;* for sensation requires new physical stimulations to produce it, and no alteration of a purely mental threshold can create these. Only in case the physical stimuli were already at work subliminally, preparing the next sensation, would whatever sub-sensation was already prepared reveal itself when the threshold fell. But with the memories, concepts, and conational states, the case is different. Nobody knows exactly how far we are "marginally" conscious of these at ordinary times, or how far beyond the "margin" of our present thought transmarginal consciousness of them may exist.[1] There is at any rate no definite bound set between what is central and what is marginal in consciousness, and the margin itself has no definite bound *a parte foris.* It is like the field of vision, which the slightest movement of the eye will extend, revealing objects that always stood there to be known. My hypothesis is that a movement of the threshold downwards will similarly bring a mass of subconscious memories, conceptions, emotional feelings, and perceptions of relation, etc., into view all at once; and that if this enlargement of the nimbus that surrounds the sensational present is vast enough, while no one of the items it contains attracts our attention singly, we shall have the conditions fulfilled for a kind of consciousness in all essential respects like that termed mystical. It will be transient, if the change of threshold is transient. It will be of reality, enlargement, and illumination, possibly rapturously so. It will be of unification, for the present coalesces in it with ranges of the remote quite out of its reach under ordinary circumstances; and the sense of *relation* will be greatly enhanced. Its form will be intuitive or perceptual, not conceptual, for the remembered or conceived objects in the enlarged field are supposed not to attract the attention singly, but only to give the sense of a tremendous *muchness* suddenly revealed. If they attracted attention separately, we should have the ordinary steep-waved consciousness, and the mystical character would depart.

Such is my suggestion. Persons who *know* something of mystical experience will no doubt find in it much to criticize. If any such shall do so with definiteness, it will have amply served its purpose of helping our understanding of mystical states to become more precise.

The notion I have tried (at such expense of metaphor) to set forth was originally suggested to me by certain experiences of my own, which could only be described as very sudden and incomprehensible enlargements of the conscious field, bringing with them a curious sense of cognition of real fact. All have occurred within the past five years; three of them were similar in type; the fourth was unique.

In each of the three like cases, the experience broke in abruptly upon a perfectly commonplace situation and lasted perhaps less than two minutes. In one instance I was engaged in conversation, but I doubt whether the interlocutor noticed my abstraction. What happened each time was that I seemed all at once to be reminded of a past experience; and this reminiscence, ere I could conceive or name it distinctly, developed into something further that belonged with it, this in turn into something further still, and so on, until the process faded out, leaving me amazed at the sudden vision of increasing ranges of distant fact of which I could give no articulate account. The mode of consciousness was perceptual, not conceptual—the field expanding so fast that there seemed no time for conception of identification to get in its work. There was a strongly exciting sense that my knowledge of past (or present?) reality was enlarging pulse by pulse, but so rapidly that my intellectual processes could not keep up the pace. The *content* was thus entirely lost to retrospection—it sank into the limbo into which dreams vanish as we gradually awake. The feeling—I won't call it belief—that I had had a sudden *opening*, had seen through a window, as it were, distant realities that incomprehensibly belonged with my own life, was so acute that I cannot shake it off today.

This conviction of fact-revealed, together with the perceptual form of the experience and the inability to make articulate report, are all characters of mystical states. The point of difference is that in my case certain special directions only, in the field of reality, seemed to get suddenly uncovered, whereas in classical mystical experiences it appears rather as if the whole of reality were uncovered at once. *Uncovering* of some sort is the essence of the phenomenon, at any rate, and is what, in the language of the Fechnerian wave-metaphor, I have used the expression "fall of the threshold" to denote.

My fourth experience of uncovering had to do with dreams. I was suddenly intromitted into the cognizance of a pair of dreams that I could not remember myself to have had, yet they seemed somehow to connect with me. I despair of giving the reader any just idea of the bewildering confusion of mind into which I was thrown by this, the most intensely peculiar experience of my whole life. I wrote a full memorandum of it a couple of days after it happened, and appended some reflections. Even though it should cast no light on the conditions of mysticism, it seems as if this record might be worthy of publication, simply as a contribution to the descriptive literature of pathological mental states. I let it follow, therefore, as originally written, with only a few words altered to make the account more clear.

"San Francisco, Feb. 14th 1906.—The night before last, in my bed at Stanford University, I woke at about 7:30 A.M., from a quiet dream of some sort, and whilst gathering my waking wits, seemed suddenly to get mixed up with reminiscences of a dream of an entirely different sort, which seemed to telescope, as it were, into the first one, a dream very elaborate, of lions, and tragic. I concluded this to have been a previous dream of the same sleep; but the apparent mingling of two dreams was something very queer, which I had never before experienced.

"On the following night (Feb. 12–13) I awoke suddenly from my first sleep, which appeared to have been very heavy, in the middle of a dream, in thinking of which I became suddenly confused by the contents of two other dreams that shuffled themselves abruptly in between the parts of the first dream, and of which I couldn't grasp the origin. Whence come *these dreams?* I asked. They were close to *me,* and fresh, as if I had just dreamed them; and yet they were far away *from the first dream.* The contents of the three had absolutely no connection. One had a cockney atmosphere, it had happened to some one in London. The other two were American. One involved the trying on of a coat (was this the dream I seemed to wake from?) the other was a sort of nightmare and had to do with soldiers. Each had a wholly distinct emotional atmosphere that made its individuality discontinuous with that of the others. And yet, in a moment, as these three dreams alternately telescoped into and out of each other, and I seemed to myself to have been their common dreamer, they seemed quite as distinctly *not* to have been dreamed in succession, in that one sleep. *When,* then? Not on a previous night, either. *When,* then, and *which* was the one out of which I had just awakened? *I could no longer tell:* one was as close to me as the others, and yet they entirely repelled each other, and I seemed thus to belong to three different dream-systems at once, no one of which would connect itself either with the others or with my waking life. I began to feel curiously confused and *scared,* and tried to wake myself up wider, but I seemed already wide-awake. Presently cold shivers of dread ran over me: *am I getting into other people's dreams?* Is this a 'telepathic' experience? Or an invasion of double (or treble) personality? Or is it a thrombus in a cortical artery? and the beginning of a general mental 'confusion' and disorientation which is going on to develop who knows how far?

"Decidedly I was losing hold of my 'self,' and making acquaintance with a quality of mental distress that I had never known before, its nearest analogue being the sinking, giddying anxiety that one may have when, in the woods, one discovers that one is really 'lost.' Most human troubles look towards a terminus. Most fears point in a direction, and concentrate towards a climax. Most assaults of the evil one may be met by bracing oneself against something, one's principles, one's courage, one's will, one's pride. But in this experience all was diffusion from a centre, and foothold swept away, the brace itself disintegrating all the faster as one needed its support more direly. Meanwhile vivid perception (or remembrance) of the various dreams kept coming over me in alteration. Whose? *whose?* WHOSE? Unless I can *attach* them, I am swept out to sea with no horizon and no bond, getting *lost*. The idea aroused the 'creeps' again, and with it the fear again of falling asleep and renewing the process. It had begun the previous night, but then the confusion had only gone one step, and had seemed simply curious. *This* was the second step—where might I be after a third step had been taken? My teeth chattered at the thought.

"At the same time I found myself filled with a new pity towards persons passing into dementia with *Verwirrtheit*, or into invasions of secondary personality. We regard them as simply *curious;* but what *they* want in the awful drift of their being out of its customary self, is any principle of steadiness to hold on to. We ought to assure them and reassure them that we will stand by them, and recognize the true self in them to the end. We ought to let them know that we are with *them* and not (as too often we must seem to them) a part of the world that but confirms and publishes their deliquescence.

"Evidently I was in full possession of my reflective wits; and whenever I thus objectively thought of the situation in which I was, my anxieties ceased. But there was a tendency to relapse vividly; and then the confusion recommenced, along with the emotion of dread lest it should develop farther.

"Then I looked at my watch. Half-past twelve! Midnight, therefore. And this gave me another reflective idea. Habitually, on going to bed, I fall into a very deep slumber from which I never naturally awaken until after two. I never awaken, therefore, from a midnight dream, as I did tonight, so of midnight dreams my ordinary consciousness retains no recollection. My sleep seemed terribly heavy as I woke to-night. Dream states carry dream memories—why may not the two succedaneous dreams (whichever two of the three *were* succedaneous) be memories of *twelve o'clock dreams of previous nights*, swept in, along with the just-fading dream, into the just-waking system of memory? Why, in short, may I not be tapping, in a way precluded by my ordinary habit of life, *the midnight stratum* of my past experiences?

"This idea gave great relief—I felt now as if I were in full possession of my *anima rationalis*. I turned on my light, resolving to read myself to sleep. But I didn't read, I felt drowsy instead, and, putting out the light, soon was in the arms of Morpheus.

"I woke again two or three times before daybreak with no dream-experiences, and finally, with a curious, but not alarming, confusion between two dreams, similar to that which I had had the previous morning, I awoke to the new day at seven.

"Nothing peculiar happened the following night, so the thing seems destined not to develop any further."[2]

The distressing confusion of mind in this experience was the exact opposite of mystical illumination, and equally unmystical was the definiteness of what was perceived. But the exaltation of the sense of relation was mystical (the perplexity all revolved about the fact that the three dreams *both did and did not belong in the most intimate way together*); and the sense that *reality was being uncovered* was mystical in the highest degree. To this day I feel that those extra dreams were dreamed in reality, but when, where, and by whom, I can not guess.

In the *Open Court* for December, 1909, Mr. Frederick Hall narrates a fit of ether-mysticism which agrees with my formula very well. When one of his doctors made a remark to the other, he chuckled, for he realized that these friends "believed they saw real things and causes, but they *didn't,* and I did. . . . I was where the causes *were* and to see them required no more mental ability than to recognize a color as blue. . . . The knowledge of how little [the doctors] actually did see, coupled with their evident feeling that they saw all there was, was funny to the last degree. . . . [They] knew as little of the real causes as does the child who, viewing a passing train and noting its revolving wheels, supposes that they, turning of themselves, give to coaches and locomotive their momentum. Or imagine a man seated in a boat, surrounded by dense fog, and out of the fog seeing a flat stone leap from the crest of one wave to another. *If he had always sat thus,* his explanations must be very crude as compared with those of a man whose eyes could pierce fog, and who saw upon the shore the boy skipping stones. In some such way the remarks of the two physicians seemed to me like the last two 'skips' of a stone thrown from my side. . . . All that was essential in the remark I knew before it was made. Thus to discover convincingly and for myself, that the things which are unseen are those of real importance, this was sufficiently stimulating."

It is evident that Mr. Hall's marginal field got enormously enlarged by the ether, yet so little defined as to its particulars that what he perceived was mainly the thoroughgoing casual integration of its whole content. That this perception brought with it a tremendous feeling of importance and superiority is a matter of course.

I have treated the phenomenon under discussion as if it consisted in the uncovering of tracts of *consciousness*. Is the consciousness already there waiting to be uncovered? and it is a veridical revelation of reality? These are questions on which I do not touch. In the subjects of the experience the "emotion of conviction" is always strong, and sometimes absolute. The ordinary psychologist disposes of the phenomenon under the conveniently "scientific" head of *petit mal*, if not of "bosh" or "rubbish." But we know so little of the noetic value of abnormal mental states of any kind that in my opinion we had better keep an open mind and collect facts sympathetically for a long time to come. We shall not *understand* these alterations of consciousness either in this generation or in the next.

NOTES

1. Transmarginal or subliminal, the terms are synonymous. Some psychologists deny the existence of such consciousness altogether (A. H. Pierce, for example, and Münsterberg apparently). Others, e.g., Bergson, make it exist and carry the whole freight of our past. Others again (as Meyers) would have it extend (in the "telepathic" mode of communication) from one person's mind to another's. For the purposes of my hypothesis I have to postulate its existence; and once postulating it, I prefer not to set any definite bounds to its extent.

2. I print the rest of my memorandum in the shape of a note:—

"Several ideas suggest themselves that make the observation instructive.

"First, the general notion, now gaining ground in mental medicine, that certain mental maladies may be foreshadowed in dream-life, and that therefore the study of the latter may be profitable.

"Then the specific suggestion, that states of 'confusion,' loss of personality, *apraxia*, etc. so often taken to indicate cortical lesion or degeneration of dementic type, may be very superficial functional affections. In my own case the confusion was *foudroyante*—a state of consciousness unique and unparalleled in my sixty-four years of the world's experience; yet it alternated quickly with perfectly rational states, as this record shows. It seems, therefore, merely as if the threshold between the rational and the morbid state had, in my case, been temporarily lowered, and as if similar confusions might be very near the line of possibility in all of us.

"There are also the suggestions of a telepathic entrance into someone else's dreams, and of a doubling up of personality. In point of fact I don't know how 'who' had those three dreams, or which one 'I' first woke up from, so quickly did they substitute themselves back and forth for each other, discontinuously. Their discontinuity was the pivot of the situation. My sense of it was as 'vivid' and 'original' an experience as anything Hume could ask for. And yet they kept telescoping!

"Then there is the notion that by waking at certain hours we may tap distinct strata of ancient dream-memory."

15

The Meaning of Mysticism as Seen through Its Psychology

WILLIAM ERNEST HOCKING

Metaphysics has all but ceased to draw water from the copious historic well of mysticism; theology with growing conviction warns against it: but today psychology begins to come in their place—first of course simply as an analyst, yet often lingering as something more than an analyst. What psychology inclines to appreciate is not wholly the same as that which the others have first drunk, then tasted, then thrown away. They were naturally interested in mysticism for the sake of its theory or doctrine; and the doctrine which they have thus far got from it has proved unsound beyond defense. It is one of the clear achievements of philosophy to have diagnosed and refuted this negative theory of reality, which crowns as its absolute the vanishing object of an experience approaching perfect immediacy. This work does not need to be done over again. But psychology, looking with a different interest, may find that the whole meaning of mysticism has not been exhausted in this discarded doctrine.

Psychology looks first to the experience and its effects, more or less careless of its objects or lack of objects: sometimes it seems to intimate that the objects make no difference, the essence of religion being in the experience as subjective fact; but without falling into that gratuitous and damnable mistake, we may well believe that for finding the meaning of mysticism psychology has advantages. For where self-expression falters the signs of meaning may still be read in causes and effects. The thread of meaning, often lost to the mystic himself in his ecstatic moment, may at that very moment appear, so to speak, on the reverse of the cloth, as something accomplished in the active disposition of the subject. Self-interpretation has always been a weak point in mysticism: it has never done well to put its speculative foot forward: eloquent in psychology, it is a stammerer in metaphysics. Many of its negative speculations are confessions of theoretic failure parading as dogmatic results. On its noetic side relatively helpless and plastic, mysticism has lived under all religions—hence with the stamp of various metaphysical conceptions. Have there not been mystics within orthodox Christianity, a religion in no sense a partisan of the "abstract universal"? We should then be nearer the historic truth, as well as more liberal, to regard mysticism first as an experience, and let its metaphysics come as a resultant, an inference, a presupposition. There is a minimum of theory without which mysticism cannot develop even as an experience—perhaps this: that God is one, and that it is possible to be one with him. Beyond this minimum, it is a community of experience that united the mystics rather than any community of explicit doctrine.

But it will be still nearer the truth, I believe, to regard mysticism (primarily) neither as a metaphysics, nor as an experience, but as an art: namely, as the fine art, almost the lost art, of worship. Historically the mystics are those who have carried the common art of worship to the degree of virtuosoship, they are those who have won eminent experimental knowledge of the way to God. And their technique which is the refinement of worship, often the exaggeration of worship, is at the same time the essence of all worship. In the course of their devotions the mystics report that remarkable experiences have befallen them, and that equally remarkable cognitions have come to them: but these have taken them, as it were, by surprise—they are by-products of their deeds, not their great ends. The mystic in his own first intention is he who approaches and acknowledges God in an immediate action called worship; and mysticism must be understood by way of this intention.

If this is a true principle of interpretation, it will bring about some revision of what both psychology and metaphysics have hitherto had to say of mysticism. Particularly, it seems to me, would the contribution of psychology be cleared if attention were given first to the motive of the mystic as an active individual, and then only secondarily to the various phenomena of the ecstasy of the mystic as a passive individual. The conception of the "mystical experience" must widen out, to include its intentional backbone; for the continuity of motive is the only thing that can determine the identity of the experience, and afford a definite ground for separating the abnormal from the normal.[1] And further, in the purpose and motive of the mystic we have the point at which the metaphysical (and ethical) judgment of mysticism naturally joins the work of psychology and completes it. The bold intention of the mystic to establish some immediate conscious relation with the most Real, and his firm belief in his own experience as fulfilling his intention, make it necessary for psychology and epistemology to work closely together in interpreting that experience. A revision in the one must bring about a revision in the other. It is the purpose of this article to contribute a few positive theses, chiefly to the psychology of mysticism, to its metaphysics only by implication. But first I have to record more definitely the ground of my objection to the prevailing metaphysical interpretation.

I

A philosophy does not supply the thinker *ipso facto* either with the incentive to worship or with the power to worship. Thought may perhaps persuade us of God's immediate presence in experience, and yet it leaves us empty of the idea of "approach"; it may even exclude such idea (for how can one who is universal be either approached or fled from?). Philosophy finds its Real in the third person, not in the second: it ends in the announcement, "Lo, he is there," not in the address, "Lo, Thou art here." Before that presence, we, as philosophers, stand dumb and awkward—we have nothing to say. The mystic is he who, finishing his philosophy, or more frequently, anticipating its conclusion, breaks through the film of objectivity involved in the theoretical relation and adopts toward his God the *vocative case*. In that new relation lies all that is distinctive of mysticism.

The possibility of such a relation must of course be provided for also by our philosophy—or rejected: and especially the possibility, in any such momentary act, of gaining a *knowledge* of the Real—a knowledge which outruns reason, and presents to the subject, prophetically and in an infinite synthesis, the Whole, as in its heart it is. It is to this point that pertinent attack must be directed. In the meantime the mystic, as a rule, does not try to explain *how* these things can be. He calls us to witness that they are so, and are plentifully illustrated in experience.

* * *

Mysticism as a practical attitude, while it involves cognition, is thus apparently different from discursive thought; it has some priority, even as a means of cognition, over the philosophic accomplishment *at any time accessible;* it seems to effect a *rapport* between the individual and his object in its integrity, and thus to look toward its future as well as toward its past: but in any case the defining mark of mysticism lies in this other-than-theoretical relation to the object, this quasi-destruction of objectivity seen quite simply in the conscious transition from "he" to "thou."

It is one thing to point out and illustrate the mystical relation; to analyze it is more difficult. It seems to be a kind of primitive, total apprehension introduced into the region of social and spiritual realities.[2] It seems to apply to reason's own world some more instantaneous equivalent of reason, taken from the resource of the moral man. In the attempt to characterize mystical experience, one naturally falls upon such words as "unitary," "total," "immediate"; and then since it is after all unique and fundamental to consciousness, one insists that it is not wholly describable. I am not now interested in pursuing this analysis. What I want to point out is, that these words, unitary, immediate, ineffable, which at all events apply to the mystic's *experience*, are precisely the words which the metaphysician applies to the mystic's *doctrine*. And I suggest that the misinterpretation of mysticism here in question is due to the fact that *what is a psychological report* (and a true one) *is taken as a metaphysical statement* (and a false one). From the fact that one's experience of God has been "one, immediate, and ineffable," it does not follow that God himself is merely "one, immediate, and ineffable"—and so a Being wholly removed from all concrete reality. It is true that this inference from the nature of the experience to the nature of its object is here of the closest order; and it is also true that many a mystic has committed himself to that inference. But it is possible, and necessary, to reject it. Let me attempt to show this.

If the experience is one, its object is one. True: for the unity of an experience is a unity of attention, and unity of attention implies some kind of unity in its object. And so reality must have for knowledge some unitary handle if a unitary experience of it is possible. It must have something like a "self," in which it is all represented or *resumed,* so that in the presence of that self we are, for our purposes, in presence of the whole. One's purposes might be satisfied if reality could be resumed in an "essence" or in a "formula"; but most mystics either assume or know that reality is resumed in a self of more concrete description. Now while such unity is indeed implied, the mystic is not concerned either to deny or to explain any plurality that may be compatible therewith. An "immediacy" does not legislate about what is beyond itself either to deny it or to affirm it. Reality may have innumerable branches and growing tips; any such variety is for the moment simply undetermined and out of mind.

If the experience is ineffable, the object is ineffable. True: for every unity, insofar as it is unique, is ineffable: the One has always to be expounded by what it is not—the many, the singular by the general. A certain formal ineffableness belongs therefore to the object of every unitary experience. But unities, we have just seen, are various in kind and degree. And insofar as the unity of the object has its *kind*, the object escapes from the ineffableness which may still cleave to the experience. Probably all experience in its immediate quality is incommunicable; but the arts of communication draw infinite material from the region nearer and nearer the heart of this immediacy. Immediacy and idea are not disparate stuff, they are different stages of the same stuff, the same meaning: and the individuals historically most active and fertile in this ideal exploitation of immediacy are none but the poets and mystics themselves. Have the Christian mystics ever refrained from trying to coin their experiences, their "revelations," into Latin or Spanish or German? Can we forget the bulky manuscripts of Boehme (who tells us that he spent twelve years in bringing to pen the burden of two such "ineffable" experiences), or the voluble recitements of Teresa? Consider the state of mind of Angèle de Foligno, of whom it is said that while dictating his [her] revelations to his [her] amanuensis he [she] would frequently break off, crying: "I blaspheme, brother, I blaspheme. All that I have said is nothing;—and there is nothing that I can say,"—and then continue his [her] dictation. Here is no simple ineffableness, but a very double state of mind: a mighty difficulty in expression, together with an even mightier impulse to express. As far, then, as the content of mystical experience is concerned, the word ineffable may often tell but half the truth, and a temporary half-truth, or again, it may wholly apply to that content; but in its first intention it is an expression of psychological difficulty, not rashly to be crystallized into metaphysical doctrine: the two questions are separable.

I judge, then, that the metaphysics of mysticism (for it most certainly has a metaphysics) may be richer and freer than we have been accustomed to think; and that the marks commonly attributed to the mystic absolute are in the first place so many contributions to mystic psychology. I may now turn to consider that psychology on its own ground.

II

The work of William James is the natural point of departure. For the *Varieties of Religious Experience* is very largely a treatise on religion in its mystical aspect, that is, as unreasoned personal intercourse with unseen reality.[3] James's main interest is not in explaining religious experience, but in proposing canons for judging it on the basis of its effects: hence his analyses may be broad and summary. Of mystical experience he says simply that it is ineffable and noetic, usually also transient and passive.[4] In adopting the hypothesis of the subconscious as the immediate seat of the activity before which the mystic is passive, he appeals to it only as "a mediating term," as indicating the direction for further research, not as a finished result. Thus he gives the conception, I think, its right place and proportion: for the subconscious is still more in need of illumination than in a position to give it. Whatever else is done toward the psychological interpretation of religious experience is shedding light on the problem of the subconscious; hence I may the more willingly forgo, as I must, any detailed reference to it in this paper. I shall consider first what has been added and is still to be added to James's account of mystical experience, simply as a psychological event; and then, secondly, come to the question of the motive of mysticism.

What James has spoken of as the transiency of the mystical experience may be brought under a wider category—that of rhythm, or of the alternation of states. That is, the mystic's elevation may be transient *because* it is a phase in an organic wave or sequence of some sort: and if so, it would be of decided advantage to study such wave or sequence in its totality. Any rhythmic movement in experience confesses an organic bond, indicates a causal law, and brings the fact at once within the field of the psycho-physical, offering perhaps the most favorable angle for scientific approach. Suggestions have never been lacking that the mystic's intense experiences are concomitant with certain physiological ups-and-downs, more or less vaguely defined; but the scientific development of these suggestions has been for the first time really begun by recent French students, notably Delacroix and De Montmorand.

The mystic himself is keenly conscious that with the entrance of these experiences his life is bound in a remarkable alternation: but he might well object at the outset to the theory conveyed in the idea of rhythm. For what is this elevation if not the moment of freedom from all ties of nature? Has he not in his preparation painfully put off these ties, so far as his human will could carry him, and has not the divine power finished the work which he himself could not accomplish? In short, is it not essential to the internal meaning of mysticism that this moment shall be regarded as a moment of just that absolute freedom which the psychologist cannot find anywhere else in nature? I bring up this question in order to point out that quite within the meaning of the mystic there are certain indications that the idea of rhythm need not be so alien thereto as it at first seems. In the first place, he has no positive reason derived from this meaning why his moment of union should pass, and is himself inclined to attribute this transiency to the weakness of nature. Then, again, even in the upward movement, there is a certain justice upon which the mystic depends, which blends with and gives regularity to the grace of God there found. The logic of the relation between the worshiper and his God is indeed wholly personal and particular (not magical), but the worshiper still relies upon a steadfastness in the Being worshiped; he frequently comes to look upon his elevation as a response to the right approach on his part, as some function of the moral condition of his own heart. The words of Plotinus in his letter to Flaccus seem to show well this quasi-natural adjustment of attitude to the supernatural. "But this sublime condition," he writes, "is not of permanent duration. It is only now and then that we can enjoy this elevation (mercifully made possible for us) above the limits of the body and the world. I myself have realized it but three times as yet. . . . All that tends to purify and elevate the mind will assist you in this attainment, and facilitate the approach and the recurrence of these happy intervals."[5] Thus the mystic himself is often disposed to read his experience as a course of interaction between a higher and a lower law. And it is noteworthy that while many a mystic has expressed regret that his joy could not endure, not one (so far as I have found) has expressed surprise. This surprising absence of surprise may indicate that the immediacy of the state is never so complete as to be wholly without fringes—that some awareness of the empirical self and of its ties remains. The mystic has found himself in a region where the gravitation of earth operates but slowly; but that it still operates and must claim its own, he himself seems by this silent confession to be aware. So much by way of helping the adjustment of internal meaning to the attempts of psycho-physical explanation.

It is of course clear that no rhythm of a wholly simple outline exists in this case. Hence those who look for the ground swell of the wave of mystic exaltation in some flux of that subtle quantum once called animal spirits, later, vital tone, and now coenesthesia, solve the problem too easily. There are two plain reasons for regarding variations of this type as external to the matter in hand.

First, the irregularity of the experiences in question, the absence of anything like periodicity in their occurrence. Since mystical experience ordinarily presupposes an initial act of will, and often an extended moral preparation, our theory must at least show how the rhythm appealed to involves the history of the worshiper's conscience. The internal logic of the event is so far personal that its external shape must be that of a history rather than that of a process, the semblance of periodicity obscured or lost in the movement of the individual will. This means simply that if there is any psycho-physical circuit concerned it must be one in which the "will" is interpolated as it is in the circuit of nutrition; it must be one which has as one segment a free connection with the whole system of higher centers. And the analogy of the circuit of nutrition, which does indeed require an interposed voluntary undertaking, is still too restricted; for it is no matter of life and death to the individual that his mystical cravings, if he has them, should be satisfied regularly, or ever. In this respect the movement of mystical life would more resemble the irregular curve of the life of sex; and, still more, the movement of those love-like hungers, for beauty, for society, for solitude, and the like, toward all of which, although some over-individual life may be vitally concerned, the individual may hold himself quite free.

Second, there is no depression so far as "vital tone" is concerned which corresponds in constancy and prominence to the elevation. The elevation is not in this sense above-normal that it must be compensated by a corresponding below-normal. On the contrary the elevation presents certain claims to be, as it were, another normal; some of its elements, for instance, tend to become permanent characters of consciousness, which could not be the case if they were simply extremes of "hyper-tensions." This is the point well made by Delacroix, when in commenting on the theory of Maine de Biran he says: "A *la rigeur*, the alternative of excitement and depression may be able to explain, and does explain in part, those conditions of enfeeblement, sadness, horror of self, which generally succeed the period of ecstasy among the mystics; it may explain also those passing 'aridities' which trouble the expansive beginnings of the mystic's life, aridities which the mystics signalize but which are lost in the expansion they for the moment interrupt. But it must never be forgotten that in the group of mystics here studied (Teresa, Guyon, Suso, and others) the last period of their career, wholly expansive, one of exaltation and activity, seems final. The systematization of mysticism is more complicated than this elementary rhythm."[6]

* * *

The work of Delacroix is in the highest degree masterly, and admirable in its union of sympathetic understanding with critical rigor. To my mind, however, he has mistaken the nature of the minor rhythm, and is thus in some danger of eliminating what is characteristic of mysticism. I should agree with Delacroix that the pathological fluctuations often associated with mystical experience are not essential parts of it; but I should not agree that the elementary alternation is essentially pathological, or that it is ever overcome. For whatever the psychological phenomena associated with mystical experience may be, the thread upon which they are hung is—as I must insist—the mystic's intention; and if that intention is at all fairly conceived as an intention to worship, it involves an occupation of attention which in the nature of the case must alternate with attention to other affairs. I am driven therefore, in the search for a psychology of mysticism, to look for further analogies among those normal alternations such as sleeping and waking, work and recreation, competition and cooperation, the hungers and satisfactions already referred to, conception and gestation, etc. In this respect, De Montmorand seems to me nearer the truth than any other writer. . . . Alternation lies deep in the nature of things psychical as well as physiological: it is the fundamental method of growth, of the influx of new freedom; and I am inclined to regard the mystical experience as an incident in the attainment of a new psychical level, and one which in various forms and degrees is a manifoldly recurrent event in every person's life. So much for general orientation as to the nature of the rhythm in mystical experience: I believe that it will now be possible by a nearer view of the facts to state with some degree of accuracy the *principle of alternation* here involved.

III

A radical alternation in consciousness may involve the disconnection of the two alternate strands one from another, as in the case of sleeping and waking. In the traditional type of ecstasy, the mystic is as thoroughly detached from his waking world as is the sleeper: and there are certain features of this disconnection which I beg leave to recall, in the hope of catching a glimpse in this pronounced form of the principle of alternation which pervades all mysticism.

In this detachment of the ecstatic from his world there is an interesting union of voluntary and involuntary factors, which closely resembles the case of sleep. It is a part of the mystic's voluntary preparation to evade the insistence of the senses, to withdraw his thoughts and desires from the interests of current living, to enter into solitude and silence, to turn his attention within. In a measure this turning away is usually guided by a positive direction of the mind to some object—say the passion of Christ—and is sustained by a lively religious impulse which rather engulfs the other desires than destroys them: to this extent it more resembles the intense and pointed absorption of the abstracted thinker than the willing laxity of the wooer of sleep. But while the rapt thinker may be lost to his surroundings, his "absence of mind" remains within control, he does not drift beyond the point of recoverable self-direction: the object of the mystic's meditation however becomes a living current which carries him away beyond the reach of life—he is given over, like the sleeper, to the movement of forces which must run their own course. The period of absence from life is like a temporary loss of life, an obliteration of some elements of complete personality; and as the loss of life in sleep is regarded as a means of keeping it, so the mystic often looks upon his self-abandonment as a paradoxical condition, not more remarkable than sleep, for maintaining his spiritual integrity.

It may be worth while to remark in passing that the idea of mystery connected with what we call mysticism is largely due to this disconnection rather than to any inherent mysteriousness in the content of the experience. In the historical origins of the word "mystic," the thing signified was a certain *social* disconnection—the initiate unable to communicate his knowledge to the world, the world unable to make connections with the initiate. But the underlying fact is psychological: mystery is felt whenever there are two bodies of experience not in perfect communication, quite apart from the question whether the one or the other is inherently wonderful or weird. Mystery does not lie in either of those two bodies alone; it expresses the state of mind of one who *begins to see*, that is, who begins to see one experience in terms of another. It is thus the characteristic quality of any new idea, not wholly naturalized in the mind. The mystic is presented with two experiences neither of which he can doubt; both must be true, and he does not understand *how* both are true. Here for instance is a typical mystical revelation of a mild order, and a typical expression thereof: "How came this creation so magically woven that nothing can do me mischief but myself. . . . If I will stand upright the creation cannot bend me." Here stands Emerson with the weight of appearances against him, sure of creation and sure of his idea, yet confessing that the mode of weaving the two into one fabric is beyond his penetration, and so, "magical." From this point of view, the mystic might be defined as the man who is willing to drop one world of assurance while he seizes another, confident that the fabric of the world will harmonize them both. Inability to bring the two experiences together tends, it is true, to cast doubt for a time on the reality of the one and the other; and the religious mystic is one for whom another world has gained such substantiality that the reality of everyday experience has suffered this kind of passing doubt. But even when the doubt passes he remains a mystic so long as the union of one with the other is not perfectly solved.

Having in the last paragraph been using the word mystic in a somewhat loose and generalized fashion, I now return to the mystic in our special sense, the man whose particular dissociation is between the *whole* of the system of things temporal on one side, and on the other the heart of the eternal, which he hopes to make empirically present to his consciousness. This involves an emphatic separation from his visible social world as well as from his physical world—a phase of the matter that needs special mention, because we are not inclined in our time to rate highly any solitary aspect of religious thought or practice, and because there is much in modern times as in ancient times that looks like mass-mysticism. I refer of course to religious dances, dramas, festivals, revivals, in which the white-heat of social consciousness seems to become the generator and sustainer of mystical enthusiasms. But I submit that even in these somewhat tumultuous and disorderly variations of our theme, the mass-consciousness forms the level from which the individual departs: he is not a mystic until his own spirit has made its solitary leap to God, like a tongue of flame out of the midst of the fire. Much of what we call "social" life moves on a similar principle, that of passing from hand to hand a function which, in any one hand, is a solitary function: each one in turn becomes "it," i.e. takes upon himself alone the difficulty in question, learning by his own experience what otherwise he sees only from outside. Whoever helps to sustain any "social" structure is alone just insofar as he is responsible; and he comes for the most part to his solitary social position through having wrestled with some angel or other in more literal isolation from other human ken. The initiate must go down alone into the grave, though initiation, on the whole, is a social ceremony. And so whether we have in mind an orgy of Dionysus or a meeting of the Society of Friends, it is individual seizure by the spirit which marks the moment of religious success. We do not understand solitude until we see that it can ride on the back of any whirl of sociality however furious: and that its pang may be the more poignant because the utmost limit of common possession has been tested in an immediately preceding moment. He who merely imitates is but a false mystic, for the thing to be imitated is the burst of original impulse; he who is entranced by social suggestion is but a false mystic, for the inner core of all that his environment presses upon him is the violent subdual of the social bond by the superior energy of the divine *rapport*. He alone is utterly unsocial who refuses, when his own watch comes, to go out and meet the absolute in the darkness. Solitude, I say, is the essence of mysticism; and I add the basis of its supreme social importance.

For it is the most dangerous things that are the most important. We of this age have come to fear solitude and with it mysticism, because solitude is the home of stagnant growths and morbid-consciousness, because it is the crowning curse of all vices. We see in it only the danger of losing objectivity, which is indeed its essential peril. But it is the intention, and so the defining character, of the mystic solitude, that its absolute object develops in strength *pari passu* with the entrance into subjectivity. Mysticism in its true character, is just the redemption of solitude: it is a process which enters one step further into the heart of our own infinite subjectivity and reclaims it for social service in the form first of a deepened morality and art. If our own age with its growing sociality and immersion in the manifold is little mystical, it is because the power of evaluating solitude, and with it the depth of self-consciousness, is so little developed. And insofar as it has flattened and shallowed out, it is because it has so far lost its mystical instincts. Mysticism, as an identifying of the subjective with the absolute-universal, might be described as an organic cultivation of reason—though not of the "reason which can (as yet) be reasoned": its fruit is an insight without reasons (without palpable roots in other insights), and without friends. The vital function of mysticism is *origination*, the creation of novelty. Of the two enemies to this pure originality the friends are perhaps more seductive than the reasons. Inevitably then, the blade of the mystic's disconnection must pass through the whole sheaf of his social ties.

Can we now state the *principle of alternation* in any definite form? Most generally put, it seems to me this: Concrete living is a condition in which we pursue some total good under shapes and by means which are inadequate to it, and so partly false to it. We are from time to time obliged to reject what we have done, to withdraw our forward moving efforts, and revert to the Whole. This necessity is due not simply to the fact of error—which might conceivably be remedied on the spot by some moving compensation—but to the type of error: it involves not only our tools, but our empirical selves, the operators. Take the case of intellectual originality. One wishes to know the whole truth—some unknown truth. The best means to that end are—reason, and social reason; he who would originate must fill himself as full as possible of science, history, social motives, the whole world: but there comes a moment when these very things, his necessary means, become, as we said, his enemies—his poisons. This is the moment at which they become *himself*. It is this self which must be withdrawn and reoriented; it must turn its back upon itself, and lose itself in the unknown whole. Every detail of psychical operation shows this method of action. Attention is a rapidly alternating current, perpetually withdrawn from its object and instantaneously replaced: but in the instant of withdrawal having recovered a better poise and a steadier termination, having wiped away the film of relativity with which self and object had begun to infect each other. The mystic only does consciously and totally that which we are all continually doing in the minuter movement of psychical life, that which we all resort to in fragmentary and instinctive manner.

Thus, at the bottom of the psychological alternation there lies an epistemological principle, which deserves to be called the Principle of Alternation. It is the counterpart and corrective of the Principle of Relativity. It is not knowledge that is relative, but the act of knowing. It is my concrete historical nature which determines that at any moment I may see but one side of the shield; it is my knowledge of the whole which leads me, by an alternation of position, to repair the defect of my knowing. In all science we recognize the alternate use of categories which are singly imperfect, but mutually corrective. The concept of substance, whether in the form of atom, or of energy, or of soul, may be inadequate for knowledge, but is indispensable for knowing. It is the same with social knowledge. Do I wish to know a person? I must pursue acquaintance in two antithetical directions: I must learn to know him in what he does, at his periphery, in the various expressions of his life that manifest themselves in my temporal world—and I must also learn to know him by the pursuit of his central "substance," by the mystical seizure in intimacy of that unity from which all these plural deeds are deposited. It is by a similar interplay of categories that I must reach a concrete knowledge of my world as a whole: at its periphery, it is "experience," "life"—at its center it is "substance," "reality," "God." My total picture of this world is drawn like an artist's sketch: not by a line continuous in the field of vision, but by a series of lines which err and which are broken in their course by reversion to the—undrawn—idea. The plural and visible aspect of things is divine also—that is, if we are able to see it so. But we need at least to have caught the idea of the original in some experience, in order to flourish with our interpretation. He who knows God at his periphery alone, or through morality and "social service," is using but one of a necessary pair of categories. He has what we might call an honorable business acquaintance with his universe. But he has no home.

IV

In what has already been said about the mystical experience simply as a psychological event, we have been foreshadowing a definition of the mystic's purpose. It only remains to bring this into tangible form. The mystic who knows himself is a mystic, not because he finds his world so bad that he must effect a spiritual retreat from it; but because he finds his world so good that he must perform a spiritual journey to the heart of it. He is not content, nor able, to hammer away at the circumference without sometime catching a glimpse of the moving principle of his labor: and whether or not he can yet grasp that principle in philosophic expression, he can at least grasp it in an experience which is immediate without being irrational. Philosopher or not, he finds that his Reality must be known by alternate exposure to its peripheral and its central aspects, to its moving and its eternal categories; and he finds that in his knowledge of this central Substance, there must be included the empirical element, present also at the periphery. The impulse of worship may thus be understood as an impulse toward *integrity* in one's relation to his absolute: no matter in how many other ways he may know the real and the good, the worshiper desires to complete his relation by knowing them also in immediate individual presence.

On its subjective side, this impulse toward integrity has a twofold character. The mystic is moved by ambition and by love. His ambition is to perfect himself, to clear his head and to purify his character. This ambition though it impels to the movement of mind we call worship is still touched by a sense of the importance of work, the world's work, as if it were for the sake of those ends that one turned his back upon them, because he must first unify himself. But when the absolute which one approaches is able to drain into its own vortex all the meanings of that work, and so to abolish the independent worth of that work, the zealot becomes the lover. When fear and hope have thus disappeared from the impulse of worship we have mysticism in its purity.

*   *   *

It is from this point of view that I would judge the theory of Leuba, who in several well-known articles[7] has done much to supply the lack of a psychology of the mystic's motive. He has rightly distinguished the two sides of this motive. The ambitious element appears to him as a fixed necessity for moral perfection, a "tendency to the universalization of action," amounting almost to "hyperaesthesia of the moral sensibility," in many historic instances. The element of love appears to him under a very earthly guise, as a need for satisfying the instinctive affections, a need for "organic enjoyment" in which a thwarted human desire finds an ideal route to its satisfaction. The divine love, on this basis, is a form of the pursuit of pleasure; no wonder that it seems to him inconsistent with that other fundamental motive, the moral ambition so often expressed in the severe asceticism of the mystic's self-discipline; no wonder that the mystic's development is read by him as an elimination of Eros, a conquering of love by moral ambition, "a reconstruction of the individual under the influence of the disposition toward universalized action, wherein he may reach entire deliverance from the desires of the natural man." I cannot but believe that this alleged incompatibility has been created by Leuba himself, through the view he takes of the nature of the divine love.

At the same time, Leuba is fundamentally right in recording the contrast between these two motives; incompatible they are not, but antithetical they assuredly are. And it is easy for the antithesis to become an antagonism. On the organic level, love and ambition look in opposite directions. The element of love may make its beginnings felt in the midst of work as a sense of the aimlessness of work, a questioning of worthwhileness, a feeling of *moral wear-and-tear* in the determined pursuit of things whose value is not wholly convincing, a need for recovering sincerity by spiritual repose: and this desire, still of the same moral stuff that first launched the work, now reverses the direction of action, and turns naturally to "pleasure," as a thing convincing without effort, especially to companionship and the friendship of the sexes. Practically, one turns away from work; and the motive which is at bottom a moral demand for the renewal of worth may easily be taken for a denial of worth: love, ignoring its own nature as transmuted ambition, enters into false competition with duty. And duty may respond by forgetting that it is nothing but transmuted love.

This is true in things total as in things partial: hence it entangles the mystic as well as other men. It is true that the love of God may become a path of dissipation, antagonizing moral ambition: but it is not true that this is its natural character. We are bound to define the motive of mysticism by its normal condition, if it has one—even though this normal condition had never yet been realized. And we are still more bound to give the mystics credit for their best achievements, and for their deepest discriminations. No one who reads the mystics can suppose that they have been unaware of precisely this danger; nor that they have been undiligent in guarding against it. They have seen and exactly stated the truth that the highest possibilities of experience are also the most perilous.

* * *

It has never been easy for human nature to sustain its love at the level of true worship; it has never been easy to keep integrity in presence of that seductive movement of reflection which seizes upon an experience and forgets its first intention; there is a statistical certainty of lapse, and this, if Delacroix is right, necessitates the long agonies of the second stadium of the mystic's life-cycle. The important point for a fair scientific theory is: that mysticism has its own corrective within itself. It recurs to the essential identity of its love and its ambition.

To know that the love of God is of the same substance with moral ambition decides some questions about the psychological nature of that love. But it does not decide the worth of Leuba's thesis that it has close psychological kinship with the love of man and woman. It would be necessary in a complete theory to show the wide differences of these two loves as well as their striking likenesses; but there is no greater scientific service than to define with accuracy the extent of this likeness so universally recognized in literature and history. To my mind this can only be done with the aid of the principle of alternation. Beyond doubt the mystic exaltation sweeps up into its current whatever in the thousandfold alternate swingings of human nature moves in its own direction—not, however, as their product but as their master. It would indeed be surprising if the sexual nature of man, with its movement away from the sphere of deeds to the sphere of substance, with its strong tide toward the over-individual and racial, with its suggestion of total, infinite, and yet immediate worth, did *not* more quickly and completely than any other human impulse discover in worship its ultimate meaning and law. And this, not because the love of God is at bottom sexual love, but because sexual love is potentially love of the divine. As to the details of Leuba's theory, I leave them to be dealt with by his competent critic, De Montmorand.[8] But the main criticism to be passed upon that theory is only that it is not the whole truth; and that in this case anything short of the whole truth is untrue.

The whole truth lies in this direction—that *all* of our human impulses and loves are akin. And the psychology of mysticism waits less for an analysis of the love of God than for an analysis of all other human desires. It is not this love, but those that need explanation. The love of God is the one natural instinct of man: worship is the one deed which answers as an echo all other deeds of history. Upon one point the psychologies of Plato, Augustine and Spinoza are agreed: that all special desires are refracted desires for the absolute good. We moderns with superior analysis have not yet regained in our own tongue these results. We need to know the "laws of transformation and equivalence" of desires and values: then we should see how they may be one and all not suppressed by, but paid-over into, the all-consuming passion of religion. Both Leuba and his critic fall into the error of supposing that in the perfecting of mysticism some side of human nature is put under, some dissociation or amnesia has been accomplished, so that the "lower centers" never again assert themselves. All this seems foreign to the facts. I like better the theory that in mysticism the needs of sex together with all needs are understood and satisfied; that all of the hundred voices of human desire are here brought to unison. With this understanding and not otherwise can I see how religion is to fulfill its assumed functions: To keep from mutual estrangement the primitive in us and the far-civilized. To offer individual souls—malformed in the specialization of our social order, or mutilated in its accidents—the possibility of complete personality. To unify in wish and will, as reason does in principle, the whole moral existence of man.

Mysticism, as worship, is only a moment of reflux in the movement of living: but in that moment human nature is dissolved and recreated, shattered and remolded—a little nearer to the heart's desire.

NOTES

1. It may be true, and I believe that it is true, that the motive presupposes an experience (in the relatively passive sense), i.e. that the impulse to worship God, whatever that may mean, is due to some perception of God as already in a degree present. The impulse of worship in its more instinctive forms is quite analogous to the quick movement of the mind toward the source of an agreeable or emotionally warming suggestion, to increase it, to lift as much of it as possible out of the region of idea into the region of empirical presence. But as experience may determine motive, so motive in turn develops experience; the two factors are in continuous and instantaneous interaction during the whole movement of consciousness to its culmination, and it is only because the initial experience has a value, i.e. takes to itself a motive, that it has a career in consciousness. What I maintain is only that we cannot understand that career apart from the motive, that our notion of the experience must include it. . . .

2. Josiah Royce's often-quoted phrase which described the mystic as the "thoroughgoing empiricist" is strikingly true of the mystic's method of knowing;

but the mystic's peculiarity is that he applies this method to objects which empiricists generally insist *cannot be given* in any such immediate, unreasoned manner, namely to totals—not to elements; to souls—not to sensations; to resultants (like "history" or "society")—not to factors; and finally, to God himself.

3. Every treatment of the psychology of religion tends for obvious reasons to become a psychology of mysticism; and there were further reasons in James's own temperament why this should be markedly the case with his own work. His interest was held by everything individual, original, and instinctive, especially if it tended to sway away from the institutional, and to renounce the support of reasons: hence he naturally finds in his net those who make their private way to God, and reach an empirical assurance of their soul's security, apart from the sanction of authority. These are mystics; and this original, untamed, God-seeking element is the mystical element in every religious nature.

4. *Varieties,* pp. 380–81.

5. Translated by Henry Vaughan, in *Hours with the Mystics,* Vol. I, p. 81.

6. *Études d'histoire et de psychologie du mysticisme* (Paris, 1908), p. 415.

7. *Revue Philosophique* 54 (1902, ii.) 1ff., 441ff.; 57 (1904, i.) 70. *Mind,* N.S., 14 (1905), 15–27.

8. *Revue Philosophique* 56 (1903) 382ff.; 57 (1904) 242ff.; 58 (1904) 602ff.; 60 (1905) 1ff.

16

Deautomatization and the Mystic Experience

ARTHUR J. DEIKMAN, M.D.

To study the mystic experience one must turn initially to material that appears unscientific, is couched in religious terms, and seems completely subjective. Yet these religious writings are data and not to be dismissed as something divorced from the reality with which psychological science is concerned. The following passage from *The Cloud of Unknowing*, a fourteenth-century religious treatise, describes a procedure to be followed in order to attain an intuitive knowledge of God. Such an intuitive experience is called mystical because it is considered beyond the scope of language to convey. However, a careful reading will show that these instructions contain within their religious idiom psychological ideas pertinent to the study and understanding of a wide range of phenomena not necessarily connected with theological issues:

> . . . forget all the creatures that ever God made and the works of them, so that thy thought or thy desire be not directed or stretched to any of them, neither in general nor in special. . . . At the first time when thou dost it, thou findst but a darkness and as it were a kind of unknowing, thou knowest not what, saving that thou feelest in thy will a naked intent unto God . . . thou mayest neither see him clearly by light of understanding in thy reason, nor feel him in sweetness of love in thy affection . . . if ever thou shalt see him or feel him as it may be here, it must always be in this cloud and in this darkness. . . . Smite upon that thick cloud of unknowing with a sharp dart of longing love (Knowles, 1961, p. 77).

Specific questions are raised by this subjective account: What constitutes a state of consciousness whose content is not rational thought ("understanding in thy reason"), affective ("sweetness of love"), or sensate ("darkness," "cloud of unknowing")? By what means do both an active "forgetting" and an objectless "longing" bring about such a state? A comparison of this passage with others in the classical mystic literature indicates that the author is referring to the activities of renunciation and contemplative meditation. This paper will present a psychological model of the mystic experience based on the assumptions that meditation and renunciation are primary techniques for producing it, and that the process can be conceptualized as one of deautomatization.

PHENOMENA OF THE MYSTIC EXPERIENCE

Accounts of mystic experiences can be categorized as (a) untrained-sensate, (b) trained-sensate, and (c) trained-transcendent. "Untrained-sensate" refers to phenomena occurring in persons not regularly engaged in meditation, prayer, or other exercises aimed at achieving a religious experience. These persons come from all occupations and classes. The mystic state they report is one of intense affective, perceptual, and cognitive phenomena that appear to be extensions of familiar psychological processes. Nature and drugs are the most frequent precipitating factors. James cites the account of Trevor to illustrate a nature experience:

> For nearly an hour I walked along the road to the "Cat and Fiddle," and then returned. On the way back, suddenly, without warning, I felt that I was in heaven—an inward state of peace and joy and assurance indescribably intense, accompanied with a sense of being bathed in a warm glow of light, as though the external condition had brought about the internal effect—a feeling of having passed, beyond the body, though the scene around me stood out more clearly and as if nearer to me than before, by reason of the illumination in the midst of which I seemed to be placed. This deep emotion lasted, though with decreasing strength, until I reached home, and for some time after, only gradually passing away (James, *The Varieties of Religious Experience*, 1929 ed., p. 388).

More recent accounts of experiences with LSD-25 and related drugs fall into the same group (Watts, 1962).

The "trained-sensate" category refers to essentially the same phenomena occurring in religious persons in the West and in the East who have deliberately sought "grace," "enlightenment," or "union" by means of long practice in concentration and renunciation (contemplative meditation, Yoga, and so forth). One example of this group is Richard Rolle, who wrote:

> . . . I was sitting in a certain chapel, and while I was taking pleasure in the delight of some prayer or meditation, I suddenly felt within me an unwonted and pleasant fire. When I had for long doubted from whence it came, I learned by experience that it came from the Creator

and not from creature, since I found it ever more pleasing and full of heat . . . (Knowles, 1961, p. 57).

A more elaborate experience is recorded by Julian of Norwich:

> In this (moment) suddenly I saw the red blood trickle down from under the garland hot and freshly and right plenteously. . . . And in the same shewing suddenly the Trinity fulfilled my heart most of joy. And so I understood it shall be in heaven without end to all that shall come there (Warrack, 1952, p. 8).

Visions, feelings of "fire," "sweetness," "song," and joy are various accompaniments of this type of experience.

The untrained-sensate and the trained-sensate states are phenomenologically indistinguishable, with the qualification that the trained mystics report experiences conforming more closely to the specific religious cosmology to which they are accustomed. As one might expect, an experience occurring as the result of training, with the support of a formal social structure, and capable of being repeated, tends to have a more significant and persisting psychological effect. However, spontaneous conversion experiences are also noteworthy for their influence on a person's life. Typical of all mystic experience is a more or less gradual fading away of the state, leaving only a memory and a longing for that which was experienced.

Mystics such as St. John of the Cross and St. Teresa of Avila, commentators such as Poulain, and Eastern mystic literature in general, divide the effects and stages through which mystics progress into a lesser experience of strong emotion and ideation (sensate) and a higher, ultimate experience that goes beyond affect or ideation. It is the latter experience, occurring almost always in association with long training, that characterizes the "trained-transcendent" group. The trans-sensate aspect is stated specifically by a number of authors, such as Walter Hilton and St. John of the Cross:

> From what I have said you may understand that visions of revelations by spirits, whether seen in bodily form or in the imagination, and whether in sleeping or waking, do not constitute true contemplation. This applies equally to any other sensible experiences of seemingly spiritual origin, whether of sound, taste, smell or of warmth felt like a glowing fire in the breast or in other parts of the body, anything, indeed, that can be experienced by the physical senses (Hilton, 1953, pp. 14–15).

> . . . that inward wisdom is so simple, so general and so spiritual that it has not entered into the understanding enwrapped or clad in

any form or image subject to sense, it follows that sense and imagination (as it has not entered through them nor has taken their form and color) cannot account for it or imagine it, so as to say anything concerning it, although the soul be clearly aware that it is experiencing and partaking of that rare and delectable wisdom (St. John of the Cross, 1953, Vol. I, p. 457).

A similar distinction between lower (sensate) and higher (transcendent) contemplative states may be found in Yoga texts. "Conscious concentration" is a preliminary step to "concentration which is not conscious (of objects)."

For practice when directed towards any supporting-object is not capable of serving as an instrument to this [concentration not conscious of an object]. . . . Mind-stuff, when engaged in the practice of this [imperceptible object], seems as if it were itself non-existent and without any supporting-object. Thus [arises] that concentration [called] seedless, [without sensational stimulus], which is not conscious of objects (Woods, 1914, p. 42).

In the transcendent state, multiplicity disappears and a sense of union with the One or with All occurs. "When all lesser things and ideas are transcended and forgotten, and there remains only a perfect state of imagelessness where Tathagata and Tathata are merged into perfect Oneness . . ." (Goddard, 1938, p. 322).

Then the spirit is transported high above all the faculties into a void of immense solitude whereof no mortal can adequately speak. It is the mysterious darkness wherein is concealed the limitless Good. To such an extent are we admitted and absorbed into something that is one, simple, divine, and illimitable, that we seem no longer distinguishable from it. . . . In this unity, the feeling of multiplicity disappears. When, afterwards, these persons come to themselves again, they find themselves possessed of a distinct knowledge of things, more luminous and more perfect than that of others. . . . This obscurity is a light to which no created intelligence can arrive by its own nature (Poulain, 1950, p. 272).

This state is described in all the literatures as one in which the mystic is passive in that he has abandoned striving. He sees "grace" to be the action of God on himself and feels himself to be receptive. In addition, some descriptions indicate that the senses and faculties of thought feel suspended, a state described in Catholic literature as the "ligature."

Human variety is reflected in the superficial differences between the various mystic records. However, perusal of these accounts leads one to agree with Maréchal when he writes,

> A very delicate psychological problem is thus raised: the consensus of the testimonies we have educed is too unanimous to be rejected. It compels us to recognize the existence in certain subjects of a special psychological state, which generally results from a very close interior concentration, sustained by an intense affective movement, but which, on the other hand, no longer presents any trace of "discursiveness," spatial imagination, or reflex consciousness. And the disconcerting question arises: after images and concepts and the conscious Ego have been abolished, what subsists of the intellectual life? Multiplicity will have disappeared, true, but to the advantage of what kind of unity? (Maréchal, 1964, p. 185.)

In summary, mystic literature suggests that various kinds of people have attained what they considered to be exalted states of mind and feeling, states that may be grouped in three divisions: untrained-sensate, trained-sensate, and trained-transcendent. The most important distinction would appear to be between an experience grounded in customary affect, sensations, and ideations, and an experience that is said to transcend such modalities.

BASIC MYSTIC TECHNIQUES

How is the mystic experience produced? To answer this question I will examine the two basic techniques involved in mystical exercises: contemplation and renunciation.

Contemplation is, ideally, a nonanalytic apprehension of an object or idea—nonanalytic because discursive thought is banished and the attempt is made to empty the mind of everything except the percept of the object in question. Thought is conceived of as an interference with the direct contact that yields essential knowledge through perception alone. The renunciation of worldly goals and pleasures, both physical and psychological, is an extension of the same principle of freeing oneself from distractions that interfere with the perception of higher realisms or more beautiful aspects of existence. The renunciation prescribed is most thorough and quite explicit in all texts. The passage that begins this paper instructs, "Forget all the creatures that ever God made . . . so that thy thought . . . be not directed . . . to any of them. . . ." In the Lankavatra Scripture one reads, ". . . he must seek to annihilate all vagrant thoughts and notions belonging to the externality of things, and all ideas of individuality and generality, of suffering and impermanence, and cultivate the noblest ideas of egolessness and emptiness and imagelessness . . ." (Goddard, 1938, p. 323). Meister Eckhart promises: "If we keep ourselves free from the things that are outside us, God will give us in exchange everything that is in heaven, . . . itself with all its powers . . ." (Clark and Skinner, 1958, p. 104). In Hilton one reads, "Therefore if you desire to discover your soul, withdraw your thoughts from outward and material things, forgetting if possible your own body and its five senses . . ." (Hilton, 1953, p. 205). St. John calls for the explicit banishment of memory:

> Of all these forms and manners of knowledge the soul must strip and void itself, and it must strive to lose the imaginary apprehension of them, so that there may be left in it no kind of impression of knowledge, nor trace of aught soever, but rather the soul must remain barren and bare, as if these forms had never passed through it and in total oblivion and suspension. And this cannot happen unless the memory be annihilated as to all its forms, if it is to be united with God (St. John of the Cross, 1953, p. 227).

In most Western and Eastern mystic practice, renunciation also extends to the actual life situation of the mystic. Poverty, chastity, and the solitary way are regarded as essential to the attainment of mystic union. Zen Buddhism, however, sees the ordinary life as a proper vehicle for "satori" as long as the "worldly" passions and desires are given up, and with them the intellectual approach to experience. "When I am in my isness, thoroughly purged of all intellectual sediments, I have my freedom in its primary sense . . . free from intellectual complexities and moralistic attachments . . ." (Suzuki, 1959, p. 19).

Instructions for performing contemplative meditation indicate that a very active effort is made to exclude outer and inner stimuli, to devalue and banish them, and at the same time to focus attention on the meditative object. In this active phase of contemplation the concentration of attention upon particular objects, ideas, physical movements, or breathing exercises is advised as an aid to diverting attention from its usual channels and restricting it to a monotonous focus.[1] Patanjali comments,

> Binding the mind-stuff to a place is fixed-attention. . . . Focusedness of the presented idea on that place is contemplation. . . . This same [contemplation] shining forth [in consciousness] as the intended object and nothing more, and, as it were, emptied of itself, is concentration. . . . The three in one are constraint. . . . Even these [three] are indirect aids to seedless [concentration] (Woods, 1914, pp. 203–8).

Elaborate instructions are found in Yoga for the selection of objects for contemplation and for the proper utilization of posture and breathing to create optimal conditions for concentration. Such techniques are not usually found in the Western religious literature except in the form of the injunction to keep the self oriented toward God and to fight the distractions which are seen as coming from the devil. (*The Spiritual Exercises of St. Ignatius* [Puhl, 1962] is a possible exception.)

The active phase of contemplative meditation is a preliminary to the stage of full contemplation, in which the subject is caught up and absorbed in a process he initiated but which now seems autonomous, requiring no effort. Instead, passivity—self-surrender—is called for, an open receptivity amidst the "darkness" resulting from the banishment of thoughts and sensations and the renunciation of goals and desires directed toward the world.

> When this active effort of mental concentration is successful, it is followed by a more passive, receptive state of *samadhi* in which the earnest disciple will enter into the blissful abode of noble wisdom . . . (Goddard, 1938, p. 323).

> For if such a soul should desire to make any effort of its own with its interior faculties, this means that it will hinder and love the blessings which . . . God is instilling into it and impressing upon it (Hilton, 1953, p. 380).

It should not be forgotten that the techniques of contemplation and renunciation are exercised within the structure of some sort of theological schema. This schema is used to interpret and organize the experiences that occur. However, mere doctrine is usually not enough. The Eastern texts insist on the necessity for being guided by a guru (an experienced teacher), for safety's sake as well as in order to attain the spiritual goal. In Western religion, a "spiritual advisor" serves as guide and teacher. The presence of a motivating and organizing conceptual structure and the support and encouragement of a teacher are undoubtedly important in helping a person to persist in the meditation exercises and to achieve the marked personality changes that can occur through success in this endeavor. Enduring personality change is made more likely by the emphasis on adapting behavior to the values and insights associated both with the doctrinal structure and with the stages of mystical experience.

How can one explain the phenomena and their relation to these techniques? Most explanations in the psychological and psychoanalytic literature have been general statements emphasizing a regression to the early infant-mother symbiotic relationship. These statements range from an extreme position, such as Alexander's (1931), where Buddhist training is described as a withdrawal of libido from the world to be reinvested in the ego until an intrauterine narcissism is achieved—"the pure narcissism of the sperm"—to the basic statement of Freud's (1961, vol. 21, pp. 64–73) that "oceanic feeling" is a memory of a relatively undifferentiated infantile ego state. Lewin (1950, pp. 149–55) in particular has developed this concept. In recent years hypotheses have been advanced uniting the concepts of regression and of active adaptation. The works of Kris (1952, p. 302), Fingarette (1963), and Prince and Savage (1965) illustrate this approach to the mystic experience. This paper will attempt an explanation of mystic phenomena from a different point of view, that of attentional mechanisms in perception and cognition.

DEAUTOMATIZATION

In earlier studies of experimental meditation, I hypothesized that mystic phenomena were a consequence of a *deautomatization* of the psychological structures that organize, limit, select, and interpret perceptual stimuli. I suggested the hypotheses of sensory translation, reality transfer, and perceptual expansion to explain certain unusual perceptions of the meditation subjects (Deikman, 1966b). At this point I will try to present an integrated formulation that relates these concepts to the classical mystic techniques of renunciation and contemplation.

Deautomatization is a concept stemming from Hartmann's (1958, pp. 88–91) discussion of the automatization of motor behavior:

> In well-established achievements they [motor apparatuses] function automatically: the integration of the somatic systems involved in the action is automatized, and so is the integration of the individual mental acts involved in it. With increasing exercise of the action its intermediate steps disappear from consciousness . . . not only motor behavior but perception and thinking, too, show automatization. . . .
>
> It is obvious that automatization may have economic advantages, in saving attention cathexis in particular and simple cathexis of consciousness in general. . . . Here, as in most adaptation processes, we have a purposive provision for the average expectable range of tasks.

Gill and Brenman (1959, p. 178) developed the concept of deautomatization:

> Deautomatization is an undoing of the automatizations of apparatuses—both means and goal structures—directed toward the environment. Deautomatization is, as it were, a shake-up which can be followed by an advance or a retreat in the level of organization. . . . Some manipulation of the attention directed toward the functioning of an apparatus is necessary if it is to be deautomatized.

Thus, deautomatization may be conceptualized as the undoing of automatization, presumably by *reinvesting actions and percepts with attention.*

The concept of psychological *structures* follows the definition by Rapaport and Gill (1959, pp. 157–58):

> Structures are configurations of a slow rate of change . . . *within which, between which, and by means of which mental processes take place.* . . . *Structures are hierarchically ordered.* . . . This assumption . . . is significant because it is the foundation for the psychoanalytic propositions concerning differentiation (whether resulting in discrete structures which are then co-ordinated, or in the increased internal articulation of structures), and because it implies that the quality of a process depends upon the level of the structural hierarchy on which it takes place.

The deautomatization of a structure may result in a shift to a structure lower in the hierarchy, rather than a complete cessation of the particular function involved.

Contemplative Meditation

In reflecting on the technique of contemplative meditation, one can see that it seems to constitute just such a manipulation of attention as is required to produce deautomatization. The percept receives intense attention while the use of attention for abstract categorization and thought is explicitly prohibited. Since automatization normally accomplishes the transfer of attention *from* a percept or action to abstract thought activity, the meditation procedure exerts a force in the reverse direction. Cognition is inhibited in favor of perception; the active intellectual style is replaced by a receptive perceptual mode.

Automatization is a hierarchically organized developmental process, so one would expect deautomatization to result in a shift toward a perceptual and cognitive organization characterized as "primitive," that is, an organization preceding the analytic, abstract, intellectual mode typical of present-day adult thought. The perceptual and cognitive functioning of children and of people of primitive cultures have been studied by Werner, who described primitive imagery and thought as (a) relatively more vivid and sensuous, (b) syncretic, (c) physiognomic and animated, (d) dedifferentiated with respect to the distinctions between self and object and between objects, and (e) characterized by a dedifferentiation and fusion of sense modalities. In a statement based on studies of eidetic imagery in children as well as on broader studies of perceptual development, Werner (1957, p. 152) states:

. . . The image . . . gradually changed in functional character. It becomes essentially subject to the exigencies of abstract thought. Once the image changes in function and becomes an instrument in reflective thought, its structure will also change. It is only through such structural change that the image can serve as an instrument of expression in abstract mental activity. This is why, of necessity the sensuousness, fullness of detail, the color and vivacity of the image must fade.

Theoretically, deautomatization should reverse this development in the direction of primitive thought, and it is striking to note that classical accounts of mystic experience emphasize the phenomenon of Unity. Unity can be viewed as a dedifferentiation that merges all boundaries until the self is no longer experienced as a separate object and customary perceptual and cognitive distinctions are no longer applicable. In this respect, the mystic literature is consistent with the deautomatization hypothesis. If one searches for evidence of changes in the mystic's experience of the external world, the classical literature is of less help, because the mystic's orientation is inward rather than outward and he tends to write about God rather than nature. However, in certain accounts of untrained-sensate experience there is evidence of a gain in sensory richness and vividness. James (1929, pp. 243–44), in describing the conversion experience, states: "A third peculiarity of the assurance state is the objective change which the world often appears to undergo, 'An appearance of newness beautifies every object.' . . ." He quotes Billy Bray: ". . . I shouted for joy, I praised God with my whole heart. . . . I remember this, that everything looked new to me, the people, the fields, the cattle, the trees. I was like a new man in a new world." Another example, this one from a woman, "I pled for mercy and had a vivid realization of forgiveness and renewal of my nature. When rising from my knees I exclaimed, 'Old things have passed away, all things have become new.' It was like entering another world, a new state of existence. Natural objects were glorified. My spiritual vision was so clarified that I saw beauty in every material object in the universe. . . ." Again, "The appearance of everything was altered, there seemed to be as it were a calm, a sweet cast or appearance of divine glory in almost everything."

Such a change in a person's perception of the world has been called by Underhill (1955, p. 235), "clarity of vision, a heightening of physical perception," and she quotes Blake's phrase, "cleanse the doors of perception." It is hard to document this perceptual alteration because the autobiographical accounts that Underhill, James, and others cite are a blend of the mystic's spiritual feeling and his actual perception, with the result that the spiritual content dominates the description the mystic gives of the physical world. However, these accounts do suggest that a "new vision" takes place, colored by an inner exaltation. Their authors report perceiving a new brilliance to the world, of seeing everything as if for the first time, of noticing beauty which for the most part they may have previously passed by without seeing. Although such descriptions do not prove a change in sensory perception, they strongly imply it. These particular phenomena appear quite variable and are not mentioned in many mystic accounts. However, direct evidence was obtained on this point in the meditation experiments already cited (Deikman, 1963, 1966b). There it was possible to ask questions and to analyze the subjects' reports to obtain information on their perceptual experiences. The phenomena the subjects reported fulfilled Werner's criteria completely, although the extent of change varied from one subject to the next. They described their reactions to the percept, a blue vase, as follows: (a) an increased vividness and richness of the percept—"more vivid," "luminous"; (b) animation in the vase, which seemed to move with a life of its own; (c) a marked decrease in self-object distinction, occurring in those subjects who continued longest in the experiments: ". . . I really began to feel, you know, almost as though the blue and I were perhaps merging, or that vase and I were. . . . It was as though everything was sort of merging . . ."; (d) syncretic thought and a fusing and alteration of normal perceptual modes: "I began to feel this light going back and forth," "When the vase changes shape I feel this in my body," "I'm still not sure, though, whether it's the motion in the rings or if it's the rings [concentric rings of light between the subject and the vase]. But in a certain way it is real . . . it's not real in the sense that you can see it, touch it, smell it or anything but it certainly is real in the sense that you can experience it happening." The perceptual and cognitive changes that did occur in the subjects were consistently in the direction of a more "primitive" organization.[2]

Thus, the available evidence supports the hypothesis that a deautomatization is produced by contemplative meditation. One might be tempted to call this deautomatization a regression to the perceptual and cognitive state of the child or infant. However, such a concept rests on assumptions as to the child's experience of the world that cannot yet be verified. In an oft-quoted passage, Wordsworth (1904, p. 353) writes:

> There was a time when meadow, grove, and stream,
> The earth, and every common sight,
> To me did seem
> Apparelled in celestial light,
> The glory and the freshness of a dream.

However, he may be confusing childhood with what is actually a reconstruction based on an interaction of adult associative capacities with the *memory* of the more direct sensory contact of the child. "Glory" is probably an adult product. Rather than speaking of a return to childhood, it is more accurate to say that the undoing of automatic perceptual and cognitive structures permits a gain in sensory intensity and richness at the expense of abstract categorization and differentiation. One might call the direction regressive in a developmental sense, but the actual experience is probably not within the psychological scope of any child. It is a deautomatization occurring in an adult mind, and the experience gains its richness from adult memories and functions now subject to a different mode of consciousness.

Renunciation

The deautomatization produced by contemplative meditation is enhanced and aided by the adoption of renunciation as a goal and a life style, a renunciation not confined to the brief meditative period alone. Poverty, chastity, isolation, and silence are traditional techniques prescribed for pursuing the mystic path: To experience God, keep your thoughts turned to God and away from the world and the body that binds one to the world. The meditative strategy is carried over into all segments of the subject's life. The mystic strives to banish from awareness the objects of the world and the desires directed toward them. To the extent that perceptual and cognitive structures require the "nutriment" of their accustomed stimuli for adequate functioning, renunciation would be expected to weaken and even disrupt these structures, thus tending to produce an unusual experience (Rapaport, 1951). Such an isolation from nutritive stimuli probably occurs internally as well. The subjects of the meditation experiment quoted earlier reported that a decrease in responsiveness to distracting stimuli took place as they became more practiced. They became more effective, with less effort, in barring unwanted stimuli from awareness. These reports suggest that psychological barrier structures were established as the subjects became more adept (Deikman, 1963, p. 338). EEG studies of Zen monks yielded similar results. The effect of a distracting stimulus, as measured by the disappearance of alpha rhythm, was most prominent in the novices, less prominent in those of intermediate training, and almost absent in the master (Kasamatsu & Hirai, 1963). It may be that the intensive, long-term practice of meditation creates temporary stimulus barriers producing a functional state of sensory isolation.[3] On the basis of sensory isolation experiments it would be expected that long-term deprivation (or decreased variability) of a particular class of stimulus "nutriment" would cause an alteration in those functions previously established to deal with that class of stimuli (Schultz, 1965, pp. 95–97; Solomon et al., 1961, pp. 226–37). These alterations seem to be a type of deautomatization, as defined earlier—for example, the reported increased brightness of colors and the impairment of perceptual skills such as color discrimination (Zubek et al., 1961). Thus, renunciation alone can be viewed as producing deautomatization. When combined with contemplative meditation, it produces a very powerful effect.

Finally, the more renunciation is achieved, the more the mystic is committed to his goal of Union or Enlightenment. His motivation necessarily increases, for having abandoned the world, he has no other hope of sustenance.

PRINCIPAL FEATURES OF THE MYSTIC EXPERIENCE

Granted that deautomatization takes place, it is necessary to explain five principal features of the mystic experience: (a) intense realness, (b) unusual sensations, (c) unity, (d) ineffability, and (e) trans-sensate phenomena.

Realness

It is assumed by those who have had a mystic experience, whether induced by years of meditation or by a single dose of LSD, that the truthfulness of the experience is attested to by its sense of realness. The criticism of skeptics is often met with the statement, "You have to experience it yourself and then you will understand." This means that if one has the actual experience he will be convinced by its intense *feeling of reality.* "I know it was real because it was more real than my talking to you now." But "realness" is not evidence. Indeed, there are many clinical examples of variability in the intensity of the feeling of realness that is not correlated with corresponding variability in the reality. A dream may be so "real" as to carry conviction into the waking state, although its content may be bizarre beyond correspondence to this world or to any other. Psychosis is often preceded or accompanied by a sense that the world is *less real* than normally, sometimes that it is more real, or has a different reality. The phenomenon of depersonalization demonstrates the potential for an alteration in the sense of the realness of one's own person, although one's evidential self undergoes no change whatsoever. However, in the case of depersonalization, or of derealization, the distinction between what is external and what is internal is still clear. What changes is the quality of realness attached to those object representations. Thus it appears that (a) the *feeling* of realness represents a function distinct from that of reality *judgment,* although they usually operate in synchrony; (b) the feeling of realness is not inherent in sensations, per se; and (c) realness can be considered a quantity function capable of displacement and therefore, of intensification, reduction, and transfer, affecting all varieties of ideational and sensorial contents.[4]

From a developmental point of view, it is clear that biological survival depends on a clear sense of what is palpable and what is not. The sense of reality necessarily becomes fused with the object world. When one considers that meditation combined with renunciation brings about a profound disruption of the subject's normal psychological relationship to the world, it becomes plausible that the practice of such mystic techniques would be associated with a significant alteration of the feeling of reality. The quality of reality formerly attached to objects becomes attached to the particular sensations and ideas that enter awareness during periods of perceptual and cognitive deautomatization. Stimuli of the inner world become invested with the feeling of reality ordinarily bestowed on objects. Through what might be termed "reality transfer," *thoughts and images become real* (Deikman, 1966b, pp. 109–11).

Unusual Percepts

The sensations and ideation occurring during mystic deautomatization are often very unusual; they do not seem part of the continuum of everyday consciousness. "All at once, without warning of any kind, he found himself wrapped around as it were by a flame colored cloud" (Bucke, 1961, p. 8). Perceptions of encompassing light, infinite energy, ineffable visions, and incommunicable knowledge are remarkable in their seeming distinction from perceptions of the phenomena of the "natural world." According to 'mystics, these experiences are different because they pertain to a higher transcendent reality. What is perceived is said to come from another world, or at least another dimension. Although such a possibility cannot be ruled out, many of the phenomena can be understood as representing *an unusual mode of perception*, rather than an unusual external stimulus.

In the studies of experimental meditation already mentioned, two long-term subjects reported vivid experiences of light and force. For example:

> . . . shortly I began to sense motion and shifting of light and dark as this became stronger and stronger. Now when this happens it's happening not only in my vision but it's happening or it feels like a physical kind of thing. It's connected with feelings of attraction, expansion, absorption and suddenly my vision pinpointed on a particular place and . . . I was in the grip of a very powerful sensation and this became the center (Deikman, 1966b, p. 109).

This report suggests that the perception of motion and shifting light and darkness may have been the perception of the *movement* of attention among various psychic contents (whatever such "movement" might actually be). "Attraction," "expansion," "absorption," would thus reflect the dynamics of the effort to focus attention—successful focusing is experienced as being "in the grip of" a powerful force. Another example: ". . . when the vase changes shape . . . I feel this in my body and particularly in my eyes . . . there is an actual kind of physical sensation as though something is moving there which recreates the shape of the vase" (Deikman, 1966b, p. 109). In this instance, the subject might have experienced the perception of a resynthesis taking place following deautomatization of the normal percept; that is, the percept of the vase was being reconstructed outside of normal awareness and the *process* of reconstruction was perceived as a physical sensation. I have termed this hypothetical perceptual mode *"sensory translation,"* defining it as the perception of psychic *action* (conflict, repression, problem solving, attentiveness, and so forth) via the relatively unstructured sensations of light, color, movement, force, sound, smell, or taste (Kris, 1952; Deikman, 1966b, pp. 108–9). This concept is related to Silberer's (1951) concept of hypnagogic phenomena but differs in its referents and genesis. In the hypnagogic state and in dreaming, a *symbolic* translation of psychic activity and ideas occurs. Although light, force, and movement may play a part in hypnagogic and dream constructions, the predominant percepts are complex visual, verbal, conceptual, and activity images. "Sensory translation" refers to the experience of nonverbal, simple, concrete perceptual equivalents of psychic action.[5]

The concept of sensory translation offers an intriguing explanation for the ubiquitous use of light as a metaphor for mystic experience. It may not be just a metaphor. "Illumination" may be derived from an actual sensory experience occurring when in the cognitive act of unification, a liberation of energy takes place, or when a resolution of unconscious conflict occurs, permitting the experience of "peace," "presence," and the like. Liberated energy experience as light may be the core sensory experience of mysticism.

If the hypothesis of sensory translation is correct, it presents the problem of why sensory translation comes into operation in any particular instance.

In general, it appears that sensory translation may occur when (a) heightened attention is directed to the sensory pathways, (b) controlled analytic thought is absent, and (c) the subject's attitude is one of receptivity to stimuli (openness instead of defensiveness or suspiciousness). Training in contemplative meditation is specifically directed toward attaining a state with those characteristics. Laski (1961) reports that spontaneous mystic experiences may occur during such diverse activities as childbirth, viewing landscapes, listening to music, or having sexual inter-

course. Although her subjects gave little description of their thought
processes preceding the ecstasies, they were all involved at the time in
intense sensory activities in which the three conditions listed above
would tend to prevail. Those conditions seem also to apply to the mystical experiences associated with LSD. The state of mind induced by
hallucinogenic drugs is reported to be one of increased sensory attention
accompanied by an impairment or loss of different intellectual functions
(Crocket et al., 1963; Watts, 1962; Michaux, 1963). With regard to the
criterion of receptivity, if paranoid reactions occur during the drug state
they are inimical to an ecstatic experience. On the other hand, when
drug subjects lose their defensiveness and suspiciousness so that they
"accept" rather than fight their situation, the "transcendent" experience
often ensues (Sherwood et al., 1962). Thus, the general psychological
context may be described as *perceptual concentration*. In this special
state of consciousness the subject becomes aware of certain intra-psychic
processes ordinarily excluded from or beyond the scope of awareness.
The vehicle for this perception appears to be amorphous sensation, made
real by a displacement of reality feeling ("reality transfer") and thus
misinterpreted as being of external origin.

Unity

Experiencing one's self as one with the universe or with God is the
hallmark of the mystic experience, regardless of its cultural context. As
James (1929, p. 410) puts it,

> This overcoming of all the usual barriers between the individual
> and the Absolute is the great mystic achievement. In mystic states we
> both become one with the Absolute and we become aware of our
> oneness. This is the everlasting and triumphant mystical tradition,
> hardly altered by differences of clime or creed. In Hinduism, in
> Neoplatonism, in Sufism, in Christian mysticism, in Whitmanism, we
> find the same recurring note, so that there is about mystical utterance
> an eternal unanimity which ought to make a critic stop and think, and
> which brings it about that the mystical classics have, as has been said,
> neither birthday nor native land. Perpetually telling of the unity of
> man with God, their speech antedates languages, and they do not grow
> old.

I have already referred to explanations of this phenomenon in terms of
regression. Two additional hypotheses should be considered: On the one
hand, the perception of unity may be the perception of one's own psychic structure; on the other hand, the experience may be a perception of
the real structure of the world.

It is a commonplace that we do not experience the world directly. Instead, we have an experience of sensation and associated memories from

which we infer the nature of the stimulating object. As far as anyone can tell, the actual *substance* of the perception is the electrochemical activity that constitutes perception and thinking. From this point of view, the contents of awareness are homogeneous. They are variations of the same substance. If awareness were turned back upon itself, as postulated for sensory translation, this fundamental homogeneity (unity) of perceived reality—the electrochemical activity—might itself be experienced as a truth about the outer world, rather than the inner one. Unity, the idea and the experience that we are one with the world and with God, would thus constitute a valid perception insofar as it pertained to the nature of the thought process, but need not in itself be a correct perception of the external world.

Logically, there is also the possibility that the perception of unity does correctly evaluate the external world. As described earlier, deautomatization is an undoing of a psychic structure permitting the experience of increased detail and sensation at the price of requiring more attention. With such attention, it is possible that deautomatization may permit the awareness of new dimensions of the total stimulus array—a process of *"perceptual expansion."* The studies of Werner (1957), Von Senden (1960), and Shapiro (1960) suggest that development from infancy to adulthood is accompanied by an organization of the perceptual and cognitive world that has as its price the selection of some stimuli and stimulus qualities to the exclusion of others. If the automatization underlying that organization is reversed, or temporarily suspended, aspects of reality that were formerly unavailable might then enter awareness. Unity may in fact be a property of the real world that becomes perceptible via the techniques of meditation and renunciation, or under the special conditions, as yet unknown, that create the spontaneous, brief mystic experience of untrained persons.

Ineffability

Mystic experiences are ineffable, incapable of being expressed to another person. Although mystics sometimes write long accounts, they maintain that the experience cannot be communicated by words or by reference to similar experiences from ordinary life. They feel at a loss for appropriate words to communicate the intense realness, the unusual sensations, and the unity cognition already mentioned. However, a careful examination of mystic phenomena indicates that there are at least several types of experiences, all of which are "indescribable" but each of which differs substantially in content and formal characteristics. Error and confusion result when these several states of consciousness are lumped together as "the mystic experience" on the basis of their common characteristic of ineffability.

To begin with, one type of mystic experience cannot be communicated in words because it is probably based on primitive memories and related to fantasies of a preverbal (infantile) or nonverbal sensory experience.[6] Certain mystical reports that speak of being blissfully enfolded, comforted and bathed in the love of God are very suggestive of the prototypical "undifferentiated state," the union of infant and breast, emphasized by psychoanalytic explanations of mystical phenomena. Indeed, it seems highly plausible that such early memories and fantasies might be reexperienced as a consequence of (a) the regression in thought processes brought about by renunciation and contemplative meditation, and (b) the activation of infantile longings by the guiding religious promise—that is, "that a benign deity would reward childlike surrender with permanent euphoria" (Moller, 1965, p. 127). In addition, the conditions of functional sensory isolation associated with mystic training may contribute to an increase in recall and vividness of such memories (Suraci, 1964).

A second type of mystical experience is equally ineffable but strikingly different—namely, a revelation too complex to be verbalized. Such experiences are reported frequently by those who have drug-induced mystical experiences. In such states the subject has a revelation of the significance and interrelationships of many dimensions of life; he becomes aware of many levels of meaning simultaneously and "understands" the totality of existence. The question of whether such knowledge is actual or an illusion remains unanswered; however, if such a multileveled comprehension were to occur, it would be difficult—perhaps impossible—to express verbally. Ordinary language is structured to follow the logical development of one idea at a time and it might be quite inadequate to express an experience encompassing a large number of concepts simultaneously. William James suggested that "states of mystical intuition may be only very sudden and great extensions of the ordinary 'field of consciousness.'" He used the image of the vast reaches of a tidal flat exposed by the lowering of the water level (James, 1920, pp. 500–13). However, mystic revelation may be ineffable, not only because of the sudden broadening of consciousness that James suggests, but also because of a new "vertical" organization of the concepts.[7] For example, for a short while after reading *The Decline and Fall of the Roman Empire,* one may be aware of the immense vista of a civilization's history as Gibbon recreated it. That experience can hardly be conveyed except through the medium of the book itself, and to that extent it is ineffable, and a minor version of James's widened consciousness. Suppose one then read *War and Peace* and acquired Tolstoy's perspective of historical events and their determination by chance factors. Again, this is an experience hard to express without returning to the novel. Now suppose one could "see" not only each of these world views individually but also their parallel relationships to each other, and the cross connections between the individual conceptual structures. And then suppose one added to these conceptual strata the biochemical perspective expressed by *The Fitness of the Environment* (Henderson, 1958), a work which deals, among other things, with the unique and vital properties of the water molecule. Then the *vertical* interrelationships of all these extensive schemata might, indeed, be beyond verbal expression, beyond ordinary conceptual capacities—in other words, they would approach the ineffable.

Trans-Sensate Phenomena

A third type of ineffable experience is that which I have described earlier as the "trained-transcendent" mystical experience. The author of *The Cloud of Unknowing*, St. John of the Cross, Walter Hilton, and others are very specific in describing a new perceptual experience that does not include feelings of warmth, sweetness, visions, or any other elements of familiar sensory or intellectual experience. They emphasize that the experience *goes beyond* the customary sensory pathways, ideas, and memories. As I have shown, they describe the state as definitely not blank or empty but as filled with intense, profound, vivid perception which they regard as the ultimate goal of the mystic path.[8] If one accepts their descriptions as phenomenologically accurate, one is presented with the problem of explaining the nature of such a state and the process by which it occurs. Following the hypotheses presented earlier in this paper, I would like to suggest that such experiences are the result of the operation of a new perceptual capacity responsive to dimensions of the stimulus array previously ignored or blocked from awareness. For such mystics, renunciation has weakened and temporarily removed the ordinary objects of consciousness as a focus of awareness. Contemplative meditation has undone the logical organization of consciousness. At the same time, the mystic is intensely *motivated* to perceive something. If undeveloped or unutilized perceptual capacities do exist, it seems likely that they would be mobilized and come into operation under such conditions. The perceptual experience that would then take place would be one outside of customary verbal or sensory reference. It would be *unidentifiable*, hence indescribable. The high value, the meaningfulness, and the intensity reported of such experiences suggest that the perception has a different scope from that of normal consciousness. The loss of "self" characteristic of the trans-sensate experience indicates that the new perceptual mode is not associated with reflective awareness—the "I" of normal consciousness is in abeyance.

CONCLUSION

A mystic experience is the production of an unusual state of consciousness. This state is brought about by a deautomatization of hierarchically ordered structures that ordinarily conserve attentional energy for maximum efficiency in achieving the basic goals of the individual: biological survival as an organism and psychological survival as a personality. Perceptual selection and cognitive patterning are in the service of these goals. Under special conditions of dysfunction, such as in acute psychosis or in LSD states, or under special goal conditions such as exist in religious mystics, the pragmatic systems of automatic selection are set aside or break down, in favor of alternate modes of consciousness whose stimulus processing may be less efficient from a biological point of view but whose very inefficiency may permit the experience of aspects of the real world formerly excluded or ignored. The extent to which such a shift takes place is a function of the motivation of the individual, his paricular neurophysiological state, and the environmental conditions encouraging or discouraging such a change.

A final comment should be made. The content of the mystic experience reflects not only its unusual mode of consciousness but also the particular stimuli being processed through that mode. The mystic experience can be beatific, satanic, revelatory, or psychotic, depending on the stimuli predominant in each case. Such an explanation says nothing conclusive about the source of "transcendent" stimuli. God or the Unconscious share equal possibilities here and one's interpretation will reflect one's presuppositions and beliefs. The mystic vision is one of unity, and modern physics lends some support to this perception when it asserts that the world and its living forms are variations of the same elements. However, there is no evidence that separateness and differences are illusions (as affirmed by Vedanta) or that God or a transcendent reality exists (as affirmed by Western religions). The available scientific evidence tends to support the view that the mystic experience is one of internal perception, an experience that can be ecstatic, profound, or therapeutic for purely internal reasons. Yet for psychological science, the problem of understanding such internal processes is hardly less complex than the theological problem of understanding God. Indeed, regardless of one's direction in the search to know what reality is, a feeling of awe, beauty, reverence, and humility seems to be the product of one's efforts. Since these emotions are characteristic of the mystic experience itself, the question of the epistemological validity of that experience may have less importance than was initially supposed.

NOTES

1. Breathing exercises can also affect the carbon dioxide content of the blood and thus alter the state of consciousness chemically.

2. As dedifferentiation of the vase progressed, however, a fusion of background and object tended to occur with a concomitant loss of color and vividness.

3. It has been postulated by McReynolds (1960, p. 269) that a related stimulus barrier system may be operative in schizophrenia.

4. Paul Federn's (1955, pp. 241–60) idea that the normal feeling of reality requires an adequate investment of energy (libido) in the ego boundary, points toward the notion of a quantity of "realness." Avery Weisman (1958) has developed and extended this idea, but prefers the more encompassing concept of "libidinal fields" to that of ego boundaries.

5. Somewhat related concepts, although extreme in scope, are those advanced by Michaux (1962, pp. 7–9), who suggests that the frequent experience of waves or vibrations in hallucinogenic drug states is the result of direct perception of the "brain waves" measured by the EEG; and by Leary (1964, pp. 330–39), who suggests that hallucinogenic drugs permit a "direct awareness of the processes which physicists and biochemists and neurologists measure," for example, electrons in orbit or the interaction of cells.

6. Schachtel (1959, p. 284) regards early childhood, beyond infancy, as unrememberable for structural reasons: "It is not merely the repression of a specific content, such as early sexual experience, that accounts for the general childhood amnesia; the biologically, culturally, and socially influenced process of memory organization results in the formation of categories (schemata) of memory which are not suitable vehicles to receive and reproduce experiences of the quality and intensity typical of early childhood." It would follow that verbal structures would likewise be "unsuitable."

7. A similar description concerning "vertical" listening to music is made by Ehrenzweig (1964, pp. 385–87).

8. Ehrenzweig (1964, p. 382) proposes that mystic "blankness" is due to a structural limitation: ". . . the true mystic orison becomes empty yet filled with intense experience. . . . This full emptiness. . . . It is the direct result of our conscious failure to grasp imagery formed on more primitive levels of differentiation. . . . Owing to their incompatible shapes, these images cancelled each other out on the way up to consciousness and so produce in our surface experience a blank 'abstract' image still replete with unconscious fantasy."

17

Bimodal Consciousness and the Mystic Experience

ARTHUR J. DEIKMAN, M.D.

TWO MODES

Let us think of a human being as an organism composed of components having both psychological and biological dimensions. These components have two basic modes of organization: an "action mode" and a "receptive mode." The action mode is a state organized to manipulate the environment. To carry out this purpose the striate muscle system is the dominant physiological agency. Base-line muscle tension is increased and the EEG usually features beta waves. Psychologically, we find focal attention, heightened boundary perception, object-based logic, and the dominance of formal characteristics over the sensory; shapes and meanings have a preference over colors and textures.

These attributes develop together. For example, as Piaget has shown, thinking develops in association with the manipulation and perception of objects, and object-oriented thought is associated with muscle activity, especially eye muscle activity.[1] Thus, we experience "effortful" thinking —reflecting the involvement of our muscle system. Likewise we can understand the perceptual characteristics of the action mode as providing what is needed for success in acting on the world. For example, a clear sense of self-object difference is necessary to obtain food. Similarly, a variety of psychological processes are coordinated and developed together in multidimensional unity adapted to the requirements of the task; i.e. manipulating the environment.

In contrast, the receptive mode is a state whose purpose is receiving the environment, rather than manipulation. The sensory-perceptual system is usually the dominant agency rather than the muscle system. Baseline muscle tension tends to be decreased, compared to the tension found in the action mode, and the EEG tends to the slower frequencies of alpha and theta. Psychologically we find that attention is diffuse, boundary perception is decreased, paralogical thought processes are evident, and sensory qualities dominate over the formal. These functions are coordinated to maximize the intake of the environment. As growth proceeds the receptive mode is gradually dominated, if not submerged, by a natural and culturally enforced emphasis on striving activity and the action mode that serves it. The receptive mode tends, more and more, to be an interlude between increasingly longer periods of action-mode organization. One consequence of this bias is that we have come to regard the action mode as the normal one for adult life and to think of the unfamiliar receptive states as pathological.

The pervasiveness of the action mode is evident when we consider that our language is its very essence. We use language to analyze, discriminate, and divide the world into pieces or objects which we can then grasp—psychologically and physically—in order to act upon them. The richness and subtlety of our language for any particular area of our lives reflects the extent to which we apply the action mode to that sector. For example, most of us have only one word for snow; if we are skiers we may have several. The Eskimo has many words that discriminate the varieties of snow conditions which he must take into account to survive. In some cases, the issue is not how many differences we have learned to detect but the mode of consciousness in which the experience takes place. "Love," for example, is represented for the average person by only one word. Yet, each of us probably has experienced many different varieties of that condition. We have not developed a rich vocabulary for love because it is experienced in the receptive mode; indeed, it requires the receptive mode for its occurrence. Similarly, color *experience* (rather than the use of color as a sign) requires the receptive mode and colors have only a relatively few names compared to the vast variety of hues to which we are sensitive. This is true even for the artist who *works* with, *manipulates,* and *makes* color objects and therefore has an expanded color vocabulary, compared to most people.

To illustrate these modes, let us consider some extreme examples. Imagine a cab driver in heavy traffic, struggling to get a passenger to the airport in time so that he may earn a large tip. He is intentionally engaged in maneuvering among the objects of his world and is focused on a future goal, trying as best he can to control what happens. He is not occupied with the color of the automobiles, the blueness of the sky, or the esthetic qualities of the streets and buildings, but sees only openings or blockades of traffic and notes only the colors of the stop lights. He sees the shapes and understands the meanings of the various objects flashing into his narrowed attentional field while at the same time part of his attention recalls alternate routes, and he scans his memory to remember the typical traffic flows. His base-line muscle tension is high and his EEG would probably show a desynchronized, fast voltage pattern.

In contrast, consider a monk, sitting in contemplative meditation in a garden. At that moment, his organism is oriented toward *taking in* the environment, a function that is performed via the receptive mode. If he is deeply into that mode, his state of consciousness may feature a marked decrease in the distinction between himself and his environment to the extent that he merges with it or has a nonverbal (ineffable) perception of unity, or both. Sensory experience dominates his consciousness, his muscles tend toward relaxation, and his EEG is likely to show alpha and theta waves. In contrast to the cab driver, he is not concerned with the future—he is letting whatever happens happen, while language and thinking are relinquished almost entirely.

During most of our lives what occurs is probably a mixture of the two modes or at least a fluctuation between them. For the majority of us, that fluctuation is heavily dominated by the action mode. However, it is not the presence or absence of physical activity per se that determines the mode. Rather, the underlying purpose or attitude seems to be crucial. For example, a monk working in a garden or lovers in sexual intercourse ideally would be very much given up to the receptive mode. The monk's relationship to his garden environment and the lovers' relationship to each other in the receptive mode is what Buber has described as the "I–Thou," in contrast to the "I–it" of the action mode.[2] However, if the monk in the garden is thinking about how soon he will attain enlightenment or if the lovers are concerned about their performance or are treating each other as fantasy objects, quite a different experience will result —in popular terms, it would be expressed as the difference between "making love" and "screwing." These are examples of the domination of different modes. An enlightened monk working in the garden may be trained to operate in the action mode only to the extent needed to perform the work, while allowing the receptive mode to play a prominent part in his conscious experience.

Thus, we are not talking about activity versus passivity as usually conceived, or about the secondary and primary processes of psychoanalytic theory. As I stated in an earlier discussion, "There is some similarity between aspects of the receptive mode and the cognitive style associated with primary process. The bimodal model, however, addresses itself to a functional orientation—that of taking in versus acting on the environment. The receptive mode is not a 'regressive' ignoring of the world or a retreat from it—although it can be employed for that purpose, but is a different strategy for engaging the world in pursuit of a different goal."[3]

RENUNCIATION AND MONASTIC TRAINING

With this discussion in mind, we can understand renunciation as a strategy to establish the receptive mode as the dominant orientation and to intensify its effects. In most spiritual disciplines a psychosocial system has been developed for use in a monastery or ashram, where technical exercises, communal living, and ideology are integrated to bring about change. It is instructive to look closely at one example of such a system; we can consider life in a Zen monastery of the Soto Zen sect. The basic principles of its operation are similar to those of other spiritual disciplines.

The Zen monastery teaches its students (monks) a state of acceptance and "nondiscrimination." This is accomplished by meditation, communal living, an ascetic way of life, and a supporting philosophy—Buddhism. There are different forms of meditation prescribed but the purest form is called *shikan-taza,* or "just sitting." A person performing *shikan-taza* is not supposed to do anything except to *be* sitting; trying to meditate better than the day before or trying to achieve enlightenment represent incorrect attitudes. Acceptance, rather than *doing,* is the basic instruction. Even intrusive thoughts or fantasies while meditating are not struggled against, but are treated as distractions that one must be patient with until they go away. The monk is told that if he is truly sitting, he is enlightened—to just sit, to just *be,* is enlightenment, itself.

The average person finds it very difficult to just sit and not do anything. When he tries it, he begins to realize how rigorously he has been trained to be busy, to solve problems, to make objects, to look ahead, to strive toward a goal. The sitting meditation may be regarded as an experiment in which the student explores what it is like when he does not respond to the usual commands of pain, anxiety, "boredom," or desires.

One effect of this meditation is to give the student the actual experience of having his ordinary sense of linear time change to something which might be described as timeless. For brief intervals, time can be felt to disappear—and anxiety with it. Likewise, the feeling of a personal self (the core dimension of the action mode) tends to become less vivid and, in some instances, may completely disappear.

The philosophical instruction that is given in lectures or, indirectly, through the chanting of religious texts, presents a theory that the world is one of constant change, composed of a basic nothing that takes an endless variety of forms but whose essence cannot be analyzed. In particular, the usual concept of death is taught to be an illusion. In this way, the most powerful force that orients us toward the future—the fear of death—is diminished.

The social systems of the monastery also undercut the action mode by minimizing material rewards. No one accrues profits; one day is very similar to the next. The food stays the same, there are few status rewards, and, thus, there tends to be nothing very concrete to "look forward to."

In these ways, the monastic system strikes at the attempt to grasp, to cling to, to strive for, to reach ahead and possess. The psychological importance of this is readily apparent. If we examine the content of our thinking, we can see that most of our energies are devoted to prolonging or bringing back a particular pleasure that we have had, often at the expense of enjoying the pleasure available at the moment. Operating in the action mode with an orientation toward the future, we tend to lose what is available to us in the present; for example, a man taking a pleasant walk on a beautiful spring day may be unhappy because he anticipates the ending of his vacation. In contrast, a monk or a yogi is taught to accept, to allow—rather than to be concerned with seeking pleasure or avoiding pain. To the extent that he succeeds in this reorientation, he establishes the groundwork for a mode of consciousness that the mystical literature describes as timeless, nondualistic, nonverbal, and completely satisfying. I propose that they are referring to a mode of organismic being that I have called the receptive mode, one that is natural to us, but seldom employed to its full potential.

THE RECEPTIVE MODE IN EVERYDAY LIFE

Although the foregoing discussion may seem to indicate that the receptive mode is the exclusive property of monks, in actuality almost all of us make use of it to perform functions that we do not usually regard as esoteric. To take a very mundane example: trying to remember a forgotten name by a direct, conscious effort may yield nothing. In such a situation we typically remark, "It will come to me in a minute" and it usually does. We stop struggling to remember and allow ourselves to be receptive. Only then does the name pop into awareness. Our shift in attitude—a change in strategy—permitted a latent function to be exercised. *Switching to the receptive mode permits the operation of capacities that are nonfunctional in the action mode.*

This principle is illustrated further when we consider a more important use of the receptive mode: to solve problems by means of creative intuition. Typically, there is an initial stage of struggling with the problem. A sense of impasse develops and the struggle is given up. Sometime later, while completely occupied with a less important activity, or perhaps waking from sleep, the answer suddenly appears. Often, it is in a symbolic or spatial form and needs to be worked over to make it coherent and applicable. In terms of the modal model, the process begins with the use of the action mode during the preliminary or preparatory stage. When progress is blocked, a shift takes place to the receptive mode. In that mode, our capacity for creative synthesis is able to function and the intuitive leap to a new configuration takes place. Then, we shift back to the action mode in order to integrate the new formulation with our previous knowledge and to communicate it to others.

For most people, the receptive mode probably has its most important function in sexual intercourse. The capacity for a deep and satisfying sexual experience is related to a person's ability to relinquish control, to allow the partner to penetrate both physical and psychological boundaries, and to stay focused in the present. Furthermore, sexual climax in persons who are thus able to "let go" is associated with heightened sensation, diffuse attention, and a decrease in the boundaries of the self (as in meditation); and in some cases, profound experiences occur that may be properly termed mystical.[4] In contrast, persons unable to give up their customary mode of active striving and control suffer a constriction of their sexual experience; pleasurable sensations, the release of tension, and feelings of closeness tend to be minimal or absent.

KNOWLEDGE

Mystics claim to have a direct, intuitive perception of reality, and that claim is a reasonable possibility. Studies in perception and developmental psychology indicate that we have exercised a significant selection process over the array of stimuli with which we are presented. For efficiency's sake, we have to pay attention to some things and not to others, and we automatize that selection process to such an extent that we cannot recover our perceptual and cognitive options. For that reason, mystical disciplines make use of a variety of means to bring about a deautomatization so that a new, fresh perception can occur. Perhaps when this deautomatization is combined with an increased capacity for receptive-mode function (as a result of "spiritual" training), the event of "awakening" to the awareness of one's true nature can then take place.

As in the case of creative intuition, descriptions of such "enlightenment" experiences indicate that they are sudden, involuntary, and present the "answer" in a flash. They tend to follow a long period of struggle and are often triggered by something of an irrelevant nature—the same pattern noticed for creative intuition. Furthermore, accounts of enlightenment often stress that additional work was needed before the new knowledge was fully "realized." We might say that it had to be integrated through use of the action mode. Thus, mystical "enlightenment" or "awakening" may be the result of a radical use of the basic creative process with which we are already familiar.

Whether or not mystical experiences yield knowledge about the world is an interesting question about which we have little data. However, LeShan has noted the striking correspondence between the cosmology of mystics and that of a number of modern physicists who also wrestle with questions about the essential nature of the universe.[5]

COMPLEMENTARY MODES

Although our conscious experience may seem to be a mixture of these different mode components, in a certain basic sense the modes appear to be *complementary*. The term "complementarity" was introduced by Niels Bohr to account for the fact that two different conditions of observations could lead to conclusions that were conceptually incompatible.[6] For example, in one set of experiments light behaved as if it were composed of discrete particles, while in another set of experiments light behaved as if it were a continuous wave. Bohr suggested that there was no intrinsic incompatibility between the two results because they were functions of different conditions of observation and no experiment could be devised that would demonstrate both aspects under a single condition. "Enlightenment" has been likened to an open hand. When you try to grasp it, you transform your open hand into a fist. The very attempt to possess it (the action mode) banishes the state because it is a function of the receptive mode. To put it in more modern terms, if you change your own organismic program from *intake* to *manipulate*, your functional characteristics will change at the same time.

CONCLUSION

Our ordinary mode of consciousness can be called the action mode, organized to manipulate the environment and featuring an acute consciousness of past and future time. Its basic reference point is the experience of a separate, personal self. In contrast, we have the capacity for a different organization—called the receptive mode—oriented toward the present, in which the personal self as a preoccupying orientation fades away and the world tends to be experienced as more unified and satisfying. As the action mode is used for problem solving and manipulating the environment, the receptive mode is used for receiving, for providing nutrition and satisfaction.

Which mode is better or "higher"? If we think in such terms, we are missing the point. We gain nothing by restricting our functions to one mode or the other. Rather, we need the capacity to function in both modes, as the occasion demands. There is a classical story that illustrates the exercise of this option: A man fell off the edge of a cliff and managed to grasp a small tree as he plunged downward. Looking up, he saw there was no way to climb back and looking down he saw jagged boulders waiting far below. He noticed that the roots of the tree were weakening and it was starting to come loose from the side of the cliff. Nothing could save him. At the same time, he noticed a small clump of wild strawberries lodged in a crevice of the rock. Holding on to the tree with one hand, he plucked a strawberry with the other and popped it into his mouth. How sweet it tasted!

What stands in the way of our making better use of this option, this nonordinary door to satisfaction, to creativity, to life in the present? It seems to me that the first barrier is our cultural bias that tells us that mystical states are unreal, pathological, "crazy," or "regressive"; it is a bias that declares the entire area to be "subjective" and, therefore, "unscientific." We have been indoctrinated neither to make use of nor to look closely at these realms. Without knowing it, under the banner of the scientific method, our thinking has been constricted. It is time that we made the receptive mode, and the experience which it engenders, a legitimate option for ourselves and for science. Having done so, we will be able to see more clearly the psychodynamic barriers that limit this option: defenses against relinquishing conscious control, defenses against the unexpected and the unknown, defenses against the blurring and loss of boundaries defining the self. We will be able to discriminate those instances in which the pathological or regressive are indeed present, but we will not miss seeing and exploring those phenomena that are truly mature and life promoting, of real practical value to us.

At this time in our history, our biological survival may depend on being able to utilize our receptive-mode function so that we will *experience* the basis for humanitarian values. We can recognize, theoretically, that selfless actions are necessary to regulate population, to deal with problems of pollution and resources, and end the possibility of a nuclear holocaust. However, the required virtues tend to be merely abstractions if they are not based on a personal realization of their validity, meaning, and importance. The action mode that pervades our civilization does not support selflessness; the receptive mode, ordinarily the specialty of mystics, does. From this point of view, mystics have been the guardians of a potentiality that has always been ours and that it is now time for us to reclaim. We can integrate this realm with our present knowledge, making it less exotic and less alien. By doing so, we can explore and regain a functional capacity that we may now need for our very preservation, as well as for the enlargement of our knowledge.

NOTES

1. J. Piaget, *The Construction of Reality in the Child.* New York: Basic Books, 1954.

2. M. Buber, *I and Thou*. New York: Charles Scribner's Sons, 1958.

3. Arthur J. Deikman, "Bimodal consciousness." *Archives of General Psychiatry*, 1971, 45:483.

4. M. Laski, *Ecstasy: A Study of Some Secular and Religious Experiences*. London: Cresset Press, 1961.

5. Lawrence LeShan, "Physicists and mystics: similarities in world views." *Journal of Transpersonal Psychology* 1, no. 2 (1969) 1–20.

6. Niels Bohr, *Essays, 1958–1962, on Atomic Physics and Human Knowledge*. New York: John Wiley, 1963.

18

Two Sides of the Brain

ROBERT E. ORNSTEIN

Never Know When It Might Come in Useful

Nasrudin sometimes took people for trips in his boat. One day a pedagogue hired him to ferry him across a very wide river. As soon as they were afloat, the scholar asked whether it was going to be rough.

"Don't ask me nothing about it," said Nasrudin.

"Have you never studied grammar?"

"No," said the Mulla.

"In that case, half your life has been wasted."

The Mulla said nothing.

Soon a terrible storm blew up. The Mulla's crazy cockleshell was filling with water. He leaned over toward his companion. "Have you ever learned to swim?"

"No," said the pedant.

"In that case, schoolmaster, *all* your life is lost, for we are sinking."[1]

The two characters in this story represent two major modes of consciousness: the verbal, rational mode is portrayed by the pedagogue, who is involved in and insists on neat and tidy perfection; the other mode is represented here by the skill of swimming, which involves movement of the body in space, a mode often devalued by the neat, rational mind of the pedagogue.

On one level, these two characters represent different types of people. The verbal-logical grammarian can also be the scientist, the logician, the mathematician who is committed to reason and "correct" proof. The boatman, ungraceful and untutored in formal terms, represents the artist, the craftsman, the dancer, the dreamer whose output is often unsatisfactory to the purely rational mind.

But other interpretations of this story are possible. These two characters can also represent major modes of consciousness which exist across cultures (comparing the Trobrianders with the West) and which simultaneously coexist within each person. Try the following exercise. Close your eyes and attempt to sense each side of your body separately. Try to get in touch with the feelings of the left and of the right side, their strengths, their weaknesses. When you are finished, open your eyes for a moment and reflect on one of these questions. Close your eyes and sense inside for the answer, then repeat the process with the next question.

1. Which side of you is more feminine?
2. Which is more masculine?
3. Which do you consider the "dark" side of yourself?
4. Which side is the "lighter"?
5. Which is more active?
6. Which is more passive?
7. Which side is more logical?
8. Which more "intuitive"?
9. Which side of you is the more mysterious?
10. Which side is the more artistic?

If you are right-handed, most likely you felt the right side of your body as more masculine, lighter, active, and logical, the left side as more feminine, dark, passive, intuitive, mysterious, and artistic. The psychologist William Domhoff asked a large number of people to rate the concepts *left* and *right* on several dimensions. His sample regarded *left* as "bad," "dark," "profane," and "female," while *right* was considered the opposite.[2]

The difference between the left and right sides of the body may provide a key to open our understanding of the psychological and physiological mechanisms of the two major modes of consciousness. The cerebral cortex of the brain is divided into two hemispheres, joined by a large bundle of interconnecting fibers called the "corpus callosum." The left side of the body is mainly controlled by the right side of the cortex, and the right side of the body by the left side of the cortex. When we speak of *left* in ordinary speech, we are referring to that side of the body, and to the *right* hemisphere of the brain.

Both the structure and the function of these two "half-brains" in some part underlie the two modes of consciousness which simultaneously coexist within each one of us. Although each hemisphere shares the potential for many functions, and both sides participate in most activities, in the normal person the two hemispheres tend to specialize. The left hemisphere (connected to the right side of the body) is predominantly involved with analytic, logical thinking, especially in verbal and mathematical functions. Its mode of operation is primarily linear. This hemisphere seems to process information sequentially. This mode of operation of necessity must underlie logical thought, since logic depends on sequence and order. Language and mathematics, both left-hemisphere activities, also depend predominantly on linear time.

If the left hemisphere is specialized for analysis, the right hemisphere (again, remember, connected to the left side of the body) seems specialized for holistic mentation. Its language ability is quite limited. This hemisphere is primarily responsible for our orientation in space, artistic endeavor, crafts, body image, recognition of faces. It processes information more diffusely than does the left hemisphere, and its responsibilities demand a ready integration of many inputs at once. If the left hemisphere can be termed predominantly analytic and sequential in its operation, then the right hemisphere is more holistic and relational, and more simultaneous in its mode of operation. *

For over a century, neurological evidence has been slowly accumulating on the different specialization of man's two cerebral hemispheres. A very valuable part of this evidence has come from the study of people whose brains have been damaged by accident or illness, and from the surgery performed on them. It is, then, in the work of clinical neurology, and especially in the review paper of Joseph Bogen, that the primary indications of our hemispheric specialization are to be found.[3]

In 1864, the great neurologist Hughlings Jackson considered the left hemisphere to be the seat of the "faculty of expression," and noted of a patient with a tumor in the right hemisphere, "She did not know objects, persons, and places." Since Hughlings Jackson, many other neurologists, neurosurgeons, and psychiatrists have confirmed that two modes of consciousness seem to be lateralized in the two cerebral hemispheres of man. In hundreds of clinical cases, it has been found that damage to the left hemisphere very often interferes with, and can in some cases completely destroy, language ability. Often patients cannot speak after such left-hemisphere lesions, a condition known as "aphasia." An injury to the right hemisphere may not interfere with language performance at all, but may cause severe disturbance in spatial awareness, in musical ability, in recognition of other people, or in awareness of one's own body. Some patients with right-hemisphere damage cannot dress themselves adequately, although their speech and reason remain unimpaired.

Throughout the clinical and neurological reports, there exists a tendency to term the left and right hemispheres the "major" and the "minor," respectively. This seems more a societal than a neurological dis-

---

* This right-left specialization is based on right-handers. Left-handers, who are about 5 per cent of the population, are less consistent; some have reversed specialization of the hemispheres, but some have mixed specialization—e.g. language in both sides. Some are specialized in the same way as right-handers. And even in right-handers these differences are not binary, but are specializations of each "half-brain." At least in very young people, each side does possess the potential for both modes; e.g. brain damage to the left hemisphere in young children often results in the development of language in the right side.

tinction. The dominant or major mode of our culture is verbal and intellectual, and this cultural emphasis can bias observations. If an injury to the right hemisphere is not found to affect speech or reason, then this damage has often been considered minor. Injury to the left hemisphere affects verbal functions; thus it has often been termed the major hemisphere. However, the conception of the function of the two hemispheres is changing, largely because of the superb work of Bogen and the increasing evidence of the brain's lateral specialization. The position of the fussy pedagogue who devalues the nonverbal boatman becomes less and less tenable.

Each hemisphere is the major one, depending on the mode of consciousness under consideration. If one is a wordsmith, a scientist, or a mathematician, damage to the left hemisphere may prove disastrous. If one is a musician, a craftsman, or an artist, damage to the left hemisphere often does not interfere with one's capacity to create music, crafts, or arts, yet damage to the right hemisphere may well obliterate a career.

In more precise neuropsychological studies, Brenda Milner and her associates at McGill University in Montreal have attempted to correlate disorders in specific kinds of tasks with lesions in specific areas of the brain. For example, a lobectomy of the right temporal lobe severely impairs the performance of visual and tactile mazes, whereas left temporal-lobe lesions of equal extent produce little deficit. These researchers also report that lesions in specific areas of the left hemisphere are associated with specific kinds of language disorders: an impairment of verbal memory is associated with lesions in the anterior (front) left temporal lobe; speech impairment seems to result from lesions in the posterior (rear) left temporal lobe.[4] On less empirical grounds, the Russian physiologist A. R. Luria has reported that mathematical function is also disturbed by lesions of the left side.[5] Milner and her associates also report that the recognition of musical pitch seems to be in the province of the right hemisphere.

The clinical neurological research is intriguing, correlating the different functions of the hemispheres which are impaired by brain damage. More intriguing still is the research of Roger Sperry of the California Institute of Technology, and his associates, notably Joseph Bogen and Michael Gazzaniga. The two cerebral hemispheres communicate through the corpus callosum, which joins the two sides anatomically. Professor Sperry and his colleagues had for some years experimentally severed the corpus callosum in laboratory animals. This led to the adoption of a radical treatment for severe epilepsy in several human patients of Drs. Vogel and Bogen of the California College of Medicine.[6]

This treatment involved an operation on humans similar to Sperry's experimental surgery on animals—a severing of the interconnections between the two cerebral hemispheres, effectively isolating one side from the other. The hope of this surgery was that when a patient had a seizure in one hemisphere, the other would still be able to take control of the body. With this control available, it was hoped that the patient could ingest the proper medication or perhaps inform the doctor of his attack. In many cases, the severely disturbed patients were improved enough to leave the hospital.

In day-to-day living, these "split-brain" people exhibit almost no abnormality, which is somewhat surprising in view of the radical surgery. However, Roger Sperry and his associates have developed many subtle tests which uncovered evidence that the operation had clearly separated the specialized functions of the two cerebral hemispheres.

If, for instance, the patient felt a pencil (hidden from sight) in his right hand, he could verbally describe it, as would be normal. But if the pencil was in his left hand, he could not describe it at all. Recall that the left hand informs the right hemisphere, which does not possess any capability for speech. With the corpus callosum cut, the verbal (left) hemisphere is no longer connected to the right hemisphere, which largely communicates with the left hand; so the verbal apparatus literally does not know what is in the left hand. If, however, the patient was offered a selection of objects—a key, book, pencil, etc.—and was asked to choose the previously given object with his left hand, he could choose correctly, although he still could not state verbally just what he was doing. This situation resembles closely what might happen if I were privately requested to perform an action and you were expected to discourse on it.

Another experiment tested the lateral specialization of the two hemispheres using visual input. The right half of each eye sends its messages to the right hemisphere, the left half to the left hemisphere. In this experiment the word "heart" was flashed to the patient, with the "he" to the left of the eyes' fixation point, and "art" to the right. Normally if any person were asked to report this experience, he would say that he saw "heart." But the split-brain patients responded differently, depending on which hemisphere was responding. When the patient was asked to *name* the word just presented, he or she replied "art," since this was the portion projected to the left hemisphere, which was answering the question. When, however, the patient was asked to point with the left hand to one of two cards on which were written "he" and "art," the left hand pointed to "he." The simultaneous experiences of each hemisphere seemed unique and independent of each other in these patients. The verbal hemisphere gave one answer, the nonverbal hemisphere another.

Although most right-handed people write and draw with the right hand, most can to some extent write and draw with their left. After surgery, Dr. Bogen tested the ability of the split-brain patients to write and draw with either hand. The ability to write English remained in the right hand after surgery, but this hand could no longer draw very well. It seemed to have lost its ability to work in a relational, spatial manner. Given a square to copy with the right hand, the patient might draw four corners stacked together: he could draw *only* the corners; the hand seemed no longer able to link the disconnected segments. The left hemisphere, which controls the right hand, seems to be able to operate well in an analytic manner, yet poorly in a relational mode. The performance of the left hand reversed that of the right. The left could draw and could copy spatial figures, but could not copy a written word. It can operate holistically, but does not have very much capacity for verbal-analytic information processing. In these split-brain patients, the right hemisphere can understand some simple speech, though it has no capacity for verbal expression; we do not know whether this is an artifact of the surgery or whether it represents a rudimentary right-hemisphere capability in normal people.

A common test of spatial mentation requires the construction of a two-dimensional geometric figure using a set of cubes, each face painted with a different color or combination of colors. The patient's left hand could perform this task quite well; the right hand could not. Professor Sperry often shows an interesting film clip of the right hand attempting to solve the problem and failing, whereupon the patient's left hand cannot restrain itself and "corrects" the right—as when you may know the answer to a problem and watch me making mistakes, and cannot refrain from telling me the answer.

The split-brain surgery most dramatically delineates the two major modes of consciousness which seem normally to coexist within each person. Recent research with experimental split-brain monkeys indicates that the two hemispheres can function simultaneously as well as independently. At the same moment, a split-brain monkey can be trained on one learning problem with one eye-brain pair (the optic chiasm in monkeys is severed as part of the experimental procedure) and a second problem with the other eye-brain pair.[7] One experiment with the split-brain people has also indicated that their two hemispheres can simultaneously process more information than can those of a normal person. Dr. Sperry writes of the effect of the operation in humans: "Everything we have seen so far indicated that the surgery has left each of these people with two separate minds, that is, with two separate spheres of consciousness."[8]

The recognition that we possess two cerebral hemispheres which are specialized to operate in different modes may allow us to understand much about the fundamental duality of our consciousness. This duality has been reflected in classical as well as modern literature as between reason and passion, or between mind and intuition. Perhaps the most famous of these dichotomies in psychology is that proposed by Sigmund Freud, of the split between the "conscious" mind and the "unconscious." The workings of the "conscious" mind are held to be accessible to language and to rational discourse and alteration; the "unconscious" is much less accessible to reason or to the verbal analysis. Some aspects of "unconscious" communication are gestures, facial and body movements, tone of voice.

There are moments in each of our lives when our verbal intellect suggests one course and our "heart" or intuition another. Because of psychosurgery which has physically separated the hemispheres, the split-brain patients provide a clear example of dual response to certain situations. In one experimental test, Roger Sperry attempted to determine whether the right hemisphere could learn to respond verbally to different colors. Either a red or a green light was flashed to the left visual field of the patient, which is received on the right half of the retina and sent to the right hemisphere. Sperry then asked the split-brain patients to guess verbally which color was flashed to them. Since the left hemisphere controls the verbal output and the color information was sent to the right hemisphere, it was expected that the patients would not be able to guess the answer beyond chance, no matter how many guesses were allowed. The side which was doing the guessing, after all, was disconnected from the side which knew the answer.

After a few trials, however, the patients' scores improved whenever the examiner allowed a second guess. What happened was this. If a red light was flashed and the patient guessed correctly by chance, this terminated the trial. If the patient guessed incorrectly, he might frown, shake his head, and then "correct" his answer verbally. The right hemisphere had seen the light, then heard the left make an incorrect answer. Having no access to verbal output, the right hemisphere used the means at its disposal, and caused a frown and a head-shake, which informed the left hemisphere that its answer was incorrect.

In a loose way, this is an analog of the conflict between "conscious" and "unconscious" processes which Freud so compellingly described. In the split-brain patients, the verbal, rational processing system, disconnected from the source of information, was countermanded by gestures and tone of voice, as when a person may insist "I am *not* angry," yet his tone of voice and facial expression simultaneously indicate exactly the opposite feeling.

A similar situation occurred when emotion-laden information was given to the right hemisphere while the verbal hemisphere remained unaware of it. A photograph of a nude woman was shown to the right hemisphere of a patient in the course of a series of otherwise dull laboratory tests. At first, the woman viewing the nude on the screen said that she saw nothing, then immediately flushed, alternately squirmed, smiled, and looked uncomfortable and confused. But her "conscious" or verbal half was *still* unaware of what had caused the emotional turmoil. All that was accessible to the verbal apparatus was that *something* unusual was occurring in her body. Her words reflected that the emotional reaction had been "unconscious," unavailable to her language apparatus. To paraphrase her, "What a funny machine you have there, Dr. Sperry."

In this instance a clear split was observed between the two independent consciousnesses that are normally in communication and collaboration. In such an experiment with split-brain patients, we can accurately localize the split of information in the system. A similar process, although much more difficult to localize, may underlie the classic Freudian symptoms of repression and denial, both situations in which the verbal mechanism has no access to emotional information in other parts of the system. In less pathological instances, when we perform an action "intuitively," our words often make no sense, perhaps because the action has been initiated by a part of the brain little involved in language.

But these spectacular split-brain and lesion studies are not the only evidence for the physiological duality in consciousness. In general, caution should be exercised in drawing inferences on normal functioning from pathological and surgical cases alone. In dealing with these cases we must recall that we are investigating disturbed, not normal, functioning, from which inference to how normal people function may be a bit tenuous. In cases of brain damage, it is never fully clear that one hemisphere has not taken over a function from the other to an unusual degree because of the injury. It is necessary to seek out evidence from normally functioning people, even if that evidence is more indirect, since we don't go poking inside the brains of our friends. In this, we are fortunate that recent research with normal people has confirmed much of the neurosurgical explorations.

If the right hemisphere operates predominantly in a simultaneous manner, it could integrate diverse input quickly. This mode of information-processing would be advantageous for spatial orientation, when the person must quickly integrate visual, muscular, and kinesthetic cues. In a carefully controlled experiment with normal people, the right hemisphere was found to be superior in depth perception to the left.[9]

When a tachistoscope is used to introduce information to only the right hemisphere and either a nonverbal or a verbal response is required, the nonverbal response comes more quickly than the verbal one. A verbal response requires the information to be sent across the callosum to the left hemisphere, which takes some time. This indicates that the normal brain does indeed make use of the lateral specialization, selecting the appropriate area for differential information-processing.[10]

Another experiment which confirms the differential specialization of the two hemispheres uses eye movements as an indicator. Ask a friend a question such as, "How do you spell Mississippi?" The chances are that he will shift his gaze off to one side while reflecting. Marcel Kinsbourne of Duke University, and Katherine Kocel, David Galin, Edward Merrin, and myself of our research group at the Langley Porter Neuropsychiatric Institute in San Francisco, have found that which direction a person gazes in is affected by the kind of question asked. If the question is verbal-analytical (such as "Divide 144 by 6, and multiply the answer by 7"), more eye movements are made to the right than if the question involves spatial mentation (such as "Which way does an Indian face on the nickel?").[11]

Kinsbourne has performed another experiment which deserves special mention. Ask a friend to balance a wooden dowel on the index finger of each hand, one hand at a time. Generally, the preferred hand is more adept at this balancing. Ask the person then to speak while balancing this dowel, and time the length of the balancing. In Kinsbourne's experiment, the balancing time of the right hand decreased, as would be expected, since the addition of a task interferes with performance in most situations. But the balancing time of the left hand *increased* with concurrent verbalization.[12]

The right hand, recall, is predominantly controlled by the left hemisphere. When the left hemisphere is engaged in speech, its control of the right hand suffers. While the left hand is balancing, the left hemisphere may still intrude on its performance. When the left hemisphere is occupied in speech, it no longer seems to interfere with the left hand and the balancing time of the left improves.

The normal brain constantly exhibits electrical activity, in the form of very low voltages, as recorded at the scalp by the electroencephalograph or EEG. If the EEG is recorded from both hemispheres of a normal person during the performance of verbal or spatial information-processing tasks, different "brain-wave" patterns result. During a verbal task, the alpha rhythm in the right hemisphere increases relative to the left, and in a spatial task the alpha increases in the left hemisphere relative to the right. The appearance of the alpha rhythm indicates a "turning off" of information-processing in the area involved. As if to reduce the interference between the two conflicting modes of operation of its two cerebral hemispheres, the brain tends to turn off its unused side in a given situation.[13]

But how do these two modes interact in daily life? My opinion, and that of David Galin, is that in most ordinary activities we simply alternate between the two modes, selecting the appropriate one and inhibiting the other. It is not at all clear how this process occurs. Do the two systems work continuously in parallel, and merely alternate control of the body, or do they truly time-share the control? Clearly each of us can work in both modes—we all speak, we all can move in space, we all can do both at once; yet in skiing, for instance, an attempt to verbally encode each bodily movement would lead to disaster. The two modes of operation *complement* each other, but do not readily substitute for one another. Consider describing a spiral staircase. Most would begin using words and quickly begin to gesture in the air. Or consider attempting to ride a bicycle purely from a verbal instruction.

This lateral specialization of the brain seems to be unique to humans and related to the evolution of language. There is no evidence that the two cerebral hemispheres of other primates are specialized, although it would be reasonable to assume some evolutionary precursor of man's hemispheric asymmetry. Jerre Levy-Agresti and Roger Sperry have suggested that humans have evolved in this manner because the sequential information-processing which must underlie language, mathematics, and "rational" thought is not readily compatible with the more simultaneous mode of information-processing which underlies relational perception, orientation in space, and what our verbal intellect can only term "intuition."[14]

Within each person the two polarities seem to exist simultaneously as two semi-independent information-processing units with different specialties. There is some suggestive evidence that the modes of physiological organization may be different in the two hemispheres. Josephine Semmes, of the National Institute of Mental Health, has found that damage to the left hemisphere results in quite localized disturbance of function, whereas damage to the right interferes less focally with performance. Semmes and her co-workers studied 124 war veterans who had incurred brain injuries. They tested the effects of brain injury on simple motor reactions, somatosensory thresholds, and object discrimination—testing each hand-hemisphere pair separately. Studying the right hand, they found that injuries in quite specific areas of the left hemisphere interfered with performance of specific tasks, but no such focus of localization could be found with right-hemisphere lesions.[15] This evidence seems to indicate that the left hemisphere is more anatomically specialized for the discrete, focal information-processing underlying logic, and that the right hemisphere is more diffusely organized, which is advantageous for orientation in space and for other situations which require simultaneous processing of many inputs.

It is the polarity and the integration of these two modes of consciousness, the complementary workings of the intellect and the intuitive, which underlie our highest achievements. However, it has often been noticed that some persons habitually prefer one mode over the other, for example, our pedagogue at the beginning of this article. The exclusively verbal, logical scientist manifests a similar dominance, and may often forget and even deny that he possesses another side; he may find it difficult to work in the areas of the right hemisphere, in art, crafts, dance, sports. But this other mode, although less logical and clear, is important for creativity: "combinatory play" was Einstein's phrase. "Have you ever learned to swim?" asks the boatman.

This duality in human consciousness has long been recognized in other cultures. For instance, the Hopi Indians of the American Southwest distinguish the function of the two hands, one for writing, one for making music. The French word for Law, that most linear and rational of human pursuits, is *droit*, which literally means "right." For the Mojave Indians, the left hand is the passive, maternal side of the person, the right, the active father. William Domhoff concludes his interesting survey of the myth and symbolism of *left* and *right* by noting that the left is often the area of the taboo, the sacred, the unconscious, the feminine, the intuitive, and the dreamer. And we do find that the symbolism of the two sides of the body is quite often in agreement with these ideas. In myth, the feminine side is most often on the left, the masculine on the right.[16]

On this right-left duality, we have scientific evidence only for dreaming, and it is not too strong. In a report on three cases, Humphrey and Zangwill have found that damage to the right parietal lobe of the brain seems to interfere with dreaming. Bogen notes that his split-brain patients tend to report the absence of dreams after the operation, perhaps because of the disconnection of the verbal output from the right hemisphere. In a study with normal subjects, Austin reports that people who tend to specialize in analytic thinking (convergers) are less likely to recall dreams than those with the opposite bias (divergers), whom he characterized as more imaginative and more able to deal with the nonrational.[17]

In Vedanta, the duality in consciousness is said to be between intellect (Buddhi) and mind (manas). Such a distinction may be hard for us to state clearly, for when we say, "This person has a fine mind," we are usually referring only to the verbal and intellectual portion of the mind. The Chinese Yin-Yang symbol neatly encapsulates the duality and complementarity of these two poles of consciousness.

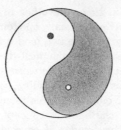

The Yin-Yang symbol

Facing out, on the figure's left is the "night," the dark side named *K'un* in the *I Ching*. On the figure's right is the "day," the light, *Ch'ien*, the creative, sometimes translated as the active or the originating principle. Here are the two polarities of man (and all creation) as represented in the Wilhelm-Baynes translation of the *I Ching*:

Ch'ien, The Creative

The first hexagram is made up of six unbroken lines. These unbroken lines stand for the primal power, which is light-giving, active, strong, and of the spirit. The hexagram is consistently strong in character, and since it is without weakness, its essence is power or energy. Its image is heaven. Its energy is represented as unrestricted by any fixed conditions in space and is therefore conceived of as motion. Time is regarded as the basis of this motion. Thus, the hexagram includes also the power of time and the power of persisting in time, that is, duration.

K'un, The Receptive

This hexagram is made up of broken lines only. The broken line represents the dark, yielding, receptive primal power of yin. The attribute of the hexagram is devotion; its image is the earth. It is the perfect complement of *The Creative*—the complement, not the opposite, for the Receptive does not combat the creative but completes it. It represents nature in contrast to spirit, earth in contrast to heaven, space as against time, the female-maternal as against the male-paternal. However, as applied to human affairs, the principle of this complementary relationship is found not only in the relation between man and woman, but also in that between prince and minister and between father and son. Indeed, even in the individual this duality appears in the coexistence of the spiritual world and the world of the senses.[18]

Note that one pole is in time, the other in space; one is light, one dark; one active, one receptive; one male, one female.

It is the complementarity of these two modes of consciousness which is a central consideration . . . as they manifest themselves on several levels simultaneously—within each person, between different persons, within different disciplines such as scientific inquiry (psychology in particular), and in the organization of cultures. In his review on the "other" side of the brain, Joseph Bogen clarifies the concept by presenting a set of dichotomies between the two modes of consciousness. Following him, I present one such table, but only for purposes of suggestion and clarification in an intuitive sort of way, not as a final categorical statement of the conception. Many of the poles are, of course, tendencies and specializations, not at all binary classifications. Examination of the table may also make the Day-Night metaphor I am using a bit clearer.

THE TWO MODES OF CONSCIOUSNESS:

A *Tentative Dichotomy*

Who Proposed It?		
Many sources	Day	Night
Blackburn	Intellectual	Sensuous
Oppenheimer	Time, History	Eternity, Timelessness
Deikman	Active	Receptive
Polanyi	Explicit	Tacit
Levy, Sperry	Analytic	Gestalt
Domhoff	Right (side of body)	Left (side of body)
Many sources	Left hemisphere	Right hemisphere
Bogen	Propositional	Appositional
Lee	Lineal	Nonlineal
Luria	Sequential	Simultaneous
Semmes	Focal	Diffuse
I Ching	The Creative: heaven masculine, Yang	The Receptive: earth feminine, Yin
I Ching	Light	Dark
I Ching	Time	Space
Many sources	Verbal	Spatial
Many sources	Intellectual	Intuitive
Vedanta	Buddhi	Manas
Jung	Causal	Acausal
Bacon	Argument	Experience

Many different occupations and disciplines involve a concentration in one of the major modes of consciousness. Science and law are heavily involved in linearity, duration, and verbal logic. Crafts, the "mystical" disciplines, music, are more present-centered, aconceptual, intuitive. A complete human consciousness involves the polarity and integration of the two modes, as a complete day includes the daylight and the darkness.

. . . Even scientific knowledge, largely a linear and rational pursuit, also relies heavily on intuition for completeness. W. I. B. Beveridge, in his *The Art of Scientific Investigation*, stresses the need for the development of the intuitive side in scientists. He defines "intuition" in science as "a clarifying idea which comes suddenly to mind." Intuitive knowledge complements the normal, rational scientific knowledge, much as the paradigm change is the complement to the normal progress of scientific thought.[19]

According to Beveridge, intuitions have most often come to scientific investigators when the normal rational processes are temporarily suspended. The French mathematician Poincare, after dismissing his work from his rational mind, went for a drive in the country. "Just as I put my foot on the brake, the idea came to me." Many others have stressed this point, that reason in science must be complemented by the "other" mode. Albert Einstein, for instance, said of his own creative processes, "The really valuable thing is intuition." The realm of the paradigm *maker* is the "other" side of science. The complete scientific endeavor, then, involves working in both modes.

To take a similar example quite close to hand. In writing . . . I have had vague idea after idea at different times: on the beach, in the mountains, in discussion, even while writing. These intuitions are sparse images—perhaps a connection which allows a new gestalt to form—but they are never fully clear, and never satisfactory by themselves. They are incomplete realizations, not a finished work. For me, it is only when the intellect has worked out these glimpses of form that the intuition becomes of any use to others. It is the very linearity of a book which enables the writer to refine his own intuitions, and clarify them, first to himself, and then if possible to the reader.

The process of building a house provides another example. At first, there may be a sudden inspiration of the gestalt of the finished house, but this image must be brought to completion, slowly, by linear methods, by plans and contracts, and then by the actual construction, sequentially, piece by piece.

The idea of the complementarity of two major modes of consciousness is hardly new. It antedates the *I Ching* and is found in many forms of philosophical, religious, and psychological endeavor. It was emphasized in physics by Robert Oppenheimer and in metaphysics by many. What is new now is a recognition that these modes operate physiologically as well as mentally and culturally. With a recognition of the physiological basis of the dual specializations of consciousness, we may be able to redress the balance in science and in psychology, a balance which has in recent years swung a bit too far to the right, into a strict insistence on verbal logic that has left context and perspective undeveloped.

NOTES

1. From Idries Shah, *The Exploits of the Incomparable Mulla Nasrudin* (New York: E. P. Dutton, 1972), p. 18; London: Jonathan Cape, 1966.

2. G. William Domhoff, "But Why Did They Sit on the Kin's Right in the First Place?" *Psychoanalytic Review* 56 (1969–70) 586–96.

3. Perhaps the best review of right-hemisphere functions is Joseph E. Bogen, "The Other Side of the Brain, I, II, III," *Bulletin of the Los Angeles Neurological Societies,* Vol. 34, no. 3 (July 1969). Reprinted in part in Robert Ornstein, ed., *The Nature of Human Consciousness* (San Francisco: W. H. Freeman and Co.; New York: The Viking Press, 1973).

4. Brenda Milner, "Brain Mechanisms Suggested by Studies of Temporal Lobes" in F. L. Darley and C. H. Millikan, eds., *Brain Mechanisms Underlying Speech and Language* (New York: Grune & Stratton, 1965). Also Brenda Milner, "Interhemispheric Differences in the Localization of Psychological Processes in Man," *British Medical Bulletin* 27, no. 3 (1971) 272–77.

5. A. R. Luria, *Higher Cortical Functions in Man* (New York: Basic Books, 1966).

6. R. W. Sperry, "The Great Cerebral Commissure," *Scientific American* (Jan. 1964), pp. 42–52. Offprint no. 174. Michael S. Gazzaniga, "The Split Brain in Man," *Scientific American* (Aug. 1967), pp. 24–29. Offprint no. 508.

7. Ibid.

8. Roger Sperry, "Problems Outstanding in the Evolution of Brain Function," James Arthur Lecture, American Museum of Natural History, New York, 1964.

9. Margaret Durnford and Doreen Kimura, "Right-Hemisphere Specialization for Depth Perception Reflected in Visual Field Differences," *Nature* 231 (June 11, 1971) 394–95.

10. R. A. Filbey and Michael Gazzaniga, "Splitting the Normal Brain with Reaction Time," *Psychonomic Science* 17 (1969) 335–36.

11. Marcel Kinsbourne, unpublished manuscript, Duke University, 1971. Katherine Kocel, David Galin, Robert Ornstein, and Edward Merrin, "Lateral Eye Movements and Cognitive Mode," *Psychonomic Science* (1972), in press.

12. Marcel Kinsbourne and Jay Cook, "Generalized and Lateralized Effects of Concurrent Verbalization on a Unimanual Skill," *Quarterly Journal of Experimental Psychology* 23 (1971) 341–45.

13. David Galin and Robert Ornstein, "Lateral Specialization of Cognitive Mode: An EEG Study," *Psychophysiology* (1972), in press.

14. J. Levy-Agresti and Roger Sperry, "Differential Perceptual Capacities in Major and Minor Hemispheres," *Proceedings of the National Academy of Sciences* 61 (1968) 1151.

15. Josephine Semmes, "Hemispheric Specialization: A Possible Clue to Mechanism," *Neuropsychologia* 6 (1968) 11–16.

16. Domhoff, op. cit.

17. M. E. Humphrey and O. L. Zangwill, "Cessation of Dreaming after Brain Injury," *Journal Neurol. Neurosurg. Psychiatry* 14 (1951) 322–25. Bogen, "The Other Side of the Brain, II," loc. cit. M. D. Austin, "Dream Recall and the Bias of Intellectual Ability," *Nature* 231 (May 7, 1971) 59.

18. R. Wilhelm, trans., and C. F. Baynes, ed., *I Ching* (Princeton, N.J.: Princeton University Press, 1950), pp. 3, 10–11.

19. W. I. B. Beveridge, *The Art of Scientific Investigation* (New York: Random House, 1950).

A Cartography of the Ecstatic and Meditative States

ROLAND FISCHER

In this age so concerned with travel in outer as well as inner space, it is strange that, while we have detailed charts of the moon, we have no cartography of the varieties of human experience. In order to draft a map of inner space, I am ready to be your travel guide and take you on two voyages: one along the perception-hallucination continuum of increasing ergotropic arousal, which includes creative, psychotic, and ecstatic experiences; and another along the preception-meditation continuum of increasing trophotropic arousal, which encompasses the hypoaroused states of Zazen and Yoga samadhi.[1]

Along the perception-hallucination continuum of increasing arousal of the sympathetic nervous system (ergotropic arousal), man—the self-referential system—perceptually-behaviorally (cortically) interprets the change (drug-induced or "natural") in his subcortical activity as creative, psychotic, and ecstatic experiences.[2] These states are marked by a gradual turning inward toward a mental dimension at the expense of the physical. The normal state of daily routine, our point of departure, is followed by an aroused, creative state, which can be characterized by an increase in both data content (a description of space) and rate of data processing "flood of inner sensation,"[3] or most intense time.[4] However, in the next aroused state on the continuum, the acute schizophrenic or rather, "hyperphrenic"[5] state, a further increase in data content may not be matched by a corresponding increase in the rate of data processing. While the creative state is conducive to the evolution of novel relations and new meaning, the psychotic "jammed computer" state interferes with the individual's creative interpretation of the activity of his central nervous system (CNS). At the peak of ecstatic rapture, the outside (physical) world "retreats to the fringe of consciousness,"[6] and the individual reflects himself in his own "program." One can conceptualize the normal, creative, "hyperphrenic," and ecstatic states along the perception-hallucination continuum as the ledges of a homeostatic step function.[7] While the creative person may travel freely between "normal" and creative states, the chronic schizophrenic patient is stranded in the "jammed computer" state. And the talented mystic, of course, does not need to go through every intermediate step to attain ecstasy.

The mutually exclusive relationship between the ergotropic and trophotropic systems[8] justifies a separate perception-meditation continuum of increasing trophotropic arousal (hypoarousal) that is continuous with, and to the right of, the perception-hallucination continuum (Fig. 1). The course of our second trip, therefore, will take us in the opposite direction, along the tranquil perception-meditation continuum, where man may symbolically interpret his gradually increasing trophotropic arousal as Zazen, and, ultimately, samadhi.

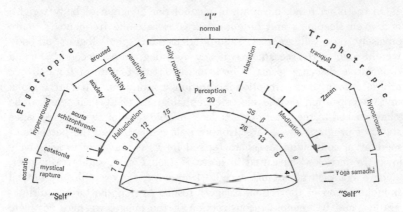

Figure 1. Varieties of conscious states mapped on a perception-hallucination continuum of increasing ergotropic arousal (left) and a perception-meditation continuum of increasing trophotropic arousal (right). These levels of hyper- and hypoarousal are interpreted by man as normal, creative, psychotic, and ecstatic states (left) and Zazen and samadhi (right). The loop connecting ecstasy and samadhi represents the rebound from ecstasy to samadhi, which is observed in response to intense ergotropic excitation. The numbers 35 to 7 on the perception-hallucination continuum are Goldstein's coefficient of variation (see note 56), specifying the decrease in variability of the EEG amplitude with increasing ergotropic arousal. The numbers 26 to 4 on the perception-meditation continuum, on the other hand, refer to those beta, alpha, and theta EEG waves (measured in hertz) that predominate during, but are not specific to, these states (see note 18).*

* Ed. note: This chart should be compared with that in the article following by Fischer.

That the two continua in Fig. 1 represent two mutually exclusive states of arousal has been well documented by Hess and Gellhorn.[9] The mutual exclusiveness of the ergotropic and trophotropic systems can also be illustrated by characteristic changes in the frequency of the small, involuntary, micronystagmoid movements of the eye. These rapid scanning movements (with a mean frequency of one per second and an amplitude of 5 to 10 minutes of arc) are regarded as a prerequisite for the fixation of an object in physical space-time.[10] The frequency of saccadic movements is increased five- to eightfold in response to the ergotropic arousal induced by moderate doses of mescaline, psilocybin, or LSD (D-lysergic acid diethylamide).[11] This increase is also present without drugs in acute schizophrenics,[12] that is, patients in a state of ergotropic arousal, the "alarm reaction"[13] stage of Selye's general adaptation syndrome.[14]

On the other hand, 0.9 gram of alcohol per kilogram of body weight, and even sleepiness and fatigue, decreases saccadic frequency;[15] more precisely, 0.01 milligram of Valium (diazepam) per kilogram of body weight reduces the saccadic frequency by 9 degrees per second.[16] Such a progressive decrease seems to be a characteristic feature of trophotropic arousal along the perception-meditation continuum. That the alpha rhythm appearing on the electroencephalogram (EEG) appears to be phase-locked to the onset of saccades[17] may also be of significance, since states of progressively greater trophotropic arousal along the perception-meditation continuum are characterized by EEG waves of progressively lower frequencies (measured in hertz)[18] (see Fig. 1, right). Moreover, since a complete arrest of saccadic frequency, for example, by optical immobilization of the retinal image[19] results in periodic fading, disintegration, and fragmented reconstruction of the image, we may postulate that reduced saccadic frequency may be linked with the Yogi's comment that, at the peak of a meditative experience, he can still see "objects," but they have no predicative properties.[20]

WHAT ARE HALLUCINATIONS AND HOW CAN THEY BE MEASURED?

The hallucinatory or waking-dream states along the perception-hallucination continuum can best be described as experiences of intense sensations that cannot be verified through voluntary motor activity. Note that such a definition does not differentiate between dreams and hallucinations. . . .

We can describe verifiable perceptions, therefore, by assigning to them low sensory-to-motor (S/M) ratios,[21] while nonverifiable hallucinations and dreams can be characterized by increasing S/M ratios as one moves along the perception-hallucination or perception-meditation continuum toward ecstasy or samadhi, the two most hallucinatory states[22] (Fig. 1, left and right, respectively). Moderate doses of the hallucinogenic drugs LSD, psilocybin, and mescaline[23] can get one "moving" along the perception-hallucination continuum, whereas minor tranquilizers and some muscle relaxants may initiate travel along the perception-meditation continuum.

If high S/M ratios do, indeed, reflect hallucinatory experiences, as my definition of hallucinations would imply, it would be important to quantify S/M ratio as a measure of hallucinatory intensity. In fact, a quantitative meaning has been given to the S/M ratio by measuring the components of a psychomotor performance, specifically, handwriting area and handwriting pressure,[24] in volunteers during a psilocybin-induced waking-dream state.

The techniques for measuring handwriting area (S) (in square centimeters), as well as for obtaining handwriting pressure (M) (in 10^4 dynes averaged over time), with an indicator that operates on a pressure-voltage-to-frequency basis, have been described elsewhere.[25] Using these two parameters prior to (T_1) and at the peak (T_2) of a psilocybin-induced experience [160 to 250 micrograms of psilocybin per kilogram of body weight], we found in a sample of forty-seven college-age volunteers a 31 per cent ($T_2 - T_1$) increase in mean S/M ratio.[26]

SPACE AND INCREASING HYPER- AND HYPOAROUSAL

We call man's symbolic interpretation of his CNS activity "perception-behavior" and regard creative, "hyperphrenic," and ecstatic states, as well as Zazen and samadhi, as perceptual-behavioral interpretations of ergotropic and trophotropic arousal, respectively. We may now consider some of the perceptual-behavioral changes, or transformation, that gradually develop as the level of arousal increases and decreases along each continuum. One of the most conspicuous transformations is that of "constancies"[27] which in the normal state of daily routine form a learned structure of primary ordering of space and time "out there." Although the newborn infant's only reality, in the beginning, is his CNS activity, he soon learns by bumping into things, to erect a corresponding model "out there." Ultimately, his forgetting that his CNS activity had been the only reality will be taken by society as proof of his maturity, and he will be ready to conduct his life "out there" in (container) space and (chronological) time.[28] This gradually learned and projected model, then, is the representation of a world ordered and stabilized by self-programmed invariances. The adult interprets his CNS activity within this structure of similarity criteria, or "constancies," and thus experience can be said to consist of two processes: the programmed (subcortical) CNS activity; and the symbolic or perceptual-behavioral (cortical) interpretation, or metaprograms, of the CNS activity.

I have studied the transformation of certain constancies along the perception-hallucination continuum and find, for example, that the ability to readapt to optically induced spatial distortions, or to maintain the constancy of the visual world, gradually diminishes as a subject turns inward under the influence of psilocybin.[29] Another finding revealed that the preferred level of (the constancy of) brightness increases under the influence of hallucinogenic drugs,[30] but only in "variable" subjects[31]— that is, those subjects whose large standard deviations on a variety of perceptual and behavioral tasks indicate a large and varied interpretive repertoire. However, in "stable" subjects, who are characterized by small standard deviations and, thus, by smaller and more predictable interpretive repertoires, the level of perferred brightness decreases when they are under the influence of hallucinogenic drugs. In addition, nearby visual space was found to gradually close in as subjects moved along the perception-hallucination continuum under the influence of moderate doses of psilocybin. This contraction of nearby visual space was observed with two different techniques: monitoring the apparent fronto-parallel plan,[32] and handwriting measurements.[33]

The transformation of constancies under ergotropic arousal—specifically, as manifested in the psilocybin-induced contraction of nearby visual space—can also be observed in acute schizophrenics under "natural" ergotropic arousal (that is, without hallucinogenic drugs). The transformation of constancies during acute psychotic episodes apparently gives rise to a "vertical displacement of the visual angle," which is implicit in a contraction of visual space and which results in an elevation of the horizon.[34] Rennert,[35] who for years has studied the angle of perspective in the drawings of schizophrenic patients, finds the acuteness of a schizophrenic episode to be significantly related to the height of the horizon in the patient's drawings. In fact, using a ruler, Rennert can predict remission or relapse from the position of the horizon in a drawing: the more severe the schizophrenic episode, the higher the position of the horizon—ultimately, it may even disappear. At the same time a map-like perspective, or bird's-eye view, of the landscape results, with houses and other significant figures appearing in the foreground. . . .[36]

I have also observed that the just-noticeable difference (JND) in taste, expressed as Weber fraction, becomes smaller with increasing ergotropic arousal: subjects need fewer molecules of a sapid substance (such as sucrose, quinine, and so on) to taste a JND in sweetness or bitterness. On the other hand, under the influence of tranquilizers of the phenothiazine type, the Weber fraction becomes larger: more molecules are needed to taste a JND.[37] Since the Weber fraction is constant at levels of arousal associated with daily routine (within the customary middle range of taste sensitivity),[38] I interpret the above as examples of arousal-induced transformations of constancies. Because the number of molecules necessary to elicit the sensation of a JND gradually decreases during a voyage from the physical to the mental dimension along the perception-hallucination continuum, it might be extrapolated that no sapid molecules at all are needed for the experience of taste during ecstasy, the most hyperaroused hallucinatory state.

It should be emphasized that the projection of our CNS activity as location in the physical dimension of space and time "out there" was learned at, and is hence bound to, the lower levels of arousal characteristic of our daily survival routines. That this projection is gradually learned can be supported by Bender's observation that schizophrenic children "do not experience hallucinations of the projected type like adults, but only of the introjected type. They hear voices inside their head or other parts of the body, feel that they originate inside themselves and to not feel persecuted by them."[39]

The constancy of corporeal awareness also undergoes transformations as one moves along the perception-hallucination continuum. For instance, phantom sensations [that is, readaptation phenomena compensation for and correcting distortions of corporeal awareness in physical space-time[40]] gradually diminish and disappear as one moves into the mental dimension under the influence of hallucinogenic drugs.[41] Depersonalization phenomena, on the other hand, manifest themselves as changes in body image, and usually accompany the dissolution of ego boundaries during creative, psychotic, ecstatic, or meditative states—whether "natural" or drug-induced—as well as while falling asleep. All of this is to say that the constancy of the "I" is interfered with as one moves along the perception-hallucination continuum from the "I" of the physical world to the "Self" of the mental dimension. Analogously, the perception-meditation continuum (Fig. 1, right) also involves a departure from the "I" to the "Self." These two continua can thus be called "I-Self" continua. As will become clear later, the "Self" of ecstasy and the "self" of samadhi are one and the same "Self."

The further we progress on the perception-hallucination continuum from the normal through the creative, psychotic, and, ultimately, to the ecstatic state (Fig. 1), the more complete is the transformation, or "unlearning," of the constancies of the physical dimension. Input, or outside information in general, is gradually reduced along this continuum. Thus, St. Teresa of Avila tells us in her autobiography that, at the peak of a mystical experience, ". . . the soul neither hears nor sees nor feels. While it lasts, none of the senses perceives or knows what is taking place."[42] Space, then, which was gradually established in ever widening circles during childhood, gradually contracts with increasing arousal and ultimately disappears.

A gradual contraction and ultimate disappearance is also the fate of chronological time in the physical dimension (of the "I" state) as one progresses along the perception-hallucination or the perception-meditation continuum. In particular, we find that LSD[43] and psilocybin[44] cause an overestimation of time, the magnitude of which is related to a subject's variability on a perceptual or behavioral test before ingesting the given drug. The greater a subject's variability before ingesting a drug— for example, the retest-variance on his quinine taste-threshold or the standard deviation on his handwriting area—the greater will be his contraction or overestimation of time at drug peak [that is, 150 minutes after the oral administration of 160 to 200 micrograms of psilocybin per kilogram of body weight, when 63 minutes of chronological time (in geometrically increasing intervals) are estimated and recorded].[45] Moreover, the greater the subject's variability, and thus his contraction of time, the greater will be his "rebound effect" twenty-four hours after; that is, his underestimation or expansion of time.[46]

Dividing people, according to the magnitude of their perceptual variability, into "maximizers" ("stable" subjects) and "minimizers" ("variable" subjects) assists one in resolving the hotly debated question of whether time "flies" or "drags" during a hallucinogenic drug-induced experience. Actually, as we have found, it does both: it is overestimated (it "flies" or "contracts") by the minimizers, the subjects with a large standard deviation, who prefer to decrease (visual) sensory data content and its rate of processing at drug peak; and it is underestimated (it "drags" or "expands") by the maximizers, the subjects with a small standard deviation, who prefer to increase data content and its rate of processing at drug peak.

Such contraction of time parallels the already described contraction of nearby visual space. By "time-contraction," I mean an increase in data content within a chronological time span, or, in experiential terms, "the flood of inner sensation";[47] and I imply that, during such an experience, the subject, if without a watch, would arrive early for an appointment. Under the impact of an acute, hallucinogenic drug-induced experience, the subject usually compares the time-contraction or increased data content of the mental dimension with his past and present routine performance in physical space-time and has, therefore, to conclude that "time" passes slowly. Note, for instance, Hofmann's classical description of rid-

ing home on his bicycle under the influence of LSD: "The trip is about
four miles and I had the feeling of not getting ahead, whereas my escort
stated that we were rolling along at a good speed."[48] By comparing the
usual rate of revolution of the spokes, as well as the usual rate at which
the roadside "passed him by," with his experience of an increased data
content of "flood of inner sensation," he had to conclude that he was not
getting ahead and that time was dragging. Thus, there is only an apparent contradiction in terms: while experience is shifting from the physical
toward the mental dimension, physical or chronological time becomes
less and less important. Still, this transitional state can only be described
in Aristotelian [dualistic, or two-valued (true-false)] terms of chronological time[49] and by comparing experimental with experiential data.
This contradiction resolves itself at the peak of ergotropic or trophotropic
arousal, since these purely mental states are timeless and spaceless and
in no need of comparative verification.

INCREASING CORTICAL-SUBCORTICAL INTEGRATION
WITH INCREASING AROUSAL

If we assume that man, the self-referential system, creates experience
through the cortical (that is, perceptual-behavioral) interpretation of his
subcortical activity, we may ask about the extent of freedom, or relative
independence, of the mind (cortex) from the subcortical substratum. Indeed, man is to a large extent free to interpret his subcortical activity in
a variety of ways at levels of arousal associated with daily routine. That
this freedom is implicit in the functional independence of the limbic and
neocortical systems is dramatically demonstrated by the fact that the
electrical discharges resulting from hippocampal seizures are confined to
the limbic system.[50]

We can find no relation between the extent of psilocybin-induced perceptual and behavioral (or cortical) change and a drug-induced increase
in pupillary diameter,[51] which is a drug dose-dependent parameter of
autonomic activity.[52] This lack of a relation points to a large degree of
freedom of cortical interpretive activity, even under moderate hyperarousal.

The cortical-subcortical independence at the level of daily routine and
even moderate levels of arousal is also implicit in the results of
Marañon's[53] and Schachter and Singer's[54] experiments, in which the set
and setting determined the particular cortical interpretation (from "good
trip" to "bad trip") of each subject after his subcortical activity had been
altered by an injection of 0.5 cubic centimeter of a 1 : 1000 solution of
epinephrine.

It is now common knowledge that the set and setting, as well as the personality, decisively influence the cortical interpretation of hallucinogenic drug-induced changes in subcortical activity.[55] What is not fully realized is that set, setting, personality, expectations, and past experiences determine the cortical "effects" of most of the psychoactive drugs when they are used in medically endorsed dosages. In fact, except for the anesthetics and hypnotics, there are no drugs that selectively direct human cognitive (psychological, or, in our terms, cortical) functions.

With rising levels of ergotropic and trophotropic arousal, however, perception-behavior becomes increasingly dependent upon (or less free of) the subcortical substratum that generates it. A cat responds to ergotropic hyperarousal with rage, while at the peak of trophotropic arousal the animal always yawns, curls up, and falls asleep. But man may be compelled to interpret these two extreme states of hyper- and hypo-arousal as ecstasy and samadhi. This increasing stereotypy (loss of freedom) with increasing ergotropic arousal can be observed, for example, as a decrease in the variability of the EEG amplitude, which Goldstein and others have measured with a Drohocki integrator.[56] A decrease in variability is expressed as the coefficient of variation (see the coefficient of variation values for states ranging from relaxation to catatonia in Fig. 1).[57] Increasing stereotypy also manifests itself as an increase in the S/M ratio,[58] thus indicating an intensification of inner sensations, accompanied by a loss in the ability to verify them through voluntary motor activity. Such high S/M ratios are implicit in the statements uttered during both drug-induced hallucinations and the hallucinations of schizophrenics: "of being hypnotized," "of being not free," "of being overpowered," "of being paralyzed," and so on, and in the mystic's inability to experience the subject-object dichotomy of daily routine in the physical dimension.

Apparently, then, an increase in ergotropic arousal is paralleled by a restriction in the individual's repertoire of available perceptual-behavioral interpretations. This restriction implies that certain levels can *only* be interpreted as creative (artistic, scientific, religious) or psychotic experiences.[59] Although religious interpretation is a common feature of catatonia,[60] ecstasy, which is the mystical experience of the Oneness of everything, results from a creative breakthrough out of catatonic hyperarousal. During the ecstatic state, there is neither capacity nor necessity for motor verification of the intense sensations. In the mental dimension, in contrast to the physical, the all-pervasive experience of absolute certainty does not require further verification[61] and will be structured according to current mythology or the belief system of a St. Francis, Pascal, or Ramakrishna. What is one man's loss of freedom, therefore, may be another's gain in creativity.

An increasing stereotypy can also be observed along the perception-meditation continuum of increasing trophotropic arousal (see Fig. 1, right); this enables one to gradually exclude stimulation from without and turn attention inward. Continuous trains of alpha waves accompany these changes, and the dominant frequency of the alpha pattern decreases toward the alpha-theta border region, until some subjects, in a state of reverie, produce long trains of theta waves[62] [see the beta, alpha, and theta waves,[63] measured in hertz, in Fig. 1, right]. According to Green et al.,[64] the "alert inner-focused state is associated with the production of alpha rhythm"; in this state Zen masters show an alpha-blocking response to auditory clicks, but, in contrast to normal controls, do not habituate to these stimuli.[65] Since the alpha rhythm is not altered or blocked by flashing lights, sounding gongs, or the touch of a hot test tube during the deep meditation of Indian Yoga masters,[66] the Yoga samadhi apparently represents a more intense state of trophotropic arousal than Zazen does and must also express a greater inability to function in physical space-time than Zazen does. In fact, a Yoga master denies noticing *any* outside stimuli during deep meditation, whereas control subjects show alpha-blocking with as little stimulus as a flashing light (as do the Yoga masters themselves when not meditating).

"SELF": THE KNOWER AND IMAGE-MAKER AND
"I": THE KNOWN AND IMAGINED

We have seen that the departure from the physical dimension during a voyage on the perception-meditation continuum is accompanied by a gradual loss of freedom, which is manifested in the increasing inability to verify the experience through voluntary motor activity.[67] At the peak of trophotropic arousal, in samadhi, the meditating subject experiences nothing but his own self-referential nature, void of compelling contents. It is not difficult to see a similarity between the meditative experience of pure self-reference and St. Teresa's description of her ecstasy: in both timeless and spaceless experiences, the mundane world is virtually excluded. Of course, the converse is true of the mundane state of daily routine, in which the oceanic unity with the universe, in ecstasy and samadhi, is virtually absent. Thus, the mutual exclusiveness of the "normal" and the exalted states, both ecstasy and samadhi, allows us to postulate that man, the self-referential system, exists on two levels: as "Self" in the mental dimension of exalted states; and as "I" in the objective world, where he is able and willing to change the physical dimension "out there." In fact, the "I" and the "Self" can be postulated on purely logical grounds. See, for instance, Brown's reasoning[68] that the universe is apparently

> . . . constructed in order (and thus in such a way as to be able) to see itself. But in order to do so, evidently it must first cut itself up into at least one *state which sees,* and at least one other *state which is seen.* In this severed and mutilated condition, whatever it sees is only partially itself . . . but, in any attempt to see itself as an object, it must, equally undoubtedly, act so as to make itself distinct from, and therefore, false to, itself. In this condition it will always partially elude itself.

In our terminology, the "Self" of exalted states is that which sees and knows, while the "I" is the interpretation, that which is seen and known in the physical space-time of the world "out there." The mutually exclusive relation between the "seer" and the "seen," or the elusiveness of the "Self" and the "I," may have its physiological basis in the mutual exclusiveness of the ergotropic and trophotropic systems.[69]

A discernible communication between the "Self" and the "I" is only possible during the dreaming and hallucinatory states, whether drug-induced or "natural." These states can be located approximately between coefficients of variation 10 and 13 on the perception-hallucination continuum (Fig. 1, left) and in the 9 to 12 hertz EEG range on the perception-meditation continuum (Fig. 1, right). Such "I"-"Self" communication is the creative source of art, science, literature, and religion.

In spite of the mutually exclusive relation between the ergotropic and trophotropic systems, however, there is a phenomenon called "rebound to superactivity," or trophotropic rebound, which occurs in response to intense sympathetic excitation,[70] that is, at ecstasy, the peak of ergotropic arousal.[71] A rebound into samadhi at this point can be conceived of as a physiological protective mechanism; Gellhorn[72] was among the first to notice that the rebound of the trophotropic system is not confined to the autonomic branches, but also causes significant changes in behavior. Thus, repetitive stimulation of the reticular formation in the midbrain increases the arousal level in awake cats, but this phase is followed by one in which the animal yawns, lies down, and finally falls asleep. This rebound phase is associated with the appearance of theta potentials in the hippocampus,[73] just as the corresponding human trophotropic rebound-samadhi is characterized by theta potentials[74] (see Fig. 1, right). These rebound or reversal phenomena between ecstasy and samadhi[75] are illustrated by the loop[76] connecting the two extreme exalted states in Fig. 1.

The "Self" of ecstasy and samadhi are one and the same, as if the reflecting surface of a lake in Fig. 1 embraced both exalted states. If the level of water in such a lake were gradually raised, it would intersect successive and corresponding hyper- and hypoaroused states. The intersected states represent levels of gradually diminishing subjectivity (less "Self") and increasing objectivity (more "I"), until eventually the objective "I"-state of the world is reached. Thus, each level of water would connect a hyper- and hypoaroused state with a specific subjectivity/objectivity (or "Self"-to-"I") ratio, implying a similarity between those pairs of hyper- and hypoaroused states that are connected by gradually raised levels of water. This similarity might, for example, be used to account for the success of the widely practiced narcoanalytic technique of abreacting a traumatic, hyperaroused experience in a hypoaroused state of similar "Self"-to-"I" ratio. The similarity between corresponding hyper- and hypoaroused states could also account for the hypermnesic phenomena of the hypoaroused elderly, who clearly recall the hyperaroused experiences of their youth, but do not recall more recent experiences.[77]

During the "I"-state of daily routine, the outside world is experienced as separate from oneself, and this may be a reflection of the greater freedom (that is, separateness or independence) of cortical interpretation from subcortical activity. With increasing ergotropic and trophotropic arousal, however, this separateness gradually disappears, apparently because in the "Self"-state of ecstasy and samadhi, cortical and subcortical activity are indistinguishably integrated. This unity is reflected in the experience of Oneness with everything, a Oneness with the universe that is oneself.

SIGN-SYMBOL-MEANING TRANSFORMATIONS

The separateness of subject and object during the daily routine levels of arousal (in the "I"-state) has been elaborated in our customary, rational, Aristotelian logic and language—a two-valued (either-or, true-false) logic that discounts the interaction between observer (subject) and observed (object).[78] This separateness of object and subject, as we have seen, is a reflection of the relative independence of cortical interpretation from subcortical activity and is of survival value in the "I"-state, where the subject must make decisions of life and death by manipulating objects (through voluntary motor activity).

But when we depart along either continuum from the "I" toward the "Self," the separateness of object and subject gradually disappears and their interaction becomes the principal content of the experience. This interaction, again, is a reflection of the gradually increasing integration of cortical and subcortical activity. In this state of Unity, the separateness of subject and object that is implicit in dualistic, Aristotelian logic and language becomes meaningless; only a symbolic logic and language can convey the experience of intense meaning. Apparently, then, meaning is "meaningful" only at that level of arousal at which it is experienced, and every experience has its state-bound meaning. During the "Self"-state of highest levels of hyper- or hypoarousal, this meaning can no longer be expressed in dualistic terms, since the experience of unity is born from the integration of interpretive (cortical) and interpreted (subcortical) structures. Since this intense meaning is devoid of specificities, the only way to communicate its intensity is the metaphor; hence, only through the transformation of objective sign into subjective symbol in art, literature, and religion can the increasing integration of cortical and subcortical activity be communicated.

The transformation of sign to symbol is also apparent in the visual realm, where the constancies of space and time are replaced by geometric-ornamental-rhythmic structures, the "hallucinatory form constants" of Klüver.[79] In the light of my own experience, I would extend Klüver's observations to include hyper- and hypoaroused hallucinatory experiences in general, whether electrically,[80] "naturally," or drug-induced.[81] The hallucinatory constancies are "magical symbols," visible or audible metaphors within a structure of symbolic logic and language, the language of hyper- and hypoaroused hallucinatory states, and are at the base of the general tendency toward geometric-rhythmic ornamentalization. For example, both the rose windows of Gothic cathedrals and the mandalas of Tantric religious art[82] are ritualized hallucinatory form constants. The tendency toward ornamentalization, however, is not reserved to visual imagery but also governs the order of poetic and musical rhythm, imposing an all-pervasive metrum and harmony on the hallucinatory creative-religious states[83] the rhythm of music, poetry, and language corresponds to the geometric-ornamental rhythm of the visual realm. Therefore, the manneristic[84] hallucinatory-creative style of art and literature is regarded as a projection and elaboration of the geometric-rhythmic-ornamental fabric of hyper- and hypoaroused states.

STATE-BOUNDARIES

Inasmuch as experience arises from the binding or coupling of a particular state or level of arousal with a particular symbolic interpretation of that arousal, experience is state-bound; thus, it can be evoked either by inducing ("naturally," hypnotically, or with the aid of drugs) the particular level of arousal, or by presenting some symbol of its interpretation, such as an image, melody, or taste. "Acquired aversions to tastes following illness are commonplace in humans. The knowledge that the illness was caused by the stomach flu and not the sauce béarnaise does not prevent the sauce from tasting bad in the future."[85]

Alcohol induces the state of arousal necessary for the recall of a state-bound experience in the film *City Lights*. Here, Charlie Chaplin saves a drunken millionaire from attempted suicide, and so becomes his good friend. When sober, however, the millionaire does not remember Charlie. However:[86]

> . . . the millionaire does not stay sober long. When he is drunk again, he spots Charlie and treats him like a long-lost friend. He takes Charlie home with him, but in the morning, when he is again sober, he forgets that Charlie is his invited guest and has the butler throw him out.

Evidently, consciousness extends either between states of drunkenness, or between states of sobriety, but there is complete amnesia between the two discontinuous states of sobriety and drunkenness, states with characteristic and different "Self"-to-"I" ratios.

Charlie's story has been recently remodeled and scientifically validated by Goodwin et al.,[87] who had forty-eight subjects memorize nonsense syllables while drunk. When sober, these volunteers had difficulty recalling what they had learned, but they could recall significantly better when they were drunk again. Bustamante et al.[88] also observed amphetamine-induced (20 milligrams) excitatory, and amobarbital-induced (200 milligrams), "inhibitory," state-dependent recall of geometric configurations. His volunteers both memorized and later recalled the configurations under one of the two drugs. I submit, however, that while remembering from one state to another is usually called "state-dependent learning"[89] (implying that the individual was confronted with a learning task), extended practice, learning, or conditioning is *not* necessary for producing "state-boundness." On the contrary, a single experience may be sufficient to establish state-boundness.

Déjà vu experiences and the so-called LSD flashbacks are, I believe, special cases of the general phenomenon of state-boundness. Note that neither focal lesions nor molecules of a hallucinogenic drug are necessary for the induction of a flashback—a symbol evoking a past drug experience may be sufficient to produce an LSD flashback.[90]

> An eighteen-year-old boy had a "bum trip" on "acid" and could not "come down" for two weeks. After he drank wine with a group of friends and was told by one of them that the wine contained a high dose of LSD (which it did not), he experienced hallucinations continuously for fourteen days.

And here is the story of a "flashback" involving no drugs whatsoever.[91]

> I was in love with a college classmate, but he married someone else. I also married, and even after four years and a beautiful baby I still

dreamed about this fellow. When I saw a car like his, my heart would pound even though he had left town years before and I knew it couldn't possibly be his.

It follows from the state-bound nature of experience, and from the fact that amnesia exists between the state of normal daily experience and all other states of hyper- and hypoarousal, that what is called the "subconscious" is but another name for this amnesia. Therefore, instead of postulating *one* subconscious, I recognize as many layers of self-awareness as there are levels of arousal and corresponding symbolic interpretations in the individual's interpretive repertoire. The many layers of self-awareness, each with its characteristic "Self"-to-"I" ratio, remind one of the captain with girl friends in many ports, each girl unaware of the existence of the others, and each existing only from visit to visit (that is, from state to state). This is how multiple existences become possible: by living from one waking state to another waking state; from one dream to the next; one amobarbital narcoanalysis session to the next;[92] from LSD to LSD;[93] from epileptic aura to aura;[94] from one creative, artistic, religious, or psychotic inspiration or possession to another creative, artistic, religious, or psychotic experience; from trance to trance; and from reverie to reverie.[95]

NOTES

1. W. Hess, *Das Zwischenhirn und die Regulierung von Kreislauf und Atmung* (Leipzig: Thieme, 1938); *Das Zwischenhirn* (Basel: Schwabe, 1949). Ergotropic arousal denotes behavioral patterns preparatory to positive action and is characterized by increased activity of the sympathetic nervous system and an activated psychic state. These states may be induced either naturally or, for example, through hallucinogenic drugs. Trophotropic arousal results from an integration of parasympathetic with somamotor activities to produce behavioral patterns that conserve and restore energy, a decrease of sensitivity to external stimuli, and sedation. During ergotropic and trophotropic arousal, "alterations in autonomic activity are not confined to the visceral organs, but induce changes in cortical activity" [W. Hess, cited by Gellhorn (9)].

2. R. Fischer, in *Psychiatry and Art*, Vol. 2, *Art Interpretation and Art Therapy*, ed. I. Jakab (Basel: Karger, 1969), p. 33.

3. R. Gelpke, quoted by A. Hofmann, in *Sonderabdruck aus dem Basler Stadtbuch* (Basel, 1964).

4. R. Fischer, in *Proceedings of the Fourth International Congress of Pharmacology* (Basel: Schwabe, 1970), Vol. 3, p. 28; *Ann. N.Y. Acad. Sci.* 138 (1967) 440.

5. The word "hyperphrenic" was suggested to me by Dr. Alfred Bader, Lausanne, Switzerland.

6. Saint Teresa, *The Life of Saint Teresa*, tr. J. M. Cohen (Baltimore: Penguin, 1957), p. 142.

7. W. Ashby, *Design for a Brain* (New York: Wiley, 1960), p. 88.

8. E. Gellhorn, *Psychol. Forsch.* 34 (1970) 48.

9. Hess, op. cit. and E. Gellhorn, *J. Nerv. Ment. Dis.* (1968) 147, 148.

10. E. Hebbard and R. Fischer, *Psychopharmacologia* 9 (1966) 146.

11. Ibid.

12. J. Silverman and K. Gaarder, *Percept. Mot. Skills* 25 (1967) 661.

13. R. Fischer, *J. Nerv. Ment. Dis.* 119 (1954) 492.

14. H. Selye, *J. Clin. Endocrinol. Metab.* 6 (1946) 117.

15. M. C. Franck and W. Kuhlo, *Arch. Psychiat. Nervenkr.* 213 (1970) 238.

16. J. Aschoff, ibid. 211 (1968) 325.

17. K. Gaarder, R. Koreski, W. Kropfi, *Electroencephalogr. Clin. Neurophysiol.* 21 (1966) 544.

18. E. Green, A. Green, E. Walters, *J. Transpersonal Psychol.* 1 (1970) 1.

19. R. Ditchburn and D. Fender, *Opt. Acta* 2 (1955) 128. Immobilization is accomplished by attaching a tiny mirror to a contact lens in such a way that the image will follow the micronystagmoid movements of the eye. Also see R. Pritchard, W. Heron, D. Hebb, *Canadian Journal of Psychology* 14 (1960) 67.

20. K. Behanan, *Yoga, A Scientific Evaluation* (New York: Dover, 1937), p. 223. The cobra has fixed eyes to begin with; therefore, to compensate for the lack of scanning eye movements, it must sway its head rhythmically to fixate the image of its victim. (If nothing else, one practical application of this paper may be the following: whenever you meet a cobra, swing along with him and he won't be able to locate you.)

21. R. Fischer, T. Kappeler, P. Wisecup, K. Thatcher, *Dis. Nerv. Syst.* 31 (1970) 91; K. Thatcher, T. Kappeler, P. Wisecup, R. Fischer, ibid., 181.

22. R. Fischer, ibid. 30 (1969) 161. J. Strauss's evidence also supports this concept of the continuous, nondiscrete nature of perceptual and hallucinatory experience [*Arch. Gen. Psychiat.* 21 (1969) 581]. Our definition of hallucinations or dreams as experiences characterized by a high S/M ratio is free of value judgment, thus implying that hallucinatory experience can be labeled pathological, artistic, religious, and so on, according to one's taste [and taste threshold: see R. Fischer, in *Gustation and Olfaction*, eds. G. Ohloff and A. E. Thomas (New York: Academic Press, 1971), pp. 187–237].

23. The cross-tolerance between LSD, psilocybin, or mescaline [H. Isbell, A. Wolbach, A. Wikler, E. Miner, *Psychopharmacologia* 2 (1961) 147; A. Wolbach, H. Isbell, E. Miner, ibid. 3 (1962) 1] as well as the characteristic square-wave pattern of saccadic movement they elicit [E. Hebbard and R. Fischer, ibid. 9 (1966) 146] mark these drugs as *the* hallucinogenic, psychotomimetic, psychedelic, or psychodysleptic drugs. It is implied, therefore, that any state which can be induced by one of these drugs can be duplicated by the others as well.

24. Cf. note 21.

25. Ibid.

26. I should note that the standard deviation on handwriting area at T_1 is significantly related to the S/M at T_1 ($r = 0.4888$, $P < .01$m $N = 47$) and that the standard deviation is a simple and useful indicator of the ensuing drug-induced increase in S/M ratio ($r = 0.372$, $P < .01$, $N = 47$). Moreover, subjects with a large standard deviation on handwriting area at T_1 (that is, "variable" subjects), tend to be "perceivers," whereas volunteers with a small standard deviation at T_1 ("stable" subjects) tend to be "judgers," in terms of the Myers-Briggs Type Indicator. This self-reporting, Jungian-type

personality indicator yields simple, continuous scores on four dichotomous scales: extroversion-introversion, sensation-intuition, thinking-feeling, and judging-perceiving. [R. Corlis, G. Splaver, P. Wisecup, R. Fischer, Nature 216 (1967) 91.] The perceivers also overestimate or contract time more than judgers do at the peak of a psilocybin-induced experience [cf. note 4]; this implies that perceivers move faster and further along the perception-hallucination continuum than do judgers, who apparently require a larger dose for a comparable experience.

27. "Constancies" assure the recognition of identity; they refer to what Piaget meant by the "conservation" of area, distance, length, volume, and so on [J. Piaget, B. Inhelder, A. Azeminska, The Child's Conception of Geometry, tr. E. A. Luzer (London: Routledge, 1960), p. 390]. For example, wearing prism spectacles results in a variety of visual distortions which, due to the cortical transformation of subcortical (retinal) information, gradually disappear with time. Perceptual-behavioral constancies can be formalized as information (or signal to noise) ratios; that is, as dimensionless quantities [R. Fischer, F. Griffin, R. C. Archer, S. C. Zinsmeister, P. S. Jastram, Nature 207 (1965) 1049].

28. Cf. note 4.

29. R. Hill, R. Fischer, D. Warshay, Experientia 25 (1969) 171.

30. R. Fischer, R. Hill, D. Warshay, ibid. (1969) 166.

31. Cf. note 21. R. Fischer, P. Marks, R. Hill, M. Rockey, Nature 218 (1968) 296; R. Fischer, in Origin and Mechanisms of Hallucinations, ed. W. Keup (New York: Plenum 1970), pp. 303–32.

32. R. Fischer, R. Hill, K. Thatcher, J. Scheib, Agents Actions 1 (1970) 190.

33. R. Hill and R. Fischer, Pharmakopsychiat. Neuro-Psychopharmakol. 3 (1970) 256.

34. H. Rennert, Confin. Psychiat. 12 (1969) 23.

35. Ibid.

36. L. Navratil, ibid., 30.

37. R. Fischer and R. Kaelbling, in Recent Advances in Biological Psychiatry, ed. J. Wortis (New York: Plenum, 1967), Vol. 9, p. 183; R. Fischer, L. Ristine, P. Wisecup, Biol. Psychiat. 1 (1970) 209.

38. R. Fischer, H. Dunbar, A. Sollberger, Arzneimittel-forschung 21 (1971) 135.

39. L. Bender, in Psychotomimetic Drugs, ed. D. Efron (New York: Raven, 1969), p. 267.

40. R. Fischer, Perspect. Biol. Med. 12 (1969) 259. The loss of a limb or an organ, for instance, can be regarded as a distortion of corporeal awareness; the phenomenon that corrects for this distortion results in a very real feeling that the lost limb or organ is still there, but this is only a phantom sensation.

41. S. Kuromaru, S. Okada, M. Hanada, Y. Kasahara, K. Sakamoto, Psychiat. Neurol. Jap. 64 (1962) 604.

42. Cf. note 6.

43. R. Fischer, Ann. N.Y. Acad. Sci. 96 (1962) 44.

44. Cf. note 4.

45. Ibid.

46. Ibid.

47. Cf. note 3.

48. A. Hofmann, in Discoveries in Biological Psychiatry, eds. F. Ayd and Blackwell (Philadelphia: Lippincott, 1970), chap. 7.

49. R. Fischer, in *The Voices of Time,* ed. J. Fraser (New York: Braziller, 1966), p. 357.

50. P. MacLean, *J. Neurosurg.* 29 (1954) 11; *Amer. J. Med.* 25 (1958) 611.

51. The mean increase in pupillary diameter induced by 160 micrograms of psilocybin per kilogram of body weight in thirty-four college-age male volunteers was 0.93 millimeter, standard deviation - ± 0.52; whereas in thirteen females, the mean increase was 0.56 millimeter, standard deviation - ± 0.27.

52. Cf. note 21 and R. Fischer and D. Warshay, *Pharmakopsychiat. Neuro-Psychopharmakol.* 1 (1968) 291; R. Fischer, *Perspect. Biol. Med.* 12 (1969) 259.

53. G. Marañon, *Rev. Fr. Endocrinol.* 2 (1924) 301.

54. S. Schachter and J. Singer, *Psychol. Rev.* 69 (1962) 379.

55. H. Lennard, L. Epstein, A. Bernstein, D. Ransom, *Science* 169 (1970) 438.

56. L. Goldstein, H. Murphree, A. Sugerman, C. Pfeiffer, E. Jenney, *Clin. Pharmacol. Ther.* 4 (1963) 10.

57. Ibid.; also K. Thatcher, W. Wiederholt, R. Fischer, *Agents Actions* 2 (1971) 21; G. Marjerrison, A. Krause, R. Keogy, *Electroencephalogr. Clin. Neurophysiol.* 24 (1967) 25.

58. Cf. note 21.

59. R. Fischer, in *Genetic Factors in "Schizophrenia,"* ed. A. Kaplan (Springfield, Ill.: Thomas, in press).

60. B. Pauleikhoff, *Fortschr. Neurol. Psychiat.* 37 (1969) 476. The distinction between a genuine religious and a psychotic religious conversion experience is pointed out by H. Weitbrecht [*Beiträge zur Religionspsychopathologie, insbesondere zur Psychopathologie der Bekehrung* (Heidelberg: Scherrer, 1948)]. His four schizophrenics experienced a religious conversion during their psychoses. Although after remission they had insight into the diseased nature of their psychoses, they continued to regard their conversion experiences as valid turning points. We conceptualize conversion experiences as confrontation and dialogue between a man's worldly "I" and his ecstatic (or meditative) "Self," resulting in the creation of a more consistent personality—one that has "found its style" [R. Fischer, *Confin. Psychiat.* 13 (1970) 1; ibid., in press].

61. Pascal recorded, at the peak of his decisive religious illumination: "Fire. / God of Abraham, God of Isaac, God of Jacob, / not of the philosophers and the scientists. / Certainty. Certainty" [M. Arland, *Pascal* (Paris: L'Enfant Poète, 1946), pp. 120–21].

62. A. Kasamatsu and T. Hirai, *Psychologia* 6 (1963) 89; *Folia Psychiat. Neurol. Jap.* 20 (1966) 315.

63. It is likely that these parietal, low-frequency EEG waves are related to dendritic field-potential charges.

64. Cf. note 18.

65. Cf. note 62.

66. B. Anand, G. Chhina, B. Singh, *Electroencephalogr. Clin. Neurophysiol.* 13 (1961) 452.

67. Ibid.

68. G. Brown, *Laws of Form* (London: Allen, 1969), p. 105. Saint Teresa elegantly expressed this partial elusiveness: "There remains the power of seeing and hearing; but is as if the things heard and seen were at a great distance far away" [in E. Underhill, *Mysticism* (London: Methuen, 1912), p. 450].

69. Cf. note 8.

70. E. Gellhorn, *Acta Neuroveg.* 20 (1959) 181.

71. Such rebound would be called "inhibition" in Pavlovian terminology; I. Pavlov, in C. Murchison, *Psychologies of 1930* (Worcester, Mass.: Clark University Press, 1930), p. 213, and "phase of resistance" by Selye [*Stress* (Montreal: ACTA, 1950), pp. 15–43]. It can also be accounted for within the frame of Wilder's Law of Initial Value, which states that "the higher the initial value of a measured function, the lower is the tendency of the system to respond to furthering stimuli, while the highest as well as the lowest values tend to result in a *reversal of action* (italics mine)" [J. Wilder, *J. Psychother.* 12 (1958) 199].

72. Cf. notes 8 and 9.

73. P. Parmeggiani, *Brain Res.* 7 (1968) 350.

74. Cf. note 18.

75. Cf. notes 8 and 9.

76. The "loop" in Fig. 1 has also been independently suggested to me (on experiential grounds alone) by both Dr. J. H. M. Whiteman, University of Cape Town, South Africa, and Marilyn Delphinium Rutgers, Glen-Ellen, California. I am gratefully indebted to them, as well as to Primarius Dr. Leo Navratil, Gugging, Austria, for sharing with me their intuition and scholarship.

77. This example was suggested to me by Primarius Dr. Leo Navratil, Gugging, Austria.

78. For example, neither quinine molecules nor a subject's taste receptors are bitter per se—bitterness results only during interaction of the two. Therefore, no taster, no bitterness (just as there can be no image or sound of a falling tree without a viewer or listener). [See R. Fischer, *Dis. Nerv. Syst.* 30 (1969) 161] The interactional nature of reality is already implicit in the fact that the brain is the only organ that develops through experiencing itself. [See H. Ey, *La Conscience* (Paris: Presses Universitaires de France, 1963), p. 64]

79. H. Klüver, *Mescal and Mechanism of Hallucinations* (Phoenix, Chicago: University of Chicago Press, 1966), p. 66.

80. M. Knoll, J. Kugler, D. Höfer, S. Lawder, *Confin. Neurol.* 23 (1963) 201.

81. W. Keup, ed., *Origin and Mechanisms of Hallucinations* (New York: Plenum, 1970), pp. 95–210.

82. A. Mookerjee, in *Tantra-Kunst*, ed. R. Kumar (Basel: Basilius, 1967–68), p. 11.

83. R. Fischer, *Confin. Psychiat.* 13 (1970) 1.

84. See L. Navratil, *Schizophrenie und Kunst* (München: Deutsches Taschenbuch Verlag, 1965), p. 35; *Schizophrenie und Sprache* (München: Deutsches Taschenbuch, 1966), p. 162.

85. M. Seligman, *Psychol. Rev.* 77 (1970) 416.

86. G. McDonald, M. Conway, M. Ricci, eds. *The Films of Charlie Chaplin* (New York: Citadel, 1965), p. 191.

87. D. Goodwin, B. Powell, D. Bremer, H. Hoine, J. Stern, *Science* 163 (1969) 1358.

88. J. Bustamante, A. Jordan, M. Vila, A. Gonzalez, A. Insua, *Physiol. Behav.* 5 (1970) 793.

89. R. Fischer, *Dis. Nerv. Syst.* 32 (1971) 373; R. Fischer and G. M. Landon, *Brit. J. Psychiat.*, in press. The latter paper also includes an extensive discussion of state-dependent learning in human beings and animals. Note that this term could just as well be "state-dependent adaptation," since learning and adaptation are as indistinguishable from each other as hallucinations and dreams.

90. L. Tec, *Journal of the American Medical Association* 215 (1971) 980.

91. From "Dear Abby," in *Citizen Journal*, Columbus, Ohio, 13 January 1971, p. 21.

92. Primarius Dr. Raoul Schindler, Vienna, informed me at Linz in 1969 that a patient's thread of thought in narcoanalysis resumes, after an injection of amobarbital, exactly where it left off at the end of the previous session.

93. Dr. Hancarl Leuner, Göttingen, Germany, also confirms (1970) that his patients in LSD-supplemented or psycholytic therapy regard each LSD experience as a continuation of the last.

94. M. Horowitz, J. Adams, and B. Rutkin [*Arch. Gen. Psychiat.* 19 (1968) 469] report from the case history of an epileptic girl that the imagery of every aura consisted of "pigs walking upright like people." In early grade school the girl would rip open her blouse during a seizure, but, of course, she would not remember this after the seizure. Nevertheless, her classmates called her a pig, and it was this pig which she saw "walking upright" in each aura.

95. Supported in part by National Institute of Mental Health grant 1 RO3 MH17633-01 and general research support grants. I am indebted to Sandoz Pharmaceuticals, Basel, Switzerland, and to Dr. John A. Scigliano, former executive Secretary, FDA-PHS Psychotomimetic Agents Advisory Committee, Bethesda, Maryland, for generously providing me with psilocybin (under IND-3530). I am also grateful to Dr. Peter Gwynne, James Scheib, and Pamela Furney for their devoted competence and to my creative artist wife, Trudy, for vital perceptual as well as cognitive illumination.

20

State-Bound Knowledge:
"I Can't Remember What I Said Last Night, but It Must Have Been Good"

ROLAND FISCHER

In the film *City Lights*, Charlie Chaplin saves a drunken millionaire from an attempted suicide and becomes his friend. When sober, the millionaire has no memory of Charlie. But he soon gets drunk and again spots Charlie, treats him like a long-lost friend, and takes him home to his mansion. Sober the next morning, the millionaire forgets Charlie is his invited guest and has the butler throw him out.

Charlie's story illustrates an amnesia between states of mind that most of us may have experienced. Like the drunken millionaire, we may forget on a sober morning what we did or said at a party the night before. Or the memory of a relaxing vacation fades as we slide back into the frenetic pace of a working day. In both cases, our experience is state-bound, i.e. tied to a particular state of consciousness. The reality of the event is most vivid in the state it was first experienced, and less so in other states.

States of consciousness depend on the level of arousal in both brain and body. The level fluctuates greatly during the day. When we are anxious or excited, the brain speeds up its rate of information processing—that is, how it organizes and reacts to what it takes in through the senses. At the same time, the body quickens its autonomic activity, speeding up heart rate, sweat levels, and other systems. When we relax, these rates slow down.

The brain processes and stores information differently at each level of arousal. The same event is very different in our perception, depending on whether we are calm, in a panic, or in between. Our memory of events, I believe, is distributed over a variety of arousal states. Each bit of knowledge is bound to, and most easily retrieved at, a particular level of arousal. The greater the difference between these states, the more difficult it is to recall in one state specifics learned in another.

LOST ACCESS. The difficulty in remembering events that occurred in another state of arousal has long posed a problem in court cases. Witnesses to violent crimes, for example, often produce vague or incorrect testimony because of amnesia between states. Witnessing a robbery, rape, or murder can put a person into a state of extreme arousal. When the witness later tries to recall the crime in court, he is no longer aroused and so does not have free access to his memory of the crime. The closer the states of arousal are, the easier it is to remember from one to the other. I have developed a diagram of arousal states (see chart).

THE RANGE OF MENTAL STATES

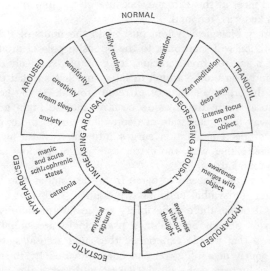

The diagram above shows various states of brain activity. Along the left side of the circle, arousal increases from normal daily activity to ecstasy. Along the right side, arousal decreases from waking relaxation to deepest meditation. We do not necessarily pass from one state to another step by step; for instance, we can move from creativity to anxiety without passing through dream sleep. An everyday example every parent has experienced is that of the shrieking baby who plummets from full cry to sound sleep.

It helps us see which states are near each other, and which deviate most from our normal waking state.

Beyond normal busy alertness, the person moves through more intense levels of sensitivity, creativity, and then anxiety. Then come conditions of hyperarousal, which include manic or acute schizophrenic episodes. Catatonia, oddly enough, is the height of schizophrenic brain arousal. The catatonic sits frozen because his brain is racing so fast he cannot keep up with his own thoughts enough to make a move. Going still further, there is the arousal peak of the mystic's ecstasy.

THE REBOUND PHENOMENON. In the opposite direction, arousal sinks beyond simple relaxation into the tranquillity of Zen meditation, where the mind is in a quiet state of alertness. In deeper meditation, body and mind become progressively more quiescent as concentration becomes more focused. At first, the person's attention focuses on a single object. Later the mind seems to merge with the object; there are no other thoughts whatever. Finally, the mind, though alert, is without a single thought, not even the original point of focus. Paradoxically, low and high arousal states meet at this extreme, because of the phenomenon psychophysiologists know as "rebound."

In rebound, a biological system pushed to the limits of stillness or of aroused excitation will snap back to the opposite pole of arousal. An infant breathless and red from tantrum, for example, suddenly drops off to sleep. Rebound seems to be a built-in safety mechanism that protects our bodies from the adverse effects of extreme arousal. At the height of increasing arousal, as in the mystic's ecstasy, intense brain activity suddenly gives way to a quiet state of deep calm. Or, in the opposite case, low arousal of deep meditation surges into the ecstatic awakening of kundalini yoga. Either way, the extremes of high and low arousal connect through rebound.

Conscious awareness seems to come from the combination of our state of arousal and the symbol or labels we connect with that state. In the normal arousal range, there is flexibility in the interpretations we attach to arousal levels. Stanley Schachter, a psychologist at Columbia University, has shown that people experience the same arousal state as either pleasure or anger, depending on the cues provided by their surroundings. When volunteers Schachter injected with adrenalin were with a happy, joking stooge, they reported feeling pleasantly aroused; when other volunteers given the same injection were with a hostile stooge they felt angry. In both situations the physiological arousal was the same, but the person's interpretations of the physical effects of the drug varied with the situation.

TEA-SOAKED CAKE. As a person approaches the extremes of high or low arousal, he has fewer labels available for interpreting his state. At the most extreme levels, there is a virtual loss of freedom in interpretation, since meaning is only meaningful at that level of arousal at which it is experienced. The enraptured mystic and entranced meditator have few words with which to label their altered state. Only the creative mystic has no difficulty describing his transcendental experience. Creativity is the ability to recollect thoughts or images experienced at a variety of arousal levels. For this reason mystics have always had difficulty describing transcendental experiences.

Since experience is the product of both arousal and the symbol or label for that level of arousal, the full memory of an experience can be triggered either by duplicating the original level or by evoking some symbol of it. A famous example is Proust in *Swann's Way,* when he tastes a tea-soaked cake like those of his childhood and is instantly flooded with a stream of early memories. One of the oldest descriptions of the symbolic triggering of a state-bound memory comes from the Spaniard Juan Luis Vives, who wrote in 1538, "When I was a boy in Valencia, I was ill of a fever; while my taste was deranged I ate cherries; for many years afterwards, whenever I tasted the fruit I not only recalled the fever, but also seemed to experience it again."

T. S. Eliot consciously used symbols to evoke arousal states. In his theory of the "objective correlative," he proposed that the poet elicits specific emotions in his audience by his use of symbols. In a set of objects, a situation, or a chain of events, the poet creates a formula for evoking a particular emotion. I extend Eliot's idea to all the arts. Specific emotions can be evoked by a melody or image as well as by a flow of words. We feel very different about the calm placidity of a Constable landscape, the sensual richness of Rousseau's plush jungles, and the tortured faces of Munch's portraits. Each of these visual images triggers a specific emotional state.

PARTIAL AMNESIA. The other route to re-experiencing the state-bound past is through duplicating the arousal level of the previous experience. One therapist says that when he uses sodium amytal ("truth serum") as part of psychotherapy, his patient picks up his narrative each time exactly where he left off at the close of the previous session.

Alcohol is the most common route to an altered state, and provides the best documentation of state-bound memory. Research headed by Herbert Weingartner at the National Institute of Mental Health in Bethesda may explain the erratic actions of Charlie Chaplin's drunken millionaire. Weingartner's team wondered if we don't remember things in different ways when we are drunk or sober, so that a partial amnesia exists between these states. They had volunteers learn a list of ten words, then asked them to recite the words when they were either in the same state as when they learned them or in the opposite state. Recall was best when a volunteer was in the same state as when he learned the words, whether drunk or sober. This partial amnesia between states means that people do not necessarily remember events better when they are sober than when they are drunk. They remember best when they are in the same state as when the original event occurred. Other studies have shown that this rule of thumb also holds for altered states induced by amphetamines, barbiturates and marijuana.

Weingartner's study of state-bound memory suggests a general principle for increasing our memory of things. We should reenter the state we were in during the original moment. This principle may explain why psychoanalysts since Freud have had their patients lie on a couch and free-associate as they search back to childhood's traumas and triumphs. The reverie of the free-associating patient produces a slowed brain-wave rhythm, typical of that of children when they are awake and alert. By slowing their brain waves to the rate of a child's, the patients in analysis may have increased their chances of recalling events from childhood.

I carry the same-state, better-memory rule a step further. Since some degree of amnesia exists between our normal everyday state and other states of increased or decreased arousal, it may be that what is called the "subconscious" is but another name for this amnesia. Instead of there being just one subconscious, therefore, there are as many layers as there are arousal levels. These many layers remind me of a captain with girl friends in several ports, each unaware of the existence of the others, and each existing for him from visit to visit—that is, from state to state.

Some of us can travel on the continuum of increasing and decreasing arousal more easily than others. I have identified the kind of person who moves most freely between arousal levels. I used a simple test in which a person copies a twenty-eight-word text four times on separate sheets of paper, and then computes the differences among the four sheets in the area covered by his handwriting. If the handwriting area varies greatly from sheet to sheet, the writer is likely to vary his behavior and perception often. This simple index of variability, we found, predicts the intensity of changes the person will experience on a psychedelic drug like psilocybin; the more variation his writing shows, the more intense his trip will be.

About one third of the population falls into the variable category, but only about one third of these can be easily hypnotized. The variability of this one ninth of the population seems to indicate fluidity within mental states that allows them to flashback, that is, re-experience an altered state rather than simply remember it. For these people, movies, novels, and the like may be especially gripping, and the moods they evoke particularly real.

The richness of our daily experience is not limited to what we see and hear. Our lives are enriched also by the range of internal states from which we witness the seen and heard. In the words of Octavio Paz, "Memory is not that which we remember, but that which remembers us. Memory is a present that never stops passing."[1]

NOTES

1. For further reading see:
R. Fischer, "On Creative, Psychotic and Ecstatic States," and "Consciousness as Role and Knowledge" in *Readings in Abnormal Psychology, Contemporary Perspectives*, eds. Lawrence Allman and Dennis Jaffe, Harper and Row, 1976.

—— "A Cartography of Inner Space" in *Hallucinations: Behavior, Experience and Theory*, R. K. Siegel and L. J. West, eds., John Wiley, pp. 197–239, 1975.
—— and G. Landon, "On the Arousal State-Dependent Recall of 'Sub-Conscious' Experience: Stateboundness," *British Journal of Psychiatry*, Vol. 120, no. 555 (1972) 159–72.

21

The Creative Personality:
Akin to Madness

FRANK BARRON

Is reason the enemy of poetic imagination? Some poets might say that reason is *always* the enemy of the creative spirit, and some rationalists might agree. We exercise our powers of logic, abstract thought, and law-making at the expense of whimsy, impulse, intense feelings, the vivid disconnected image or emotion, or the sense of validity of the singular event or the eccentric person or passion. At the expense of part of ourselves—would that be too much to say?

The artist often sees rational thought not merely as an enemy but as a prison from which he must struggle to get free. We are both rational and nonrational, sometimes in order and sometimes in disorder, as indeed the world itself is. The artist's peculiar fate, occupational hazard, and private joy is that he creates order out of images that play under quite different rules from the rules of logic, though they exist in the same house of self.

FRAME. Freud was keenly aware of the task of the artist. He suggested that poetic imagination expressed a separate mode of thinking, more closely related to pleasure-seeking than to reality-testing. He divided mental activity into two areas and called them primary-process thinking and secondary-process thinking.

We use primary-process thinking in part because of the urgency of instinctual drives or impulses and their demand for immediate gratification. Primary process will displace or condense the impulse, and find substitute or symbolic objects to meet our needs. In contrast, secondary-process thinking enables us to delay gratification voluntarily, while we make plans for obtaining satisfaction directly with the object of the drive in real life. It does not permit us to deflect the drive by fantasy, displacement, or substitute objects. It may renounce the drive altogether. Secondary-process thinking is tolerant of frustration, and flexible in finding real alternatives.

These two principles of mental activity provide a framework for a look at the nature of creative activity. With them we can avoid the boundary disputes and difficulties that accompany terms like unconscious process and preconscious process. Primary-process phenomena include the following kinds of cognitive activities that fall outside the realm of the rational: recurring dreams, prophetic dreams, and dreams of a preternatural vividness and intensity; precognitions, telepathy, clairvoyance; unusual coincidences; falling in love, mystical experiences of oneness with the universe, or its negative side, total forlornness; and fantasies of an archetypal or mythological sort. At Berkeley my colleagues and I have tested these Freudian ideas. We conducted a study of writers to determine the importance of nonrational experience in creative activity. We evaluated these experiences through psychological interviews, personality tests, and self reports. We found that creative writers are, as Freud had hypothesized, unusually open to nonrational experience. They report a very high frequency of primary-process activities that range from recurring dreams to transcendental visions. But the creative writer by no means sacrifices secondary-process thinking to primary-process activities. In fact, he utilizes both modes freely and to great effect.

Fifty-six professional writers took part in the study. Their work covered a wide spectrum of artistic purpose and esthetic quality. We were not concerned with individual differences, but with characteristics of creative writers as a class. All of our subjects were capable of writing phrases, essays, stories, novels, poems or plays that communicated personal experience in an original manner. In this sense, all were agents of the creative spirit.

We studied most of these writers individually by means of intensive interviews about their lives and their work. We later asked the psychologists who got to know them to give personal impressions of them individually through use of a standard deck of one hundred cards printed with phrases that could be used to describe a person. We asked the observer to arrange the cards in nine piles. We assumed that the placement of the cards represented a continuum of saliency of the traits in the personality of the individual being described. We then averaged the item placements for all observers to arrive at a composite description of each other, and then averaged these findings to arrive at a composite description of the group.

QUALITIES. We found that five items most characterized the group. The observers thought that the creative writer:
1 Appears to have a high degree of intellectual capacity.
2 Genuinely values intellectual and cognitive matters.
3 Values his own independence and autonomy.
4 Is verbally fluent; can express ideas well.
5 Enjoys esthetic impressions; is esthetically reactive.

In addition, the observers thought that the creative writer:

1 Is productive; gets things done.

2 Is concerned with philosophical problems; for example, religion, values, the meaning of life, and so forth.

3 Has a high aspiration level for himself.

4 Has a wide range of interests.

5 Thinks and associates to ideas in unusual ways; has unconventional thought processes.

6 Is an interesting, arresting person.

7 Appears straightforward, forthright, candid in dealings with others.

8 Behaves in an ethically consistent manner; is consistent with own personal standards.

SCORES. The writers supported these descriptions by achieving very high scores on tests of conceptual thinking, esthetic judgment, originality, and personal effectiveness and flexibility.

In spite of this picture of personal, intellectual and social effectiveness, the writers earned rather high scores on the Minnesota Multiphasic Personality Inventory (MMPI), a questionnaire designed to measure psychopathological tendencies. Specifically, they were well above the average of the general-population on measures of schizophrenic tendency (the schizophrenia scale) and depression, and moderately high also on hysteria and psychopathic deviation. This finding fascinated us because at the same time (and on the same test) the writers scored well above average in ego strength. A high score on this measure almost never occurs with a high score in any of the psychopathology measures. (For the general population the correlation is $-.70$.)

RANGE. It is especially difficult to apply psychopathological indices to groups of persons who are not clinically ill. We know that the items in the clinical scales differentiate psychiatric patients of the named diagnostic class (depressives, hypochondriacs, hysterics, psychopaths, schizophrenics, and so on) from people in general, but whether the scales measure dispositions toward such psychopathology throughout the total range of variation is another question.

It is quite possible, for example, that such diseases as schizophrenia and paranoia are not extreme examples of tendencies present continuously throughout the total range of behavior, but are really different in kind from any normal tendencies, however superficially analogous they are. If such discontinuities do exist, scales constructed by comparing the responses of diseased persons with those of normal persons could not be valid measures within the normal range of the tendencies that they identify in the abnormal.

MATCH. In an effort to explore this matter further, S. H. Fritz and I located a group of young artists highly regarded for their creativity and then we established a comparison group of hospitalized mental patients who had been diagnosed as schizophrenic. We matched the groups quite precisely in terms of age, sex, education, and scores on the schizophrenia scale of the MMPI, so that they differed only in that one group was in a mental hospital and the other group in an art school. We then analyzed the schizophrenia scale, item by item, to discover what items the two groups answered differently. (It must be remembered that all items on the schizophrenia scale presumably distinguish "schizophrenics" from "normals.")

Of the seventy-eight items in the scale, we found that eighteen helped differentiate the artists from the hospital patients. A subjective analysis of the importance of these items suggests to me that the following factors are involved:

1 Clinical schizophrenia, in contrast to artistic unconventionality or oddness, is marked by apathy, despair, dread, and a sort of spiritual death.

2 In schizophrenia there is confusion, bizarre ideation, delusion of control by others, and loss of stable self-regulation of mood.

3 The artist, by contrast, finds joy in life, is not self-pitying, is reasonably worried about practical matters, and functions well physically.

LOCKS. It must be noted that an art school is enough different, as an institution, from a mental hospital to produce through sheer environmental effects a different sort of mood in the persons who are enrolled. Who would not be more cheerful in an art school than in the locked ward of a psychiatric hospital? What could be more supportive of the bizarre in oneself than a community of artists? Conversely, what worse social judgment can be passed upon one than to be locked up and labeled insane?

It must be remembered too that the particular artists we studied were selected for high scores on the schizophrenia scale. For this reason, they could be expected not to differ much from patients in the way they answered specific items, so that the differences we found take on added importance.

The similarities are worth noting, however. They occurred usually on items that only a small minority of either group answered in the symptomatic direction. The textbook schizophrenic, like the textbook artist, is an idealized type, if not a myth, and in real life only a few of the many traits attributed to the type will be found in individuals. Keeping this in mind, let us look at the results in a preliminary way.

About an equal number of artists and schizophrenic patients report odd sensations—ringing in their ears, peculiar odors, unaccountable numbness in parts of their body at times. They were equal too in often preferring solitude to the company of other persons. They shared to the same extent a feeling of lack of love from parents, a rejection of home and of many common values of society. Finally, both groups expressed high levels of tension, restlessness, a feeling of strain, a proneness to impulsive outbursts.

MATRIX. These findings suggest an unusual state of psychic affairs in creative artists. They seem to be able to incorporate psychotic-like experiences and tendencies in a matrix of rationality, very high conceptual intelligence, honesty, and personal effectiveness.

Let us now turn to the reports, in their own words, of the kinds of experiences that lead us to rate creative writers high in primary-process thinking, even while they are notably efficient in secondary-process thinking as well.

We begin with the most commonplace example of primary-process activity, the dream. What is a dream? Put simply, dreaming is thinking under the condition of sleep. And because we are asleep, we may in dreams be irrational at no cost to our survival.

In the life of the creative individual, this safe irrationality of dreaming becomes the unsafe mode of thought that permits wild hunches, censorable images, unprintable words, unthinkable ideas, to merge with the day's thinking. "Dreaming awake" may be an apt description of the creative reverie and of the creative person's ordinary mental life.

SELF. The dream may be a song, a painting, a solution to a problem, a drama, an expression of love. The dream process is nonrational in the sense that it does not obey the rules of waking logic, but it is not unconscious and it need not stand for something unconscious. It may in fact be an expression of the self at a very high level of integration and wholeness. Indeed, there are some who believe that in dreams we may reach out with a higher self beyond the limits of our ordinary world.

Seventy per cent of the sample had had recurring dreams. One writer had dreamt at least once a week for the past fifteen years that he was swallowing something indigestible, "usually watch gears or glass." The dreams were so vivid and realistic that often he awakened his wife and urged her to get help. Built into the dream was a rather complex mechanism: "This has always been just a dream before, but this time it has really happened."

Another writer had a dream that had recurred for thirty years: "Since the time my eldest son started to walk, I had dreamed that he was walking around the cornice of a high building; the wind is blowing a gale; he is balancing himself unsteadily. I try to speak quietly but I can make no sound. I am so frightened that I want to rush and grab him, but caution myself to move slowly. Then, as I am creeping carefully toward him, the dream fades. He has never fallen and I have never rescued him."

TERROR. In almost all cases, the writers' dreams had an intensely unpleasant, nightmarish quality, and often they terrified the dreamers. Something in the dreams threatened the physical safety of the dreamers; this was an especially common characteristic of dreams that recurred from childhood on. In several of the dreams, the assault upon the dreamers was psychological rather than physical. One woman had two recurring dreams of this nature: "I wandered around from floor to floor of a large hotel, wearing a shabby bathrobe, unable to remember the number of my room." In the second dream, "I find myself in a college class without pen, pencil, notebook or textbooks. These are agonizing dreams."

Two of the women writers had recurrent dreams that ceased after they dreamed resolutions to the problems in the dreams. One was a fairly simple and lucid example of this kind of resolution. "I often dreamed of being stranded in the middle of a collapsing bridge, the Golden Gate Bridge, to be exact. The flooring of the bridge would be torn away. Finally one night I dreamed that I personally built myself a path of planks over the remaining framework of the bridge, and got across. The dream never recurred after that."

ESC. Just under 20 per cent of the writers reported that they had had dreams that proved prophetic.

We asked the writers: "Have you ever had an experience that made you think that extrasensory communication is possible?"

The experiences they reported ranged from relatively common interpersonal exchanges to much more unusual psychic occurrences. One writer gave the following account:

"Once when in the Navy I was to be sent for several months to the South Pacific and the Orient. My mother had fallen in love with a man who disappeared the day before I left. I was deeply disturbed, leaving my mother in a desperate brokenhearted condition. About two months later, I was tending a midnight searchlight watch. Suddenly, almost as if I heard someone plainly speaking, I was informed of this man's whereabouts, and before retiring, I wrote my mother, telling her she could meet him at the Navy gate in Brooklyn, giving the exact hour and day she would meet him. My mother immediately went to Brooklyn and met her fiancé exactly as I had described, and they were married."

Two women writers described experiences of extrasensory perception.

One writer told of an automobile trip, on which she was reading *Crime and Punishment:*

"We parked and locked the car," she reports. "Just previous to this, I thought, 'If we stop in this town and leave the car, it will be broken into, and my new coat will be stolen.' When we returned, this had happened. . . ."

We also asked: "Can you remember any especially peculiar coincidence that has occurred in your life? If so, how do you explain it?" Nearly two thirds of the writers reported unusual coincidences, but they attributed nine tenths of these coincidences to chance. There were some striking exceptions, however.

One writer had made an agreement with his best friend, immediately prior to the friend's embarkation on a naval ship, to meet in a certain place at a certain date and hour five years hence "no matter how hard it would be to do so." The appointed date and location was noted on the two halves of a card.

Sometime after this agreement was made, the writer received word from his friend that he was sailing for home. But the ship never made port. "It is believed she carried nitrates and blew up. . . ." Nevertheless the writer kept his word. He went to the agreed location and waited for an hour, fully aware he could not expect to see his friend. He did find, however, in the "accumulation of papers, dust and rubbish" at the appointed place a "stained square of business card paper that had once been white." It was the other half of the card—his friend's half.

The writer pondered over this incident: "Had W. dropped his half (I thought I had seen him place it in his wallet) and had the wind blown it into a crevice to rest there five years to the day we were to meet and match the torn edges of the two halves? Or—was there some other explanation, wherein we can say he *was* there in some form—spiritual or otherwise?"

GHOSTS. We asked the writers: "Have you ever had a vivid sensory experience of something which wasn't really there? What were the circumstances of the experience?"

More than half of the male writers reported vivid sensory experiences of something that wasn't really there. Most of these experiences were visual. One respondent was sitting by a radio that was turned off; around the switch and speaker he seemed to see a blue flickering light. At times he also saw a disappearing figure who, he felt, was not unfriendly. Another respondent recounted an experience that occurred one moonlit night while he was sitting on a rock on Glacier Point above Yosemite Valley.

"Several ghostlike figures floated past, white, one- to three-feet tall, vague of outline. . . . I was with another man who saw these figures as vividly as I did! The night was cloudless and (there was) no apparent mist. Reason tells me there's a logical explanation for this, but I've never been able to pin it down."

Women writers seemed to be even more susceptible than men; two thirds of them reported such possibly illusory sensory experiences.

AWE. Half of the writers, men and women, reported that they had had intense experiences of mystical communion. One writer remarked tersely that he experienced a mystical communion whenever he painted. A second had had several experiences "consisting primarily of a consciousness of 'belonging'" while he was studying Hatha Yoga.

One woman reported that when she was with her husband on their first pack trip into the Sierras, "we were so breathless with awe and the vision of beauty before us that we almost ceased to exist." She has had other such experiences in the mountains since then but never one of quite such intensity.

We also asked our subjects: "Have you ever experienced an overwhelming sense of emptiness, desolation, aloneness, forsakenness?"

More than half of the writers of both sexes responded affirmatively. Again, the nature of the experiences was varied. One man has a feeling of emptiness and desolation "often, when the day ends, when the sun sets, when the evening comes on." Another told of having such an experience when he faced death in the crash of a military plane.

Freud believed that primary-process thinking occurred earlier than secondary-process thinking, and that it predominated in infancy and earlier childhood, yielding gradually to domination by secondary-process thinking. The distinction is analogous to that proposed by Jean Piaget between animistic and scientific modes of thought, the animistic being characteristic of young children and gradually being supplanted, beginning around age five or six, by the scientific mode.

This temporal sequence and its occasional reversal suggested the concept of regression. The psychoanalytic theorist Ernst Kris introduced the memorable phrase "regression in the service of the ego" to describe the origin of the sort of phenomena that we have presented as examples of primary-process activity. This theory supports the commonplace concept that artistic perception is childlike and that genius is "to madness near allied."

GROWTH. To apply the concept of regression to artistic activity seems to me to be misleading. Primary-process thinking is a *capability* that *may* be weakened in some individuals as they grow from childhood to adulthood. I emphasize *may* because we do not know that this is the case.

Primary-process activity *may* also simply become muted, or be altogether behaviorally silent, while the capability remains. This is an empirical question, and one badly in need of basic research by psychologists.

Creative power increases from childhood to adulthood in about the same way that general intelligence does. Creative individuals retain qualities of freshness, spontaneity and joy, as well as a certain lack of cautious reality-testing—openness to the nonrational, if you will. They are in that sense childlike. But this is not regression; it is progression with courage. They bring their childhood along instead of leaving it behind.

In the creative act we witness neither dissociation nor mere bisociation. But integration and synthesis. The tendency toward centering goes hand in hand with the tendency toward divergence. The whole self creates.

22

Mysticism and Schizophrenia[1]

KENNETH WAPNICK

INTRODUCTION

Mysticism and schizophrenia have often been linked in psychiatric literature. Some writers have suggested that mystics demonstrate a special form of schizophrenia or other psychopathology. (See, for example, Alexander, 1931; Freud, 1961; and Menninger, 1938.) Others write of schizophrenia in highly metaphorical, quasi-mystical language focusing on the experience of psychosis, which leads many to conclude that they are proselytizing for schizophrenia as a valuable and even desirable experience (Bateson, 1961; Laing, 1965, 1967). In a more objective tone, William James noted the similarity between the mystic and schizophrenic experience as far back as 1902. He distinguished between two kinds of mysticism; a higher and a lower. The former included the classic mystical experiences, while the latter James identified with insanity, which he termed a "diabolical mysticism." James (1958) concluded that in both forms is found,

> The same sense of ineffable importance in the smallest events, the same texts and words coming with new meanings, the same voices and visions and leadings and missions, the same controlling by extraneous powers. . . . It is evident that from the point of view of their psychological mechanism, the classic mysticism and these lower mysticisms spring from the same mental level, from that great subliminal or transmarginal region of which science is beginning to admit the existence, but of which so little is really known. That region contains every kind of matter: "seraph and snake" abide there side by side [p. 326].

In a 1965 paper delivered before the R. M. Bucke Memorial Society, Prince and Savage discussed the mystical experience in terms of Kris's concept of regression in the service of the ego (Prince and Savage, 1965). Almost parenthetically, the authors noted a "plausible link" between psychosis and mysticism, and suggested that psychosis was a "pressured withdrawal" with an incomplete return, while the mystic's withdrawal was more controlled and his return more complete.

Though the similarity of many aspects of these two experiences is striking, it should not obscure the significant differences between them. It is the purpose of the present paper to clarify these similarities and differences so as to more fully understand the nature of these two processes. The nature of mysticism will be presented through an outline of the "typical" mystical experience and the mystical life of St. Teresa of Avila, a sixteenth-century Spanish Catholic. The schizophrenic experience will be illustrated by excerpts from a first-person account of a schizophrenic episode.

Due to the nature of the experiences to be described below, it will be necessary to use the original metaphoric language of the reported experiences. These words and terms, though personal and experiential, are nonetheless more expressive of the particular experiences than precise, objective language that inevitably transforms the experience.

However, it must be remembered that words like "inner," "outer," "death and rebirth of self," "God," etc. are metaphors that attempt to express the experience in words, but are not to be taken literally as the experience itself. Indeed, the very struggle of John Perceval during his psychosis was to realize that the voices he heard were metaphorical, not literal. As he wrote:

> The spirit speaks poetically, but the man understands it literally. Thus, you will hear one lunatic declare that he is made of iron, and that nothing can break him; another, that he is a china vessel, and that he runs in danger of being destroyed every minute. The meaning of the spirit is that this man is strong as iron, the other frail as an earthen vessel; but the lunatic takes the literal sense [Bateson (1961), p. 271].

MYSTICISM

Mysticism is usually characterized as the experience of Unity, or what Stace (1960) has called, "the apprehension of *an ultimate nonsensuous unity in all things*, a oneness or a One to which neither the sense nor the reason can penetrate (pp. 14–15)." Equally characteristic, however, is the orderly quality of the mystic's development. In a classic statement, Underhill (1961) described mysticism as:

> the name of that organic process which . . . is the art of [man's] establishing his conscious relation with the Absolute. The movement of the mystic consciousness towards this consummation, is not merely the sudden admission to an overwhelming vision of Truth: though such dazzling glimpses may from time to time be vouchsafed to the soul. It

is rather an *ordered movement* towards ever higher levels of reality, ever closer identification with the Infinite [author's emphasis; pp. 81–82].

Every mystic appears to undergo the same basic "ordered movement," and it is this commonality that binds the Christian mystic to the Hindu, the atheist to the Sūfī. For purposes of discussion, commentators have found it convenient to delineate the successive stages of this movement. These stages, which as described in the literature vary in number from three to eight, are not to be taken literally, nor as descriptive of the experience of any one mystic; rather, they are intended to be diagrammatic of the "typical" mystical experience. The five stages described by Underhill (1961) provide a framework that lends itself to a workable outline of the mystic's experience and is used as the basis for the present discussion. A sixth stage seems necessary to describe the process completely and is added to Underhill's five stages.

1. As experienced and reported by the mystics, this is the sudden conversion that follows a long period of great unrest and disquiet. Known as "The Awakening of the Self," it is the sudden realization of a strikingly new and different emotional experience that seems to exist beyond sensation, and that carries with it the awareness of a "higher," more desirable level of experience. James referred to this conversion as the "breakthrough" of the transmarginal consciousness, the sudden "possession of an active subliminal self."

2. After the mystic experiences this deeper level of consciousness, he finds that his former patterns of living are no longer satisfying. He feels that they must be purged or mortified, what Underhill refers to as "The Purification of the Self." In the language of James's dichotomy of levels of consciousness, the new subliminal consciousness with which the person has just come into contact is markedly different from the everyday consciousness of his ordinary experience. Thus, the behaviors that involved his everyday functioning in the social world are not applicable to this more personal experience and so must be discarded.

The extreme ascetic practices of many mystics that occur during this stage are designed to purge the individual of his need for his old connections to the social reality. Once this is accomplished, the process of purgation or mortification ceases. As Underhill points out, despite its etymology, the goal of mortification for the mystic is life, but this life can only come through the "death" of the "old self."

3. After the person has purged himself of his former interest and involvement with the social world, he enters the third stage of what Underhill terms "The Illumination of the Self." Here, he experiences more fully what lays beyond the boundaries of his immediate senses. The main

reported characteristic of this stage is the joyous apprehension of what the mystic experiences to be the Absolute, including effulgent outpourings of ecstasy and rapture in which the individual glories in his relationship to the Absolute. What distinguishes this stage from later stages, however, is that the person still experiences himself as a separate entity, not yet unified with what he considers to be the Ultimate. There is yet a sense of I-hood, of ego, of self.

4. This is perhaps the most striking stage of the mystical process. Although it may be found in all mystic experiences, its emotional expression appears only in the Western tradition, where it has taken its name from the evocative phrase of St. John of the Cross: "The Dark Night of the Soul." Here, there is the total negation and rejection of the joy of the preceding stage. The person feels totally removed and alienated from his previous experiences and feels very much alone and depressed. It is as if he were thrown into the middle of a vast wasteland or desert, with no hope of survival.

During the first purgative period, the individual had to purge himself of his former attachments to the social world. Now, he must purge himself of his experience of self. His very will must become totally submerged to the unknown "force" he experiences to be within. As long as he asserts his own will or individuality, he is maintaining distance or separateness from what he feels to be the Ultimate.

5. Though not the final stage, this is the culmination of the mystic's quest: the complete and total absorption in the asocial, personal world, what has been called "The Unitive Life." It consists of the obliteration of the senses, and even the sense of self, resulting in the experience of unity with the universe. This state has been described as a state of pure consciousness, in which the individual experiences nothing—no thing. The individual has seemingly made contact with the deepest regions of his consciousness and experiences the process as having been completed. Emotionally, the person feels totally tranquil and at peace.

6. *Though not mentioned as an independent stage by commentators the return of the mystic from the experience of oneness with the universe to the requirements of social living constitutes the most important part of his path. In most mystics, it may be observed that they renew their practical involvement in social situations with a new vitality and strength. As St. Teresa observed: "Martha and Mary must work together when they offer the Lord lodging," implying that material and spiritual involvement are equally important* (St. Teresa [1961], p. 231). *The lives of Sts. Teresa, Francis and Ignatius, to name just three, bear testimony to the important practical role the mystics have played in the world. In the classical Eastern tradition, the same emphasis on returning to the world is found. The prime example is the Buddha, who returned from his ec-*

stasy underneath the Bo tree to the social world from which he had "fled" (Campbell, 1956).

The mystic now no longer finds his involvement with the world to be abhorrent, but, in fact, seems to welcome the opportunity to move in the social world he had abandoned. This seeming paradox becomes understandable when one considers that it was not the world that the mystic was renouncing, but merely his attachments and needs relating to it, which precluded the development of his personal, asocial experience. Once he was able to abandon these dependent, social needs, and felt freed of the pull of the social world, he experienced the freedom to live within society in conjunction with his inner strivings, rather than experiencing society's customs and institutions as obstacles to his self-fulfillment.

The following review of St. Teresa's mystical experiences is largely based upon her *Interior Castle,* one of the most widely known mystical treatises, written in 1577. Using the metaphor of a castle and writing in the third person, Teresa systematically described her own mystical development.

As Teresa experienced it, inside of herself was a soul that she represented as a castle in which there were many rooms or mansions, at the innermost of which was God. The castle was constructed like a palmito— a Spanish shrub consisting of several thick layers of leaves enclosing a succulent kernel at its center, and whose layers had to be removed before the kernel could be eaten. In like manner, the room where God dwelt was surrounded by many mansions, and to reach the center, Teresa had first to travel through the surrounding rooms. Teresa believed that despite the great beauty of these rooms most people chose not to enter the castle, which Teresa equated with being interested and involved in the social world. The path outlined by Teresa corresponds in general to the one outlined above. To avoid confusion, however, Teresa's stages will be referred to by her descriptive names, rather than by number.

Teresa's early mansions correspond roughly to the period of disquiet that precedes the conversion labeled above as the first stage. As Teresa experienced the conversion, the feeling seemed to radiate from deep within her, from a source beyond her awareness and control. This source Teresa called God.

Teresa's preparation for her further experiences was called the Prayer of Recollection. For her it consisted of abandoning her involvement with the social world as a source of pleasure and gratification and concentrating (recollecting) her faculties and attention inward to this inner source.

[The person] involuntarily closes his eyes and desires solitude; and, without the display of any human skill, there seems gradually to be built for him a temple in which he can make the prayer already described; the senses and all external things seem gradually to lose their hold on him, while the soul, on the other hand, regains its lost control [p. 85].[2]

Through the Prayer of Recollection, Teresa prepared herself for movement into the next mansion, what she referred to as the Prayer of Quiet, comparable to the "Illumination" described above. She likened the indescribable feelings of great joy that resulted from her withdrawal of concern in matters external to her to the water in an overflowing basin:

. . . as this heavenly water begins to flow from this source of which I am speaking—that is, from our very depths—it proceeds to spread within us, and cause an interior dilation and produce ineffable blessings, so that the soul itself cannot understand all that it receives there. The fragrance it experiences, we might say, is as if in those interior depths there were a brazier on which were cast sweet perfumes; the light cannot be seen, nor the place where it dwells, but the fragrant smoke and the heat penetrates the entire soul, and very often, as I have said, the effects extend even to the body [p. 82].

Teresa cautioned others to be wary of the good feeling of this mansion because they might believe that the Ultimate had been achieved and leave the castle without progressing further.

For as yet the soul is not even weaned but is like a child beginning to suck the breast. If it be taken from its mother, what can it be expected to do but die? That, I am very much afraid, will be the lot of anyone to whom God has granted this favor if he gives up prayer. . . . [p. 91]

As the delights of this period increased, Teresa moved into the next mansion, the Prayer of Union. Here, she completely gave up all investments in the social world, and totally surrendered herself to what she experienced as God. It was as if she were asleep to everything external to her, and even to herself. She was without consciousness and had seemingly "completely died to the world so that . . . she may live more fully in God [p. 98]."

Because of her great difficulty in verbalizing her experiences during this period and those to follow, Teresa employed the metaphor of the Spiritual Marriage to aid her in communicating. The marriage is between herself and God, and was a "union of love with love." During the Prayer of Union, the two met for the first time, became acquainted, and drew up the marriage contract: A Spiritual Betrothal. After those brief "encounters," Teresa experienced a hunger and yearning for the experience of God.

> . . . the soul has been wounded with love for the Spouse and seeks more opportunity of being alone, trying, so far as is possible to one in its state, to renounce everything which can disturb it in this its solitude [p. 126].

However, in the words of the metaphor, God was still withholding the consummation of the Betrothal and, instead, inflicted great pain and trials on Teresa,

> [disregarding her] yearnings for the conclusion of the Betrothal, desiring that they should become still deeper and that this greatest of all blessings should be won by the soul at some cost to itself [p. 126].

These trials—the most difficult and painful that Teresa had yet to experience ("The Dark Night of the Soul")—included the following: people accusing her of being deceitful or collaborating with the devil; rejection by her friends; tremendous bodily pains; and feelings of great loneliness, when she felt herself apart, not only from others, but from herself. During the latter times, she would be unable to pray, not to experience God inside of her.

Some of her most excruciating physical pains came during these moments known as "Raptures," when Teresa would experience a "meeting with God." At those moments, she would feel physically freed of her body. This experience brought with it a strange kind of detachment, more than what Teresa experienced during earlier periods. It produced a profound loneliness, as she had severed all attachments to the social world, but was still, in the metaphor of Marriage, not united with God:

> no comfort comes to it [Teresa] from Heaven, and it is not in Heaven, and when it desires no earthly comfort and is not on earth either, but is, as it were, crucified between Heaven and earth; and it suffers greatly, for no help comes to it either from the one hand or from the other [St. Teresa (1957), p. 123].

Teresa experienced this period as the most difficult for her because it required that she completely relinquish control over herself and be able to withstand the complete independence from the social world.

> For, happen what may, we must risk everything, and resign ourselves into the hands of God and go willingly wherever we are carried away [St. Teresa (1957), p. 120].

Once Teresa was able to do this, she experienced the final union, the consummation of the Spiritual Marriage, the state of "pure spirituality." This experience of union was markedly different from that of the earlier "betrothal." There, although there was an experience of union, there was still separation between herself and the innermost source. Not so, however, in the final stage:

> . . . it is like rain falling from the heavens into a river or a spring; there is nothing but water there and it is impossible to divide or separate the water belonging to the river from that which fell from the heavens. Or it is as if a tiny streamlet enters the sea, from which it will find no way of separating itself, or as if in a room there were two large windows through which the light streamed in: it enters in different places but it all becomes one.

Teresa found herself in an almost perpetual state of tranquillity, even when performing social functions. She now no longer felt overwhelmed by what she previously experienced as the evil in the world. Contrary to what had existed to date, Teresa fervently desired to live in the world and spread the word of God. The remainder of her life was spent in active participation in the Reform of the Spanish Carmelites, which included the founding of eighteen convents. Throughout, Teresa's inner experiences continued and she would frequently feel herself to be at one with God.

Summarizing the crucial aspects of Teresa's experience, it is found that as she was able to abandon her dependent involvements with the social world, she had more lasting contact with the asocial, personal experience of herself that she called God. The process was lifelong, entailed tremendous pain, both physical and mental, and culminated in the complete cessation of external involvement and the experience of "Union with God." The most painful stage of the process occurred immediately before the experience of Union. At this time Teresa had severed her ties with the social world, but had yet to experience the Unity with God. She felt tremendous panic and fear of being completely alone, but this feeling was soon replaced by the experience of Union and feelings of the highest peace and joy. Teresa was then able to renew her activity in the social world, deriving greater satisfaction and fulfillment in these activities than before.

SCHIZOPHRENIA

Schizophrenia is a condition wherein the individual experiences himself and the world about him in a manner distinctly different from that of most members of society. The schizophrenic's conception of time, space, and the relationship between social situations and inner feelings are often not those shared by the social world. His behavior, accordingly, is often socially inappropriate and strange and incomprehensible to others. The intensely personal, asocial quality of this experience has made schizophrenia most resistant to consensus concerning its etiology and treatment. Indeed, there are almost as many theories and therapeutic approaches as there are theorists and therapists.

Recently in psychology a new direction in the understanding and treatment of schizophrenia has developed. A primary tenet of this position is that the psychosis is part of an ongoing, constructive process, wherein the individual attempts to correct the inadequacy of his functioning. This position has been summarized by Kaplan (1964), who writes that the

so-called "symptoms," rather than being ego-alien manifestations of a disease process that has somehow gotten a grip on the person, are instead purposeful acts of the individual, which have intentionality and are motivated. The "illness" is something the individual "wills" to happen [p. x].

Similarly, Bateson (1961), in his introduction to John Perceval's autobiographical account of his psychosis, writes of the *process* of schizophrenia and its purposeful quality: ". . . the mind contains, in some form, such wisdom that it can create that *attack* upon itself that will lead to a later resolution of the pathology [p. xii]."

Perhaps the most prominent spokesman of this position is Laing. In his 1966 lectures before the William Alanson White Institute, Laing proposed a new name for schizophrenia: "metanoia," which translated literally from the Greek means "beyond the mind." (In the King James version of the New Testament, "metanoia" is translated as "redemption." See Lara Jefferson's account of her psychosis in the following discussion.) Schizophrenia, thus redefined, denotes a process or experience of the individual that moves beyond the mind or what we conceptualize as the ego, "beyond the horizons of our communal sense [Laing, 1967, p. 92]." The behavioral accompaniments to this movement according to Laing are neither unintelligible nor bizarre, but are rather expressive of the unusual experiences the individual is undergoing; moreover, Laing (1967) states, these experiences sometimes "appear to be part of a potentially orderly, natural sequence of experiences . . . the behavioral expressions of an experiential drama [p. 85]."

One of the principal contributions of this movement has been to focus attention on the experiences of the schizophrenic as being expressive of the individual's personal, asocial, "otherworldly" experiences, rather than merely the manifestations of a deranged mind. As Haley (1959) demonstrated, when the behavior and communications can be understood in the context of the individual's own personal logic and situation, as opposed to that of social convention, they become meaningful and comprehensible. Publications containing firsthand accounts of psychotic episodes and phenomenological analyses of these experiences have advanced the understanding of this condition, as well as having fostered its identification with mystical experiences that are also movements "beyond the horizons of our communal sense." (See, for example, Bateson, 1961; Coate, 1964; Kaplan, 1964; and Laing, 1965, 1967.) The following excerpt from a first-person account of a schizophrenic episode will demonstrate the phenomenological similarity between aspects of the schizophrenic and mystic experiences, as well as illustrate the differences between them in terms of the meaning each experience has within the context of the individual's life.

Lara Jefferson was a psychiatric patient in a Midwestern state hospital during the 1940s. During her psychosis, she wrote of her experiences. These were subsequently found and published as *These Are My Sisters*. Substantial excerpts from this book are contained in Kaplan's anthology (1964), from which this digest is taken.

Lara's experience of her psychosis was that "something has broken loose within"; and what differentiated her from most other psychotics was that she was aware of this process taking place.

> Something has happened to me—I do not know what. All that was my former self has crumbled and fallen together and a creature has emerged of whom I know nothing. She is a stranger to me. . . . My whole former life has fallen away. . . . All I could do was to feel— startingly—nakedly—starkly—things no words can describe [pp. 6–8].

This former self was as:

> a pitiful creature who could not cope with life as she found it—nor could she escape it—nor adjust herself to it. So she became mad, and died in anguish—of frustration and raving [p. 9].

Thus, madness became the agent of the "death" of her "former self." With this "death,"

> There is nothing solid to stand on—nothing beneath me but a vast treacherous quagmire of despondency—followed by periods of exultation and ecstasy; and neither condition has any foundation in logic. . . . Reason has slipped—altogether . . . [p. 9].

Through her madness, Lara understood that the reason her former self had to be abandoned was because it was ignorant of the true meaning of living:

. . . I have concerned myself with externals only, and have missed all the meanings of the great inner significance . . . I became mad—not because of some inner deformity—but because of too close supervision and trying. . . . Trying to force the thing I was into an unnatural mold [p. 11].

The "second self" that had been created in the madness now suggested to Lara that "the best weapon with which to fight fire—is fire."
And suggests "fighting madness with madness."

Perhaps she is not so insane as I think—perhaps she is saner than I was before she came to me. She presents her idea with so much logic she makes me think that instead of losing reason in madness—and finding insanity on the other side—that, in reality, I will lose insanity in madness—and find a sound mind on the other side [p. 10].

The consequences of this decision:

I cannot escape from the Madness by the door I came in, that is certain. . . . I cannot go back—I shall have to go onwards—even though the path leads to "Three Building"—where the hopeless incurables walk and wail and wait for the death of their bodies. I cannot escape it—I cannot face it—how can I endure it? [p. 7]

Having "decided" to pursue this course, despite its "intolerable horror," Lara experienced a five-day period of "total madness." It began with the feeling that something was about to erupt inside her.

So the monster was out and the ghost of some old beserker ancestor rose up within me and suggested that I could do something about it, and the fierce hatred exalted that it had possessed itself of a massive and powerful body. And the thing that was in me was not I at all—but another—and I knew that no power on earth but a straitjacket could hold her [p. 33].

Lara requested a jacket, and it was granted to her. Now protected against herself and secure in the feeling that she could not harm or destroy others, Lara could release the bonds that were holding her back.

And once the great Madness in me found a voice, there was no stopping it. It rolled out in such a tumult I was amazed at it myself; wondered where it all came from. It seemed obscene and terrible that I should answer in adult language, things said to me in my childhood. Things I had forgotten, until they again began to pour about me in a flood of bitter memories. Even incidents I remembered clearly came back so warped and twisted they seemed like evil changelings. . . .

I felt so much better that I had at last found the courage to look and see things as they were (not camouflaging them in the rosy light of a meaning they did not have) that I wanted to shout and sing.

That voice was reason making a last desperate stand—but it was just a shadow and had no power to check the things I was feeling. Still it held me silent for a few short minutes and forced me to consider the thing I knew was happening to me. . . .

But not for long.

All my human fear of pain and death and loss of reason was drowned in wild exultation. . . . So the last connected and coherent thing in my thinking gave way—and the Madness filling me rejoiced. Because at last there was nothing to stay it, it shouted and exulted with a noise that tore my throat out, charging through me till it nearly dragged the life out of me. Part of my mind stood there and took in the whole situation, yet could know nothing about it. The thing that was raging did not seem wrong to me then—but the rightest thing in the world—a magnificent accomplishment [pp. 36–37].

Lara hardly slept through the night, despite two shots of morphine. But after finally falling asleep near morning she was awakened by a patient screaming about wanting to be on a lake. And then suddenly Lara felt herself alongside a lake:

It was not imagination—but something stronger. Mere imagination, however vivid, cannot transport a person tied down hand and foot in an insane asylum to set them free in some far place. I found I was standing somewhere on a pebbly beach at dawn. . . . I had never seen a dawn so lovely. For I had never been on a lake before which did not exist—nor had I ever experienced a dawn that had not reached me through my dull sense organs—and this was something different—so poignant and perfect it was an ecstasy. . . .

There was such rest and freedom in floating in the current of my thoughts without the struggle of forcing my thinking to continue in the channels I had been taught were right! So I let them run wild and free. . . .

As singing is the natural, spontaneous expression of freedom, I felt an urge to sing—for I was free. And I did sing—song after song. Nothing mattered [pp. 37–39].

The nurses came in at this point, transferred Lara to solitary confinement, and placed her into a new straitjacket, extra-strong, and strapped her to the bedrail. However, the flow continued unabated. Lara began to hallucinate and this continued for at least a day. Then, despite the tight binding of the jacket, she felt a sense of liberation and experienced her arms as free. By the morning of the third day, Lara "was far away in the real heights of ecstasy" and she began to emerge from the Madness.

By the morning of the fourth day I had settled down into something of the person I still am to this day. . . .

The fifth morning they took me out of the jacket. I had been wringing wet with perspiration most of the time during those five days and nights and the odor . . . which assailed me when that jacket was loosened, was asphyxiating. Truly, something had died, and was decomposing! There was a timbre to the odor of that perspiration which was totally unfamiliar. Even the sweat glands had become a voice in that conflict. My hands were filled with a heavy glutinous substance. Every nerve and fibre in my whole body registered the effect of what I had been through. My whole chemistry was changed. Truly I was a different person [p. 41].

Reflecting back on her experience, Lara offered the following advice to those who one day may undergo a similar experience:

I who stand on the other side of this phenomenon called Madness, would like to stretch a hand across to those who may some day, go through it. . . .

To those I would speak and say (because I know, I have been there): "Remember, when a soul sails out on that unmarked sea called Madness they have gained release. . . . Though the need which brought it cannot well be known by those who have not felt it. For what the sane call 'ruin'—because they do not know—those who have experienced what I am speaking of, know the wild hysteria of Madness means salvation. Release. Escape. Salvation from a much greater pain than the stark pain of Madness. Escape—from that which could not be endured. And that is why the Madness came. Deliverance; pure, simple, deliverance. . . . Nothing in this world can stay it when it has claimed its own. . . . I have felt it sweep me and take me —where—I do not know (all the way through Hell, and far, on the other side, and give me keener sense of feeling than the full edge of reason has)"—still, I have no way of telling about the things experienced on that weird journey [pp. 31–32].

In summary, Lara reported a dichotomy between two levels of experience; one was identified with the pre-psychotic self—concerned with reason and "externals only"—while the other was the intense emotions Lara had never expressed. Her psychosis consisted of the breakdown of her control, which enabled these feelings to emerge. These impulses erupted with an explosive power that terrified her; at the same time their liberation filled her with exultation. This loss of control marked the complete withdrawal of her involvement with the social world. Lara expressed this shift in attitude toward her relationship to society as the death of her former self. With the end of the five-day "total madness," Lara felt an inner peace, which she described as the emergence of a new self. She was now able to "return" to the social world, and was subsequently released from the hospital.

DISCUSSION

Though coming from vastly different cultures and separated in time by almost four centuries, the experiences of St. Teresa and Lara Jefferson appear to have much in common. These include: their experience of a dichotomy between two levels of experience—the outer or social, as opposed to the inner or personal; the breakdown of their attachments to the social world; their experience of pain and terror as they "entered the inner world"; their feeling of peace following the end of the terror; and their "return" to the social world, deriving more satisfaction in their social functioning than before their experiences.

However, there were important differences as well: the mystical process of St. Teresa was lifelong, whereas Lara Jefferson's experience of the "inner world" was compressed into a much shorter period of time. Teresa's mystic life culminated in the experience of Unity, while Lara had no such experience.[3] Throughout the process, Teresa was able to maintain some degree of social contact, though living in a cloister. Moreover, her decisions to isolate herself were within her conscious control. Lara, on the other hand, experienced a loss of conscious control and breakdown in her social functioning, necessitating her hospitalization.

Though Lara Jefferson is an example of a schizophrenic who "came back" to the social world from the terrors of the personal world, her experience of the overwhelming power of its fantasies and images totally incapacitated her from functioning socially during the psychosis. The schizophrenic's inability to manage this inner experience and his break with social reality strikingly contrasts with the mystic's tolerance for the inner experience. This becomes understandable in light of the differing preparations for the experience.

The entire mystic path may be understood to be a strengthening process whereby the mystic gradually develops the "muscles" to withstand the experiences of this "inner world." It is this strengthening that is responsible for the long periods of suffering and fallowness that are often the mystic's fate, as well as the mystic's faith in the positive outcome of his experience. Al Ghazzali, eleventh-century Persian mystic, writes of his seclusion and purgation

I went to Syria, where I remained more than two years; without any other object than that of living in seclusion and solitude, conquering my desires, struggling with my passions, striving to purify my soul, to perfect my character, and to prepare my heart to meditate upon God [Underhill, 1961, p. 226].

Underhill, employing the metaphor of the child, describes the strengthening process thus:

. . . the Divine Child which was, in the hour of the mystic conversion, born in the spark of the soul, must learn like other children to walk. Though it is true that the spiritual self must never lose its sense of utter dependence on the Invisible; yet within that supporting atmosphere, and fed by its gifts, it must "find its feel." Each effort to stand brings first a glorious sense of growth, and then a fall: each fall means another struggle to obtain the difficult balance which comes when infancy is past. There are many eager trials, many hopes, many disappointments. At last, as it seems suddenly, the moment comes: tottering is over, the muscles have learnt their lesson, they adjust themselves automatically, and the new self suddenly finds itself—it knows not how —standing upright and secure.

The schizophrenic undergoes no such training or strengthening. His "muscles" are undeveloped and when "thrown" into this "inner world" he is overwhelmed, with no means of dealing with his experience and no conviction that he will survive it.

Writing of the mystic's renunciation of his societal attachments that insulate him from the experience of God, Underhill (1961) uses the image of the mollusk with its hard shell, thereby illustrating the nature of the person's "shell of attachments (pp. 98–99)." Likewise, Schachtel (1959) employs Hebb's image of a cocoon to describe the world of embeddedness that seals off the person's capacity for growth. *Borrowing this imagery, it can be seen that the schizophrenic is one whose protective shell has been suddenly and prematurely broken.* (The etiology of this break will not be discussed in the present paper.) Because of this, he is totally unable to deal with the sudden onrush of the asocial, personal feelings he experiences and his social functioning breaks down. The mystic, on the other hand, through his long training process, is able to slough the shell off gradually. As he increases his tolerance for those new feelings, he is able to incorporate them into his social living. As the mystic becomes strengthened, he becomes ready for the next step and removes another part of his shell.

In writing of his own experiences of the terror of his "confrontation with the unconscious," Jung (1961) stressed the importance of his external life in protecting him from the too-sudden exposure to the inner world of the unconscious.

> Particularly at this time, when I was working on the fantasies, I needed a point of support in "this world," and I may say that my family and my professional work were that to me. It was most essential for me to have a normal life in the real world as a counterpose to that strange inner world. My family and my profession remained the base to which I could always return, assuring me that I was an actually existing, ordinary person. The unconscious contents could have driven me out of my wits . . . (as they did Nietzsche) who was a blank page whirling about in the winds of the spirit . . . (who) had lost the ground under his feet because he possessed nothing more than the inner world of his thoughts—which incidentally possessed him more than he it. He was uprooted and hovered above the earth, and therefore he succumbed to exaggeration and irreality. For me, such irreality was the quintessence of horror, for I aimed, after all at *this* world and *this* life. No matter how deeply absorbed or how blown about I was, I always knew that everything I was experiencing was ultimately directed at this real life of mine [p. 189].

These differences in the preparation reflect the essential difference between the mystic and the schizophrenic. The mystic's goal, as manifested in his lifelong dedication to the Absolute, is to gradually expand his consciousness by moving more deeply into the "inner world" of his personal feelings, until its innermost depth is reached, what he usually refers to as the Self or God, wherein he feels at one with the universe. Though the mystic and schizophrenic ostensibly share the same flight from the social world, the mystic's abandonment is merely of his own dependent attachments to it. Thus, the mystic's life is in essence a process of freeing himself from those habits and customs that had been adopted as security measures to protect against the anxiety that inevitably accompanies any growth or movement toward independence.[4] Once the state of total freedom has been achieved, the mystic is able to once again involve himself in social activities. (To a certain degree, such participation is always necessary. A life lived totally in the "inner world," with no contact with the "outer world," would inevitably lead to physical death, as there could be no search for protection against overexposure or acquisition of food or drink.)

The schizophrenic, on the other hand, has as the "purpose" of his psychosis the escape from the social world within which he is totally unable to function. The "inner world" becomes his refuge from the impossibility of existing in the "outer world." Unlike the mystic, whose inner experiences are consciously chosen over a period of time and developed within the cultural context, the schizophrenic's experience of his deepest feelings is sudden and occurs in the denial of his social functioning. The flight into psychosis, if successful, restores his capacity to function as a productive member of society, but it does not necessarily prepare him for the lifelong process of movement between inner experience and social functioning, nor for the elimination of those learned habits that preclude the development of his inner potential. There is nothing in the reports of recovered schizophrenics to suggest that once having freed themselves from the pathological patterns of their pre-morbid living they continue to explore those inner experiences that had previously overwhelmed them.

In summary, the mystic's life may be seen as a recognition of the existence of the inner, personal experience, which though independent of, and even antagonistic to, the social reality, cannot be fully developed unless the individual also affirms his role in society. Beautiful and powerful feelings are not sufficient to improve one's functioning in the social world. What is needed is the integration of these inner experiences with the various social roles one adopts. The mystic provides the example of the method whereby the inner and outer may be joined; the schizophrenic, the tragic result when they are separated.

NOTES

1. I am grateful to Drs. Gordon F. Derner, Kenneth A. Fisher, and Joel Rudley for their comments on an earlier version of the manuscript. The paper in its present form benefited greatly from the suggestions of Dr. Paul Z. Frisch.

2. Unless otherwise noted, all quotes from this section are from St. Teresa (*St. Teresa*, 1961).

3. At least one self-report of a schizophrenic episode included an awareness of a greater experience—perhaps the experience of Unity—which the person did not allow to occur (Laing, 1967, pp. 108–12).

4. For an excellent discussion of how these habits prevent one's development, see Schachtel, 1959. A more extensive discussion of the mystic process from this and other points of view may be found in Wapnick, 1968.

23

Cocoon Work: An Interpretation of the Concern of Contemporary Youth with the Mystical

RAYMOND H. PRINCE

The most striking element in the American metaphysical movement today is the preoccupation of middle-class youth with mystical experience. Mysticism is strongly linked with the use of psychedelic drugs on the one hand, and with a variety of contemplative religious traditions on the other. And, as have mystics in other times and places, today's psychedelic youth is antimaterialistic and caught up in experiments with communal styles of living. In this paper I will discuss the development of this movement and attempt to interpret it as a self-imposed *rite de passage*. To choose a different image, it is a metamorphic struggle, a kind of "cocoon work" which, unlike the insect analogue and unlike the situation in other cultures, lacks a clear and acceptable image of the adult.

What Is Mystical Experience?

Mystical states are alterations of consciousness characterized by a radical change in the everyday sense of self and experience of time and space; a feeling of heightened significance attaches to the episode or its content; the mood is one of ecstasy; invariably, the subject is left dissatisfied with the adequacy of ordinary language to describe his experience (James 1961; Stace 1960:11). These states vary greatly in mode of onset, intensity, duration, and susceptibility to recall. Some occur spontaneously (Bucke 1901; Laski 1961); others represent the culmination of a prolonged quest; still others may be the result of the use of psychedelic substances or form part of the phenomenology of a functional psychotic episode (Custance 1951; Prince and Savage 1966) or a toxic or organic brain disturbance (Ludwig 1968). Stace (1960:15) has conveniently divided these states into those in which the awareness of the environment persists—the extrovertive group—and those in which the awareness of environment is lost—the introvertive.

In extrovertive experiences the individual feels himself to have become part of surrounding nature and, in addition to the general mystical characteristics noted above, there is usually a heightened intensity of visual or auditory perception, and a quality that suggests the use of the word "religious." The experiences often light up the surroundings, so to speak, so that many years later they can be recollected complete with the setting in which they occurred. Other terms for extrovertive experiences include peak experiences, nature mysticism, or adamic experiences; the last of these suggests that during the episode the world appears as it did to Adam on the day of creation.

Introvertive experiences are more intense and for the most part occur to those who have adopted an ascetic way of life and have practiced meditation or other techniques in order to achieve them. The environment is lost and there remains in consciousness only the sense of one pervading aspect or, in the Judeo-Christian and Islamic traditions, the sense of two things, the self and God.

For some, these various kinds of mystical experience, including both the introvertive and extrovertive, are part of a single continuum of increasing intensity with aesthetic experiences and adamic states at one end and the high-powered introvertive experiences at the other. But others like Zaehner (1957) see a distinct difference between the adamic and monistic experiences on the one hand and the dualistic self-in-the-presence-of-God experiences on the other: according to him, only the latter are of supernatural origin. For myself, I accept the continuum view and like to think of mystical states as in some ways like a television screen: "The image on the screen is the picture of the world. The set is turned off and the picture collapses to become a point of intense light—a ball of pure meaning. With the mystical state, the perceiving ego also collapses into the globule of undifferentiated meaning and all is one. When ordinary perception returns, the globule of meaning is once again diffused over the world . . . in the transitional stages before the complete collapse of the ego and the world and the culmination in the all-is-one, there are regions of experience where the mystic finds himself interfused with the surroundings; he is part of all mankind, and of the animal world and the universe" (Prince 1968).

Mystical states especially of the introvertive type, have of course provided inspiration for most of the world's religions. Mystical states are the origin of Shelley's "white radiance" which transmitted through the "dome of many-coloured glass," expresses itself in the world in the multifarious imagery of the institutionalized religions.

How does the psychologist regard mystical states? Two main interpretations have been offered: (1) that mystical states represent regressions in the service of the ego (Prince and Savage 1966), and (2) they represent de-automatizations of ego functions (Deikman 1966). The regression explanation holds that mystical states occur when an individual or group is confronted with a problem which seems insoluble by habitual means. The individual's (or group leader's) ego regresses to earlier levels of adaptation in an attempt to discover an alternative solution. It is as though the ego has an elevator which can descend to several lower levels in which prior experience and earlier coping mechanisms are stored. The mystical descent is to the earliest level of experience, before the creation of the world as it were, in the primal chaos, long before self and other have become differentiated, before space and time, before language, when the only coping mechanism, the panacea for all ills and discomforts, was sucking at the breast. The mystical state is a "flash-back" of that primal experience. The mystic returns from his descent with the perennial mystical message:[1] at the root of things all is one, all is good, the universe may be trusted; salvation lies in simplification, in de-institutionalization, and above all in love.

The de-automatization hypothesis is based upon the observation that in the early stages of the learning process a good deal of attention energy is required. But with practice, the motor and perceptual patterns become automatic with attendant energy conservation. Deikman (1966) believes that through the mystic's life style of renunciation and in the process of meditation he is reinvesting attention energies in these automatic actions and returning them to awareness. The resulting relation with the world may be less efficient from a biological point of view but may permit the experience of aspects of the real world formerly ignored. The undoing of automatic structures permits a gain in sensory intensity and richness at the expense of abstract categorization and differentiation. As regards the relation between the two hypotheses, Deikman writes, "One might call the direction regressive in a developmental sense, but the actual experience (i.e. mystical experience) is probably not within the psychological scope of any child. It is a de-automatization occurring in an adult mind, and the experience gains its richness from adult memories and functions now subject to a different mode of consciousness."

History of the Movement: Some Landmarks

Writing of a visit of Swami Jogut Sangooly to her father in Concord, Massachusetts, in 1858, Emerson's daughter (Rusk 1949:397) expressed delight "to have a real live Brahmin, brought up a priest to Kreeshna etc., knowing Sanskrit and all the Vedas and able to tell father all he wanted to know." We should probably look to Emerson and the New England Transcendentalists for the early traces of the present youth movement, for the Transcendentalists, like today's youth, drew their mystical insights and formulations far more from the Eastern religions than from the Christian tradition. Emerson had a lifelong interest in the Hindu mystical tradition (though in his youth he called it Indian superstition). According to Greenland (1965) the Transcendentalists were among the first in North America to peruse translations of the *Bhagavad-Gita* and the *Vedas*. The group's interests appear to have been intellectual rather than experiential. They did not experiment with drugs; indeed, at the time of the greatest cohesion of the group between 1840 and 1850, awareness of the possible mystical effects of drugs was just beginning to dawn; Moreau brought *hashish* back from his Persian journeys and introduced it to Europe in the early 1840s (De Ropp 1957:66; Holmstedt 1967); the pioneer American *hashish* enthusiast Fitzhugh Ludlow (De Ropp 1957:77) did not publish his work until 1857. And, in spite of their keen interest in Indian religions, the Transcendentalists do not appear to have practiced meditation. Thoreau, and probably some of the other Transcendentalists however were subject to spontaneous adamic states (Bucke 1901:244). Emerson wrote in his essay "The Oversoul":

> There is a difference between one and another hour of life, in their authority and subsequent effect. There is a depth in those brief moments which constrains us to ascribe more reality to them than to all other experiences. . . . In ascending to this primary and aboriginal sentiment, we have come from our remote station on the circumference instantaneously to the centre of the world, where, as in the closet of God, we see the cause and anticipate the universe, which is but a slow effect.

But Bucke (1901:240) was skeptical. If Emerson had experienced such moments himself he would never have used such moderate and cold language!

The Transcendentalists did experiment with communal living. Brook Farm (1841–47), which Ripley (Rusk 1949) in his founding charter felt "would prepare a society of liberal, intelligent and cultivated persons whose relations with each other would permit a more simple and wholesome life than can be led amidst the pressure of our competitive society," was not very successful.

Another important early figure was the poet-prophet of democratization and de-institutionalization, Walt Whitman (1819–92). Several passages of his *Leaves of Grass* are probably expressions of his own intense mystical experiences (Bucke 1901:178; James 1961). To explain the difference between Whitman's tedious early writings and the inspired *Leaves of Grass*, Braden (1967:71) has speculated that Whitman may have used marihuana while on his visit to New Orleans in 1849!

An unusual and influential figure in the story of North American mysticism is Richard Maurice Bucke (1837–1902). A Canadian psychiatrist who was for many years the superintendent of a mental hospital in London, Ontario, Bucke was the subject of a powerful spontaneous mystical experience at the age of thirty-five and spent the rest of his life puzzling over its meaning (Greenland 1965). A year before he died he published his famous pioneer study of comparative mysticism, *Cosmic Consciousness*. In it he expressed his belief in the evolution of human consciousness—from simple consciousness (as possessed by animals and infants), through the self-consciousness of adults, to cosmic consciousness which he felt had been experienced by a few in the past, Buddha, Paul, Christ, and was being increasingly experienced by contemporary man. Bucke's book has been very influential. Since the publication of five hundred volumes in 1901, there have been twenty-one further editions and recently the work has appeared in paperback. Bucke would not entertain the idea that chemical substances could reproduce genuine mystical states: "Just as the drinking of alcohol induces a kind of artificial and bastard joy, so the inhalation of ether and chloroform induces (sometimes) a kind of bastard and artificial cosmic consciousness."

William James published his Gifford Lectures of 1901–02 as the famous *Varieties of Religious Experience*. For the first time, James clearly separated off mystical states from other types of religious experience, clarified their defining characteristics, and illustrated them with a wealth of descriptive documents that have never been superseded. James was, moreover, willing to concede that chemical substances might produce genuine mystical states. After reading the nitrous oxide explorations of Benjamin Blood in *The Anaesthetic Revelation and the Gist of Philosophy* (1874), James himself sampled (James 1882) the gas and found that the "keynote of the experience is the tremendously exciting sense of intense metaphysical illumination." In 1896, Weir Mitchell ate a few buttons of the psychedelic cactus, peyote, and described the remarkable effects in the *British Medical Journal* (1896). Mitchell passed some buttons on to James, but they only gave him a stomach ache. "I ate one bud three days ago," he wrote to his brother, "was violently sick for twenty four hours, and had no other symptoms whatever. . . . I will take the visions on trust."

It is interesting to observe the extent to which the lives and ideas of these early American mystics intertwined. Whitman was very much influenced by reading *The Dial*, the publication of the Transcendentalists (published between 1841 and 1847). Emerson's influence was important to Whitman: "I was simmering, simmering, simmering; Emerson brought me to a boil" (Rusk 1949:374). *Leaves of Grass* was published in the summer of 1855, and before the year was out, Thoreau, Emerson, and several other Transcendentalists had made the good gray poet's personal acquaintance. Throughout the prolonged storm of protest raised by Whitman's earthy *Leaves,* Emerson was one of the very few eminent literary figures to defend him. Bucke too admired Whitman enormously. He considered Whitman to be the most developed example of cosmic consciousness to have appeared in history! Bucke became Whitman's official biographer and, after Whitman's death, his literary executor. James made extensive quotes from the work of Emerson, Thoreau, Whitman and Bucke in his *Varieties of Religious Experience.*

James's work marked the end of an era in American mysticism. For the next forty years, the major explorations of consciousness, particularly of drug-induced states, took place in Germany and France. Holmstedt (1967) has provided us with an excellent description of this period; suffice it here to mention Lewin (1924), Beringer (1927), and Kluver (1928), who made major contributions to our knowledge of mescaline, cocaine, kava, and other consciousness-influencing substances. An interesting and little known contribution was made by Philippe de Félice in his *Poisons sacrés, ivresses divines* (1936). He documented extensively the now familiar theme of the relationship between religious experiences and the ingestion of drugs. He proposed that the divine soma plant of the Vedic hymns may have been an important factor in the development of Yoga. Soma was brought by the Aryan invaders into India from central Asia in about 1500 B.C. As they moved deeper into India, the plant proved increasingly difficult to find. De Félice suggests that the exercises and meditation practices may have been developed in an effort to contact the gods by a different route. In 1945, Hoffman, working on ergot alkaloids in the Sandoz laboratories in Switzerland, accidentally discovered the most potent of the psychedelics, LSD.

The beginning of the new era of widespread interest in mysticism in America can probably be dated to the arrival of Aldous Huxley in California just before the second world war. Huxley had always been fascinated by the mystical, but, as he wrote of his early Oxford days, he read "Western and Eastern (mystic) writings, always with intense interest, but always with a wish to debunk them" (Clark 1968:302). Perhaps as part of his escapist response to the horrors of the war, soon after settling in California he began to express decidedly mystical convictions. This was first evident in the novel *Time Must Have a Stop* (1944), but most clearly in the didactic *The Perennial Philosophy* (1945), which, as Huxley explains in the opening paragraph, is the metaphysic that recognizes "a divine Reality substantial to the world of things and lives and minds; the psychology that finds in the soul something similar to, or even identical with, divine Reality; the ethic that places man's final end in the knowledge of the imminent and transcendent Ground of all being—the thing is immemorial and universal."

Huxley tells us in *The Doors of Perception,* that until he used mescaline he had never experienced a state which he could call mystical or
religious, but he was in fact capable of voluntarily entering a rather unusual trance-like alteration of consciousness that has been described by
Milton Erikson (1965). In any case, his intellectual absorption with
things mystical induced a longing for a personal experience of the
Beatific Vision. It was with considerable enthusiasm then, that when
Humphry Osmond[2] visited him in California in 1953 he accepted Osmond's offer to initiate him into the mysteries of mescaline (Clark
1968:347). The result was the highly potent little book *The Doors of
Perception* (1954). The title comes from William Blake: "If the doors of
perception were cleansed, everything will appear to man as it is,
infinite." In this book, Huxley unequivocally equated the drug-induced
experience with the mystical states of the Perennial Philosophy. This
doctrine, perhaps because it was so convincingly presented, or because
the times were ripe, spread rapidly throughout the American intellectual
world. Many were launched on their psychedelic adventures by this
book.

It was the sacred mushrooms of the Aztecs—*teonanactl* or god's flesh—
that launched Timothy Leary (1970) on his psychedelic career: "On a
sunny afternoon in the garden of a Cuernavaca villa, I ate seven of the
so-called sacred mushrooms which had been given to me by a scientist
from the University of Mexico. During the next five hours, I was whirled
through an experience which could be described in many extravagant
metaphors but which was, above all, and without question, the deepest
religious experience of my life." The story of Leary's expulsion from Harvard and his continuing jousts with the legal windmills is too well known
to narrate here. More than any other, Leary has attempted to cast the
movement in religious terms. Unlike the novelist Kesey's invitation to
LSD as the portal to fun and games (Wolfe 1968), Leary promised enlightenment. Leary's career (up to 1966) as the high priest of the psychedelic movement is well described in *The Politics of Ecstasy* (1970).

As we have seen, exchange visits between mystics of the East and
West go back at least as far as the era of the New England Transcendentalists. At first, the major North American relationships seem to
have been with India. Documentation is scanty, but we have from Isherwood (1965:318) in his biography of Ramakrishna an interesting picture
of the visits of some of Ramakrishna's disciples during the 1890s. Japanese influences began even before the second world war in the writings
of Daisetz Suzuki on Zen Buddhism. But these influences intensified
remarkably in the postwar period due to the popular writings of another
English *émigré,* Alan Watts (1957) and to such poets as Gary Snyder
(1969). Zen ideas and practices form an important element in the cur-

rent youth movement. Since the invasion of Tibet by China, there has been an influx of Tibetan holy men with their special type of Buddhism. There have also been exchange visits with the Sūfī mystics of North Africa. A host of centers for the study and practice of Eastern religions has recently mushroomed. A 1970 directory of "Light Centers" (Mishra 1970) lists some 190 centers in the U.S.A. and Canada, and these no doubt represent only the tip of the iceberg. Two Indian groups seem particularly well organized and influential. The Hare Krishna movement founded in 1966 by Bhaktivedanta Swami Prabhupada claims ancestry from the earliest Hindu tradition of the *Bhagavad-Gita* and Krishna. It is a dualistic, devotional kind of mysticism which most Westerners would not associate with the East. It does not accept chemical ecstasies as valid: "One is frustrated . . . and perhaps takes LSD and tries to become one with the void. But this nonsense cannot bring happiness . . . it will end in LSD frustration and roaming in impersonal void concepts" (Bhaktivedanta 1970a). The group publishes a magazine, *Back to Godhead*. Perhaps even better organized is the School of Transcendental Meditation launched by Maharishi Mahesh Yogi fifteen years ago; this group has recently focused upon students and in 1966 launched the Student's International Meditation Society (Maharishi 1966). The Maharishi's is a monistic mysticism of the type we more commonly associate with Hindu belief: "Underneath the subtlest layer of all that exists in the relative field is the abstract, absolute field of pure Being, which is unmanifested and transcendental. It is neither matter nor energy. It is pure Being, the state of pure existence." Although Hindu philosophy is generally one of withdrawal, the Maharishi feels that this tendency is to be decried; it is one of the main reasons that India has remained economically backward. He feels that there is no contradiction between the mystic way and full involvement in life. On the contrary, as one of his students, Jerry Jarvis (1970), U.S. leader of the S.I.M.S., rather startlingly proclaimed, "If everyone in NASA had been meditators, we would have been on the moon years ago." Transcendental meditation requires no philosophical or religious commitment; it is simply a technique for accomplishing peace of mind, an increased ability to mobilize one's energy and to be more effective in the world. Recent neurophysiological studies (Kamiya 1969) have gone further to demystify the mystical and give surprising support to the notion that meditation really does promote serenity and can be learned quickly and painlessly.

The Current Scene

With this background, let us now try to tie down a little more firmly the particular religious movement we are here trying to describe and interpret. Let us, for a start, give the movement a name: Neotranscendentalism. It includes the ever increasing number of people who (1) reject traditional Western acquisitive and economic values, (2) are concerned with the mystical, (3) wish to develop more direct, less role-oriented interpersonal relationships, and (4) are interested in communal and cooperative styles of living rather than isolationist, competitive patterns. As with all religious movements, there is of course a core of dedicated practitioners and a much larger number of sympathizers. A characteristic which distinguishes Neotranscendentalism from most other religious movements, however, is its lack of homogeneity and dogma. Neotranscendentalists are allergic to structure or standardization. They are young, mostly under thirty. They are clearly distinguishable from other youth movements—the activist maoists and yippies for example and the "delinquent" groups of motorcycle gangs. The Neotranscendentalists derive usually from affluent homes, are often attending universities or are university dropouts. Although their symbolism and ideas are all-pervasive, and no doubt there are pockets of practicing groups in all the big North American cities, the major centers of the movement continue to be New York and southern California.

The Neotranscendentalists clearly have their parallels in the bohemians of earlier eras, most directly in such bohemian groups as those which occupied Greenwich Village during the twenties and thirties. Cowley's (1934) list of "philosophical principles" of the Villagers of the twenties has a familiar ring: the idea of self-expression—each man's purpose in life is to express himself; the idea of paganism—the body is a temple in which there is nothing unclean, a shrine to be adorned for the ritual of love; the idea of living for the moment; the idea of liberty—every law or rule that prevents self-expression should be shattered. But some principles are different: the Villagers believed "that they do things better in Europe. By expatriating ourselves and living in Paris, Capri, or the south of France we can break the Puritan shackles and become creative and free." The Neotranscendentalists, however, do not see salvation as a matter of changing locale but of changing consciousness.

Clearly, parts of the Neotranscendentalist movement were the beatniks of the 1950s and, of course, the hippies of the 1960s. The differences between these groups have been described by Gould (1971). In brief, the beat (short for beatific) scene was dominated by the novels of Kerouac, the poetry of Ginsberg, and the mysticism of Huxley. The beat was a wanderer who dropped out of life and claimed the right not to raise a family, or work, or become a status seeker; bearded, dirty, living in poverty, he lived a life of tentative personal relationships and held onto life with his fingertips. The hippie scene launched by Kesey's celebrated trip across the United States in the Day-Glo bus (Wolfe 1968), saw an intensification of interest in the mystical, dominated by Leary and the

Maharishi. Relationships became more important, and communes both rural and urban proliferated, particularly in California, Colorado, and New York.

Individual and Cultural "Cocoon Work"

Van Gennep (1960) in his *Rites of Passage,* was the first to draw attention to the significance and ubiquity of the religious symbolism associated with changes of social state in primitive societies, e.g. birth, puberty, marriage, changes of occupation, death, etc. Primitive society was like a series of plateaus separated by sacred and perilous crevasses that required religious ritual for a safe crossing. Of special relevance to our present study, he analyzed in detail the initiation rites at puberty. These last anywhere from a few days to several years and are generally more elaborate for men than for women. Typically, the young men are isolated in a holy place—a remote grove or a sacred hut. Removal from the secure world of women and children is usually accompanied by terror tactics, nocturnal visits by terrifying masqueraders and often from circumcision or other disfiguration. Then follows a period of limbo often associated with the symbolism of infancy; the initiate does not speak, goes around naked, crawls rather than walks, and is fed baby foods. The reintegration into the group as an adult occurs through the teaching of secret adult lore; often the initiates are shown the reality of the fearful masks used during the early stages of the initiation. The exposing of these bogeymen of their childhood is one of the central features of the ritual. The pervasive symbolism is that of the death of the old self and rebirth of the new.

Psychoanalysts have always taken an interest in these puberty rites, for they seem to confirm some of their hypotheses about the universality of the Oedipus complex. The circumcision for example was regarded as the symbolic castration of their sons by the jealous father. Bettelheim (1954), however, observed that even when these rites were not imposed by the adult world, American adolescents would often rediscover rites of passage themselves. He studied several groups which, as part of their struggle for maturation, developed their own rites, complete with real or symbolic disfigurement.

It is clear that we can derive some insight into the Neotranscendentalist movement if we regard it as a rite of passage. The crevasse between the plateaus of childhood and adulthood in America have always seemed especially wide and deep. It required Margaret Mead's voyage to Samoa in the 1920s to show that adolescence is not universally a highly turbulent life crisis. We used to regard the commencement of schizophrenia in adolescence as a distinctive part of the disease; now it is clear that the age of onset varies a good deal depending upon the stress configurations peculiar to the given culture (Murphy 1968).

Neotranscendentalism, then, can be regarded as a self-imposed rite of passage. Instead of the secret grove or sacred hut, contemporary youth remove themselves to pads in the dim hearts of our large cities, or to communes in the California hills. They may withdraw for periods of months or years. The essential task is a psychological metamorphosis—a kind of cocoon work—shucking parental authority and making ready to accept the responsibilities for a spouse and family. Brainwashing is a major feature of the task: the freeing of the initiate from his childish attitudes, beliefs, and fears. As we have seen, in primitive societies this brainwashing is accomplished through a regression induced by fear and clothed and interpreted by symbols of infancy. The initiate's ego with its childish concepts and emotional sets is reduced to a kind of primal egoplasm by terror at the hands of masqueraders wielding circumcision knives. Then the adult identity can be imprinted like a seal in wax.

Our own youth have discovered different methods for returning to the "root." They produce regressions by psychedelic drugs or through meditation. There is an interesting parallel between the primitive youth's discovery of the reality of the bogeyman in tribal society and some to the Neotranscendentalist leader's assertions about seeing through society's games. This is a major theme in Leary's writings for example: "All behavior involves learned games. But only that rare Westerner we call 'mystic' or who has had a visionary experience of some sort sees clearly the game structure of behavior. Most of the rest of us spend our time struggling with roles and rules and goals and concepts of games which are implicit and confusedly not seen as games, trying to apply the roles and rules and rituals of one game to other games" (Leary 1964:106).

This analysis permits us to see a little more clearly why the crevasses between society's plateaus are so often regarded as dangerous and awesome and in some sense religious. The passage from one stage of life to another presents the ego with a major problem of adaptation. The mechanisms of its current stage will no longer equip it to cope on the new level. As we have seen, under these circumstances a common ego reaction is to seek a solution by regression. Regression may result in a mystical state of some kind; or on the other hand it may result in a psychiatric disorder—even a major psychosis. Bridging the crevasse then excites both fear and religious awe.

Contemporary Western psychiatry has recently rediscovered the special significance of these developmental crises. Adolescence, marriage, childbirth, retirement, etc., are now recognized as periods in life when individuals are especially vulnerable to psychiatric disorders. Preventive methods in psychiatry are brought to bear at the time of the developmental crises.

If we are to regard the Neotranscendentalist movement as a rite of passage, we would expect that young people would continue their cocoon work for a period and that they would then emerge as adults ready to take up their positions in adult society. The following description of a participant in a beat commune seems to indicate that this may in fact occur.

We had a commune of sorts in the '50s. We rented a large old dilapidated house in the center of the city. Most of us were between about eighteen and twenty-five, and most worked during the day or went to school—we were just beatniks in the evenings and on weekends. We didn't dress differently, except that we were rather careless perhaps. Quite a few of us entered the commune after a breakup in our marriages—as if we were depressed and had to work something out. It was rather an intellectual group—there was much poetry reading and giving of papers and endless discussion. Perhaps most important were our parties—there was a great sense of the festive. They would have a theme—like a death and rebirth theme—Persephone returning from the Underworld and we would paint huge murals on the walls and make clay sculptures and there would be daffodils and dancing all night. There was a fair amount of free love, though not as much as the neighbors suspected. Of course we all read *The Doors of Perception* and many of us had psychedelic trips on mescaline and LSD.

There were perhaps fifty people who went through the commune at one time or other. Most of them have married successfully and on the whole have become highly successful people—professors of biochemistry, philosophy, English—mostly academics but a few business people —only one I know of is in a mental hospital.

The rite of passage interpretation seems applicable for the Greenwich Villagers of the twenties and thirties and even perhaps for the beatniks of the fifties. But the movement during the sixties seems more pervasive and more fundamental than during those earlier eras. The rite of passage interpretation is most applicable when considering a relatively stable society, when the culturally prescribed image of the adult is clear and acceptable for the majority of the young. The ideal is given; the problem is simply to achieve it. Such does not seem to be the case today. Youth is not satisfied with the adult models available. Let us turn to other possible explanations for the Neotranscendentalists.

Wallace's (1970:188) concept of revitalization movement should be considered. He has defined revitalization movements as "deliberate, organized attempts by some members of a society to construct a more satisfying culture by rapid acceptance of a pattern of multiple innovations." Wallace sees revitalization movements as a response to pervasive social disorganization. Using several Amerindian movements as a basis for his analysis, he points out that disorganization may be brought about by a variety of forces which push a given society beyond the limits of its ability to preserve equilibrium—natural disasters, epidemic diseases, warfare with defeat and colonization perhaps, and also such internal forces as "conflict among interest groups, which results in extreme disadvantage for at least one group; and, very commonly, a position of perceived subordination and inferiority with respect to an adjacent society."

He describes the various steps through which the culture passes on the road to revitalization: from its original steady state through a period of increased individual stress, with widespread anomie and disillusionment; a period of cultural distortion in which piecemeal and ineffectual individual solutions are attempted, such as alcoholism, "black market," breaches of kin or sexual mores, gambling, etc.; and finally the period of revitalization. He points out that revitalization depends on the successful completion of a number of stages. First, there is the formulation of a code. An individual or group must construct a new utopian image of cultural organization. Not infrequently the new code is formulated during the course of a hallucinatory revelation or a mystical experience. The second step is the communication of the new code to a band of followers. The code is usually offered as a means of spiritual salvation for the individual and of cultural salvation for the society. Finally, as the movement gains momentum new institutions based on the code are organized, with subsequent widespread acceptance and routinization.

Can we regard Neotranscendentalism as a revitalization movement? Clearly the Neotranscendentalists are not responding to social disorganization as outlined by Wallace. If the movement has anything to do with organization, it is a response to overorganization. As Roszak (1969:5) emphasizes, youth is revolting against the technocracy, "that social form within which an industrial society reaches the peak of its organizational integration. It is the ideal men usually have in mind when they speak of modernizing, up-dating, rationalizing, planning. Drawing upon such unquestionable imperatives as the demand for efficiency, for social security, for large-scale coordination of men and resources, for ever higher levels of affluence and even more impressive manifestations of collective human power, the technocracy works to knit together the anachronistic gaps and fissures of the industrial society." We may say then that Neotranscendentalism has some of the attributes of a revitalization movement in its form but is responding to an unprecedented degree of overorganization and affluence rather than to social disorganization and poverty.

Recently Turner (1969) has presented us with another model. He studied the Ndembu of East Africa for many years and became interested in their rites of passage, particularly in the boundary stages of the rites, the period of limbo during which, as we have seen, the initiate is stripped of symbols both of youth and of adulthood and resumes the role of infant. Turner became impressed with the significance of this boundary stage or *limen* for a wider social interpretation. He described the boundary stage as a period of *communitas*, which he sees as a type of egalitarian relationship typical of all groups stripped of status and property. He proceeds to show how social life generally is an oscillation between periods of *communitas* and structure:

> It is as though there are here two major "models" for human interrelatedness, juxtaposed and alternating. The first is of society as a structured differentiated and often hierarchical system of politico-legal-economic positions with many types of evaluation, separating men in terms of "more" or "less." The second which emerges recognizably in the liminal period, is of society as an unstructured or rudimentarily structured and relatively undifferentiated *communitas*, community, or even communion of equal individuals who submit together to the general authority of the ritual elders.

He characterizes these modes by the following sets of dichotomies: *communitas*/structures; absence of property/property; nakedness or uniform clothing/distinctions of clothing; minimization of sex distinctions/maximization of sex distinctions; humility/just pride of position; disregard for personal appearance/care for personal appearance; simplicity/complexity; continuous reference to mystical powers/intermittent reference to mystical powers; and many others.

Turner makes a brief excursion into our contemporary world and draws the beat and hippie phenomena into his analysis. These he sees as clear examples of communitas and liminality on the part of the participants, who, however "do not have the advantages of national *rites de passage*—who 'opt out' of the status-bound social order and acquire the stigmata of the lowly." He also points out that the sacred properties often associated with communitas are evident in the hippie movement in their preoccupation with the mystical.

Why does society oscillate between these states of structure and anti-structure? Turner seems at a loss to answer, other than that it is a kind of balancing act to preserve equilibrium:

> Society seems to be a process rather than a thing—a dialectical process with successive phases of structure and communitas. There would seem to be—if one can use such a controversial term—a human "need"

to participate in both modalities. Persons starved of one in their functional day-to-day activities seek it in ritual liminality. The structurally inferior aspire to symbolic structural superiority in ritual; the structurally superior aspire to symbolic communitas.

For Turner, then, the explanation of the Neotranscendentalist movement is that middle-class American youth, by the age of eighteen, is glutted with organization and structure. Neotranscendentalism answers the need for a period of communitas. Presumably, after the communal need is satisfied for a few years, they will happily return to the old world of structure, organization, and status.

With these various explanations in mind, I would like to put forward a somewhat rephrased interpretation of the Neotranscendentalists. American society has, in the past, neglected religious ritual in the passage from childhood to adulthood. Casualties of the crisis have been treated by psychotherapy or mental hospitalization. But in the past twenty-five years a series of unprecedented factors have appeared on the scene: the population explosion, lethal pollution levels, automation and computerization, nuclear weapons, the pill, universal education, and instant communication. These combine to render virtually irrelevant the basic values of yesterday's adult:

> What is it to be a man or a woman, a father or a mother? Educated side by side and equipped for identical roles in the same universities, how can male and female find difference and sexual identity? And the pill has radically altered the sexual game. What is the rationale for "attack" and "defense" and what now is the case for chastity?
>
> Nor are such role changes the most fundamental. Once unquestioned concepts and values require radical revision. War and peace, nationalism, pride in the large family, the virtue of work and other ideals which once gave meaning and purpose are no longer valid. In fact some have become positively malignant. We must not be taken in by words; they are no longer the solid cobblestones of our world; they have become quicksand which will no longer bear our weight. We can no longer ask, "Do you think war is ever justified?" For we are instead inadvertently asking, "Is annihilation justified?" Nor can we ask, "Ought we ever to compromise for the sake of peace?" The question has become, "What sacrifices will we make for survival?" (Prince 1968).

Many of today's youth sense that a perpetuation of the present social order is the blueprint for disaster. They must not only navigate the perilous, age-old crossing between childhood and adulthood, but they feel called upon to create almost overnight an entire new social order and world view. To the individual cocoon work is added the enormously more complicated cultural cocoon work.

Is it possible to say anything about the new society which the Neotranscendentalists have in mind? This is difficult, for they deny that they have any specific program: "My generation does not have goals. We are not goal-directed. We just want to know what is going on" (Messer 1968). Carey (1968) points out that the "new bohemians" feel part of a widespread movement which is only beginning to take shape: "At present there is little indication of where it is going. It tends to be unorganized; there is little official leadership or recognized membership. Progress toward whatever the goal seems to be is uneven. But of one thing these young people are sure: it represents an extraordinarily powerful force."

In spite of this vagueness, something can perhaps be said about the new butterfly that is emerging from its cultural cocoon. Let us consider three basic social aspects: the family, the relation between the sexes, and the problem of work. The family in primitive society consisted of a group of kin which provided a rudimentary kind of welfare system; when young, members invested their labor with an expectation that when they became old or infirm they would be cared for. The next family style was the nuclear family which was adapted to competitive industrial society. The next term in the series is a return to the extended type of family, but with the member families not necessarily kin but families sharing common interests. The function of the grouping is not economic but a remedy for the isolation of the nuclear family; the aim is enrichment of the intellectual and emotional quality of life. Related to this evolution of the family is an alteration in the relations between the sexes. Relations between the sexes in primitive societies are often I-it, with the spheres of male and female kept quite distinct and separate. Next came the era of romantic love with a possessive I-Thou relationship and often a dominant-submissive quality. The new term in the series is the I-Thou relationship without personal jealousy, the possibility of sharing mates without individual possessiveness and with group care of children and egalitarian status between the sexes. Finally, in the sphere of work the Protestant ethic is passing away and repetitive work is seen as the proper function of machines. The Neotranscendentalists believe that it is time to "live off machines rather than live like machines" (Messer 1968). One must "be" rather than "do."

But whether these implicit goals of the Neotranscendentalists will be found widely acceptable or socially viable is another question. And how far they will get with such a Herculean task, even armed with that most powerful of metamorphotic engines—the mystical state—only the future can tell.

NOTES

1. Given, of course, that his primal experience was satisfactory. If it was not, the result may be psychosis rather than mystical experience (Prince and Savage 1966).

2. Osmond, like Huxley, was an English *émigré* in the New World. He is one of the major intellectuals in the psychedelic movement. He in fact coined the word "psychedelic," which means "mind manifesting," to avoid the impression that the drugs were specifically related to psychoses, as was implied by the earlier designations "psychotomimetic" or "hallucinogenic."

PART IV

Philosophical and Aesthetic Evaluations

24

Mysticism, Action and Philosophy

HENRI BERGSON

In defining mysticism by its relation to the vital impetus, we have implicitly admitted that true mysticism is rare. We shall deal presently with its significance and its value. Let us confine ourselves for the moment to noting that it lies, according to the above, at a point which the spiritual current, in its passage through matter, probably desired to reach but could not. For it makes light of obstacles with which nature has had to come to terms, and, on the other hand, we can understand the evolution of life, setting aside any bypaths it has been compelled to follow, only if we view it as seeking for something beyond its reach, something to which the great mystic attains. If all men, if any large number of men, could have soared as high as this privileged man, nature would not have stopped at the human species, for such a one is in fact more than a man. The same can be said of other forms of genius: they are all equally rare. It is not by chance, then, it is by reason of its very essence that true mysticism is exceptional.

But when it does call, there is in the innermost being of most men the whisper of an echo. Mysticism reveals, or rather would reveal to us, if we actually willed it, a marvelous prospect: we do not, and in most cases we could not, will it; we should collapse under the strain. Yet the spell has worked; and just as when an artist of genius has produced a work which is beyond us, the spirit of which we cannot grasp, but which makes us feel how commonplace were the things we used to admire, in the same way static religion, though it may still be there, is no longer what it was, above all it no longer dares to assert itself, when truly great mysticism comes on the scene. . . . Thus may arise a mixed religion, implying a new direction given to the old, a more or less marked aspiration for the ancient god who emanated from the myth-making function to be merged into the God Who effectively reveals Himself, Who illuminates and warms privileged souls with His presence. Thus do we find interposed, as we were suggesting, transitions and differences, ostensibly of degree, between two things which are as a matter of fact radically different in nature and which, at first sight, we can hardly believe deserve the same name. . . . And yet we should not, on the strength of this contrast, disparage religions born of mysticism, which have generalized the use of its formulae and yet have been unable to pervade all humanity with the full measure of its spirit. It sometimes happens that well-nigh empty formulae, the veriest magical incantations, contrive to summon up here and there the spirit capable of imparting substance to them.

Yet . . . we shall notice, in the matter of religion, a gradual disappearance of the contrast between the static and the dynamic, on which we have just insisted in order to bring out the characteristics of the two religions. The great majority of men may very well know practically nothing about mathematics and yet admire the genius of a Descartes or a Newton. But those who have, from afar off, bowed their heads to the mystic word, because they heard a faint echo of it within themselves, will not remain indifferent to its message. . . . A religious historian will have no difficulty in discovering in the material form of a vaguely mystic belief, which has spread far and wide among mankind, some mythical and even magic elements. He will prove thereby that there exists a static religion, natural to man, and that human nature is unchanging. But, if he stops at that, he will have overlooked something, and perhaps the essential. At any rate he will, unwittingly perhaps, have bridged the gulf between the static and the dynamic, and justified the use of the same word in such widely different instances. One will indeed be still dealing with a religion, but with a new one.

We shall be still more convinced of this, we shall see from another angle how these two religions are antagonistic and yet come together, if we take into consideration the attempts of the second to lodge within the first, preparatory to supplanting it.

. . . Among the tentative efforts leading to the mysticism which was to come, certain aspects of the pagan mysteries occupy a foremost position. We must not allow ourselves to be led astray by the term: there was nothing mystic about most of the mysteries. They were connected with the established religion, which considered it perfectly natural that they should exist along with it. They glorified the same gods, or gods originating from the same myth-making function. They merely strengthened the religious spirit among the initiate by adding to it that satisfaction which men have always had in forming little societies within the larger one, and setting themselves up as privileged beings on the strength of an initiation kept jealously secret. The members of these closed societies felt as if they were nearer to the god upon whom they called, if only because the performance of mythological scenes played a greater part here than in the public ceremonies. . . .

At first sight then there would seem to be no more mysticism about this religion than the other. But we must not confine ourselves to that aspect which was probably the only one to interest most of the initiates. We must ask ourselves if some at least of these mysteries did not bear the stamp of this or that great personality whose spirit they claimed to recall to life. We must also note the importance most of the authors give to scenes of religious enthusiasm, where the soul was thought to become really possessed by the god it invoked. In fact the most conspicuously alive of them, those which ended by attracting into their orbit the mysteries of Eleusis themselves, were those of Dionysos and his continuator, Orpheus. As a foreign god from Thrace, Dionysos was by his violence a sharp contrast to the serenity of the gods upon Olympus. He was not originally the god of wine, but he easily became so, because the intoxication of the soul he produced was not unlike that of wine. We know how William James was treated for having described as mystical, or at least having regarded as such for purposes of study, the condition induced by inhaling protoxide of nitrogen. People took this to be a profanation. And they would have been right, if the philosopher had made the protoxide a psychical equivalent of the "interior revelation," the protoxide then being, as the metaphysicians say, the efficient and sufficient cause of the result produced. But in his eyes the intoxication was presumably the occasion rather than the cause. The psychic disposition was there, potentially, along with the others, only awaiting a signal to express itself in action. It might have been evoked spiritually by an effort made on its own spiritual level. But it could just as well be brought about materially, by an inhibition of what inhibited it, by the removing of an obstacle, and this effect was the wholly negative one produced by the drug; the psychologist preferred making use of the latter, which enabled him to obtain his result whenever he wished. It is possible that no more important role attached to wine, when its effect was compared to the Dionysiac frenzy. But that is not the main point. What we want to find out is whether this frenzy can be considered, in retrospect, and once mysticism has come on the scene, as heralding certain mystic states. In order to answer this question, we need but glance at the evolution of Greek philosophy.

. . . Two points must be noted. The first is that at the origin of this great movement there was an impulsion or a shock which was not of a philosophic nature. The second is that the doctrine in which the movement culminated, and which brought Greek thought to a climax, claimed to transcend pure reason. . . . We do, as a matter of fact, see a first wave, purely Dionysiac, merging into Orphism, which was of a higher intellectual character; a second wave, which we might call Orphic, led to Pythagoreanism, that is to say, to a distinct philosophy; in its turn Pythagoreanism transmitted something of its spirit to Platonism, and the latter, having adopted it, in time expanded naturally into Alexandrine mysticism. But in whatever form we imagine the relation between the two currents, the one intellectual, the other extra-intellectual, it is only by placing ourselves at the terminal point that we can call the latter supra-intellectual or mystic, and regard as mystic an impulsion which originated in the mysteries.

It remains to be seen, in this case, whether the final stage of the movement was complete mysticism. One may give words whatever connotation one likes, provided one begins by defining that meaning. In our eyes, the ultimate end of mysticism is the establishment of a contact, consequently of a partial coincidence, with the creative effort which life itself manifests. This effort is of God, if it is not God himself. The great mystic is to be conceived as an individual being, capable of transcending the limitations imposed on the species by its material nature, thus continuing and extending the divine action. Such is our definition. We are free to posit it, provided we ask ourselves whether it ever finds its application, and then whether it fits such and such a particular case. As regards Plotinus, there is no doubt about the answer. It was granted to him to look upon the promised land, but not to set foot upon its soil. He went as far as ecstasy, a state in which the soul feels itself, or thinks it feels itself, in the presence of God, being irradiated with His light; he did not get beyond this last stage, he did not reach the point where, as contemplation is engulfed in action, the human will becomes one with the divine will. He thought he had reached the summit: in his eyes, to go further would have meant to go downhill. This is what he expressed in language of rare beauty, yet which is not the language of thoroughgoing mysticism. "Action," he said, "is a weakening of contemplation."[1] Therein he remains faithful to Greek intellectualism, he even sums it up in a striking formula; and at any rate he did contrive to impregnate it with mysticism. In short, mysticism, in the absolute sense in which we have agreed to take the word, was never attained by Greek thought. . . .

There is a radical distinction, in this case, between the mystical and the dialectical; they only come together at long intervals. Elsewhere, on the contrary, they have been constantly intermingled, in appearance helping each other, perhaps in actual fact mutually preventing each other from attaining full maturity. This is what appears to have happened in Hindu thought.

*   *   *

We are considering, of course, ancient India only, alone with herself, untouched by the influences which have since been brought to bear on her by Western civilization, or by the impulse to resist them. For, be it static or dynamic, we take religion at its origins. We have found that the first was foreshadowed in nature; we see now that the second is a leap beyond nature, and we study the leap in those cases where the impetus was unsufficient or thwarted. The Hindu soul seems to have striven for this impetus in two different ways.

One of them is at the same time of a physiological and psychological character. Its remotest origin is to be found in a practice common to Hindus and Iranians, previous, therefore, to their separation: the recourse to an intoxicating drink which they both call *soma*. It produced a divine rapture, somewhat like that which the devotees of Dionysos sought in wine. Later came a set of practices designed to inhibit all sensation, to dull mental activity, in a word to induce states similar to hypnosis; these became systematized into the *yoga*. Should this be called mysticism in our sense of the word? There is nothing mystical in hypnotic states as such, but they may become so, or at least herald true mysticism and pave the way for it, through the suggestions which creep into them. And they will become so very easily, their form will be predisposed to fill out with this matter, if they already entail visions, ecstasies, which suspend the critical functions of intelligence. Such must have been, in one aspect at least, the significance of the practices which culminated in *yoga*. Here mysticism was no more than outlined; but a more marked mysticism, a purely spiritual concentration, could utilize the *yoga* in its material elements, and by that very operation spiritualize it. In fact, the *yoga* seems to have been, according to the time and place, a more popular form of mystic contemplation or else a complete system which included this contemplation.

We must ascertain then what this contemplation was, as also what connection there can have been between it and mysticism as we understand it. From the most remote times, the Hindu speculated on being in general, on nature, on life. But his effort, sustained through many centuries, has not led, like the effort of the Greek philosophers, to a knowledge susceptible, as was Greek science, of unlimited development. The reason lies in the fact that to him knowledge was always rather a means to an end. The problem for him was to escape from life, which he felt to be unremitting cruelty. And suicide would not have provided this escape, for the soul has to pass into another body after death, and this would have meant a perpetual round of living and suffering. But from the very beginnings of Brahmanism, he drifted into the belief that deliverance could be won by renunciation. This renunciation was absorption in the Whole as well as in self. Buddhism, which gave a new turn to

Brahmanism, did not modify it in essentials. It made it, above all, into something much more elaborate. Till then human experience had shown indeed that life meant suffering; the Buddha worked back to the cause of this suffering; he found it in desire of every kind, in the craving for life. Thus the road to deliverance could be more accurately traced. Brahmanism, Buddhism, even Jainism, therefore preached with increasing vehemence the extinction of the will to live, and this preaching strikes us at first as a call on intelligence, the three doctrines differing only in a greater or lesser degree of intellectuality. But on looking closer, we perceive that the conviction they aimed at implanting was far from being a purely intellectual state. Already in antique Brahmanism it was neither by reasoning nor by study that the ultimate conviction was obtained; it consisted in a vision, passed on by him who *had* seen. Buddhism, more philosophical on the one hand, is still more mystical on the other. The state toward which it guides the soul is beyond joy and pain, beyond consciousness. It is by a series of stages, and by a whole system of mystical discipline, that it leads to Nirvana, to the abolition of desire during life and of Karma after death. We must not forget that the origin of the Buddha's mission lies in the illumination that came to him in his early youth. Everything in Buddhism which can be put into words can doubtless be considered as a philosophy; but the essential is the final revelation, transcending both reason and speech. It is the conviction, gradually neared and suddenly attained, that the goal is reached: man's sufferings, the only certainty, and consequently, the only living thing in life, are over. If we consider that we are here dealing, not with a theoretical view, but with an experience closely resembling ecstasy, that in an effort at oneness with the creative impetus a soul might indeed take the path thus described and only fail because it stopped halfway, dangling all dizzy in the void between two activities, between the human life it has left behind and the divine life it has not reached, then we shall not hesitate to see mysticism in the Buddhist faith. But we shall understand why it is not complete mysticism. This would be action, creation, love.

Not that Buddhism ignored charity. On the contrary it recommended it in the most exalted terms. And it joined example to precept. But it lacked warmth and glow. As a religious historian very justly puts it, it knew nothing "of the complete and mysterious gift of self." Let us add—and it comes perhaps to the same thing—that it did not believe in the efficacy of human action. It had no faith in such action. And faith alone can grow to power and move mountains. A complete mysticism would have reached this point. It is perhaps to be met with in India, but much later. That enthusiastic charity, that mysticism comparable to the mysticism of Christianity, we find in a Ramakrishna or a Vivekananda, to take only the most recent examples. But Christianity, and this is just the point, had come into the world in the interval. Its influence on India—gone over meanwhile to Islamism—was superficial enough, but to the soul that is predisposed a mere hint, the slightest token, is enough. But let us suppose even that the direct action of Christianity, as a dogma, has been practically nil in India. Since it has impregnated the whole of Western civilization, one breathes it, like a perfume, in everything which this civilization brings in its wake. Industrialism itself, as we shall try to prove, springs indirectly from it. And it was industrialism, it was our Western civilization, which unloosed the mysticism of a Ramakrishna or a Vivekananda. This burning, active mysticism could never have been kindled in the days when the Hindu felt he was crushed by nature and when no human intervention was of any avail. What could be done when inevitable famine doomed millions of wretches to die of starvation? The principal origin of Hindu pessimism lay in this helplessness. And it was pessimism which prevented India from carrying her mysticism to its full conclusion, since complete mysticism is action. But then, with the advent also of political and social organizations which proved experimentally that the mass of the people was not doomed, as though by some inexorable necessity, to a life of grinding labor and bitter poverty, deliverance became possible in an entirely new sense; the mystical impulse, if operating anywhere with sufficient power, was no longer going to be stopped short by the impossibility of acting; it was no longer to be driven back into doctrines of renunciation or the systematic practice of ecstasy; instead of turning inwards and closing, the soul could open wide its gates to a universal love. Now these inventions and organizations are essentially Western; it is they who, in this case, have enabled mysticism to develop to its fullest extent and reach its goal. We may therefore conclude that neither in Greece nor in ancient India was there complete mysticism, in the one case because the impetus was not strong enough, in the other case because it was thwarted by material conditions or by too narrow an intellectual frame. It is its appearance at a given moment that enables us to follow in retrospect its preparatory phases, just as the volcano, bursting into activity, explains a long series of earthquakes in the past.[2]

For the complete mysticism is that of the great Christian mystics. Let us leave aside, for the moment, their Christianity, and study in them the form apart from the matter. There is no doubt that most of them passed through states resembling the various culminating phases of the mysticism of the ancients.[3] But they merely passed through them; bracing themselves up for an entirely new effort, they burst a dam; they were then swept back into a vast current of life; from their increased vitality there radiated an extraordinary energy, daring, power of conception and realization. Just think of what was accomplished in the field of action by a St. Paul, a St. Teresa, a St. Catherine of Siena, a St. Francis, a Joan of Arc, and how many others besides! Nearly all this superabundant activity was devoted to spreading the Christian faith. Yet there are exceptions, and the case of Joan of Arc will suffice to show that the form can be separated from the matter.

When we grasp that such is the culminating point of the inner evolution of the great mystics, we can but wonder how they could ever have been classed with the mentally diseased. True, we live in a condition of unstable equilibrium; normal health of mind, as, indeed, of body, is not easily defined. Yet there is an exceptional, deep-rooted mental healthiness, which is readily recognizable. It is expressed in the bent for action, the faculty of adapting and readapting oneself to circumstances, in firmness combined with suppleness, in the prophetic discernment of what is possible and what is not, in the spirit of simplicity which triumphs over complications, in a word, supreme good sense. Is not this exactly what we find in the above-named mystics? And might they not provide us with the very definition of intellectual vigor?

If they have been judged otherwise, it is because of the abnormal states which are, with them, the prelude to the ultimate transformation. They talk of their visions, their ecstasies, their raptures. These are phenomena which also occur in sick people and which are part of their malady. . . . But there exist morbid states which are imitations of healthy states; the latter are none the less healthy, and the former morbid. . . . Yet there is no denying that ecstasies, visions, raptures, are abnormal states, and that it is difficult to distinguish between the abnormal and the morbid. And such indeed has been the opinion of the great mystics themselves. They have been the first to warn their disciples against visions which were quite likely to be pure hallucinations. And they generally regarded their own visions, when they had any, as of secondary importance, as wayside incidents; they had had to go beyond them, leaving raptures and ecstasies far behind, to reach the goal, which was identification of the human will with the divine will. The truth is that these abnormal states, resembling morbid states, and sometimes doubtless very much akin to them, are easily comprehensible, if we only stop to think what a shock to the soul is the passing from the static to the dynamic, from the closed to the open, from everyday life to mystic life. When the darkest depths of the soul are stirred, what rises to the surface and attains consciousness takes on there, if it be intense enough, the form of an image or an emotion. The image is often pure hallucination, just as the emotion may be meaningless agitation. But they both may express the fact that the disturbance is a systematic readjustment with a view to equilibrium on a higher level: the image then becomes symbolic of what is about to happen, and the emotion is a concentration of the soul awaiting transformation. The latter is the case of mysticism, but it may partake of the other; what is only abnormal may be accompanied by what is distinctly morbid; we cannot upset the regular relation of the conscious to the unconscious without running a risk. So we must not be surprised if nervous disturbances and mysticism sometimes go together; we find the same disturbances in other forms of genius, notably in musicians. They have to be regarded as merely accidental. The former have no more to do with mystical inspiration than the latter with musical.

Shaken to its depths by the current which is about to sweep it forward, the soul ceases to revolve round itself and escapes for a moment from the law which demands that the species and the individual should condition one another. It stops, as though to listen to a voice calling. Then it lets itself go, straight onward. It does not directly perceive the force that moves it, but it feels an indefinable presence or divines it through a symbolic vision. Then comes a boundless joy, an all-absorbing ecstasy or an enthralling rapture: God is there, and the soul is in God. Mystery is no more. Problems vanish, darkness is dispelled; everything is flooded with light. But for how long? An imperceptible anxiety, hovering above the ecstasy, descends and clings to it like its shadow. This anxiety alone would suffice, even without the phases which are to come, to distinguish true and complete mysticism from what was in bygone days its anticipated imitation or preparation. For it shows that the soul of the great mystic does not stop at ecstasy, as at the end of a journey. The ecstasy is indeed rest, if you like, but as though at a station, where the engine is still under steam, the onward movement becoming a vibration on one spot, until it is time to race forward again. Let us put it more clearly: however close the union with God may be, it could be final only if it were total. Gone, doubtless, is the distance between the thought and the object of the thought, since the problems which measured and indeed constituted the gap have disappeared. Gone the radical separation between him who loves and him who is beloved: God is there, and joy is boundless. But though the soul becomes, in thought and feeling, absorbed in God, something of it remains outside; that something is the will, whence the soul's action, if it acted, would quite naturally proceed. Its life, then, is not yet divine. The soul is aware of this, hence its vague disquietude, hence the agitation in repose which is the striking feature of what we call complete mysticism: it means that the impetus has acquired the momentum to go further, that ecstasy affects indeed the ability to see and to feel, but that there is, besides, the will, which itself has to find its way back to God. When this agitation has grown to the extent of displacing everything else, the ecstasy has died out, the soul finds itself alone again, and sometimes desolate. Accustomed for a time to a dazzling light, it is now left blindly groping in the gloom. It does not realize the profound metamorphosis which is going on obscurely within it. It feels that it has lost much; it does not yet know that this was in order to gain all. Such is the "darkest night" of which the great mystics have spoken, and which is perhaps the most significant thing, in any case the most instructive, in Christian mysticism. The final phase, characteristic of great mysticism, is imminent. To analyze this ultimate preparation is impossible, for the mystics themselves have barely had a glimpse of its mechanism. Let us confine ourselves to suggesting that a machine of wonderfully tempered steel, built for some extraordinary feat, might be in a somewhat similar state if it became conscious of itself as it was being put together. Its parts being one by one subjected to the severest tests, some of them rejected and replaced by others, it would have a feeling of something lacking here and there, and of pain all over. But this entirely superficial distress would only have to be intensified in order to pass into the hope and expectation of a marvelous instrument. The mystic soul yearns to become this instrument. It throws off anything in its substance that is not pure enough, not flexible and strong enough, to be turned to some use by God. Already it had sensed the presence of God, it had thought it beheld God in a symbolic vision, it had even been united to Him in its ecstasy; but none of this rapture was lasting, because it was mere contemplation; action threw the soul back upon itself and thus divorced it from God. *Now* it is God who is acting through the soul, in the soul; the union is total, therefore final. At this point words such as mechanism and instrument evoke images which are better left alone. They could be used to give us an idea of the preliminary work. They will teach us nothing of the final result. Let us say that henceforth for the soul there is a superabundance of life. There is a boundless impetus. There is an irresistible impulse which hurls it into vast enterprises. A calm exaltation of all its faculties makes it see things on a vast scale only, and, in spite of its own weakness, produce only what can be mightily wrought. Above all, it sees things simply, and this simplicity, which is equally striking in the words it uses and the conduct it follows, guides it through complications which it apparently does not even perceive. An innate knowledge, or rather an acquired ignorance, suggests to it straightaway the step to be taken, the decisive act, the unanswerable word. Yet effort remains indispensable, endurance and perseverance likewise. But they come of themselves, they develop of their own accord, in a soul acting and acted upon, whose liberty coincides with the divine activity. They represent a vast expenditure of energy, but this energy is supplied as it is required, for the superabundance of vitality which it demands flows from a spring which is the very source of life. And now the visions are left far behind: the divinity could not manifest itself from without to a soul henceforth replete with its essence. Nothing remains to distinguish such a man outwardly from the men about him. He alone realized the change which has raised him to the rank of *adjutores Dei,* "patients" in respect to God, agents in respect to man. In this elevation he feels no pride. On the contrary, great is his humility. . . .

Even in the mysticism which went only as far as ecstasy, that is to say contemplation, a certain line of action was foreshadowed. Hardly had these mystics come back from Heaven to earth, when they felt it incumbent on them to teach mankind. They had to tell all men that the world perceived by the eyes of the body is doubtless real, but that there is something else, and that this something is no mere possibility or probability, like the conclusion of an argument, but the certainty of a thing experienced: here is one who has seen, who has touched, one who knows. And yet these were but the tentative beginnings of an apostolate. The enterprise was indeed discouraging: how could the conviction derived from an experience be handed down by speech? And, above all, how could the inexpressible be expressed? But these questions do not even present themselves to the great mystic. He has felt truth flowing into his soul from its fountainhead like an active force. He can no more help spreading it abroad than the sun can help diffusing its light. Only, it is not by mere words that he will spread it.

For the love which consumes him is no longer simply the love of man for God, it is the love of God for all men. Through God, in the strength of God, he loves all mankind with a divine love. This is not the fraternity enjoined on us by the philosophers in the name of reason, on the principle that all men share by birth in one rational essence: so noble an ideal cannot but command our respect; we may strive to the best of our ability to put it into practice, if it be not too irksome for the individual and the community; we shall never attach ourselves to it passionately. Or, if we do, it will be because we have breathed in some nook or corner of our civilization the intoxicating fragrance left there by mysticism. Would the philosophers themselves have laid down so confidently the principle, so little in keeping with everyday experience, of an equal participation of all men in a higher essence, if there had not been mystics to embrace all humanity in one simple indivisible love? This is not, then, that fraternity which started as an idea, whence an ideal has been erected. Neither is it the intensification of an innate sympathy of man for man. . . . The mystic love of humanity is a very different thing. It is not the extension of an instinct, it does not originate in an idea. It is neither of the senses nor of the mind. It is of both, implicitly, and is effectively much more. For such a love lies at the very root of feeling and reason, as of all other things. Coinciding with God's love for His handiwork, a love which has been the source of everything, it would yield up, to anyone who knew how to question it, the secret of creation. It is still more metaphysical than moral in its essence. What it wants to do, with God's help, is to complete the creation of the human species and make of humanity what it would have straightaway become, had it been able to assume its final shape without the assistance of man himself. Or to use words which mean, as we shall see, the same thing in different terms: its direction is exactly that of the vital impetus; it *is* this impetus itself, communicated in its entirety to exceptional men who in their turn would fain impart it to all humanity and by a living contradiction change into creative effort that created thing which is a species, and turn into movement what was, by definition, a stop.

Can it succeed? If mysticism is to transform humanity, it can do so only by passing on, from one man to another, slowly, a part of itself. The mystics are well aware of this. The great obstacle in their way is the same which prevented the creation of a divine humanity. Man has to earn his bread with the sweat of his brow; in other words, humanity is an animal species, and, as such, subject to the law which governs the animal world and condemns the living to batten upon the living. Since he has to contend for his food both with nature and with his own kind, he necessarily expends his energies procuring it; his intelligence is designed for the very object of supplying him with weapons and tools, with a view to that struggle and that toil. How then, in these conditions, could humanity turn heavenwards an attention which is essentially concentrated on earth? If possible at all, it can only be by using simultaneously or successively two very different methods. The first would consist presumably in intensifying the intellectual work to such an extent, in carrying intelligence so far beyond what nature intended, that the simple tool would give place to a vast system of machinery such as might set human activity at liberty, this liberation being, moreover, stabilized by a political and social organization which would ensure the application of the mechanism to its true object. A dangerous method, for mechanization, as it developed, might turn against mysticism: nay more, it is by an apparent reaction against the latter that mechanization would reach its highest pitch of development. But there are certain risks which must be taken: an activity of a superior kind, which to be operative requires one of a lower order, must call forth this activity, or at least permit it to function, if necessary, even at the cost of having to defend itself against it. . . . However that may be, this means could only be utilized much later; in the meantime an entirely different method had to be followed. This consisted, not in contemplating a general and immediate spreading of the mystic impetus, which was obviously impossible, but in imparting it, already weakened though it was, to a tiny handful of privileged souls who together would form a spiritual society; societies of this kind might multiply; each one, through such of its members as might be exceptionally gifted, would give birth to one or several others; thus the impetus would be preserved and continued until such time as a profound change in the material conditions imposed on humanity by nature should permit, in spiritual matters, of a radical transformation. Such is the method followed by the great mystics. It was of necessity, and because they could do no more, that they were particularly prone to spend their superabundant energy in founding convents or religious orders. For the time being they had no need to look further. The impetus of love which drove them to lift humanity up to God and complete the divine creation could reach its end, in their eyes, only with the help of God Whose instruments they were. Therefore all their efforts must be concentrated on a very great, a very difficult, but a limited task. Other efforts would be forthcoming, indeed others had already been; they would all be convergent, since God imparted to them their unity.

We have, indeed, simplified a great deal. To make things clearer, and, above all, to take the difficulties one by one, we have reasoned as though the Christian mystic, the bearer of an inner revelation, had made his appearance in a humanity utterly ignorant of such a thing. As a matter of fact, the men to whom he spoke already had their religion, the same, moreover, as his own. If he had visions, these visions showed him, in the form of images what his religion had impressed on him in the form of ideas. His ecstasies, when they occurred, united him to a God probably greater than anything he had ever conceived, but who did nevertheless correspond to the abstract descriptions with which religion had supplied him.

* * *

A doctrine which is but a doctrine has a poor chance indeed of giving birth to the glowing enthusiasm, the illumination, the faith that moves mountains. But grant this fierce glow, and the molten matter will easily run into the mold of a doctrine, or even become that doctrine as it solidifies. We represent religion, then, as the crystallization, brought about by a scientific process of cooling, of what mysticism had poured, while hot, into the soul of man. Through religion all men get a little of what a few privileged souls possessed in full. True, religion had to accept a great deal to get itself accepted. Humanity really understands the new only when it inherits much of the old. Now the old was, on the one hand, what had been built up by the Greek philosophers, and, on the other hand, what had been imagined by ancient religions. That Christianity received or derived a great deal from both there is no doubt. It is permeated with Greek philosophy, and has preserved many rites, many ceremonies, many beliefs even, from the religion we called static or natural. It was in its interest to do so, for its partial adoption of the Aristotelian Neoplatonism enabled it to win over philosophic thought, and its borrowings from ancient religions were bound to help this new religion—with its marked tendency in the opposite direction, having hardly anything in common with past religions but the name—to become popular. But none of all that was essential; the essence of the new religion was to be the diffusion of mysticism. . . .

What the mystic finds waiting for him, then, is a humanity which has been prepared to listen to his message by other mystics invisible and present in the religion which is actually taught. Indeed his mysticism itself is imbued with this religion, for such was its starting point. His theology will generally conform to that of the theologians. His intelligence and his imagination will use the teachings of the theologians to express in words what he experiences, and in material images what he sees spiritually. And this he can do easily, since theology has tapped that very current whose source is the mystical. Thus his mysticism is served by religion, against the day when religion becomes enriched by his mysticism. This explains the primary mission which he feels to be entrusted to him, that of an intensifier of religious faith. He takes the most crying needs first. In reality, the task of the great mystic is to effect a radical transformation of humanity by setting an example. The object could be attained only if there existed in the end what should theoretically have existed in the beginning, a divine humanity.

So then mysticism and religion are mutually cause and effect, and continue to interact on one another indefinitely. Yet there must have been a beginning. And indeed at the origin of Christianity there is Christ. From our standpoint, which shows us the divinity of all men, it matters little whether or no Christ be called a man. It does not even matter that he be called Christ. . . . Let us merely say that, if the great mystics are indeed such as we described them, they are the imitators, and original but incomplete continuators, of what the Christ of the Gospels was completely.

He Himself may be considered as the continuator of the prophets of Israel. There is no doubt but that Christianity was a profound transformation of Judaism. It has been said over and over again: a religion which was still essentially national was replaced by a religion that could be made universal. A God who was doubtless a contrast to all other gods by His justice as well as by His power, but Whose power was used for His people, and Whose justice was applied, above all, to His own subjects, was succeeded by a God of love, a God Who loved all mankind. This is precisely why we hesitate to classify the Jewish prophets among the mystics of antiquity: Jehovah was too stern a judge, Israel and its God were not close enough together for Judaism to be the mysticism which we are defining. And yet no current of thought or feeling has contributed so much as the thought and feeling of Jewish prophets to arouse the mysticism which we call complete, that of the Christian mystics. The reason is that, if other currents carried certain souls toward a contemplative mysticism and thereby deserved to be regarded as mystic, pure contemplation they remained, and nothing more. To cover the interval between thought and action an impetus was needed—and it was not forthcoming. We find this impetus in the prophets: they longed passionately for justice, demanded it in the name of the God of Israel; and Christianity, which succeeded Judaism, owed largely to the Jewish prophets its active mysticism, capable of marching on to the conquest of the world.

If mysticism is really what we have just said it is, it must furnish us with the means of approaching, as it were experimentally, the problem of the existence and the nature of God. Indeed we fail to see how philosophy could approach the problem in any other way. Generally speaking, we look upon an object as existing if it is perceived, or might be perceived. Such an object is therefore presented in actual or possible experience. No doubt you may construct the idea of an object or of a being, as the geometrician does for a geometrical figure; but experience alone will decide whether it actually exists outside the idea thus constructed. Now, you may assert that this is just the question, and that the problem precisely is to know whether a certain Being is not distinctive from all other beings in that He stands beyond the reach of our experience, and yet is as real as they are. Granted, for this once; although an assertion of this kind, with its attendant arguments, appears to me to imply a fundamental illusion. But then you must prove that the Being thus defined, thus demonstrated, is indeed God. You may argue that He is so by definition, and that one is at liberty to confer any meaning one likes on words, provided one defines them first. Granted again; but if you attribute to a word a radically different meaning from that which it usually bears, it will apply to a new object; your reasoning no longer refers to the former one; it is therefore understood that you are speaking to us of something else. This is precisely what occurs in most cases when the philosopher speaks of God. So remote is this conception from the God most men have in mind that if, by some miracle, and contrary to the opinion of philosophers, God as thus defined should step down into the field of experience, none would recognize Him. For religion, be it static or dynamic, regards Him, above all, as a Being who can hold communication with us: now this is just what the God of Aristotle, adopted with a few modifications by most of his successors, is incapable of doing.

＊　　＊　　＊

The God of Aristotle has nothing in common with the gods worshiped by the Greeks; nor has he much more in common with the God of the Bible, of the Gospels. Religion, whether static or dynamic, confronts the philosopher with a God who raises totally different problems. Yet it is to Aristotle's God that metaphysical thought has generally attached itself, even at the price of investing him with attributes incompatible with his essence.

*   *   *

Now, is mystical experience able to solve these problems? It is easy to see the objections that such a notion will arouse. We have disposed of those which consist in asserting that no mystic is sound in the head and that all mysticism is a pathological state. The great mystics, the only ones that we are dealing with, have generally been men or women of action, endowed with superior common sense; it matters little that some of them had imitators who well deserved to be called "crazy," or that there are cases when they themselves felt the effect of extreme and prolonged strain of mind and will; many a man of genius has been in the same condition. But there is another series of objections, which it is impossible to overlook. For it is alleged that the experiences of great mystics are individual and exceptional, that they cannot be verified by the ordinary man, that they cannot therefore be compared to a scientific experiment and cannot possibly solve problems.

*   *   *

We must first note the fact that mystics generally agree among themselves. This is striking in the case of the Christian mystics. To reach the ultimate identification with God, they go through a series of states. These may vary from mystic to mystic, but there is a strong resemblance between them. In any case, the path followed is the same, even admitting that the stopping places by the way are at different intervals. They have in any case the same terminal point. In the descriptions of the final state we find the same expressions, the same images, the same comparisons, although the authors were generally unknown to each other. It will be replied that in some cases they had known one another, that furthermore there is a mystic tradition, and that all mystics may have felt its influence. We grant this, but the fact must be noted that the great mystics give little thought to this tradition; each one has his own originality, which is not intentional, which he has not sought, but which we feel is of fundamental importance to him; it means that he is the object of an exceptional favor, unmerited though it be. Now it may be objected that a community of religion suffices to explain the resemblance, that all Christian mystics have lived on the Gospels, that they all received the same theological teaching. But this would be to forget that, if the resemblance between the visions is indeed explainable by a common religion, these visions occupy but a small place in the lives of the great mystics; they are soon left behind, and treated as if they had been merely symbolical.

As to theological teaching in general, it is true that they seem to accept it with utter docility, and in particular to obey their confessors; but, as has been shrewdly remarked, "they obey themselves alone, and a sure instinct leads them straight to the very man who can be relied upon to guide them in the way they want to go. If he should happen to depart from it, our mystics would not hesitate to shake off his authority, and, on the strength of their direct contact with the Deity, place their own liberty above all else."[4] . . . All we want to make clear is that, if external resemblances between Christian mystics may be due to a common tradition or a common training, their deep-seated agreement is a sign of an identity of intuition which would find its simplest explanation in the actual existence of the Being with whom they believe themselves to hold intercourse. So much the more so, then, if we consider that the other mysticisms, ancient or modern, go more or less far, stopping at this or that stage, but all point in the same direction.

Yet we may admit that mystical experience, left to itself cannot provide the philosopher with complete certainty. It could be absolutely convincing only if he had come by another way, such as a sensuous experience coupled with rational inference, to the conclusion of the probable existence of a privileged experience through which man could get into touch with a transcendent principle. The occurrence in mystics of just such an experience would then make it possible to add something to the results already established, whilst these established results would reflect back on to the mystical experience something of their own objectivity. Experience is the only source of knowledge. But, since the intellectual record of the fact inevitably goes further than the raw fact, all experiences are far from being equally conclusive and from justifying the same certainty. Many lead us to merely probable conclusions. Yet probabilities may accumulate, and the sum total be practically equivalent to certainty. We have alluded elsewhere to those "lines of fact" each one indicating but the direction of truth, because it does not go far enough: truth itself, however, will be reached if two of them can be prolonged to the point where they intersect. . . . Now it so happens that a thorough study of a certain order of problems, entirely different from religious problems, has led us to a conclusion which makes probable the existence of a singular privileged experience, such as a mystic experience. And, on the other hand, the mystical experience, studied for its own sake, supplies us with pointers that can be added and fitted to the knowledge obtained in an entirely different method. It is a case, then, of one supporting and complementing the other. Let us begin with the first point.

It was by following as closely as possible the evidence of biology that we reached the conception of a vital impetus and of a creative evolution. As we set it out . . . this conception was by no means a hypothesis, such as can be found at the basis of any metaphysical system: it was a condensation of fact, a summing up of summings up. Now, whence came the impetus, and what was the principle behind it? If it sufficed unto itself, what was it in itself, and what meaning were we to ascribe to its manifestations as a whole? To such questions the facts under consideration supplied no direct answer; but we saw clearly from what direction the answer might come. For the energy thrown through matter appeared to us, as it were, below or above consciousness, in any case of the same order as consciousness. It had had to get round many obstacles, squeeze itself through others, above all, divide itself between diverging lines of evolution: at the extremity of the two main lines we ultimately found two modes of knowledge into which it had resolved itself in order to materialize; the instinct of insects, the intelligence of man. Instinct was intuitive; intelligence reflected and reasoned. . . . But just as there subsisted around animal instinct a fringe of intelligence, so human intelligence preserved a halo of intuition. The latter, in man, had remained fully disinterested and conscious, but it was only a faint glow and did not radiate very far. Yet it is from this that the light must come, if ever the inner working of the vital impetus were to be made clear in its significance and in its object. For this intuition was turned inward; and if, in a first intensification, beyond which most of us did not go, it made us realize the continuity of our inner life, a deeper intensification might carry it to the roots of our being, and thus to the very principle of life in general. Now is not this precisely the privilege of the mystic soul?

This brings to what we have just stated as our second point. The first question was to find out whether or no the mystics were merely "queer," if the accounts of their experiences were purely fanciful or not. But the question was soon settled, at least as far as the great mystics were concerned. The next thing was to find out whether mysticism was no more than a more fervent faith, an imaginative form such as traditional religion is capable of assuming in passionate souls, or whether, while assimilating as much as it can from this religion, while turning to it for confirmation, while borrowing its language, it did not possess an original content, drawn straight from the very wellspring of religion, independent of all that religion owes to tradition, to theology, to the churches. In the first case, it would necessarily stand aloof from philosophy, for the latter ignores revelation which has a definite date, the institutions which have transmitted it, the faith that accepts it: it must confine itself to experience and inference. But, in the second case, it would suffice to take mysticism unalloyed, apart from the visions, the allegories, the theological language which express it, to make it a powerful helpmeet to philosophical research. Of these two conceptions of the relation that it maintains to religion, the second seems to us indubitably the right one. We must then find out in what measure mystic experience is a continuation of the experience which led us to the doctrine of the vital impetus. All the information with which it would furnish philosophy, philosophy would repay in the shape of confirmation.

Let us first note that the mystics ignore what we have called "false problems." . . . We have shown elsewhere that part of metaphysics moves, consciously or not, around the question of knowing why anything exists—why matter, or spirit, or God, rather than nothing at all? But the question presupposes that reality fills a void, that underneath Being lies nothingness, that *de jure* there should be nothing, that we must therefore explain why there is *de facto* something. And this presupposition is pure illusion, for the idea of absolute nothingness has not one jot more meaning than a square circle. The absence of one thing being always the presence of another—which we prefer to leave aside because it is not the thing that interests us or the thing we were expecting—suppression is never anything more than substitution, a two-sided operation which we agree to look at from one side only: so that the idea of the abolition of everything is self-destructive, inconceivable; it is a pseudo-idea, a mirage conjured up by our imagination. But, for reasons we have stated elsewhere, the illusion is natural: its source lies in the depths of the understanding. It raises questions which are the main origin of metaphysical anguish. Now, for a mystic these questions simply do not exist, they are optical illusions arising, in the inner world, from the structure of human intelligence, they recede and disappear as the mystic rises superior to the human point of view. And, for similar reasons, the mystic will no more worry about the difficulties accumulated by philosophy around the "metaphysical" attributes of Deity: he has nothing to do with properties which are mere negations and can only be expressed negatively; he believes that he sees what God is, for him there is no seeing what God is not. It is therefore on the nature of God, immediately apprehended on the positive side, I mean on the side which is perceptible to the eyes of the soul, that the philosopher must question him.

The philosopher could soon define this nature, did he wish to find a formula for mysticism. God is love, and the object of love: herein lies the whole contribution of mysticism. About this twofold love the mystic will never have done talking. His description is interminable, because what he wants to describe is ineffable. But what he does state clearly is that divine love is not a thing of God: it is God Himself. It is upon this point that the philosopher must fasten who holds God to be a person, and yet wishes to avoid anything like a gross assimilation with man. He will think, for example, of the enthusiasms which can fire a soul, consume all that is within it, and henceforth fill the whole space. The individual then becomes one with the emotion; and yet he was never so thoroughly himself; he is simplified, unified, intensified.

*   *   *

An emotion of this kind doubtless resembles, though very remotely, the sublime love which is for the mystic the very essence of God. In any case, the philosopher must bear the emotion in mind when he compresses mystic intuition more and more in order to express it in terms of intelligence.

He may not write music, but he generally writes books; and the analysis of his own state of mind when he writes will help him to understand how the love in which the mystics see the very essence of divinity can be both a person and a creative power. He generally keeps, when writing, within the sphere of concepts and words. Society supplies ideas ready to hand, worked out by his predecessors and stored up in the language, ideas which he combines in a new way, after himself reshaping them to a certain extent so as to make them fit into his combination. This method will always produce some more or less satisfactory result, but still a result, and in a limited space of time. And the work produced may be original and vigorous; in many cases human thought will be enriched by it. Yet this will be but an increase of that year's income; social intelligence will continue to live on the same capital, the same stock. Now there is another method of composition, more ambitious, less certain, which cannot tell when it will succeed at all. It consists in working back from the intellectual and social plane to a point in the soul from which there springs an imperative demand for creation. The soul within which this demand dwells may indeed have felt it fully only once in its lifetime, but it is always there, a unique emotion, an impulse, an impetus received from the very depths of things. To obey it completely new words would have to be coined, new ideas would have to be created, but this would no longer be communicating something, it would not be writing. Yet the writer will attempt to realize the unrealizable. He will revert to the simple emotion, to the form which yearns to create its matter, and will go with it to meet ideas already made, words that already exist, briefly social segments of reality. All along the way he will feel it manifesting itself in signs born of itself, I mean in fragments of its own materialization. How can these elements, each unique of its kind, be made to coincide with words already expressing things? He will be driven to strain the words, to do violence to speech. And, even so, success can never be sure; the writer wonders at every step if it will be granted to him to go on to the end; he thanks his luck for every partial success, just as a punster might thank the words he comes across for lending themselves to his fun. But if he does succeed, he will have enriched humanity with a thought that can take on a fresh aspect for each generation, with a capital yielding ever-renewed dividends, and not just with a sum down to be spent at once. These are the two methods of literary composition. They may not, indeed, utterly exclude each other, yet they are radically different. The second one, as providing the image of the creation of matter by form, is what the philosopher must have in mind in order to conceive as creative energy the love wherein the mystic sees the very essence of God.

Has this love an object? Let us bear in mind that an emotion of a superior order is self-sufficient. Imagine a piece of music which expresses love. It is not love for any particular person. Another piece of music will express another love. Here we have two distinct emotional atmospheres, two different fragrances, and in both cases the quality of love will depend upon its essence and not upon its object. Nevertheless, it is hard to conceive a love which is, so to speak, at work, and yet applies to nothing. As a matter of fact, the mystics unanimously bear witness that God needs us, just as we need God. Why should He need us unless it be to love us? And it is to this very conclusion that the philosopher who holds to the mystical experience must come. Creation will appear to him as God undertaking to create creators, that He may have, besides Himself, beings worthy of His love.

We should hesitate to admit this if it were merely a question of humdrum dwellers on this corner of the universe called Earth. But, as we have said before, it is probable that life animates all the planets revolving round all the stars. It doubtless takes, by reason of the diversity of conditions in which it exists, the most varied forms, some very remote from what we imagine them to be; but its essence is everywhere the same, a slow accumulation of potential energy to be spent suddenly in free action. . . . Though there were other lines of evolution running alongside the line which led to man, and though much is incomplete in man himself, we can say, while keeping closely to what experience shows, that it is man who accounts for the presence of life on our planet. [Thus] there is nothing to prevent the philosopher from following to its logical conclusion the idea which mysticism suggests to him of a universe which is the more visible and tangible aspect of love and of the need of loving, together with all the consequences entailed by this creative emotion: I mean the appearance of living creatures in which this emotion finds its complement; of an infinity of other beings without which they could not have appeared, and lastly of the unfathomable depths of material substance without which life would not have been possible.

. . . Here we are in the field of probabilities alone. But we cannot reiterate too often that philosophic certainty admits of degrees, that it calls for intuition as well as for reason, and that if intuition, backed up by science, is to be extended, such extension can be made only by mystical intuition.

* * *

Beings have been called into existence who were destined to love and be loved, since creative energy is to be defined as love. Distinct from God, Who is this energy itself, they could spring into being only in a universe, and therefore the universe sprang into being. In that portion of the universe which is our planet—probably in our whole planetary system —such beings, in order to appear, have had to be wrought into a species, and this species involved a multitude of other species, which led up to it, or sustained it, or else formed a residue. . . . It would never for an instant have thought of becoming completely itself, if certain representatives of it had not succeeded, by an individual effort added to the general work of life, in breaking through the resistance put up by the instrument, in triumphing over materiality—in a word, in getting back to God. These men are the mystics. They have blazed a trail along which other men may pass. They have, by this very act, shown to the philosopher the whence and whither of life.

NOTES

1. Ἐπεὶ καὶ ἄνθρωποι, ὅταν ἀσθενήσωσιν εἰς τὸ θεωρεῖν, σκιὰν θεωρίας καὶ λόγον τὴν πρᾶξιν ποιοῦνται (*Enneads* III. viii. 4).

2. We are perfectly aware of the fact that there existed other mysticisms in antiquity besides Neoplatonism, and Buddhism. But, for the object we have in view, we need only take those that advanced furthest.

3. M. Henri Delacroix, in a book which deserves to become a classic (*Études d'histoire et de psychologie du mysticisme*, Paris, 1908), has called attention to the essentially active element of the great mystics. Similar ideas will be found in the remarkable works of Evelyn Underhill (*Mysticism*, London, 1911; and *The Mystic Way*, London, 1913). The latter author connects certain of her views with those we expressed in *L'Evolution Créatrice*, and which we have taken up again, to carry them further, in the present chapter. See, in particular, on this point, *The Mystic Way*.

4. M. De Montmorand, *Psychologie des mystiques catholiques orthodoxes* (Paris, 1920), p. 17.

25

Four Kinds of Mystical Experience

W. H. AUDEN

I

. . . We are created animals gifted with intelligence, that is to say, we cannot be content merely to experience but must seek to make sense of it, to know what is its cause and significance, to find the truth behind brute fact. Though some individuals have greater intelligence and curiosity than others, the nature of intelligence is identical in every individual. It is impossible for something to be true for one mind and false for another. That is to say, if two of us disagree, either one of us is right or both of us are wrong.

In our relation to one another as intelligent beings, seeking a truth to which we shall both be compelled to assent, We is not the collective singular We of tradition, but a plural signifying a You-and-I united by a common love for the truth. In relation to each other we are protestants; in relation to the truth we are catholics. I must be prepared to doubt the truth of every statement you make, but I must have unquestioning faith in your intellectual integrity.

The basic stimulus to the intelligence is doubt, a feeling that the meaning of an experience is not self-evident. We never make a statement about what seems to us self-evidently the case. That is why the positive content of a proposition, what it asserts to be true, is never so clear as what it excludes as being false. Dogmatic theology, for example, came into being more to exclude heresy than to define orthodoxy, and one reason why theology must continue to be and grow is that the heresies of one age are never the same as the heresies of another. The Christian faith is always a scandal to the imagination and reason of the flesh, but the particular aspect which seems most scandalous depends upon the prevailing mentality of a period or a culture. Thus, to both the Gnostics of the fourth century and the liberal humanists of the eighteenth, the Cross was an offense, but for quite different reasons. The Gnostic said: "Christ was the Son of God, therefore He cannot have been physically crucified. The Crucifixion was an illusion." The liberal humanist said:

"Christ was physically crucified, therefore He cannot have been the Son of God. His claim was a delusion." In our own day, the stumbling block is again different. I think most Christians will find themselves in understanding sympathy with Simone Weil's difficulty: "If the Gospels omitted all mention of Christ's resurrection, faith would be easier for me. The Cross by itself suffices me."

Besides defending the Church against heresy, theology has another perennial task to perform, instructing the devout, both the institutional authorities and the mass of the laity, in the difference between the things of God and the things of Caesar. In addition to the absolute presuppositions which we consciously hold by faith as necessary to salvation, we all of us hold a large number of notions about what constitutes the beautiful in art, what is the just form of social structure, what the natural universe is like, etc., which we hold not by faith but by habit—they are what we are used to and we cannot imagine them otherwise. Along comes a new style of art, a social change, a scientific discovery, and our immediate reaction is to think that such changes are contrary to our faith. It is one of the tasks of the theologian to show that this is not the case, and that our fright is unnecessary. If this is not done, we shall presently find that we have changed either our faith or our God.

Whatever the field under discussion, those who engage in debate must not only believe in each other's good faith, but also in their capacity to arrive at the truth. Intellectual debate is only possible between those who are equal in learning and intelligence. Preferably they should have no audience, but if they do have one, it should be an audience of their peers. Otherwise, the desire for applause, the wish, not to arrive at the truth but to vanquish one's opponent, becomes irresistible.

* * *

In addition to being members of a species gifted with intelligence, each of us is created in the Image of God, that is to say, each is a unique person who can say *I*, with a unique perspective on the universe, the exact like of whom has never existed before nor will again. As persons, each of us has his biography, a story with a beginning, middle and end. As St. Augustine, following St. James, says: "Man was created in order that a beginning might be made." The dogma of the descent of all mankind from a single ancestor, Adam, is not, and should never have been imagined to be, a statement about man's biological evolution. It asserts that, insofar as he or she is a unique person, every man and woman, irrespective of race, nation, culture, and sex, *is* Adam, an incarnation of all mankind; that, as persons, we are called into being, not by any biological process but by other persons, God, our parents, our friends and enemies. And it is as persons, not as members of a species, that we become guilty of sin. When we speak of being "born in sin," of inheriting the original sin of Adam, this cannot mean, it seems to me—I speak as a fool—that sin is physically present in our flesh and our genes. Our flesh, surely, is not in itself sinful, but our every bodily movement, touch, gesture, tone of voice is that of a sinner. From the moment consciousness first wakes in a baby (and this may possibly be before birth) it finds itself in the company of sinners, and its consciousness is affected by a contagion against which there is no prophylaxis.

The personal I is by necessity protestant (again with a small p), for no one else can have my experience for me or be responsible for my history. This I, though, exists only in the present instant: my past memories are never of myself alone. Toward my immediate experience, what is required of me is neither faith nor doubt but a self-forgetful concentration of my attention upon the experience which is only mine in the sense that it has been given to me and not to someone else. The I is only truly itself when its attention to experience is so intense that it is unaware of its own existence. I must not ask whether the experience is like or unlike the experience of others, a hallucination or objectively real, expected or unexpected, pleasant or painful. All these questions are to be asked later, for the answers are bound to be erroneous if, through distraction of attention, I fail to experience fully. When I do ask them, I shall usually find, of course, that however novel the experience may have been to me, most people have had similar experiences, and that the explanation and significance have long been known. But, occasionally, there may have been some element in it which is really novel. In that case, though I must beware of exaggerating its importance simply because it happened to me, I must neither deny it nor hug it as private secret, but make it public though all the authorities on earth, administrative or intellectual, should laugh at me or threaten me with penalties. In any case, it is only through the sharing of personal experience, important or trivial, that our relation with others ceases to be that of one member of a social species to another and becomes that of one person to another. So, too, in my relation to God; it is personal experience which enables me to add to the catholic *We believe still* the protestant *I believe again.*

When von Hügel calls all that is not institutional or intellectual "mystical," he obviously includes under this division many experiences which are not, in a technical sense, mystical. He includes any firsthand religious experience. But mystical experiences, whether concerned with God or with his creatures, have, of all experiences, the most right to be called firsthand, as owing least to either tradition or impersonal ratiocination.

II

There seem to be four distinct kinds of mystical experience:

> The Vision of Dame Kind
> The Vision of Eros
> The Vision of Agape
> The Vision of God

Before considering the differences between them one should consider what they have in common which makes comparison possible.

1. The experience is always "given," that is to say, it cannot be induced by an effort of will. In the case of the Vision of Dame Kind, it can in some cases, it seems, be induced by chemical means, alcohol or the hallucinogenic drugs. (I have myself taken mescaline once and LSD once. Aside from a slight schizophrenic dissociation of the I from the Not-I including my body, nothing happened at all.) In the case of the Vision of God, it does not seem to be granted to anyone who has not undergone a long process of self-discipline and prayer, but self-discipline and prayer cannot of themselves compel it.

2. The experience seems to the subject not only more important than anything he experiences when in a "normal" state, but also a revelation of reality. When he returns to a normal state, he does not say: "That was a pleasant dream but, of course, an illusion. Now I am awake and see things as they really are"; he says: "For a moment a veil was lifted and I saw what really is. Now the veil has fallen again and reality is again hidden from me." His conclusion is similar to that of Don Quixote who in his bouts of madness sees windmills as giants, but when in his lucid intervals he sees them as windmills, says: "Those cursed magicians delude me, first drawing me into dangerous adventures by the appearance of things as they really are, and then presently changing the face of things as they please."

3. The experience is totally different from that of "seeing things" whether in dreams or waking visions. In the case of the first three kinds which are concerned with visible creatures, these are seen with extraordinary vividness and charged with extraordinary significance, but they are not physically distorted; square objects do not become round or blue ones red, nor does the subject see objects which are not there when the vision fades. Again one thinks of Don Quixote. He may see a windmill as a giant, but he doesn't see a giant unless there is a windmill there. In the case of the Vision of God, in which, whatever explanation one cares to make, what the subject encounters is not a visible creature; the mystics are unanimous in saying that they do not see anything in a physical

sense. Thus St. Teresa says that in her true visions and locutions "she never saw anything with her bodily eyes, nor heard anything with her bodily ears." Sometimes they do "see and hear" things, but they always recognize these as accidental and irrelevant to the real experience, and to be regarded with suspicion. When his followers came to St. Philip Neri to tell him about their delightful visions of the Blessed Virgin, he ordered them the next time they had such a vision to spit in her face, and it is said that, when they did so, a devil's face was at once revealed.

4. Though the experience is always given and surprising, its nature is never entirely independent of the subject. In the case of the Vision of Dame Kind, for example, it is commoner in childhood and adolescence than in maturity, and the actual content of the vision, the kind of creatures transformed and the hierarchy of importance among them seem to vary from person to person. To one color is the most significant, to another form, and so on. In the case of the Vision of God, the religious beliefs of the subject seem to play a part. Thus, when one compares the accounts given by Christian, Mohammedan, and Indian mystics, it is impossible to say with certainty whether they are accounts of different experiences or accounts of the same experience described in different theological languages, and, if the first, whether the differences are due to the mystic's beliefs. If a Hindu mystic, for example, were to become converted to Christianity, would his mystical experience show a change?

As an example of the difficulty of separating observation from interpretation of experience, let me take a trivial personal one. Many people have given accounts of what they experienced while having a tooth extracted under nitrous oxide, and these show close similarities. Thus William James says:

> The Keynote of it is invariably a reconciliation. It is as if the opposites of the world, whose contradictions and conflict make all our difficulties and troubles, were melted into unity.

My experience, like his, was of two opposites, love in the sense of agape, and hate, but in my case they did not melt into a unity. I felt an absolute conviction about two things: (a) that, ultimately the power of love was greater than the force of hate; (b) that, on the other hand, however great any human being might estimate the force of hate to be, he would always underestimate it. The actual quantity of hate in the universe was greater than any human imagination could conceive. Nevertheless, the power of love was still greater. Would I, I ask myself, have had precisely *this* experience if I had not been brought up in a Christian home and therefore been a person to whom the Christian notion of agape was a familiar one, and I find myself unable to say yes or no with any certainty.

5. From a Christian point of view, all four kinds of experience are, in

themselves, blessings and a good; there is nothing in any of them that is contrary to Christian doctrine. On the other hand, all of them are dangerous. So long as the subject recognizes them as totally unmerited blessings and feels obligated by gratitude to produce, insofar as it lies in his power, works which are good according to their kind, they can lead him toward the Light. But if he allows himself either to regard the experience as a sign of superior merit, natural or supernatural, or to idolize it as something he cannot live without, then it can only lead him into darkness and destruction.

III

The Vision of Dame Kind

The objects of this vision may be inorganic—mountains, rivers, seas—or organic—trees, flowers, beasts—but they are all non-human, though human artifacts like buildings may be included. Occasionally human figures are involved, but if so, they are invariably, I believe, strangers to the subject, people working in the fields, passersby, beggars, or the like, with whom he has no personal relation and of whom, therefore, no personal knowledge. The basic experience is an overwhelming conviction that the objects confronting him have a numinous significance and importance, that the existence of everything he is aware of is holy. And the basic emotion is one of innocent joy, though this joy can include, of course, a reverent dread. In a "normal" state, we value objects either for the immediate aesthetic pleasure they give to our senses—this flower has a pleasant color, this mountain a pleasing shape, but that flower, that mountain are ugly—or for the future satisfaction of our desires which they promise—this fruit will taste delicious, that one horrid. In the Vision of the Dame Kind, such distinctions, between the beautiful and the ugly, the serviceable and the unserviceable, vanish. So long as the vision lasts the self is "noughted," for its attention is completely absorbed in what it contemplates; it makes no judgments and desires nothing, except to continue in communion with what Gerard Manley Hopkins called the inscape of things:

> Each mortal thing does one thing and the same:
> Deals out that being indoors each one dwells;
> Selves—goes itself; *myself* it speaks and spells
> Crying *What I do is me: for that I came.*

In some cases, the subject speaks of this sense of communion as if he were himself *in* every object, and they in him. Thus Wordsworth in *The Ruined Cottage*:

> . . . sensation, soul and form
> All melted in him. They swallowed up
> His animal being; in them did he live
> And by them did he live.

In his book *Mysticism Sacred and Profane*, Professor Zaehner calls this the pan-en-henic vision, which he considers the definitive sign of the natural mystic; for him, an account which does not speak of this fusion of identities cannot be an account of a genuinely mystical experience. I think Professor Zaehner is mistaken. In their accounts of the Vision of God, Christian mystics sometimes seem almost to say that they *became* God, which they cannot, of course, have believed; they are trying to describe, presumably, a state in consciousness so filled with the presence of God that there is no vacant corner of it detachedly observing the experience. The natural mystic who speaks in pan-en-henic terms does not really mean that he becomes a tree or that a tree becomes him. No one, for example, was more convinced than Richard Jefferies, who does speak in these terms, that "there is nothing human in nature." He would certainly say that in the vision he feels capable of imaginatively entering into the life of a tree, but that no more means he becomes a tree than imaginatively entering into the life of another human being means that one ceases to be oneself and becomes him.

The joy felt by the natural mystic may be called innocent. While the vision lasts, the self and its desires are so completely forgotten that he is, in fact, incapable of sin. On the other hand, unlike the religious mystic, he is unaware of sin as a past fact and a future possibility, because his mystical encounter is with creatures who are not persons, and to which, therefore, the terms moral good and moral evil do not apply. For the same reason, Eros plays no conscious role. No accounts of the Vision of Dame Kind ever use, as accounts of the Vision of God often do, the experience of sexual union as an analogy.

The interpretations of the Vision of Dame Kind and even the language in which it is described vary, of course, according to the religious beliefs of the subject, but the experience itself seems to be independent of them, though not entirely independent, I think, of either the personality or the culture of the subject. In our own culture, in various degrees of intensity, many persons experience it in childhood and adolescence, but its occurrence among adults is rare. In so-called primitive cultures it may persist longer. Colonel Van Der Post's account of the African Bushmen suggests to me that among them it may persist uninterrupted throughout life. Even in our Western culture, its frequency is not evenly distributed. It is to be observed that nearly all the accounts have been written by members of the Northern peoples—the Mediterranean countries have contributed very little—which means that in fact, though the fact may be irrelevant, most of them have been written by persons with a Protestant upbringing. My own, very tentative, explanation for this is that in the Mediterranean countries the individual experience of Nature as sacred is absorbed and transformed into a social experience, expressed by the institutional cults, so common around the Mediterranean, of the local Madonna and the local saint. Whether it is possible completely to Christianize in spirit what is plainly polytheistic in form, I shall not presume to say. If I have my doubts, it is because of the enormous aesthetic pleasure such cults give me and my nostalgic regret when I am in countries which lack them.

Though the Vision of Dame Kind is not specifically Christian, there is nothing in it incompatible with the Christian belief in a God who created the material universe and all its creatures out of love and found them good: the glory in which the creatures appear to the natural mystic must be a feeble approximation to their glory as God sees them. There is nothing to prevent him from welcoming it as a gift, however indirect, from God. To a Gnostic for whom matter is the creation of an evil spirit, it must, of course, be a diabolic visitation, and to the monist who regards the phenomenal world as an illusion, it must be doubly an illusion, harmless, maybe, but to be seen through as soon as possible. To a philosophical materialist for whom the notion of glory has no meaning, it must be an individual delusion, probably neurotic in origin, and to be discouraged as abnormal and likely to lead the patient into the more serious and socially harmful delusion of some sort of theism. When such a staunch atheist as Richard Jefferies can speak of praying "that I might touch the unutterable existence even higher than deity," the danger of allowing people to take solitary country walks becomes obvious.

Believing Christians who have had the vision have always been explicit as to what it was *not*. Thus Wordsworth:

> He did not feel the God; he felt his works;
> Thought was not. In enjoyment it expired.
> Such hour by prayer or praise was unprofaned.
> He neither prayed, nor offered thanks or praise,
> His mind was a thanksgiving to the power
> That made him. It was blessedness and love.

And thus George Macdonald:

> I lived in everything; everything entered and lived in me. To be aware of a thing was to know its life at once and mine, to know whence it came and where we were at home—was to know that we are all what we are, because Another is what He is.

And they give thanks to God for it, not only for the joy that accompanies it, but also because it safeguards them, as even the Vision of God cannot, against a Gnostic undervaluation of the creaturely. Even in the Vision of God, the Christian must remember that, as Suso says:

> The being of the creatures in God is not that of a creature, but the creatureliness of every creature is nobler for it, and more useful, than the being it has in God. For what advantage has a stone or a man or any creature in its status as a creature, from the fact that it has been eternally in God?

To those who have never been Christians or, for one reason or another, have lost their faith, the very innocence of the experience can be an occasion of error. Since it involves neither the intellect nor the will, it is always possible for the intellect to misunderstand and the will to abuse it. The intellect can take the encounter with a numinous creature for an encounter with deity itself. Hence animism, polytheism, idols, magic and the so-called natural religions in which the non-human creation, including, of course, those physical and biological elements and forces which man shares with all other creatures, is the ultimate source of power and meaning and, therefore, responsible for man. Pantheism, as we find it in Goethe and Hardy, is really a sophisticated and sensitive form of humanism. Since man is, at present and so far as we know, the only creature in nature with consciousness, moral conscience, reason, will and purpose, a God (or Goddess) solely immanent in Nature must, unless He can create a new species, be at man's mercy; only man can tell Him what his will is or carry it out; one can pray to an idol, but it is difficult to see how one could *pray* to His Immanence, though one might revere Him.

The other temptation, more dangerous in a culture like ours than it was to the pagan world because in ours the experience is probably rarer and more temporary, is to idolize the experience itself as the summum bonum and spend one's life either gloomily regretting its loss and so falling into a state of accidie, or trying by artificial means, like alcohol and drugs, to recapture and prolong it. The hallucinogenic drugs are not, so far as we know, habit-forming, but no one has yet made a habit of taking them day after day for years. When this has been done, as it surely will be, I suspect that the law of diminishing returns will be found to apply to them as it applies to the more traditional artificial aids. If this should not turn out to be the case, if it should become possible for anyone to enjoy the Vision of Dame Kind whenever he wishes, the consequences might be even more serious. It is a characteristic of the world which this vision reveals that its only human inhabitant is the subject himself, and a continual indulgence in it could only lead to an increasing indifference toward the existence and needs of other human beings.

The vision of the splendor of creation, like all kinds, lays a duty upon one who has been fortunate enough to receive it, a duty in his turn to create works which are as worthy of what he has seen as his feeble capacities will permit. And many have listened and obeyed. It has been, I am quite certain, the initial cause of all genuine works of art and, I believe, of all genuine scientific inquiry and discovery, for it is the wonder which is, as Plato said, the beginning of every kind of philosophy.

IV

The Vision of Eros

Half the literature, highbrow and popular, produced in the West during the past four hundred years has been based on the false assumption that what is an exceptional experience is or ought to be a universal one. Under its influence so many millions of persons have persuaded themselves they were "in love" when their experience could be fully and accurately described by the more brutal four-letter words, that one is sometimes tempted to doubt if the experience is ever genuine, even when, or especially when, it seems to have happened to oneself. However, it is impossible to read some of the documents, *La Vita Nuova*, for example, many of Shakespeare's sonnets or the *Symposium* and dismiss them as fakes. All accounts of the experience agree on essentials. Like the Vision of Dame Kind, the Vision of Eros is a revelation of creaturely glory, but whereas in the former it is the glory of a multiplicity of non-human creatures which is revealed, in the latter it is the glory of a single human being. Again, while in the vision of Nature, conscious sexuality is never present, in the erotic vision it always is—it cannot be experienced by eunuchs (though it may occur before puberty) and no one ever fell in love with someone they found sexually unattractive—but physical desire is always, and without any effort of will, subordinate to the feeling of awe and reverence in the presence of a sacred being: however great his desire, the lover feels unworthy of the beloved's notice. It is impossible to take such accounts as a fancy poetization of any of the three kinds of unmystical erotic experiences with which we are all familiar. It is not simple lust, the detached recognition of another as a desirable sexual object, for in relation to anything one regards as an object one feels superior, and the lover feels inferior to the beloved. Nor is it sexual infatuation, the experience of *Venus toute entière à sa proie attachée*, in which desire has invaded and possessed the whole self until what it craves is not sexual satisfaction only but a total absorption of the other self, body and soul, into itself; in this condition the dominant feeling is not of unworthiness but of anguish, rage and despair at not being able to get what one craves. Nor, again, is it that healthy mixture of mutual physical desire and *philia*, a mutual personal liking based on common interests and values, which is the securest foundation for a happy marriage for, in this state, the dominant feeling is of mutual respect between equals.

Moreover, all the accounts agree that the Vision of Eros cannot long survive if the parties enter into an actual sexual relation. It was not merely the social conditions of an age in which marriages were arranged by the parents which made the Provençal poets declare that married couples could not be in love. This does not mean that one must under no circumstances marry the person whose glory has been revealed to one, but the risk in doing so is proportionate to the intensity of the vision. It is difficult to live day after day, year after year, with an ordinary human being, neither much better nor much worse than oneself, after one has seen her or him transfigured, without feeling that the fading of the vision is the other's fault.

*　　*　　*

The effect of the vision on the lover's conduct is not confined to his behavior toward his beloved. Even in his relations to others, conduct which before he fell in love seemed natural and proper, judged by his new standard of what he feels it should be to be worthy of her, now seems base and ignoble. Further, in most cases, the experience does not lead, as one might expect, to a sort of erotic quietism, a rapt contemplation of the beloved to the exclusion of others and the world. On the contrary, it usually releases a flood of psychic energy for actions which are not directly concerned with the beloved at all. When in love, the soldier fights more bravely, the thinker thinks more clearly, the carpenter fashions with greater skill.

The Church, whose institutional and intellectual concern in sexual matters is, and must be, primarily with marriage and the family, has always, very understandably, regarded the Vision of Eros with utmost suspicion. Either she has dismissed it as moonshine, or condemned it offhand, without trying first to understand it, as idolatry of the creature and a blasphemous parody of the Christian love of God. Knowing that marriage and the vision are not compatible, she has feared that it will be, as it very often is, used as an excuse for adultery. Condemnation without understanding, however, is seldom effective. If the lover idolizes the beloved, it is not what we ordinarily mean by idolization, in which the worshiper makes his idol responsible for his existence. . . .

The two most serious attempts to analyze the Vision of Eros and give it a theological significance are Plato's and Dante's. Both agree on three points: (a) the experience is a genuine revelation, not a delusion; (b) the erotic mode of the vision prefigures a kind of love in which the sexual element is transformed and transcended; (c) he who has once seen the glory of the Uncreated revealed indirectly in the glory of a creature can henceforth never be fully satisfied with anything less than a direct encounter with the former. About everything else they disagree radically. One of the most important differences between them is obscured by the inadequacy of our vocabulary. When I say, "X has a beautiful profile," and when I say, "Elizabeth has a beautiful face," or "the expression on Mary's face was beautiful," I have to use the same adjective, though I mean two totally different things. Beauty in the first statement is a given public quality of an object; I am talking about a quality the object *has,* not about what it *is.* If (but only if) a number of objects belong to the same class, I can compare them and arrange them in order according to the degree of beauty they possess, from the most beautiful to the least. That is why, even among human beings, it is possible to hold beauty contests to elect Miss America, and possible for an experienced sculptor to state in mathematical terms the proportions of the ideal male or female figure. Beauty in this sense is a gift of Nature or of Chance, and can be withdrawn. . . .

When I say, "Elizabeth has a beautiful face," I mean something quite different. I am still referring to something physical—I could not make the statement if I were blind—but this physical quality is not a gift from Nature, but a personal creation for which I hold Elizabeth to be responsible. The physical beauty seems to me a revelation of something immaterial, the person whom I cannot see. Beauty in this sense is unique in every case: I cannot compare Elizabeth and Mary and say which has the more beautiful face. The emotion aroused by it is personal love, and again, this is unique in every case. To the degree that I love both Elizabeth and Mary, I cannot say which I love more. Finally, to say that someone is beautiful in this sense is never simply a favorable aesthetic judgment; it is always a favorable moral judgment as well. I can say, "X has a beautiful profile but is a monster," I cannot say, "Elizabeth has a beautiful face but is a monster."

As creatures, human beings have a double nature. As members of a mammalian species which reproduces itself sexually, each of us is born either male or female and endowed with an impersonal need to mate with a member of the opposite sex; any member will do so long as he or she is not immature or senile. As unique persons we are capable of, but not compelled to, enter voluntarily into unique relations of love with other persons. The Vision of Eros is, therefore, double too. The beloved always possesses some degree of that beauty which is Nature's gift. A girl who weighs two hundred pounds and a woman of eighty may both have beautiful faces in the personal sense, but men do not fall in love with them. The lover is, of course, aware of this, but what seems to him infinitely more important is his awareness of the beloved as a person. Or so, at least, Dante says. What is so puzzling about Plato's description is that he seems unaware of what we mean by a person. By beauty, he always seems to mean impersonal beauty and by love impersonal admiration.

*　　*　　*

How different, and much more comprehensible, is Dante's account. He sees Beatrice, and a voice says, "Now you have seen your beatitude." Dante certainly thinks that Beatrice is beautiful in the public sense that any stranger would call her beautiful, but it would never enter his head to ask if she were more or less beautiful than other Florentine girls of her age. She is Beatrice and that is that. And what is the essential thing about her is that she is, he is absolutely certain, a "graced" person, so that after her death, he is convinced, as a believing Christian, that her soul is among the redeemed in Paradise, not among the lost in Hell. He does not tell us exactly what the sins and errors were which has brought him near to perdition nor, when they meet again, does Beatrice, but both speak of them as acts of infidelity to her, that is to say, if he had remained faithful to his vision of one human creature, Beatrice, he would not have committed offenses against their common Creator. Though unfaithful to her image, he has, however, never completely forgotten it (the Platonic ladder makes the forgetting of an image on a lower rung a moral duty), and it is this memory, the fact that he has never completely ceased to love her, which makes it possible for Beatrice to intervene from Heaven to save his soul. When, at last, they meet again in the earthly paradise, he reexperiences, though infinitely more intensely, the vision he had when they first met on earth, and she remains with him until the very last moment when he turns toward "the eternal fountain" and, even then, he knows that her eyes are turned in the same direction. The Vision of Eros is not, according to Dante, the first rung of a long ladder: there is only one step to take, from the personal creature who can love and be loved to the personal Creator who is Love. And in this final vision, Eros is transfigured but not annihilated. On earth we rank "love" higher than either sexual desire or sexless friendship because it involves the whole of our being, not like them, only a part of it. Whatever else is asserted by the doctrine of the resurrection of the body, it asserts the sacred importance of the body. As Silesius says, we have one advantage over the angels: only we can each become the bride of God. And

Juliana of Norwich: "In the self-same point that our Soul is made sensual, in the self-same point is the City of God ordained to him from without beginning."

v

The Vision of Agape

The classic Christian example of this is, of course, the vision of Pentecost, but there are modes of it which are not overtly Christian. Since I cannot find a specific description among these selections, I shall quote from an unpublished account for the authenticity of which I can vouch.

One fine summer night in June 1933 I was sitting on a lawn after dinner with three colleagues, two women and one man. We like each other well enough but we were certainly not intimate friends, nor had any one of us a sexual interest in another. Incidentally, we had not drunk any alcohol. We were talking casually about everyday matters when, quite suddenly and unexpectedly something happened. I felt myself invaded by a power which, though I consented to it, was irresistible and certainly not mine. For the first time in my life I knew exactly—because, thanks to the power, I was doing it—what it means to love one's neighbor as oneself. I was also certain, though the conversation continued to be perfectly ordinary, that my three colleagues were having the same experience. (In the case of one of them, I was able later to confirm this.) My personal feelings toward them were unchanged—they were still colleagues, not intimate friends—but I felt their existence as themselves to be of infinite value and rejoiced in it. I recalled with shame the many occasions on which I had been spiteful, snobbish, selfish, but the immediate joy was greater than the shame, for I knew that, so long as I was possessed by this spirit, it would be literally impossible for me deliberately to injure another human being. I also knew that the power would, of course, be withdrawn sooner or later and that, when it did, my greeds and self-regard would return. The experience lasted at its full intensity for about two hours when we said good-night to each other and went to bed. When I awoke the next morning, it was still present, though weaker, and it did not vanish completely for two days or so. The memory of the experience has not prevented me from making use of others, grossly and often, but it has made it much more difficult for me to deceive myself about what I am up to when I do. And among the various factors which several years later brought me back to the Christian faith in which I had been brought up, the memory of this experience and asking myself what it could mean was one of the most crucial, though, at the time it occurred, I thought I had done with Christianity for good.

Compared with the other kinds of vision, the Vision of Agape has several peculiarities. In the Vision of Dame Kind, there is one human person, the subject, and a multiplicity of creatures whose way of existence is different from his. The relation between him and them is therefore one-sided; though they are transfigured for him, he does not imagine that he is transfigured for them. In the Vision of Eros two human persons are involved, but the relation between them is unequal; the lover feels unworthy of the beloved. If it should so happen that both experience the vision simultaneously in regard to each other, both will still feel unworthy. In the Vision of God, two persons are again involved, the soul and God, and the relation of creature to Creator is utterly unequal, but it is a mutual one; the soul is conscious of loving God and being loved by Him in return. Like the Vision of Dame Kind, the Vision of Agape is multiple, but it is a multiplicity of persons; like the Vision of Eros, it involves human persons only; like the Vision of God it is of a mutual relation; but unlike any of the others, this relation is a relation between equals.

Not the least puzzling thing about it is that most of the experiences which are closest to it in mode, involving plurality, equality and mutuality of human persons, are clear cases of diabolic possession, as when thousands cheer hysterically for the Man-God, or cry bloodthirstily for the crucifixion of the God-Man. Still, without it, there might be no Church.

VI

The Vision of God

No one could be less qualified than I to discuss what the bulk of these selections are concerned with, the direct encounter of a human soul with God. In the first place because I lead an ordinary sensual worldly life, so that I can scarcely be surprised if I have never seen the God whom no man has seen at any time, a vision which is reserved, the Gospels tell us, for the pure in heart. In the second place, because I am an Anglican. Of all the Christian Churches, not excluding the Roman Catholic, the Anglican Church has laid the most stress upon the institutional aspect of religion. Uniformity of rite has always seemed to her more important than uniformity of doctrine, and the private devotions of her members have been left to their own discretion without much instruction or encouragement from her. Her intellectual temper is summed up in a remark by one of her bishops, "Orthodoxy is reticence," and the frigid

welcome she offers to any kind of religious "enthusiasm" in a sentence of
C. D. Broad's: "A healthy appetite for righteousness, kept in due control by good manners, is an excellent thing; but to 'hunger and thirst'
after it is often merely a symptom of spiritual diabetes."

*   *   *

In every sphere of life, when we read or listen to accounts of experiences which are completely strange to us, we tend either to be bored or,
if they make us envious, to try and explain them away, and in reading
the Christian mystics, Catholic or Protestant, I have, as a worldly man,
to be constantly on my guard about this tendency. Then, as an Anglican
with an Anglican's prejudices, I must not pretend that I do not have
them, but I must pray that the evidence these writers present will refute
them.

The first thing which disturbs me is the number of mystics who have
suffered from ill-health and various kinds of psychophysical disturbances.
I am aware, of course, that many, perhaps the majority, of those whose
achievements in this world, in art, in science, in politics, have earned
them the right to be called great men, have suffered from physical and
psychological abnormalities, and that to dismiss their achievements on
that account as "sick" is the cheapest kind of philistine envy. I cannot
help feeling, however, that there is a fundamental difference between a
great man and a mystic. In the case of the latter, what matters, surely, is
not what he or she outwardly "achieves"—the vision of God cannot be a
"work" like a poem—but what they are. The vision is only granted to
those who are far advanced in the practice of the Imitation of Christ. In
the Gospels, there is no suggestion that, in his human nature, Christ was
anything but physically and psychologically normal, no reports of any
mental crisis such as we read of in the life of Mahomet. Even more im-
portantly, since the God-Man is a unique case, the twelve Apostles
whom he chose seem to have been equally healthy. The mystics themselves do not seem to have believed their physical and mental sufferings
to be a sign of grace, but it is unfortunate that it is precisely physical
manifestations which appeal most to the religiosity of the mob. A woman
might spend twenty years nursing lepers without having any notice
taken of her, but let her once exhibit the stigmata or live for long periods
on nothing but the Host and water, and in no time the crowd will be
clamoring for her beatification.

Then I am a little disturbed by the sometimes startling resemblances
between the accounts of their experiences given by mystics and those
given by persons suffering from a manic-depressive psychosis. The
differences between them are, of course, obvious too. The inflated egoism
of the manic-depressive is always conspicuous, whether, in his elated

phase, he thinks that, unlike other folks, he is God, or, in his depressed phase, he thinks that, unlike other folks, he has committed the Sin against the Holy Ghost. The genuine mystics, on the other hand, always interpret their ecstasy as a gratuitous blessing from God which they have done nothing to deserve and their dark night of the soul not as evidence of their extraordinary wickedness, but as a period of trial and purgation. Thus speaking of the two phases, the Arab mystic Qushayri says:

> There are cases of contradiction the cause of which is not easily ascertainable by the subject . . . the only remedy for this condition is complete submission to the will of God until the mood passes. . . . Expansion, on the other hand, comes suddenly and strikes the subject unexpectedly, so that he can find no reason for it. It makes him quiver with joy, yet scares him. The way to deal with it is to keep quiet and observe conventional good manners.

A similarity, however, remains. This suggests to me two possibilities. Is it not possible that those who fall into a manic-depressive psychosis are persons with a vocation for the Via Negativa which they are either unaware of or have rejected? In the late Middle Ages there were, no doubt, many persons in monasteries and convents who had no business there and should have been out in the world earning an honest living, but today it may well be that there are many persons trying to earn a living in the world and driven by failure into mental homes whose true home would be the cloister. Secondly, though no one in this life can experience the Vision of God without having, through a life of prayer and self-mortification, reached a high level of spiritual life, is it not possible that certain psychophysical human types are more likely to have such experiences than others who have reached the same level? Whether this is so or not, both the ecclesiastical authorities and the mystics themselves have always insisted that mystical experience is not necessary to salvation or in itself a proof of sanctity. St. John of the Cross, for instance, says:

> All visions, revelations, heavenly feelings, and whatever is greater than these, are not worth the least act of humility, being the fruits of that charity which neither values nor seeks itself, which thinketh well, not of self, but of others. . . . many souls, to whom visions have never come, are incomparably more advanced in the way of perfection than others to whom many have been given.

Certainly, in reading accounts of the early life of those who have chosen the Via Negativa, whether or not their choice was later rewarded by visions, how often one comes across the same kind of character, a man or woman who seems, both by talent and temperament, born to command, to wield power either in the temporal or the spiritual sphere, a person, that is, for whom the Third Temptation of Christ can be, as it cannot for most of us, a real temptation. (If Satan were to promise me all the kingdoms of the earth on condition that I bowed down and worshiped him, I should laugh because I should know that, given my limited capacities, he could not fulfill his promise.) Their rejection of what one would have thought to be their natural destiny may have been occasioned by an awareness that, in their case, their gift for power and domination, if exercised, could only bring disaster to others and themselves. As Goethe, who certainly felt no natural sympathy for the Via Negativa, observed about St. Philip Neri:

> Only superior and essentially proud men are capable of choosing on principle to taste the enmity of a world which is always opposed to the good and the great, and empty the bitter cup of experience before it is offered to them.

In this selection of writings by Protestants, practicing or lapsed, I can find little which a Catholic reader will consider alien to his experience or contrary to faith and morals. (He may find Swedenborg rather hard to swallow but so, as a Protestant, do I.) Many of them are concerned with visions of nature, at which level theological doctrine is irrelevant, though it is relevant to any interpretation of their significance. Among those directly concerned with man's relation to God, more attention is paid, as one would expect, to the Pauline conversion experience than one would find in a similar collection written by Catholics, for it is this experience upon which most of the Protestant churches have based their claims. There are two kinds of conversion, the conversion from one faith—it may be atheism—to another, and the transformation of an unthinking traditional faith into a personal conviction. Here we are only concerned with the second. It would be nonsense to say either that this experience does not occur among Catholics or that the Catholic Church, institutionally and theologically, does not pray that it shall occur and welcome it when it does: she certainly does not desire, and never has, that her children should go through their lives attending Mass and going to confession as she prescribes without this ever becoming more than a ritual routine in which they experience nothing for themselves. But she has been, perhaps, overly aware, as the Protestant churches have certainly been insufficiently aware, of the spiritual danger implicit in all firsthand experience, the temptation to imagine one is a special person to whom the common rules do not apply, the temptation intellectually to suppose that since an experience is new to oneself, it is new to the human race, the thinkers of the past cannot possibly throw light on it, and one must construct a new philosophy of one's own.

But, at least during her post-tridentine phase, now happily over, the Catholic Church seemed more or less to take the view that the proper place for her protestants, those who claimed firsthand experience, was the priesthood or the cloister where she could keep a sharp eye on them, and that no more could be asked of the laity than obedience to her rules. The Protestant churches, on the other hand, probably asked more of the average layman than is, humanly speaking, possible. Kierkegaard, himself a Protestant, put the difference neatly:

> Catholicism has the universal premise that we men are pretty well rascals. . . . The Protestant principle is related to a particular premise: a man who sits in the anguish of death, in fear and trembling and much tribulation—and of those there are not many in any one generation.

Aside from this difference in emphasis, the main difference seems to be one of vocabulary. The language of the Catholic mystics shows an acquaintance with a whole tradition of mystical literature, that of the Protestant is derived almost entirely from the Bible. The former, living in monastic orders and, usually, under the spiritual direction of a confessor, have at their disposal a highly developed technical theological language, which the latter, except for the Calvinists, have lacked. Consequently one might say that the Catholic writes like a professional, the Protestant like an amateur.

The virtue of the amateur is freshness and honesty, his defect a clumsiness in expression; the difficulty for a professional is that he may be unaware that the traditional language he has inherited is falsifying what he means to say. One sometimes comes across passages written by Catholic mystics which, taken out of the context of their whole writings and their lives, seem to be not Christian but monist or manichaean, and I think the reason for this is probably the influence on the Catholic vocabulary of certain writers, in particular Plotinus and Pseudo-Dionysius, who were not Christians but Neoplatonists.

VII

Even among the most ignorant, there can be very few Protestants today who still think that Rome is the Scarlet Woman, or Catholics who think, like the officer Goethe met in Italy, that Protestants are allowed to marry their sisters. And among the more thoughtful, there can be few, no matter what church they belong to, who do not regard the series of events in the sixteenth and seventeenth centuries whereby the Western Church became divided into Catholics and Protestants with capital letters, hating and despising each other, as a spiritual tragedy for which all parties concerned must bear some of the blame. Looking back, there seems no *ra-*

tional reason why the habits of reading the Bible and family prayers from which Protestants have obviously derived so much strength and refreshment could not have been added to the sacramental habits from which Catholics have, as obviously, derived so much, instead of both parties regarding them as incompatible. There seems no *rational* reason why a return to St. Paul and St. Augustine could not have rescued theology from its sterile debate between Realism and Nominalism without leading to Calvinism and, as a defense reaction, to the adoption by Rome, understandably but still, to my mind, mistakenly, of Thomism as the official Catholic philosophy. But history, of course, is not rational nor repeatable. (For me the most mysterious aspect of the whole affair is not theological or political but cultural. Why was it that the peoples and nations who became Protestant were precisely those who, before Christ was born, had been least influenced by the culture of *pagan* Rome?)

That Protestant and Catholic no longer regard each other as monsters is a reason for thanking God, but also a reason to be ashamed of ourselves that we, as Christians, have contributed so little to this more charitable atmosphere. If we have learned that it is wicked to inflict secular penalties on heresy, to keep people in the faith by terror, we have learned it from skeptical rationalists who felt, like Earl Halifax, that "Most men's anger about religion is as if two men should quarrel for a lady they neither of them care for." Even after the burnings stopped, the religious minority, Catholic or Protestant, still continued to suffer sufficient civil disabilities to ensure that to a great extent religious boundaries would coincide with state boundaries and prevent the average Protestant and Catholic from ever meeting. Defoe says that in the England of his time "there were a hundred thousand fellows ready to fight to the death against popery, without knowing whether popery was a man or a horse," and the situation in Catholic countries can have been no better. Again, the campaign to make the secular authorities grant equal rights to all citizens, irrespective of their religious beliefs, was certainly not headed by Christians. Even when equality in law had been granted, class barriers remained which have only begun to disappear in my own lifetime. Among the English middle classes, thanks to the existence of old Catholic families whose social status was unimpeachable, it might be eccentric or immoral to be a Catholic, but it was not "infra dig" like being a Dissenter. When I was young, for an Anglican to "go over to Rome" was rather like having an illegitimate baby, an unfortunate event but something which can happen in the best families. But for an Anglican to become a Baptist would have been unthinkable: Baptists were persons who came to the back door, not the front. Once again, the part played by Christians in fighting against social injustice and snobbery has not been a conspicuous one. Lastly, whether we desire it or not, we are being brought closer together by simple physical fear. There are large areas of the globe where it is now a serious worldly disadvantage, and sometimes dangerous, to be a Christian of any kind, and these areas may very well increase.

When all fleshly and worldly circumstances favor a greater mutual understanding, any failure of charity on our part becomes all the more inexcusable. As I write, it is but a few days to Pentecost, the Ecumenical Feast, in what the Pope has proclaimed an Ecumenical Year. As a preliminary we might start by thanking each other, and the modern secular culture against which we both inveigh, for the competition. It is good for Protestant minister and Catholic priest to know that there is a church of another persuasion round the corner and a movie-house across the way from them both, to know that they cannot hold their flocks simply because there is no other place of worship to attend, or because not attending some place of worship will incur social disapproval. I have often observed how much more vital, liturgically, both Catholic and Protestant services become in countries with religiously mixed populations than in countries which are overwhelmingly one or the other. Then, after this exchange of compliments, we might reread together the second chapter of Acts. The miracle wrought by the Holy Spirit is generally referred to as a gift of tongues: is it not equally a gift of ears? It is just as miraculous that those in the parts of Libya about Cyrene and strangers from Rome should be able to listen to Galileans, as that Galileans should be able to speak to them. The Curse of Babel is not the diversity of human tongues —diversity is essential to life—but the pride of each of us which makes us think that those who make different verbal noises from our own are incapable of human speech so that discourse with them is out of the question, a pride which, since the speech of no two persons is identical—language is not algebra—must inevitably lead to the conclusion that the gift of human speech is reserved for oneself alone. It is due to this curse that, as Sir William Osler said, "Half of us are blind, few of us feel, and we are all deaf." That we may learn first how to listen and then how to translate are the two gifts of which we stand most urgently in need and for which we should most fervently pray at this time.

26

The Mystic as Creative Artist

EVELYN UNDERHILL

Hostile criticism of the mystics almost invariably includes the charge that their great experiences are in the nature of merely personal satisfactions. It is said that they stand apart from the ruck of humanity, claiming a special knowledge of the supersensual, a special privilege of communion with it; yet do not pass on to others, in any real and genuine sense, the illumination, the intuition of Reality, which they declare that they have received. St. Bernard's favorite mistranslation from Isaiah, "My secret to myself," has again and again been used against them with damaging effect; linked sometimes with the notorious phrase in which Plotinus defined the soul's fruition of Eternity as "a flight of the alone to the Alone."

It is true that these hints concerning a solitary and ineffable encounter do tally with one side of the experience of the mystic; do describe one aspect of his richly various, many-angled spiritual universe, one way in which that divine union which is his high objective is apprehended by the surface-consciousness. But that which is here told, is only half the truth. There is another side, a "completing opposite," to this admittedly indescribable union of hearts; a side which is often—and most ungraciously—forgotten by those who have received its benefits. The great mystic's loneliness is a consecrated loneliness. When he ascends to that encounter with Divine Reality which is his peculiar privilege, he is not a spiritual individualist. He goes as the ambassador of the race. His spirit is not, so to speak, a "spark flying upwards" from this world into that world, flung out from the mass of humanity, cut off; a little, separate, brilliant thing. It is more like a feeler, a tentacle, which life as a whole stretches out into that supersensual world which envelops her. Life stretches that tentacle out, but she also draws it in again with the food that it has gathered, the news that it has to tell of the regions which its delicate tactile sense has enabled it to explore. This, it seems to me, is the function of the mystic consciousness in respect of the human race. For this purpose it is specialized. It receives, in order that it may give. As the prophet looks at the landscape of Eternity, the mystic finds and feels it: and both know that there is laid on them the obligation of exhibiting it if they can.

If this be so, then it becomes clear that the mystic's personal encounter with Infinite Reality represents only one of the two movements which constitute his completed life. He must turn back to pass on the revelation he has received: must mediate between the transcendent and his fellow men. He is, in fact, called to be a creative artist of the highest kind; and only when he is such an artist, does he fulfill his duty to the race.

It is coming to be realized more and more clearly that it is the business of the artist not only to delight us, but to enlighten us: in Blake's words, to "Cleanse the doors of perception, so that everything may appear as it is—infinite." Artists mediate between the truth and beauty which they know, and those who cannot without their help discern it. It is the function of art, says Hegel, to deliver to the domain of feeling and delight of vision all that the mind may possess of essential and transcendent Being. In this respect it ranks with religion and philosophy as "one of the three spheres of Absolute Spirit." Bergson, again, declares that it is the peculiar business of art to brush aside everything that veils reality from us, in order to bring us face to face with the real, the true. The artist is the man who sees things in their native purity.

"Could reality," he observes in a celebrated passage, "come into direct contact with sense and consciousness, could we enter into immediate communion with things and with ourselves—then, we should all be artists. . . . Deep in our souls we should hear the uninterrupted melody of our inner life: a music often gay, more often sad, always original. All this is around and within us: yet none of it is distinctly perceived by us. Between nature and ourselves—more, between ourselves and our own consciousness—hangs a veil: a veil dense and opaque for normal men, but thin, almost transparent, for the artist and poet." He might have added, for the mystic too.

This veil, he says again, is woven of self-interest: we perceive things, not as they are, but as they affect ourselves. The artist, on the contrary, sees them for their own sakes, with the eyes of disinterested love. So, when the mystics declare to us that the first conditions of spiritual illumination are self-simplification, humility and detachment, they are demanding just those qualities which control the artist's power of seeing things in their beauty and truth. The true mystic sees Reality in its infinite aspect; and tries, as other artists, to reveal it within the finite world. He not only ascends, but descends the ladder of contemplation; having heard "the uninterrupted music of the inner life," he tries to weave it into melodies that other men can understand.

Bergson's contemporary, Eucken, claims—and I think in one of his most striking doctrines—that man is gradually but actually bringing into existence a spiritual world. This spiritual world springs up from within through humanity—that is, through man's own consciousness—yet at the same time humanity is, as it were, growing up into it; finding it as an independent reality, waiting to be apprehended, waiting to be incorporated into our universe. In respect of man's normal universe, this spiritual world is both immanent and transcendent: "Absent only from those unable to perceive it," as Plotinus said of the *Nous*. We are reminded of the Voice which said to St. Augustine, "I am the Food of the Full-grown."

This paradox of a wholly new order of experience thrusting itself up through the race which it yet transcends, is a permanent feature in the teachings of the higher religions and philosophies, and is closely connected with the phenomena of inspiration and of artistic creation. The artist, the prophet, the metaphysician, each builds up from material beyond the grasp of other souls, a world within which those other souls can live and dream: a world, moreover, which exhibits in new proportions and endows with new meanings the common world of daily life. When we ask what organ of the race—the whole body of humanity—it is, by and through which this supernal world thus receives expression, it becomes clear that this organ is the corporate spiritual consciousness, emerging in those whom we call, preeminently, mystics and seers. It is, actually and literally, through them that this new world is emerging and being built up; as it is through other forms of enhanced and clarified consciousness, in painters, musicians, philosophers, and the adepts of physical science, that other aspects of the universe are made known to men. In all of these, and in the mystic too, the twin powers of a steadfast, selective attention and of creative imagination are at work. Because of their wide, deep, attention to life they receive more news from the external world than others do; because of the creative cast of their minds, they are able to weave up the crude received material into a living whole, into an idea or image which can be communicated to other men. Ultimately, we owe to the mystics all the symbols, ideas and images of which our spiritual world, as it is thought of by the bulk of men, is constructed. We take its topography from them, at secondhand; and often forget the sublime adventures immortalized in those phrases which we take so lightly on our lips—the Divine Dark, the Beatific Vision, the Eternal Beauty, Ecstasy, Union, Spiritual Marriage, and the rest. The mystics have actually created, from that language which we have evolved to describe and deal with the time-world, another artistic world; a self-consistent and spiritually expressive world of imaginative concepts, like the world of music or the world of color and form. They are always trying to give us the key to it, to induct us into its mysterious delights. It is by means of this world, and the symbols which furnish it, that human consciousness is enabled to actualize its most elusive experiences; and hence it is wholly due to the unselfish labors of those mystics who have struggled to body forth the realities by which they were possessed, that we are able, to some extent, to enter into the special experiences of the mystical saints; and that they are able to snatch us up to a brief sharing of their vision, to make us live for a moment "Eternal Life in the midst of Time."

How, then, have they done this? What is the general method by which any man communicates the result of his personal contacts with the universe to other minds? Roughly speaking, he has two ways of doing this, by description and by suggestion; and his best successes are those in which these two methods are combined. His descriptions are addressed to the intellect, his suggestions are appeals to the imagination, of those with whom he is trying to communicate. The necessities which control these two ways of telling the news—oblique suggestion and symbolic image—practically govern the whole of mystical literature. The span of this literature is wide. It goes from the utterly formless, yet infinitely suggestive, language of certain great contemplatives, to the crisply formal pictorial descriptions of those whose own revelations of Reality crystallize into visions, voices, or other psychosensorial experiences. At one end of the scale is the vivid, prismatic imagery of the Christian apocalypse, at the other the fluid, ecstatic poetry of some of the Sūfī saints.

In his suggestive and allusive language the mystical artist often approaches the methods of music. When he does this, his statements do not give information. They operate a kind of enchantment which dilates the consciousness of the hearer to a point at which it is able to apprehend new aspects of the world. In his descriptive passages, on the other hand, he generally proceeds, as do nearly all our descriptive efforts, by way of comparison. Yet often these comparisons, like those employed by the great poet, are more valuable for their strange suggestive quality than for any exact parallels which they set up between the mystic's universe and our own. Thus, when Clement of Alexandria compares the Logos to a "New Song," when Suso calls the Eternal Wisdom a "sweet and beautiful wild flower," when Dionysius the Areopagite speaks of the Divine Dark which *is* the Inaccessible Light, or Ruysbroeck of "the unwalled world," we recognize a sudden flash of the creative imagination; evoking for us a truth far greater, deeper and more fruitful than the merely external parallel which it suggests. So too with many common metaphors of the mystics: the Fire of Love, the Game of Love, the Desert of God, the Marriage of the Soul. Such phrases succeed because of their interior and imaginative appeal.

We have numerous examples of this kind of artistic language—the highly charged imaginative phrase—in the Bible; especially in the prophetic books, and the Apocalypse.

> Ho, every one that thirsteth, come ye to the waters.
> I will give thee treasures of darkness and hidden riches
>   of secret places.
> The Lord shall be a diadem of beauty.
> He showed me a pure river of the water of life.
> I heard a voice from heaven, as the voice of many waters.
> I saw a new heaven and a new earth.

Whereas the original prophetic significance of these phrases is now meaningless for us, their suggestive quality—their appeal to the mystic consciousness—retains its full force. They are artistic creations; and have the enormous evocative power proper to all great art. Later mystics use such passages again and again, reading their own experiences into these traditional forms. The classic example of this close alliance between poetic readings of life and practical mysticism is of course the mystical interpretation of the Song of Songs, which appears in Christian mysticism at least as early as the fourth century. But there are many other instances. Thus St. Macarius finds in Ezekiel's vision of the Cherubim a profoundly suggestive image of the state of the deified soul, "all eyes and all wings," driven upon its course by the Heavenly Charioteer of the Spirit. Thus in "The Mirror of Simple Souls," another of Ezekiel's visions —that of the "great eagle, with great wings, long wings, full of feathers, which took the highest branch of the cedar"—becomes the vivid symbol of the contemplative mind, "the eagle that flies high, so right high and yet more high than does any other bird, for she is feathered with fine love, and beholds above other the beauty of the sun."

When we pass to the mystical poets, we find that nearly all their best effects are due to their extraordinary genius for this kind of indirect, suggestive imagery. This is the method by which they proceed when they wish to communicate their vision of reality. Their works are full of magical phrases which baffle analysis, yet, as one of them has said:

> Lighten the wave-washed caverns of the mind
> With a pale, starry grace.

Many of these phrases are of course familiar to everyone. Vaughan's

> I saw Eternity the other night
> Like a great ring of pure and endless light.

Blake's

> To see the world in a grain of sand,
>   And a heaven in a wild flower;
> Hold infinity in the palm of your hand,
>   And eternity in an hour.

Whitman's

> Light rare, untellable, lighting the very light.

Thompson's

> Ever and anon a trumpet sounds
> From the hid battlements of Eternity.

These are artistic, sidelong representations of the mystic's direct apprehension of the Infinite on, so to speak, its cosmic and impersonal side. Others reflect the personal and intimate contact with the Divine Life which forms the opposite side of his complete experience. Thus Francis Thompson:

> With his aureole
> The tresses of my soul
> Are blent
> In wished content.

So, too, St. John of the Cross:

> All things I then forgot,
>   My cheek on him who for my coming came;
> All ceased, and I was not,
>   Leaving my cares and shame
>   Among the lilies, and forgetting them.

Best of all, perhaps, Jalāluddin Rūmi:

> In a place beyond uttermost place, in a tract without shadow of trace,
>   Soul and body transcending I live, in the soul of my loved one anew.

Sometimes the two aspects, personal and impersonal, are woven together by the poet: and then it is that we come nearest to an understanding of the full experience he is trying to express. A remarkable example of this occurs in Gerard Hopkins, perhaps the greatest mystical poet of the Victorian era:

> Thou mastering me
> God! giver of breath and bread;
> World's strand, sway of the sea;
> Lord of living and dead;

Thou hast bound bones and veins in me, fastened me flesh,
And after it almost unmade, what with dread,
　　Thy doing: and dost thou touch me afresh?
Over again I feel thy finger and find thee.

❋　　❋　　❋

　　I kiss my hand
　　To the stars, lovely-asunder
　Starlight, wafting him out of it; and
　　Glow, glory in thunder;
Kiss my hand to the dappled-with-damson west;
Since, tho' he is under the world's splendor and wonder,
　　His mystery must be instressed, stressed;
For I greet him the days I meet him, and bless when I understand.

So much for the poets. In the prose writings of the mystics we find again the same characters, the same high imaginative qualities, the same passionate effort to give the ineffable some kind of artistic form. This effort includes in its span a wide range of literary artifices; some endeavoring to recapture and represent in concrete symbols the objective reality known; some, like one dominant art movement of the present day, trying to communicate it obliquely, by a representation of the subjective feeling-state induced in the mystic's own consciousness. At one end of the scale, therefore, we have the so-called negative language of mysticism, which describes the supersensuous in paradox by refusing to describe it at all; by declaring that the entry of the soul upon spiritual experience is an entry into a Cloud of Unknowing, a nothing, a Divine Darkness, a fathomless abyss. The curious thing is that though here, if anywhere, the mystic seems to keep his secret to himself, as a matter of fact it is just this sort of language which has been proved to possess the highest evocative power. For many types of mind, this really does fling magic casements wide; does give us a momentary glimpse of the perilous seas. I am inclined to think that, many and beautiful as are the symbolic and pictorial creations of mystical genius, it is here that this genius works most freely, produces its most magnificent results. When Ruysbroeck speaks of the boundless abyss of pure simplicity, that "dim silence where all lovers lose themselves"; when he assures us that, "stripped of its very life," the soul is destined to "sail the wild billows of that Sea Divine," surely he effects a true change in our universe. So, too, the wonderful series of formless visions—though "vision" is a poor word for intuitive experience of this sort—experienced by Angela of Foligno, far exceed in their suggestive power her vividly pictured conversations with Christ, when she declares that she beheld "those eyes and that face so gracious and so pleasing."

"I beheld," she says of her ultimate experience of the Absolute, "a Thing, as fixed and stable as it was indescribable; and more than this I cannot say, save what I have often said already, namely, that it was all good. And though my soul beheld not love, yet when it saw that ineffable Thing it was itself filled with unutterable joy, and it was taken out of the state it was in, and placed in this great and ineffable state. . . . But if thou seekest to know that which I beheld, I can tell thee nothing, save that I beheld a Fullness and a Clearness, and felt them within me so abundantly that I cannot describe it, nor give any image thereof: for what I beheld was not bodily, but as though it were in heaven. Thus I beheld a beauty so great that I can say nothing of it save that I saw the Supreme Beauty, which contains in itself all goodness."

In the end, all that Angela has said here is, "Come and see!" but in saying this, she tells us far more than many do who go about to measure the City of Contemplation. Here words suggest, they do not tell; entice, but do not describe. Reminding us of the solemn declaration of Thomas à Kempis, that "there is a distance incomparable between those things that imperfect men think, and those that men illumined by high revelation behold," they yet extend to other minds a musical invitation to intercourse with new orders of reality.

This sort of language, this form of paradoxical, suggestive, allusive art is a permanent feature in mystical literature. It is usually supposed to be derived through Dionysius the Areopagite from the Platonists, but is really far older than this. As it comes down the centuries, it develops in depth and richness. Each successive mystic takes up the imagery of negation where the last one leaves it—takes it, because he recognizes that it describes a country where he too has been—and adds to it the products of his own most secret and august experiences. As in the torch-race of the antique world, the illuminating symbol, once lit, is snatched from hand to hand, and burns ever brighter as it is passed on.

I take one example of this out of many. Nearly all the great mystics of the later Middle Ages speak of the Wilderness or Desert of Deity; suggesting thus that sense of great, swept spaces, "beyond the polar circle of the mind"—of a plane of experience destitute of all the homely furniture of thought—which seems to characterize a certain high type, or stage, of contemplation. It represents the emergence of the self into a real universe—a "place beyond uttermost place"—unrelated to the categories of thought, and is substantially the same experience which Dionysius the Areopagite and those mystics who follow him call the Divine Ignorance or the Dark, and which his English interpreter names the Cloud of Unknowing, where the soul feels itself to be lost. But each mystic who uses this traditional image of amazement—really the description of a psychological situation, not of an objective reality—gives to it a characteristic touch; each has passed it through the furnace of his own passionate imagination, and slightly modified its temper and its form. This place, or state, says Eckhart, is "a still wilderness where no one is at home." It is "the quiet desert of the Godhead," says Tauler; "So still, so mysterious, so desolate! The great wastes to be found in it have neither image, form, nor condition." Yet, says Richard Rolle—suddenly bringing the positive experience of the contemplative heart to the rescue of the baffled contemplative mind—in this same wilderness consciousness *does* set up an ineffable correspondence with Reality.

"There speaks the loved to the heart of the lover; as it were a bashful lover, that his sweetheart before men entreats not, nor friendly-wise but commonly and as a stranger kisses . . . and anon comes heavenly joy, marvelously making merry melody."

Here the mystic, with an astonishing boldness, weaves together spatial, personal and musical imagery, positive and negative experience, in order to produce his full effect.

Finally, St. John of the Cross, great thinker, manly and heroic mystic, and true poet, effects a perfect synthesis of these positive and negative experiences—that apparent self-loss in empty spaces which is also, mysteriously, an encounter of love.

"The soul in dim contemplation (he says) is like a man who sees something for the first time, the like of which he has never seen before . . . hence it feels like one who is placed in a wild and vast solitude where no human being can come; an immense wilderness without limits. But this wilderness is the more delicious, sweet and lovely, the more it is wide, vast and lonely; for where the soul seems most to be lost, there it is most raised up above all created things."

All this language, as I have said, belongs to the oblique and paradoxical side of the mystic's art; and comes to us from those who are temperamentally inclined to that pure contemplation which "has no image." Psychologically speaking, these mystics are closer to the musician than to any other type of artist, though they avail themselves when they wish of material drawn from all the arts. But there is another kind of mystic, naturally inclined to visualization, who tends to translate his supersensual experience into concrete, pictorial images; into terms of color and of form. He uses, in fact, the methods of the painter, the descriptive writer, sometimes of the dramatist, rather than those of the musician or the lyric poet. He is, I think, as a rule much less impressive than the artist of the illusive kind, and is seldom so successful in putting us into communion with reality. On the other hand—and partly because of his more concrete method—he is the more generally understood. For one person to whom Plotinus or Ruysbroeck communicates his sublime intuition of reality, a hundred accept at their face value, as true "revelations," the visions of St. Gertrude or St. Teresa.

The picture-making proceedings of this type of mystical artist are of two kinds. Sometimes they are involuntary, sometimes deliberate. Often we find both forms in the same individual; for instance, in Mechthild of Magdeburg and in Suso, where it is sometimes extremely difficult to find the dividing line between true visionary experience entirely outside the self's control, and the meditation, or poetic apprehension of truth, which demands a symbolic and concrete form for its literary expression. In both cases an act of artistic creation has taken place; in one below, in the other above, the normal threshold of consciousness. In true visionaries, the translation of the supersensual into sensual terms is uncontrolled by the surface intellect; as it is indeed in many artists. Without the will or knowledge of the subject, intuitions are woven up into pictures, cadences, words; and, by that which psychologists call a psychosensorial automatism, the mystic seems to himself to receive the message of Reality in a pictorial, verbal, dramatic or sometimes a musical form—"coming in to his body to the windows of the wits," as one old writer has it.

Thus the rhythmic phrases in which the Eternal Wisdom speaks to Suso or the Divine Voice to St. Catherine of Siena verge on poetic composition; but poetic composition of the automatic type, uncontrolled by the mystic's surface-mind. Thus, too, the great fluid visions of the prophets, the sharply definite, often lovely, pictures which surge up before the mind of Suso, the Mechthilds, St. Gertrude, Angela of Foligno, of the great St. Teresa herself, are symbolic pictures which represent an actual interior experience, a real contact with the supersensual; exhibiting the interpretative power inherent in the mystical imagination. These pictures are seen by the mystic—sometimes, as he says, within the mind, sometimes as projections in space—always in sharp definition, lit by that strong light which is peculiar to visionary states. They are not produced by any voluntary process of composition, but loom up, as do the best creations of other artists, from his deeper mind, bringing with them an intense conviction of reality. Good instances are the visions which so often occur at conversion, or mark the transition from one stage of the mystic way to another: for example, the mystic marriage of St. Catherine of Siena, or that vision of the Upper School of True Resignation, which initiated Suso into the "dark night of the soul." I believe that we may look on such visions as allied to dream-states; but in the case of the great mystics they are the richly significant waking-dreams of creative genius, not the confused and meaningless dreaming of normal men. Suso himself makes this comparison, and says that none but the mystic can distinguish vision from dream. In character they vary as widely as do the creations of the painter and the poet. The personal and intimate, the remote and metaphysical, sides of the spiritual life are richly represented in them. Sometimes the elements from which they are built up come from theology, sometimes from history, legend, nature, or human life. But in every case the "glory of the lighted mind" shines on them.

Often a particularly delicate and gay poetic feeling—a faëry touch—shows itself in the symbolic pictures by which these mystics try to represent their encounter with the spiritual world. Coventry Patmore once spoke of a "sphere of rapture and dalliance" to which the great contemplatives are raised; and it is from such a sphere that these seem to turn back to us, trying, by direct appeals to our sense of joy, the most stunted of our spiritual faculties, to communicate their exultant experience of that Kingdom of Reality which is neither "here" nor "there" but "everywhere."

Music and dancing, birds and flowers, the freshness of a living, growing world, all simple joyous things, all airy beauties, are used in the effort to tell us of that vision which Clement called the privilege of love. When we read these declarations we feel that it is always springtime in those gardens of the soul of which they tell. St. John of the Cross, who described those spiritual gardens, said that fragrant roses brought from strange islands grew there—those strange islands which are the romantic unexplored possibilities of God—and that water lilies shine like stars in that roaring torrent of supernal glory which pours without ceasing through the transfigured soul. This is high poetry; but sometimes the mystic imagination shows itself under simpler, more endearing forms, as when St. Mechthild of Hackeborn saw the prayers of her sisters flying up like larks into the presence of God; some soaring as high as His countenance and some falling down to rest upon His heart. An angel carried the little, fluttering prayers which were not strong enough to rise of themselves. Imagery less charming than this has gone to the making of many a successful poem.

Between the sublime intensity of St. John and the crystalline simplicity of St. Mechthild, mystical literature provides us with examples of almost every type of romantic and symbolic language; deliberate or involuntary translation of the heavenly fact into the earthly image. True, the earthly image is transfused by a new light, radiant with a new color, has been lifted into a new atmosphere; and thus has often a suggestive quality far in excess of its symbolic appropriateness. In their search for such images the mystics explore the resources of all the arts. In particular, music and dancing—joyous harmony, unceasing measured movement—have seemed to them specially significant *media* whereby to express their intuitions of Eternal Life. St. Francis, and after him Richard Rolle, heard celestial melodies; Kabir, the "Unstruck Music of the Infinite." Dante saw the saints dancing in the sphere of the sun; Suso heard the music of the angels, and was invited to join in their song and dance. It was not, he says, like the dancing of this world, but was like a celestial ebb and flow within that incomprehensible Abyss which is the secret being of the Deity. There is no need to dwell upon the remarkable way in which mystics of all countries and periods, from Plotinus to Jakob Boehme, resort to the dance as an image of the glad harmonious movements of liberated souls. I will take two characteristic examples, from the East and from the West. The first is a poem by Kabir:

Dance, my heart! dance to-day with joy.
The strains of love fill the days and the nights with music, and the world
    is listening to its melodies;
Mad with joy, life and death dance to the rhythm of this music. The hills
    and the sea and the earth dance. The world of man dances in
    laughter and tears. . . .
Behold! my heart dances in the delight of a hundred arts, and the Crea-
    tor is well pleased.

The next is the German mystic and poetess, Mechthild of Magdeburg, whose writings are amongst the finest products of mystical genius of the romantic and emotional type. This Mechthild's book, *The Book of the Flowing Light of the Godhead*, is a collection of visions, revelations, thoughts and letters, written in alternate prose and verse. The variety of its contents includes the most practical advice on daily conduct, the most sublime descriptions of high mystical experience. Mechthild was an artist, who was evidently familiar with the literary tradition and most of the literary expedients of her time. She uses many of them in the attempt to impart to others that vision of Life, Light and Love which she knew. I take, as an example of her genius, and a last specimen of the mystic's creative art, the celebrated letter addressed to a fellow pilgrim on that spiritual "Love path" which she trod herself with so great a fortitude. It represents not only the rich variety of Mechthild's literary resources, but also those several forms of artistic expression which the great mystics have employed. Here, concrete representation is perpetually reinforced by oblique suggestion; the imagery of the poet is double-edged, evoking moods as well as ideas. We observe that it opens with a spiritual love scene, closely related in style to the secular and romantic literature of Mechthild's time; that this develops to a dramatic dialogue between soul and senses—another common artifice of the medieval author—and this again leads by a perfectly natural transition to the soul's great acclamation of its destiny, and the crowning announcement of the union of lover and beloved.

The movement of this mystical romance, then, like the movement of ascending consciousness, goes from the concrete image to the mysterious and sidelong apprehension of imageless facts. First we have picture, then dialectic, then intuitive certitude. Here, too, we find both those aspects of experience which dominate mystical literature: the personal and intimate encounter of love, and the self-loss of the soul in an utterly transcendent Absolute. Surely the union of these "completing opposites" in one work of art must rank as a great imaginative achievement.

Mechthild tells her story of the soul's adventure in snatches of freely rhymed verse, linked together by prose narrative passages—a form which is not uncommon in the secular literature of the Middle Ages.[1] We are further reminded of that secular literature by the imagery which she employs. The soul is described as a maiden, the Divine Lover is a fair youth whom she desires. The very setting of the story is just such a fairy landscape as we find in the lays and romances of chivalry; it has something of the spring-like charm that we feel in Aucassin and Nicolette—the dewy morning, the bird-haunted forest, the song and dance. It is, in fact, a love story of the period adapted with extraordinary boldness to the purposes of mystical experience.

When the virgin soul, says Mechthild at the opening of her tale, has endured all the trials of mystical purification, she is very weary, and cries to her Love, saying, "Oh, beautiful youth! I long for thee. Where shall I find thee?" Then the Divine Youth answers:

> A gentle voice I hear,
> Something of love sounds there:
> I have wooed her long and long,
> Yet not till now have I heard that song.
> It moveth me so,
> Towards her I must go.
> She is the soul who with pain is torn,
> And love, that is one with the pain.
> In the early dew of the morn,
> In the hidden depths, which are far below,
> The life of the soul is born.

Then her vassals, which are the five senses, say to the soul, "Lady, adorn thyself."

> We have heard the whisper clear;
> The Prince is coming towards thee here,
> In the morning dew, in the bird's song.
> Ah, fair Bride, tarry not long!

So the soul adorns herself with the virtues, and goes out into the forest: and the forest, says Mechthild, is the company of the saints. Sweet nightingales sing there night and day of true union with God, and there in the thicket are heard the voices of the birds of holy wisdom. But the youth himself comes not to her. He sends messengers to the intent that she may dance: one by one he sends her the faith of Abraham, the aspirations of the Prophets, the pure humility of our Lady Saint Mary, all the virtues of Christ, and all the sanctity of His elect; and thus there is prepared a most noble dance. And then comes the youth and says to the soul, "Maiden, as gladly shouldst thou have danced, as mine elect have danced." But she replies:

> Unless thou lead me, Lord, I cannot dance;
> Would'st thou have me leap and spring,
> Thou thyself, dear Lord, must sing,
> So shall I spring into thy love,
> From thy love to understanding,
> From understanding to delight.
> Then, soaring human thought far, far above,
> There circling will I dwell, and taste encircling love.

So sings the Bride; and so the youth must sing, that she may dance. Then says he:

"Maiden, thy dance of praise was well performed. Now thou shalt have thy will of the Virgin's Son, for thou art weary. Come at midday to the shady fountain, to the resting-place of love: and with him thou shalt find refreshment."

And the maiden replies:

> O Lord, it is too high, too great,
> That she should be thy chosen mate,
> Within whose heart no love can be
> Till she is quickened, Lord, by thee.

By this romantic, storytelling method Mechthild has appealed to the fancy and emotion of the reader, and has enticed him into the heart of the spiritual situation. Next, she passes to her intellectual appeal; the argument between the soul and the senses. From this she proceeds, by a transition which seems to be free and natural, yet is the outcome of consummate art, to the supreme declarations of the deified spirit "at home with the Lord," as St. Paul said.

The dialogue moves by the process of reduction to a demonstration of God as the only satisfaction of the questing soul which has surrendered to the incantations of Reality.

      ❋   ❋   ❋

This is the end of all mysticism. It is the term to which all the artistic efforts of the mystics have striven to lead the hearts of other men.

NOTES

1. For the verse translations in the following extracts I am indebted to the great skill and kindness of Mrs. Theodore Beck, who, possessing a special talent for this difficult art, has most generously made for me these versions of Mechthild's poetry.

27

Mysticism and Rationalistic Metaphysics

CHARLES HARTSHORNE

"Mystics" are persons who say, or of whom it is said, that they have had immediate experience of God—or of the eminent, supreme, or unsurpassable Reality; but the term mystic is also used to denote a person who insists that this Reality is ineffable or can only be characterized in paradoxical or, at least seemingly, contradictory ways.[1] The two aspects, immediate experience and ineffability, seem quite distinct and I shall discuss them separately.

So far from finding any severe paradox in the idea of direct experience of deity, or the unsurpassable, it is in my view a paradox to suppose that such a reality could be known or truly affirmed only on the basis of indirect evidence. The Unsurpassable must be unsurpassably pervasive, that is to say, ubiquitous. It must be where anything is. Moreover, Its existence must be the essential factor in the existence of all lesser realities. Hence to be anywhere is to be in the right place to experience It; to experience anything is to experience an X-related-to-It, thus to experience It. It cannot be merely behind, but must be in, everything; not merely in the reality which appears but in the appearance itself; not merely in the world experienced but in the experience. Thus to claim not to experience God—or Brahman—is no less paradoxical than the contradictory claim.

The foregoing can be made more precise. I hold that the direct data of experience coincide with its independent causes or grounds. Consciously detectable data are but a subclass of experienced data, and the wider class is defined as those factors necessary to the experience but independent of it. How far they are introspectively accessible depends upon several conditions, including the level of awareness attained by the individual. Infants and subhuman animals do little introspecting, and the rest of us are more like them in this than we usually admit. If my definition of givenness, or being a direct datum, is accepted, then from this and most definitions of the divine or eminent reality it follows that that reality is a datum of all experience. For the unsurpassable is essential to all lesser realities, including nondivine experiences, but exists independently of them.

The definition of givenness is simply the formal statement of the central intuition of all realism, that things are experienced because they exist, they do not exist because they are experienced. An experience depends upon a world or reality that does not depend upon it. Whitehead's concept of "prehension" is precisely this formalization of the central realistic tenet. I believe that the lack of a clear formal concept of this kind in nearly all modern epistemology is a radical defect, clearly exhibited in a variety of ways in the systems of Berkeley, Leibniz, Kant, and many others.

That the data of experience coincide with its independent causes is readily overlooked for several reasons. There is the feebleness of human introspective powers, a feebleness some take satisfaction in denying. The obvious, readily detectable data are those that are sometimes present and sometimes not, thus, for instance, the sensation of red or of pain, or the appearance of an elephant. What is always given tends to escape notice. Thus some claim not to experience spatial extension in sounds, although they experience it in colors. But in fact (as it seems to me) spatiality is given in all experience, including auditory, though in different aspects and degrees of distinctness. This furnishes at least a remote analogy for the difference between the mystic and the rest of us.

Another reason for the failure to detect the coincidence of causes and data of experience is the belief in naïve realism just where that deviates from a reasonably sophisticated form of realism. In vision, and to a lesser extent in hearing and touch, we seem to experience directly the world outside the body. It is an open secret of genetic psychology that in fact this sense of extra-bodily reality is mediated by what we have learned in infancy and childhood about the meaning of inner-bodily changes. It is these bodily changes that are given, but it is the extra-bodily processes or objects that are thought. Normal adult perception is as truly thought as it is direct experience. The inner-bodily changes are given, but not necessarily *as* inner bodily. Naïve realism is in error, not in the realistic assumption that something independently real is given, but in the spatial location of the something outside the body. This location is learned and thought rather than directly given, and is partly an error insofar as the element of mediation is lost for introspection. True enough, what we see is the extra-bodily world, but "see" is one function, "directly intuit or experience" is another.

A third reason for confusion about causes and data is the assumption, natural enough but, I hold, unjustified, that the data of sensory experience are simultaneous with their being experienced. In that case they could not be causes of experience in the normal sense of "antecedent conditions." The argument that what is intuited now must be happening now merely begs the question about the temporal structure of experience, as can be seen by recalling that a parallel argument would entail that in memory there is no intuition of past experience, a consequence which opens the door . . . a "solipsism of the present moment" opens and is exposed to other objections. In Husserl we see a philosopher who, on the one hand, insists that past experience is immediately given in present experience, but on the other hand denies that in perception the data are past. How he knows that they are not past is his secret. No time lapse is clearly given as such; however, the failure to introspect a presence is not always the intuition of an absence.

I believe Whitehead to have been right, against an entire tradition, in denying that any direct data of experience are simultaneous with the experience for which they are data, or by which they are prehended. The way is thus opened for the immensely fruitful and illuminating principle: To be independent, antecedent condition of an experience is to be immanent in the experience, to qualify its objective content, whether or not introspection can detect its presence there. And then, insofar as divine reality is conceived as independent cause of all things and all experiences it must also be conceived as given in all experiences. I have discussed in many writings the need to distinguish, in the idea of the Unsurpassable, between that in it which is cause and that which is effect, both in relation to things in general and in relation to particular things or happenings. The divine reality which is given in this or that experience is not the entirety of all that has been or can ever be divine, but only so much of divinity as is antecedent condition of the experience.

There are ways of making somewhat more detectable the presence of Deity in all experience. We are all naïvely aware that other people exist, that they have their own feelings and thoughts, partly hidden from us at any given time. Our experience is somewhat paradoxical in respect to these "other minds." On the one hand, they seem mere background for our own existence, important because we need and enjoy their presence; on the other hand, so far as we are rational or ethical we know that it is just as true that our importance is measured by what we contribute to the lives of others as that their importance is measured by what they contribute to our own lives. The relativity can be taken either way. This suggests that the true measure of importance is Something that quite transcends "I" and "you." What is this Something? Is it the entire human group? There are reasons to the contrary. For one thing, the value of a group seems simply the sum of the values which life in the group affords the individual members. Value, in the intrinsic sense, is enjoyment, happiness, bliss, satisfaction; but only individuals literally enjoy or are satisfied, not groups. And so the Something which measures importance cannot be the group, for this would be circular. As Whitehead and the late Henry Simons (an economist I admired) almost alone in my experience have pointed out, the greatest happiness of the greatest number is not itself an actual happiness of anyone, and so is not a value in a clearly intelligible sense, unless in relation to something other than human individuals or groups. The economist suggested that only a theist, which I suspect he was not, could identify this additional factor.

Whitehead, in a near-mystical passage, profoundly intimates that our realization that solipsism is absurd is inseparable from the realization that our basic intuition of value, from which, he holds, our intuition of reality cannot be radically distinguished, is also the intuition that "importance" is not merely for ourselves or our neighbors, but for That which adequately and impartially measures all reality and value, that is, Deity, with its primordial and imperishable "Ideals" for the cosmos.[2] Objectivity is the sense that we are "there" not merely for ourselves or for each other, but for the impartial, cosmically concerned, and eminent reality. Objectivity is also the sense of being object for that for which all other subjects are likewise objects.

One can also argue that spatiality, about which something was said above, is, as Newton and Clarke held, intelligible only in terms of the all-inclusive unity of the Divine Life, to which every lesser life is a contribution. Whitehead's "objective immortality" makes this contribution explicit. It has often seemed to me, I think largely apart from any influence coming from the two writers just mentioned, that space and deity are somehow inseparable ideas. Thinking physicalistically we picture space as an emptiness in which material processes go on. We tend to think of these processes in visual or tactual terms. But not only has physics rejected the applicability of these images, they never did do justice to what space intuitively means for us. There confronting me in space are you. It has never seemed to me admissible to say, "What confronts me is but your body; your mind or soul, by contrast, is not in space." Rather, you, mind and body, or "minded body," are there in space. But materialistic images for this fail to fit even the bodily aspect, let alone the entire psychophysical reality. The only proper images or analogues for another's feelings or thoughts must themselves be feelings or thoughts. The only way to imagine another's feelings is to empathize with the other, to participate imaginatively in his feelings. So, there in space are your feelings and thoughts. But then what is the difference between space occupied by human or animal feelings, or other psychical processes, and those empty of such processes? Materialistic pictures do not adequately characterize this difference.

If space containing a certain kind of feeling differs from space not containing that kind, then we need a nonmaterialistic conception of space. I am not forgetting "identity theories." In their true version they concern only certain feelings, those we call sensations, which on my view belong, in the first instance, to cellular or subcellular members of the body and become our feelings only by a kind of innately grounded empathy on our part with these members.

With Peirce and Whitehead we can think of the extended cosmos as a society of sentient creatures whose influences upon one another, via empathic prehensions, conform largely to the patterns traced by physics. We can then say that space not occupied by human feelings is occupied by some other sort of feelings—unless there can be strictly empty space. But then questions arise about the self-sufficiency of such a society, if there is no supreme Socius to impose limits upon mutual conflict and disorder, or to measure relative importance. And how is truth to be conceived? Inadequate partial perspectives do not add up to definite truths. I hold, with Peirce, Royce, and others, that neither "reality" nor "truth" can be defined except in relation to knowledge and that our always partial and fallible kind of knowledge presupposes a higher kind as its measure. And so I incline to think of the pervasive unity of space as somehow an aspect of the divine unity, sensitive to all feeling and value, and the measure of its contribution. We do not merely infer space, we intuit it— not distinctly and completely in its geometrical structure, but still directly and always.

When I was a student at Harvard it occurred to me that solipsism contradicts the intuition of space. For according to solipsism it is false that "I am here and you are there" (*you* can be a subhuman creature). Rather, according to solipsism, I am everywhere; or, there is nowhere except where I am. But we directly experience space as ourselves and other things or creatures coexistent with us. Apart from this intuition "space" is but a word. I still believe that solipsism is incompatible with this intuition. And so I suggest that deity as the inclusive, ordering, and definitive unity of coexisting things is the full reality of what is directly given as spatiality.

The well-known Quaker mystic and scholarly writer on mysticism, Rufus Jones, whom I knew as my teacher at Haverford, held that the difference between mystics and others was a relative not an absolute one. The mystic is one who is aware of experiencing what we all do experience, whether aware of the fact or not. In mystics unconscious intuition, in the sense in which infants and the lower animals are unconscious, that is, without introspective judgments, becomes also conscious. It hardly seems possible that our common human nature could embrace so absolute a difference as that between the presence and the sheer absence of That without which there could, if mysticism is valid, be nothing at all.

The real problem about mysticism for the rationalistic metaphysician is not the givenness but the alleged ineffability of what is given. Here too it seems that absolute differences can hardly be involved. If we can speak of Supreme Reality only in contradictions, shall we say that Supreme is also inferior, or vicious, reality, or that it is no more to be admired than to be despised? Some Buddhists do talk almost in this way. But what limits, if any, to absurdity are here in order?

There is another consideration. Just how can direct experience rule out every possible nonparadoxical description? While having the experience, has the mystic run through in his mind every possible nonparadoxical description and seen its inapplicability? This seems implausible. Has he, after the experience, found that no description that he is familiar with fits his memory of the experience? But then perhaps either his memory or his knowledge of possible descriptions is inadequate. Historically there have been certain rather pervasive biases in metaphysical traditions, and mystics show signs of being limited by these biases. If Process Philosophers are right, it is only in the last few decades that an adequate metaphysics has been available.

If nonparadoxical descriptions are unsuitable, are they all equally so, or are some better than others? In the latter case, there must be some value in knowing which are the least unsuitable accounts.

We also have the problem of evaluating the contrasting mystical traditions, e.g. Vedantism and Buddhism. How can these be evaluated unless rationally? Or are they essentially the same? I incline to think that the differences are significant.

The older cultures that have depreciated rationalistic metaphysics, chiefly those of India, Southeast Asia, and Japan, have had to turn to more rationalistic cultures for much of their science and technology. Perhaps this implies that mysticism alone is not enough. This seems all the more likely when we consider that China has turned to a radically nonmystical philosophy as basis for its striking advances in practical matters.

It is indeed true that the mystical (especially Buddhist) cultures have been less militaristic, with the temporary and problematic exception of Japan, whose Shintoism is perhaps hard to classify in this regard. For this reason alone we should take seriously the possibility that we have something to learn from these cultures.

So far I have neglected an important distinction. If "ineffable" means not exhaustively describable, then everything concrete or actual is ineffable in that sense. It follows that, a fortiori, the Eminent Actuality is describable only in radically incomplete fashion. This has always been obvious from the idea of omniscience. If to know God is to know One Who Knows All, then to know God fully would simply mean to know all. Of course we do nothing like that when we describe God. In addition, language is only a powerful, not an infinitely powerful or absolute means of expression, and human discriminations are in various respects imperfect. And so what we fail to know about the Eminent Actuality can scarcely be exaggerated.

There are grounds for distinguishing, as I have done in many writings, between the abstract, eternal, necessary essence of deity and the concrete, contingent, partly temporal divine actuality. The abstract essence need not transcend language, at least not for the same reason as the actuality. Nor does referring to the essence as an object of thought reduce deity to a mere object rather than subject, an *it* rather than a *thou*. God's eternal character is indeed an it, essentially an object. However, God is incomparably more than his mere eternal character, for that is an abstraction for his concrete and developing Life. Any person, and anything at all comparable to a person, has a character distinguishable from his or her concrete experiences and actions. The *thou* is never the mere character but is the character as now embodied in experiences and actions which express, but are not in their particularity necessary to, the character. (The previous sentence will not be acceptable to absolute determinists, Spinozists, or Leibnizians. But I do not regard this as a defect of the sentence.)

The challenge of mysticism needs to be taken seriously. Yet it seems to me unlikely that metaphysicians attempting to be rational can be dispensed with. Merely to mediate between religion, however mystical, and science, or between widely different religions, or widely different sciences, such as physics and psychology, we must have such metaphysicians. What is perhaps needed is that more of us moderns and Westerners should undergo forms of disciplinary meditation, Buddhist or Vedantist. (Heidegger's recommendations in this direction seem too lacking in any traditional disciplinary guides, especially of an ethical character, to be very promising, if they are not downright dangerous.) Apart from such efforts, how shall we be sure we have not missed some "pearl of great price"? Possibly we need to devote more time to meditation and less (though at present it is no vast amount) to rationalistic metaphysics.

NOTES

1. See W. T. Stace, *Religion and the Modern Mind* (Philadelphia, New York: J. B. Lippincott Company, 1960), part III.

2. A. N. Whitehead, *Modes of Thought* (New York: The Macmillan Company, 1938), pp. 140–42.

28

Mystical Experience as Cognition

JOHN HICK

I

Our "practicing mystics" have spoken both of mystical experience and of the mystic's practices and disciplines. I should like to discuss the former, the religious experience and its significance, rather than the practices and techniques which serve it. Mystical experience, as our mystics (and others as well) describe it, does not seem to me to be anything other than firsthand religious experience as such. This is however, I believe, the core of religion. Religion has often been understood, particularly within our modern science-oriented Western culture, as an attempt (though a primitive and unsuccessful attempt) to explain certain puzzling phenomena, from perennial puzzles concerning the origin of the world and the source of its order, to cosmic puzzles concerning the origin of the world and the source of its order, to local puzzles about why the rains are late this year or what last night's thunder signified. There is, certainly, an explanatory side to religion, although recent religious thought has tended to apply these explanatory resources to the existence or the meaning of the world as a whole rather than to the occurrence of particular events within it. How far this movement away from a theological explanation of the genesis of particular events can or should be taken is an important open question which, however, I shall not be taking up here. The point I wish to make is rather that the explanatory function of religion is secondary and derivative. Religion consists primarily in experiencing our life in its relation to the Transcendent and living on the basis of that experience. And mysticism, I take it, is simply religion understood in this way. Or, rather, it is a name for one, but the most important, aspect of the total phenomenon of religion. In terms of Ninian Smart's six-dimensional analysis—distinguishing the ritual, mythological, doctrinal, ethical, social, and experiential dimensions of religion—mysticism is a general name for religious experience together with part at least of the network of religious practices which support it.

I am emboldened to equate mysticism in this way with the experiential

core of religion by the fact that two of our practicing mystics have said
something very like this, whilst nothing was said by the other three to
suggest dissent. Brother David [Steindl-Rast] defined mysticism as "experience of communion with the source of meaning"; and he stressed
that all who worship, and indeed all who are conscious of the divine, are
mystics. And Swami Prabuddhananda defined mysticism as the realization of relationship between the individual soul and the infinite reality,
and again, as being consciously in relation to God or to Brahman. This
would mean that all who are conscious of existing in the presence of the
divine are mystics. This would in turn mean, in both cases, that rather
than religious people being divided into a small minority of mystics and
a large majority of nonmystics, we should equate mysticism with religious experience or religious consciousness as such, but recognizing, of
course, many degrees of consciousness of the Transcendent, as well as
many forms which this consciousness can take.

Thus far it is not very clear why we need the term "mysticism" in addition to "religious experience" and "devotional practice." Nevertheless,
we do have the word, and its use in the title of this Conference is a sign
of its continuing life. The word clearly meets a need; and that need is, I
think, twofold. There is first the inevitable distinction between what can
be variously called conventional, nominal, external or secondhand religion on the one hand, and real, true, or firsthand religion on the other.
The former has always, in all large traditions, been the major part of the
total phenomenon of religion. And it has seemed convenient, and perhaps reassuring, to the mass of ordinary adherents of a religious tradition, to whom their faith means conformity to the customary creed and
ritual of their society, to bestow a special label upon the minority among
them who live by a firsthand experience of the Transcendent, with the
implied suggestion that the latter follow a special and peculiar way
which is not for everyone. And second, there is the fact that mysticism,
in the broad sense of what may be called firsthand religion as such, is
continuous with rare forms of religious experience which are reported by
a minority within the minority and which involve the paranormal or supernatural, in the seeing of visions or the hearing of voices, in yet rarer
experiences of oneness with the Transcendent which language can barely
begin to express.

Any full theory of mysticism, or of religious experience, must take account both of the kind of experiences reported by our practicing mystics
and also of the rarer experiences of visions and voices and of the unitive
life to which the label "mysticism" is sometimes restricted. However, I
shall confine myself here to the level or stage of religious experience described by our three reporters, this constituting—as I presume—a stage on
a spiritual journey which leads eventually to the unitive life in God; or to

Azilut, the highest world, in which "there is only One and no other and the soul is a moment of God"; or is *moksha;* or *nirvana.*

II

Let us reserve for later the question, which is of course ultimately all-important, whether it is reasonable for those who experience life religiously to base their beliefs upon this experience. For, as we must all be well aware in this skeptical age, it is always in principle possible to dismiss religious experience as a fantasy or projection; and I shall in due course come to this crucial issue. But for the moment let us bracket off that question and assume that the several reports of the mystics, and the wider traditions of belief out of which they come, are substantially true. Let us assume that these are substantially accurate accounts of experiences on the interface between the human and the divine. What metaphysical hypotheses, or picture of the universe, is implied in this supposition? Any answer, within the confines of this paper, must of course be in very large and general terms.

First, the Transcendent of which the mystics speak is of the nature of mind rather than of matter; and accordingly a distinction between matter, on the one hand, and spirit, soul, mind or consciousness on the other, is implicit in a great deal that they have said. The Transcendent, let us then say, is infinite Spirit.

It follows, second, that the material universe is other than the infinite Spirit, or at any rate other than the infinite Spirit per se. Matter may (as the Semitic religions teach) be wholly other than, and created out of nothing by, the infinite Spirit, or (as the religions of Indian origin teach) it may be a kind of illusion or dream experienced at some level of the infinite Consciousness, or again it may be related to that Consciousness somewhat as body to mind. But on any of these views, matter is not simply identical with the infinite Spirit as such. And because the material universe is thus either really or illusorily other than the eternal Spirit, its real existence, or its existence as a real illusion, is not self-explanatory. Indeed, so far from being self-explanatory, its existence constitutes for us, who are parts of it, the ultimate mystery. There seems to be a metaphysical analogue of Gödel's theorem, to the effect that, from the point of view of a consciousness which is part of the universe, any systematic interpretation of the universe must generate at least one question which that system can never answer. And for the religious systems it is essentially the same question, though posed in different terms within the different traditions. For the theistic religions it is the question why a perfect and self-sufficient God has created something other than, and of necessity inferior to, himself. For the nontheistic system of Advaita Vedanta it is the question why the illusion of finite and material existence occurs at all—for an illusion is just as truly something whose occurrence demands an explanation as is a nonillusion: the existence of the material world has not become any less problematic when it has been labeled an illusion. For nontheistic Buddhism, the unanswerable question is why the wheel of *samsara* turns. (One has to define the problem as its turning rather than its existing; for *samsara* is a process, consisting wholly in a series of events.) The immediate answer is that it turns by the power of *tanhā* (craving, thirst, desire); but why is there this apparently otiose phenomenon of finite consciousness and its cravings? This is the Buddhist form of the unanswerable question which appears elsewhere as the questions why there is *maya* and why there is a created universe.

There is, then, the mysterious fact of material existence. And accepting it as a fact, we can see that, whether or not by design, it has the effect of allowing a plurality of finite individuals existing over against one another. We are distinct beings because consciousness is exercised in us through separate bodily organisms in virtue of which we are aware of the world from particular positions within it. Further, we are conscious from the point of view of living organisms each programmed for its own survival. And whether we are parts or aspects of the infinite Spirit, somehow separated from it (even though the separation be an illusion of our finite consciousness) or are real beings created ex nihilo by the infinite Spirit, we have in either case a certain all-important affinity with that supreme infinite Spirit. And such conscious relationship, which Schleiermacher called God-consciousness, and which more broadly we can call consciousness of the Transcendent, is as it seems to me, the essential religious or mystical experience.

III

What is the nature of our human consciousness of the Transcendent?

In the mysticism of our reporters, it occurs within the context of this world, for they are men living on this earth. And the epistemological character of this experience enjoyed by the soul *in via* is not, I suggest, peculiar to religious consciousness. On the contrary, what is going on is not fundamentally different in character from what is going on in other forms of awareness which we take to be awareness of our environment. For in all our conscious experiencing there is an important element of cognitive choice, and this element in religious awareness is continuous with the element of subjective interpretation in our other awarenesses. I mean by this that when we are aware of a thing (such as this pen) or aware of being in a particular kind of situation (such as our present situation of participating in a Conference) we are interpreting what is before us, or around us, in terms of concepts. And by "interpreting" here I do not mean the intellectual exercise of conscious theory-construction, as when we speak of the prosecution's interpretation of the evidence in a court of law, or, on a grander scale, of a philosopher's interpretation of the universe. I am referring to interpretation in the sense in which this enters continuously into our ordinary sense experience. For it is a commonplace today that in our ordinary everyday perception of our physical environment as having the character that we perceive it to have, the mind is constantly active—comparing, remembering, selecting, grouping, presuming, and, above all, recognizing—that is to say, being aware of our environment as having the particular character that we perceive (and of course often misperceive) it to have.

For example, I want to say that in seeing this biro [ball-point] pen, I am seeing what is before me *as* a biro—borrowing and extending the notion of "seeing-as" which Wittgenstein discussed in the *Philosophical Investigations*. Wittgenstein himself thought that the notion only applies to special cases, like puzzle pictures: for example, you can see Jastrow's duck/rabbit *as* a picture of a duck or *as* a picture of a rabbit. But I want to say that *all* seeing-as, or more broadly that all conscious experiencing, is experiencing-as. That is to say, it involves *recognizing* objects and situations by means of concepts; or in other words, perceiving them as having this or that particular character or significance. For consider this biro. Surely, you might say, it is impossible to see it as anything other than a biro; and therefore the idea of seeing-*as*, implying as it does some sort of ambiguity in what is seen, is not appropriate. But to be conscious of seeing a biro, to be identifying *this* as a biro, is to be using a concept which has been created within a particular culture and which functions within certain cultures and not in others. We in North America and Europe see certain things as biro pens; but doubtless in rural Tibet they do not. And in Europe and North America a century ago they did not. Of course those who lack this concept could soon acquire it, and would then be able to see this as a biro pen. But the dispositional capacity to recognize it as such, to see it in this way, is not innate to the human mind but is on the contrary a cultural product. Again, to experience what is now going on as a seminar discussion presupposes a certain cultural background: beings from the planet Mars might well suppose something quite different to be taking place.

This second example, of being aware of the nature of a situation, is more to the point than the previous example of recognizing an individual object. For we are all the time within situations of various kinds, indeed usually within a number of different situations at the same time—for example, the situation of being in this room (on which our attention might become focused if someone were to shout out that there is a bomb concealed in it); the situation of participating in a discussion (on which our attention is I hope in fact concentrated); the situation of being a Canadian or American or British citizen; the situation of being father, mother, son or daughter, brother or sister, or colleague; of being a human being over against the mystery of existence; or—could it be?—the .situation of being in the presence of God, or of being part of the *samsaric* process which leads to eventual oneness with the eternal reality. And these are not mutually exclusive situations; someone could be in all of them at once but with the spotlight of his attention moving back and forth amongst them.

Let us speak, then, of our experiencing situations as having this or that character, it being always the case that in order so to experience we have to have a certain conceptual and interpretative equipment, often a very complex equipment. And one feature of situational awareness to which I should like to draw attention is that it involves tendencies or dispositions to act in ways appropriate to the perceived character of the situation. For one important thing about a situation in which we find ourselves is that we are *in* it, part of it, and have therefore to conduct ourselves in terms of its character as we perceive it. The appropriate action may of course often be inaction, or just going on doing the same thing. For example, consciousness of our present situation as being the situation of my reading a paper on a subject which we are all going to discuss together involves, on my part, that I go on reading my paper, and on your parts that you go on listening and preparing points for the later discussion. Every form of situational awareness has its own practical dispositional aspect. Thus, to be conscious of being in a certain kind of situation is, amongst other things, to be in a dispositional state to act in this rather than in that way or range of ways. And this is as true of religious as of secular cases. To be conscious of living in the presence of the Transcendent has all kinds of practical implications. For example, to be conscious of existing in the presence of God as Jesus depicted him, is not to be anxious about the future, not to be afraid of other people but on the contrary full of love for them all, and it is to believe that whatever happens to one, one is in the divine presence and within God's loving providence. Again, to be conscious of being a "spark of divinity," wrapped in illusion but struggling toward the clear light of reality, is to be set upon overcoming one's own egoity and upon breaking the many threads of selfish desire which hold one back.

I have been suggesting, then, that religious experience exhibits a common structure, which it shares with all our other cognitive experience, and that this is the experiencing of situations in terms of certain concepts. And awareness of a situation as having a certain character includes an appropriate dispositional stance. We can call the experienced

character of a situation, in virtue of which we are in a certain dispositional state in relation to it, its meaning—or, more precisely, the meaning
that we have found in it. Meaning, then, is the experienced character of
a situation such that to experience it as having that character is to be in
a distinctive dispositional state in relation to it. And so we can speak of
the different meanings of human life—of the global human situation—
which different religious traditions enable men to be aware of and to live
in terms of.

IV

This diversity of religious meanings is brought out by comparing the reports of our practicing mystics. If we assumed that they were all
deluded, the differences between their delusions would not present any
basic problem. But assuming, as I am, that they are not deluded, one has
to consider whether the diversity of these experiences is compatible with
their all being experiences of the same transcendent reality.

Clearly, the possibility to be explored is that the concepts, which we
have seen to be involved in all experience, may account for the same
transcendent reality being experienced in different ways.

Does Christian consciousness differ from Hindu, and Jewish from
Buddhist, because in these different traditions different concepts of the
Transcendent enter into the formation of one's religious experience? And
if so, how is it that the Transcendent is capable of being conceptualized
in such different ways?

In order to answer these questions we need, I think, a broadly Kantian
epistemology.

There are, of course, many difficult and disputed questions of Kantian
interpretation. But the main outlines of his epistemology are clear
enough. He distinguished between the noumenal world, which exists independently of man's perception of it, and the phenomenal world, which
is that world experienced in terms of the various forms and categories
that constitute the structure of our human consciousness. All that we
know about the noumenal world is that it is the unknown reality whose
impact upon us produces the phenomenal world of conscious experience.
An analogous distinction has to be drawn, and has indeed often been
drawn, in man's thought of the Transcendent. Perhaps its most explicit
form is the Hindu distinction between *nirguna* Brahman, Brahman without attributes, beyond the scope of human language, and *saguna* Brahman, Brahman with attributes, known within human religious experience
as Ishvara, the personal creator and governor of the Universe. In the
west the Christian mystic Meister Eckhart distinguished between the
Godhead (*Deitas*) and God (*Deus*); and Rudolf Otto, in his comparative

study of Eckhart and Shankara, says, "Herein lies the most extraordinary analogy between Eckhart and Sankara: high above God and the personal Lord abides the 'Godhead,' having an almost identical relationship to God as that of Brahman to Isvara" (*Mysticism East and West*, p. 14). More recently, Paul Tillich has spoken of the "God above the God of theism" (*The Courage to Be*, p. 190) and has said that "God is the symbol of God" (*Dynamics of Faith*, p. 46). Whitehead, and the process theologians who have followed him, distinguish between the primordial and the consequent natures of God, the former being his nature in himself, and the latter being formed by his response to and inclusion of the world. And Gordon Kaufman distinguishes between the "real God" and the "available God," the former being an "utterly unknowable X," and the latter "essentially a mental or imaginative construction" (*God the Problem*, p. 86). A more traditional form of the distinction is that between God in himself, in his infinite self-existent being, beyond the grasp of the human mind, and God in relation to mankind, revealed as creator and redeemer. In one form or another the distinction seems unavoidable for any view which is not willing to reduce God to a finite being who can, in principle, be wholly known by the human mind and defined within human concepts. If God is infinite, he must pass out into sheer mystery beyond the reach of our knowledge and comprehension, and in his limitless transcendence he is *nirguna*, ultimate Godhead, the God above the God of theism.

But if we see such concepts as *nirguna* Brahman, the Godhead, and the God above God, as pointing to the unknowable divine noumenon, we need not necessarily follow the advaitist Hindu thinkers in equating the divine noumenon with impersonal reality, in contrast to personal deities who are merely phenomenal. The personalist-dualist experience of I-Thou encounter between a human self and the transcendent Self, and the monistic or advaitic consciousness of oneness with infinite nonpersonal being, are alike experiences of divine phenomena. All that we can say of the divine noumenon is that it is the source and ground of all those experienced realities, as also of human minds in their awareness of these different phenomenal forms.

The thesis we are considering, then, is that religious experience is experience of the Transcendent, not however as divine noumenon but as divine phenomenon. The Transcendent as phenomenal object of man's religious experience is a joint product of the divine noumenon itself and the various human concepts of the Transcendent which have developed within different human cultures. These concepts have a common source in man's innate religiousness—that is, in our tendency to experience religiously, or in terms of the Transcendent; and the specific forms taken by the generic concept of the Transcendent arise from the manifold influences which have produced the varied ways of thinking and feeling that are characteristic of different human cultures.

But why are there these different human concepts of the Transcendent, correlated with different forms of religious awareness, different kinds of cult, and different ways of living and worshiping? To answer this question in detail is the task of the historians, anthropologists and sociologists of religion, and is a task which they may or may not ever be able fully to discharge. But the general conclusion seems inevitable that concepts of the Transcendent are related to the conditions of human life in different ages and different parts of the world—in short, to different human cultures.

As earnest of more fully developed theories for which we may hope in the future, such suggestions as the following have been made: "In nomadic, pastoral, herd-keeping societies, the male principle predominates; among agricultural peoples, aware of the fertile earth which brings forth from itself and nourishes its progeny upon its broad bosom, it is the mother principle which seems important. Among Semitic peoples therefore, whose traditions are those of herdsmen, the sacred is thought of in male terms: God the father. Among Indian peoples whose tradition has been for many centuries, and even millennia, agricultural, it is in female terms that the sacred is understood: God the mother" (Trevor Ling, *Religion East and West*, p. 27).

I am not equipped either to criticize or to contribute to this work of relating the several kinds of religious experience and thought to the different circumstances of man's life. But it seems clear that, whether or not we can successfully trace them, all manner of environing influences have gone into the formation of the different human cultures; and that many of these same influences must have affected the religions which are aspects, and indeed usually central aspects, of those cultures. And once a broad cultural stream is flowing, even the new revelatory experiences and insights of the great spirits who arise within it are bound to share the basic character of that stream. Thus, it is not surprising that Gautama the Buddha lived in India and Jesus the Christ in Palestine.

There is a very important difference to be noted between our awareness of the Transcendent and our awareness of our material environment, with our awareness of other human selves standing somewhere between these extreme cases. This is a difference within the dimension which has been thought of as the degrees of value and also as the degrees of reality or being—although in the Platonic tradition these two scales are identified as one. When we add that it is of the essence of human existence—whether as child of God or as divine spark—to be finitely free, we see that our relationship to that which is superior to ourselves in value or in fullness of being will differ in character from our relationship to that which is inferior to ourselves, with our relationship to that which is on the same level as ourselves falling between these two extremes. We are not diminished in our essential dignity or freedom by being aware of the existence of realities below ourselves in the scale of value or of reality. The power of storm and earthquake, or the strength of elephant or tiger, dwarfs my own strength; and the vastness of the universe around us shows us by comparison as microscopically small. But man nevertheless transcends the whole world of nature, with all its immensity of power, by his consciousness of it; as Pascal said, "if the universe were to crush him, man would still be more noble than that which killed him, because he knows that he dies and the advantage which the universe has over him; the universe knows nothing of this" (Pensées, no. 347). And in relation to other human beings, whilst many are more successful, or more intelligent, or more wealthy, or more powerful, etc., yet they are still in the end only fellow mortals and thus ultimately on the same level as myself. But in relation to absolute value or absolute reality I am nothing, and can have no personal being and freedom in relation to it, unless the infinitely good reality allows me largely to shut it out of my consciousness. Accordingly, we preserve our freedom over against that which is infinitely superior to ourselves by being aware of it, not in its infinite fullness, but in terms of limited and limiting concepts.

In theistic terms, to be directly confronted by infinite goodness and love, infinite knowledge and power, infinite fullness of being and life, would deprive us of any independence. There would be no room for a free human response of faith and love, or of trust and obedience. Indeed, the disparity between our finite selves and the infinite divine reality would exclude our very existence as relatively autonomous centers of finite freedom. Therefore God has to be the hidden God, veiling himself by creating us at an epistemic distance in order that he may then progressively reveal himself to us in limited ways which respect and preserve our own human freedom as persons. Again, in nontheistic terms, it is the finite individual's relative ignorance (avidya) of Brahman that constitutes his own finite individuality. As he rightly exercises his freedom through the long process of samsara, separate individuality is eventually transcended and he becomes the infinite Spirit. (Why, in view of this, there should be finite centers of freedom at all is the ultimate mystery that we noted earlier as fulfilling the metaphysical analogue of Gödel's theorem.)

It has been suggested, for example by Bergson, that one function of the brain is to filter out the virtual infinity of information reaching us through our senses, so that what comes to consciousness is the relatively simple and manageable world which we perceive and can successfully inhabit. We also have a system for filtering out the Transcendent and reducing it to forms with which we can cope; for "human kind cannot bear very much reality." This system is religion, which is our resistance (in the electronic sense) to the infinite Transcendent. In the earliest stages of man's development, the Transcendent was reduced in human awareness to the dimensions of man's own image, so that the gods were, like human kings, often cruel and bloodthirsty; or to the dimensions of the tribe or nation, as the symbol of its unity and power; or again to the more ample dimensions of the forces of nature, such as the life-giving and yet burning radiance of the sun, or the destructive power of storm and earthquake, or the mysterious pervasive force of fertility. And the response that was required, the way of life which such awareness rendered appropriate, was a communal response. For the anthropologists have shown us how closely knit primitive societies have been, and how little scope they offered for individual thought, whether in religion or in other aspects of life. As Robertson Smith wrote long ago, "Religion in primitive times was not a system of belief with practical applications: it was a body of fixed traditional practices, to which every member of society conformed as a matter of course" (*The Religion of the Semites*, 3d ed., p. 20). It was with the gradual emergence of individuality, in what Jaspers has called the axial period, particularly during the second half of the first millennium B.C., that higher conceptions of the Transcendent developed in correlation with a deeper sense of moral claim upon human life, and upon the individual as well as the collectivity.

For it was the emergence of the individual, and in particular of the religious individual, that made possible those great souls or *mahatmas* on whose consciousness the Transcendent impinged in new ways or with new intensity and power. The greatest of these became founders of religious traditions—Moses, Zoroaster, Confucius, Gautama, Jesus, and later Mohammed. Others effected important developments within existing traditions—the Hebrew prophets, the writers of the Upanishads and of the Bhagavad Gita, Pythagoras, Socrates, Plato. Each of the great religious traditions has of course continued to develop in larger and smaller ways through the centuries. . . .

The broad hypothesis which I am suggesting, then, is that the infinite Spirit presses in all the time upon the multiplicity of finite human spirits, and yet always so that our finite awareness of this encompassing reality is filtered through a set of human religious concepts. When the developing human race produces a spirit who is able to respond to the Transcendent in a new and fuller way, his (or her) experience of the Transcendent overflows or breaks the system of religious concepts inherited from his culture, and he proclaims a new truth about God or about the meaning of the process of existence, bringing with it new demands for the living of human life.

V

All this is hypothesis, of the kind which we are led to develop when we accept as true the religious-experience reports of the mystics. But can we, and indeed can they, properly have confidence in those reports? Let us, in this last section, consider the question of the cognitive value of religious experience.

The central feature of the mystics' reports is that they speak of a divine reality other than the human mind and other than the material universe which is our present environment. This transcendent reality is experienced as the God of the theistic religions and as Brahman or the Void in the nontheistic religions; and I have suggested that these are all divine phenomena constituting forms in which the unknown divine noumenon impinges upon human consciousness. The status of these divine phenomena (which I am generically calling the Transcendent) is thus comparable with that of the phenomenal world in Kant's critical philosophy. That world exists independently of the individual consciousness, being common to a community of minds functioning in the same way—this community being, in the case of the phenomenal world, coextensive with the human race. But the perceived world, although thus objectively real in relation to ourselves, is still a phenomenon constituting the particular way in which the noumenal reality becomes the object of our finite human consciousness. In an analogous way, God, Yahweh, Allah, Brahman, the Void, insofar as these are objects of man's religious experience, are divine phenomena constituting ways in which the unknown divine noumenon impinges upon human consciousness within different religious communities, with their different concepts of the Transcendent.

Our question now concerns the reality, over against our human consciousness, of God, Brahman, and the other divine phenomena. Can we properly claim to know that God exists, or that Brahman is real?

We must be careful to pose the question rightly. Whenever we ask whether x exists—whether x be an electron, a tree, a house, a human consciousness, or Brahman, or God—we must not exclude ourselves, as the cognizing minds asking the question, from the picture. The apparently purely objective question, Does x exist? is always in reality the objective/subjective question, Do I know that x exists; Is the existence of x an item of knowledge, i.e. of *my* knowledge? But even this reformulation is not yet quite right. For most philosophers prefer to define knowledge in ideal terms so that "I know p" entails p, and there can thus be no knowing p except when p is in fact the case. This ideal definition has many advantages, but it also has the inconvenience that we are never entitled to certify definitely that we know, but only to register claims to know.

We can claim to know that *p*, i.e. claim that what we present as our well-warranted belief that *p* corresponds with the facts. But this claim must necessarily be made from the perspective of our own finite range of data. And it is not open to us, having made that claim from our own particular and limited standpoint, to go on to certify it from an unlimited or ideal perspective. Only omniscience could know that a human being's claimed knowledge is indeed knowledge in the ideal sense. We have the data on the basis of which we claim to have knowledge, but we do not have further data, or knowledge that there are no further data, such as only omniscience could have. And therefore if we are to speak strictly, we must speak not of *knowledge* that the Transcendent exists, but of a well-grounded knowledge claim. This is the same as a well-grounded belief that the Transcendent exists; and I shall accordingly speak interchangeably of well-grounded beliefs and well-grounded knowledge claims. Our question is thus not properly formulated as "whether the Transcendent exists" but "whether there is well-grounded human belief that the Transcendent exists."

At this point we turn to the mystics, and above all to the great souls whose religious experience lies at the origin of the major world faiths. I shall put the argument in terms of the theistic experience of living in the presence of God; but a parallel argument will apply to the nontheistic forms of religious experience. In the theistic world, then, such a person as Jesus was as powerfully conscious of being in the presence of God as he was of the presence of other human beings and of his physical environment. And so let us ask: is it rational for such a person, experiencing in this way, to believe and to claim to know, on the basis of his own experience, that God is real?

I suggest that it *is* rational for him to make such a claim, and indeed that it would be irrational on his part not to. We have to trust our own experience for otherwise we have no basis on which to believe anything about the nature of the universe in which we find ourselves. Of course we also know that sometimes particular parts of our experience are delusory, so that experience is not *always* to be trusted. But we only know this on the basis of trust in the general veracity of our experience. We cannot go beyond our experience as a whole; for there is no "beyond" for us to go to, since any further data that we may come to have must, when we have it, form part of our experience as a whole. And if some aspect of our experience is sufficiently intrusive and persistent, and coherent with the rest of our experience, then to reject it would be in effect to doubt our own sanity and would thus amount to a kind of cognitive suicide. One who has a powerful and continuous sense of existing in the presence of God *must*, as a rational person, claim to know that God exists; and he is as entitled to make this claim as he and the rest of us are to claim to know that the physical world exists and that other people exist. In each case doubt is theoretically possible: a solipsism which reduces the world, or other minds, or God, to a modification of one's own private consciousness remains a logical possibility. But we are so made that we live, and can only live, on the basis of our experience and on the assumption that it is generally cognitive of reality transcending our own consciousness. Indeed, what we call sanity consists in acting on the basis of our putatively cognitive experience as a whole. And this being so, the religious man, experiencing life in terms of the presence of God, is rationally entitled to believe what he experiences to be the case—namely that God is real, or exists.

But having said this one must immediately add certain qualifications. For we cannot say that *all* religious and quasi-religious experiences, without exception, provide a good grounding for knowledge-claims. Just as there are illusions and delusions in other fields of experience, so also in religious experience. Suppose, for example, someone experiences his life in terms of witchcraft, or astrology, or alchemy, or influences from extragalactic intelligences who visit this earth in flying saucers, or in some other way which most of us regard as perverse or crazy. What are we to say about such a form of experience?

Let us suppose that the person concerned makes a knowledge-claim on the basis of his experience. Are we to hold that he is rationally entitled to make such a claim? The question, I would suggest, becomes the question whether we regard him as a fully sane, sober and rational person. If we do so regard him, we must also regard him as entitled to trust his own experience and to base knowledge-claims upon it. And our judgment as to whether he is fully sane, sober and rational will have two dimensions. One will be our estimate of the person himself; and here our assessment is partly psychological and partly moral. The criteria for such judgments are of course very hard to formulate; and yet it is clear that we are accustomed to make judgments in this area almost every day of our lives. The other dimension concerns the content of the knowledge-claim. It can only be rational to base a knowledge-claim upon some aspect of our experience if that claim is consistent with our other knowledge, based as this is upon the rest of our experience. And it may well be that knowledge-claims about the truth of witchcraft, or astrology, or alchemy, or about the existence of extragalactic intelligences who visit the earth in flying saucers, fail to cohere with what we know on the basis of our experience as a whole. In particular, such claims may clash with our scientific knowledge. In that case the wider experience will, in a rational person, provide a context within which the special experience is criticized, and bracketed as peculiar and suspect. And when, in hearing reports of astrological or other eccentric experience-reports, we judge the beliefs based upon such experience to be incompatible with public scientific knowledge, we shall probably hold that the person holding the belief is irrational or eccentric and that his special form of experience is not to be relied upon. For it is only if we can accept both that his special beliefs *may* be true and that he is a sane and well-balanced human being, that we feel obliged to take his experience-reports seriously.

How does all this apply to the religious case? It means that a rational person will only trust his own religious experience, and will only trust the religious experience reports of others, if the beliefs to which they give rise are beliefs which he judges *may* be true. In the theistic case, the existence of God must be judged to be possible if the "experience of living in God's presence" is to be taken seriously. This is where rational theology, or natural theology, comes into its own. Its office, I would suggest, is not to prove that God exists, or even that God's existence is probable; but to establish the possibility of divine existence. Without arguing the matter here I believe that reason can ascertain that it is *possible* that there is a God; and in that case theistic religious-experience has to be taken seriously. But whether experiences in terms of witchcraft, astrology, alchemy, flying saucers, etc. are to be taken seriously depends upon a corresponding rational scrutiny of the content of the knowledge-claims to which they give rise.

The final question that I must briefly raise is this: suppose, for the sake of argument, we accept the right of the great theistic mystics to believe in the reality of God on the basis of their own religious experience. We shall then be prepared to acknowledge that such a person as Jesus or St. Paul or St. Francis or Martin Luther, or again Mohammed, or Ramanuja, or Guru Nanak, have been entitled, as rational persons, to claim on the basis of their own experiences to know that God exists. But what about ordinary religious believers, who do not enjoy the same overwhelmingly powerful forms of theistic experience? Does our line of thought point to any justification for belief in the existence of God (or the reality of Brahman) on the part of ordinary people? Not, I would say, if they do not experience religiously in any degree whatever. For the absolutely unmystical—if such there are—there can be no good grounds for religious belief. However, the ordinary believer does, I would think, have some at least remote echo within his own experience of the much more momentous experience of the great religious figures. And it is this that makes him take their reports seriously. If he experiences his own life religiously at least to some slight extent, this makes it possible, and I would suggest reasonable, for him to be so impressed by the reports of the great souls that he comes to share their belief in the reality of the Transcendent. His belief is not *as* well-grounded as theirs is. But I would suggest that it is well enough grounded for it to be reasonable for him to proceed in faith in the footsteps of a religious leader, anticipating the full confirmation which his faith will ultimately receive if it does indeed correspond with reality.

29

Unity and Diversity in the Interpretation of Mysticism

TERENCE PENELHUM

I

The philosopher is never where the action is. He is always someone who tries to interpret and evaluate the activities and experiences of others. This conference gives us, as philosophers, an unusual opportunity of being closer to the action than usual.

Two opposite things strike a philosopher about what our practitioners have said. The first is a remarkable similarity in what they say about their experience and techniques. The second is the presence, throughout, of apparently radical differences. Philosophical discussions of mysticism have tended to concentrate around two questions. First, how real are the differences, and can they be interpreted in a manner which allows us to talk of mystical experience as a distinct and fundamentally single form of consciousness? Second, if we can talk of it in this way, is it, in philosophical jargon, cognitive, or noetic, rather than delusory?

II

Let me begin by mentioning some of the likenesses that I think we all find in the accounts before us. Each practitioner speaks of the highest experience vouchsafed to him in the language of union. Each speaks of it as something which is vouchsafed—the passive voice seems necessary when speaking of it. Yet it comes only after dedicated spiritual activity, which involves moral discipline, the negation of distraction and spiritual clutter, and the invocation and assertion of the presence of the transcendent in the self. These, broadly, are the likenesses; and they are the likenesses which have always served to distinguish mystical experience from religious experience of other kinds. Insofar as these other kinds are included in what our mystics speak of to us, they appear as preparatory to the unitive experience. They may indeed be part of the mystic way, but it is not their presence that makes the mystic way *mystical*. The differences are all differences in what Professor Smart has called doctrinal presuppositions. Each speaks to us of his experience and practice in the language of a particular religious tradition, which embodies doctrines about the relation of man to the transcendent. These doctrines have some likenesses (Rabbi Schachter is particularly concerned to draw attention to these, in order to contest W. T. Stace's claim that Jewish mysticism is not mystical) but analogy is far from identity in doctrinal matters.

Now there is an implied assumption in the way in which both Professor Hick and Professor Smart approach this combination of likeness and difference. It is one which philosophers generally make when they talk about the second of my two questions. The assumption is this: that the presence of doctrinal diversity in the language the mystics use, to themselves and to us, represents a barrier to a positive estimate of their experience and practice. Professor Smart tells us not to be disheartened by it; Professor Hick classifies the differences as merely phenomenal. Both seem to say that if we accept that there is a distinctive mystical form of consciousness, we can only be confident that it is not delusory through and through if we can reconcile the differences between what one mystic says and what another says. I think this is a most unrealistic assumption. I want to put a question mark against it, and to suggest that it, too, is culturally conditioned.

Let me make a couple of simple comparisons. The first comparison is this. Moral thinkers have been struck by the fact that men in many times and places manifest a sense of duty or obligation: that they feel themselves bound in one way or another to put aside their personal wishes and follow their consciences. Some thinkers have gone on to say that this widespread phenomenon shows men to have a special moral sense that alerts them to their duties; and they have given it an honored place in their analyses of human nature. Others, however, have been struck by the fact that what men's consciences tell them to do varies enormously from place to place—think only of our attitudes to practices like infanticide and senicide: and they have gone on to say that the moral sense is wholly delusory, that the wise man will not accept it as his guide to action at any time. Now one can defend morality against this form of skepticism by underplaying the differences between different moral codes, or by saying that it is not morally important what you think your duty is, provided you do whatever you think to be your duty. But one does not have to proceed this way, because there is another possibility. Perhaps there is indeed a specifically moral form of consciousness, and it is potentially a source of truth, but not a guaranteed source of truth. Perhaps it can sometimes go wrong. Perhaps the other forms of belief and attitude that coexist with it must be the right ones before conscience itself can be a reliable guide to moral choice.

My second comparison is this. Plato, Aristotle, Spinoza and Leibniz all created metaphysical systems which evaluate man's place in the universe, place scientific knowledge in a wider context, and support moral conclusions. Each system can provide the person who has done the intellectual and imaginative labor necessary to understand it with a profound vision that he could not get otherwise. All these systems are distinguishable in these respects from the undeveloped and unsystematic reflections of common sense, and from the skeptical and anti-metaphysical philosophies of (say) a Hume or a Wittgenstein. It would not naturally occur to us to say, as a result of these similarities, that the doctrinal differences between them are merely superficial differences that mask a deeper identity of intent. For the similarities are the similarities that exist between those who accept a certain manner of proceeding in philosophy but get different results from it. If Spinoza is right, then what Leibniz says is false. Profound, yes, but you can be profound and wrong. If you say that the differences between Spinoza and Leibniz are in some way not real differences, this is a way of rejecting both, not of accepting either.

Suppose we now agree that there is a distinct mystical mode of consciousness that is integrated with other forms of religious experience but is not identical with any of them. Suppose we also agree that these connections result in substantial doctrinal differences. I agree that these differences do not show that mystical consciousness is delusory. But in order to reject this negative conclusion we do not have to say that all mystical experience is experience of a reality to which the varying doctrinal responses are somehow ultimately equivalent. We *can* say this, but there is another possibility: that this mode of consciousness can sometimes lead to real union and sometimes only to the semblance of it. Perhaps doctrine is not an obfuscatory set of pointers to a higher reality that cannot be doctrinally understood, but mystical experience is a reward which is only noetic when sought and found in the context of the right set of doctrines.

If we reject this possibility a priori, why do we? I would like to suggest that we must at least be on our guard against a form of cultural conditioning of our own that makes us too readily angry with doctrinal differences, and makes us a little too ecumenical for our own good. In our day and age we are apt to be struck primarily by the difference there is between those who are willing to participate in the mystical (or for that matter, any other) form of religious consciousness, and those who reject it altogether. So keen are we to assert the importance of openness to the mystical way that we are quite unwilling to accept the theoretical possibility that one can follow it and go wrong; and the only way of not conceding this is to deny the ultimate importance of the different directions followed by those whose forms of experience are psychologically similar to one another. Negatively, this often takes the form of equating secularity with frivolity and closed-mindedness. Positively, it often takes the form of equating the religious consciousness with seriousness and openness. While such connections do, in my view, exist, they are not universal. But the temptation to make the equations is a natural response to an era in which adherents of all religious traditions are faced with the spread of secularity, and want to believe that the doctrinal differences that separate them can be put aside to enable them to face a common enemy. I think that this is an invasion of religion by the criteria of secular politics, but I will not try to argue this. The moral I do want to draw is this: let us not assume the differences between our respondents are necessarily less fundamental than their similarities, or that a philosophical interpretation of what they have said must presuppose a unitary significance. Let us proceed in hope; and let us, as philosophers, take with deep seriousness the recognition which the practicing mystics show for one another. But let us not assume that reality must accord with our spiritual preferences. Or that he who feels he has to reject, however respectfully, what a fellow seeker has to say is, for that reason, not listening.

III

I would now like to make a second, related point about the significance of the differences between mystical experiences as they are found in varied religious traditions. The problem of unity and diversity does not just arise in relation to the significance of what the mystic says, but arises equally in connection with the significance of ritual and worship, prophecy and vision. It is therefore quite natural to find Professor Hick electing to treat the question of the cognitive character of mystical experience in the wider context of religious experience in general. He appears to prefer a very wide understanding of the word "mysticism" which includes not only unitive experience but also all firsthand religion. Professor Smart concerns himself particularly with the interrelationship between contemplative techniques and worship, confining the word "mystical" to the former. There is no harm in this semantic difference when the context tells us which use is intended. I myself shall use the word "mystical" and its cognates in the more restricted way. But the difference can serve to draw our attention to a very important fact about the relationship between the special questions concerning the nature and status of mystical experience in the special sense, and the general questions to which Professor Hick has addressed himself about the nature and status of all forms of religious experience. The fact is this: the major religious traditions of the world do not merely differ in the doctrinal interpretations they offer of religious experience. They also differ markedly in the relative importance or centrality accorded to one sort of religious experience as opposed to another.

Mystical experience issues, as we have seen, in utterances of a special kind, that say that the one vouchsafed it is one with, is a moment of, is not set in duality over against, the Transcendent. This language demarcates *mystical* experience from religious experience of other kinds. But it does not come to us "neat." It comes mixed with speech that emanates from a tradition that also incorporates other practices and experiences. And each tradition places a different value on one kind of experience and practice relative to another. There is a very great difference between thinking of worship and devotional practice as primarily a mode of disciplining and liberating the soul for the ultimate reception of the unitive experience, and thinking of the latter experience as one available to a minority as a special divine dispensation to a soul that has already attained spiritual resolution in some other mode of religious life. Associated with this difference there will be a difference in the centrality accorded the great mystical figures in the determination of the character of the religious traditions to which they belong, and a difference in the importance attached to the precise nature of the pronouncements they make. While I am subject to authoritative contradiction in a gathering such as this, it can hardly be doubted that the importance accorded the mystic in the Hindu and Buddhist traditions is vastly greater than that accorded the mystic in any of the three major Western traditions; that in the three Western traditions the mystic does not determine, but merely enriches, the tradition; that what he says deepens, but does not fundamentally redirect, the religious experience sought after as a norm by others in the tradition; and that insofar as his experience requires him to bend and twist the language that the tradition provides him to talk of it, what he then says will be something that the tradition will not try to direct itself by, but merely to *accommodate*—and in the end may accommodate, if it must, by treating as an anomaly. On the other hand, a tradition like that represented by Swami Prabuddhananda, which regards the mystic as the normative spiritual figure, will interpret doctrinal differences as of little consequence if they express diverse ways of preparing men to follow in his footsteps.

I would infer two things. First, that even if we find the most striking similarities between mystics of different traditions, we cannot happily deduce that this shows a corresponding unity of significance or ultimate meaning between the *traditions,* for these traditions vary in how much the mystic represents them. Second, even though Professor Hick may be wise in raising questions about the significance of religious experience in general, rather than mystical experience per se, we are more likely to follow him in stressing the unity against the diversity if we sit among a group of mystics than if we compare religious traditions in their totality.

IV

Having made all these remarks in order to emphasize the diversity we find among mystics, and its potential importance for the philosopher of religion, I want to turn to the unity we also find. I want to suggest that the very unity that we find among the mystics is itself a barrier to a particular way of coming to terms with the diversity! I am sorry to spin conceits: let me explain what I mean.

Professor Hick has introduced here a notion which he has put to very penetrating use elsewhere in the analysis of religious experience—the notion of "experiencing-as." I do not need to repeat his explanation, but it is a development, as he says, of some remarks of Wittgenstein. Wittgenstein comments on the fact that an ambiguous picture can be "seen as" quite different things by different people—and also can be "seen as" different things by one and the same person at different times. Hick widens the notion from "seeing-as" to "experiencing-as," in order to incorporate within it our power to interpret all aspects of our common experience in different ways. The application of the notion of experiencing-as requires the postulation of three elements: a common or shared *object* to be interpreted (to correspond to the picture that is to be seen one way or another), two or more individual *subjects* to do the interpreting, and finally, of course, two or more resultant interpretations *by* the subjects *of* the object. I do not think it would be a fair criticism of this model to say that it requires that there be some neutral description of the common object which both subjects could accept before moving to their alternative interpretations—even though there would be such a common description in the case of ambiguous pictures. But it does seem to follow from this model that the object can be in some manner *identified* in common by those who understand it in different ways: though this would be a very sticky requirement to spell out.

The experiencing-as model is very helpful in expressing the difference between the mode of experience of the religious believer and that of the secular man or woman. Here the common object is our common perceptible environment, with all its goods and evils; and each interprets it in differing ways, while continuing to coexist with the other within it. The model also leaves it open to say, as Hick does, that each of us can exercise some degree of *choice* whether to interpret this common world in a secular or a religious fashion. The model also has a natural use in representing the differences between alternative religious traditions. Here one can go in two directions. One can either take the common object to be, once again, our common world or some part of it, in which case (say) the Christian and Islamic world views would be two interpretations, and the secular world view a third one alongside them; or one can say instead that the common object is one whose existence or reality is only recognized by religious believers and is not even open for interpretation by the secular man. Each way has difficulties, because each seems to jeopardize the neutrality of the model. To say that the object is once again the common world or some part of it seems to concede too much to the secularist, who is insisting all along that there is no possible object beyond the common world; but to say that the object is something beyond the common world concedes him too little. Professor Hick actually uses his experiencing-as model in both ways. He uses it in the first way when he takes as the common object religious *experience*. This is something which the unbeliever will regard as delusory, but he will agree that it exists in our common world, so he and the believer can disagree about how to interpret it, while agreeing on what it is that they are differently interpreting. Hick argues persuasively for the view that a positive interpretation of it is at least rational. I hasten past the difficult question: can an unbeliever interpret religious experience negatively while at the same time himself *having* it? Or is it a necessary truth that anyone who has it will interpret it in some positive manner? But while I hasten past this, I must linger a little on an allied question.

This question is the following. If one takes the common object that is differently interpreted to be some kind of *experience*, this seems to imply too neat a distinction between an experience and the interpretation of it. Is this really possible for anyone other than a person who regards it as an illusion? To explain: the secularist will reject mystical experience, while agreeing that it happens *to others*. So for him the experience and the interpretation are obviously distinct. But what about the two mystics who speak of their experience in doctrinally opposite ways, e.g. in personal or impersonal language? Can we glibly say that they are offering different interpretations of *one and the same experience*? Do we have a common object of interpretation at all? How do we tell? What is to correspond to the independently identifiable ambiguous picture? When someone tells me that two friends have been presented with the same ambiguous picture and one has seen it as a duck and the other as a rabbit, I want to say that although they have been looking at the same object, they have had different experiences. But in our present case we have to locate one and the same experience in order to have a common object. Most of us, reading and listening to our practicing mystics, will feel somewhat torn, but will indeed want to say that they share experiences which they are interpreting differently. Here I think Professor Smart's distinction between ramified and unramified descriptions is important. If we wanted to prove to someone that the mystics had the same experience we would have to produce, from their statements, a number of closely similar unramified descriptions—descriptions that did not contain much language that entailed one doctrinal scheme and excluded another. If we were able to do this, then we could reasonably say that each was having the same (i.e. a phenomenologically similar) experience that the other was having, and interpreting it in different ways. This would leave it open, of course, for the skeptic to say that this shared experience was interpreted mistakenly by all of them, and offer his own negative reading of it.

While reasonable, this application of the idea of experiencing-as does leave some philosophical difficulties behind it. In the first place, it is always somewhat arbitrary to decide when an experience ends and an interpretation begins, and it is in consequence always open to someone to insist that the line cannot be drawn anywhere. More important, however, is this: there is, in one obvious sense, no such thing as one common experience, in the sense of one numerically identical experience shared by several people. There are at best several numerically distinct but exactly similar experiences. The single common object in the case of the ambiguous picture is the picture—something drawn on paper or projected on a screen. Philosophers present will no doubt recall all the difficulties that arise in the philosophy of perception if one tries to say that there is also some mental element that is common to all the percipients who see the picture, in addition to their differing perceptions of it as a duck or a rabbit. Even though they can give a neutral common description of the picture, this does not yield a common mental object, but an agreed abstraction from a diverse set of differing interpretations, which is not the same thing.

Yet all these difficulties are merely that—difficulties. I myself think that they do not prevent one from using the experiencing-as model to talk of mystical experience as containing a common core of phenomenologically similar elements that are fairly described as one and the same experience variously interpreted. On the whole, however, this is not the way in which Professor Hick chooses to use his experiencing-as model of analysis. He does not, for most of his paper, talk of the common object as the mystics' shared *experience*. Instead he talks of the common object as the Transcendent. This immediately excludes the secular interpretation as an interpretation of a common object, since the secularist cannot admit that religious experience, *defined as experience of the Transcendent*, ever occurs. I can only speculate on Hick's reasons for choosing to talk in this way, but two possible ones occur to me. The first is that he might feel that if he did not talk in this way—in a way, that is, which presupposes in identifying the common object which all mystics experience that there is indeed a Transcendent reality—he would yield a point to the skeptic. The skeptic might say that the very variety of mystical interpretations was itself an argument against accepting the truth of any of them. If one defines the experience as experience of the Transcendent then of course one blocks that contention. The second reason he might have is one I have already expressed anxiety about: he might feel that by identifying the common object of interpretation as the Transcendent he will also weaken the suggestion that one form of mystical experience is more nearly veridical than another. I do not myself feel persuaded by either consideration, if either did in fact move him. The fact that the skeptic cannot admit the existence of that which you define as the common object of religious experience is not a philosophical advantage, but the contrary, and the fact that your identification of the common object entails that all the diverse interpretations are partially right seems to me to be an advantage only from the point of view of considerations other than that of truth.

But let us leave all this, and consider the suggestions that Professor Hick does make. He says that different forms of religious experience are different ways of experiencing the Transcendent, or Infinite Spirit. To accommodate the most radical of these differences, such as the interpretation of it as personal and impersonal, he invokes the Kantian distinction between noumenon and phenomenon—the distinction between that which is independent of human consciousness and yet appears to it, and the interpreted appearance that it presents to a particular consciousness. He amends Kant in more than one way, the primary way being the claim that the forms of phenomena are not universal, but culturally conditioned. The ultimate object of religious experience is beyond human description, but is experienced as the varyingly described Absolutes of the different religious traditions. It can be shut out of the consciousness of a person (or a culture) altogether; but if it is admitted, if it is allowed to appear to human consciousness, it does so in the manner determined by the traditional influences that have helped to mold that particular consciousness.

Attractive and valuable though this is in other contexts, I think that *mystical* experience does not admit this sort of understanding. My reason is that the unity of which the mystics speak calls into question the whole framework within which it is here being understood. The difference between other forms of religious experience and the claims of the mystics seems to me to matter critically here. For worship and devotional experience do indeed seem to occur in a manner which necessarily preserves the distinctness and otherness of men and the divine, and here it is

wholly intelligible to say that the way the Other divine is perceived is a
result of the particular situation of the human consciousness that perceives it and worships it. But does one not claim to be beyond this if one
claims to experience mystic union? To use Kantian language a little
more: a phenomenon is, according to Kant, necessarily that which appears to a human conscious subject. Without a conscious individual subject, or a multiplicity of them, there would be no phenomena. There
would, of course, "be" noumena. But the distinction between the noumenon, and that to which it appears so that it is experienced as a phenomenon, is essential. (In Kantian language, the self is noumenal also.)
It is this very distinction which is characteristically denied in those accounts of mystical experience in which the diverse mystics most regularly
agree. My point is simply that distinctively mystical experience is the
one sort of religious experience where the duality of subject and noumenon seems not to be applicable. Mystical experience may indeed be
experience of the Transcendent, but not (necessarily not) *as phenomenon*. The use of the Kantian framework may be wholly correct in helping
us cope with the variety of perceptions of the Transcendent with which
men's religious life abounds. But it cannot assume within it the distinctive experience of the mystic. For the mystic does not seem to be "experiencing-as" at all.

v

If these comments on Professor Hick's argument are sound ones, it seems
to me that we are left with the problem of diversity in a very intractable
form. Let me restate it. It does seem that there is a common core of experience and interpretation that is distinctively mystical; but that it is always found in those who experience it interlocked with doctrinal commitments that vary to the point of apparent incompatibility between one
person and another, and which affect the perception of the personal disciplines that mystical experience requires. Unless we are willing to dismiss all mystical experience as delusory, the unity we find makes us look
for some way of reducing the doctrinal differences, of making the discord concordant, as Zaehner might say. As far as I can see, there are
only two ways, and one has to choose between them.

1. The first way is to work from within a doctrinal framework, interpret the mystics' experiences in the language of that doctrinal framework,
and say that the experience of mystics in *other* traditions, though it parallels the experience of mystics in the one within which you work, is nevertheless incomplete, misleading, or noncognitive to the very extent to
which it is interpreted in ways inconsistent with the doctrines you hold.
This way forces us into different judgments upon similar experiences in

the light of their doctrinal contexts, and consequently presupposes in an obvious way the primacy of doctrine over mystical experience.

2. The alternative way is to insist that the common features of the mystics' experiences must override the differences between the doctrines that interlock with them in the traditions where they are found; and that the various incompatible doctrines are all expressions of the varying ways men have experienced the Transcendent reality which is known and shared directly in the mystics' experience. This way requires us to subordinate all doctrinal requirements to the recognition of the common features of the mystics' experience, in a very strong manner: we have to say that the mystic, insofar as he does not himself indulge in doctrinal pronouncements of the kind which divide the traditions, has transcended the limitations which the differences between the doctrines reveal. *His* experience is not phenomenal, but literally unitive in the way he is impelled to say it is.

Which way one chooses will depend on many factors. One of these, no doubt, will be the presence or absence of mystical experience in one's own life. Another will be the relation one has to a particular religious tradition, and whether it is itself one which gives a central or peripheral place to mystical experience. But whatever the causes, no philosopher can invent any *grounds* for decision that do not beg all the questions.

30

The Mystical Experience of the Self and Its Philosophical Significance

LOUIS DUPRÉ

Much of what is written in the philosophy of religion deals with abstract generalities and makes exceedingly tedious reading. It is as if philosophers had not yet learned to apply to religion what they do as a matter of course in the area of science: to acquaint themselves thoroughly with the subject. Since this subject includes full rational articulation as much as prereflective experience, it requires a detailed study of particular theologies. Religious categories are not trans-historical concepts: they originate in specific religious cultures and develop with those cultures. What we need far more than the current analysis of presumably universal concepts, is a philosophical equivalent of Bremond's *Histoire littéraire du sentiment religieux*. This is particularly true for the entire area of mystical experience and its systematic expression. Here more than anywhere else the principle holds: There is no mysticism; there are only mystics and specific mystical theologies. This is not to deny the existence of a common element in the variety of experience. Indeed, one of philosophy's main tasks is precisely to discover this element—but on the actual texts in their historical setting.

The significance of such a study is not restricted to the sole area of philosophy of religion. It would affect other, more general philosophical notions which have developed on the basis of a too limited reflection. A primary instance is that of the notion of the self. Philosophy, particularly empiricist philosophy, has largely been satisfied with describing and cataloging the content of ordinary consciousness. Some suspected long ago that there might be more to the self than what the unperceptive eye so easily detects. In his distinction between *"apperceptions"* and *"petites perceptions"* Leibniz attempted to go beyond consciousness by introducing elements which, although not fully conscious themselves, nevertheless play a constitutive role in consciousness. His simple juxtaposition of both elements is inadequate to explain the structure of selfhood. Yet it reveals an amazing awareness of the difficulty created by the interrupted consciousness (in states of sleep or sickness), to any theory which attempts to interpret the self as a string of phenomena united by means of a common memory. Memory itself, in spite of total discontinuity, is what most urgently needs to be explained. To bridge the gaps of consciousness the self clearly requires a subphenomenal dimension.

William Ernest Hocking was one of the few to heed this requirement. Interestingly enough, he was led to do so by reflecting on the religious concept of immortality.[1] He posits two "selves," the excursive self which is conscious of the world in which it lives, and the reflective self which transcends worldly flux and thereby enables the other self to become conscious. The reflective self is not subject to the lapses of the excursive one: steadfastly it maintains itself through the blackouts of consciousness and connects the intermittent stretches of consciousness. The body may be an indispensable instrument in this constant identification process, but it cannot provide its ultimate foundation since the body itself needs to be recognized as identical from one stretch to another. The self, then, surpasses the sum total of psychic phenomena. Indeed, the phenomena themselves remain unintelligible unless we accept a subphenomenal source from which they spring and which gives them their coherence. The founding self depends considerably less upon its bodily environment than the phenomenal self. The former's activity continues uninterruptedly after a withdrawal from the physical world in sleep, in trance, in artistic creation or even in daydreams. Particularly in the latter two states we notice a strange interference of the unconscious with the conscious self. At such occasions, the self appears to be led beyond the boundaries of its ordinary world and to escape its ruling laws. It becomes expressive rather than reactive, revealing the workings of an inner power instead of those of its bodily world.

Such a view is, of course, not proper to modern philosophy. It was anticipated in Kant's transcendental ego, Fichte's pure I, Schelling's Absolute and, more recently, Husserl's transcendental reduction. Yet on the whole philosophers have seldom attempted to give this deeper self a positive content and, in the case of Kant and his followers, have explicitly denied that such a content could be given. The subphenomenal self remained mostly a condition of the phenomenal self.

Indeed, the exploration of the self as it extends beyond consciousness has been done outside the realm of philosophy proper. Whatever little scientific knowledge of it we possess, we owe to the psychological investigations of conscious behavior that could not be explained in terms of consciousness alone. Unfortunately, the therapeutic success of depth psychology has become one of the main obstacles preventing a full theoretical exploration of the unconscious self. The unconscious part of the self is obviously more than a storage place for what the mind has forgotten or blocked out. Nor must it be regarded as merely the more "primitive" part of the self in which the more instinctual conflicts take place. Primitive it may be in the sense in which the "lower" is said to precede the "higher."

> What we call subconsciousness, far from being a sort of mental sub-basement, is at the center of selfhood, and the invidious term "subconsciousness" is an inept recognition of the fact that the primary springs of selfhood are not habitually at the focus of its outgoing interests.[2]

Nor can one unqualifiedly maintain that a self which is not conscious cannot be known and is therefore no legitimate object of discussion. Although the unconscious as such undoubtedly escapes the direct glance of perceptive awareness, it may well manifest itself indirectly, as the achievements of depth psychology have proven. Moreover, those who reached for the most intensive experience of the self have at all times believed that they would attain in the end a self no longer circumscribed by the bounds of ordinary consciousness. The very purpose of the mystical journey is to surpass consciousness and to rest in the dark source of the conscious self.

If we may attach any credence to the revelations of the mystics—and the universal nature of their experience forces us at least to consider their claims seriously—an altogether different layer of selfhood hides underneath the familiar succession of outward-oriented phenomena. Behind the gates to this restricted area the laws ruling ordinary consciousness seem to be suspended. Space and time recede or are transformed from a priori forms of outward perception into vistas of an inner realm with unknown rhythms and successions. From archaic depths the imagination (if it has not taken leave altogether) conjures well-structured visions known to the dream consciousness only through fragments and to the waking consciousness not at all. In privileged instances the intellectual intuition, so preemptorily exorcized by Kant's critique, reasserts its rights and the mind literally *perceives* as directly as the senses ordinarily do. The intellectual visions described by John of the Cross and Ignatius of Loyola are truly visions in that they belong to the order of perception, even though all sensory input and perhaps all images have been halted. Does all this not support William James's observations that the ordinary, rational consciousness is only one kind of consciousness while all around it, separated from it by the flimsiest screens, there are potential forms of consciousness of a completely different nature? To James, the psychologist, a full knowledge of the self requires the contribution of the peak religious experience.[3]

Religious Origin of the Concept of Soul

The exceptional character of the mystical experience tempts us to isolate it from all others. But if its vision is unique, its foundation is not, for the mystical experience merely brings to full awareness the common religious principle that the soul itself rests on a divine basis. To the religious mind the soul is always more than it is: it transcends itself so that the way inward must eventually become the way upward or downward, depending on the schema one adopts. This transcendence becomes manifest in the mind's self-understanding when the ordinary consciousness starts loosening its grip. At this point, religious man claims, we enter the sanctuary where God and the soul touch. It is also the very core of the self, as Eckhart so daringly expressed:

> There is something in the soul so closely akin to God that it is already one with him and need never be united to him. . . . If one were wholly this, he would be both uncreated and unlike any creature.[4]

To lose one's God, then, is to lose one's deepest self, to become "unfree" and to be reduced to a "substance," a part of the world. The power of the soul to surpass the world altogether lies only in its capacity to transcend itself. The religious mind will find it symptomatic that even a creative theory of man, such as that of Marx, runs into difficulties with a concept of freedom that lacks true transcendence.

The concept of soul is originally religious. According to Tylor's theory, religion originates with the awareness of a ghost-soul that is able to wander away while the body remains stationary, and that eventually will leave the body altogether. Although Tylor's simplistically evolutionist and intellectualist interpretations of the primitive mind were later rejected, on one crucial issue he was undoubtedly right: the idea of soul itself emerges as a religious notion and remains so long after it has ceased to be primitive. Plato's view that the soul longs to rejoin the divine forms to which it is related sinks its roots into primary beliefs that long preceded philosophical reflection. To most North American Indians the soul was created separately by a god. Aake Hultkranz, the Swedish student of native American religions, does not hesitate to generalize:

> As a rule, the Indians of North America believe that man's spirit has its ultimate origin in the deity himself, either through creation or partial emanation. . . . A soul that is commonly considered to derive from the gods is *ipso facto* not an ordinary profane creation. Whether it is conceived to be a gift of the deity or an emanation of his being, it belongs through its origin to the supernatural world. The supernatural

origin of the human soul finds particularly clear expression in the idea of pre-existence.[5]

We find similar concepts among Australian natives. To the Murngin tribe the soul is what lifts man above the profane existence and allows him to participate in the sacred values of an eternal civilization.[6] In the Greek mystery cult the soul is above all a subject of ecstasy, first in this life and eventually in the afterlife.[7] According to Rhode the awareness of this ecstatic quality is what led to the belief in immortality.[8] The notion of a substantial soul itself may have been born out of the ecstatic experience and the concomitant belief in immortality.[9] In any event, it is certain that the archaic notion of the soul is mainly characterized by what Rudolf Otto calls "the element of feeling—stupor—which it liberates, and the character of 'mystery' and 'wholly otherness' which surrounds it."[10]

Even developed religious cultures have preserved this numinous quality. Thus, much in the Upanishadic movement may be regarded as an attempt to penetrate that point of the soul where Atman is Brahman. The absolute is what I am in my true self: *Tat tvam asi*. The Bhagavad Gita describes the Atman in terms of the sacred: "marvelous,"[11] "indestructible," "immutable," "incomprehensible."[12]

Christian theology regards the soul as created and is therefore more reserved, at least in its orthodox expression. Yet by no means does this "desacralize" psychology. The concept of the soul as an image of God determines the development of Christian mysticism as much as the notion of the Atman determines the Vedantic vision. The divine "character" of the redeemed soul, clearly present in St. Paul, was developed into a Christian psychology by the Capadocians in the East and by St. Augustine in the West. The religious origin of their theories makes us all too easily overlook their psychological significance. To Gregory of Nyssa and Augustine the fundamental structure of the soul can be understood only from a transcendent perspective. Thus, the first theologies of the soul were also the first attempts at depth psychology. Nor should we dismiss them as purely theoretical speculations. Whatever the quality of their interpretations may be, they were primarily attempts to articulate and to justify an experience.

The Deeper Self of the Mystics

In accordance with the principle stated at the beginning of this paper I shall abstain from attributing more than a "characteristic" or typological significance to each particular mystical description of the self. Nor do I expect my elementary remarks in any way to disclose the phenomenological essence of the experiences. At this initial stage of what Whitehead called "descriptive generalization" I feel unable to do more than to point at some striking differences between the ordinary self and the mystical self.

In fact the very existence of an essential difference presents the most salient point in mystical literature on the soul. Thus Ruusbroec clearly distinguishes the mystical awareness from the ordinary one: in the former, reason is suspended and the mind is emptied of all objects.

> Here our reason must be put aside, like every distinct work; for our powers become simple in love, they are silent and bowed down in the presence of the Father. This revelation of the Father, in fact, *raises the soul above reason, to an imageless nakedness.* The soul there is simple, pure and spotless, empty of all things, and it is in this state of absolute emptiness that the Father shows his divine brightness. To this brightness neither reason nor sense nor remark nor distinction may serve; *all that must remain below;* for the measureless brightness blinds the eyes of the reason and compels them to yield to the incomprehensible light.[13]

A difference between two levels is universally suggested by metaphors of isolation, secrecy, height and, of course, depth. St. Teresa speaks of the inner castle, Catherine of Siena of the interior home of the heart, Eckhart of the little castle, Tauler of the ground of the soul, the author of *The Cloud of Unknowing* of the closed house, Plotinus of the innermost sanctuary in which there are no images.[14] St. John of the Cross combines several metaphors in the second stanza of his famous poem:

> In darkness and secure
> By the secret ladder, disguised—oh happy chance—
> In darkness and in concealment
> My house being now at rest.[15]

Omnipresent are the images of depth.[16] Almost equally common is the image of height. The soul must "ascend" beyond images and understanding. In Plotinus this metaphor dominates and the term "beyond" is the most significant one in the *Mystical Theology* of Pseudo-Dionysius, his Christian interpreter.

What characterizes the new state of consciousness above all is its qualitative distinctness. Ordinary psychic activity ceases to function and the mind is "taken" into the ground of itself to which it has no independent access. In the *Katha Upanishad* we read:

> Atman is not to be obtained by instruction, nor by intellect, nor by much learning. He is to be obtained only by the one whom he chooses; to such a one Atman reveals his own essence.[17]

Even the most cautious interpreters speak of "passive" states and "infused" contemplation. In the so-called quietist school passivity became the overriding characteristic of spiritual life.[18] In some texts of the Vedanta this mental passivity appears to exclude consciousness. Thus in the *Brihad-Aranyaka Upanishad* we read:

> As a man, when in the embrace of a beloved wife, knows nothing within or without, so this person, when in the embrace of the intelligent soul, knows nothing within or without.[19]

But no description ever surpassed the one found in the *Mandukya Upanishad* of the fourth state of being, beyond dreamless sleep, in which all awareness of world and multiplicity totally vanishes.[20]

> Into this Dark beyond all light, we pray to come and, unseeing and unknowing, to see and to know Him that is beyond seeing and beyond knowing precisely by not seeing, by not knowing.[21]

Johann Tauler equally stresses the discontinuity with ordinary thought.

> This inner ground of the soul is only known to very few people . . . ; it has nothing to do with thinking or reasoning.[22]

St. Augustine's distinction between the discursive *ratio* and the *intellectus* which is directly illumined by God's light[23] will be adopted by numerous spiritual writers after him. Richard of St. Victor describes the mystical ecstasy as a state of consciousness in which the soul is "cut off from itself."[24]

The Ligature of the Faculties

As reflection on the distinct states of consciousness increased, a theory of the activity of the "faculties" in the mystical consciousness emerged. In *Dark Night of the Soul* St. John describes the transition from the ordinary to the spiritual level:

> In this state of contemplation which the soul enters when it forsakes meditation for the state of the proficient, it is God who is now working in the soul; *He binds its interior faculties* and allows it not to cling to the understanding, nor to have delight in the will, nor to reason with the memory.[25]

St. Teresa frequently refers to the paralyzation of the ordinary psychic functions, as in the following passage:

> When all the faculties of the soul are in union . . . they can do nothing whatever, because the understanding is as it were surprised. The will loves more than the understanding knows; but the under-

standing does not know that the will loves, nor what it is doing, so as to be able in any way to speak of it. As to the memory, the soul, I think, has none then, nor any power of thinking, nor are the senses awake, but rather as lost. . . .[26]

The preceding texts must not be understood as if all "faculties" ceased to function at once. We noticed St. Teresa's hesitation when she comes to memory. A nineteenth-century spiritual writer states explicitly: "The soul's powers are not always in the same degree of drowsiness. Sometimes the memory remains free, with the imagination."[27] Most of the time the "faculties" do not cease to function at all. They are "bound," which means that they no longer function in the ordinary way. The Spanish mystics insist that the will always continues to function, even though free choice no longer exists. But, above all, mystical states remain states of awareness, i.e. cognitive states. Some mystics, especially in the Dominican school, consider ecstasy primarily an intellectual act, though not a discursive one. By several accounts also the imagination and the senses may become endowed with new powers. Thus the mystic in certain cases *sees* visions and *hears* voices, either with the senses or the imagination, which others do not perceive.[28] Are sensations which are not supported by ordinary sensory stimuli simply "illusions" as the term "hallucination" commonly implies, or can they refer to a different kind of reality? This is not the proper place to discuss this epistemological question, but for an authoritative treatment of the problem I refer [the reader] to Joseph Maréchal's remarkable essay "On the Feeling of Presence in Mystics and Non-Mystics."[29]

Yet a great deal of caution is required in interpreting references to mystical sensations. What John of the Cross describes as "touches" (*toque*) appears to be totally unrelated to those hallucinatory experiences in which the senses play a direct part and which remain therefore subject to errors of interpretation.

> When God himself visits it [the soul] . . . it is in total darkness and in concealment from the enemy that the soul receives these spiritual favors of God. The reason for this is that, as his Majesty dwells substantially in the soul, where neither angel nor devil can attain to an understanding of that which comes to pass, they cannot know the intimate and secret communications which take place there between the soul and God. These communications, since the Lord Himself works them, are wholly divine and sovereign, for they are all substantial touches of Divine union between the soul and God.[30]

Repeatedly St. John insists that those touches occur "in the substance" of the soul, not in its faculties, and, consequently, that they have neither form nor figure.[31] He seems to use the term "touches" to denote an experience unrelated to sensation but analogous to it by its directly intuitive character. The sense of touch was probably selected because of its greater immediacy and lesser distinctness.

As for the imagination, many spiritual writers attribute a new function to it in the visions and voices which usually precede the higher states of union. Imaginary visions may appear with the intensity of actual sensations, yet without any hallucinatory sensory experiences and often in phantastic or unprecedented forms.[32] It is as if images and symbols normally restricted to the unconscious are released when the mind first penetrates into the unknown depths of itself.[33] Jung has written memorable pages on this release of unconscious types and symbols.[34] The mystical vision structures this "unconscious" material according to its own intentionality. It would therefore be mistaken to place those visions on a par with ordinary dreams in which the same or similar material may appear. Indeed, St. Teresa points out that the imaginary vision is often accompanied by an "intellectual" one which it renders more vivid and to which it gives a more lasting impact.[35] Nevertheless the upper levels of the unconscious appear to be more autonomous here than at any other stage of the mystical experience. Spiritual directors almost universally adopt a critical attitude toward this most sensational aspect of the mystical life. Zen masters as well as Christian directors caution the novice not to attach any importance to those apparitions.[36] Even if they come from God, St. John of the Cross warns us, they are "curtains and veils covering the spiritual thing."[37] True spiritual communication takes place on a deeper level and all attention spent on those intermediate phenomena detracts from the direct contemplation of what remains beyond perception and imagination. Nevertheless, St. John attempts to justify the existence of those imaginary visions and, in so doing, approaches a modern psychological interpretation of the phenomenon.

> If God is to move the soul and to raise it up from the extreme depth of its lowliness to the extreme height of His loftiness, in Divine union with Him, He must do it with order and sweetness and according to the nature of the soul itself. Then, since the order whereby the soul acquires knowledge is through forms and images of created things, and the natural way wherein it acquires this knowledge and wisdom is through the senses, it follows that, if God is to raise up the soul to supreme knowledge, and to do so with sweetness, He must begin to work from the lowest and extreme end of the senses of the soul, in order that He may gradually lead it, according to its own nature, to the other extreme of His spiritual wisdom, which belongs not to sense.[38]

A further discussion of those states belongs to the psychology of mysticism. Our present purpose is merely to explore what the mystical experience contributes to the knowledge of the self as such. From that point of view the highest states of mysticism in which the so-called intellectual visions take place are the most important ones, because they are totally unique and incomparable to any other experiences.

First it must be emphasized that there is more to those states than visions, even though we shall concentrate on them for practical reasons. Next, "intellectual visions" are not visions proper, since they do not consist of perceptions or images. Nor are they "intellectual" in the ordinary sense, since they are entirely nondiscursive and contribute nothing to the subject's "understanding" of himself and his world. Nevertheless, their main impact is one of insight and even of all-surpassing insight. Since the reader may not be familiar with descriptions of this kind of experience, I here relate two clear instances of it taken from Teresa and Ignatius of Loyola. Teresa writes:

> I once had such great light from the presence of the Three Persons which I bear in my soul that it was impossible for me to doubt that the true and living God was present, and I came to understand things which I shall never be able to describe. One of these was how human flesh was taken by the Person of the Son and not by the other Persons. As I say, I shall never be able to explain any of this, for there are some things which take place in such secret depths of the soul that the understanding seems to comprehend them only like a person who, though sleeping or half asleep, believes he is understanding what is being told him.[39]

Even more typical is Ignatius' description of what he experienced at the river Cardoner:

> As he sat there, the eyes of his understanding began to open. Without having any vision he understood—knew—many matters both spiritual and pertaining to the Faith and the realm of letters and that with such clearness that they seemed utterly new to him. There is no possibility of setting out in detail everything he then understood. The most that he can say is that he was given so great an enlightening of his mind that if one were to put together all the helps he has received from God and all the things he has ever learned, they would not be the equal of what he received in that single illumination. He was left with his understanding so enlightened that he seemed to be another man with another mind than the one that was his before.[40]

The only mystic who has attempted to explain those experiences is John of the Cross. If I understand his interpretation correctly, the purely intellectual "apprehensions" may still have a certain sensory orientation in the sense that some affect the subject as visions would affect him, others as voices and still others as touches, yet always "without any kind of apprehension concerning form, images or figure of natural fancy or imagination."[41] If this is the case then Teresa's words make sense when she writes that "the Lord Himself in an *intellectual vision so clear that it seemed almost imaginary,* laid Himself in my arms."[42]

Still for our purpose it may be more profitable to concentrate on the purely spiritual content. All visions of this nature are short, ecstatic and, in spite of their abundant spiritual light, somewhat obscure. Among the visions of incorporeal substances St. John of the Cross mentions a direct vision of the soul. He also claims that the intellectual experiences are "felt in the substance of the soul."[43] "God works then in the soul without making use of its own capacities."[44] From all evidence, we confront here unified states of consciousness which allow the soul to contact its own core. Let us subject this metaphorical language to a critical analysis.

The Substance of the Soul

First, even those unified states of consciousness retain a noetic quality which allows the mystics to refer to them as intellectual.[45] Yet the mind escapes the duality of ordinary consciousness. Taken literally the expression "beyond dreamless sleep" in the *Mandukya Upanishad* would place the highest mystical state outside consciousness altogether. Yet the *Brihad-Aranyaka* explains: "Verily while he does not think, he is verily thinking."[46] However, the thought is not a second thing different from the thinker. This is indicated by John's claim that intellectual visions take place "in the substance of the soul" and the various other expressions referring to substance at the end of *The Dark Night,* such as "His Majesty dwells substantially in the soul" and "substantial touches of Divine union between the soul and God."[47] Clearly the term *substance* alone appeared appropriate for that coincidence of being and knowing which precedes all mental differentiation.

Whatever else this knowledge may contain, it includes a unique and direct awareness of the self. Its direct character is all the more remarkable, since it is described entirely in negative terms. One attentive reader of the Christian mystics writes:

> The soul empties itself absolutely of every specific operation and of all multiplicity, and knows negatively by means of the void and the annihilation of every act and of every object of thought coming from outside—the soul knows negatively—but nakedly, without veils—that metaphysical marvel, that absolute, that perfection of every act and of

every perfection, which is *to exist,* which is the soul's own substantial existence.[48]

Whether the right term is existence as Maritain claims, or essence as it is called by many mystics, all agree that we have here a direct, although negative, knowledge of ultimate selfhood—an immediate awareness of presence to oneself and to the transcendent source of the self. Such a direct intuition bypasses the channels of sensation and judgment by which the awareness of the self is usually attained. It neither needs nor provides any rational justification of itself. Confronted with statements such as "I felt that God was there: I saw Him neither with my bodily eyes nor through my imagination, nevertheless His presence was certain to me,"[49] it is difficult not to accept the existence of a direct mental intuition in the mystical state. Most epistemologists have followed Kant in denying that the human mind ever attains such a direct insight into the presence of the real as such. Yet even Kantian students of the mystical experience are forced to admit that no other explanation remains.[50] For this fully conscious being-with-oneself cannot be accounted for by the categories of ordinary consciousness. The ordinary awareness of the self is achieved indirectly through a reflection upon its operations. Yet in mystical states we attain a direct, explicit awareness of the self *as such.*

And this knowledge shows itself so radically different from ordinary knowledge, from the threefold standpoint of immediateness, mode and content, that the contemplative remains in the deepest stupefaction thereat. For in this case it is not amnesia which appears after the ecstasy any more than it was complete consciousness during it; the mystic remembers perfectly, but he does it through the belittling and dividing forms of the understanding which once more oppress him.[51]

Those words of Maréchal echo the conclusion of John of the Cross: "It is like one who sees something never seen before, whereof he has not even seen the like. . . . How much less, then, could he describe a thing that has not entered through the senses."[52]

Some of the insight into the self, acquired through mystical experience, was thematized in various developments of Augustine's theory of memory. In *De Trinitate,* XIV. 13.17, memory is said to contain the mind's latent knowledge of itself and of God. By wisdom (*sapientia*) "distinct from knowledge, conferred by God's gift through a partaking in God himself"[53] the mind *recognizes* what it knew implicitly. The knowledge of God here coincides with the ultimate knowledge of the self. Even in Augustine this theory is more than a Christian adaptation of Plato's theory of *anamnesis,* because the religious experience in Augustine always precedes the categories, borrowed or invented, in which he expresses it. Mystical writers will adopt this theory of memory and develop its Trinitarian aspect. Thus for William of St. Thierry, just as the Father is the silent source of the Word, memory is the silent ground of the soul from which the work of cognition proceeds.[54] This theory is developed more systematically by the Franciscans Alexander of Hales and Bonaventure. In the third chapter of his *Itinerarium Mentis ad Deum* Bonaventure concludes:

> And thus through the operation of the memory, it appears that the soul itself is the image of God and His likeness, so present to itself and having Him present that it receives Him in actuality and is susceptible of receiving Him in potency, and that it can also participate in Him.[55]

In the Vedantic tradition the mystical knowledge of a self that remains hidden from ordinary awareness is all the more emphasized since the duality between man and Brahman is abolished. This fundamental self, unknowable yet attainable, is the ultimate reality. Shankara built his entire mystical philosophy on it. The "ground" of the soul, the Atman beyond all functions of consciousness, is the locus of mystical truth. This ground of selfhood is experienced by the mystics not only as hidden but also as transcendent. It is the very point in which the soul is more than an individual soul. Thus in the Vedantic tradition this deeper self is at once the core of all that is.

> The Inner Soul of all things, the One Controller,
> Who makes his one form manifold—
> The wise who perceive Him as standing in oneself,
> They, and no others, have eternal happiness.[56]

> Now, he who on all beings
> Looks as just in the Self,
> And on the Self as in all beings—
> He does not shrink away from Him.[57]

Texts such as these clearly indicate that the ground of the Self far surpasses the boundaries of individual personhood.

Christians tend to write this off as Oriental pantheism. But upon careful scrutiny they will find that their own mystics assert the transcendence of the mystical self. To them also at one point the soul and God are not two but one. In Eckhart's daring language: "There is something in the soul so closely akin to God that it is already one with Him and need never be united to Him. . . . If one were wholly this, he would be both uncreated and unlike any creature."[58] Most Christian mystics have been less radical in their expression but not in their meaning. Thus Johann Tauler refers to the soul as a creature, but one standing between eternity and time, and with its supernatural part entirely in eternity.[59] Yet no one has elaborated the theme of self-transcendence more consistently and with more theological strength than Jan Ruusbroec. According to the Flemish mystic, man's true essence (*wesen*) is his super-essence (*over-wesen*). Before its creation the soul is present in God as a pure image: this divine image remains its super-essence after its actual creation.[60] The mystical conversion, then, consists for Ruusbroec in regaining one's uncreated image. Through the mystical transformation (which Ruus-broec calls "overformation") the soul surpasses its createdness and par-ticipates actively in God's uncreated life.

> All those men who are raised up above their created being into a contemplative life are one with this divine brightness and are that brightness itself. And they see, feel and find, even by means of this Divine Light, that, as regards their uncreated nature, they are that same simple ground from which the brightness without limit shines forth in a godlike manner, and which according to the simplicity of the essence remains in everlasting, mode-less simplicity.[61]

To Ruusbroec the soul is from all eternity an archetype within God. To the extent that its actual existence in time is essentially connected with this archetypal image, it "dwells in God, flows forth from God, depends upon God and returns to God."[62] The nobleness which the mind possesses by its very nature, it cannot lose without ceasing to exist alto-gether. Now free, created mind may actualize the dynamic tendency of its nature "toward the Image" through a virtuous and God-seeking life. Yet a total identification can occur only through the passive graces of the "God-seeing" life. In the mystical state the mind comes to live "above nature" "in the essential unity of God's own being, at the summit of his spirit."[63]

Thus the ultimate message of the mystic about the nature of selfhood is that the self is essentially more than a mere self, that transcendence belongs to its nature as much as the act through which it is immanent to itself, and that a total failure on the mind's part to realize this tran-scendence reduces the self to less than itself. It is in this dynamic view of a potentially unlimited mind that I find the most significant contri-bution to a philosophical understanding of the self.

NOTES

1. William Ernest Hocking, *The Meaning of Immortality in Human Experi-ence* (New York: Harper & Brothers, 1957), pp. 44–59.

2. Ibid., p. 50.

3. Obviously I do not accept Erich Neumann's interpretation of the mystical types as corresponding to the three stages of life ("Mystical Man," in *The Mystical Vision*, ed. by Campbell, Princeton University Press, 1958, pp. 375–415). Such a reductionist projection is the exact opposite of what I have in mind. Instead of subsuming the unknown under the known, I want to expand the known by adding the novel in its own right.

4. *Meister Eckhart*, tr. Raymond Bernard Blakney (New York: Harper & Brothers, 1957), p. 205.

5. *Conceptions of the Soul among North American Indians* (Stockholm: Statens etnografiska Museum, 1964), pp. 412–24.

6. W. Lloyd Warner, *A Black Civilization* (New York: Harper, 1964), p. 436.

7. William Bousset, "Die Himmelsreise der Seele," *Archiv für Religionswissenschaft* 4 (1901) 253ff.

8. Erwin Rhode, *Psyche*, tr. W. B. Hillis (New York: Harper Torchbooks, 1966), pp. 264–91.

9. Th. K. T. Preuss, *Tod und Unsterblichkeit in Glauben der Naturvölker* (1930), p. 17, cited in Gerardus van der Leeuw, *Religion in Essence and Manifestation* (New York: Harper Torchbooks, 1963), p. 311.

10. Rudolf Otto, *The Idea of the Holy*, tr. John Harvey (New York: Oxford University Press, 1958), p. 194.

11. *The Bhagavad Gita* 2.29, tr. Eliot Deutsch (New York: Holt, Rinehart and Winston, 1968), p. 49. R. C. Zaehner translates the term *ascaryam* (marvelous) as *"By a rare privilege* may someone behold it . . ." (New York: Oxford University Press, 1969), p. 50, while Rudolf Otto reads "As *wholly other* does one gaze upon it . . ." *The Idea of the Holy*, p. 195.

12. *The Bhagavad Gita* 2.17–18, Deutsch, p. 38. A similar idea is expressed in the *Visnu-smrti* 20.53.

13. *De Spieghel der Ewighe Salicheit*, in *Werken*, III (Tielt: Lannoo, 1947), p. 212.

14. *Enneads* VI. 9.11.

15. *Dark Night of the Soul*, tr. E. Allison Peers (New York: Doubleday, 1959), p. 34.

16. William Johnston describes the mystical process in *The Cloud of Unknowing* as a descent to "the still point or the ground of the soul" in which the mind goes silently down into its own center, revealing cavernous depths ordinarily latent and untouched by the flow of images and concepts that pass across the surface of the mind." *The Still Point* (New York: Harper and Row, 1971), p. 132.

17. R. E. Hume, *Thirteen Principal Upanishads* (New York: Oxford University Press, 1931). *Katha* 2.23, p. 350.

18. One of the propositions endorsed by Molinos and condemned by Pope Innocent XI reads: "Doing nothing the soul annihilates itself and returns to the source and origin, the essence of God, in which it remains transformed and deified. God remains in Himself because then there are no longer two things united but one sole thing. In this way God lives and reigns in us and the soul annihilates itself in the very source of its operations." Denzinger-Bannwart, *Enchiridion Symbolorum*, n. 1225. Translation from Elmer O'Brien, *Varieties of Mystic Experience* (New York: Rinehart, Holt, 1964), p. 304.

19. *Brihad-Aranyaka* 4.3.21; Hume, p. 136.

20. *Mandukya* 5; Hume, p. 392.

21. *Mystical Theology*, Migne, P.G., III, 1000. Translation by Elmer O'Brien in *Varieties of Mystic Experience*, p. 83.

22. *Sign Posts to Perfection: A Selection from the Sermons of Johann Tauler*, ed. and tr. Elizabeth Strakosch (St. Louis: Herder, 1958), pp. 95–96.

23. *In Joan. Evang.*, 15.4.19. On this distinction, cf. Etienne Gilson, *The Christian Philosophy of St. Augustine*, tr. L. E. M. Lynch (New York: Vantage Books, 1967), p. 270.

24. On the basis of the Vulgate translation of Hebrews 4:12 he distinguishes *anima* and *spiritus*. Cf. *Selected Writings on Contemplation*, ed. and tr. Clare Kirchberger (London: Faber and Faber, 1957), p. 204.

25. *Dark Night of the Soul*, I 9.7; Peers, p. 67.

26. *Relations* v, in *Works*, tr. E. Allison Peers (New York: Sheed and Ward, 1946) I, 328.

27. Picot de Clorivière, *Considérations sur l'exercise de la prière* (1802), quoted in A. Poulain, *The Graces of Interior Prayer* (St. Louis: Herder, 1950), p. 78. Why so much special attention is given to memory will appear later in this paper.

28. Scaramelli in his renowned *Directorio mistico* (1754) (Treatise 3, no. 32) does not hesitate to use the term sensation for those direct perceptions. Luis de la Puente distinguishes separate senses: "As the body has its exterior senses, with which it perceives the visible and delectable things of this life, and makes experience of them, so the spirit with its faculties of understanding and will, has five interior acts corresponding to these senses, which we call seeing, hearing, smelling, and delectable things of Almighty God, and makes experience of them." *Meditations*, as quoted in Poulain, *op. cit.*, p. 101.

29. In *Studies in the Psychology of the Mystics*, tr. Algar Thorold (Albany: Magi Books, 1964), pp. 55–146.

30. *Dark Night of the Soul*, II 23.11. Cf. also II 23.5 and *The Living Flame of Love*, tr. E. Allison Peers (New York: Doubleday, 1962), stanza 11.16, pp. 67–68.

31. *The Living Flame of Love*, stanza 11.7, p. 62.

32. Teresa describes the imaginary vision as being "so clear that it seems like reality" and "a living image" which imagination is unable to produce in its ordinary functioning. "How could we picture Christ's Humanity by merely studying the subject or form any impression of His great beauty by means of the imagination"? *The Autobiography of St. Teresa of Avila*, tr. and ed. E. Allison Peers (New York: Doubleday, 1960), pp. 268, 261, 262.

33. In writing "first" I do not wish to imply that those states are restricted to one particular stage of development. They may be part of a recurring experience, as they clearly were in St. Teresa's case.

34. *Psychology and Religion: West and East*, tr. R. F. C. Hull (New Haven: Yale University Press, 1938), pp. 542–52. Jung's interpretation was vaguely anticipated in 1902 by William James, in 1902, *The Varieties of Religious Experience* (New York: Collier Books, 1961), p. 375, and, uncritically, by H. Delacroix, *Études d'histoire et de psychologie du mysticisme; les grands mystiques chretiens* (Paris: F. Alcan, 1908).

35. "Through the former type of vision [the intellectual] which, as I said, reveals God without presenting any image of Him, is of a higher kind, yet, if the memory of it is to last . . . it is a great thing that so divine a Presence should be presented to the imagination and should remain within it. These two kinds of vision almost invariably occur simultaneously." *The Autobiography of St. Teresa of Avila*, Peers, p. 263.

36. William Johnston, explaining the suspicion with which the phenomena of the "makyo" stage in the developing Zen enlightenment are regarded, interprets it as the rising of the unconscious into the conscious mind. *The Still Point: Reflections on Zen and Christian Mysticism,* pp. 10 and 60. St. John of the Cross claims that "both God and the devil can represent the same images and species." *The Ascent of Mount Carmel,* tr. and ed. E. Allison Peers (New York: Doubleday, 1958), II. 16.3. Even Teresa who reports some of her most striking visions as having been of this kind, nevertheless adds that they are open to "illusions of the devil" and that she herself has been deceived by them. *Autobiography,* ch. 28, esp. Peers, pp. 259 and 263.

37. *The Ascent of Mount Carmel,* II. 16.11. Also: II. 19.

38. Ibid., II. 17.3.

39. *Relations,* in *Works,* tr. E. Allison Peers (New York: Sheed and Ward, 1946), I, 362.

40. *Obras Completas de san Ignacio de Loyola* (Madrid: B.A.C., 1952), pp. 49–50; tr. from *Varieties of Mystic Experience,* O'Brien, p. 247.

41. *The Ascent of Mount Carmel,* II. 23.3.

42. *Relations,* in *Works,* I, Peers, p. 364.

43. *The Ascent of Mount Carmel,* II. 24.4 and II. 24.2.

44. Ibid., II. 26.5.

45. William James was undoubtedly right in ascribing this quality to all mystical states. Cf. *Varieties of Religious Experience,* 1961 edition, p. 300.

46. *Brihad-Aranyaka* 4.3.28 in Hume, *Thirteen Principal Upanishads.* Teresa in a text which strongly emphasizes the total passivity of the experience, qualifies her assertion about the lack of knowledge: "Here we are all asleep, and fast asleep to the things of the world, and to ourselves." *Interior Castle* (Fifth Mansions), tr. E. Allison Peers (New York: Doubleday, 1961), p. 97.

47. *Dark Night of the Soul,* II 23.11.

48. Jacques Maritain, *Redeeming the Time* (London: Geoffrey Bles, 1946), p. 42. Maritain distinguishes between the "natural" mystical experience in which the soul is attained directly and God indirectly, and the "supernatural" in which God is attained directly (p. 246). I am not sure that such a distinction can be maintained consistently on a theological level, much less on a philosophical level. In all religious mysticism the self is immediately perceived in its transcendent dimension or, in Maritain's language, in its sources.

49. Luis de la Puente, *Vida del P. Balthasar Alvarez* (Madrid, 1615), ch. XV, tr. and quoted in Poulain, *The Graces of Interior Prayer,* p. 83.

50. This is especially the case for Joseph Maréchal; cf. *op. cit.,* pp. 102 and 196. But we find it also in Rudolf Otto, *Mysticism East and West,* tr. Bertha L. Bracey and Richenda C. Payne (New York: Macmillan, 1932 and 1970), pp. 50–88, and, with some qualifications, in the Thomist Jacques Maritain, *The Degrees of Knowledge,* tr. Gerald Phelan (New York: Scribner, 1959), pp. 261ff, and 446–50. Compare with St. Thomas, *Summa Theologiae,* II–II, q. 180, a. 5.

51. Joseph Maréchal, *op. cit.,* p. 192.

52. *Dark Night of the Soul,* II 17.3.

53. *De Trinitate,* XV. 3.5.

54. O. Brooke, "The Trinitarian Ascent of the Soul to God in the Theology of William of St. Thierry," *Recherches de théologie ancienne et medievale* 26 (1959) 85–127.

55. *The Mind's Road to God,* tr. George Boas (Indianapolis: Bobbs-Merrill, 1953), p. 23.

56. *Katha Upanishad* 5.12; Hume, p. 357.

57. *Isa Upanishad* 6; Hume, p. 363.

58. Sermon "Qui audit me, non confundetur," in *Meister Eckhart*, tr. Raymond Bernard Blakney (New York: Harper & Brothers, 1957), p. 205.

59. "Sermon for Christmas" in *Signposts to Perfection*, selected and tr. Elisabeth Strakosch (St. Louis: Herder, 1958), pp. 3–4.

60. *Spieghel der eeuwigher salicheit* in Jan Van Ruusbroec, *Werken* (Tielt: Lannoo, 1947), Vol. III, p. 167.

61. *Die gheestelike brulocht* in *Werken*, I, p. 246. *The Adornment of Spiritual Marriage*, tr. Wynschenck (New York: E. P. Dutton, 1916), p. 174.

62. *The Adornment of Spiritual Marriage*, p. 127.

63. Ibid., p. 130.

PART V
Theological Appraisals

31

Ontology and Theology of Christian Mysticism

JOSEPH MARÉCHAL, S.J.

One preliminary remark.

Even supposing that a *purely psychological* (*phenomenal*) theory of the states of prayer could be perfected on all points, there would always remain room beside it for a theological interpretation of the nature and causes of these states. For without question God can act supernaturally in the human soul after an empirical manner capable of reduction to the classical forms of psychology. The doctrine of grace remains in any case untouched. We have elsewhere insisted on the distinction of points of view which is here imposed.[1]

Therefore, if we take the trouble to form an ontological and theological conception of the mystical states (one which is likewise in positive harmony with their positive phenomenology and with the indications of psychology), this is assuredly not in order to save the dogma of supernatural grace, which is in no wise threatened, but from a purely personal concern to come to grips as closely as possible with the "integral" truth.

Let us then, from this complete point of view, once more examine our problem on all sides to enumerate its data.

I. THE INTEGRAL DATA OF THE PROBLEM

1. First of all, as we have seen, the most authoritative witnesses of Catholic mysticism unanimously affirm the existence of a strictly intellectual intuition in the high states of contemplation, the object whereof is not the pantheistic Absolute, but the personal God of Christianity, the indivisible Trinity.

2. This intellectual intuition, in spite of its sovereign liberty, is very generally prepared for by a progressive "unification" of the complete psychological and moral life of the contemplative.

3. On the other hand, from the standpoint of purely profane psychology, the life of the mind in man consists entirely, with the fettering but

necessary collaboration of the body and the sense-life, in an effort of *indefinite co-ordination,* whose limit is the possession of the absolute Good. This twofold effort represents the two aspects of the fundamental tendency of all intelligent nature to the immediate assimilation of Being in an intuition. The radical finality of the human individual, then, is wholly directed toward the Absolute, although it only contrives to display itself here on earth in the plane of quantity. Being is never naturally presented to our intelligence apart from material symbolism, although the interior movement of our intelligence carries it beyond matter; and though even if we had the immediate, intellectual intuition of created "intelligibles," our radical capacity for embracing *being* would not be satisfied. All our psychology is contained in this natural inadequation of the fundamental tendency and the possible realization.

4. Let us pass to the point of view of Catholic theology. The inadequation whereof we have just spoken is the connecting link, the "stepping-stone," as Cardinal Dechamps said, of supernatural grace in human nature. We must not indeed forget that the bestowal of grace supposes an *aptitude* in the subject for its reception; a stone or a vegetable is of its nature inapt for this purpose. Now what is supernatural grace? It is a help, a gratuitous gift of God, which is marked by its finality; it is essentially and directly ordained to the supernatural end of man—that is, the "beatific vision," the intuition of God in the other life. Grace renders our acts "meritorious"—that is to say, able to bring about the vision of God under given conditions; it establishes a real, ontological relation between our activity and our supernatural end.

Thus it will be seen how "nature" and "grace" suppose and complete each other. The Christian God is not really distinct from the philosophical Absolute. The intuition of the divine Being, which constitutes, in the natural order, for the mind left to its own powers, an ever-receding limit, an inaccessible ideal, becomes, in the order of grace, the real and efficaciously procured end. Truth to tell, the natural activity of the mind is already seized upon, orientated and constantly stimulated by the implicit desire—*desiderium naturale,* as St. Thomas dares to call it[2]—for absolute Being; but this obscure desire hurls itself against the barriers of quantity and falls powerless; it grasps of Being only an image refracted in sense-perception, and all its effort has to be limited to refining a symbol. Let "Grace" supervene to compenetrate this effort, and the symbolic unity which it prepares in us will take on an ontological value; it will become an efficacious preparation, a real and internal title, to supreme unification in the intuition of God. Much more, it is a teaching of Catholic dogma that the very degree of charity—that is to say, in empirical language, the degree of unification of the interior man by love—is in a very real sense the measure of final beatitude, of the supernatural possession of God.

In sum, Grace completes and crowns Nature by transforming into an *end* properly so called what was only the superior and inaccessible *limit* of a radical tendency, or, if you prefer, by building up into *efficacious means of attaining an explicit end* psychological activities which by themselves were but the *impotent expression of a hidden tendency*. The unifying development of the psychological life in natural ascesis, and the intimate development of the religious life in supernatural *ascesis*, then, work in a parallel fashion, in conformity with a single ideal of unity; it may be said that they are identical save in *value*. And this gives the explanation of many analogies which might otherwise seem disconcerting.

But in what can this "supernatural value," this "lived title" to divine intuition, really consist? One aspect of the problem alone concerns us here. It is quite evident that this "title" supplies for a natural insufficiency in us. What? There is one which immediately comes to mind. The human mind cannot, any more than any other creature, have the smallest "right" to God; sovereign independence is a primordial attribute, if not of the pantheistic Absolute, at least of the true Absolute, transcendent in relation to the world. But the intuition of God supposes the intimate and immediate union of the divine Being with the human intelligence, the direct "information" of the latter by the former; and this kind of taking possession by created passivity of uncreated activity is only conceivable as the effect of a benevolent initiative, an active and absolutely free "presentation," on God's part. We foresee here at the crown of supernatural destiny a "complementary event," at the same time withdrawn from the natural exigency of the human mind and indispensable for the latter's integration into an "absolute unity," for making its indefinite progression "proceed to the limit." What, then, does supernatural grace bring about? It gives, here below, for the future life, the certain pledge, the real title, of that benevolent initiative of a God who wills to communicate himself to saintly souls according to their capacity to receive him; it is, so to say, a "right" which God confers on them over himself, in the measure of their good works; or again, a proximate possibility of "seeing God" as soon as the veil of matter is torn away.

Now the Christian mystics have believed that their ecstatic intuition afforded a foretaste, a pale and fugitive anticipation, of the face-to-face vision of eternity.

II. SOME ESSENTIAL CHARACTERS OF CHRISTIAN MYSTICISM

Here, then, if we are not mistaken, are the principal data which the mystical documents, general psychology and Catholic theology in turn supply to us; the agreement of these data is so evident that a few words will be enough to enable us to bring to light a few really distinctive characteristics of Christian mysticism.

1. The first and most fundamental of these characteristics resides in *supernatural grace,* which compenetrates the whole religious life of the Christian. Truth to tell, this is an ontological characteristic inaccessible to direct experience. In fact, from the empirical and external point of view, all the isolated religious manifestations—lower than the mystical states described as immediate union with God—seem identical from one religion to another; there is certainly a difference in their combination and harmonization, but not in the psychological types to which they are individually reducible. On the contrary, from the interior, from the ontological standpoint, there is a radical difference between purely natural religious activity and that which grace—as is normally the case in Christianity—supernaturalizes; it is, as we have seen, nothing less than a difference of value and finality.

When we say that grace is not the object of direct experience, we by no means claim that grace has no empirical object. Quite on the contrary, in the terms of Catholic doctrine, the supernatural elevation of acts which have become "meritorious" (*gratia elevans*) is not separated from a powerful aid (*gratia adjuvans*) lent by God to the effort of the human freewill in pursuit of moral Good. The "supernatural finality" then can betray itself, to the psychological experience, by the particularly strong and elevated orientation of a whole of acts. But as this whole may always, in the eyes of a psychologist, be explained also by purely empirical antecedents, it is a chimæra to wish to *demonstrate* the influence of grace by way of pure induction. The role of actual grace must already be admitted in order that its concrete traces in personal experience may be recognized.

The first distinctive characteristic of Christian mysticism, then, is principally theological.

2. The second distinctive mark of Christian mysticism is drawn from the states of union; it is at the same time phenomenological and ontological. Not everyone will admit its reality; for it is not forbidden even to Catholics to reduce the higher mystical states to a simple quantitative increase of normal psychological potentiality and ordinary supernatural grace, or, if you will, in theological language, to a pure intensification of the infused virtues communicated at baptism.

We consider, however, basing ourselves on the unanimous declarations of contemplatives—the sole witnesses of their inner experiences—that high contemplation implies a new element, qualitatively distinct from the normal psychological activities and from ordinary grace; we mean the active, nonsymbolic presentation of God to the soul, with its psychological correlative: the *immediate intuition of God* by the soul.[3]

This literal interpretation of the texts alone furnishes a clear demarcation—and not merely a difference of degree—between the mystical states and ordinary contemplation. The hypothesis, moreover, does not seem exorbitant from the point of view of Catholic dogma, since the life of grace by which the mystic lives is an efficacious preparation for, and a title to, the vision of God; why should not God sometimes grant an anticipation of the other life, when the subject shows himself physically and morally susceptible of that anticipation? From the point of view of psychology even, the hypothesis does not seem so very strange; we have seen how the intuition of Being—the implicit ideal and latent regulator of all the mind's undertakings—is, so to speak, the center of perspective of human psychology.

3. If the interpretation that has just been proposed be admitted, we possess the most decisive differential character—phenomenological and ontological, necessary and sufficient at the same time—of a definition of Christian and supernatural mysticism. It will not be useless, however, to complete it by some *secondary characters*, which are mostly only corollaries. Let us posit first of all that supernatural ecstasy possesses all the psychological efficacy of natural ecstasy.

It may be asked indeed, since the essential of ecstasy depends upon God's free initiative, what role the psychological unification brought about by asceticism still has in it. This role, we think we may affirm without boldness, is very important. Let us not insist on the moral preparation which it seems in God's designs to require as a preliminary condition of his favors. There is another point of view, very often neglected—namely, that God, in ecstasy, communicates himself, not to a soul separated from a body, but to a "man," whose spiritual form has not ceased to be the very act of the body and the principle of sensibility. It may be imagined, then, that the repose of the ecstatic vision cannot fail to require a fitting adaptation of the lower functions; now is not the adaptation which will best favor for it the transcendent operation of the soul, a harmonious unification, analogically realizing here in the lower parts in diversity the very type of unity which the summit of the organism enjoys? The whole man must be "prepared" for the divine communications by his natural dispositions or by the training of ascesis. And if God, by an exception of which his providence is not lavish, choose suddenly to ravish to himself a soul still in prey to exterior agitation, to the conflict of tendencies and the play of scattered impressions, it will never be without at the same time reducing that tumultuous diversity to harmony and silence.

However, God is not accustomed to do violence to our natural mechanism. The normal predisposition for mystical favors will always remain, with a privileged physical temperament, the perseveringly progressive ascesis of recollected prayer and moral action.

4. The preceding remarks supply the key to a problem set us by the affirmations of the Christian mystics themselves. On the one hand they demand of the contemplative the assiduous practice of asceticism, renunciation, prayer; and they make of this not only a salutary exercise of moral perfection, but also, and especially, a prerequisite condition for the states of union. A superficial reader might believe that they profess, in these passages, to supply an efficacious method of training for ecstasy. On the other hand, they insist, with even greater energy, on the absolute powerlessness of the contemplative to attain to mystical union by his own strength; it is a free and gratuitous gift of God, a favor *independent of any law, withdrawn from human will* and consequently impossible to foresee.

The conciliation of these characteristics, so easy from the point of view of Christian mysticism, is doubtless also a differential note thereof.

In fact, in profane or pantheistic, and, it would seem, in Buddhist mysticism, *ascesis* appears to be the necessary and sufficient condition of ecstasy. The texts of the Moslem mystics are less affirmative on this point; while the God of their ecstasies is transcendent Being, the true God, the processes of training seem to possess in their eyes, if not a proper and independent, at least an infallible efficacy. The Christian mystics, however, formally vindicate the sovereign liberty of the divine initiative; for them the *ascesis* constitutes a condition normally necessary for ecstasy, doubtless, but it is never a sufficient one.

5. If mystical activity in Christianity is informed by grace, and constitutes therefore, relatively to our supernatural destiny, either a superior stage or the imperfect and transitory anticipation of the term itself, we may deduce from this necessary finality a new characteristic—rather negative, but very important—of true mysticism: *its entire agreement with Christian dogma and morals*. A complete concordance, it is true, would constitute only a presumption of its supernatural value; but a real disharmony would evidently ruin on the very point of conflict all claim to a supernatural value. Such is the exact bearing of the "moral" and "ecclesiastical" criteria applied to the mystical states.

We now understand the point of view of the Catholic Church in the valuation of states of this kind. Doubtless she admits, in a general way, their possibility and even their existence. But how is she going to diagnose concrete cases? Their mechanism does not interest her. Authorized guide of our ascent to God as she is, she is especially preoccupied with the relation of our proceedings to that supreme end; her appreciations and approvals have no other law. Were the mystical steps for a pious person a ladder of sanctity? Do they conform to the Gospel ideal? The

Church will approve, convinced that every good and salutary effect was seconded by divine grace. But she does not claim either to solve the "how" of this influence, nor to side with the particular interpretations, the subtle teachings, the true or pretended revelations which the writings of an approved mystic may contain; all these are "guaranteed" only in the exact measure of their supernatural value, a measure very different from that of human curiosity. Again, in the terms of Benedict XIV's formal declaration,[4] and in agreement with the most assured principles of theology, the guarantee given by the Church to particular revelations cannot compel the belief of the individual Christian; it is only a datum, eminently worthy of respect, whereof Christian prudence requires us to take account. The most entire liberty, therefore, is here left to the Catholic psychologist; all that is asked of him is to avoid levity, and when he wishes to judge, to put all the weights in the scale.

6. In conclusion, we ought to reply to a question which has probably arisen in the minds of some of our readers. Where is that supernatural ecstasy, whose general features we have outlined, to be met with? Above all, doubtless, in the princes of orthodox Catholic mysticism; but do all the high ecstasies attributed to Catholic contemplatives answer to this type? It is very probable that they do not; and we see no inconvenience in admitting that many descriptions of pretended mystical states cover in reality only more or less high stages of ordinary contemplation. But it will readily be seen that an attempt at particular qualification will often meet with insurmountable difficulties.

Are there, outside Catholicism, among Christian dissidents, true supernatural ecstasies?

Since everyone agrees that they share, if they are in good faith, in the grace of Christ, there is nothing to prevent, in principle, their benefiting, on a personal title, by the highest mystical favors.

But contemplatives outside Christianity: Moslems, Brahmans, Buddhists—or even mere philosophers without any positive religion?

We will not speak of the shocking practices of numerous "professionals," who lower mysticism to the level of a very material game. We willingly recognize that there are others whose relations of their experiences or theoretical writings bear such a seal of honesty and spiritual elevation that it would be repugnant to us to deny to their ecstasies all religious value. But we must not forget either that simple natural contemplation—even if it should, by excess of concentration, finally lapse into total unconsciousness—may already present a very high religious efficacy, since it ameliorates the moral life and thus prepares the ways for supernatural grace.

No doubt; but does not Catholic theology teach that supernatural grace, whatever be the manner of its bestowal, is not refused to any soul of good will? Why deny, then, that God may manifest himself sometimes even more directly, even outside Christianity, to some devout ascetic, who seeks him haltingly, with humble and persevering energy, perhaps by means of proceedings of a touching and exotic quaintness?

Let us hope, dear reader, that it may be so, but as to this you are asking us much more than we can know.

NOTES

1. *Studies in the Psychology of the Mystics* (1927), pp. 3–54.
2. St. Thomas Aquinas, *Summa contra Gentiles,* iii, cap. 50. (See the commentaries of Francisco de Sylvestris of Ferrara.)
3. As is shown by the very expressions we use, we only apply the hypothesis of an "immediate intuition of God" to the *higher* mystical states, which represent the complete perfection of infused contemplation. For more exact details, see the study entitled "On the Feeling of Presence in Mystics and Non-Mystics," in *Studies in the Psychology of the Mystics,* pp. 55–145.
4. Benedictus XIV, *De beatificatione et canonisatione servorum Dei.* Vermeersch, S.J., *Quaestiones morales,* Tomus prior, quaest. i, ch. ii: *De oratione,* pp. 64–109 (*De oratione extraordinaria seu de theologia mystica:* a sober and very explanation of the point of view of Catholic theology). Brugis, 1912.

32

The Natural Mystical Experience and the Void[1]

JACQUES MARITAIN

Classification of Knowings by Connaturality

This study is in the philosophical order. I have attempted to arrange in some sort of synthetic *schema* the principal elements of interpretation and of classification which it seems possible to me to propose concerning the difficult subject of the natural mystical experience and of the void. The background for this study consists of the historical and experimental data which seemed to me the most significant in my random reading over many years and of reflections which I have long since pursued concerning the discrimination of the typical forms of knowing by means of connaturality. . . .

May I add, in order to give precision to my language in a manner which I believe conformable to reality, but which in any case may be granted me as a convention of speech, that in general by the phrase "mystical experience" I mean a *possession-giving experience of the absolute?*

. . . I shall first set forth in a few words the manner in which I believe it is proper to classify the various types of knowledge by means of connaturality. We are here dealing with a classification which is not empirological, but ontological and metaphysical.

1. I should like in the first instance to single out that type of knowledge by means of *affective connaturality* which in the most general and the most common fashion concerns human life, because it is in the practical and ethical order. It is knowledge by means of an affective and tendential connaturality *with the ends of human action*—a knowledge which is at the heart of *prudential* knowledge. For the moral virtues being conjoint with one another and a prudent man being prudent only if he is also temperate, just, etc., such a man will form his prudential judgments not only in the mode of pure knowledge, after the fashion of a moral philosopher, but also in the mode of instinct or inclination and guided by his interior leanings—those very *habitus* of temperance or of justice

which are present in him and which are himself or something of himself. This knowledge of the things of human life by means of instinct or of inclination covers an immense territory. By the very fact that it is in the practical and ethical order and specifically concerns action, it does not belong to the world of contemplation. And if it can be integrated with the mystical life properly so called (to the extent that human action itself, among those who have entered into mystical state, is dependent upon the gifts of the Holy Spirit, particularly the gift of counsel), nevertheless this prudential knowledge by means of connaturality remains as such on an altogether different level from that of mystical experience, understood as being a possession-giving—and hence contemplative—experience of the absolute. But here is the *basal* type, the type best proportioned to human beings, of knowledge by means of affective or tendential connaturality, and you will observe that St. Thomas, in order to explain how the mystic "suffers divine things rather than learns them," refers to the case of the chaste man who knows the things of chastity, not by means of knowledge, but by means of inclination.

2. In contrast to this fundamental type of knowledge through affective connaturality, and to all knowledge of this sort, I must now call attention to knowledge through a connaturality which is not affective but intellectual, which is due to the *habitus* proper to speculative man as such, philosopher or scientist. Every *habitus* creates a proportion to the object, as well as a connaturality. But it is the intelligence of the mathematician or of the metaphysician, which is thus connaturalized with the things of mathematics or metaphysics, and this intellectual connaturalization acts only to perfect and facilitate the play of knowledge in the mode of pure knowledge, by concepts and by notions. We have here a knowledge through *intellectual* connaturality with reality as possible of *conceptualization* and made proportionate in act to the human intellect. It goes on an even footing with the development of the *habitus* or proper virtues of the intelligence, and it is here that belongs the intellectual intuition—abstractive and eidetic (concept-forming) and capable of expression in a mental "word"—of the philosopher or the scientist, of him who knows in the mode of pure knowledge.

Is it possible that by following this road a metaphysician can arrive at a *natural contemplation* of divine things? I believe so. Is this natural contemplation of divine things a *mystical experience* in the natural order? I believe not.

Certain thinkers, who in my opinion somewhat dramatize and push to the extreme Aristotelian tendencies and the *nihil est in intellectu quod non prius fuerit in sensu*, would like to say, with Father Thomas Philippe,[2] that metaphysical effort, far from preparing us in some fashion for union with God, would rather make us despair of such a union, and throw us back to earth, broken rather than unified, after having caused us to cast ourselves against the barrier of the steely sky which cuts off divine transcendence from every means of human knowing. The philosopher as such cannot contemplate divine things; he is, as it were, an Icarus of contemplation, and the movement proper to him hopelessly casts him down into the realm of the multiple and the created. Others, on the contrary, follow Platonic tendencies, even if they do not go so far as to admit that there is in the soul a door other than the senses whereby the soul naturally opens out over the real by an immediate existential contact; they believe with Father Rousselot and his school or with Father Festugière (author of a recent and much praised study on Plato) that metaphysical effort can lead (exceeding itself, but moving always in the same direction—the direction of the intelligible reality to be conquered—and by virtue of the same initial eros) either to a mystical experience in the natural order, a natural mystical union with that One or that Good which Plato placed above being, or else at least to a contemplation which, by its specific dynamism and in order to satisfy its constituent desire, demands that it pass over the threshold of supernatural realities and that it become, by means of the gifts of grace, the supernatural mystical union, conceived above all as an intellectual intuition of the absolute Being.

If we turn to St. Thomas, we find that he is less pessimistic with regard to philosophy than is Father Thomas Philippe. And indeed how should ananoetic or analogical intellection, set in motion by the natural movement of metaphysical thought toward the cause of being, and well aware, although welded to human means of knowing, that the divine reality infinitely exceeds these means and is not circumscribed by any of our concepts—how should this intellection not seek to make itself more stable in a more and more simplified and in a better and better savored meditation of that prime reality? Have we not here a normal effect of the intensive increase of the *habitus* of natural wisdom, especially if, with regard to the conditions of its exercise, it dwells in a climate of grace's strengthening? Doubtless such a contemplation is more speculation than contemplation, and its fixity remains very imperfect with respect to the superior fixity of supernatural contemplation. "It flies, it is not at rest," whereas of mystical contemplation one must say: *Et volabo et requiescam.* Yet on its own account it merits the name of contemplation, albeit in an *analogical* fashion. St. Thomas admits the existence of such a philosophical contemplation, and he admits that it has God for its object. "For, according to the Philosopher in the Tenth Book of the *Ethics,* this contemplation consists in the action of the highest power there is in us, that is to say the power of the intellect, and in the most noble *habitus,* that is to say wisdom, and also in the most worthy object, who is God.

This is why the philosophers used to set aside the last days of their lives for the contemplation of divine things, employing their earlier days in the other sciences, in order to become thereby more capable of considering that which is divine."3

On the other hand this natural contemplation of God is not a mystical experience, even in the natural order. It is not a possession-giving experience, it occurs at the summit of the powers of the abstractive ideation of the intellect, it knows God by means of things, at a distance, and in an enigmatic fashion; doubtless an eidetic intuitivity can develop there by means of the habit of meditation, of recollection, and of metaphysical serenity, and receive from the natural love of God an affective and experiential coloring, and in some sort mimic a true experience thanks to a high intellectual taste and to a certain simplification; this intuitivity remains, however, far removed, either from an intellectual intuition of the *esse divinum* which is possible only by means of the illumination of the light of glory, or from the unitive experience of the depths of God which is possible only by means of the gifts of grace. Of itself the philosopher's contemplation stops short at a feeling of presence which, however exalted, however powerful, however illuminating it may be, so far only concerns God the Cause of things, attained from a distance in the mirror of things and as present to them. It is not the hidden God attained in His uncommunicable life by the experience of union. Knowledge through intellective connaturality with reality as capable of conceptualization, knowledge *per modum cognitionis*, this knowledge remains such even when it makes use—dialectically and notionally—of the *via negationis*."4 In short there is no natural intuition, as Plato would have had it, of the supersubstantial One. And the philosophical contemplation of divine things doubtless corresponds—albeit in an extremely imperfect and deficient fashion, which merely makes one's thirst the greater—to that natural desire to see the First Cause, which, although conditional and inefficacious, is at the deepest depth of spiritual creatures.5 But this desire itself is essentially distinct from the natural tendency of the created intelligence toward its proper and specifying object, which is being *in communi*, not the Cause of being. The natural desire to see the Cause of being *derives* from the natural desire of knowing being; it is a corollary thereof; it is in no way identified therewith. From this it follows that every great metaphysic is indeed pierced by a mystical aspiration, but is not built thereon. By an at least theoretically normal effect, the philosophic contemplation of God indeed implants in the soul a longing which mystical union alone will satisfy. In this sense it aspires to such a union, as a lower thing aspires to a higher, but it does not seek to pass into mystical union by virtue of its specific dynamism and of its own constitutive desire.

That there could exist in the proper sense of the word a natural mystical experience, which prolongs and consummates a metaphysical élan is what I shall undertake to show in the second portion of this chapter. But —and this is the point which in my opinion the school of Father Rousselot does not sufficiently stress—this philosophic overreaching of philosophy, this metaphilosophical contemplation does not continue the natural movement of philosophy in its own direction, which, according to Aristotle, and according to the truth of our nature, is a movement toward things and toward reality to be grasped by eidetic intuition; on the contrary it inevitably presumes a kind of reversal, a reversal against the grain of nature; and hence the bursting forth of a desire which is surely not the constitutive desire of philosophy itself, the intellectual desire of knowing being, but a deeper desire suddenly set free in the soul and properly religious, a desire which is no longer that of the intellect wishing to see the first Cause, to which I referred a moment ago as a sequel of the intellectual desire of knowing being. The desire of which I am now speaking is one more radical than the natural desire of the intelligence for being and than its natural desire for the Cause of being, for this is the natural desire not of a special faculty, but of the whole man, body and soul. This is, I believe, the desire essential to every creature to join again *its* sources and the principle of *its* individual being, in other words, that natural love of the part for its Whole—for the divine and separate Whole—which St. Thomas[6] finds in every creature; in a stone, a rose, a bird, as well as in a rational creature, and which implants in the heart of all things, tending toward their principle and toward the good of the whole even more than toward their own specific action and their own good, a sort of hyper-finality.

3. A third category of knowledge by means of connaturality is that of *poetic* knowledge, or knowledge in the mode of creation. I believe it to consist in a knowledge by means of *affective* connaturality with reality as *non-conceptualizable,* because awakening to themselves the *creative depths of the subject.* Stated in other words, this is a knowledge by connaturality with reality according as the latter is emboweled in subjectivity itself in so far as intellectually productive existence, and according as reality is attained in its concrete and existential consonance with the subject *as subject.*

Raissa Maritain and I have tried, in a recently published essay,[7] to characterize this sort of knowledge and its relationship to mystical knowledge; therefore I can here treat the matter very briefly. Let it suffice to note that poetic knowledge is indeed, and preeminently, an experience, and is more an experience than it is a knowledge. But on the one hand let it be noted that, being placed within practical lines, like knowledge by means of prudential connaturality (not in the lines of *agibile*, but in those of *factibile*) it doubtless disposes the mind to contemplation, and it is full of contemplative flashes, but it is not properly contemplative nor possession-giving; it is situated at the minimum of knowledge and the maximum of germinative power; it does not have its goal and its fruit in itself, it does not tend toward silence, it tends toward utterance *ad extra*, it has its goal and its fruit in an external work in which it objectifies itself and which it produces. On the other hand that which is typically *grasped* or *apprehended* in this experience is not the absolute but rather the intercommunion of things which themselves and with the subjectivity they reveal to itself, in the spiritual flux from which existence derives. Thus poetic knowledge is truly experience, but it is not mystical experience, it is not possession-giving experience of the absolute, even though we are justified in recognizing "the proximity, in the same divine source, of the experience of the poet and of that of the mystic."[8]

4. I come now to the fourth sort of knowledge by means of connaturality, and it is this sort which interests us here. It takes place by means of connaturality which reality as *non-conceptualizable* (and in this it is the same case as poetic experience). But, and here is the distinguishing feature, this reality grasped according as it is non-conceptualizable is at the same time grasped *as the ultimate goal of the act of knowing in its perfect immanence,* an interiorized goal in which knowledge has its fulfillment, its fruit and its living repose. In other words, this is a knowledge by means of connaturality with reality as *non-objectivable in notions,* and yet *as goal of objective union.* Here is the mode of knowing which to my mind characterizes the mystical experience in general: knowledge of contemplation (the philosophic contemplation to which I referred earlier in this chapter being the inferior analogue of contemplation, and mystical contemplation, under present discussion, the superior analogue, itself hierarchically diversified). Knowledge not in the mode of practical inclination, like prudential experience; not in the mode of pure knowledge, like the natural contemplation of philosophers; not in the mode of creation, like poetic experience; but in the mode of nescience, of possession-giving not-knowing.

This sort of knowledge is in turn divided, I believe, into two essentially distinct types, according as the connaturality which it involves is itself either *affective* or *intellectual.*

It must be noted that, as I have sought to explain elsewhere, supernatural charity alone is capable of connaturalizing the soul with the divine. Therefore in the first instance—affective connaturality—we are dealing with supernatural mystical experience, with a supernatural contemplation which, by means of the union of love (*amor transit in conditionem objecti*) and of a specific resonance in the subject itself, becomes an instrument of knowing, attains as its object the divine reality, of itself inexpressible in any created word. The problems relating to this supernatural contemplation are not germane to the subject of this chapter. The short formulas which I have just used in their connection sufficiently indicate that while I have a high regard for the researches of Father Maréchal,[9] researches which supply us with so much precious data on comparative mysticism, I think that the truer theology of supernatural contemplation is to be found less in a theory of the *intuition* of God than in the substantially converging views of John of St. Thomas and of St. John of the Cross regarding divine experience by means of the union of love.

In the second case—intellectual connaturality—we are dealing (I come to the subject at last!) with a natural contemplation which by means of a supra- or para-conceptual intellection attains a transcendent reality, of itself inexpressible in any human mental word. There we have the typical mode of knowing in the natural mystical experience.

Before concerning myself more closely with this natural mystical experience, I must make two more digressions.

In the first place I should like to make myself clear concerning the words *object, objective union,* of which I have made use in connection with the knowledge of contemplation and with the mystical experience in general. These words have the disadvantage of bothering a certain number of philosophers from the outset, be they idealists or existentialists (existentialists formerly idealists) and I am afraid that these words will be disapproved by Hindu thinkers, whose evidence is particularly important in the present discussion. Why is this the case? Because in the eyes of an idealist the object is a product of the mind which separates the being from the subject, and in any case object signifies duality of the known and of the knowing, whereas in the mystical experience there is a sovereign unity. With perfect exactitude St. John of the Cross says: "Two natures in a single spirit and love"; and the teachers of the Vedanta might like to say, "Identity pure and simple," using a language which is doubtless monist only for lack of ability better to conceptualize the experience in question. Well, then, what I merely wish to point out is that I am herein using the words *object* and *objective union* in a strictly Aristotelian and Thomist sense and that under these conditions the difficulties and anxieties to which I refer lose their reason for existence. For in this case the object is only reality itself, according as it is present in act to the soul, and abolishing all separation in such a manner that the soul *is* intentionally the known reality, and that, while being specified by the object, in this very fact the soul indeed itself specifies itself. Objective union is the very consummation of the unity between the knowing and the known, according as the latter is the goal in which the knowing flowers forth in its own specific actuality, and rests therein. For Thomists the intentional identification of sense and of its object is so strong that pure sensation is in itself an unconscious process, so strongly does it absorb the sentient in the sensed; and the notion of object so little implies duality that God, the subsistent Simplicity (but a transcendent and infinitely rich Simplicity) is to Himself His own object, in an intuition which is His very being and the triumph of most perfect unity.

My second digression relates to the existence of a great zone of natural pre-mysticism—in the intellectual as well as in the affective order—which is not to be confused with the natural or supernatural mystical experience; this zone of natural pre-mysticism is the province of the intuitions, warnings, forebodings, premonitions, divinations which bear on the individual and the concrete and whereof the noetic world of practical affectivity supplies us with so many examples. The province, again, of certain metaphysical intuitions vouchsafed after the fashion of natural illuminations or revelations;[10] and the province of certain exalted states of philosophic contemplation. Here also is the province of other states of contemplation which have a strongly affective hue and which, without being poetic experience itself, are very common with poets (I am here thinking of Keats, Shelley, and many others) and which poetic experience induces or presumes. Here is finally the province of the numerous cases of "religious experience" of which William James has collected so many examples, and of the luxuriance of "religious phenomena," often more or less aberrant, in which the Orient seems even richer than the Occident. Moreover, all such are not typical and specific forms, but rather accidental manifestations or general and inchoate dispositions of natural spirituality.

The Possibility of an Intellectual (Negative) Experience of the Substantial Esse of the Soul

I have just said that the problems which concern supernatural contemplation are foreign to the subject of this chapter. Nevertheless, it is necessary that I summarily refer to these problems in order to find an easier introduction to the ideas which I should like to propose.

The supernatural mystical experience, by means of affective connaturality with the deity, not only finds a natural analogy in the prudential experience of the things of human action, in the knowledge in the mode of inclination, for example, which the chaste man has for everything which concerns chastity. This experience has many another natural analogue, especially poetic experience. But that which I should like to point out is that, being at once a contemplative knowledge and a contemplation by means of love, the typical value of this experience as contemplative *knowledge* will prove deficient the best natural analogies one can find with it in the world of inclination and of affectivity, while, inversely, the essential role which *love* plays in this same experience will prove deficient the best natural analogies one can find for it in the world of contemplative knowledge.

The love of the creature for the creature is thus a natural analogue of the most obvious sort for the supernatural mystical experience. Bergson, in his lectures at the College de France, liked to refer to this sentence: "I have suffered enough from my friend really to know him"; and he would also invoke the intimate knowledge which a mother has of her child. If the child, he said, stirs in its cradle, she wakes up, whereas the discharge of a cannon might perhaps not even half-waken her. The experience of profane love is of the same sort; suffice it to remember that the *Song of Songs* is the supreme image, consecrated by Scripture—and also largely used in the annoying rhetoric of mystical platitudes—of the trials and progress which pertain to supernatural mystical experience. But whatever incidence the love of the creature for the creature may involve as regards knowledge, its own proper constituent element is not contemplation and contemplative fruition, its specifying object is not a reality to be contemplated.

In the world of contemplative knowledge there is another natural analogue, preeminently valuable, which Father Gardeil has admirably expounded in his great book, *La Structure de l'âme et l'expérience mystique*. It is the knowledge of the soul through itself, the inner and obscure experience of myself, through myself. But if this analogue makes us experience better than any other that value of unitive contemplation and obscure intellective transparency which is characteristic of the supernatural mystical experience, such an analogue in itself alone, however, tells us nothing of the part played by love as proper means of knowledge in this experience. Moreover, in the last analysis, this analogy enlightens us by means of a sort of *as if* rather than by means of a fact, and it presents us only with a virtual image of the supernatural mystical experience: because the specific case to which it relates—the even partial actualization of the latent self-intellection of the soul reflecting upon itself—cannot, in fact, be realized in the present life.

John of St. Thomas, in fine sentences of which Father Gardeil has made use,[11] indeed tells us that the soul, to the extent that it is a spirit, has an habitual or latent knowledge of itself—because the intellect, emanating from the substance of the soul, is intelligibly informed by the latter as by a *species intelligibilis:* here is the permanent privilege of spirituality which the human soul has in common with other spirits. But John of St. Thomas at once adds that the actualization of this latent autointellection is impeded and prevented by the state of union with the body. Besides it could not be actualized except as an intuitive vision of the essence of the soul, a vision whereof it is clear that the soul is lacking in this world.

These objections are opposed to certain elements of the conceptualization proposed by Father Gardeil, not to the substance of his thought and of his views. Concerning both the structure of the soul *ut mens,* and its latent intellection of itself through itself, the recognition of the obstacle which the state of union with the body offers for their intuitive actualization is not enough to warrant our considering them as of slight account and no longer being concerned with them. These data, on the contrary, are something fundamental, and it is impossible that so important an ontological privilege should not have a primordial significance for human psychology, especially for everything which touches upon natural spirituality. And here especially we have the metaphysical condition and the first foundation for the faculty of perfect reflection upon its own acts which the soul enjoys by title of its spirituality, and which is the proximate reason for the experience which the soul has of itself through reflection upon its own acts. For in this reflection we are dealing with a true experience, attaining in its singular existentiality the principle of *my own* singular operations.

In accordance with the most natural exercise of our faculties and the most natural leanings of the soul and of the "communings of common life," there is a universal, a daily experience of the soul through itself, thanks to reflection upon its own acts. "Such an experiential apprehension of the soul, not through its essence but through its acts, can be called immediate, in the sense that the reality it attains is known by means of no other intermediary than its own actuation."[12] Here, then, is for each man a true experience of the singular *existence* of his soul, through and in its operations.

But concerning *what is* our soul, concerning its essence, or its quiddity, this experience tells us nothing. The existence which it grasps is indeed the existence of something, but of a something of which we are made aware only through the glimmering of the phenomena which emanate therefrom; it is the existence of the principle, unknown in itself, of the operations and psychic states grouped together in the conscious synthesis. In short, my experience of myself has, in the order of *suchness* or of essentiality, no more content than my own operations, the flux of more or less profound phenomena grasped through reflection. It is of altogether central importance to understand that my experiential knowledge of my soul (or rather of my substance, which is soul and body, but which is grasped by means of a spiritual activity, of an activity of the soul alone) thus remains in an order *purely existential* and implies no other *quid* offered to my mind than my own operations, grasped reflexively in the emanation of their principle. My soul (or my substance) cannot be experienced by myself in its essence; a *quidditative* experience of the soul is possible only for a separated soul, wherein, from the very fact of the state of separation, the latent self-intellection to which I have already alluded proceeds into act. Doubtless, the more my attention comes to bear upon the *existential* experience of my soul, the more shall I tend to neglect the diversity of objects and of operations the reflexive grasp of which is nevertheless the very condition for such an experience. Yet it remains true that as long as we go in the direction of nature, the experiential folding back of which I speak, however powerful it may be in certain "interior" souls, leaves the soul prisoner of mobility and multiplicity, of the fugitive luxuriance of phenomena and of operations which emerge in us from the darkness of the unconscious—prisoner of the apparent ego, if we agree thus to describe the phenomenal content which occupies the stage and indeed is the only set of qualities to be grasped in the existential experience of ourselves. Then, too, concern with the external world is a natural condition of mental equilibrium, and it often appears that the more man observes himself (observes himself psychologically, which is an altogether different thing from descending into himself metaphysically or mystically than to a disciplined and purified procedure) the more he runs the risk of dispersion or of *acedia*, if he does not indeed become a victim of schizophrenia and of the illusions of some pathological introversion.

Well then, let us suppose for a moment that the soul be by force constrained decidedly and absolutely to have reflexivity set the pace, but this time by means of an ascesis and a technique appropriate to a radical stripping of oneself, and by going deliberately against the grain of nature: supposing all this, would it not be possible—even risking all the dangers—to pass over from the common experience of the soul's existence (of which I have just been speaking) to an exceptional and privileged experience leading into the abyss of subjectivity? Would it not be possible to escape the apparent ego to attain the absolute *self?* Modified as we have sought to modify it, reworked and developed, Father Gardeil's *schema* could thus explain what I here set up as the typical case of natural mystical experience—Yoga mysticism—at least of the sort the best Hindu witnesses have lived and expressed. This mysticism, reduced to its essential kernel, would above all be a metaphysical experience of the substantial *esse* of the soul by means of negative, or rather annihilating, intellectual connaturality. I remember having put this question to Father Gardeil a few months before his death. He had not thought of such an application of his views. I, for my part, believe that this application is possible and is required by reality and that Father Gardeil has opened here an extremely valuable line of thought. For it would be an inestimable advantage to be able, at least in the classical case, to give to the natural mystical experience, and especially to that which we associate with India, an interpretation that respects its authenticity and its truth and that circumscribes with precision its proper domain.

I readily grant that the various recipes of Yogism can lead to all sorts of illusions and psychological extrapolations. But counterfeits, however swarming, must be counterfeits of something authentic. Moreover, it does not seem to my mind possible to reduce to a psychological aberration—however respectfully one does it—the age-old and manifold testimony, the testimony in the last analysis concordant, and very intelligent, of men who, in order to achieve a certain deliverance, have sacrificed everything else, and whom we have no reason either to consider sick or unbalanced. In all this there must be, at least for certain unexceptionable personalities (whatever may be the case with the camp followers and their repetitious verbalism, or even trickery), a real, not a misleading experience. I know very well that the economy of causes is a good principle, but it is such only on condition that with the explanatory material at our command we in no way warp the data of experience. It is also a principle of sound method not to challenge the integrity of testimony such as is here in case, unless we are constrained and forced to do so. It would be singularly unreasonable for us to refuse to non-Christian mystics the rules of objectivity upon which we properly insist in the study of Christian mystics. What do the men we are discussing themselves say? They say that they have experience of the absolute. And what name do they give to this absolute? They call it *atman,* that is to say, the Self.

I do not mean to say, of course, that these Hindu ascetics achieve a realization of that which I have just said was metaphysically impossible—an actualization, however imperfect, however partial, of the latent self-intellection of the soul. That possibility is excluded by reasons I have already stated.

What I am inclined to believe is, on the contrary, that these ascetics so thoroughly rid themselves of every image, of every particular representation, and of every distinct operation of the mind that they themselves in some fashion reduce, always by means of an act but of a negative act, an act of supreme silence—their souls and their intellects to such a latent, not-actualized autointellection. In short, the idea I am proposing is that they attain not at all the *essence* of their souls, but the *existence* thereof, the substantial *esse* itself. And how do they do this? They do it by drastically purifying and pushing to the extreme limit that ordinary experience of the existence of myself to which I have alluded. This ordinary experience, taking place by means of operations and acts, usually remain immersed in their phenomenal multiplicity; and it remains veiled because of this multiplicity. Now, on the contrary, risking everything to gain everything, and thanks to assiduous exercise reversing the ordinary course of mental activity, the soul empties itself absolutely of every specific operation and of all multiplicity, and knows negatively by means of the void and the annihilation of every act and of every object of thought coming from outside—the soul knows negatively—but nakedly, without veils—that metaphysical marvel, that absolute, that perfection of every act and of every perfection, which is *to exist*, which is the soul's own substantial existence.

Thus to drain oneself of every image, is this not rather to end with pure and simple nothingness? Doubtless this is often the case, whenever the operation involved misses fire, and then calls upon some illusion or other to substitute itself for the missing authentic result. But in itself such an operation, by the very fact that it starts from the normal activity and the immensity, in some fashion infinite, of the universe of psychic multiplicity in order actively to reduce and concentrate all this immensity (to an extraordinary degree exalting, through this very death, the vitality of the soul and the intellect), must, it seems to me, ends up in something altogether different from pure and simple nothingness, I mean in a negation, a void, and an annihilation which are in no sense nothingness.

We are here, then, in the presence of a negative and apophatic experience—I do not say of a dialectic and conceptual *via negationis*, as is the case with philosophers, but rather a lived *via negationis*, aneidetic and para- or supra-conceptual—which no more attains (for if it did it would not be negative) the intuitive vision of the essence of the soul than does supernatural mystical contemplation the beatific vision, but which makes use of the void and of abolition in order to know as unknown the substantial existence of the soul (which is the existence of the subject as a whole, for man exists through the existence of his soul). In like fashion supernatural mystical contemplation makes use of the connaturality of love in order to know as unknown the Godhead—*in finem nostrae cognitionis Deum tamquam ignotum cognoscimus*. It is necessary to point out, as I have indicated in passing, that the words void, abolition, negation, riddance, in reality signify an act which continues to be intensely vital, the ultimate actuation whereby and wherein the void, abolition, negation, riddance, are consummated and silence is made perfect. Coming at the end of a very long ascetic process in which the intellect more and more connaturalizes itself with silence and negation, it can happen that in certain instances this actuation finally surges up after so spontaneous a fashion that it seems altogether a gift from without and passively received; and that it can from the psychological point of view lose every active and voluntary appearance. Nevertheless, it in reality finds its source in an ascending movement which is fundamentally active[13] and in a supreme tension of the forces of the soul. Even from the psychological point of view the active and voluntary aspect must therefore remain predominant;[14] and furthermore, here is ontologically, of itself, an act, an ἐνέργεια, a vital and sovereign immanent act. Hence the principle which asserts that the soul knows itself by means of its acts is still herein preserved—paradoxically, since the act in question is the act of abolition of all act. Properly speaking, it is this act of abolition and of annihilation which is, I believe, the formal means of the experience under discussion. And it is in this sense that the void is the goal to which this experience tends, is not merely its condition but its proper medium, thanks to which the deep, fathomless "to exist" of the subjectivity is—negatively—transferred into the status of an object, not indeed of an object expressible in a concept and appearing before the mind, but an object entirely inexpressible and engulfed in the night wherein the mind engulfs itself in order to join it. Instead of saying: *amor transit in conditionem objecti*, in this case we should have to say: *vacuitas, abolitio, denudatio transit in conditionem objecti*. Here is the most purely existential experience possible, and it is an experience by means of not-knowing.[15] In the supernatural mystical experience, the void is a *condition* of contemplation (a condition actively prepared by the soul and, much more, passively received from divine influence) but its *formal means* is sovereignly positive: it is union of love under the inspiration of the Holy Spirit. In the case in discussion, the void is not only a condition but also the formal means of the experience.

I should like to indicate three other characteristics among the ontological notes of this experience.

In the first place, and as I have already hinted, the way of the void deliberately works against the grain of nature—hence the host of techniques. It requires the soul to forswear every movement toward things, which amounts to leaving the world. Whereas in poetic recollection the world is drawn into the subjectivity and awakens it to itself, here, on the contrary, the subjectivity separates itself from the world, in order to seek within itself alone a sleep more intense than all awakenings. Then again it may be pointed out that the mystical experience of the Self requires the soul to leave the world after an altogether different fashion from that required by Christian ascesis and contemplation. In both cases the crucial step must be taken, as Father Lallemant used to say, but in the natural effort against the grain of nature, it is to satisfy the demands of an ascesis entirely ordered to gnosis[16]—demands at once more negative and less profound than those of evangelic perfection. More negative demands: for that which is required of the Christian is the utter detachment of the heart from a world for which he, more than ever, continues to exist, a world which he continues to know and to love and for the salvation of which he suffers; but that which is required of the soul in the other case is that it purely and simply suppress the world, that it no longer exist to the world, at least until it reaches the state of deliverance and of "realization." Demands less profound: for a detachment which goes to the very roots of freedom itself and which causes man not only to leave the world but even leave himself (I do not mean merely egoism, the passions, etc.; I mean the supreme governance of self) is deeper than a detachment which goes to the roots of the intelligence. And a void and a dispossession which take place through the Holy Spirit and through grace should create suppleness and abandonments and a pliability toward that Spirit which bloweth where it listeth, and a real passivity with regard to God, and a freedom, which are altogether different from the burning immobility, the unbending confidence in the techniques of heroism, the victory over the attractions of multiplicity which result from the most tenacious of active tensions, from that concentration and liberation of which nature is capable at its own highest point.

In the second place we are here dealing, indeed, with a metaphysical experience in the strongest sense. The effort of the Oriental contemplatives seems indeed from this point of view to be an effort to follow the line proper to philosophic intellection over and beyond philosophy itself: but by means of that reversal of which I spoke at the outset and of the intervention of a natural desire, deeper and more total than that of the philosophic intelligence for the intellectual conquest of being. The proof of this is that many Yogis—such as Ramana Maharshi, of whom Olivier Lacombe wrote a few years ago[17]—did not begin with philosophy, but with a first experience of a metaphilosophical character. The metaphysical effort against the grain of nature which is thus required is a slow labor of death, which Plato also knew, but in which India particularly excels, an art of entering while living into death, into a death which is not evangelic death, intended to give place to the life of Another, but a metaphysical death, intended to winnow spiritual activities away from the body.

In the third place and finally—and this is a major matter, but one difficult to express in a few words—from the very fact that the experience here discussed is a (negative) purely existential experience, and from the fact that existence is transcendental and polyvalent, and is limited only by the essence which enjoys it, of which in this case we indeed know nothing, it is comprehensible that this negative experience, in attaining the existential *esse* of the soul, should at the same time attain, indistinctly, both this same existence proper to the soul and existence in its metaphysical amplitude, and the sources of existence. All this, according as the existence of the soul, taken concretely and to the extent that it is an act of effectuation *extra nihil*, is something emanating from and suffused by an influx wherefrom it obtains its all. This influx is not experienced in itself, of course, but rather in the effect which it produces, and itself in and through this effect. This is why the experience we are discussing in a certain way answers (as much as that is possible in the natural order) to the desire of all things to return to their sources and the principle of their being. Man thus attains to the sources of being in his soul, thanks to the techniques through which nature reverts toward the spirit against the grain of nature and in a certain way disjoints its own proper metaphysical texture. The Hindu experience appears therefore to be a mystical experience in the natural order, a possession-giving experience of the absolute, of that absolute which is the existential *esse* of the soul and, in it and by it, of the divine absolute.[18] And how could this experience, being purely negative, distinguish one absolute from the other? Inasmuch as it is a purely negative experience, it neither confuses nor distinguishes them. And since therein is attained no content in the "essential" order, no *quid,* it is comprehensible that philosophic thought reflecting upon such an experience fatally runs into danger of identifying in some measure one absolute with the other, that absolute which is the mirror and that which is perceived in the mirror. The same word "atman" designates the human Self and the supreme Self.

In this attempt at analysis of the intellectual experience of the existential *esse* of the soul by means of not-knowing, as in the classification of the various sorts of knowledge by means of connaturality which I proposed at the outset, what I have attempted to winnow out have been certain pure types. In fact, as regards mystical experience, I think that the purest specimens of natural mystical experience must be sought in India (the Buddhist Nirvana doubtless corresponding to the same basic experience as the *mukti,* or Brahmanic deliverance, but understood in a deficient fashion, and more easily lending itself to impurities, by reason of the phenomenalist philosophy of Buddhism); whereas the purest cases of supernatural mystical experience should be sought in the Christian contemplatives, particularly in those of the spiritual family of St. Teresa and of Marie de l'Incarnation (Ursuline), of St. John of the Cross, of Tauler, of Father Lallemant. To the extent that supernatural mysticism requires human preparation, involves structures and disciplines, one should find therein structures analogically similar to those of natural mysticism—yet transposed toward a specifically different finality, and hence specifically different themselves.

It is scarcely necessary to add that the contingencies of history and of the concrete present us with every kind and every degree of mixture and juxtaposition of natural with supernatural contemplations (leaving to one side parasitic phenomena, mimetic aberrations, or simple neuropathic interferences, which are not here under discussion). So also are there mixtures of the various types of knowledge by means of connaturality which

I have distinguished one from another. But I believe that one of the advantages of the distinctions which I propose here is precisely that they permit a more exact analysis of complex cases. In Plato and Plotinus is to be found, I believe, a combination of philosophic contemplation, of the poetic experience and of the natural mystical experience, the role of the latter being, although more or less hidden, far greater with Plotinus than with Plato. With many Sūfis it could be asked if faith in the divine transcendence joined to the natural mystical experience (which of itself alone would lead rather to a monist conceptualization) does not explain certain traits of Mohammedan mysticism. While the poetic experience with its own proper affectivity adds its complications among the Persians. Among Christian contemplatives, St. Augustine is a great example of the meeting of philosophic or theological contemplation with the supernatural mystical experience. And among Christian mystics of a Platonic cast—even in the case of a Ruysbroeck, but much more in the case of a Boehme—could there not be found a singularly exalting combination (but sometimes muddy) of the supernatural mystical experience with the poetic experience and with the natural mystical experience? In the orchestration made possible by these mixtures lies the charm—and also the danger—of all these great spirits.

I should like also to point out that in authentically contemplative souls, the poetic experience—withdrawn from its proper sphere and carried away by contemplation—can, it would seem, engage extremely complex relationships of mutual concurrence with the supernatural mystical experience, thus powerfully helping the soul to enter into the experience of union and also somewhat concealing the real extent of this union. For not only poetic *expression*, but the poetic *experience* itself can, by means of its discoveries and its intuitions, outstrip the mystical experience. And thanks thereto precious illuminations and spiritual lessons can be given by contemplatives whose dealings with their neighbors—and this is the great criterion—still betray hardnesses of nature and ignorances of self which the grace of supernatural contemplation, achieved in the same degree, should have reduced.

A Few Conclusions after the Fashion of Hypotheses for Research

It remains for me only to propose a few of the consequences which seem to me to spring from the preceding analyses, and which above all I submit as hypotheses for research.

1. What relationship is it suitable to set up between the *void* of the natural mystical experience and the supernatural night of the spirit? It seems to me first of all that the distinction made by St. John of the Cross between the night of the senses and the night of the spirit has not only a theological value but also, and first, a philosophical value. By this I mean

that this distinction is based upon the nature of the human being, and upon the double disproportion on the one hand between the senses (imagination, sensible affectivity, rational discursus immersed in signs) and the spirit (in the purely metaphysical sense of the word), and on the other hand between the spirit itself and things divine (even leaving to one side the supernatural).

But there is not correspondence or parallelism between the two nights of St. John of the Cross, nights which relate to certain painful phases of the perfecting and transfiguring of nature by grace, and the void of the natural mystical experience, which relates to the essential requirements of a movement against the grain of nature. This void, whatever suffering and terror it may carry with it, does not go so far as the night of the spirit, inasmuch as the latter dries up, disorganizes, and in some way "destroys" the spirit (not doubtless physically, but in all its operative measures and proportions and in its natural vital urge) in order that it may be made proportionate to the Godhead. For the void of the natural mystical experience does not make the soul proportionate to the supernatural, to God in His inner life; moreover, it is accomplished by means of the spirit itself, by means of the effort of the spirit, and it remains altogether intellectual, whereas the night of the spirit is brought about by means of *gratia operans* and by means of love, both of which know how to be as cruel as the grave. And this void is not, like the night of the spirit, a step on the road toward a better state (the transforming union), but the very goal to which one tends, since it is the formal means of the experience of the Self, and of the deliverance.

At the same time this void goes a great deal further than the night of the senses, inasmuch as the latter "destroys" the senses in order to make them proportionate to the spirit. The void of the natural mystical experience makes the spirit proportionate to itself. It is like an excess and a paroxysm of a night of the senses on the natural level, ordered toward passing beyond the purification of the senses, and toward a metaphysical death.

Nor is there any correspondence or parallelism between the nights which correspond in the natural order to the nights of St. John of the Cross and the void of the natural mystical experience.

Finally, I have already indicated what a fundamental difference in my opinion separates the void—metaphysical, and by means of suppression and concentration—proper to the natural mystical experience from the void, or rather the process of stripping which is evangelic, and in the mode of a gift of oneself, of a dispossession in favor of Another, more loved—such an evangelic stripping constitutes, moreover, not the formal means, but the condition (itself attributable to cooperating or operating grace) of the supernatural mystical experience. In order to avoid all misunderstanding may I point out that this evangelic dispossession of one-self, this void, or this evangelic stripping is linked in an altogether general fashion, in accordance with differing modalities and degrees, with all the states of supernatural contemplation. Here is something different from the night of the spirit and the special void which it involves, the two latter being a very special and even violent form of dispossession—torturing and altogether passive—and produced as an effect by the implacable light of contemplation itself and of the wisdom of love.

2. The distinction between the intellectual union and the union of love must be held as fundamental.

An altogether intellectual union does not go beyond the order of nature (in the sense that Christian philosophy and theology give to this word), even when such a union goes against the grain of nature.

In the case of love, we are dealing either with experiences and modes of contemplation which are pre-mystical, or else with incidences of poetic experience, or with a supernatural mystical experience.

Wherever there really exists a mystical experience by means of union of love, this experience is supernatural (be it typical or atypical, and perhaps more or less hidden or even more or less reduced, deformed, or "crushed" by the effect of environmental conditions, and in the absence of a proportionate mental regime).

The case of bhakti, once more to take an example from India, is one of those which in this connection presents us with the greatest number of problems; for such of the Hindu contemplatives as thus place piety in the position of first importance attribute a major role to love. To the extent that here we have authentic experiences—particularly those which probably came with the origin of the doctrine of bhakti—the testimony is such that it must be admitted, if we are to give credence to Professor Olivier Lacombe, that these experiences involve, at least participatively, a union of love with the Supreme Being, whose grace the soul awaits. Here is something which goes beyond the experience of the Self. Since we believe that sanctifying grace is offered to all men, and that souls which do not visibly belong to the Church can effectively receive this grace and with it the organism of the virtues and the gifts which are linked to it; since, moreover, it is not believable that God should refuse Himself to souls in good faith who, even if the idea of grace is with them only a natural product of the interpretation of psychological phases of aridity and fullness, nevertheless, by means of this manufactured idea of grace, call upon grace itself, which has not been revealed to them—in view of all these things, I do not see why one should deny that the mystical experience such as is found in the school of bhakti can depend upon a sort of *composition* of the upward movement of Yoga and of the disciplines of the natural contemplation of the Self combined with supernatural touches, and with the love of charity. Explicit knowledge of the mysteries of the redemptive Incarnation and of the gifts of supernatural life creates that mental and moral regime which is proportionate to the normal development of the supernatural mystical experience. In a regime on the other hand, where this supernatural mystical experience can gain admittance only as a stranger, and in disguise, it is possible to believe that there are many substitutions, and notably that graces by attraction from a distance come to impart to the natural mystical experience a higher value and a participation in the supernatural union of love. We are here confronted with the unexplored realm of questions concerning the state of the gifts of grace in non-Christian climates.

3. In order to survive the supernatural night of the spirit, which is a death and a despair of *everything* (even of God)—a lived, not a voluntarily suffered despair—at the heart of which grace alone maintains a secret hope—in order to survive such a night, divine power is necessary.

In the natural state there are nights of the spirit which are also death and despair, and, in the sense defined a few lines back, "destruction" of the spirit even unto its natural desire and its consubstantial taste for its own proper operative ends—a radical horror at its own life. This kind of frightful and suicidal disjunction between the immutable ontological structure of the spirit, with which is identified its natural appetite, and that same natural appetite, to the extent that it is grasped and assumed by the movement of the whole conscious appetitiveness and of the will, in any case bears witness, along abnormal lines, as does reflectiveness along normal lines, to the freedom of the spirit with regard to itself and to what might be called the fourth dimension in spiritual things. Are these nights the result of some great abuse, causing a passage into accursed regions? In any case they are, in their own special order, like unto a hell.[19]

One could cite many examples of these nights of the spirit in the natural order. May I point out that they can be found in the realm of pure intellectual knowledge, be it metaphysical or moral (such is the case with Faust, *drum hab' ich mich der Magie ergeben*), in the realm of poetic experience (one naturally thinks of Rimbaud), in a mixture of these two realms (here one thinks of Nietzsche, and those words which are so astonishing coming from his pen: *Crux mea lux, lux mea crux*). It should also be possible to find such nights in the realm of the natural mystical experience (I wonder whether tantrism has not some relationship with such a night?), it being understood that this night is an altogether different thing from the void which constitutes the formal means of the natural mystical experience, and of which this night would tend to induce despair.

For such nights there is no recourse. For here despair reaches, as in the supernatural night, the very ligature of the soul with the spirit. But being in the natural order and hence not including in their depths the secret power of a superhuman help, these nights of themselves end in a catastrophe of the spirit (an annihilation in the sensual; magic; insanity; moral or physical suicide). The supernatural night of the spirit is the only night from which the spirit can emerge alive.

The trials and torments of profane love are a natural analogy or an image of this supernatural night; but this love, as I have pointed out, is not a contemplative experience, and in it are not to be found natural nights *of the spirit*.

4. Is it possible to try to set forth the differential ontological characteristics of the supernatural night of the spirit? This question goes beyond the limits of the present study. Yet I shall be forgiven if I indicate that in my opinion three characteristics, when they are all present at once, and are joined to the anguish and shadows which strike at the root of the higher faculties, would seem to be characteristic of this supernatural night:

1. Mystical experience through union of love;
2. Transcendence with regard to all technique;
3. Evangelical behavior, or detachment of perfection in perfection. I here make reference to the fact that evangelic perfection is not perfection of some spiritual athleticism wherein a man would make himself faultless, indeed impeccable, but rather the perfection of love, of love toward Another whom the soul loves more than itself, and whom it concerns the soul above all ever more to love and to join, even though the soul in the process carries with it imperfections and weaknesses, deficiencies of the body and spirit, even sins which it detests and which it also gives Him, together with all that which He undertakes to clean away. This detachment of perfection in perfection is, it seems to me, the secret of the souls who have passed over the threshold of union; and this invisible behavior is reflected, as in a visible mirror, in a certain typical behavior toward one's neighbor.

NOTES

1. Based on a communication to the Fourth Congress of Religious Psychology, Avon-Fontainebleau, September 21–23, 1938 (*Études Carmélitaines*, "Nuit Mystique," October 1938).

2. Cf. R. P. Thomas Philippe, "Spéculation métaphysique et contemplation chrétienne," *Angelicum* (*Strena Garrigou-Lagrange*), Vol. XIV (1937), fasc. 1–2.

3. In III *Sent.*, dist. 35, q. I, a. 2, sol. 3.

4. Cf. *Les Degrés du Savoir*, Paris, p. 470, note 1; *The Degrees of Knowledge*, New York, p. 292, note 3.

5. Ibid., Paris, pp. 527–32; New York, pp. 327–31. Also see ibid., Paris, p. 562, note 1; New York, p. 350, note 1, which is not complete.

6. Cf. *Sum. theol.*, I, 60, 5.

7. *Situation de la Poésie*, Paris, 1938.

8. Raissa Maritain, "Magie, Poésie et Mystique," *Situation de la Poésie*, p. 67.

9. J. Maréchal, *Études sur la Psychologie des Mystiques*, 2 vol., Desclée De Brouwer.

10. Cf. *Les Degrés du Savoir*, Paris, p. 552; *The Degrees of Knowledge*, New York, p. 343.

11. John of Saint Thomas, *Curs. phil.*, t. III, q. 9, a. 1; *Curs. theol.*, t. IV, disp. 21, a. 2, n. 13. (. . . .)

12. *Les Degrés du Savoir*, Paris, p. 861. This reference not included in English edition. "Here the object of direct knowledge is merely like the necessary condition for the reflection of the mind upon itself; and its *species*, which as Father Roland-Gosselin properly observes, does not prevent the object being immediately known, no more prevents the soul, having become intelligible in act thanks to this species, from being immediately known in so far as it knows. We thus have a true *experience* of the singular existence of our soul, that is to say, through and in its operations, and the concept which we form of ourselves is an *experiential* concept."

13. *Science et Sagesse*, Paris, Labergerie, 1935, pp. 24–27; *Science and Wisdom*, London and New York, 1940, pp. 7–10.

14. As Marcel De Corte points out in his report (*Études Carmélitaines*, October, 1938) the Plotinian void is "entirely active." . . . "Obtaining the vision of God is the proper work of whoever has desired to obtain it." (*Enneads*, VI, 9; 4 and 7.) Such also, I believe, is the common doctrine of the Hindu *samnyasin*, making exception of the school of bhakti.

15. Neither in conceptual and abstractive knowledge nor in any experience of a positive sect (as, for example, poetic experience) is it possible to isolate existence by perfectly "prescinding" it from the essence. But the experience here under discussion being negative and by means of not-knowing, it can attain—as unknown—existence alone, without moreover knowing anything, precisely because it attains existence by means of the act of abolition of everything else.

16. That love for the supreme Lord or for lesser lords should be joined among Yogis to this intellectual contemplation is not extraordinary, but it is not the formal means of their experience, and the latter remains essentially gnosis.

17. Cf. *Études Carmélitaines*, "Illuminations et Secheresses," October, 1937, p. 173.

18. In terms of our own philosophic vocabulary and in accordance with distinctions which Hindu thought does not know, let us indicate more precisely that we are here concerned with the divine absolute as the cause of being, not as giving Himself as an object of possession. In the experience here analyzed, the divine absolute is not, Himself, properly speaking an object of possession. It is the substantial *esse* of the soul which is the object of (negative) possession; and by this negative experience of the self God is attained at the same time, without any duality of act, though attained indirectly. God being, then, not known "by His works," that is to say by His effects as by things known beforehand and which discursively make us pass to the knowledge of their cause, but God being known (1) by and in the substantial *esse* of the soul, itself attained

immediately and negatively by means of the *formal medium* of the void; (2) in the negative experience itself of that substantial *esse* (just as the eye, by one and the same act of knowing, sees the image, and in the image the signified)— all this being the case, I think it is permissible in such an instance to speak of a "contact" with the absolute, and of an improperly "immediate" experience (that is to say, one wrapt up in the very act of the immediate experience of the self) of God creator and author of nature. To explain this we must fall back on considerations *analogous*, on an essentially different level, to those considerations which make it possible in the supernatural order—and without falling back on a partial or transitory *intuition* of the divine essence—to speak of a truly "immediate" experience (in this case, by the union of love) of God, author of grace and dweller in the soul as in His own temple. (Cf. *Les Degrés du Savoir*, Paris, pp. 509–12, page 652, note 2; *The Degrees of Knowledge*, New York, pp. 317–19, page 403, note 4.)

In natural mystical experience we do not have an experience of the *depths of God*, an experience of the Godhead, and *in this sense* I still insist upon everything I wrote in the above cited work (pp. 532–34) against the possibility of an authentic mystical experience in the natural order. But here we have an experience of God *inquantum infundens et profundens esse in rebus*, indirectly attained in the mirror of the substantial *esse* of the soul; and in this sense the case of the negative experience of this *esse*, obtained by means of the void and against the grain of nature (and wherein God, without being Himself an object of possession, is attained by this same act of the experience of the self), brings further matter and correction to these pages in my book, for it seems to me this constitutes an authentic mystical experience in the natural order. I had not taken this case into account in Chapter vi of *Les Degrés du Savoir*, because at that time I had in mind only the mystical experience of the *depths of God*, and I considered the word mystical only in this major meaning. I now believe that a sufficiently careful reflection upon Hindu contemplation requires us to recognize the possibility, under the conditions herein analyzed, of a negative mystical experience of the *presence of immensity* itself.

May I here point out the distinction established by Ramanuja, which supplies, it seems to me, a remarkable confirmation of the views proposed in these pages—distinction between salvation by bare knowledge (the path of immanence and of indifferentiation with the universal Brahman—here is the natural mystical experience as we have sought to describe it), and salvation by grace (the path of love, and of access to the very Personality of the Brahman)? See the recent book of Olivier Lacombe—a contribution of capital importance to our knowledge of Vedantic Philosophy—*L'Absolu selon le Vedanta*, Paris, Geuthner, 1937, p. 372.

19. One could here revert to the remarks made by John of Saint Thomas concerning the state of lived contradiction wherein the spirit of the fallen angel finds itself, and concerning the kind of radical asthenia with which that spirit is stricken; *Curs. theol.*, t. IV, disp. 24, a. 2 and 3.

33

Unitas Spiritus

ETIENNE GILSON

First of all . . . let us examine the question of "pantheism" or the supposed "pantheistic tendencies" of the Cistercian mysticism; observing at once that while, as a matter of right, the very conception of a pantheistic Christian mysticism is a contradiction in terms, the mysticism of St. Bernard, as a matter of fact, is in radical opposition to all pantheism.[1]

As regards the first point, its settlement obviously depends on our definitions. Mysticism may be conceived in an endless variety of ways, some wide enough to embrace in their scope the vague poetical emotions of a Wordsworth or a Lamartine, others leaving no room for anything save the rigorous terms of a St. Thomas Aquinas or a St. John of the Cross. That is so much the more reason for taking up a position—we must offer our opponents a clear concept to discuss. Now in the present instance it is of the first importance to grasp that wherever there is any trace, how slight soever, of pantheism, there the problem of Christian mysticism ceases to arise.

By way of hypothesis, let us admit one of these poetico-metaphysical states,[2] in which is effected a sort of fusion of the soul and God, as if the two substances were henceforth one, were it only in a certain respect. Explain their nature as you will, such states always presuppose that the divine being is in no real and irreducible transcendence with respect to the human being. No one doubts, of course, that even for the poet or metaphysician who sets his face in this direction the states he takes for mystical are rare, exceptional, open only to an élite, and then only at the price of a severe discipline. But the question does not lie there, for what we want to know is simply this: whether, yes or no, we can admit the possibility of a coincidence, even partial, between the human substance and the Divine substance—whether we can admit it to be then in fact realized. To admit this is to evacuate the conception of mysticism of all its content for a Christian. For the Christian God is Being—*Ego sum qui sum*—and this creative being is radically other than the being of His creatures. The whole drama of Christian mysticism lies in the fact that the creature feels a need for his Creator much more absolute than that of any being for his god in any other metaphysical economy, and in the fact that, for the same reason, a Creator is much less accessible to his creature than is any god to beings less radically dependent on him. The Christian asks, and always asks: How can I rejoin Being, I, who am nothing? If you lower, were it but for an instant and at any point, the barrier set up by the contingence of being between man and God, then you rob the Christian mystic of his God, and you rob him therefore of his mysticism. He can do without any god who is not inaccessible; the sole God Who by nature is inaccessible is also the sole God he can in no wise do without.

The fact is, of course, that no other God exists. St. Bernard puts it clearly enough for those who are willing to listen. No matter how the mystical union may be interpreted in his doctrine, this at least must be laid down before everything else: that it absolutely excludes all confusion, all substantial unification, between the Divine *Being* as such, and the human *being* as such, and conversely. Had we no knowledge of the general tendency of his mysticism, or of the wholehearted Christianity it expresses, we should have, if we needed them, his own explicit declarations to assure us of this. Never, in any event, will the substance of the mystic himself become the substance of God; never, in any event, not even in that of the beatific vision—which otherwise would abolish the thing it is destined to perfect and fulfill—will any part of the human substance coincide with that of God; never, in any event, will that part of the substance of the soul we call the human will, coincide with this substantial Divine attribute: the will of God. *Manebit quidem substantia,*[3] the text is formal. There are others of the same kind, as we shall show farther on; but before coming to this point we must set out in detail a second thesis that flows at once from the foregoing.

Without going so far as to detect pantheist tendencies in St. Bernard, without even dreaming of such absurdities, some historians have credited him with a vague tendency to conceive the mystic union as an annihilation of the human personality, as if this were destined to be wholly dissolved in God. Here again the interpretation does not survive examination of the very texts which suggested it. Everybody thinks in this connection of the famous comparisons proposed by St. Bernard between the soul "deified" by ecstasy and the drop of water diluted in wine, or the air transfigured into light, or the glowing iron that becomes fire. But let us consider these expressions attentively; for never does his ardor tempt him to lose sight of that careful measure which is the true theologian's golden rule. What happens to the drop of water? "Deficere a se tota *videtur"*; it seems, but we know that even when indefinitely diluted it does not cease to exist. What happens to the glowing iron? *"Igni simillimum* fit"; it becomes as like it as possible, but it *is* not it, nor indeed could it possibly be it if it is to be free to become like it. What happens to the air illuminated by the sun? It is so penetrated with its light, "ut non tam illuminatus, quam ipsum lumen esse *videatur*." Here again we have a mere appearance, a transfiguration of an indestructible substance by the glorious form in which it is henceforth arrayed. St. Bernard therefore never spoke of any abolition of the creature, but of a transformation.

It is true that this transformation may appear at first glance as the equivalent of an abolition: *pene adnullari;* but that, in truth, is mere appearance. To what extent it is illusory, how far it corresponds to a reality, we shall have to consider. For the moment, however, we must particularly note that it can mean neither a destruction of the soul by the ecstatic union, nor even any diminution of its individuality. Quite the contrary. With its face set toward the beatific vision, ecstasy, although essentially distinct from that vision, prefigures and partakes of its characteristics. Now the beatific vision is the crowning of the whole work of creation. It consummates it. It is the establishment of the creature in a divine state of glory, in which it is borne to a supreme point of perfection such as only a God could gratuitously bestow. *Creatio, reformatio, consummatio,*[4] these are the three great stages of the Divine plan; and just as the "reformation" is that of the creation corrupted, so the "consummation" is that of the creation restored. It is already the same in the case of the mystic union, where the soul is borne, for short instants, to a perfection that is more than human, a perfection which, far from annihilating it, only exalts and glorifies.

Thus we are already assured of two closely connected points: the soul does not become the substance of God, neither does it lose its own being in ecstasy. Let us turn now to the positive side of these states and try to explain their nature without falsifying St. Bernard's expressions, retaining them all and weakening none. For observe—he does not hesitate to speak of a "deification": *sic affici, deificare est.*[5] What then are we to make of such a state? Undoubtedly it is a union, and the resultant unity. But of what nature is this union?

The answer can be put in a few lines. The mystical union integrally respects this real distinction between the Divine substance and the human substance, between the will of God and the will of man; it is neither a confusion of the two substances in general, nor a confusion of the substances of the two wills in particular; but it is their perfect accord, the coincidence of two willings. Two distinct spiritual substances—two substances even *infinitely* distinct—two wills no less distinct as far as concerns the existential order, but in which intention and object coincide to such an extent that the one is a perfect image of the other, there we have the mystical union and unity as St. Bernard conceived them. We have only to compare them with the union and unity of the Divine Persons and we shall see at once how far they go and where also they stop short. The unity of God is that of the *consubstantiale*, the unity of man with God is limited to the *consentibile:*

> Between man and God, on the contrary, there is no unity of substance or nature, and it cannot be said that they are One, albeit it may be said with certainty and perfect truth that if they are attached to each other and bound together by the tie of love, then they are one spirit. But this unity results rather from a concurrence of wills than from a union of essences. By which is made sufficiently clear, if I do not mistake, not only the difference but the disparity of these unities, the one existing is the same essence, the other between distinct essences. What could be more different than the unity of that which is one, and the unity which is merely the unity of several?
>
> Thus it is with these two unities. The thing that delimits their respective spheres is, as I have said, the line that separates "to be one" (*unus*) from "to be the One" (*unum*). For the word One designates the unity of essence in the Father and the Son, but to be one, when we speak of God and man, designates quite a different kind of unity, a tender consent of affections. Undoubtedly we may very well say that the Father and the Son are one (*unus*) if we add some defining word, as, for example, one God, one Lord, and so forth, for then we speak of Each with respect to Himself and not with respect to the Other. For their Godhead or their Majesty is no more diverse in Each than is their Substance, their Essence, or their Nature; and none of these last, if you consider it with due piety, is a thing diverse in Them, or distinct, but altogether One. I say too little; they are One also with Them. What shall we say of that other unity whereby many hearts may be reputed one, and many souls one? I think it does not deserve the name of unity when compared with this, which instead of being a union of plurality, marks the singularity of One. That, therefore, is a unity unique and supreme, not brought about by any unifying act but existing from all eternity. . . . But as to God and man each subsisting separately in his own proper substance and his own proper will, if they abide mutually in each other we understand it quite differently: they are not one by confusion of two substances but by the accord of two wills. In that then consists their union, a communion of wills and their accord in charity. Happy that union if you experience it; but if you compare it with this other, nothing.[6]

Words heavily charged with meaning, admirably defining the position of St. Bernard. The promised deification of the *De diligendo Deo* is nothing less, but also nothing more, than a perfect accord between the will of the human substance and the will of the Divine substance, in a

strict distinction of the substances and the wills. And let it not be supposed that here we have to do with any minimizing interpretation of the
doctrine of St. Bernard; to refuse to accept it under the pretext that it
wears the air of a *pia interpretatio* would amount to a refusal to grasp
anything whatever in his thought. Nor let us imagine, that if it is not to
be charged upon the timidity of the interpreter, it gives us any right to
denounce a constraint or embarrassment in St. Bernard's thought itself.
Harnack thought so, and would persuade us to the same opinion. Seeing
in St. Bernard an ardent mystical piety—the true piety—beating vainly
against the obstacles heaped in its path by the rigidity of dogma, he
could not but see in his doctrine the concrete expression of that conflict
between the interior life of the soul on the one hand and dogma on the
other, in which, according to him, the whole history of medieval theology may be summed up.[7] Strange subjective illusion in a scholar whose
work, so highly praised for its objectivity, is more deeply involved than
any other in the personal faith of its author. For there we have a complete misconception of the facts. St. Bernard is no mystic of love forced
against all his real inclinations to stop short of his aim by the dogma of
the Divine transcendence; the three points we have touched on in succession are strung upon an unbroken thread which, when followed out,
will lead us on to a fourth: the substance of God will never be our substance, the will of God will never be our will, union with God can never
be anything but the accord of two distinct wills, and *therefore* this union
with God can be effected in no other way than by and through love.
Here is no case of a love resigning itself to the transcendence of its object. If its object were not transcendent there would be no basis for the
existence of the love.

Here too we are in no need to fall back upon one of those logical re-
constructions with which history has perforce at times to content itself.
St. Bernard is not only fully capable of grasping his own thought but
excels in formulating it:

> God, the same God Who has said: *Ego sum qui sum,* in the true
> sense of the term *is,* because He is Being. What participation, what
> conjunction can there be between him who is not and Him who is?
> How can things so different be joined together? *For me,* says the
> Saint, *to adhere to my God is my good.* Immediately united to Him
> we cannot be, but this union may be effected perhaps through some
> intermediary.[8]

What is this intermediary, this middle term, between the creature and
Being? We might perhaps be tempted to think of cupidity or of fear, but
we know already why these must be considered as merely temporary expedients. The sole truly sure and indestructible bond is charity, for the

man in whom it dwells *tam suaviter quam secure ligatus, adhaerens Deo, unus spiritus est cum eo.*

Hence we may be well assured that the thought of St. Bernard is all of a piece; it is not in the least in the nature of a compromise between his deepest aspirations and any kind of external pressure or constraint. On the contrary, love is there inserted between Being and beings as called for by the gulf which otherwise would separate the creature from his Creator; it pours itself out in order to fill it. But observe well the way in which it fills it: the man who loves God becomes *unus spiritus cum eo.* Unity of spirit, therefore, is the sole bond of unity conceivable between creature and Creator. What are we to understand by that?

A unity of spirit is a unity, first of all, which is no more than the unity of two spirits, that is to say it is not that identity of substance we have explicitly excluded above, but only the perfect accord of their structures and lives. The true nature of this unity is expressed unequivocally in the word "likeness." The only way in which one spirit can become another without ceasing to be itself, is by way of perfect resemblance to this other. The thing that invests St. Bernard's mysticism with its distinctive character is the manner in which the mystical union is linked up with the nature of the divine image in man,[9] for it is just this that makes all the difficulties with which his mystical theology has been encumbered move toward the solution he provides. Let us go over the objections charged against it and see what becomes of them when looked at from the true center of everything—the fact that man is an image of God.

Cistercian ecstasy, it is said, and precisely in virtue of its ecstatic character, tends toward a sort of loss of the individual in God.[10] That love, whose so great vehemence precipitates the soul toward its divine object, can by no means attain it save by total self-renunciation—and exigence at issue with the very foundations of the doctrine, since love of self is there laid down as primary and indestructible. The objection is feeble. What is the object of the Cistercian ascesis? Progressively to eliminate the *proprium* in order to install charity in its place. What is this *proprium?* Unlikeness—that in virtue of which man wills to be different from God. But what, on the other hand, is man? A divine likeness. It is therefore perfectly clear that in such a doctrine there is a coincidence between the loss of "proper will" and the restoration of our true nature. To eliminate from self all that stands in the way of being really oneself, that is not to lose but to find oneself once more. The whole difficulty in which St. Bernard is here supposed to be involved is therefore simply due to a misconception. The soul that forsakes itself, detaches itself from self, far from renouncing its own being, is merely reestablished on the contrary in its own proper substance under the transforming influence of divine love. For what in fact is the true meaning of such expressions as *"deficere a se tota videtur,*" "*a semetipsa liquescere*" and others of the same kind? Always it is twofold. In the first place St. Bernard would say that the soul empties itself of this false ego, this illusory personality of self-will, brought into it by sin. In so doing, far from annihilating itself, it restores itself to its own nature. A disfiguring mask falls away, revealing the true countenance of a soul whose nature it is to have been made to the image of God. In the second place, such expressions have always a positive meaning as well, which is indicated by St. Bernard when he adds this commentary: "*a semetipsa liquescere, atque in Dei penitus transfundi voluntatem.*" A commentary, for the rest, with which we might easily find fault on account of its brevity, were it not in turn commented [upon] by the entire mystical work of St. Bernard. For this transfusion into the will of God is unity of spirit itself, and it is so moreover in a twofold sense.

Ontologically the soul henceforth lives by the spirit of charity, by way of grace, which in us is the gift of the Holy Spirit. The life of the soul has therefore become, in virtue of and by right of this gift, what the life of God is by nature. Unity of spirit, because by this same Spirit by which God lives in Himself, we live now by grace. Impossible to unite more closely two subjects that must needs remain substantially distinct. But unity of spirit once more, because since the soul is a likeness to God, the more it conforms itself in will to God's will so much the more does it become itself. Then the soul knows itself as God knows it, loves itself as God loves it, and loves God as He loves Himself. It subsists, but now it is to be considered as a substance which, although irreducibly distinct from that of God, had no other function than to be the bearer of the Divine likeness. This likeness is its "form"; the more it is enveloped by this form, as it is here below by charity and is destined to be the more so in glory, so much the more does it become indistinguishable from God. And so much the more is it itself. Of man, then, it may be said that he tends in effect, by way of love, to make himself invisible; for this image of God will never be fully itself till nothing is any longer to be seen in it save only God: *et tunc erit omnia in omnibus Deus.*[11]

And now perhaps we may read one of these much-debated texts with some little hope of understanding it more or less as St. Bernard did.

But flesh and blood, this vessel of clay this earthen dwelling-place, when shall it attain at last to this [*sc.* this love by which a man loves not even himself save for the sake of God]? When shall it feel affection like this [*affectum:* i.e., here, love], so that inebriated with divine love, forgetful of self, and become to its own self *like a broken vessel* (Ps. 30, 13), it may utterly pass over into God, and so adhere to Him as to become one spirit with Him, and say: *My flesh and my heart hath fainted away, thou art the God of my heart, and the God that is my portion for ever?* (Ps. 72, 26) Blessed and holy should I call that man to whom it has been granted to experience such a thing in this mortal life, were it only rarely or even but once, and this so to speak in passing and for the space of a moment. For in a certain manner to lose thyself, as though thou wert not [*quandamodo*, for man does not lose himself], and to be utterly unconscious of thyself and to be emptied of thyself and brought almost to nothing [*pene*, for the substance endures]—that pertains to the life of heaven and not to the life of human affection. And if, indeed, any mortal is occasionally admitted to this, in passing, as I have said, and only for a moment, then straightway the wicked world begins to envy him, the evil of the day disturbs,[12] this body of death becomes a burden,[13] the necessity of flesh provokes,[14] the weakness of corruption does not endure it, and what is even more insistent than these, fraternal charity recalls.[15] Alas! he is compelled to return into himself, to fall back into his own,[16] and miserably to exclaim: *Lord, I suffer violence, answer thou for me;* and this: *Unhappy man that I am, who shall deliver me from the body of this death?* (Rom. 7, 24)

Nevertheless, since the Scripture says that God *hath made all things for Himself* (Prov. 16, 4), the creature will surely at some time conform itself and bring itself into harmony with its Author. Some day, then, we shall come to love as He loved; so that, even as God willed all things to exist only for Himself, so we too may will to have been and to be, neither ourselves nor aught else save equally for His sake, to serve His will alone and not our pleasure.[17] Truly not the appeasing of our necessity,[18] nor the obtaining of felicity,[19] will delight so much as that His will shall be fulfilled in us and concerning us;[20] which, too, we daily ask in our prayers when we say: *Thy will be done on earth as it is in heaven.*

O holy[21] and chaste[22] love! O sweet and tender affection! O pure and perfect intention of the will!—surely so much more perfect and pure as there is in it nothing now mixed of its own,[23] the more sweet and tender, as nought is felt but what is divine. Thus to be affected is to become Godlike (*deificare est*).[24] As a small drop of water mingled in much wine seems to be wholly lost and to take on the color and taste of the wine; as a kindled and glowing iron becomes most like to fire, having put off its former and natural form;[25] and as the air, when flooded with the light of the sun is transformed into the very brightness of light, so that it seems to be not so much illumined as to be the light itself, and be entirely poured over into the will of God. Otherwise how will *God be all in all,* if in man somewhat remains

over of man?[26] The substance indeed will remain but in another
form, another glory, and another power.[27]

Let us now consider the problem of love in the light of the foregoing
conclusions. We know that man is an indestructible substance, resistant
to the fusion of ecstasy or even to that of the beatific vision. But we
know also that the end for which this substance was created is to realize
a perfect divine likeness. Now if it be true that in virtue of its form it
tends to differ from God in ever less and less degree than any given degree, then it is very evident that, at the limit, the famous antinomy between love of self and pure love disappears—at the limit it has neither
meaning nor *raison d'être*. God is a Love of Himself for Himself. Man is
so much the more himself as he is the more like God. Since he is an
image, the less he is distinguishable from the original the more he exists.
If then we eliminate from his nature this *proprium* which is no part of
his nature but corrupts it, what remains is a perfect image of God, that is
to say of an infinite good that loves itself only for itself. What difference
is there then, at the limit, between loving God and loving oneself, then,
when one is no longer anything but a participation in the love which
God bears Himself? In the soul which loves itself no longer save for
God's sake, the love it bears itself is englobed in God's love for Himself,
since God loves it only as a likeness to Himself and it loves itself only as
a likeness to God.[28]

*   *   *

The first characteristic of pure love in the doctrine of St. Bernard lies
in the exclusion of every other affection. I put it as St. Bernard puts it,
but what he means to say is rather that pure love is *inclusive* of all the
other affections. The reason is this. The purity of love is one and the
same thing with its intensity; let us say, if we want at any price to maintain a distinction between the two conceptions, that its purity is the first
and most immediate effect of its intensity. That is why the reference to
ardent love recurs so incessantly in his writings. The ardor of love,
pushed to the last degree of intensity, has for apparent effect the elimination from the soul of all that is not itself. There is no longer any room
left for the rest. But we have to remember on the other hand that love is
essentially the very opposite of a destroying force, and that the only
thing that it really eliminates is nonbeing—the rest it transforms and
brings to fulfillment. That is what takes place in the case of all the other
affections. As regards what is positive in them none is destroyed. Thus
cupidity survives in respect of the whole positivity of its essence; it is
"ordered," that is to say when everything that would falsify it is eliminated then no more of it remains save that element which was capable of

being set in order: love. It is just the same in the case of fear and hope; love consumes all, but only to consummate.[29]

In the second place, since all the other affections are reabsorbed in the ardor of love, it is at once evident that pure love is disinterested. Its very definition itself demands it, but far from excluding the substance of the other affections which the creature owes to his Creator, it absorbs and exalts them by bringing them to their point of perfection.[30] This is especially to be noted as regards the desire of beatitude. Pure love neither desires nor hopes for any reward, but it enjoys it; it is essentially fruition of the Divine good. It may be asked perhaps how this character can be added to love without vitiating its purity. But it is not added; it is of the very essence of love, and that is why St. Bernard says that love is itself its own reward.[31] Being by its very nature a participation in the Divine life, which is beatitude, it is a participation in beatitude. To say therefore that love carries with it its own reward is to say simply that its purity is that of the fruition of God.

To historians of spirituality such phrases as "pure love," "disinterested love" almost always seem to carry a suggestion of quietism. The specter of Mme. Guyon flits around a truth and makes the place uninhabitable. It is true that pure love, as St. Bernard conceives it, is a love that looks for no recompense; but we have just seen why. At the root of the whole question we must put the Scriptural phrase so often cited: love drives out fear. Throughout the course of all St. Bernard's meditations we watch the gradual elimination of the fear of Divine chastisement by certitude of the possession of God in love. Insofar as the thought of the contemplative is still busied with consideration of Divine Providence, or of Divine Judgment on our conduct,[32] it has not yet arrived at its term: it has not yet attained to pure love. But suppose, on the contrary, that the intensity of love has invested it with this purity which absorbs all other affections into itself, then, from that very moment, it is married to the Word, it rejoices therefore in God; it achieves this state of *fiducia* which is but the very consciousness of being united with the Divine beatitude. Obviously, from that moment also it can no longer stand in any fear of chastisement. Absorbed as it is in its joy, it can no longer even *think* of chastisement. And this St. Bernard indicates in the text [of *De diligendo Deo*] where he says that the soul that loves thus no longer looks for reward, *nor does it feel any mistrust*. This is the point that decides all, and it is precisely for lack of taking it into account that the Quietists have raised questions of which the very enunciation is excluded by St. Bernard's doctrine in the most formal manner.

To be assured on the point we have only to resume the key positions of St. Bernard touching the nature and conditions of pure love. If we turn to the fundamental text of the *De diligendo Deo* 7, 17, we see there first that love of God cannot go unrewarded, and then, next, that pure love of God is nevertheless a love without any thought of reward: *non enim sine praemio diligitur Deus, etsi absque praemii intuitu diligendus est.* Now what does that mean?

It means that pure love, as conceived by St. Bernard is essentially a mystical experience. What we have to do with here is neither an idea, nor an habitual disposition, but the brief and perpetually interrupted *excessus* of the soul of the mystic, when God unites it with Himself by exceptional graces. This primary difference between St. Bernard and the Quietists is important and should never be lost sight of. The former speaks of a momentary ecstasy—*rara hora, sed parva mora*—in no way of a state; when he deals with the habitual state he calls it, not *amor purus,* but *vicissitudo.*[33] A continual pining desire, interrupted by the fleeting and always unforeseeable joys of the divine union—there we have the picture of his life. And he knows moreover that even his pure love, when it brings its joyous reward, is far from being absolutely pure. There will never be any love that is purely pure save in heaven.

This point decides a second. Since pure love is a mystical experience, it is an affection and nothing else; or nothing else at any rate for the consciousness of him who experiences it. By that let us understand that at the moment when he experiences it the ecstatic is integrally occupied by it, no room being left in his soul for anything else whatever. In the forefront of all that love by its very intensity expels stand the considerations of the reason, and this exclusion takes effect against two possible orders of rational calculation, the calculations of cupidity and the calculations of fear.

First those of cupidity; for in fact the soul that rejoices in God no longer thinks of Him as of a recompense in prospect since she possesses Him already—that absurdity is at once excluded by the very nature of ecstasy, which is beatifying. But neither does she think of Him as of a present recompense, because now she does not represent Him to herself in any way whatever; she loves Him, and that is all. St. Bernard says precisely: "absque praemii *intuitu* diligendus." In other words, the idea of recompense is then no longer in the mind's eye. The ecstatic no longer says to himself: "I find blessedness in this love, and therefore I must feel it"; or again: "If God makes me blessed in His love, as He does, then I must continue in this love so that He may continue to bestow this blessedness." All that has now fallen away. Love is not a contract, it is an affection: "Affectus est, non contractus." It is not a "contractus," but an "amplexus." That is why, in virtue of its very nature, it can be neither empty-handed nor mercenary: "Vacua namque vera charitas esse non potest nec tamen mercenaria est." It never goes empty-handed because it is an embrace, but neither is it ever mercenary, because it is nothing but an embrace. Either then there is a rational calculation, and then we are no longer in the presence of a simple *affectus*, a love that is nought but love; and then it merits no reward, or rather cannot have it since the reward is precisely the simple embrace of love—and if it is not there, how should the recompense be there? Or else on the other hand there is no longer any rational outlook, any contractual calculation, but only the pure affection of a soul that loves and *knows* nought else; and then the affection merits recompense, or rather it is it, since it is the *amplexus*— which is much less an embrace of God by the soul, than an embrace of the soul by God. "Verus amor seipso contentus est. Habet praemium, sed id quod amatur."[34]

Consider now the relation between pure love and fear. It must of necessity amount to an exclusion of fear, and for the same reasons. Pure love cannot be a love that still keeps fear in view any more than it can be a love that has reward in view, and this simply because it excludes all "views." It is in no wise a contract, neither to obtain joy, nor to avoid pain; it is an affection. St. Bernard's *fiducia* therefore no more expresses a satisfaction at the prospect of avoiding an only too well-merited punishment, than his *amplexus* expresses the joy of holding at last the long-desired reward. The one excludes all thought of punishment, as the other excludes all thought of reward. Literally, according to the word of Scripture, fear has just been turned out of doors, and there it remains as long as the ecstasy endures; but no longer. The spontaneity of love—*sponte afficit, et spontaneum facit*—therefore presupposes a thoroughgoing elimination of any motive other than itself as long as it subsists in its purity, and in proportion to this purity itself. We are just as far from Luther's state of *fiducia* as from the state of pure love imagined by the followers of Fénelon. St. Bernard's *fiducia*, without doubt, is a certitude of salvation, but it would be much better to say that it marks the point where the question of salvation ceases to arise either one way or the other. The Lutheran *fiducia* is a faith in which the sinner feels himself a sinner and nevertheless feels that he is saved by Jesus Christ.[35] St. Bernard's confidence is a charity which, not by any means for a whole lifetime, but for short instants, succeeds in transcending the normal state in which the question of punishment still arises. When a soul thinks of punishment she can think of it in no way if not as deserved; when she no longer sees that she deserves it, that is not because she knows herself guilty but pardoned, but because she no longer thinks of it at all. That is why forgetfulness of the God of power and justice and judgment can be the work of nothing but pure love. None but pure love has power to lay hold, without shame and without fear, of this subsistent Beatitude, in whose possession the very notions of promise, of hope, of threat, or of punishment become void of meaning.

Hence we may also perceive at the same time how far removed from St. Bernard was even the genius of St. Francis de Sales when he declared himself ready to love hell with the will of God even above heaven without it.[36] There is naturally no question of objecting to him here that heaven is the very will of God itself. St. Francis de Sales was not such a novice as all that; he is perfectly well aware that his hypothesis is "an imagination of an impossible thing"; but what has to be brought out on the other hand, since this is precisely the starting point of the whole Fénelonian mistake, is that inasmuch as a man is still capable of imagining, whether possible things or impossible, he has not yet arrived at pure love. For pure love imagines nothing, it possesses. St. Francis de Sales is quite well aware that love is not to be divorced from the joy that it gives,[37] but perhaps he never knew the joy of the ecstatic in actual love of God for God's sake; and that is why he still reasons and argues when the time has gone by for anything but love. A doubly fatal illusion, for it was to lead the Fénelonians to miss the essence of pure love itself; an illusion that was inevitable, however, from the moment the attempt was made to make the language of St. Bernard express the spiritual life of Mme. Guyon or of Fénelon. Pure love may be taken to mean either the Cistercian ecstasy or the Fénelonian state, but it cannot possibly be both at once. Fénelon, of course, was free to adopt the definition he preferred, but when he cites St. Bernard in support of his own thesis we can but choose between two hypotheses: either he failed to understand him, or he falsified. I have no doubt at all that he failed to understand. The plain fact is that the definition of pure love for the Quietists is the definition of impure love for St. Bernard. Purify your love still more, he would say to them, and then you will see that the problem that worries you no longer arises. To ask whether we could love God when certain of never possessing Him—that is certainly a question; on condition, however, that love has not yet filled the whole soul. Let it put forth all its power and then it will forget all about chastisements to the point of feeling no fear of them; and all about rewards to the point of renunciation.[38]

Thus, to whatever side we turn, we must always come back to the image of God in man, if the problems involved in the interpretation of the doctrine are to be solved. Move away from this central point, and everything is shifted out of perspective, difficulties and apparent contradictions accumulate; return, and everything falls back into order. It remains to verify this in connection with the famous doctrine of charity as knowledge of God. St. Bernard says and repeats, appealing moreover expressly to Gregory the Great,[39] that charity is knowledge or even vision of God. What are we to understand by these formulae?

One might be tempted to take them quite literally as meaning that love exerts a cognitive function properly so-called, and is strictly a "sight." That would amount to a formal identification of knowledge and love. On the other hand, this thesis seems at first sight so paradoxical that we might be tempted to take it for no more than a metaphor, without any definite doctrinal content. But St. Bernard's expressions are so formal that this will soon appear a mere shift to evade the difficulty. Doubtless the true solution is equally removed from either extreme; love undoubtedly for St. Bernard is a genuine sight of God, but only in a certain sense.

We may remark in the first place that although he has left us but few indications as to how he understood cognition, we know at least this, that for him it is based entirely on a likeness of the subject knowing to the object known. Where such likeness is wanting, knowledge is impossible. How did St. Bernard picture the assimilation of subject and object in sensible or intellectual cognition? We do not know. . . . It may be that St. Bernard did not think about it at all. But what on the contrary is of the highest importance is to note that, with him, the resemblance of subject and object is the indispensable condition of any knowledge of the one by the other.

Once that has been laid down the thesis in question is forced upon us as an unavoidable conclusion. In whatever way the intellectual cognition of objects be interpreted, it is possible only if some action proceeding from the object has transformed the knowing subject to its likeness. On the other hand, when once the likeness between subject and object has been set up, the knowledge of the object by the subject follows of itself. We may therefore say that the likeness is the knowledge itself, at least in the sense that it is the indispensable and sufficient condition of the knowledge. Now, in the case of knowledge of God, what is it that transforms the soul to the likeness of God? Charity, love, and nothing else. In the precise measure in which love shall have transformed the soul to the likeness of God, Whose name is charity, in that same measure it will be in a position to know Him and will indeed know Him effectively.[40]

But then, it will be said, with what kind of knowledge will it know Him? It will know Him by feeling Him. The affection of love of God for God's sake is, to the soul that loves, if not the equivalent at least the succedaneum, of her vision of bodies. God is neither perceptible to our senses nor conceivable by our intellects, but He is sensible to the heart. To love Him as He loves Himself, to love Him as He loves us, and by the gift of that very love with which He loves Himself and loves us—that truly, as St. Augustine has already said, is to have God in us. To perceive within itself this divine love which circulates in the soul henceforth one in spirit with God, is to perceive God in the sole manner in which this Spirit is perceptible here below to ours: in charity. Thus, for the soul reformed to the Divine likeness by love, the very affection of love is the sole possible substitute here below for the vision of God which we lack, and love therefore in us stands for vision.

And this St. Bernard will explain to us if we allow him to speak for himself once more; and thus we may watch his master-theses as they pass beneath our eyes for the last time in one of the most highly condensed syntheses he has left us.

When the soul discerns in her own nature two things so opposed [the likeness of the image and the unlikeness of sin] how should it not cry out between hope and despair: *Lord, who is like unto Thee?* Drawn toward despair by so great an evil [unlikeness] it is recalled to hope by this great good [the persistence of the image].[41] Thence it is that the more it is offended by the evil within it the more ardently it aspires to the good which equally it sees there, and desires to become what it was meant to be [not simply an image, but a likeness], that is to say simple [by absence of cupidity] upright [by absence of fear[42]] yet fearing God [but not God's chastisements] and departing from evil. Why should it not be able to depart from that which it has been able to approach, or to draw near to that from which it has been able to withdraw? This it can do, be it noted, if it relies on grace, not on nature, nor even on its own zeal (*industria*). For it is wisdom that conquers evil (Wis. 7, 30), not nature, nor zeal. Nor does it count on grace without reason, for its conversion is to the Word [now the Word is precisely Wisdom]. This noble kinship of the soul to the Word, of which for three days we have discoursed, is not barren [*kinship*, since the Word is *Imago*, and the soul is *ad imaginem*], nor is the persistent likeness, the witness of this kinship [the *imago*]. The Spirit [introduced by the Word] will deign to admit into His fellowship this soul so like to Him by nature; and that for a natural reason, for like seeks like. Hear the voice of One who calls: *Return, return, O Sulamitess, return that we may look upon thee* (Cant. 6, 12). He will look upon her now that she is in His likeness, she whom when she was unlike He saw not, but He will admit her also to the vision of Himself. For we know that when He shall appear [beatific vision] we shall be like Him; for we shall see Him as He is (I John 3, 2). Rather hold it then for a thing difficult, not a thing impossible, when thou hearest what is asked: *Lord, who is like unto Thee?* (Ps. 34, 10)

Or again, if you will have it so, let us call this a cry of admiration. For surely most wonderful and admirable is that likeness from which there springs the vision of God, or rather which is that vision of God; but this I speak of is that vision which is in charity. For charity is that vision, charity is that likeness [for it reestablishes the likeness which determines the vision]. Who does not stand amazed at beholding the charity of a God despised, Who nonetheless recalls us to Himself? Well therefore did that wicked one of whom I spoke a while ago deserve the reproach addressed to him in that he would usurp the likeness of God to his own profit [by willing to give himself his own law, which is God's privilege], since in loving iniquity [his "proper will"] he could love neither himself [for he is no longer himself now that he is no longer like God], nor God [because he prefers himself to God]. Thus must we understand the word: *He that loveth iniquity hateth his own soul* (Ps. 10, 6). When then this iniquity shall be taken away, which is the cause of our part in unlikeness, then will there be union of spirit [since union between two spirits is made of their very likeness], then will there be mutual vision [since each may know the other in knowing himself], and mutual dilection [like loving his like]. When that which is perfect is come [charity] then that which is in part [unlikeness] shall be done away; and then between God and the soul shall be nought but a mutual dilection chaste and consummated, a full mutual recognition, a manifest vision, a firm conjunction, a society undivided, and a perfect likeness. Then shall the soul know God even as she is known (I Cor. 13, 10); then shall she love as she is loved; and over his Bride shall rejoice the Bridegroom, knowing and known, loving and beloved, Jesus Christ Our Lord, Who is over all things, God blessed for ever. Amen (*In Cant. Cant.*, Sermo 82, 7 and 8).

Thus have we tried to pass in review the chief ideas that enter into the composition of the mysticism of St. Bernard, and to suggest the manner in which they are interconnected. Perhaps it would be better to say that we have tried to suggest some of their more frequent interconnections—for nothing can equal the easy mastery with which their author works them into combination. It would be illusory and altogether unjust to St. Bernard to take such analyses—even supposing them to be always exact—for the equivalent of his mystical theology. For they stand to that much as an anatomical specimen would stand to the living organism whence it was taken. To understand it as it truly is we should have to be able to seize in one unique and simple intuition the work of a God who creates man in order to associate him, by way of beatitude, with His own likeness, Who gives man back the lost likeness that he may give back the lost beatitude, and Who, while awaiting the day when the work shall be fully accomplished, gratuitously raises to like felicity souls whom the gift of charity has already made conformable to His nature—*Deus charitas est*—closely enough to enable them to taste even here below of the blessedness of His life. And then it is that there reigns between God and the creature made to His image, this perfect conformity, this unity of spirit, in which the human substance finds at last its full actuality; and in that creature the great work of creation is completed, for he becomes at last that very thing for which he was made—a translucid mirror in which God now sees nought but Himself, and in which the soul now sees nought but God: a created participation of His glory and of His beatitude.

NOTES

1. Since the Cistercian mysticism is sometimes accused of pantheistic tendencies, it will not perhaps be superfluous to note that it consists in a full development in us of the life of grace. Now grace is not God save in the sense that it is a "gift" of God. The distinction is strongly marked in St. Bernard between God, Who is substantial Charity, and grace, a quality of charity. The metaphysical gulf between God, Who is Charity, and man, who receives a created charity, is therefore clearly delineated: "Dicitur ergo rectae et charitas, et Deus, et Dei donum. Itaque caritas dat caritatem, substantiva accidentalem. Ubi dantem significat, nomen substantiae est; ubi donum qualitatis" (St. Bernard *De diligendo Deo*, 12, 35; PL [*Patrologia latina*, ed. J. Migne], 182, 996). William of Saint-Thierry has the same distinction expressed in very similar terms: "Quidquid de Deo potest dici, potest dici et de caritate; sic tamen ut, considerata secumdum naturas doni et dantis, in dante nomen sit substantiae, in dono qualitatis" (William of Saint-Thierry *De nat. et dignit. amoris*, 5, 12; PL, 184, 587–88). Since the two works are almost contemporary we cannot tell here, any more than we can elsewhere, whether the coincidence indicates an influence, or in which direction such influence went.

2. Cf. Margaret Smith, *An Introduction to the History of Mysticism*, London: S.P.C.K., 1930. There is no question here of denying the existence of poetic sentiments corresponding, on quite another plane, of course, to the mystic states. But there we have something very different, and not to be termed mystical without radical impropriety.

3. St. Bernard *De diligendo Deo*, 10, 28; PL, 182, 991B.

4. St. Bernard *De gratia et libero arbitrio*, 14, 49; PL, 182, 1027C.

5. Numerous references to the use of this phrase may be found in W. W. Williams, p. 50, note 1.

6. St. Bernard *In Cantica Canticorum*, Sermo 71, 9–10; PL, 183, 1125–26.

7. See on this point A. Harnack, *Lehrbuch der Dogmengeschichte*, III, 342.

8. "Ille autem qui idem ipse est, qui dixit: *Ego sum qui sum* (Exod. 3:14), veraciter est, cui est esse quod est. Quae ergo participatio, quae convento, illius qui non est ad illum qui est? Quomodo possunt tam diversa conjungi? *Mihi*, ait sanctus, *adhaerere Deo bonum est* (Ps. 72:28). Immediate ei conjungi non possumus, sed per medium aliquod poterit fieri fortassis ista conjunctio" (St. Bernard *De diversis*, Sermo 4, 2–3; PL, 183, 552CD). For the formula which follows see ibid., 553A. The source of the formula is evidently St. Paul, I Cor. 6:17: "Qui autem adhaeret Domino, unus spiritus est." This text alone would have sufficed to determine one of the fundamental positions of the Cistercian mysticism; love alone is capable of establishing between God and man the unity of spirit which is the term of the spiritual life. Let us add that the Pauline text

was an irresistible invitation to Bernard to comment on the Canticle of Canticles in this sense. St. Paul (I Cor. 6:16) compares carnal union of man and wife with spiritual union: the Canticle then could be interpreted in the same way. It happened, on the other hand, as we have already seen, that Cicero had described friendship as the sentiment which makes of two minds one. . . . Bernard therefore had a double reason for seeing in love the principle of the spiritual unification of the creature with the Creator.

9. I say the manner in which they are linked up, not the mere fact that they are so. William of Saint-Thierry equally links up the mystical union with image of God in man, but his doctrine is rather a description of the manner in which the "memory" of God, obliterated by sin, is gradually recovered by the soul. The likeness is restored in two different ways in the two doctrines, because it is not situated exactly at the same point. In St. Bernard it lies in a good use of free will, and the restoration effected is therefore essentially the restoration of liberty. In William it is especially in the Augustinian "memory" of God, which gives birth to reason; therefore the presence of God. Each doctrine reaches the same conclusions and leaves room for all the essentials of the other, but each travels by its own particular route.

10. Père Rousselot, *Pour l'histoire du problème de l'amour au moyen âge*, pp. 53–54. It is of great interest to read these two pages closely, for their author never ceases to correct himself line by line, and lastly corrects the whole text by a note (p. 53, note 1), which contains the essential elements of the solution. Père Rousselot clearly sees that St. Bernard speaks of an annihilation and that nevertheless the individual personality, which *seems* an obstacle to the mystic union, is carefully safeguarded. Further, if "the undoing of souls is their state of perfection" (p. 54, note) it is because what is undone in them is unlikeness. Père Rousselot puts his finger on the true reply when he writes, "that amounts to saying that one cannot fully possess God without fully possessing oneself, and that this *proprium* that has to be got rid of in order to arrive at the perfection of love, is not the natural appetite, but a solicitude that impedes, contracts and restrains the natural appetite" (p. 53, note 1). True, and if Père Rousselot had reconstructed the whole book on this basis, many of the contradictions he believed himself to have discovered would at once have vanished. They were, in large measure, of his own making.

11. Père Rousselot very clearly sees that thus it must be in St. Bernard: "There is no longer any *suum*, the being is emptied of itself; the man who loves God is carried away into the very center of all; he has no longer any other inclinations save those of the absolute spirit; he must needs in any event love what is better; he has become identified with the pure Reason" (op. cit. [n. 10], p. 70). Let us leave on one side a terminology that makes of the *Deus charitas* a Pure Reason; that is a detail. What is important is to see what is meant by *suum*. If you are imprudent enough to understand it as involving the very personality of the ecstatic, you are led, like P. Rousselot, to set up the "graeco-Thomist" conception of love in strong opposition to the "ecstatic," and moreover to destroy the unity of Cistercian thought. If what is eliminated is only the false *suum*, that of unlikeness, then it follows at once that the most ecstatic of loves excludes neither the subsistence of the part as part, nor the inclusion of the love that the part bears itself in that which it bears to the whole. The soul then loves itself only for God's sake. What needs to be added is that in this case the words *part* and *whole* are equivalent to *image* and *original*, a remark that avails equally for St. Thomas and for St. Bernard. The opposition proposed to be set up between the two schools on this point entails,

as a first consequence, the ruin of the coherence of both; their differences are real, but they lie elsewhere, and moreover are incomparably less deep-seated than that would amount to.

12. *Malitia diei:* a Scriptural metaphor of technical significance. It means, in St. Bernard, the duties of the active life insofar as they obstruct the free development of the contemplative life. See *In Cant. Cant.*, Sermo 3, 7; *PL*, 183, 796BC.

13. *Corpus mortis:* the concupiscence engendered by sin. Cf. Wis. 11:15, cited in *In Cant. Cant.*, Sermo 16, 1; *PL*, 183, 848–49.

14. *Carnis necessitas:* the natural necessity, the needs of nature, as contrasted with sinful cupidity.

15. The duty of spiritual charity for his brethren, and from taking care for their souls, snatches the contemplative from his joys. See *In Cant. Cant.*, Sermo 9, 9; *PL*, 183, 818–19.

16. To fall back *in sua,* into that whereby it is not one spirit with God and separates itself from the Divine life.

17. The whole substructure of St. Bernard's mysticism is here revealed. God created all things for Himself; the last end of man is conformity with God; ecstasy brings this conformity to the highest point it can attain in this life; mystical union consists therefore in realizing the closest conformity possible between the created image of God and its Exemplar.

18. That is, our ceasing to feel the need to which the natural necessity of the body subjects us in this life.

19. For then we shall have obtained it, but we shall no longer think of it as a reward, any more than God, to whose will [we] shall then be united, considers His eternal beatitude as a reward for His perfection. We shall return again to the question of the disinterestedness of love.

20. *In nobis,* because henceforth there is perfect accord between His will and ours; *de nobis,* because the realization of this accord is the end for which God created us.

21. *Sanctus, Sancte.* Holy love (*amor sanctus, sancte amare*) is spiritual love of God, as contrasted with the concupiscence of the flesh—"Amat sancte, quia non in concupiscientia carnis, sed in puritate spiritus" (St. Bernard, *In Cant. Cant.*, Sermo 7, 3; *PL*, 183, 807).

22. *Castus. Caste. Chaste,* in St. Bernard, means always *disinterested.* Here then it means that a love in this state, turns toward its object for the sake of the object itself, to the exclusion of every other consideration and every other affection. For this reason *amor castus* is synonymous with *amor purus.* "Amat profecto caste, quae ipsum quem amat quaerit; non aliud quidquam ipsius" (ibid.).

23. That is, of the *proprium:* of the proper will which constitutes our unlikeness.

24. This expression, as well as the following comparisons, was taken by St. Bernard from Maximus the Confessor *Ambigua,* loc. cit., p. 26.

25. Remember that in St. Bernard's terminology the form is *never* the substance of which it is the form, so that a change of form implies no change of substance.

26. Whether natural necessity of the *proprium;* that is, something of that whereby man is unlike God.

27. St. Bernard *De diligendo Deo,* 10, 27–28; *PL*, 182, 990–91.

28. This is elaborated minutely and at length in another text which by

reason of the very closeness of its condensation ought to be read and meditated by everyone who seriously desires to enter into the thought of St. Bernard: *In Cant. Cant.*, Sermo 83. This most remarkable text contains not only an outline of the theological principles governing the question of ecstasy as St. Bernard conceives it, but sets forth also with all desirable precision his conception of love. The formulae that define a pure love have certainly not passed without remark, for we know to what use, not to say abuse, they were to be put by the Quietists. For indeed any number of texts in support of Quietism might be cited from St. Bernard—provided only that care be taken to make them say the opposite of what they mean.

29. This is the famous doctrine of *cupiditas ordinata*, so dear to the heart of Fénelon; but what does it mean? We must scrutinize the inner significance of the chief words involved:

Ordinatus, Ordinare. The affections are ordered when they follow each other in the order that favors the attainment of love. St. Bernard *De diversis*, Sermo 50, 2; *PL*, 183, 673. The doctrine means therefore that cupidity is evil if not preceded by fear of God. It is evil because it does not tend to lead us to our end. If, on the contrary, fear precedes it, then it becomes good because it becomes love.

The ordering of the affections is moreover closely akin to their "purgation." See the following expressions:

Purgatus, Purgare. The purgation of the affections consists in referring them to their appointed end. Love what ought to be loved, and love more what ought to be loved more; fear what ought to be feared, and fear more what ought to be feared more, etc.

30. St. Bernard here moreover places himself in direct opposition with one of Abelard's theses condemned in 1140 at the Council of Sens. In accordance with the spirit of his doctrine Abelard taught: "Quod etiam castus timor excludatur a future vita" (see in P. Ruf and M. Grabmann, *Ein neuaufgefundenes Bruchstück der Apologia Abaelards*, I, 24–25 [Munich, 1930], p. 10). Cf. J. Riviere, "Les 'capitula' d'Abélard," *Recherches de theologie ancienne et médiévale*, 5 (1933), 17.

31. The most important text on this point is the fully developed meditation to be found in *In Cant. Cant.*, Sermo 23, 11–16; *PL*, 183, 890–93. It proceeds entirely on the mystical plane, not, that is to say, by way of simple "consideration," but of "contemplation" properly so-called (see, as to the meaning of these terms, *De consideratione*, Lib. II, cap. 5; *PL*, 182, 745. *In Cant. Cant.*, Sermo 52, 5; *PL*, 183, 1031). It consists therefore of a series of glimpses, of intuitive certitudes, putting the soul in the presence of facts which it intuitively grasps. Cf. *In Cant. Cant.*, Sermo 16, 7; *PL*, 183, 851–52; Sermo 6, 8–9; 806; *De diversis*, Sermo 16, 7; *PL*, 183, 582–83.

32. St. Bernard *De diligendo Deo*, 7, 17; *PL*, 182, 984–85.

33. This inevitable alternation of ecstasy and languor is therefore at the opposite pole to pure love. St. Bernard calls it:

Vicissitudo: Alternate presences and absences of the Bridegroom, due to the fact that the soul is united to a nonglorified body. St. Bernard *In Cant. Cant.*, Sermo 32, 2; *PL*, 183, 946.

34. St. Bernard *De diligendo Deo*, 7, 17; *PL*, 182, 984D.

35. On the radical distinction between the nonimputation of sin according to St. Bernard on the one hand and Luther on the other, see the excellent remarks of W. W. Williams, to which I have nothing essential to add: *De diligendo*

Deo, ed. cit., p. 6. St. Bernard, says his editor, "has no notion of a mere forensic righteousness." It is the least that can be said, but it suffices.

36. St. Francis de Sales, *Traite de l'amour de Dieu,* bk. IX, chap. IV. Translated by the Rev. H. B. Mackey, O.S.B., 3d ed. (London: Burns & Oates), p. 375. Cf. Fénelon, *Explication des Maximes des saints,* ed. A. Chérel, pp. 136–38.

37. St. Francis de Sales, *Treatise on the Love of God,* Mackey translation, bk. IX, chap. X, p. 392; bk. IX, chap. XII, p. 395.

38. This initial difference of standpoint explains why the citations from St. Bernard with which Fénelon so plentifully strews his writings are almost always given a sophistical twist. It is not done intentionally, but was simply bound to happen because pure love does not mean the same thing in the two doctrines. I would not intrude into the *hortus conclusus* where I have no right of access, but perhaps it is permissible to say that the spiritual life of Fénelon, and even the tenderness of a St. Francis de Sales, would have appeared to St. Bernard as nothing but permanent states of *languor.* That is the reason why, lacking the triumphant certainty that ecstasy alone can bring, the only means left to them to persuade themselves of the purity of their love lay in the acceptance of dryness. St. Francis de Sales himself relies only on *anguishes* to make love *pure* and *clear;* this pure love seems more like that of the courtly poets or of the *Astraea* than of St. Bernard, for whom love is purified, not by dryness or languor, but by ardor.

39. "Exponit beatus Gregorius, quia amor ipse, notitia est" (St. Bernard *De diversis,* Sermo 29, 1; *PL,* 183, 620C). Cf. Gregory the Great *Hom.* 27 *in Evang.; PL,* 76, 1207; "Dum enim audita supercaelestia amamus, amata jam novimus, quia amo ipse notitia est." Note moreover that Gregory, like Bernard, depends here on I John 4:7–8.

40. St. Bernard *In Cant. Cant.,* Sermo 31, 2; *PL,* 183, 941.

41. This great good is that which St. Bernard sometimes designates in a single word, recalling that in virtue of this we are made to the image of God:

Dignitas: Emphatically, free will. "Dignitatem in homine liberum arbitrium dico: in quo ei nimirum datum est non solum caeteris praeeminere, sed et praesidere animantibus" (*De diligendo Deo,* 2, 2; *PL,* 182, 976). Cf. *De gratia et libero arbitrio,* 9, 28; *PL,* 182, 1016.

The expression is probably of Stoic origin. On the "preeminence" conferred on man by free will, see Cicero *De natura Deorum,* 2, 11 (cited by W. W. Williams, ed. cit., p. 11, note 15).

42. On the meaning of "recta" and "curva"—state of the soul which has lost the divine likeness and stoops to earth—see St. Bernard, *In Cant. Cant.; PL,* 183, 897–98.

34

What Is Mysticism?

DAVID KNOWLES

Everyone in our day who proposes to speak or to write of mysticism must begin by deploring both the ambiguity of the word itself and the difficulty of defining it in any of its meanings. Yet without some sort of definition and some kind of understanding between writer and reader as to what is being discussed no progress of any kind can be hoped for. Consequently, before attempting to answer the question that forms the heading to this chapter it will be well to say that in this book we are primarily concerned with traditional Christian mysticism. [Elsewhere] we shall take a wider view, and try to decide to what extent, if at all, the various apparently mystical experiences found outside Christianity and indeed outside any religious context are in fact identical with or similar to Christian experience. But for the moment, writing as Catholic Christians committed by our faith to a belief in the direct communication between God and the soul of man, we cannot proceed in any other way than that of defining first of all what we hold to be the veritable form and end of the mystical experience in its purest form.

This explanation is necessary because, for historical reasons which would need a lengthy exposition and which need not be elaborated here, all general interest in mysticism was absent both within and without the Catholic Church for some two centuries before the twentieth. Mystics, hidden and not so hidden, certainly existed and even wrote of their experiences, but outside Catholic circles such people were widely regarded as instances of the abnormal or of the occult, if not as simply hysterical or fraudulent, and within the Church they were left to their spiritual directors and to the small group of theologians interested in such things. A revival of interest began simultaneously toward the end of the nineteenth century in two quarters for different reasons. Outside the Catholic Church the scientific study of psychology, largely in its morbid and abnormal, or at least in its subliminal and pre-rational manifestations, became common. This was conducted primarily by nonbelievers or those unorthodox by traditional theological standards, and was directed princi-

pally towards psychiatry and the establishment of a balanced personality. Its adepts proceeded by way of observation and empirical
methods, and were interested in religious phenomena only as providing
further instances of unusual psychological conditions. It must be added,
that this psychology, though preserving the traditional name of a department of philosophy very closely connected with theology, had an entirely
different subject matter. To the Christian (and, though with wide
differences, to many schools of philosophy) the human soul is an entity
in its own right, directly created by God to "inform" the body and to
make up with it the human being. This soul, of itself a spiritual being,
gives actuality to all the powers and faculties of the body, but has also,
of itself, intellectual and volitional powers which make it capable of rational knowledge of the universe about it and of free will to direct its activities and to control and direct its love. Its natural capacities are indeed
limited to a knowledge of beings of which it has experience or of which
it can by reason and intuition deduce the existence and nature, but the
Christian knows that his soul was created "in the likeness of God" in
order that it might be raised, by means of what theologians call the potentiality of obedience, to a far higher and more intense knowledge and
love, that of God as he is in himself. And as love implies union with its
object, and knowledge if adequate implies equality in some degree, God
can be known and loved in himself only by a being to whom he has
given something of his own divine nature.

The modern psychologist, as such, has no such wide view. By the
psyche he understands simply the active principle that manifests itself in
all the cognitive, volitional and emotional movements of the human
being. It is not part of his science to assume the data of philosophy or
theology, and indeed philosophy, in the world of today, would provide
no firm basis of any kind. In consequence, the psychologist can do no
more than treat what he hears of mysticism as one among many of the
"varieties of religious experience."

While psychology was developing as a science by observation, Catholic thinkers, for the most part not expert in technical theology, were re-
acting against the prevalent arid rationalism and materialism by interesting themselves in the direct, personal experiences and writings of the
celebrated mystical saints of the past. Some were drawn by devotional
motives, others hoped to use the mystical experience as an argument for
the truth of Christian belief, but most of these Catholic thinkers, in this
resembling the psychologists, approached the subject from outside, with
a quasi-scientific technique of observing and comparing phenomena in
hope of arriving at general conclusions and a definition of their subject.
Gradually, and especially in England, mysticism became a subject of
study and research, and came to embrace a wide arc of experience as

treated by William James, Evelyn Underhill and Baron Friedrich von Hügel. While many of these writers and thinkers were believing Catholics, they made no attempt at a theological analysis of the mystical experience. They might judge mysticism to be a true and valuable "element of religion," and even consider that the experiences of the Catholic mystics were the deepest and most spiritually significant, but they remained on the phenomenal level, amassing and comparing the accounts of the mystics themselves. One result, or it may have been the manifestation, of this new interest was a shift in devotional and even of popular interest toward mystical writings of all ages and countries. Works unpublished or long out of print became, and have remained, popular.

As a result, there was for long no consensus of opinion, even among the best qualified writers on mysticism, as to what precisely mysticism or contemplation might be. One has only to glance at the writings of Abbot Cuthbert Butler, in the editions of the 1920s and 1930s, to see the extent of "theological agnosticism" on the subject even in a scholar long interested in the subject, whose findings and conclusions on the mystics have found acceptance at the highest level of Catholic and non-Catholic scholarship. Such an "agnostic" attitude is naturally even more common among non-Catholics, and is both comprehensible and indeed inevitable among nonbelievers, to whom mysticism must always remain as something to be treated on the phenomenal level, but it is far from uncommon among Catholics, and the revulsion from systematic, scholastic theology, so prevalent at the present moment, will doubtless help to perpetuate it.

Mysticism, both as a word and as a topic of discussion, is of relatively recent birth, and has developed new shades of meaning in the past fifty years. No English dictionary attains absolute precision in its definition. The Oxford English Dictionary gives, among others, the following entry for "mystic": "One who seeks by contemplation and self-surrender to obtain union with or absorption into the Deity, or who believes in the spiritual apprehension of truths inaccessible to the understanding." And for "mysticism" it gives a corresponding entry: "Belief in the possibility of union with the divine nature by means of acquiring knowledge of mysteries inaccessible to the understanding." These definitions are certainly faulty both from lack of technical precision and mutual agreement (the former has "truths" where the latter uses "mysteries"), and in their use of words that are either otiose (e.g. "ecstatic") or practically synonymous with the word that is being defined (e.g. "contemplation"), but they indicate well enough two fields in which the word commonly occurs, as also the basic element common to both. The basic element is the inaccessibility to the human understanding of the knowledge acquired or received. The two fields are those in which God and Nature respectively are the dominating objects of attention.

. . . We shall be concerned primarily with theological mysticism or, to use the term consecrated by tradition, "mystical theology," and this may be defined as "an incommunicable and inexpressible knowledge and love of God or of religious truth received in the spirit without precedent effort or reasoning." More loosely used, it may comprehend the normal conditions, accompaniments and side effects of such knowledge, and a description of the circumstances of its reception, and of the attempts made to receive it and to convey its meaning and effects to others.

It may be said, and with some truth, that such a definition begs the whole question. Granted that mystics assert the inexpressibility and incommunicability of their experiences, it is for others to inquire, to discover and to criticize their nature and value, and therefore it is intellectually misleading, even dishonest, to assume their transcendental, or in theological language their supernatural, origin. To this we can only answer that mystical theology is but a corner of a large field, that of theology in all its branches, and that it is intimately linked with the whole body of Christian revelation. If it were necessary to prove at every point the existence and truth of that revelation before considering any particular consequence of it—let us say, the theology of grace, or of the sacraments—the burden would be intolerable. The definition given above must suffice as an indication of our subject, and no attempt will be made to prove the validity of the mystics' claim. On the other hand, it is part of [my] purpose . . . to explain the mystical experience by showing what it has in common with the theology of grace considered as the principle of the Christian life. This in its turn can be understood and analyzed only from above, so to say, that is, in the light of the common and traditional Christian teaching whose authority must be sought in the teaching of Christ and his apostles. To say this may surprise many, and will certainly not meet with agreement from those (and nowadays they are many) who are interested in mysticism as psychologists or students of religious experience, and who regard mysticism either as a purely subjective activity, or as the outward appearance of powers rare in themselves or at least normally overlaid by superficial activity or, finally, as a purely natural contact with a power or spirit within the framework of the universe. Such disagreement is inevitable if we hold that the true mystical experience is an instance of the (normally imperceptible) action of God within the soul and powers of a human being. If we hold this, any consideration of it must pass, so to say, from God downwards before we are in a position to look at the visible evidence and consequences of God's action. God is Spirit; what is born of the spirit is itself spirit also.

The end of human life, the purpose for which each human soul was created, is to give glory to God, at the elementary level by being what God creates it to be, at a higher level by seeing and acknowledging in thought and action the sovereignty of God, and at the highest level, itself infinitely diversified in degree, by loving God as revealed by Christ in three Persons, Father, Son and Holy Spirit, and by fulfilling in all ways the will of God as known and loved. The first and last purpose of human life as seen by Christ is to do the will of God. To do the will of the Father always, to be and to remain one with the Father, was Christ's *raison d'être* on earth, and it is the Christian's also, whether the Father is seen as one to be feared and obeyed or one to be loved even to spiritual union. The greatest commandment is to love God with every power of mind and soul, to show this love by keeping the commandments of Christ, to abide in Christ, and to be perfect as our heavenly Father is perfect. Union with Christ, which he himself compares to the union of his own human soul with the Father or, in other words, the attainment within the limits of a creature of the divine perfection, is the end of human endeavor as seen by Christ. It need scarcely be said that such an end, such an achievement is, to purely human eyes, extravagant to absurdity.

Christ stands alone as one who could claim complete sinlessness and harmony of will with God, and who appears perfect with divine perfection. Such perfection was possible only because his human nature shared in his divinity through his personal and essential union with God. It is only possible, in an infinitely lower degree, to a mere creature through a direct gift of divine powers; one can even say, using the words of Scripture and of the daily liturgy of the Mass, by a sharing of the divine nature.[1] Such a gift, such a consortium, seems the height of extravagance or, alternatively, a meaningless, if not hypocritical or blasphemous, use of words. Yet the words stand, and if we do not acknowledge the power and the love of God which they express, it is because we do not in common life realize even what a likeness of the divine powers we have been given as human beings by our capacity to know and to love. But it is also because we find it hard to acknowledge in thought and word, what we hourly allow in practice, that perfection is of infinitely varying kinds and is reached by a seemingly slow and endless advance. Moral perfection—as indeed also the perfection of art—is not reached as one reaches the terminus of a railway, but as a flower develops from a seed. The flower has already something of its final beauty as a living creature when the first recognizable green shoot appears. But besides this, we do not find it easy to isolate love, the one thing needful, from all other human qualities and activities, nor do we give a real, as distinct from a notional, assent to the presence and power of sanctifying grace, which by definition is the invisible force which raises the human mind and will to a power beyond anything they could obtain of themselves.

Christ, as we hear and see him in the Gospels, does more than demand our love and obedience for himself and for the Father, he offers and prays for an identity of knowledge and love between the believer and himself. "That they all may be one, as thou, Father, in me and I in thee; that they also may be one in us . . . that they may be one, as we also are one; I in them and thou in me; that they may be made perfect in one."[2] These words of Christ, and other similar phrases repeated by St. John the Evangelist, have been rightly called "the mystic's charter," but it is surprising how many, indeed how the majority of Christians, can read them without a realization of their mystical force and their stupendous implications. Sometimes consciously, more often unconsciously, the reader regards them as if spoken loosely or in metaphor, not as bearing the full weight of theological sublimity. Christ was speaking for the last time as a man among men, speaking with the clear sight of his redemptive death before him, speaking what was to be a message, a solemn covenant, for all time. He saw his Church, his redeemed, not as defective souls incapable of constancy in their profession of faith in him, but as sons of God who were to be in solidarity with himself, divinely gifted to be members of the Body of which he was Head. We speak of the glory and power of the human reason, clearly visible in a Plato or an Einstein, but even in its lowliest exercise transcending all the material universe. Christ was speaking of the sublimity of the eternal life he gave, recognizable in a Paul or a John, but existing darkly and in germ in every soul in grace. Supernatural indeed in the smallest act of faith or love, but visibly divine or, more correctly, wholly supernatural and thus transcending all observation, but experienced in the soul itself and radiant by its reflection on the spiritual and material faculties and actions.

The depth of Christ's calling and the practical consequences of his gifts were realized by two or three of those who stood spiritually nearest to him, the apostles Peter, John and Paul. St. Peter in his appearances in history in the Gospels and in the Acts seems to have little of the mystic about him. Yet it is he who in one place demands of Christians a holiness defined by the exemplary holiness of God, and in another speaks of Christian souls as sharers or companions of the divine nature.[3] St. John the Apostle, for his part, speaks of redeemed souls as truly the children of God who will see him as he is.[4] In St. Paul's words, the souls of the just will know God even as they are known by him.[5] The words of SS. Peter and John have been considered, as tradition has always considered them, as the authentic utterances of those who had walked with Christ and heard his words. Even if this were not so, and the words were written by an unknown hand of the second century, they would be, if anything, still more striking, as reflecting the outlook of the early generations of Christianity, an outlook wholly different from that of later Neoplatonic thinkers.

Thus the teaching of Christ, as seen in its presentation by the evangelists and apostles, puts before us a new life, the free gift of God, implying new powers and a new knowledge of God. It is a life lived wholly by virtue of the grace of Christ, without whose agency the Christian can do nothing, and leading to a clear vision of the divine Being. It implies a life of holiness, lived in union with Christ, a union both typified and fortified by the gift of himself in the holy Eucharist, and based upon the exemplar of God the Father. That the life of the great majority of Christians in every century has borne little resemblance to this ideal should not be a matter for surprise, still less for doubting its reality. Christ himself repeated more than once that many are called but few chosen, and laid down firm conditions for those who would follow him. Those who, by his grace, and by their acceptance of his gifts, have fulfilled those conditions have experienced the truth of his promises.

The term "supernatural" . . . is a word that is out of favor at the present day. It is indeed meaningless to those who do not acknowledge the existence of a God who has, in a preeminent degree, all that we mean by personality and providential care for his creatures whom he loves, and whose love in return he both invites and bestows. Some even of those who profess a belief in a personal, providential God feel an objection to any distinction between his natural and supernatural agency, either because they are unwilling to admit the possibility of any evidence for the supernatural, or because they regard all God's dealings with the universe as something transcendental and not susceptible of analysis and differentiation. All such differentiation and definition must, it is granted, be on our part only. God is absolute simplicity. Creatures have relationship to him, but he has none to them.

Nevertheless, the term "supernatural" is necessary, if only as a sumbol, in any Christian theology. Human beings, as such, have certain powers, certain potentialities, and certain modes and conditions of existence. God, on the other hand, and in particular Christ, the Son of God, has bestowed gifts, and made demands and promises, that exceed the exigencies and capabilities of human beings, and the Christian life is directed to an end beyond all human expectations, which can only be attained by powers and actions beyond unaided human capacity. Neither the end, nor the means of attaining it, are visible, save to the eye of faith. Moreover, the means of attaining to the immediate end of the Christian life, the fulfillment of the will of God, are to the outward eye identical, or at least similar, to those which form part of any ethical program. The life of Christ, to those who lived with him for the first thirty or more years of his existence on earth, was not visibly different from that of an exceptionally good man, and even during his public life those who had no insight regarded him as an ordinary, indeed as a misguided, man. Yet he could claim that those who saw him, saw the Father because, by doing always the will of his Father and seeking nothing but his glory, he was in fact presenting to the world of human beings one like themselves fulfilling exactly all that the Father could wish from a human being who was his Son.

What is strictly "supernatural" is also strictly imperceptible to the normal faculties of man. This is a principle of very great importance in any discussion of Christian mysticism. The natural faculties of man can only perceive the supernatural by its effects. Once they have been given a higher capacity, by the free gift of God that we call grace, they can perceive things above their nature in proportion to the measure of grace they have received, but they cannot express them either to themselves or to others, on the normal level of thought and speech.

NOTES

1. "Grant that by this mystery of water and wine, symbols of the human and divine natures of Christ, we may be sharers in the divine nature of him who deigned to share with us in our human nature" (Prayer at the blessing of water at the offertory of the Mass).
2. John 16:22–23.
3. I Peter 1:15–16.
4. I John 3:2–3.
5. II Cor. 13:12.

35

Liberation as an Encounter with Politics and Contemplation

SEGUNDO GALILEA

I. THE COMMITMENT TO LIBERATION AND THE CRISIS IN SPIRITUALITY

The term "commitment to liberation" can be misinterpreted because it is ambiguous. Even today in Latin American it can be utilized for ideological or party political ends. At times the impression is given that Christians committed to liberation are to be identified with revolutionary Christians of various political sectors, or even with those who accept to a greater or less degree the Marxist analysis for their diagnosis of injustice in Latin American society. The sociopolitical options involved in the acceptance of these positions limit the right meaning of commitment or the praxis of liberation. What we have to understand by this latter term—and we take the view of Gustavo Gutiérrez here—is "man's efforts to abolish the present injustice and to construct a different society, freer and more human . . . where the oppressed will be agents of their own destiny."[1] This effort not only allows many options to Christians, but is brought about in many ways—through educational work ("education for liberation"), work for cultural or socioeconomic advancement and political work. In the present state of society in Latin America, with its strong political emphasis in which changes depend enormously on political decisions, the political dimension is of first importance and in fact tends to be dominant. Hence the political aspect of our commitment to human liberation in Latin America.

The major theologians of Latin American liberation, concerned with faith and not merely with questions related to praxis, coincide in their affirmation that the experience of commitment to liberation has brought Christians into contact with a different cultural world.[2]

This "transculturization" is due to the nature of the activities followed by these committed Christians—politics with its own strategy and rationale, praxis as a criterion of action, and permanent recourse to the human sciences which control the dynamism of society. . . . The Christian is plunged into this world, which is often new to him—in the past it belonged to a few "professional politicians"—and his faith suffers and is called into question.

Generally speaking, the faith of the average Latin American has until now been very clearly defined by his culture. His family, his education, his social environment and the sociological primacy of Catholicism, which gave him a certain image of Christ, ethics and faithful practice, all formed part of this "traditional faith." But as soon as the traditional Catholic commits himself to the liberation of the workers or the peasants in tasks of an educational or political nature, he finds himself in a way exiled. The categories of his faith—sin, salvation, charity, prayer, etc.—do not inspire or illuminate sufficiently his commitments. Hence the crisis.

And so, from the pastoral angle, liberation is not only a question of temporal efficacy or of ethics. It is fundamentally also a problem of spirituality. As well as a theology, we need a spirituality of liberation. The Christian's commitment to liberation and within it this primordial sociopolitical task, is called, like every activity of the believer, to be more than a chance to put into practice the demands of faith and to apply the postulates of charity. It is more than a backdrop to the achievement of salvation. The commitment to liberation in the Christian must be a place of encounter with God, and therefore a source of inspiration to his theological life and his contemplative life. Liberation is the historical and theologico-spiritual place of encounter of the political and contemplative dimensions in the Christian.

The synthesis between "militant" and "contemplative" is urgent, due to the crisis which we indicated above. This is all the more necessary on account of the misunderstanding which arose in the last thirty years between Christians of different types of spirituality. The last few decades have witnessed two tendencies toward a Christian life style. These can be defined as "religious-contemplative" and "militantly committed." The former looked to strictly "religious" values—prayer and its practice, the liturgy and the sacraments and the transcendent dimensions of Christianity. They were less affected by the temporal or social divisions of the faith.

The latter group emphasize the commitment to historical tasks, social militancy and the praxis of liberation. To varying extents they distrust the inaccurately named "vertical" dimensions of Christianity such as sacramental life, prayer and Christian contemplation in general. One of the important reasons for this dichotomy, which we must now consider more closely, is the ambiguity of the traditional practice of contemplation. Many of its theoretical formulations have not been free of this ambiguity either.

Christian contemplation as "the tranquil dwelling of man in the presence of God"[3] has acquired two different shades of meaning from the early centuries. One came from Platonic mysticism, which in turn was in harmony with oriental mysticism stemming from Buddhism, Hinduism and later Islam. The characteristics of this Platonic contemplation and their indisputable influence, as part of the Greek spirit, on Christian formulations are well known. It has, for instance, a strongly transcendent orientation and neglects bodily, historical, temporal mediations. It tends to make of contemplation an ascent to God in which the temporal sphere is gradually left behind until an exclusive absorption in God is reached. This tendency can easily become a form of escape. This mysticism infected authentic Christian contemplation, not as an isolated fact, but as Greek thought and its dualistic ethos gained influence in the nascent Church.

In questions of spirituality, this was due to a great extent to the writings of Jerome and Cassian, which carried oriental tendencies into Latin spirituality. Cassian himself became the most widely read spiritual author of antiquity and exercised a decisive influence on monachism. For him "Contemplation is a death, an exodus from all earthly things, but at the same time it is also a new life in heaven. The contemplative, having reached the summit of the mountain of contemplation, no longer lives really in the world, but in his true homeland. Resembling the holy angels, he already enjoys their company."[4] The authentic biblical dimension of contemplation, which we call historical or the contemplation of commitment, persisted together with this view. This is the aspect of Christian contemplation which we must recover today in all its fullness, in favor of a renewal of spirituality which will reconcile the contemplative and the political elements in our continent. What is interesting at this moment in Latin America is that this recovery is beginning to be encountered in the experience of many Christians and Christian groups, including those who are committed to various tasks oriented toward liberation.

In these forms of commitment, many believers experience collaboration with the Lord in the redemptive work of building up the Kingdom of God. Many are undergoing a kind of evolution in their dedication to the sociopolitical field of action. From a tendency to question or even lose their faith they have moved to a position where they now tend to strengthen it, renew prayer and rediscover its meaning. Frequently unprepared for this by their formation, they are discovering a deep affinity between the faith and their options.

These Christians react against an ahistorical salvation. They see salvation rather as tied to temporal and political commitments, although they do not reduce it to temporal liberation. They give great importance to the praxis of liberation and discover in prayer the guarantee that evangelical values preside over that praxis. Their commitment itself, at times a very radical one, has led them in many cases to bring their faith to a high degree of Christian mysticism. (In this respect a well-known case is that of Nestor Paz, the Christian *guerrillero* who died four years ago in guerrilla conflicts in Bolivia.)

They see in the practice of their faith the guarantee that their options are governed by love, and that they preserve the ethic sense, and feeling for persons. It is also a guarantee of freedom from pragmatism and from Machiavellian political methods, but it in no way diminishes the intensity of their commitment, or their clarity of vision. Their Christian experience enables them to encounter more creative, human, brotherly ways in liberation, beyond the watchwords of the politicians. They need to experience here and now, the strength of Christian hope in the present-day Latin American historical process, which gives them the certainty that the Kingdom will come. This helps them not to lose heart, to take inspiration from beyond the frequent disillusion of immediate events. Personal, contemplative prayer ensures for them this kind of experience. The Christian committed to liberation becomes a contemplative to the extent that he grasps what God wishes for his fellow man and makes that the decisive motive for his commitment. He also becomes capable of preserving the universality of love, without renouncing his preference for the oppressed.[5]

II. CONTEMPLATION AND COMMITMENT

These experiences are not pure intuitions without Christian values. They go to meet the biblical, historical, committed dimension of contemplation, much neglected among us.

Renewal through integration is sought here, without any rejection of other traditionally valid dimensions of Christian contemplation, in particular its dimension of gratuitous adoration and the value of loving and contemplating God for himself. The dimension that concerns us now relates to the fact that contemplation is essentially linked to the vigor of faith, and to the capacity of faith to bathe life and history in a new light. Contemplation means having an experience of God, real though obscure, in all dimensions of human life. It is the capacity to encounter Christ, and the experience of encountering him, through a vigorous, incarnate faith (I John 1:1) ". . . which we have heard, which we have seen with our eyes, which we have looked upon and touched with our hands, concerning the word of life. . . ." John's witness is always found in the contemplative in the experience of his faith.

This experimental encounter with God, which is revealed to us in Christ, assumes the two contemplative encounters conveyed by the Gospel. The first is that of the person of Jesus. In the New Testament, this encounter is the root of every conversion to the faith and the contemplative life. Christ's revelation to the men of his time (Zacchaeus, the Samaritan woman, Peter, the disciples of Emmaus, etc.) created in them a contemplative encounter and experience. Each one of them is a type of the Christian, and to be a Christian and have met Jesus is one and the same thing in the New Testament. The same contemplative encounter happened to the Apostles and was expressed in the experience of I John 1:1. It appears as identified with the apostolic vocation in the Transfiguration (Matt. 17:1-8). This episode corresponds to the discovery of a new dimension of Christianity, a contemplative dimension which goes beyond action. ("It is well that we are here: if you wish, I will make three booths here.") The encounter with the person of Jesus acquires for the apostles a value in itself; it is privileged and surpasses at that moment the experience of action. Paul also had the same type of encounter (II Cor. 12; Phil. 3, 7ff) and it is found in the experience of all the saints.

The second encounter is inseparable from and complementary to that of the person of Christ. It is the contemplative experience of the presence of Christ in one's brother, particularly one's "little brother." It is typified in the famous pericope of Matthew 25:31: "I was hungry, and you gave me food . . . as you did to one of the least of these my brethren, you did it to me." Here the encounter with the needy and suffering brother (the "least") and the consequent service to him is an experience of Christ—it is contemplative in this sense of being a personal encounter with the Lord. Both encounters are inseparable. The first emphasizes that Christianity transcends any temporal reality, the second that it is incarnate and inseparable from the love for one's brother. The first recalls the first commandment of the love of God above all things, and the absolute of the person of Jesus. The second recalls the commandment similar to the first, the love of one's neighbor as oneself, and the presence of Christ in this love. The first encounter derives from contemplative prayer and the various ways of relating to God, the second from temporal commitment as a Christian experience. The second encounter "incarnates" the first, and gives an historical dimension to the encounter with God and to our life of prayer.

The experience of Jesus in service to our brother gives the Christian consciousness its social dimension and frees it of any tendency to be purely individual, private or platonic. It gives brotherly love a social, collective dimension to the extent that the "least" are not only individual persons in Latin America, but human groups—marginal subcultures, social classes or sectors. There is in them a collective presence of Jesus, the experience of which constitutes a true contemplative act.

Contemplation conceived in this way gives a sociopolitical content to

faith and itself acquires an historicosocial dimension, without being reduced to this alone. Christ encountered and contemplated in prayer is
prolonged in the encounter with our brother and, if we are capable of
experiencing Christ in our service of the "least," it is because we have already encountered him in contemplative prayer. Contemplation is not
only the discovery of the presence of Jesus in the brother ("you did it to
me") but also a call to action in his favor, to the liberating commitment
("as you did it . . ."). The contemplation of Christ in the suffering,
oppressed brother is a call to commitment. It is the historical content of
Christian contemplation in the Latin American Church.

The service-encounter with the poor is contemplative in believers, and
makes of them "contemplatives in action," in the purest Christian tradition. This is not an automatic experience—it occurs as the Christian becomes conscious of Christ encountered in prayer, as a backdrop to action. The Other experienced in contemplative prayer is also experienced
in the encounter with the others.

This encounter with Christ in others is not improvised. It assumes that
he has been contemplated in prayer and this experience is reactivated in
the service of others and so acquires a social, historical content and
purifies our orientation toward others.[6]

Dedication to our brother and his liberation, considered as a contemplative experience, implies an accompanying and intuitively illuminating
presence of that same Christ encountered in prayer. This consciousness
of Christ is the point where prayer and commitment unite, and it prevents the latter from becoming hollow and empty, by including them
both in the same contemplative experience. Christian mysticism is a mysticism of commitment.

III. THE MYSTICAL AND POLITICAL DIMENSION
OF CONTEMPLATION

These reflections call for a reformulation or perfection of the idea of
contemplation, while preserving its traditional values and especially its
gratuitous quality and its transcendence of any element of "utili-
tarianism" which may place it at the service of profane or apostolic tasks.
Contemplative prayer is not to be placed at the service of liberation. The
aim is rather to open up all its potentialities, in this case above all its dimension of commitment.

The essence of true Christian prayer has always consisted in going out
of oneself to encounter the Other who is God. Far from being a kind of
egoistic approach, an escape from realities and responsibilities, true
prayer is the supreme act of abnegation and forgetfulness of self in order
to encounter Christ and his demands in others. In this sense prayer is re-

lated to the classical themes of the cross and death. According to Paul's teaching in Romans, we were crucified with Christ and having died with him we are now alive for God in him. This implies the crucifixion of egoism and the purification of the self as a condition of contemplation. This crucifixion of egoism in forgetfulness of self in the dialectic prayer-commitment will be brought to fulfillment both in the mystical dimension of communication with Jesus in the luminous night of faith, and also in the sacrifice which is assumed by commitment to the liberation of others. The "death" of mysticism and the "death" of the militant are the two dimensions of the call to accept the cross, as the condition of being a disciple (Matt. 16:24).

Solitude, aridity and the dark night accompany the exercise of contemplation and are a means to purge egoism and go out of oneself to encounter the Other. These are also found in the commitment of the Christian to the service of the other. To discover him as the other to whom I must dedicate myself, and not as an extension of myself and my own interests, it is necessary to go out of myself, to die, to crucify egoism through a dark night of contradictions and a prolonged apprenticeship to brotherly love. We purify ourselves for God, to the extent that we purify ourselves for our brother and vice versa.

This capacity to live for one's brother, especially if he is poor and little, is the decisive source of the temporal commitment of the Christian and of the sociopolitical dimension of his faith and charity. It is the basis of the public and social dimension of contemplation, until now unduly "privatized" and wrapped in mystery. It is there, not in the dialectic of the class struggle, that believers will find the strength for their militancy and their work for liberation.

Close to the theme of purification, the cross and death, is found that of the desert, an equally traditional theme in Christian spirituality. Here also we must rediscover its double dimension, mystical and political. The desert in Christian tradition is first and foremost a spiritual attitude. However, many of the great contemplatives, including Jesus himself (Matt. 4:1), Paul (Gal. 1:17), many prophets (Ezekiel, Jeremiah, Moses and Elijah, to whom we will return later), the early monks, many contemplative orders and Charles de Foucauld in modern times, went to the geographical desert at many periods of their lives, so as to feel this attitude with the help of an external setting. The geographical desert is the symbol of an attitude of self-emptying and of taking up one's place in truth and without illusions before God. It is an attitude of radical poverty which leads one to place all one's hope in the gift of Christ, of silence in order to listen to the word of the Other.

The desert is an attitude of human powerlessness in the presence of salvation. It is a disposition to receive this salvation gratuitously in the painful experience of one's own limitations and with the obscure conviction that God seeks us out and that Christianity, rather than man's love of God, is the love of Jesus seeking out man first.

The desert has been conceived almost exclusively in relation to the mystical life of prayer and in the context of the first encounter of the New Testament to which we referred previously, which is the contemplative relationship with the person of Jesus. We believe that to rediscover the authentic concept of Christian contemplation, in a form bearing significance for those believers who are committed to liberating action, the experience of the desert would also have to be extended to the second encounter, the encounter of Christ with the least of his brethren.

The attitude of the desert, a contemplative attitude, is united to this commitment. The desert forged the great prophets, and present-day Christian prophecy in Latin America likewise needs the contemplative attitude of the desert. The attitude of going out of oneself, of reencountering the Absolute and the true reality of things appropriate to the desert allows the Christian to leave the system, to regard it as an unjust and false society, to condemn it and to become free of it. If the Christian does not withdraw to the desert in order to make an interior withdrawal from the system, he will not become free or a prophet of liberation for others. If he has not managed to create silence within himself in order to shut out the words of oppression and listen to the word of "the truth which makes us free," he will not be able to transform his milieu prophetically or politically. The desert as a political experience liberates him from egoism and from the "system," and is a source of freedom and of an ability to liberate.

Authentic Christian contemplation, passing through the desert, transforms contemplatives into prophets and heroes of commitment and militants into mystics. Christianity achieves the synthesis of the politician and the mystic, the militant and the contemplative, and abolishes the false antithesis between the religious-contemplative and the militantly committed. Authentic contemplation, through the encounter with the absolute of God, leads to the absolute of one's neighbor. It is the meeting place for this difficult symbiosis which is so necessary and creative for Latin American Christians committed to the liberation of the poor.

IV. CONTEMPLATION AND PROPHECY IN THE
BIBLICAL MESSAGE

Current Christian witness to the synthesis of commitment and contemplation and the restoration of its authentic content are rooted in the best tradition of Christianity and the Bible. The prophets follow this line and guide the people, criticize the system, act as spokesmen of a message of liberty. They do this not from the vantage point of power politics, but from the people themselves and service of the people and also from the contemplation of the Word of God which impels them to act. This is the mystical political attitude of the Christian, beginning from the people and the Word and not from the egoism of power. The prophetic figure of Elijah could be an inspiration to these Christians of today. Scripture shows this prophet on fire with God's zeal (I Kings 19:10) and this zeal and solicitude were revealed to him in the desert, where he had to flee (17:1ff; 19:4–8). From the desert, God led him to the contemplation of his face, manifesting himself in the same place where Moses saw the Lord (19:9–14). This manifestation is not spectacular but is "the sound of a gentle breeze" (19:12) like a sign of the intimacy of God with the contemplatives and prophets. Like Moses, Elijah was converted by his encounter with God into a source of justice for his people (19:15–18).

Transformed by this encounter with his Lord, Elijah was able to confront the potentates and oppressors of his time, who were intoxicated by military victories and material splendors and who wallowed in a climate of pride and national exultation (16:23–24). In the temple of Baal hundreds of false prophets sustained and propagated the worship of idols. Elijah accepted the commitment which God offered him to confront this power system and liberate the people from idolatrous oppression. The confrontation reached its crisis on Mount Carmel (18:25ff) where God was by Elijah's side, confounding the enemy with his gratuitous intervention.

Every time God's rights were at stake, Elijah once again became prophetically committed (II Kings 1). He did so not only respecting the cult of idols and questions of religion, but also respecting justice and the faith of the weak. This was the case in his prophetic denunciation of Ahab, the King of Samaria, the murderer and usurper of the possessions of the defenseless Naboth (I Kings 21). The king eventually repented and was converted.

In the New Testament, the symbol of Elijah as a contemplative and committed prophet is offered to all Christians. John the Baptist, the greatest of the prophets, is presented in this line (Matt. 11:14), and James puts him forward as a model of faith and prayer, since he was "a human being like ourselves" (James 5:17). In Matthew 17:1ff, his dialogue with the transfigured Jesus, as previously with Yahweh in the whisper of the breeze, has stood in the Christian tradition as the symbol of the contemplative prophet.[7]

The figure of Moses must also be seen in this line as typical of the mystical politician, who had a profound experience of God in the desert, and without ceasing to be guided by this experience, led a people toward their liberation.

In this enterprise, the contemplative quality of Moses led him to an encounter with the absolute of the Other in the solitude of the burning bush and with the absolute of the others in whom his experienced faith caused him to discover a people indwelt by Yahweh, to which he was to communicate the freedom of the children of God. This contemplative quality also enabled this mystic to avoid "mythifying" a people who were frequently mediocre; and to accept therefore the lonely task of prophetic guidance. "Why does Yahweh bring us to this land? Should we not do better to go back to Egypt? Let us appoint a leader and go back. Why did you lead us out of Egypt only to bring us to this wretched place" (Num. 14 and 20).

In this prophetic solitude, Moses nevertheless remained firm in hope, as if he had seen the invisible since because of his contemplative faith "he considered that the insults offered to Christ were more precious than all the treasures of Egypt" (Heb. 11:26–27).

This hope which is so characteristic of political prophecy led Moses to the limit of sacrifice in his mission and in the end he himself did not enter the promised land to which he had led the people. He sacrificed "power" to the "liberating service of the people," faithful to his mission.

The Latin American theology of liberation has restored the Exodus to its political symbolism and has seen in Moses an authentic politician, guiding the people toward a better society.[8]

If the Christian politician in Latin America has to have a spirituality adequate to his mission and commitments, he has an inspiring model in Moses. In his political activity this prophet (and the Christian politician at the present moment in the continent ought to be a prophet) kept the wide significance of his mission alive. He knew that the political liberation from Egypt fitted into a much wider and more integral divine plan for the eschatological salvation of the people. He knew that his activity would remain always incomplete, at times frustrated, at times rejected, because the unique and definitive liberator of the people was not himself, but God, whose Kingdom would have no end. So he dedicated himself up to the end, because the hope that animated him came not from himself, but was renewed daily in him, in his encounter with his Lord. And is hope not the great inspiring virtue of the politician?

In a different dimension, the message delivered to us by the Messianism of Jesus is also profoundly illuminating. In him, contemplation reverts to a commitment not directly temporal, but prophetic and pastoral, with sociopolitical consequences, more fitted for the ministry of evangelization than for temporal political action.

The commitment of the contemplative to the poor and the little can be specified along two directions. The first is the straight political option. In this, the Christian canalizes his charity—the service of Christ in the other

—through the mediation of projects. For this, he needs to share in power. That is the basis of his party political option, in which charity, for him, finds its most effective channel of liberation. Here his contemplative commitment becomes strategy and party politics.

The second direction of the commitment to the "least" is that of the prophetic pastoral option. In it charity, the source of contemplation, is channeled into the effective proclamation of the message of Christ about the liberation of the poor and the "least." The message becomes a critical consciousness, and is capable of inspiring the deepest and most decisive liberating transformations. In this sense it has social and political consequences. This option is more charismatic and therefore it is less widespread.

Committed charity needs both of these forms of expression, and one does not necessarily exclude the other. Human love also finds its expression in two ways—in marriage and in the less widespread and more charismatic modality of celibacy. Both forms of living are potent, like the two kinds of commitment which we have noted, and both are effective and legitimately Christian. The second kind, more appropriate to the pastoral ministry and the hierarchy—although it does not absolutely exclude the other forms of commitment—is the kind of militancy which Christ himself and the apostles adopted. With it, they renounced power and politics, but in return they brought about the conditions of consciousness necessary for progressive liberation from all forms of oppression.

When Christ and all the apostles revealed the presence of God in every human being, and with it the dignity and absolute destiny of man, they not merely expressed their own contemplative vision of man, but endowed this prophetic announcement with a sociopolitical content, making it incompatible with the prevailing social system and with pagan attitudes toward human beings.

By giving the poor and little a privileged place and identifying himself specially with them, Christ called the poor to the Kingdom of God and mobilized them. This is not only a mystic act—"to intuit" the presence of Jesus in the dispossessed, so discovering their dignity—but it leads to social commitment and to political consequences, since this incorporation of the poor in the Kingdom of God passes through history and implies a progressive liberation of the same poor and little from concrete social systems.

Jesus proclaimed the beatitudes. It is impossible to announce and live this message without living in hope, in other words, without being a contemplative. But the beatitudes themselves form the ethical attitude of the contemplatives. This radical modality of living and gospel is a prophecy which invariably questions individuals and societies.

Thus, the biblical message from Moses to Jesus shows us the two aspects of the liberating commitment of faith. In Moses, liberation takes on a temporal, political expression, and in Christ it shows forth the full sense of liberation.

This full meaning is established in Jesus. Liberation is seen as decisive, eschatological, saving and transforming from within man and society. It implies a sociopolitical transformation, just as the liberation of Moses implied the conversion of the heart and the eschatological vocation of Israel.

We have here incarnate the mystic-prophetic dimension and the political dimension of faith and contemplation. Latin American Christians live out these dimensions in varying degrees in their daily lives, but they always complement each other in accordance with the individual's function or vocation. The mystic and the politician are united in one same call to contemplation, since the source of their Christian vision is the same—the experience of Jesus encountered in prayer and in our brothers, particularly the "least" (Matt. 25:41).

NOTES

1. G. Gutiérrez, *A Theology of Liberation* (Maryknoll, N.Y., 1973).
2. Cf. G. Gutiérrez in "Liberation, Theology and Proclamation," in *Concilium* 6 (1974).
3. See K. Rahner and H. Vorgrimler, *Concise Theological Dictionary* (London and New York, 1965), under "Contemplation."
4. Quoted by S. Marsili, *Casiano ed Evragio* (Rome, 1936), p. 57.
5. See the report of S. Galilea, "Spiritual Awakening and the Movements of Liberation in Latin America," in *Concilium*, Nov. 1973 (American ed., Vol. 89).
6. K. Rahner and H. Vorgrimler, op. cit.
7. Cf. X. Leon-Dufour, *Dictionary of Biblical Theology* (New York, 1968).
8. G. Gutiérrez, *op. cit.*; E. Pironio, "Teología de la liberación," in *Criterio* 1606 (Buenos Aires, 1970), p. 786; H. Assmann, *Opresiónliberación, desafío a los cristianos* (Montevideo, 1971), p. 71; R. Alves, "El pueblo de Dios y la liberación del hombre" in *Fichas de ISAL* 3 (Montevideo, 1970) 9ff and many others. On this point the consensus of authors is remarkable.

36

Meister Eckhart and Karl Marx:
The Mystic as Political Theologian

MATTHEW FOX, O.P.

It is a shock to spiritualists who imagine that spirituality is a term restricted to the "inner life" to learn that the last talk the late Thomas Merton ever gave was entitled "Marxism and Monastic Perspectives." In this talk, delivered two hours before his death, Merton called the Marxist Herbert Marcuse "a kind of monastic thinker" and declared that "the whole New Testament is, in fact—and can be read by a Marxist-oriented mind as—a protest against religious alienation."[1] What the many proponents of spiritualist and sentimental spirituality fail to comprehend is the inherent politics in all mysticism. For all energy is interconnected, whether it be energy of politics *or* of the flight from politics.[2]

Equally baffling to devotees of spiritualism will be the title of this article and the suggestion that spirituality and politics might go hand in hand. They of course do. On the one hand, spirituality is often used as a weapon (and a powerful one it is) to repress political consciousness and assertiveness, as the following observation of the historian Christopher Hill makes clear, describing the role of the preacher in late medieval society.

> The common people were permanently discontented, held down only by the preaching of the clergy and the swords of the nobility. If clergy or nobility lost positive enthusiasm for government policy a popular revolt might break out, like that of the Spanish *comuneros* in 1520 or of the Norfolk peasantry in 1549. But normally, as in these cases, once the point had been made and the government had learned its lesson, the commons would be bloodily repressed and preached against.[3]

On the other hand, spirituality has supported prophetic movements as is clearly the case with Meister Eckhart (1260–1327), the German Dominican mystic and spiritual theologian. No less a disciple of Marxism than Ernst Bloch interpreted Eckhart's historical contribution to socialism in the following manner: "In Eckhart the heretical, antiecclesiastical lay movement of the late Middle Ages became articulate in German; which is a decisive factor in any socialist evaluation." Eckhart in the name of mysticism demystified the economic and political facts of life for the "common people" whom he inspired

> in the revolutions of the next two centuries, along with its predecessor, the mysticism of Joachim of Floris, Abbot of Calabrese—among the Hussites, and with Thomas Munzer in the German Peasant War; events, indeed, not notable ideologically for the rule of clarity, but ones in which the mystic fog was at least not of service to the ruling class.[4]

"To a healthy number of Marxists," writes Eckhartian scholar Reiner Schurmann, "Meister Eckhart appears as the theorician of the class struggle in the Middle Ages." His is a "mysticism of the left" that "would designate the appropriation by man of his authentic good when he is alienated by the dogma of an inaccessible heaven."[5]

In this paper I want to concentrate on three areas of political consciousness in the life and preaching of Eckhart: (1) The Merchant Mentality, (2) How Everyone is an Aristocrat, and (3) His Political Condemnation. Before we examine these three areas, however, we need to deal briefly with certain general presuppositions to Eckhart's preaching.

I. GENERAL POLITICAL-MYSTICAL PRINCIPLES IN ECKHART

To do justice to all of Eckhart's mystical-political consciousness would be impossible in the length of a single article. The following themes of Eckhart are important for grasping the groundwork of his spirituality and, what is significant for this present study, carry within themselves powerful and profound insights as to the interrelatedness of spirituality and political consciousness. Since I have dealt with them in greater length in another article,[6] I will only list them here.

1) Realized Eschatology. Heaven is not projected onto another time or place for Eckhart but has already begun within individuals. Bloch comments: "This first insight into man's alienation of himself, namely, that human treasures have been bartered for the illusion of heaven, did not come about without some contribution from mysticism."[7]

2) The spiritual journey culminates in a return to the world, not in a flight from it. The return to creation means loving one's neighbor. As Eckhart puts it:

> In contemplation you serve only yourself, in good works you serve many people.

If a person were in such a rapturous state as St. Paul once entered, and he knew of a sick man who wanted a cup of soup, it would be far better to withdraw from the rapture for love's sake and serve him who is in need.[8]

In his Commentary on the *Our Father* Eckhart explains the expression "our daily bread":

Bread is given to us not that we eat it alone but that others who are indigent might be participants. . . . He who does not give to another what belongs to another does not eat his own bread, but another's at the same time with his own. Thus, when we eat bread acquired justly, we eat our bread; but when bread is acquired by evil means and with sin, we are not eating our own but another's. For nothing that we have unjustly is ours.[9]

3) Salvation is a We, not an I, salvation for Eckhart. He says: "God has been the common Savior of the entire world, and for this I am indebted to him with much more thanks than if he had saved only me."[10]

4) Eckhart is a champion of the *via negativa* as an approach to God. He calls God the "non-God" and the "unnameable." This rejection of the language that culture or religion takes for granted for "their God" should be recognized for what it is with Eckhart: a political as well as a theological starting point. For to wipe one's mind clean of an inherited language is to wipe one's mind clean of an entire culture with its social and symbolic structures. The *via negativa* has profound political implications. It is a rejection of everything in order to start anew.

5) The Kingdom of God theme, like that of Realized Eschatology, is personalized by Eckhart. In him there is no trace of ecclesiastical triumphalism, no confusion of Church with Kingdom of God.

6) Eckhart dismisses dualistic relationships of God and people in favor of dialectical ones. All deep living is dialectical for him. He rejects subject/object relations with God that support most theisms in favor of a deeply shared panentheism. The panentheism is a political panentheism.

7) Marx objected to philosophers of contemplation who only wanted to gaze at the world as at an object. His philosophy, he insisted, would change the world. Eckhart too resists contemplation as a passive gazing at. Knowing for Eckhart is a "participation in being" and not a "gazing at" being.[11] He is a spiritual theologian and preacher which is to say he seeks not "a theoretical dogma of what man is, but . . . a practical guide to what he must become." His is an effort at getting persons to give birth, to become, to beget, to create. To change and to be changed. Our identity with God is operative and verb-oriented, not ontological or substantial.[12] Eckhart, like Marx, is action-oriented. His spirituality "is

not oriented towards contemplation. It produces a new birth: the birth of the Son. . . ."[13] It is oriented then toward creativity and giving birth.

Having considered this brief outline of themes in Eckhart's spirituality, we can now turn to the three issues on which I want to concentrate in this article.

II. THE MERCHANT MENTALITY

In his sermon based on Jesus' ejecting moneylenders from the temple,[14] Eckhart presents his case against what he calls the "merchant mentality" —a way of thinking and acting that infiltrates the deepest levels of a person, the space where God dwells or wants to dwell within us.

> This temple, in which God wants to rule in power according to His will, is the soul of man, which He formed and created just like Himself. . . . He made the soul of man so like Himself that in heaven or on earth, among all the glorious creatures that God so beautifully created, there is none which is so like Him as the human soul (*Cl*, 127).

Notice in this passage how Eckhart declares God's presence not to be in institutions however magnificent or religious, but in people. People are the New Temple for Eckhart. It is because the merchant mentality has the power to touch us at our depths that it is so insidious and demonic. It can displace God from ourselves. "That is why God wants to have this temple empty, so that He alone may dwell in it. Hence this temple pleases Him so much, because it is so like Him and He is so pleased to be in the temple if He alone dwells in it." God's dwelling with persons depends on their chasing the attitudes of buying and selling from their inner selves—a task that is not easy, for a merchant mentality will poison even good people and certainly religion itself.

> Who were the people who bought and sold, and who are they now? Take careful note of my words. This time I will only preach of good people. . . . All those are merchants who refrain from grave sins and would like to be good people and to do their good works to the glory of God, such as fasting, vigils, prayers and so forth (127*f*).

Eckhart explains here that what makes otherwise good people into merchants is an attitude of doing even pious works in order to get "something in return" from God. "All such persons are merchants" he declares elsewhere, who want to "trade with our Lord" (*Bl*, 240, 245). It is the mentality of getting that is so devastating. "As long as we perform our works for the sake of salvation or of going to heaven, we are on the wrong track" (*Cl*, 80).

What is a mercenary? What is a serf? Anyone who lives a life of means instead of ends. "Those who seek something with their works are servants and hirelings, or those who work for a Why or a Wherefore" (*Cl-Sk*, 53). In other words, the merchant mentality reduces all living and thinking to problem-solving. It robs us of mystery-living or living "without a why." It is for this reason too that living without a why lies at the very heart of Eckhart's spirituality[15] and why he himself could declare that "he who understands my teaching about justice and the just person understands everything I say."[16] Eckhart's critique of the merchant mentality becomes a criticism of religion when it is itself a quid pro quo or a God-Give-Me mentality. Why is Eckhart so disturbed by such merchant attitudes? Because they miss the "glad and gratuitous" giving of God. It is a work over a grace mentality. Above all, it signifies a lack of freedom to experience life in terms other than buying/selling, giving/getting.

Truth needs no huckstering. God does not seek His own ends; in all His works He is free and untrammeled, and performs them from pure love. So does the man who is united with God: he is free and untrammeled in all his actions and performs them to the glory of God alone.

Furthermore, a merchant mentality produces a dualistic consciousness of before and after and erases the potential for "the highest truth" which is found in unitive experiences. The subject-object relationships of dualism that the merchant mentality generates are a contradiction to the unitive experience between God and humans. Unity, not separation, is the law of life. This interplay between God and humans cannot happen without "the continuous abandonment of both human and divine *eigenschaft*, property."[17] Since the divine-human interplay is truly play, it is just as truly without dualism. Eckhart's goal, then, is that we be free from the merchant mentality to the very core of our being. When you are so free, you are in touch with the divine.

If you would be entirely free from huckstering, so that God will leave you in this temple, you should do everything that is possible in all your actions purely in praise of God, and should be as free as you were when you did not exist. You should ask for nothing in return (128*f*).

With this freedom, one is open to receiving divine gifts "anew in this Now . . . and begetting them again without hindrance" (129). All things—God included—come to those who do not fall victim to the commercial or merchandising mentality. You cannot enjoy life if your attitude is commercial.

Another objection Eckhart harbors against the merchant mentality is that the goods we buy and sell are external goods. Concentration on the external as object quite literally kills the divine in us. "Whatever motivates us other than out of ourselves is thoroughly an act of mortal sin," he declares.[18] In another sermon he develops further the lethal (mortal) aspects of materialism and how it kills even God.

> There is also a Something by which the soul lives in God, but when the soul is intent on external things that Something dies, and therefore God dies, as far as the soul is concerned. Of course, God himself does not die. He continues very much alive to himself (*Bl*, 133).

> Some people want to see God with their eyes as they see a cow and to love him as they love their cow—they love their cow for the milk and cheese and profit it makes them. This is how it is with people who love God for the sake of outward wealth or inward comfort. . . . Indeed, I tell you the truth, any object you have on your mind, however good, will be a barrier between you and the inmost truth (*Bl*, 241).

Still another objection to the merchant mentality is that it creates a false sense of ownership. We own nothing, Eckhart insists. We are wayfarers who have been lent many gifts, all of which are to be returned to the Creator. "We should have all things as if they were lent to us, without any ownership, whether they are body and soul, sense, strength, external goods or honors, friends, relations, house, hall, everything in fact" (*Cl-Sk*, 103). Once again Eckhart is getting at our relationships as being the fundament of spiritual liveliness. But economics can poison our relationships and we need to resist what merchant attitudes can do to us. God is not a giver of personal property or a canonizer of ownership, "As personal property He never gave anything either to His Mother or to any man, or to any creature in any way." Instead of ownership of things, possession of God.

> Never has anything so fully owned by anyone as God will be mind with all that He can do and is. This ownership we should earn by being here without self-seeking and without everything that is not God (*Cl-Sk*, 104).

Eckhart praises an attitude of reverence to life that is built around this consciousness of living on time that is borrowed and gifts that are borrowed from the Creator. We have been lent life from God—there lies the key to peaceful and gentle living. He has a radical sense of how being and all the gifts of living are ours *on loan* (*ze borge*).

> Everything that is good and goodness itself was lent to him by God and not given. . . . He gives no good to the creature, but bestows it on him as a loan. The sun gives the air heat, but lends light to it; and

therefore, as soon as the sun sets, the air loses the light, but the heat remains, because this is given to the air as its own (*Cl-Sk,* 128).

It follows that we are to be as lighthearted and as non-grabbing as the air is to the light that passes through it. Eckhart is deeply disturbed by a possessive instead of a "loan" mentality. In fact, he denounces *eigenschaft*—selfhood, attachment, property—"as nothingness because it darkens peregrine joy by making being into that particular being, man into that individual, and God into that divine person."[19] "Nothingness" is here used by Eckhart as a synonym for sin. We see then that the "merchant mentality" is an ultimate affront or sin to Eckhart's mystical view of living gracefully and with awareness of our receptivity.

Like his Dominican brother Aquinas who wrote that "there can be no joy in living without joy in work," Eckhart turns his attention to the important issue of finding joy in work. We do not work merely for pay but for ecstasy. He explores how "all man's suffering, all his works, all his life become happy and joyful" (*Cl-Sk,* 135*f*). Work is to be an end in itself and not just a means toward an end. For this is the way God, who "is still continually creating" the world, works.

> Whoever is born of God . . . does all his work for the sake of working. God is never weary of loving and working. . . . He loves for the sake of love, works for the sake of work, and therefore God loves and works uninterruptedly. God's work is His nature, His being, His life, His happiness (*Cl-Sk,* 134).

Our work is to be patterned after God's work. For a wise person, "to work for God's sake is his being, his life, his work, his happiness." Authentic human work comes from within a person and not from outside. "If a man's work is to live, it must come from the depths of him—not from alien sources outside himself—but from within."[20] We are to love ourselves as well as God in our work.[21] To love self is to love God and to please God.

Eckhart's vision of spirituality does not repress or ignore injustice and human suffering but in fact demands awareness of it. Yet this sensitivity and awareness is only possible where the merchant mentality is lacking.

> What do poor people do who endure the same or more severe illness and suffering, and have no one even to give them water? They must seek their very bread in rain, cold and snow from house to house. Therefore, if you would be comforted, forget those who are better placed and remember only those who are less fortunate (*Cl-Sk,* 115).

Love of neighbor is not based on society's definition of wealth but on the richness of our love of God. "The man who has Christ can give to all men of his riches and in abundance. We are to show by our good conduct that we are rich in Christ through his indwelling spirit."[22]

Eckhart does not hesitate to criticize the comfortable and the powerful.

> Some say: "Lord, I can indeed come in honor and wealth and comfort." Truly, if the Lamb had lived thus and had thus walked before us, I should rejoice to see you following Him in the same manner. But the virgin strides after the Lamb over rough and smooth ways, and wherever He steps (*Cl*, 221).

His argument against comfortable piety and spirituality is a Gospel one, namely that Jesus did not live and grow that way. Nor is philanthropy—even religious philanthropy—a substitute for love of neighbor.

> If a man were to give a thousand marks in gold, so that churches and monasteries could be built with it, that would be a great thing. Yet anyone would have given much more if he knew how to esteem a thousand marks as nothing. He would have done far more than the other (*Cl*, 173).

Even dogs, he points out, know that love is more important than authority and thus they are wise enough to put affection for their master ahead of King or Emperor (*Cl*, 147). Is wisdom to be found where there is wealth, influence and the comfort of the powerful? Hardly. "Now a master says that there is no man who is so foolish as not to desire wisdom. . . . If I am a rich man, that does not make me wise. But if I am transformed and conformed to the essence and nature of wisdom and become wisdom itself, then I am a wise man" (*Cl*, 200). It is the power of transformation and conformation, of death and rebirth that are the ingredients to authentic wisdom and not the power of having power.

Still another criticism of the merchant mentality is that it destroys our capacity to receive. "The very best and highest things are really and in the best sense free gifts" (*Cl*, 171), he insists. And these come from within us and cannot be measured by externals. In a real sense, our receiving is more important than our giving.

> I much prefer a person who can love God enough to take a handout of bread, to a person who can give a hundred dollars for God's sake. How do I explain that? . . . When the poor man extends his hand to beg the bread, he trades his honor in exchange. The giver buys the honor the receiver sells (*Bl*, 235).

Receiving, and our capacity of becoming bigger for the sake of greater receptivity, divine receptivity, is more important than giving. The problem with an activist merchant mentality is that it shrinks us up. It reduces the soul to the size of objects instead of expanding it to God-like dimensions. "The soul is like that: the more it wants the more it is given; the more it receives the more it grows" (*Bl*, 233).

In considering Eckhart's criticisms of the merchant mentality, criticisms that correspond to [those of] a Marxist like Erich Fromm at his best, we see that Eckhart is not moralizing about materialism. He is not treating the merchant mentality as an ethical problem. Rather, he sees materialism as a poisonous consciousness, a stumbling block to spiritual awareness. An alienation, to use his word. Nowhere does Eckhart complain that things are evil or immoral. Nor does he romanticize poverty (in fact, he criticizes conditions of poverty for how they degrade humanity). He directs his considerable energies instead to the heart of the demonic dimensions of materialism, that is to its thing-consciousness. Thing-consciousness is a dualistic, subject-object way of thinking and acting that destroys our greatness and our oneness with self, others, nature and God. Thus, for Eckhart it is our attitude toward things—an attitude most often taught by a merchant-mentality economic system—that makes us materialistic and, as he says, God-slayers in the process.

In Eckhart's opinion our drying up and becoming as puny as the objects we worship is not a moral fault but a spiritual catastrophe. For it means that God, who has chosen humankind in a special way to do big things within and among, is stymied. God cannot move, operate or dance in a person who is as puny as a thing or in a society that worships thing-puniness. And God does want to dance for joy, Eckhart insists. "With each deed, however trifling, done out of virtue and justice, and resulting in justice, God is made glad—glad through and through!—so that there is nothing in the core of the Godhead that does not dance for joy" (*Bl*, 246). Thus the merchant mentality stymies not only human history but divine history as well—the continual unfolding of creation that God desires to do in a constant process of birthing is stymied. "Just as little as I can do anything without Him, He cannot really accomplish anything apart from me" (*Cl*, 249). Eckhart's final word then against the merchant and materialistic mentality is not a fire and brimstone moral reprimand but an awesome, even divine, sadness. For he senses with a piercing sensitivity God's frustration that the divine work of continual loving and creating, a work that God "savors" and finds immense pleasure in, is being interfered with. It is as if God has no place to show divine love if men and women become obstacles along the way. God accomplishes through us or not at all. Eckhart's vision is staggering. No humanist ever imagined a more awesome view of the importance of human history than this.

But Eckhart does not stop with criticism of the merchant mentality. He offers an alternative way of living and of seeing, of interrelating whether by way of politics, economics or religious practice. It is the way of *Abegescheidenheit,* a term he himself coined, and *Gelazenheit.* These terms have been variously translated as detachment, disinterest, solitude, releasement, letting go, letting be. Whatever be their most acceptable translation for our culture (and I prefer "letting go" for the former and "letting be" for the latter), we know what their opposites are. Their opposites are grabbing, hoarding, possessing, clinging—in other words the way of *Abegescheidenheit* and *Gelazenheit* is meant to be an alternative way to the way of rapacious, merchant-like having and thinking and acting. This way is a way of letting go of things—even our images of things and even our images of God—in order to experience experience once again. It is a way of letting things be as well so that when we experience we truly experience what is there. This path or way of letting go and letting be is not a passive, quietistic sleep; it is an active, supremely awake and aware attitude toward all of life.

The path of letting go and letting be cuts to the quick of the merchant mentality. It is radically anti-materialistic and Eckhart insists on applying it to all forms of materialism including religious ones. It means letting go of religious forms of materialism which appear so often under the guise of pietistic exercises, clericalism, caste privileges, spiritualism or ecclesial triumphalism. Religious no less than profane power trips are to be let go of.

III. HOW EVERYONE IS AN ARISTOCRAT

Having considered Eckhart's economic consciousness, we are prepared to examine his political consciousness as well. The two are intimately related for there was in Eckhart's time and place a "merchant aristocracy."[23] Eckhart devoted an entire talk to the subject of "The Aristocrat."[24] The talk is an exegesis of the scriptural passage from Luke (19:12): "A certain nobleman went into a far country to receive for himself a kingdom, and to return."

Eckhart begins his talk insisting that everyone is a nobleman or aristocrat.

> How nobly man is constituted by nature, and how divine is the state to which he can come by grace . . . a large part of Holy Scripture is affected by these words. . . . In us is the inward man, whom the Scriptures call the new man, the heavenly man, the young man, the friend and the noble man (*Cl-Sk,* 149).

Eckhart does not hide the biblical basis for his disturbing thesis and when he claims that "within us is the aristocrat" he adds: "And this is what our Lord means when he says: 'A nobleman went out into a far country and received for himself a kingdom and returned.'" In a society that was as aware of privilege as was Eckhart's, the thesis that all are aristocrats is a far from subtle rebuke of the caste system then prevailing. But it is more than a rebuke—it is an imaginative alternative that Eckhart is suggesting. According to historian Jacques Heers, what characterized the popular uprisings of Eckhart's period and place was that even when the "people" overthrew one aristocracy another immediately took its place.[25] We see then how truly radical and imaginative was Eckhart's alternative—not to confront aristocracy but to re-create it entirely by baptizing all into it. Eckhart does not put down nobles and aristocrats and he refuses to substitute a new dualism of the lowly over the privileged. Instead, with a dialectical imagination that only a mystic could muster, he makes the peasants into nobles. Instead, therefore, of putting down anyone, he elevates all. The practical fallout from such a democratic vision would, no doubt, express itself more stridently.

He elaborates on what the consequences are if all persons are indeed aristocrats (though one suspects that detailed elaboration was hardly necessary to the populace just as, were a preacher to suggest today that "everyone is president of General Motors" the consequences would hardly demand involved elaboration). It means, says Eckhart, that "no one is nobler than you." That there are no ladders that we need to climb or no chiefs on ladder tops that we need please. It means we are equal, not ranked.

> What our Lord calls a nobleman the prophet calls a great eagle. Who then is nobler than he who is born, on one hand of the highest and the best that the creature has, and on the other hand from the inmost ground of the Divine nature and of His desert?[26]

Thus Eckhart reiterates his marvelous admiration for the nobility of the human person. Eckhart does not stop short of claiming that human beings give a home to the divine within them. For in us "God has sowed His image and His likeness, and . . . He sows the good seed, the root of all wisdom, all knowledge, all virtue and all goodness, the seed of Divine nature. The seed of Divine nature is the Son of God, the Word of God" (p. 150). Eckhart's theology of personhood does not concentrate on sin and redemption but on divinization. In this regard he drinks fully of Eastern Christian spiritual theologies.

> The seed of God is in us. If it was cultivated by a good, wise and industrious laborer, it would thrive all the more and would grow up to God, whose seed it is, and the fruit would be like the Divine nature. The seed of a pear tree grows into a pear tree, a hazel seed into a hazel tree, a seed of God into God (ibid., p. 151).

We come in touch with our own divinity when we experience ego-loss and ecstasy, provided we let ourselves go to these experiences of fullness. For the ego-suspension that ecstasy is about is at the same time our God-experience. One might say that full joy is our experience of God. Thomas Aquinas, Eckhart's brother Dominican and predecessor in the Chair of Theology for Foreigners at the University of Paris, was also roundly criticized for considering ecstasy to be a result of love and not merely "supernatural" loves.[27] "How should man know that he knows God, if he does not know himself? For certainly this man does not know himself or other things in the least, but God alone, when he becomes blessed and is blessed in the root and the ground of blessedness" (157). But getting in touch with our divine origins has profound political implications, as Bloch recognized:

> One thing is certain: Eckhart's sermon does not intend to snuff man out for the sake of an Otherworld beyond him: . . . The revolutionary Anabaptists, those disciples of Eckhart and Tauler, showed afterwards in practice exactly how highly and how uncomfortably for every tyrant. A subject who thought himself to be in personal union with the Lord of Lords provided, when things got serious, a very poor example indeed of serfhood.[28]

How regular is this God-experience for Eckhart? When does it happen? Is it only for heaven? By no means. For Eckhart, steeped in a consciousness of realized eschatology, heaven begins here on earth. The future is now. God is now. We know God (and not just about God) now. And here. "Our Lord tells us very aptly what eternal life is; to know God as the only true God . . ." (157). Notice the use of the present tense in his phrase "eternal life *is to* know God." The present-day experience of God is repeated by Eckhart. "He who follows and lives according to the spirit and according to its counsel, belongs to eternal life. It is the inward man . . . that . . . always brings forth good fruit and never evil" (151). Again eternal life has already begun for Eckhart.

The essence of the fullness of divine joy that Eckhart senses in the present life is one of cutting through the dualisms of subject-object. He insists on our cutting through the dualism implicit in our knowing *about* God, a dualism between knower and known, subject and object. "The nobleman receives and derives all his being, life and happiness solely and only from God, by God and in God, and not from knowing, contemplating or loving God, or anything of the kind" (157). Eckhart is not being anti-intellectual for he never is; but he is, one might say, being anti-academic in the sense that he rejects the notion that knowledge *of* and the social advantages that accrue to the educated ever takes precedence over knowledge *with*. He takes up the subject of the limits of knowledge that is knowledge *of* on another occasion. "One person who has mastered life is better than a thousand persons who have mastered only the contents of books . . ." (*Bl*, 236). The joy and beauty that we experience change us so that God "shines forth and sparkles" from us when we become the aristocrat we are born to be.

Eckhart recognizes two kinds of knowledge: One is characterized by "clearly distinguished ideas" (cf. Descartes' definition of truth as "clear and distinct ideas") that might be called "evening knowledge." And another that sees creatures not as separate entities that make for clear distinctions but as *interrelated,* that is in their relationship to God in whom they live and move and have their being. This panentheistic manner of seeing reality happens "when one knows the creatures in God that is called and is 'morning knowledge'; and in this way one sees the creatures without any differentiation and stripped of all images and deprived of all similarity in the One, who is God Himself" (156). Since interrelatedness, seeing the oneness of all things and their interconnections, is the essence of compassion,[29] we can call this dimension to aristocracy a compassionate consciousness. Indeed, compassion becomes the very definition of aristocrat for Eckhart. "This is also the nobleman of whom our Lord said 'A nobleman went out.' He is noble because he is one, and because he knows God and creatures in the One" (156). To know God and creatures as they are one is to know that God suffers when creatures suffer. Such knowledge is the beginning of compassion which is an active effort to relieve creaturely *and* divine suffering. To know that God *and* the universe *and* people suffer together is to know how thoroughly political and nonprivatized some mysticism can be. "Indeed *anima mea anima nostra* has seldom or never been so highly thought of" as in Meister Eckhart's mysticism.[30] The redemption of one is the redemption of all.

Eckhart does not sentimentalize compassion—compassion for him is an awareness of our ontological togetherness, of the kinship of all creation and all being. "All creatures are interdependent," he declares, and it is for this reason that we serve one another.[31] Compassion for him means justice,[32] and it is the best of the names we can assign to God. "Wisdom and justice are the same in God."[33] "Since God is justice, you must embrace justice as it is in itself, as it is in God. Consequently, where justice is at work, you are at work, because you could not but do the works of justice. Yes, even if hell would interfere with the course of justice, you would still do the works of justice, and hell itself would not constitute any pain; hell would be joy."[34]

In this exegesis of Eckhart's profoundly political talk on "The Aristocrat" we have seen how a politically conscious spirituality demands the following characteristics: A redefinition of aristocrat; a belief in the nobility and basic equality of every person regardless of class or caste distinctions of any kind; ecstasy as an experience for all; realized eschatology as a taste of the end time already begun; eschatology as personal, not institutional; interrelatedness as a way of knowing and living; and therefore compassion as the basis of human consciousness and activity, i.e. as the definition of the human person at its best (as aristocrat). We have considered in this essay Eckhart's position on capitalism (merchant mentalities kill God in us and they kill the joy of work and life); on class (there is none: we are all nobles); on democracy (all people give birth to God); on realized eschatology (heaven is now and is not to be projected into another life); on self-criticism as including a criticism of one's own institutions including religious ones; on human history as divine history. It does not take a great deal of imagination to suspect that not all of these ingredients to Eckhart's preaching would have set well with each and every member of his society. Especially is this true when one considers that Eckhart in his day was "the most popular preacher in Germany"[35] and how his renown as a theologian lent fuel and status to his preaching. Since his was not spirituality that sentimentalized the sins of society or church or their captains, it was bound to be observed closely in high places. Since his spirituality does not encourage ordinary persons to be masochistic and to be content to derive fulfillment in this life by waiting subserviently for a heaven-after-death, he was a marked man. His democratic suggestion that all are nobles and not only those born into power by blood or fortune or both, is hardly a lesson to go unnoticed by the aristocratic classes. His suggestion that the merchant mentality slays God and us must have disturbed many an influential seller since Cologne in Eckhart's period was a European trade center par excellence. Not only did [the German Emperor] Henry VII convoke an international gathering of the Lombard moneylenders there in 1309 that was attended by representatives of over seventy-seven European towns and cities, but Cologne held the key to Germany's trade with England. "Its merchants forwarded English cloth by way of the Rhine valley toward the fairs in Frankfurt, in the cities of Southern Germany, in the countries on the Danube and even to the grand fairs of Eastern Europe at Lvov and Krakow.[36]

What characterized the social problems of Eckhart's day? There was a population explosion that was especially manifest in the Rhineland area where Eckhart did the bulk of his preaching and counseling.[37] From the year 1303 until the eighteenth century a "Little Ice Age" blanketed Europe with the consequence that the growing season was shortened and food was made scarce. After torrential rains in 1315, crops failed all over Europe and famine became a reality for many. The expanding economies that characterized the twelfth and thirteenth centuries gave rise to the contracting economies of the fourteenth century, thus opening a widening division between the rich and poor. "Division of rich and poor became increasingly sharp. With control of the raw materials and tools of production, the owners were able to reduce wages in classic exploitation. The poor . . . felt a sense of injustice that finding no remedy grew into a spirit of revolt."[38] The rural poor were the first to revolt when in 1320 the Pastoureaux (the Shepherds movement) broke out in the wake of famine. They were excommunicated by Pope John XXII and were eventually suppressed. It is worth noting that this Pope, who is the same one who will play such a destiny in Eckhart's future, managed to spend 7,500 florins a year on his retinue's clothing, owned an ermine-trimmed pillow and bought as a gift for himself forty pieces of gold cloth from Damascus at the cost of 1,276 gold florins.[39]

IV. ECKHART'S POLITICAL CONDEMNATION

Meister Eckhart was subjected to an Inquisition first in Cologne and then, since that brought no substantial fruits, in Avignon where certain of his statements (or statements reportedly of his) were condemned in a Bull issued by John XXII and dated March 27, 1329. He was already dead by this time however and had defended himself stoutly at his trial. This is not the place to enter into a theological debate on fine points of Eckhart's thought since in fact, more and more scholars agree that Eckhart was not heretical and that the Inquisition would have learned this had they bothered to study his whole works including his Latin ones. Instead of theological niceties I wish to explore what might have been some other, more political and economic motives, behind Eckhart's trial and condemnation. It is not enough, for example, to demonstrate as scholars can now do how the Inquisition actually misquoted Eckhart in at least one crucial juncture and in doing so made him sound heretical when actually his very words had been employed by a Church Council centuries previously.[40] We are asking a more basic question: Why the trial? Why this energy brought together against this preacher? Why the lies and distortions in the trial? Whence such violence?

Heresy and heretical trials are invariably bound up with more than a quest for intellectual purity. As Georg Strecher has put it, the words "heresy" and "orthodoxy" are terms usually applied to "designate movements in history." The terms are "theologically loaded slogans" since traditional orthodoxy often "wields political as well as social and theological weapons."[41] What is more to the point is to put the question: What did heresy mean in Eckhart's time and place? We find a most revealing answer from the medieval scholar Jacques Heers, citing A. Borst: "Heresy is most often identified with the aspirations of the popular classes." And from another scholar: "All the movement of countryside revolts, religious and political heresies so frequent and violent in middle Germany, Thuringia and especially the Rhineland were aimed not only at the Church and its lords, but also at the bourgeois."[42] Price rises that affected all of Europe in the High Middle Ages left the nobility "extremely weak" with its "economic foundation undermined." The nobility was going through a crisis of identity and survival that included selling much of their land, often to bourgeois and marrying many bourgeois. "A strict definition of what constituted nobility" was now lacking since "the nobility in general was becoming much poorer."[43] The bourgeoisie meanwhile continued to recognize the social superiority of noble birth. It was into this milieu of town and merchant bourgeois power versus noble power that Meister Eckhart imprudently thrust his message: "Damn the merchants and everyone a nobleman." If he had done this only to academic audiences and in the clerical, Latin tongue that would have been one thing; but to preach this message in the vernacular of the peasant people was much too provocative. A heretic then is often the theologian on the losing side and in his case Eckhart was hardly on the side of the powers that were.

The least that can be said about the heresy trial of Eckhart is that the climate was hardly ripe for an objective consideration of his spiritual theology. Eckhart did not choose to teach his spirituality in a vacuum of comfort and invulnerability. He was not ensconced in an ivory tower either of academic or ecclesial protectionism. He was a preacher who preached. What were these times and what was the spirit of the times into which Eckhart threw himself in order to recreate them?

It was a period of great conflict in society and Church between ensconced and privileged institutions and movements of reform or renewal. There was a heated anti-clericalism buttressed by an anti-merchant and anti-money rhetoric that was directed against the comfortable clergy as well as certain temporal powers. The more vital of the proponents for greater justice for the poor were the Beghards and Beguines who were very active in the Cologne area where Eckhart preached and taught. Indeed, so active were they that the Archbishop of Cologne, Heinrich von Virneberg, put many of them to death by burning and drowning.[44] Eckhart himself preached in the vernacular and took the revolutionary language of the Beghards and adapted it[45] in order to reach the lower classes with the kind of messages we have considered in this article, namely, how every person is an aristocrat and how all baptized believers are "other Christs." His choice of the vernacular in preference to Latin was itself a political choice on his part. No greater proof of this is required than the prominent role this played at his trial where he was accused of corrupting the ignorant, i.e. the lower classes. Twice in the papal Bull condemning Eckhart mention is made of his "preaching per-

sistently to simple persons." Eckhart had already received this criticism
of his ministry and replied to it in the following manner:

> People will also say that such doctrine should not be spoken or written
> for the unlearned. To this I reply: if one is not to teach the unlearned,
> then no one will ever be learned and no one will be able to teach or to
> write. For one teaches the unlearned to the end that from unlearned
> persons they may become learned ones. . . . "They who are whole,"
> said our Lord, "have no need of medicine." The physician exists for
> the purpose of making the sick healthy (*Cl*, 148).

We have here a classic confrontation of those who want to control by
leaving the ignorant ignorant; and one who wants to set free by educat-
ing the ignorant. One does not trust the peasants; the other does.
Eckhart practiced the democracy he preached.

But Eckhart, poet and artist that he was, did more than just speak to
the peasants in their own tongue. He, practicing his theme of birthing,
actually created "a new vocabulary of mysticism." The German language
of the time "consisted of a mass of dialects, spoken by people who were,
for the most part, illiterate serfs."[46] Eckhart begot new words and language to correspond to the deep experience he felt was available to all.
Like St. Francis before him, the language Eckhart chose belonged to the
people he chose to reach by his language—the disenfranchised. His
choice of language reveals his ecclesiology—one that is primarily of "the
people of God," not the hierarchies of Christendom.[47]

There was an institutionalized elitism in the intellectual circles of
scholastic theology that Eckhart, like Luther who was to follow him, also
attacked. "Meister Eckhart turns against Scholasticism. His preaching is
seditious: it rises up against the project of a culture which reduces the
Indeterminate to the disposition of man, which makes it serviceable to
spiritual comfort, collective security, academic erudition, and institutions."[48] This was part of Eckhart's message in his insistence on an anti-
theism by way of a panentheism. To the extent that theologians only
reinforced the theisms and subject/object relationships of God and people and of people (the haves) and people (the have-nots)—to this extent
the anti-theism in his panentheistic God-talk was a distinct spiritual and
political threat.[49] The people no doubt understood very well Eckhart's
telling remark: "I pray God to rid me of God"[50] for they too sensed that
any God that supported the oppressive situation in which they were living was hardly worthy to be called God. He goes beyond God to the
Godhead, which is to go beyond the immediately inherited God.

Eckhart of course was not alone in efforts to renew church and society. Indeed, that was part of his problem. In the conflict that raged between German Emperor and Pope the Dominicans supported the Pope

and the Franciscans supported the Emperor. The Archbishop of Cologne was a Franciscan and an "active partisan of the imperial cause" against the papal one.[51] This would not endear the Dominican Eckhart, who favored the Pope, to him. As we saw in his reference to dogs, Eckhart was not innocent of what has been called "indiscreet references" to the Emperor-Papal struggles in his sermons. Indeed, complaints were raised at the General Chapter of the Dominican Order that was held in Venice in 1325 against unnamed German friars who were leading the simple-minded into error. The Dominican Order would itself go through the throes of corruption and reform that characterized church and society at large. Eckhart and his disciple Suso have been described as the "promoters in the German provinces"[52] of the reform movement in their century as the ill-fated Savonarola was to be the center of this movement from St. Marco in Florence in the next. In this regard it is significant that from its inception a century earlier the Dominican Order had considered its vow of poverty not so much an ascetic practice as a political one. That is to say, the vow was a socioeconomic-political one of refusing to be part of the decadent feudal economy of the time on the one hand or the rising and equally nefarious capitalism on the other.[53] Any Dominican involved in renewal of his own order would necessarily be facing the issues of capitalism head on. This the sociologist R. H. Tawney saw clearly when he declared that: "The true descendant of the doctrines of Aquinas is the labor theory of value. The last of the schoolmen was Karl Marx."[54]

There were no small numbers of peasant people who believed the world—or at least the world they knew—was coming to an end. Plagues, famines, comets, depletion of male population from ill-fated crusades, papal-imperial battles, were all seen as omens of the (or at least an) end time. "All spirituals from Suso to Catherine of Siena agree: The clergy are corrupt. What was new . . . was the spirit of revolt which fermented in the popular masses on the terrain of doctrine."[55]

Such was the cultural-religious setting for the trial of Meister Eckhart. A trial instigated by none other than the Franciscan Archbishop of Cologne whom we have seen in action three times previously. It should be remembered that the Franciscans, favoring the German Emperor, were immensely hostile to the Dominicans (and vice versa) at this time. Indeed, so deep was their split that more than one scholar feels that the real reason for the condemnation of Eckhart was that it was a Franciscan "revenge" against the recent canonization of the Dominican Thomas Aquinas.[56] Nor should this be discounted lightly since Aquinas had been under a very heavy cloud indeed since his Parisian (1277) and two Oxford (1284, 1286) condemnations. So heavy was this cloud in Germany that Dominicans there reverted to a more platonic and Augustinian spirituality in order not to be tainted with the suspect matter-oriented spirituality of Aquinas. Eckhart himself, however, tried to marry Augustine and Aquinas and it is clear from this paper alone that he certainly did not repress Aquinas' creation spirituality. Indeed, at his Defense, Eckhart compared his situation of being under suspicion to that of his recently canonized brother, Thomas Aquinas. To the Dominican Order's everlasting credit, that order never abandoned Eckhart's defense as long as he was alive.

With the condemnation much of Eckhart's holistic spirituality went underground to feed the imaginations of movements like Friends of God and the Beghards and Beguines. Some of it surfaced in his follower John Tauler in particular who in turn had a direct influence on Martin Luther. And not least among subsequent disciples, as we suggested at the beginning of this paper, was Karl Marx.

Ernst Bloch traces the Eckhartian influence on Marx in the following manner: From the revolutionary thinkers behind the Peasant Wars such as Thomas Munzer and Huss to the revolutionary Anabaptists to the mystic poet Angelus Silesius to the young Hegel to the atheist Feuerbach to Karl Marx. He sees in particular a great likeness between Angelus Silesius (who has been described as a "seventeenth century . . . Eckhart"[57]) and Ludwig Feuerbach whose position on religion Karl Marx borrowed almost in its entirety. James Clark, who is very cautious in this regard, concedes that it is "very plausible" that "some of the Beghards charged with heresy at Cologne" had quoted Eckhart in their own defense and that this "would explain Heinrich von Firneburg's attitudes toward Eckhart."[58] Thomas Merton has written his opinion of Eckhart's trial:

> He was a great man who was pulled down by a lot of little men who thought they could destroy him: who thought they could drag him to Avignon and have him utterly discredited. And indeed he was ruined, after his death in 28 propositions which might doubtless be found somewhere in him, but which had none of his joy, his energy, his freedom. . . . Eckhart did not have the kind of mind that wasted time being cautious about every comma: he trusted men to recognize that what he saw was worth seeing because it brought obvious fruits of life and joy. For him, that was what mattered.[59]

It may well be that the greatest victim of his condemnation was not Eckhart but the mainstream of Christian spirituality. I do wonder whether Eckhart's condemnation did not make Luther's institutional rebellion inevitable. And, what is more evident, the spiritualities that were to follow Eckhart, in particular the *devotio moderna*, Imitation of Christ, and flagellants would be notable mostly for their sentimentalism, which includes anti-intellectualism, masochism, lack of political-social consciousness and withdrawal from the vocation to change the world. "An entire work of interiorization is pursued at the end of the Middle Ages. The pilgrimage replaces the crusade, and the stations of the cross will soon replace the pilgrimage."[60] Henceforth privatization and spirituality would, with few exceptions, become almost synonymous terms in the West. Is Eckhart a "mystic of the left"? According to William Eckhardt in his study on *Compassion: Toward a Science of Value,* left-wing freedom as distinct from right-wing freedom means freedom for the many instead of freedom for the few.[61] Given this criterion, Eckhart is clearly a "mystic of the left."

Like his sister, Joan of Arc, Eckhart paid a prophetic price for his trust of his own experience. His mysticism became prophecy for others and a cross for him. Joan of Arc spent five hundred years in the ecclesial darkness until she emerged as a canonized saint only in our century. I hardly think that Eckhart wants or needs such honors. After six centuries of being under a shadow, however, it might now be time to open our eyes to listen to the Gospel that this man who paid the price of a prophet was preaching. Ironically, Marx may assist believers to open their eyes as Eckhart assisted Marx to open his. Spiritual-political theology akin to Meister Eckhart's is still claiming its victims in our own time. But at least they receive the support of those who went before. As Theodor Adorno has put it, "all those outside the sphere of management are pathfinders, trailblazers, and—above all—tragic figures."[62]

NOTES

1. Thomas Merton, "Marxism and Monastic Perspectives," in *A New Charter for Monasticism,* ed. John Moffitt (Notre Dame: 1970), pp. 69, 76.
2. No one has demonstrated this more convincingly than Anne Douglas in her brilliant study on sentimentalism. See Anne Douglas, *The Feminization of American Culture* (New York: 1977). For spirituality and sentimentalism, see my "On Desentimentalizing Spirituality," *Spirituality Today* (Winter 1977), pp. 64–76.
3. Christopher Hill, "Top People," *New York Review of Books,* December 8, 1977, p. 42.
4. Ernst Bloch, *Atheism in Christianity* (New York: Herder & Herder, 1972), pp. 63ff. See also: Alois M. Hass, "Maitre Eckhart dans le miroir de l'ideologie marxiste," *La Vie Spirituelle,* January 1971, pp. 62–79; H. Ley, *Studie zur Geschichte des Materialismus im Mittelalter* (Berlin: 1957).
5. Reiner Schurmann, *Maitre Eckhart ou La Joie Errante* (Paris: 1972), p. 11. Hereafter I will use the English translation of this excellent study on Eckhart, *Meister Eckhart: Mystic and Philosopher* (Indiana University Press, 1978).

6. See Matthew Fox, "Meister Eckhart on the Four-Fold Journey in Creation Spirituality," in *Western Spirituality: Historical Roots, Ecumenical Routes,* ed. Matthew Fox (Notre Dame: Fides/Claretian, 1979).

7. Bloch [n. 4], p. 65.

8. Raymond Blakney, *Meister Eckhart: A Modern Translation* (New York: 1941), pp. 244, 14. Subsequent references to this translation will be abbreviated *Bl* and will be inserted in the text. Other translations employed in this article include James M. Clark, *Meister Eckhart* (New York: 1957) abbreviated *Cl;* and James M. Clark and John V. Skinner, *Meister Eckhart* (London: 1953), abbreviated *Cl-Sk.* In this particular instance as in no. 3 (p. 543), Blakney's translation is more accurate than Clark's.

9. *LW,* V, 11. This and subsequent references to the Latin Works are from Meister Eckhart, *Die lateinischen Werke,* eds. J. Koch, et al., Kohlhammer edition, 5 vols. Stuggart: 1938*ff*.

10. *Q,* 77. ("*Q*" stands for Josef Quint, *Meister Eckhart: Deutsche Predigten und Traktate* (Munchen: 1977). Citations abbreviated *DW* are from Meister Eckhart, *Die Deutschen Werke,* ed. Josef Quint, Vols. I, II, III, V (Stuttgart: 1958–76).

11. C. F. Kelly, *Meister Eckhart on Divine Knowledge* (Yale University Press, 1977), p. 58.

12. Schurmann [n. 5], pp. 13, 23, 28, 30, 47, 92, 233.

13. Ibid., p. 38.

14. "Intravit Jesus in Templum Dei et Ejiciebat Omnes," in *Q,* pp. 153–58 and in *Cl,* pp. 127–32.

15. Cf. Schurmann, p. 113. The "without why" attitude lies at the center of Eckhart's spiritual theology—it is a mystery instead of a problem-solving attitude. It follows then that an anti-merchant mentality also lies at the core of Eckhart's spirituality.

16. *DW,* I, 105.

17. Schurmann, p. 110.

18. Eckhart's *"Defense,"* edited by Thery, *RS,* II, art. 31. Cited, ibid., p. 245.

19. Ibid., pp. 201*f*.

20. *DW,* II, 708.

21. How similar this theory of pride and work as an end in itself comes to the Buddhist philosophy of work may be seen in E. F. Schumacher, *Small Is Beautiful* (New York: 1973), pp. 53–63.

22. *LW,* IV, 195.

23. Jacques Heers, *L'Occident aux XIVe et XVe siecles: aspects economiques et sociaux* (Paris: 1970), p. 237.

24. *Q,* pp. 140–50 and in *Cl-Sk,* pp. 149–59.

25. Heers [n. 23], p. 235.

26. *Cl-Sk,* p. 159. Eckhart does a play on the German words *Adler* (eagle) and *edler* (more noble).

27. For Aquinas' concept of ecstasy, see especially *De divinis nominibus,* c. 4, nn. 427–39; *Summa theologica,* I–II, q. 28, a. 3; II–II, q. 175, a. 2 ad 1. I have developed this creation-centered and typically Dominican, ecstasy-oriented spirituality in Matthew Fox, *Whee!, We, wee All the Way Home: A Guide to the New Sensual Spirituality* (Gaithersburg, Md., 1976). Eckhart notes that "this birth does not take place once in the year or once in a month or once a day but all the time" (*DW,* II, 677).

28. Bloch, p. 65.

29. Cf. Merton [n. 1], p. 80. "The whole idea of compassion . . . is based on a keen awareness of the interdependence of all these living beings."

30. Bloch, p. 64.

31. *DW*, II, 746. Eckhart is one of the few Christian spiritual writers to truly develop a spirituality of compassion. See Matthew Fox, *A Spirituality Named Compassion* (Minneapolis: Winston, 1979).

32. *LW*, IV, 126.

33. *DW*, II, 601.

34. *DW*, II, 708.

35. James M. Clark, *The Great German Mystics* (New York: Russell and Russell, 1949), p. 9.

36. B. Kuske, *Quellen zur Geschichte*. Cited in Heers, p. 199.

37. Philippe Dollinger, "Strasbourg et Colmar Foyers de la mystique Rhénane," in *La mystique Rhenane: colloque de Strasbourg* (Paris, 1963), p. 4.

38. Barbara W. Tuchman, *A Distant Mirror: The Calamitous Fourteenth Century* (New York: Knopf, 1978), pp. 24, 38.

39. Iris Origo, *The Merchant of Prato, 1335-1410* (New York: 1957), p. 8; see Tuchman [n. 38], p. 28.

40. I am referring of course to the critical question of Eckhart's being a pantheist. The sentence condemned is "Everything that is is God"—but Eckhart did not say that. He said "Everything that is in God is God." This proposition was used as a solemn declaration by the Synod of Rheims in 1148 and is also found in Alan of Insulis, *Regulae Theologicae* IX, Patrologia latina, ed. J. Mighe, CCX 628. Thomas Aquinas, canonized three years before Eckhart's trial, also said: "That which is in God is God" (*Compendium theologiae, 37, 41*).

41. Walter Bauer, *Orthodoxy and Heresy in Earliest Christianity* (Philadelphia, 1971), pp. 313f, 312.

42. A. Borst, *Die Katherer* (Stuttgart: 1953). Referred to in Heers, p. 360.

43. David M. Nicholas, "Town and Countryside: Social and Economic Tensions in Fourteenth-Century Flanders," *Comparative Studies in Society and History* (1968), pp. 458f, 471f.

44. M. de Gandillac, *Maitre Eckhart* (Paris: 1942), pp. 10ff.

45. Ibid., pp. 23ff. Most of the Beguines were unmarried women asserting their own rights in a society that did not want them. See Norman Cohn, *The Pursuit of the Millennium* (New York: 1970), pp. 148–62. Dollinger establishes that Eckhart preached in their homes and corresponded with them (n. 37, p. 8).

46. Clark [n. 35], pp. 22f.

47. Cf. Andre Vauchez, "La spiritualité populaire au Moyen Age d'apres l'oeuvre d'E. Delaruelle," *Revue d'histoire et de la spiritualité* 51 (1975) 285.

48. Schurmann, p. 209; see J. A. Bizet, *Mystiques Allemands du XIVe siécle* (Paris: 1957), p. 14.

49. John D. Caputo says that "Eckhart proposes a kind of mystical atheism. . . ." (John D. Caputo, "Fundamental Themes in Eckhart's Mysticism," *The Thomist* [April 1978], p. 211.) For more on the relationship of atheism to politics, see Manuel-Reyes Matte, "Atheism as a Political Problem," *Listening* (Spring/Autumn 1970), pp. 97–110.

50. *Q*, p. 308.

51. *Cl*, p. 21.

52. Bizet [n. 48], pp. 12ff.

53. Cf. M. D. Chenu, *Nature, Man and Society in the Twelfth Century* (Chicago, 1968): "Poverty . . . represented both a rejection of the avarice and

vanity of the new world and a liberation from the temporal security of the old regime. . . . It involved more than moral purification . . . [it involved] rejecting out of hand an entire economic system" (pp. 235, 256).

54. R. H. Tawney, *Religion and the Rise of Capitalism* (Middlesex, England: 1969), p. 48.

55. Bizet, pp. 12*f*.

56. Cited by Gandillac [n. 44], p. 19. Clark characterizes the Franciscan-Dominican relationship at this time as one of "unconcealed hostility" (p. 15).

57. O. Karrer, *Meister Eckhart* (Munich: Muller, 1926), p. 55. Cited in Thomas F. O'Meara, "Meister Eckhart's Destiny," *Spirituality Today* (December 1978), p. 349.

58. Cited by Gandillac, p. 17. He also points out that as Provincial Minister of Saxony in Bohemia Eckhart was much immersed in the milieu of the Brethren of the Free Spirit who were so dominant a force in Bohemia at that time.

59. Thomas Merton, *Conjectures of a Guilty Bystander* (Garden City, N.Y.: Doubleday, 1968), pp. 53*f*.

60. E. Delaruelle, cited in Vauchez [n. 47], p. 287. So thoroughly has the dualism of politics and spirituality taken over that even today commentators on Eckhart miss his political-economic consciousness. C. F. Kelly would be an example. Kelly, a former monk, apparently wants to make Eckhart into a monk whereas in fact he was a very active and politically embroiled Dominican friar.

61. William Eckhardt, *Compassion: Toward a Science of Value* (Oakville, Ontario: CPRI Press, 1972), pp. 66*f*, 257*f*.

62. Theodor W. Adorno, *Philosophy of Modern Music* (New York: 1973), p. 30.

Bibliography

Alexander, F. "Buddhistic Training as an Artificial Catatonia," *Psychoanalytical Review* 18 (1931) 129–45.

Alpert, R. *Be Now Here*. San Cristobal: 1971.

Anesaki, M. *History of Japanese Religion with Special Reference to the Social and Moral Life of the Nation*. Rutland and Tokyo: 1963.

Arberry, A. J. *Sūfism: An Account of the Mystics of Islam*. London: George Allen and Unwin, 1950.

Arieti, S. *The Intrapsychic Self*. New York: Basic Books, 1967.

Barnes, Mary, and Berke, Joseph. *Two Accounts of a Journey through Madness*. Harmondsworth, England: Penguin Books, 1973.

Bateson, G., ed. *Perceval's Narrative: A Patient's Account of His Psychosis*. Stanford University Press, 1961.

Bentov, Itzhak. *Stalking the Wild Pendulum: On the Mechanics of Consciousness*. New York: Dutton, 1977.

Beringer, K. *Der Meskalinrausch*. Berlin: Springer Verlag, 1927.

Bettelheim, Bruno. *Symbolic Wounds: Puberty Rites and the Envious Male*. Glencoe, Ill.: The Free Press, 1954.

Bhaktivedanta, A. C. "The Highest Love," *Back to Godhead* 35 (1970) 4–8.

Blofeld, J. *The Tantric Mysticism of Tibet*. New York: Dutton, 1970.

Boetzelaer, J. M. van. *Sureśvara's Taittirīyopanesadbhāsyavārtikam*. Leiden: 1971.

Bohr, Niels. *Essays, 1958–1962, on Atomic Physics and Human Knowledge*. New York: John Wiley, 1963.

Braden, William. *The Age of Aquarius: Technology and the Cultural Revolution*. Chicago: Quadrangle Books, 1970. Paper: New York: Pocket Books, 1971.

———. *The Private Sea: LSD and the Search for God*. Chicago: Quadrangle Books, 1967.

Bridges, Hal. *American Mysticism from William James to Zen*. New York: Harper and Row, 1970.

Brough, J. "Soma and Amanita Muscaria," *Bulletin of the School of Oriental and African Studies* 34 (1971) 331–62.

Buber, M. *Between Man and Man*. New York: Macmillan, 1965.

———. *I and Thou*. New York: Charles Scribner's Sons, 1958.

Bucke, R. M. *Cosmic Consciousness: A Study of the Evolution of the*

Human Mind. Philadelphia: Innis and Son, 1901; Hyde Park, N.Y.: University Books, 1961.

Buitenen, J. A. B. van. *Rāmānuja on the Bhagavadgītā.* Delhi: 1968.

Burrow, T. *Preconscious Foundations of Human Experience.* New York: Basic Books, 1964.

Campbell, J. *The Hero with a Thousand Faces.* New York: Meridian Books, 1956.

Capra, Fritjof. *The Tao of Physics: An Exploration of the Parallels between Modern Physics and Eastern Mysticism.* Boulder: Shambala, 1975.

Carey, J. T. "Marijuana Use among the New Bohemians," *Journal of Psychedelic Drugs* 2 (1968) 79–92.

Castaneda, Carlos. *Journey to Ixtlan.* New York: Simon and Schuster, 1973.

———. *A Separate Reality: Further Conversations with Don Juan.* New York: Simon and Schuster, 1971.

———. *Tales of Power.* New York: Simon and Schuster, 1974.

———. *The Teachings of Don Juan: a Yaqui Way of Knowledge.* University of California Press, 1968.

Cazeneuve, J. "Le peyotisme au Nouveau-Mexique: notes sur une nouvelle religion," *Revue philosophique* 149 (1959) 169–82.

Claridge, G. *Drugs and Human Behaviour.* Penguin Books, 1972.

Clark, J., and Skinner, J., eds. *Treatises and Sermons of Meister Eckhart.* New York: Harper, 1958.

Clark, R. W. *The Huxleys.* London: Heinemann, 1968.

Clark, Walter Houston. *Chemical Ecstasy: Psychedelic Drugs and Religion.* New York: Sheed and Ward, 1969.

———. "Mysticism as a basic concept in defining the religious self," in *From Religious Experience to a Religious Attitude,* A. Godin, ed. Chicago: Loyola University Press, 1965, pp. 31–42.

———. "The Phenomena of religious experience," in *Religious Experience: Its Nature and Function in the Human Psyche,* W. II. Clark, H. N. Malony, J. Daane, and A. R. Tippett, eds. Springfield, Ill.: C. C. Thomas, 1973, pp. 21–40.

———. "The Relationship between Drugs and Religious Experience," *Catholic Psychological Record* 6 (1968) 146–55.

———. "Religious Experiences in Contemporary Perspective," in *Religious Experience: Its Nature and Function in the Human Psyche,* W. H. Clark, H. N. Malony, J. Daane, and A. R. Tippett, eds. Springfield, Ill.: C. C. Thomas, 1973, pp. 3–20.

Coate, M. *Beyond All Reason.* London: Constable, 1964.

Cohn, Norman. *The Pursuit of the Millennium: Revolutionary Mille-

narians and Mystical Anarchists of the Middle Ages. New York: Oxford University Press, rev. ed., 1970.

Cornford, F. M. *Greek Religious Thought from Homer to the Age of Alexander.* London and Toronto: 1923.

Coward, Harold, and Penelhum, Terence. *Mystics and Scholars: The Calgary Conference on Mysticism, 1976.* Waterloo, Ontario: Wilfrid Laurier University Press, SR Supplements/3, 1977.

Cowley, Malcolm. *Exile's Return: A Literary Odyssey of the 1920's.* New York: Viking Press, 1934.

Cox, Harvey. *Turning East: The Promise and Peril of the New Orientalism.* New York: Simon and Schuster, 1977.

Crockett, R., et al. *Hallucinogenic Drugs and Their Psychotherapeutic Use.* London: J. Q. Lewis, 1963.

Curle, Adam. *Mystics and Militants: A Study of Awareness, Identity and Social Action.* New York: Barnes & Noble, 1972.

Custance, J. *Wisdom, Madness and Folly: The Philosophy of a Lunatic.* London: Gollancz, 1951.

Danto, Arthur C. *Mysticism and Morality.* New York: Basic Books, Inc., 1972; Harmondsworth, England: Penguin Books, 1976.

Dasgupta, S. C. *A History of Indian Philosophy,* 2 vols. Cambridge: The University Press, 1922–32.

De Félice, Philippe. *Poisons Sacrés, Ivresses Divines: essai sur quelques formes inférieures de la mystique.* Paris: Editions Albin, 1936.

Deikman, Arthur J. "Bimodal consciousness." *Archives of General Psychiatry* 45 (1971) 483ff.

———. "Experimental meditation," *J. Nerv. Ment. Dis.* 136 (1963) 329–43.

———. "Implication of experimentally induced contemplative meditation," *J. Nerv. Ment. Dis.* 142 (1966) 101–16.

Delacroix, H. *Études d'histoire et de psychologie du mysticisme.* Paris: 1908.

DeRopp, Robert S. *Drugs and the Mind.* New York: St. Martin's Press, 1957.

———. *The Master Game.* New York: Dell, 1968.

Dodds, E. R. *Pagan and Christian in an Age of Anxiety: Some Aspects of Religious Experience from Marcus Aurelius to Constantine.* Cambridge: The University Press, 1968.

Ehrenzweig, A. "The Undifferentiated Matrix of Artistic Imagination," in *The Psychoanalytic Study of Society,* W. Neusterberger and S. Axelrad, eds. New York: International Universities Press, 1964, pp. 373–98.

Federn, P. *Ego Psychology and the Psychoses.* New York: Basic Books, 1952.

Ferguson, John. *Encyclopedia of Mysticism and the Mystery Religions.* New York: Seabury Press, 1977.

Findlay, J. N. *Ascent to the Absolute.* London: Allen & Unwin, 1970.

Fingarette, H. *The Self in Transformation: Psychoanalysis Philosophy and the Life of the Spirit.* New York: Basic Books, 1963.

Fischer, Roland. "Pharmacology and Metabolism of Mescaline," *Revue Canadienne de Biologie* 17 (1958) 389–409.

Freud, Sigmund. *Civilization and Its Discontents.* New York: Norton, 1961.

———. *The Future of an Illusion.* Garden City, N.Y.: Doubleday Anchor Books, 1964.

———. *The Interpretation of Dreams,* vol. I, tr. J. Strachey. London: 1953.

———. *Standard Edition of the Complete Psychological Works.* London: Hogarth, 1961.

Furse, Margaret Lewis. *Mysticism: Window on a World View.* Nashville: Abingdon, 1977.

Gill, M., and Brenman, M. *Hypnosis and Related States: Psychoanalytic Studies in Regression.* New York: International Universities Press, 1959.

Goddard, Dwight. *A Buddhist Bible.* Thetford, Vt.: Dwight Goddard, 2d ed., 1938.

Gould, R. E. "The Marginally Asocial Personality: The Beatnik-Hippie Alienation," in *World Biennial of Psychiatry and Psychotherapy,* Silvano Arieti, ed., vol. I, pp. 258–90.

Govinda, Lama Anagarika. *Foundations of Tibetan Mysticism.* New York: Samuel Weiser, 1969.

Graham, Dom Aelred. *Zen Catholicism.* New York: Harcourt, Brace & World, 1963.

Greeley, A. M. *Ecstasy.* New York: Prentice-Hall, 1974.

Greenland, C. "Richard Maurice Bucke, M.D., 1837–1902: Psychiatrist, Author, Mystic," in *Personality Change and Religious Experience,* R. Prince, ed. Montreal: R. M. Bucke Memorial Society, 1965.

Hacker, P. *Untersuchungen über Texte des fruhen Advaitavada,* I: *Die Schüler Sankaras.* Wiesbaden: 1950.

Haley, J. "An Interactional Description of Schizophrenia," *Psychiatry* 22 (1959) 321–32.

Hammarskjöld, Dag. *Markings,* Leif Sjöberg and W. H. Auden, trans., foreword by W. H. Auden. New York: Knopf, 1967.

Happold, F. C. *Mysticism: A Study and an Anthology.* Baltimore: Penguin Books, rev. ed., 1970.

Hara, M. "Tapo-dhana," *Acta Asiatica* 19 (1970) 58–76.

Hara, M. "Transfer of Merit," *Adyar Library Bulletin* 31-2 (1968–69) 382–411.

Harkness, Georgia. *Mysticism, Its Meaning and Message.* Nashville: Abingdon Press, 1973.

Hartmann, H. *Ego Psychology and the Problem of Adaptation.* New York: International Universities Press, 1958.

Henderson, L. *The Fitness of the Environment: an Inquiry into the Biological Significance of the Properties of Matter.* Boston: Beacon Press, 1958.

Hilton, Walter. *The Scale of Perfection.* London: Burns and Oates, 1953.

Hiriyanna, M., ed. *The Naiskarmya-Siddhi of Surésvarācārya.* Poona: 1925.

Hocking, William Ernest. *The Meaning of Immortality in Human Experience.* Westport, Conn.: Greenwood Press, 1973.

Holmstedt, B. "Historical Survey," in *Ethnopharmacological Search for Psychoactive Drugs,* D. H. Efrin, ed. Washington: U. S. Public Health Service Publication No. 1645, 1967.

Hood, R. W., Jr. "The Construction and Preliminary Validation of a Measure of Reported Mystical Experience," *Journal for the Scientific Study of Religion* 14 (1975) 29–41.

——. "Psychology Strength and the Report of Intense Religious Experience," *Journal for the Scientific Study of Religion* 13 (1974) 65–71.

——. "Religious Orientation and the Experience of Transcendence," *Journal for the Scientific Study of Religion* 12 (1973) 441–48.

——. "Religious Orientation and the Report of Religious Experience," *Journal for the Scientific Study of Religion* 9 (1970) 285–91.

Huxley, Aldous. *The Doors of Perception* and *Heaven and Hell.* New York: Penguin Books, 1963.

——. *The Perennial Philosophy.* London: 1946.

Isherwood, Christopher. *Ramakrishna and His Disciples.* New York: Simon and Schuster, 1965.

de Jaegher, Paul, ed. *An Anthology of Christian Mysticism.* Springfield, Ill.: Templegate Publishers, 1977; London: Burns and Oates, 1977.

James, William. "The Subjective Effects of Nitrous Oxide," *Mind* 7 (1882) 186–208.

——. *The Varieties of Religious Experience* (1902). Introduction by Jacques Barzun. New York: New American Library, 1958.

Jarvis, J. Quoted in *Stanford Daily,* January 8, 1967, p. 1.

John of the Cross, St. *The Complete Works of St. John of the Cross,* E. Allison Peers, trans. Westminster, Md.: The Newman Press, 1953.

Johnson, R. C. *The Imprisoned Splendor.* Madras, India: Theosophical Publishing House, 1971.

Johnston, William, S.J. *The Inner Eye of Love: Mysticism and Religion.* New York: Harper and Row, 1978.
——. *The Mysticism of the Cloud of Unknowing.* New York: Desclee, 1967. Paper: St. Meinrad, Ind.: Abbey Press, 1976.
——. *Silent Music: The Science of Meditation.* New York: Harper and Row, 1974.
——. *The Still Point.* New York: Harper and Row, 1970.
Jones, Rufus, *The Flowering of Mysticism: The Friends of God in the Fourteenth Century.* New York: Hafner, 1971.
——. *New Studies in Mystical Religion.* New York: Macmillan, 1927.
——. *Studies in Mystical Religion* (1909). New York: Russell & Russell, 1970.
Jung, C. G. *Memories, Dreams, Reflections.* New York: Pantheon, 1961.
——. "The Transcendent Function," in *The Portable Jung,* S. Campbell, ed. New York: Viking Press, 1971.
Kamiya, Joe. "Operant Control of the EEG Alpha Rhythm and Some of Its Reported Effects on Consciousness," in Tart (1972), pp. 519–29.
Kaplan, B., ed. *The Inner World of Mental Illness.* New York: Harper, 1964.
Kasamatsu, A., and Hirai, T. "Science of Zazen," *Psychologia* 6 (1963) 86–91.
Katz, Stephen, ed. *Mysticism and Philosophical Analysis.* New York: Oxford University Press, 1978.
Kee, Alistair. *The Way of Transcendence: Christian Faith Without Belief in God.* Baltimore: Penguin Books, 1971.
Keen, E. *Psychology and the New Consciousness.* Monterey: Brooks and Cole, 1972.
Kluver, H. *Mescal: The Divine Plant and Its Psychological Effects.* London: Kegan Paul, 1928.
Knowles, Dom David. *The English Mystical Tradition.* London: Burns and Oates, 1961. New York: Harper, 1961.
Knox, Ronald. *Enthusiasm: A Chapter in the History of Religion.* New York: Oxford University Press, 1951, 1961.
Kris, E. *Psychoanalytic Explorations in Art.* New York: International Universities Press, 1952.
Kuppuswami Sastri, S., ed. *Brahmasiddhi* by Ācārya Mandanamisra, Madras: 1937.
LaBarre, W. *The Peyote Cult.* New York: 1970.
Laing, R. D. *The Divided Self.* Baltimore: Penguin Books, 1965.
——. *The Politics of Experience.* New York: Pantheon, 1967.
Lamotte, E. *Le traité de la grande vertu de sagesse de Nāgārjuna,* 3 vols. Louvain: 1944–70.

Laski, Marghanita. *Ecstasy: A Study of Some Secular and Religious Experiences*. London: Cresset Press, 1961.

Leary, Timothy. *The Politics of Ecstasy*. London: Paladin, 1970.

———. "The Religious Experience: Its Production and Interpretation," *Psychedelic Revue* 1 (1964) 324–46.

LeShan, Lawrence. "Physicists and mystics: similarities in world views." *Journal of Transpersonal Psychology* 1, 2 (1969) 1–20.

———. *The Medium, the Mystic and the Medium: Toward a General Theory of the Paranormal*. New York: Viking Press, 1975.

———. *Toward a General Theory of the Paranormal*, introduced by Henry Margenau. New York: Parapsychology Foundation, Inc., Parapsychological Monographs no. 9, 1969.

Leuba, J. H. *The Psychology of Religious Mysticism*. New York: Harcourt, Brace, 1925.

Lewin, B. *The Psychoanalysis of Elation*. New York: Norton, 1950.

Lewin, L. *Phantastica*. Berlin: G. Stilke, 1924.

Ludwig, Arnold, "Altered States of Consciousness," in *Trance and Possession States*, R. Prince, ed. Montreal: The R. M. Bucke Memorial Society, 1968, and in Tart (1972), pp. 11–24.

Mahadevon, T. M. P. *The Sambandha-Vārtika of Sureśvarācārya*, Madras: 1958.

Maharishi Mahesh Yogi. *The Science of Being and the Art of Living*. London: International SRM Publications, rev. ed., 1966.

Maritain, Jacques. *The Degrees of Knowledge*, Gerald B. Phelan, trans. New York: Scribner, 1959.

Marty, Martin. "The Persistence of the Mystical," in *The Persistence of Religion*, Andrew Greeley and Gregory Baum, eds. New York: Herder and Herder, Concilium, vol. 81, 1973, pp. 36–45.

Maslow, A. H. *Religion, Values, and Peak Experiences*. Ohio State University Press, 1964.

Massignon, Louis. *Essai sur les origines du lexique technique de la mystique musulmane*. Paris: 1954.

Masters, R. E. L. and Houston, Jean. *The Varieties of Psychedelic Experience*. New York: Dell, 1966.

Maven, A. "The Mystic Union: a Suggested Biological Interpretation," in White (1972), pp. 429–35.

McReynolds, P. "Anxiety, Perception, and Schizophrenia," in *The Etiology of Schizophrenia*. D. Jackson, ed., New York: Basic Books, 1960, p. 269.

Menninger, Karl. *Man Against Himself*. New York: Harcourt, Brace & World, 1938.

Merton, Thomas. *Contemplative Prayer*. Garden City, N.Y.: Doubleday Image Books, 1971.

——. *Mystics and Zen Masters*. New York: Dell, 1967.

Messer, M. "Running Out of Era: Some Non-pharmacological Notes on the Psychedelic Revolution," *Journal of Psychedelic Drugs* 2 (1968) 157–66.

Michaux, H. *Light through Darkness*. New York: Orion Press, 1963.

Mishra, R. S. *Directory of Light Centers*. North Syracuse, N.Y.: ICSA Press, 1970.

Moller, H. "Affective Mysticism in Western Civilization," *Psychoanal. Rev.* 52 (1965) 115–30.

De Montmorand, *Psychologie des mystiques catholiques orthodoxes*. Paris: 1920.

Moraczewski, Albert, O.P. "Psychedelic Agents and Mysticism," *Psychosomatics* 12 (1971) 94–100.

Murphy, G., and Murphy, L. B., eds. *Asian Psychology*. New York: Basic Books, 1968.

Murphy, H. B. M. "Cultural Factors in the Genesis of Schizophrenia," in *The Transmission of Schizophrenia*, D. Rosenthal and S. Ketz, eds. Oxford: Pergamon Press, 1968.

Nakamura, H. *A History of the Development of Japanese Thought*, 2 vols. Tokyo: 1967.

——. *Ways of Thinking of Eastern Peoples*. Honolulu: 1964.

Needleman, Jacob. *The New Religions*. Garden City, N.Y.: Doubleday, 1970, rev. ed., 1972. Paper: New York: Pocket Books, 1972.

——. Bierman, A. K., and Gould, James A. *Religion for a New Generation*. New York: Macmillan, rev. ed., 1977.

Neumann, Erick. "Mystical Man," in *The Mystic Vision*, Ralph Mannheim, trans. Princeton University Press, 1968, pp. 375–415.

Niwa, Fumio. *The Buddha Tree*. Rutland and Tokyo: 1966.

Nowell, Robert. *What a Modern Catholic Believes about Mysticism*. Chicago: The Thomas More Press, 1975.

O'Brien, Elmer, S.J., ed. *The Varieties of Mystic Experience*. New York: Holt, Rinehart & Winston, 1964. Paper: New York: New American Library, 1965.

Ornstein, Robert. *The Mind Field: A Personal Essay*. New York: Grossman, 1976.

—— ed. *The Nature of Human Consciousness*. San Francisco: Freeman, 1973.

Otto, Rudolf. *Indiens Gnadenreligion und das Christentum*. Gotha: 1930.

——. *Mysticism East and West*, Bertha L. Bracey and Richenda C. Payne, trans. New York: Macmillan, 1932, 1970.

Ouspensky, P. D. *The Psychology of Man's Possible Evolution*. New York: Random House, 1974.

Owens, C. M. "The Mystical Experience: Facts and Values," in White (1972), pp. 135–52.

Pahnke, Walter N. "Drugs and Mysticism: An Analysis of the Relationship between Psychedelic Drugs and Mystical Consciousness." PhD. Dissertation, Harvard University, 1963.

—— and Richards, W. A. "Implications of LSD and experimental mysticism," *Journal of Religion and Health* 5 (1966) 175–218.

Panikkar, Raimundo, S.J. *The Unknown Christ of Hinduism*. London: Darton, Longman & Todd, 1964.

Piaget, J. *The Construction of Reality in the Child*. New York: Basic Books, 1954.

Poulain, Auguste, S.J. *The Graces of Interior Prayer: A Treatise on Mystical Theology*. St. Louis: B. Herder, 1950.

Prince, Raymond, ed. *Trance and Possession States*. Montreal: R. M. Bucke Memorial Society, 1968.

—— and Savage, C. "Mystical States and the Concept of Regression." Paper delivered at the First Annual Meeting, R. M. Bucke Society, Montreal, January 1965, in White (1972), pp. 114–34.

Puhl, L., trans. *The Spiritual Exercises of St. Ignatius*. Westminster, Md.: Newman Press, 1962.

Rahula, Walpola. *What the Buddha Taught*. New York: Grove Press, rev. ed., 1974.

Rapaport, D. "The Autonomy of the Ego," *Bulletin Menninger Clinic* 15 (1951) 113–23.

—— and Gill, M. "The Points of View and Assumptions of Metapsychology," *Int. J. Psychoanal.* 40 (1959) 153.

Reinhold, H. A., ed. *The Soul Afire: Revelations of the Mystics*. Garden City, N.Y.: Doubleday Image Books, 1973.

Roszak, Theodore. *The Making of a Counter Culture*. Garden City, N.Y.: Doubleday, 1969.

Rusk, R. L. *The Life of Ralph Waldo Emerson*. New York: Scribner, 1949.

Russell, Bertrand. *Mysticism and Logic*. London: George Allen & Unwin, 1917, 1963.

Ryle, G. *The Concept of Mind*. London: 1949.

Schachtel, E. G. *Metamorphosis*. New York: Basic Books, 1959.

Schachter, Zalman. "The Humanistic Transcendentalist Practice of the Kabbalah," in Coward and Penelhum (1977), pp. 31–38.

Scharfstein, Ben-Ami. *Mystical Experience*. Indianapolis: Bobbs-Merrill, 1973; Oxford: Basil Blackwell, 1973.

Schimmel, Annemarie. *Mystical Dimensions of Islam*. University of North Carolina Press, 1975.

Scholem, Gershom. *On the Kabbalah and Its Symbolism.* New York: Schocken, 1965, 1969.

Schultz, D. *Sensory Restriction: Effects on Behavior.* New York: Academic Press, 1965.

Shah, I. *The Sufis.* Garden City, N.Y.: Doubleday, 1964.

Shapiro, D. "A Perceptual Understanding of Color Response," in *Rorschach Psychology,* M. Richersman, ed. New York: Wiley 1960, pp. 154–201.

Sherwood, J., et al. "The Psychedelic Experience: a new concept in psychotherapy," *J. Neuropsychiat.* 4 (1962) 69–80.

Silberer, H. "Report on a Method of Eliciting and Observing Certain Symbolic and Hallucination Phenomena," in *Organization and Pathology of Thought,* D. Rapaport, ed. Columbia University Press, 1951, pp. 195–207.

Smart, Ninian. *Doctrine and Argument in Indian Philosophy.* London: George Allen & Unwin, 1964.

Smith, H. "Do Drugs Have Religious Import?" *The Journal of Philosophy* 61 (1964) 517–30.

Smith, John. "Is the Self an Ultimate Metaphysical Category?" in *Philosophy, Religion and the Coming World Civilization,* Essays in honor of W. E. Hocking; Leroy Rouner, ed. The Hague: Martinus Nijhoff, 1966.

Smith, Margaret. *The Way of the Mystics: The Early Christian Mystics and the Rise of the Sufis.* London: Sheldon Press, 1931, 1976.

Smythies, J. R. "The Mescaline Phenomena," *The British Journal for the Philosophy of Science* 3 (1953) 339–47.

Snyder, Gary. *Riprap and Cold Mountain Poems.* San Francisco: Four Seasons Foundation, 1969.

Solomon, P., et al. *Sensory Deprivation.* Harvard University Press, 1961.

Staal, J. F. *Advaita and Neo-Platonism: A Critical Study in Comparative Philosophy.* Madras: 1961.

———. *Nambudiri Veda Recitation.* The Hague: 1961.

———. "Negation and the Law of Contradiction in Indian Thought," *Bulletin of the School of Oriental and African Studies* 25 (1962) 52–71.

Stace, Walter T. *Mysticism and Philosophy.* Philadelphia: Lippincott, 1960; London: Macmillan, 1960, 1973.

———. *The Teachings of the Mystics.* New York: New American Library, 1960.

Starbuck, E. D. *The Psychology of Religion.* New York: Scribner, 1899.

Suraci, A. "Environmental Stimulus Reduction as a Technique to Effect the Reactivation of Crucial Repressed Memories," *J. Nerv. Ment. Dis.* 138 (1964) 172–80.

Suzuki, Daisetz T. *The Field of Zen*. New York: Perennial Library, 1970.

———. *Introduction to Zen Buddhism*. New York: Causeway Books, 1974.

———. *The Training of the Zen Buddhist Monk*. New York: University Books, 1959.

Szasz, T. *The Manufacture of Madness*. New York: Harper and Row, 1970.

———. *The Myth of Mental Illness*. New York: Hoeber-Harper, 1961.

Tart, Charles, ed. *Altered States of Consciousness*. Garden City, N.Y.: Doubleday Anchor Books, 1972.

———. *Transpersonal Psychologies*. New York: Harper and Row, 1975.

Teresa of Avila, St. *The Complete Works of St. Teresa*, E. Allison Peers, trans., 3 vols. New York: Sheed and Ward, 1957.

———. *Interior Castle*, E. Allison Peers, trans. Garden City, N.Y.: Doubleday Image Books, 1961.

Tillich, Paul. *The Courage to Be*. Yale University Press, 1952.

Trethowan, Illtyd. *Mysticism and Theology: An Essay in Christian Metaphysics*. London: Geoffrey Chapman, 1975.

Trimingham, J. Spencer. *The Sūfi Orders in Islam*. London: Oxford University Press, 1971, 1973.

Turner, Victor. *The Ritual Process: Structure and Anti-Structure*. Chicago: Aldine, 1969.

Underhill, Evelyn. *Mysticism: A Study in the Nature of Man's Spiritual Consciousness*. New York: Dutton, 1910, 1961.

———. *Practical Mysticism*. New York: Dutton, 1915.

Van Gennep, A. *The Rites of Passage*. London: Routledge and Kegan Paul, 1960.

Volken, L. *Visions, Revelations, and the Church*, E. Gallanger, trans. New York: P. J. Kenedy and Sons, 1963.

Von Senden, M. *Space and Sight*. Glencoe, Ill.: Free Press, 1960.

Walker, D. P. *The Ancient Theology: Studies in Christian Platonism from the Fifteenth to the Eighteenth Centuries*. London: Duckworth, 1972.

Wallace, Anthony F. C. *Culture and Personality*. New York: Random House, 2d ed., 1970.

Wallis, R. T. *Neoplatonism*. London: Gerald Duckworth, 1972.

Wapnick, K. "The Psychology of the Mystical Experience." Doctoral dissertation, Adelphi University, 1968.

Warrack, Grace, ed. *Julian of Norwich: Revelations of Divine Love*. London: Methuen, 1952.

Watt, W. Montgomery. *The Faith and Practice of Al-Ghazali*. London: George Allen and Unwin, 1953.

Watts, Alan W. *The Joyous Cosmology*. New York: 1962.

———. *Psychotherapy East and West*. New York: Ballantine, 1961.

———. *This is IT and Other Essays on Zen and Spiritual Experience*. New York: 1967.

———. *The Way of Zen*. New York: Pantheon Books, 1957.

Weisman, A. "Reality Sense and Reality Testing," *Behavioral Science* 3 (1958) 228–61.

Werner, H. *Comparative Psychology of Mental Development*. New York: International Universities Press, 1957.

White, John, ed. *The Highest State of Consciousness*. Garden City, N.Y.: Doubleday Anchor Books, 1972.

Wilson, Colin. *Poetry & Mysticism*. San Francisco: City Lights, 1969.

Wolfe, Tom. *The Electric Kool-Aid Acid Test*. New York: Farrar, Strauss and Giroux, 1968.

Williams, W. W., ed. *Select Treatises of St. Bernard of Clairvaux, De Diligendo Deo*. Cambridge University Press, 1926.

Wordsworth, W. "Intimations of Immortality from Recollections of Early Childhood," 1803–6, 1807, in *The Complete Poetical Works of William Wordsworth*. Cambridge, Mass.: Houghton, Mifflin, The Riverside Press, Student's Cambridge Edition, 1904, p. 353.

Woods, J. *The Yoga-System of Patanjali*. Harvard University Press, 1914.

Woods, Richard J., O.P. *The Occult Revolution*. New York: Seabury Press, 1973.

———. "The Social Dimension of Mysticism: A Study of the Meaning and Structure of Religious Experience in the Philosophy of William Ernest Hocking." Doctoral dissertation, Loyola University of Chicago, 1978.

Zaehner, R. C. *At Sundry Times*. London: Faber and Faber, 1958.

———. *Zen, Drugs, and Mysticism*. New York: Vantage, 1974.

Zubeck, et al. "Perceptual Changes after Prolonged Sensory Isolation (Darkness and Silence)," *Canad. J. Psych.* 15 (1961) 83–100.

Index